AN EARLY HISTORY

OF

MADISON TOWNSHIP

FRANKLIN COUNTY, OHIO

INCLUDING

Groveport and Canal Winchester

Re-created from and based on the original work compiled by

George F. Bareis

First published in 1902

Fully and Completely Re-Indexed Plus
Additional Photos, Illustrations and Addendums

BY

C. Stephen Badgley

2016

ISBN 978-0-9862268-7-8

George F. Bareis
1852 - 1935

I Dedicate this Book to

AMANDA J. SCHOCH,

the wife of my bosom,
whose assistance and encouragement
lightened my labor in compiling
and arranging it.

G. F. B.

NEW HIGH SCHOOL BUILDING — M. E. CHURCH — UNITED BRETHREN CHURCH — DAVIDS REFORMED CHURCH — LUTHERAN CHURCH

CANAL WINCHESTER HOME COMING OCT. 6 - 1910 - A CORDIAL WELCOME AWAITS YOU - COME HOME — THE OLD TOWN WANTS TO SEE YOU AND YOU WANT TO SEE OUR NEW TOWN

G. F. BARIES   E. C. GAYMAN   H. S. CANNON

Table of Contents

CHAPTER XXIX

CHAPTER I
PREFATORY INTRODUCTION

"And praise be theirs who plan
And fix the corner-stone
Of house or fane devote to God or man,
Not for themselves alone.
— Not for themselves alone,
The Pilgrim Fathers of the Western Wood,
Not only for themselves and for their own,
Came hither planting in heroic mood
The seeds of civil-graced society,
Repeating their New England by the sea
In the green wilderness.
From church and school, with church and school they came
To kindle here their consecrated flame:
With the high passion for humanity,
The largest light, the amplest liberty.
(No man a slave unless himself enthrall),
(The tree of knowledge no forbidden tree,)
For eager-seeking youth,
With priceless opportunity for all,
(The tree of knowledge no forbidden tree,)
Free speech and conscience free.
— Honor and praise no less
But theirs, who in the mighty forest, then
The haunt of savage men,
And tenanted by ravening beasts of prey
Only less fierce than they,
(The fever-chill, the hunger-pang they bore,
Dangers of day and darkness at their door)
Abode, and in the panther-startled shade
The deep foundations of an empire laid."
— John James Platt

The conception of this work dates back some twelve years, when the writer was persuaded to prepare a condensed narrative history of Madison Township to go into Captain A. E. Lee's *History of Columbus,*

1

Ohio. Later plans suggested the publication in separate form, and this volume is the result. To compile a history a century after the first settlement was made is no easy task, especially so when the time required must be snatched from a busy life. Three generations have lived and gone to the "great beyond" since then. Not only has the wolf, the bear, the deer, the wild-turkey, the Indian, the pioneer cabin, and all the associations of those "good old days" gone forever from view, but even the pioneers themselves are all gone — not one remains to tell the story of the hardships endured in their solitary lives in the great woods. Very few even of those who had the privilege of hearing from the first settlers' own lips the story of their struggle to subdue the wilderness, are living.

No records remain and none were made of much that goes to make up a history of those early days. Unfortunately, no newspaper was published in the township for more than sixty-five years. Scores of old account and record books have been searched for names, dates, and events. Martin's *History of Franklin County*, Scott's *History of Fairfield County*, Hill's *History of Licking County*, Williams *History of Franklin and Pickaway Counties*, Studer's *History of Columbus*, Lee's *History of Columbus*, Howe's *Historical Collections*, Graham's *Map of Franklin County*, and other similar works have been consulted. Original records have been carefully examined, such as the Plats and additions to the villages, at the County Recorder's office; the appraisement and sale of school lands at the Auditor of State's office; the bids, awards and payment of contracts on the Ohio Canal at the Ohio State Board of Public Works' office, etc. While we do not claim that every name and statement is absolutely correct in every particular, still we have spared no pains to make it as accurate as the nature of the work permitted; for *"errors will creep into history as long as the human mind is forgetful."*

Instead of giving "personal" sketches at so much per head — a thing utterly distasteful to most persons — we have aimed to mention in a thoroughly impartial way the name and work of everyone who contributed to the development of the township. In the prescribed limits of this book a host of the names of those who lived honorable and influential private lives must necessarily be omitted to give place to those who sacrificed time and personal comforts to bear the responsibilities of public trusts and criticisms.

We deemed it would be a source of satisfaction and enjoyment to our readers to see the faces of as many of the more active and influential citizens reproduced as we could secure, even though we omit a personal sketch of their lives.

It would require more space than is at our disposal to enumerate all the persons who have helped in this *"labor of love."* The compiler acknowledges himself under special obligations to the late John R. Wright, Mrs. Nathaniel Tallman and George P. Champe, and to James B. Evans, Esq., Geo. M. B. Dove, A. M. Senter, and all others who have aided him in any way, and he sincerely thanks one and all of them.

In our search we accumulated a large amount of material that we could not use in our present prescribed book; this together with all such items of personal, family and general history, illustrating in any way the development of the township, as our friends will kindly send us by-times, will be preserved for future use and reference.

Geo. F. Bareis
February 22d, 1902

CHAPTER II
DESCRIPTION AND ORGANIZATION OF MADISON TOWNSHIP

"The hills are dearest which our childish feet
Have cherished the earliest; and the streams most sweet
Are ever those at which our young lips drank.
Stooped to their waters o'er the grassy bank."

— Whittier

The most recent epoch in geology is the Glacial Period or Ice Age, although quite remote as compared with human history. During this period a vast field of ice, hundreds of feet thick, extended from the far north to Southern Ohio. This sea of ice was the accumulations of the snows of a long continued period, and possessed the properties of a solid and of a fluid. The accumulating weight of the snow above caused a slow, but steady and powerful flow, grinding mountains to powder in its path and forming great valleys and basins. It was thus that the great fresh water lakes were excavated and the wide valleys through Ohio became the water courses, the dry beds of which are now the fertile fields. For ages this powerful force was grinding and mixing the rocks into earth in such a way that no one generation can utilize all its fertility, but, as it were, locking it up that future generations may still reach down and inherit its wealth of productiveness. As the enormous weight of ice in its powerful and almost imperceptible flow moved onward, a bank of debris which resisted its flow, called a terminal moraine, was left to mark its southern progress. One of these terminal moraines, known as the Ridge road between Pickerington and Basil marks the place where an iceberg was finally resisted in its journey further southward.

As the climate became warmer this territory was in a great open sea, in which the winds and currents drifted detached mountains of ice, which when floating southward into more temperate latitudes melted, depositing boulders and ground debris, which clung to them. This deposit is called "the drift," being the earth on top of the solid rock.

Great volumes of water from the melting ice flowed southward, cutting wide rivers whose dry beds are now called second bottoms.

Madison Township with the surrounding territory must have been a great inland sea. The drift deposit is of various depths.

The drilling of the gas well at Winchester revealed that the drift was about 500 feet thick, while just south of Little Walnut Creek, not more than half a mile away, the Black Shale crops out, and only a few hundred yards farther south at the Zimmer Hill the Berea grit sandstone comes to the surface. The underlying rock bed in the remainder of the township is Huron or Black Shale; this is underlaid by the coniferous limestone, familiarly spoken of as the Columbus Limestone. Dr. Edward Orton says of this strata: *"It is one of the most remarkable store houses of ancient life in our whole series of rock formations."*

Scene on Little Walnut, Canal Winchester, O.

Circa 1908

As the climate still gradually became warmer and the expanse of ice less the streams became narrower, finally cutting deeper and narrower channels and leaving the older and higher beds dry. Then began the processes by which the fertility of these deposits should become available for the habitation of man. Nature provided seeds with the means of finding a congenial soil and climate. Vegetable growths followed each other, each enriching the soil. Worms, crabs, burrowing animals, roots, frosts, rains, all assisted in making the soil fertile.

Another element of great importance in the deposit of the drift is that it shall be of such a mixture of gravel, clay and sand that there may

6

be a good supply of water. In this respect the deposit of earth in the township is of such a character that the soil is of the most productive and the water supply of the amplest. Scarcity of water in the wells is rarely ever known. Blue clay is to be found in most localities of the township, usually from six to twenty feet under the surface. Large "nigger-heads"* are found on the surface, as also wherever a well is dug or excavations made.

*A large rock, or boulder. BPC

In 1899 the U. S. Geological Survey placed a plate in one of the stones of the creek bridge abutments near Winchester, indicating that the elevation above the sea level at that point is 758 feet. Other elevations in this section, as obtained by surveys for the Ohio Canal, Hocking Valley and the Ohio Central Railroads, are as follows: Lockbourne 688 feet. Groveport 740 feet. Winchester 768 feet. Columbus (Union Station) 744 feet. South Columbus 734 feet. Brice 765 feet. The fixed level at the Franklin County Court House is 777 1/2 feet.

The township is well watered by several good sized streams, as shown on the map: Big Walnut (also called Big-Belly and Gahanna), Blacklick, Little Walnut, and Alum Creek; there are also numerous smaller streams, among them George Creek, Spring Run and Big Run — which, with the network of tile drains, carry off the surplus water. The adjoining lowlands along the larger streams are often flooded when rich fertilizing sediment is left. Large portions of the township were originally covered with large ponds and swamps, often spoken of as prairies; especially was this true of the eastern section, giving it the name of "the flats." Scarcely a trace of these remain, the larger ditches only reminding one of them. So rich and productive is the land in this township that sections of it are referred to as the "garden spot of Franklin County." This is notably true of land in the neighborhood of Asbury Church.

Corn, wheat, grass and the cereals usually produced on rich soil grow to perfection. On the wide bottoms, which once formed the beds of the streams now narrowed down to mere rills compared to what they once were, is the richest alluvial soil, and has been in continuous cultivation in many instances for upwards of ninety years. In recent years many persons find remunerative results in raising small fruits and vegetables, especially strawberries, raspberries and nutmeg melons, for the Columbus market. The land generally having a southern slope and being of a warm nature is well adapted for market gardening.

Originally the township was densely timbered with giant oak, ash, walnut, hickory, elm, maple, beech, linden, cottonwood and other trees. Along the streams grew buckeye, pawpaw, willow and immense sycamores. Thousands of the choicest walnut and white oak logs have been shipped to eastern and foreign markets, and thousands of others were burned in great log heaps, at an early day, to get rid of them.

John Sharpe
1781 - 1863

Michael Corbett
1829 - 1901

On the first day of March, 1784, Thomas Jefferson, Samuel Hardy, Arthur Lee and James Monroe, delegates in Congress on the part of Virginia, executed a deed of cession by which they transferred to the United States all rights, titles and claims of Virginia to the country northwest of the Ohio River.

October 22, 1784, Arthur Lee, Richard Butler and Oliver Walcott met the hostile Indian tribes of the Six Nations at Fort Stanwix, and there concluded a treaty of peace with them. After the old indefinite claims of the Iroquois was thus extinguished, on January 21, 1785, negotiations with the Western Indians was begun by Arthur Lee,

Richard Butler and George Rogers Clark at Fort McIntosh. The Wyandots, Delawares, Chippewas and Ottowas were represented at this treaty.

During 1785 Brant, the great chief, formed a confederacy of the Western Indians, and on January 31,1786, a meeting was held by George Rogers Clark, Richard Butler and Samuel H. Parsons with the Delawares, Wyandots and Shawnees at the mouth of the Great Miami River. On account of the hostile attitude of the Shawnees and the absence of the Wabash tribes no treaty was signed.

The Indian wars were terminated by the treaty at Greenville in August, 1795. After the final transfer of the territory from Britain to the United States in 1796, under Jay's treaty, and the extinguishment of the Indian titles all apprehensions of danger on the part of the whites ceased and friendly intercourse with the Indians succeeded.

By the Ordinance of 1787 the territory purchased of the Indians was to be divided into townships six miles square, by north and south lines crossed at right angles by others: the first north and south line to begin on the Ohio River at a point due north of the western termination of the southern boundary of Pennsylvania, and the first east and west line to begin at the same point, and to extend throughout the territory. The ranges of townships thus formed were to be numbered from the Pennsylvania line westward; the townships themselves from the Ohio River northward. Each township was to be sub-divided into thirty-six parts or sections, each one mile square. When seven ranges of townships had been thus surveyed, the Geographer was to make a return of them to the Board of Treasury, who were to take therefrom one-seventh part, by lot, for the use of the late Continental army; and so of every seven ranges as surveyed and returned; the remaining six-sevenths were to be drawn for by the several states, in the proportion of the last requisition made on them; and they were to make public sale thereof in the following manner: Range I, Township 1, was to be sold entire; Township No. 2 by sections and so on alternately; while in Range II, Township 1, was to be sold by sections and Township 2 entire, retaining throughout, both as to ranges and townships, the principle of alternation. The price was to be at least one dollar in specie or certificate of liquidated debts of the United States. Five sections in each township were to be reserved for the United States, and one section for schools.

Madison Township is wholly composed of what is denominated *Congress Lands;* that is, land that has not been set apart for any special purpose but is sold by the government at a fixed price. Most of the land in this township was entered at the Land Office at Chillicothe, in Ross County . A good portion of it — all that purchased before 1820 — was paid for at the rate of two dollars per acre, in payments; after that date Congress fixed the price at one dollar and twenty-five cents per acre, cash to be paid when entered.

These lands were first surveyed in 1799 by John Matthews and Ebenezer Buckingham into townships six miles square and then divided into thirty-six sections one mile square, containing six hundred and forty (640) acres each. The numbering of these sections is indicated on the map of the township, and was always in the same order.

The sections were again sub-divided into four equal parts, called northeast quarter section, southeast quarter section, etc., containing 160 acres each. And by an "Act" which went into effect in July, 1820, these quarter sections are also divided by a north and south line, into two equal parts containing 80 acres each, and' called the east half of the northeast quarter of section, etc.

In establishing the township and section lines a post or stone is first planted at the point of intersection; then on the tree nearest the post or stone, and standing within the section intended to be designated, is numbered with a marking iron, in the following order:

R. (Range) No. ... T. (Township) No. ... S. (Section) No. ...

The fact that these surveyed townships, which are designated by numbers, are of different boundaries from the *civil* townships which have been otherwise named is often confusing. Thus this territory as surveyed is known as Range No. 21, Township 11. While for civil purposes it has been named after the fourth President of the United States — *Madison* — and includes parts of two other surveyed townships, viz: two tiers of sections — No. 1 to No. 12 inclusive— of Range No. 21, Township No. 10, formerly in Ross County.

On January 12, 1810, when Pickaway County was formed — *"picked away"** — from Ross, Franklin and Fairfield Counties, these sections became part of Franklin County, and the following March were included in this township; and by an act of the Legislature of 1850-51, six sections from Range No. 20, Township No. 15 — Violet Township,

Fairfield County — were added to Madison Township and this accounts for the fact that there are three sections each number 6 and 7, and two each numbers 1, 2, 3, 4, 5, 8, 9, 10, 11, 12, 18, 19, 30 and 31.

*Pickaway County was actually named after one of the five septs or bands of the native American Shawnee who occupied the area in the 18th century. Pickaway was anglicized from Peckuway, Piquay, Pekowi or one of the many other ways of spelling this name. BPC.

In the first division of Franklin County into townships, in 1803, this territory formed part of Harrison Township; there were at this time only two townships in Franklin County east of the Scioto River. Madison is now the largest township in the county, being eight miles in extent north and south, and seven miles east and west, with the exception of a gog of two sections in the southeast corner — one mile east and west and two miles north and south — belonging to Fairfield County. Madison Township was organized as a township on March 4, 1810, and Ebenezer Richards and George Hays were elected Justices of the Peace.

CHAPTER III
SOME STATISTICS

We could not ascertain the population of Madison Township for the first thirty years of its history, but to illustrate the rapid increase in population, we give the following statistics from Kilbourne's *Ohio Gazetteer: "In 1800 the territory, now the State of Ohio, contained about 45,000 inhabitants; in 1810, 230,760; in 1820, 581,434, and in 1830, 937,679."*

In 1829 Madison Township had 278 voters while the total in Franklin County was 2,312. Mr. Kilbourne makes the following suggestive observation regarding the rapid increase of the population:

"Perhaps the greatest operating cause of the more rapid increase of population in Ohio, than in some of the other Western States, is that slavery, with all its blighting evils, is here excluded."

Population

The population by decades is as follows: Madison Township in 1840, 1,815; in 1850, 2,480; in 1860, 3,395; in 1870, 3,440; in 1880, 3,859; in 1890, 3,357; in 1900, 3,217. The population of the villages is included in the above figures:

Groveport: In 1850, 438; in 1860, 540; in 1870, 629; in 1880, 650; in 1890, 578, and in 1900, 527.

Winchester: In 1850, 350; in 1860, 459; in 1870, 633; in 1880, 850; in 1890, 633; and in 1900, 666.

Madison Township had as large a population forty years ago as at present. This is also true in regard to Groveport.

Elections

The first elections in the township were held at the log tavern of Adam Rarey. Later elections were held at the offices of the Justices of the Peace; in the early fifties in a building that stood south of the Presbyterian Church; in 1852-54 in Dr. J. H. Saylor's office, which was then occupied by Esq. Jeremiah White. In 1860 the township erected the brick building on lot No. 13, West Main Street. The elections were held here until the fall of 1873 when the township was divided into

13

two voting precincts by a line beginning at the north township line, between Sections 2 and 3, thence south to the Ohio Canal, thence following the canal east one-half mile to Rager's Bridge, thence south on the quarter section line to the south line of the township. The territory west of said line was named Groveport precinct, and that east Winchester precinct.

The elections in the Groveport precinct were held in the township house until the Town Hall was erected; the elections in the Winchester precinct were held at various places, among them the Schoch office building on High Street, the Baily Brothers' building on Waterloo Street and since Winchester purchased the Town Hall, the elections are held there.

On January 25, 1896, the Board of Deputy State Supervisors of Elections of Franklin County considered the advisability of subdividing the Groveport precinct, and on February 8th following, the division was made and Zimmer precinct was established, as follows: *"Beginning at the northwest corner of Madison Township, thence south with the township line to the center of Big Walnut Creek, thence northeasterly with the meanderings thereof to the north section line of the Madison Township school lands, thence east with said section line to the line between Groveport and Winchester precincts, thence north with said precinct line to the north line of Madison Township, thence west with said line to the place of beginning. All territory within said boundary to be known as Zimmer Precinct; all territory in Groveport precinct not within above described lines to be known as Groveport precinct."*

The Zimmer voting building was erected in March, 1897.

Beginning with 1872 the vote of the township has been as follows:

For U. S. Grant 260, for Horace Greely 436; total, 696. **1876**, for R. B. Hayes, Groveport 158, Winchester 145; Samuel J. Tilden, Groveport 329, Winchester 256; total 754. **1880**, James A. Garfield, Groveport 176, Winchester 178; Winfield Scott Hancock, Groveport 332, Winchester 256; total, 948. **1884**, James G. Blaine, Groveport 184, Winchester 150; Grover Cleveland, Groveport 305, Winchester 279; total, 953. **1888,** Benjamin Harrison, Groveport 166, Winchester 161; Grover Cleveland, Groveport 294, Winchester 259; Fisk, Groveport 43, Winchester 12; total, 935. **1892**, Benjamin Harrison, Groveport 150,

14

Winchester 146; Grover Cleveland, Groveport 227, Winchester 232; People's, Groveport 14; Prohibition, Groveport 27, Winchester 9; total, 826. **1896**, Wm. McKinley, Groveport 130, Winchester 138, Zimmer 47; Wm. J. Bryan, Groveport 282, Winchester 296, Zimmer 65; total, 958. **1900**, Wm. McKinley, Groveport 123, Winchester 130, Zimmer 34; W. J. Bryan, Groveport 257, Winchester 273, Zimmer 68; total, 907.

The local elections are usually very quiet, with little rivalry; frequently the Democrats having the only tickets in the field, as was the case in the April election of 1901. The State and Presidential elections are however, quite spirited, although always orderly.

During the Vallandingham—Brough Campaign in 1863, both parties held mass meeting on the Madison Township fair grounds. The Republican meeting was held on September 19. C. P. Dildine furnished an ox that was roasted for the occasion. Thirty-six girls, one to represent each State, dressed in red skirts, white waists and blue sashes, rode from Winchester to the fair grounds on a wagon that G. M. B. Dove and Almanzor Hathaway borrowed of a man at Amanda, Ohio, which had been used at Lancaster for a similar purpose.

The Democratic meeting was held on October 13, and was addressed by Hon. S. S. Cox, Isaac W. Fry and Robt. F. Dildine canvassed the township for horses and 100 teams were hitched to a hickory wagon that , furnished.

Madison Township School Enumeration

1861, Sub-district No. 1, 65; No. 2, 65; No. 3, 7; No. 4,. 47; No. 6, 54; No. 7, 57; No. 8, 75; No. 9, 46; No. 10, 32; No. 11, 51; No. 12, 15; No. 13, 48; No. 14, 7; No. 15, 9; No. 16, 9; No. 17, 31; No. 18, 200; No. 19, 43; No. 21, 35; No. 22, 72; a total of 968. **1885**, male, white, 338; colored, 1; female, white, 276; colored, 1: total, 616. Hamilton Township, 8; Marion Township, 8. **1886**, male, 349; female, 294; total 643. **1887**, males, 329; females, 274; total, 603. **1888**, males, 326; females, 251; total, 577. **1890**, males, 288; females, 254; total 542. **1891**, males, 285; females, 250; total, 535. **1892**, males, 291; females, 242; total. 533. **1893**, males, 300; females, 241; total 541. **1894**, males, 295; females, 251; total, 546. **1895**, males, 274; females, 239; total, 513. Hamilton Township, 12. Marion Township, 19. **1896**, males, 277; females, 234; total 511. **1897**, males, 268; females, 242; total, 510. Hamilton

Township, 8. Marion Township, 15. **1898,** males, 289; females, 248; total, 537. Hamilton Township, 13. Marion Township, 15. **1899**, males, 308; females, 258; total, 566. Hamilton Township, 13. Marion Township, 14. **1900**, males, 302; females, 254; total, 556. Hamilton Township, 10. Marion Township, 14.

Enumeration of Groveport Schools

1894, males, 106; females, 99; total, 205. **1895**, males, 100; females, 95; total, 195. **1896**, males, 102; females, 90; total. 192. **1897**, males, 106; females, 85; total, 191. **1898**, males, 110; females, 88; total, 198. **1899**, males, 98; females, 85; total, 183; **1900**, males, 95; females, 73: total, 168.

Enumeration of Winchester Schools

1854, male, 90; female, 78; total, 168. **1857**, male, 102; female, 96; total, 198. **1858**, male, 101; female, 91; total, 192. 1**859**, male, 108; female, 96; total, 204. **1860**, male, 107; female, 103; total, 210. **1861**— this is the year when the union school building was erected—male, 100; female, 100; total, 200. **1862**, male, 95; female, 89; total, 184; **1863**, male, 103: female, 100; total, 208. **1864**, male, 114; female, 86: total, 200; **1865**, male, 101; female, 102; total, 203; **1866**—when district No. 18 became the Winchester Special School District—male, 117; female, 106; total, 223. * * * **1884**, male, 161; female, 135; total, 296. **1885**, male, 178; female, 127; total, 305. **1886**, male, 167; female, 127; total, 294. **1887,** male, 145; female, 121; total, 266. **1888**, male, 141; female, 104; total, 245; **1889**, male, 138; female, 97; total, 235. **1890,** male, 139; female, 90; total, 229. * * * **1893,** male, 125; 2 H M T female, 82; total, 207. **1894,** male, 104; female, 92; total, 196. * * * **1897**, male, 116; female, 89; total, 205. **1898**, male, 116; female, 98; total, 214. **1899**, male, 117; female, 97; total, 214. **1900**, male, 106; female, 95; total, 201.

Assessor's Report

1855.—Total number of acres, 33,277$^{1/2}$; number acres in wheat, 3,091; number bushels produced, 37,179; average per acre, 12 bushels; number acres in corn, 9,229; number bushels, 269,306; average per acre, 30 bushels; number of horses, 1,369; mules, 2; cattle, 2,885; sheep, 1,866; hogs, 5,423.

	Winchester Precinct.		Winchester School District.		Winchester Corporation.		Zimmer and Groveport Precincts.		Groveport School District.		Groveport Corporation.	
	No.	Value.	No.	Value.	No.	Value.	No.	Value.	No.	Value.	No.	Value.
Horses	304	$13,665	25	$1,125	41	$1,650	419	$21,295	16	$770	16	$890
Cattle	776	11,895	79	1,135	17	370	496	14,150	8	230	9	320
Mules	5	195										
Sheep	395	1,895	10	50	17	60	549	2,595				
Hogs	1,396	4,195	102	370	26	110	771	2,615			25	80
Carriages	57	1,425	6	170	30	715	9	:00				
Watches	18	210	5	80	29	280	10	109	1	10	1	10
Pianos and Organs	19	1,460	4	190	18	1,170	11	325		3	3	90
Money subject to draft		8,035		2,695		11,975		2,250				
Credits		32,770		3,110		67,800		37,650		2,800		8,200
Dogs	84		4		11		38				1	
Mdse. — average value						25,415		500				5,950
Raw materials						2,240		595				500
Total		$99,675		$10,230		$115,460		$93,680		$3,810		$16,620

Total in township, chattels ...... $ 339,475
Total in township, real estate 1,769,457

Grand total ...... $ 2,108,932

Crop Statistics Reported 1900 for Year 1899

Winchester Precinct.—Wheat, 5,689 acres, 47,083 bushels; oats, 57 acres, 1,690 bushels; corn, 2,748 acres, 134,926 bushels; potatoes, 35³/⁴ acres, 1,557 bushels; meadow, 497 acres, 648 tons; clover, 527 acres, 720 tons; apples, 158 acres, 22,520 bushels; butter, 42,560 pounds; eggs, 27,550 dozen; wool, 1,847 pounds; commercial fertilizer, used 64,800 pounds, cost $678; acres in cultivation, 6,637; in pasture, 379 acres; in woodland, 462 acres; lying waste, 943 acres; total owned in Winchester precinct, 9,421 acres.

Zimmer Precinct.—Wheat, 412 acres; 6,750 bushels; corn, 409 acres, 18,500 bushels; potatoes, 9 acres, 430 bushels; meadow, 65 acres, 71 tons; apples, 17 acres, 1,450 bushels; butter, 4,000 pounds; eggs, 2,100 dozen; Commercial fertilizer used, 40,000 pounds; cost, $389; acres in cultivation, 995; in pasture, 221 acres; in woodland, 20 acres; lying waste, 86 acres; total owned in Zimmer precinct, 1,322 acres.

Groveport Precinct.—Wheat, 4,198 acres, 72,550 bushels; oats, 67 acres, 2,670 bushels; corn, 3,661 acres, 146,800 bushels; potatoes, 120 acres, 5,710 bushels; meadow, 539 acres, 704 tons; clover, 507 acres, 632 tons; butter, 40,300 pounds; eggs, 22,700 dozen; Commercial fertilizer used, 115,600 pounds; cost, $1,179; apples, 173 acres, 15,570 bushels; wool, 2,794 pounds; acres in cultivation, 10,571; in pasture,

1,716 acres; in woodland, 299 acres; lying waste, 844 acres; total owned in Groveport precinct, 13,676 acres.

Decennial Appraisement of Real Property, 1900

In Madison Township.—Total number of acres. 33,860; value, $1,143,163; average value per acre, $34.08; value of buildings, $194,385; average value per acre, including land and buildings, $39.80; value of village lots and buildings, $225,270; aggregate value of real estate in Madison Township as equalized by county board, $1,544,187; amount on duplicate in 1900, $1,468,820; number of acres of arable or plow lands, 30,876; number acres of pasture or meadow lands, 335; number acres of uncultivated or woodlands, 2,649.

Winchester Village.—Value of lots, $29,210; value of buildings, $116,260; aggregate value, $145,470; value on tax duplicate in 1900, $167,940.

Groveport Village.—Value of lots, $21,250; value of buildings, $58,550; aggregate value, $79,800; value on tax duplicate in 1900, $83,170.

Range of Prices of Wheat and Corn per Bushel 1850-1900

Wheat. — **1850 to '59**, 58c to $2.00; **1860 to '69**, 60c to $3.50; **1870 to '79**, 85c to $2.15; **1880 to '89**, 71c to $1.50; **1890 to '99**, 48c to $1.45.

Corn. — **1850 to '59**, 24c to 90c; **1860 to '69**, 27c to $1.29; **1870 to '79**, 38c to $1.05; **1880 to '89,** 30c to 87c; **1890 to '99,** 18c to 77c.

Dr. G. L. Smith, M.D.
1824 - 1904

Dr. Abel Clark, M.D.
1812 - 1869

CHAPTER IV
NATIVE AND EARLY SETTLERS

"I hear the tread of pioneers
Of nations yet to be
The first low wash of waves where soon
Shall roll a human sea."

Whittier

The first occupancy of this continent by man is as uncertain as the date of man's origin. Many scientists now admit man's presence here as a contemporary of the mastodon and other extinct animals.

Who built the ancient mounds and earthworks with their rich store of implements and utensils is a sealed volume. To present students they are still a "nameless people" and hence for want of a better name are called Mound Builders. Where they came from, and when, are equally as mysterious and obscure problems. The Red Man's traditions shed no light and are worthless on the subject.

It is quite likely that the country was mostly open and un-wooded during the dominion of the Mound Builders, and that the center of their population was in Ohio.

It is certain that most of these ancient works have been built for more than five hundred years; this is proven by the fact that trees of five centuries' growth are found upon them. There are other circumstances that point to even a much longer period of residence here. Their influence over nature in the domestication of wild animals and in the transforming influence of certain plant life, such as maize, tobacco and cotton indicate a very long period. Some of the plants domesticated by these people have been in cultivation so long that they would perish only for the fostering care of human hands.

The fact that during the Middle Ages no investigations were tolerated and that every reference to such discovery was burned and obliterated, makes it doubly difficult to find solutions now.

Many theories have been advanced to solve the mysterious uncertainty; Bancroft, in his *Native Races*, among others mentioned the following ones: Father Duran, a native of Spain, wrote in 1585, *"My opinion and supposition is that these natives are the ten tribes of Israel that Salmanazer, king of the Assyrians, made prisoners and carried to Assyria in the time of Hoshea, king of Israel, and in the time of Hezekiah, king of Jerusalem, as can be seen in Esdras, Book Fourth. Chapter Third, they went to live in a land, remote and separated, which had never been inhabited, to which they had a long and tedious journey of a year and a half:"* L'Estrange contraverted this theory, but concluded that Shem was the progenitor of the American; and says: *"Shem was ninety-eight years old at the time of the flood and was not present at the building of Babel."*

It is claimed by some that the word Peru has the same meaning as Ophir, the grandson of Heber, from whom the Hebrews derived their name, then setting up the theory that Solomon's ships, on their voyages, which lasted sometimes for three years, went to Peru for the "gold of Ophir."

The conjecture of some has been that the Queen of Sheba came from this continent.

Others claim that Noah's long and aimless voyage in the ark encouraged his immediate descendants to construct similar vessels and undertake voyages. These falling in with adverse winds and currents were driven to these shores and being unable to return they became the colonists.

Ignatius Donnelly, in his *Atlantis,* published a score of years ago, attracted renewed attention to the theory based on Plato's *"fabled island of Atlantis."* It is related that the priests of Egypt told Solon of an island continent which furnished an almost continuous land passage across the Atlantic Ocean. The Azores Islands, it is claimed, are the mountain peaks of this submerged island.

The Book of Mormon, said to have been discovered by Joseph Smith, September 22, 1827, in a mound called Cumorah, Ontario County, New York, tells that the colonization of America took place soon after the confusion of tongues at Babel.

Some claim that a remnant of the inhabitants of Tyre, who escaped the siege of Alexander the Great, 332 B. C., sailed to America and landed in Florida, and in proof of their theory quote Ezekiel *27;26*.

Still others point to the similarity between the architecture and sculpture of Mexico and Central America and Egypt for a solution of the problem. Some advocate Carthaginian, Phoenician or Greek colonization. The narrowness of the channel at Bering Straits has invited others to look in that quarter for a solution. Among the arguments presented are for Tartar colonization, noting the resemblance in manner of life and physical appearance of the natives on both sides of the channel. Others argue for Japanese and still others for a Chinese colonization. Others refute all these theories and claim the race is indigenous; others that God created an original pair of human beings here as He did in the old world; still others look to evolution.

Most of these conclusions have very little to stand upon except the productiveness of an imaginative mind.

There are several pre-Columbian discoveries that rest on documentary evidence, although each of these have their disputants.

In the writings of the early Chinese historians is found the statement that in the year 499 A. D. Hoei Shin, a Buddhist priest, returned to China from a long journey to an island which he called Fusang, on account of the many trees of that name growing there, it has been assumed that this country was Mexico or California.

Two discoveries are accredited to the Irish; one to "White Man's Land," claimed to be located on the Atlantic coast from North Carolina to Florida, the other when St. Patrick sent missionaries to the "Isles of America." which would place the date of the latter prior to 493 A. D. The Norsemen discovery in 1002 A. D. is familiar. The Welsh discovery by Madoc in about 1170 A. D. of the coast of Mexico or California. In 1380 A. D. it is claimed the Venetians established a church in Greenland. The Portuguese date their discovery of New Foundland about 1464 A. D. The discovery by the Poles is given as 1476 A. D.

The writer has spent many of his leisure hours in the study of the earthworks and implements of these people, and has many times let his imagination look in on their domestic and outdoor life. He has often sat with a stone pipe or axe or other of their relics before him trying to lure it to unfold its mysterious history.

A conservative view of the consensus of the conclusions of those who have had the best opportunities to give these investigations intelligent study seems to be that they are of old world origin; that they came in installments, some coming from the southeast, others from the northwest, meeting in the Ohio and Mississippi valleys where they were amalgamated, as is proven by the finding of the crania of the long heads and of the short heads with their intermediate types in the same mound; that they became populous and widespread; that they evolved a system of government which controlled multitudes; that they were in the main agriculturists, although they had a division of labor by which some devoted their time to special trades; that they developed a civilization and culture of no mean type, as is shown by their domestic utensils, artistically formed and decorated vessels, cloth,. implements and earthworks; that they mined copper, which they made into ornaments and implements; that they quarried mica for mirrors; that they worked salt mines and flint quarries. The finding of copper from Lake Superior, mica from North Carolina, lead from Missouri, and shells from Florida, all in the same mound, indicates their wide-spread commerce.

The next race— the American Indian—most likely the descendent of the Mound Builders, had less fixed homes, leading nomadic lives, from the fact that most of their time was devoted to hunting and fishing. As far as we are able to learn no Indian villages were located in this township, although a flint-worker's shop must have been located in the neighborhood of Asbury Church, judging by the large number of flint chips found there. The early settlers in Violet Township, Fairfield County, remembered a small village of some twenty or thirty wigwams located on the north bank of Little Walnut Creek about one mile east of Winchester. In a year or two after the first settlements, the Indians left, and while they still occasionally passed through the township they scarcely ever molested any one or attracted any attention. One of their trails leading from *To-be-town* (Royalton) to *Crane town* (Upper Sandusky) passed over the farm of Irvin E. Stevenson. The prominent

22

imminence on this farm no doubt furnishing them a good view of the surrounding country. One thing is certain; they did not make proper use of the rich soil by cultivating it. After game sought the deeper and more unvisited forests of the unexplored and uninhabited country farther west and north, they seemed to realize the inevitable and yielded their old familiar haunts to the pale face's power to make the "desert rejoice and blossom as the rose."

Irvin E. Stevenson
1839 - 1923

The early settlers came not from wealthy and luxurious homes; neither did they come from the indolent class.

Many of them had no competence except healthy bodies and determined wills. They came seeking homes of their own, rather than continue as tenant to a class whom they feared might oppress and emaciate them, as had been done by the landlord system in Europe, with which they were familiar and which they abhorred.

They knew full well that in seeking a home in the western forest they were sacrificing many comforts, which they could not hope to secure for many years, if at all in their generation: they knew that they were facing sickness in a malarious climate; they must have, at least in part, considered the great hard ships and privations to be endured.

Congress strengthened the ordinance of 1785 by the execution of the great "Compact" of 1787 establishing, as Salomon P. Chase in his Preliminary Sketch of the History of Ohio says, *"Certain great fundamental principles of governmental duty and private right as the*

23

basis of all future constitutions and legislation, unalterable and indestructible." Mr. Chase further remarks. *"Never, probably, in the history of the world did a measure of legislation so accurately fulfill, and yet so mightily exceed the anticipations of the legislators."* Faith in a country governed by such provisions as this ordinance contained inspired a courage and hope that here, where slavery was excluded and where property rights were sacred they would perpetuate the principles of freedom and liberty that moved their ancestors to come to America. The early settler therefore came with a purpose to enter a tract of land, which at once made him an interested citizen who would have every incentive to seek and hold fast to the very best in government and morals for himself and family. They were mostly persons in the same circumstances, so very little distinction in modes of life existed among them; but had there been distinctions the perils and hardships to be mutually endured would have made them akin. Their manner of living compelled them to seek and avail themselves of each other's help. They could not erect their cabin or clear away the giants of the forest alone; they must help each other, and no one ever failed to respond unless sick or otherwise disabled. When one family would butcher or go to mill or make a successful catch of fish or game, all the near neighbors would be remembered with a portion. Many other similar neighborly acts, such as ministrations in sickness and death, and indeed, kindly assistance and sympathy in every experience of their wilderness life knit them together in a bond of friendship the durability and grace of which can only be found in a community where common privations and perils are experienced for a long time. The effects of these beautiful friendships thus formed are even now held dear and sacred among the descendants of many of the pioneer families.

The fact that they had to worship in log cabins and barns and were denied all of those peculiar comforts and conveniences, as books, pictures, etc., which cultivate and culture the aesthetic side of man's nature, gave them a characteristic frankness and bluntness, which might, in older communities appear as abrupt and unceremonious, perhaps even inelegant. In principal they were positive and firm as a rock, yet gentle and considerate to man and beast.

The great majority were Christians, members of the different denominations now represented in the township. Their Christian characters were unimpeachable, and their lives, although partaking of their surroundings and circumstances, exemplified the highest virtues of true manhood and womanhood.

Among the very first settlers was George Tongue, who located on George's Creek (perhaps this stream is named after him) on the southeast quarter of section No. 7, as early as 1802 or 1803.

By 1805 quite a number of others settled in the township, among them John Kalb, Geo. Kalb and wife, John Stevenson and family, William Stevenson and family of five boys and two girls, all from Maryland; Stauffel Kramer, Charles Rarey and sons, Adam, Benjamin, William, Charles and George, and James, Samuel and Robert Ramsey from Pennsylvania; Elias Decker and family, William D. Hendren and wife, Esau Decker and Ezekiel Groom from New Jersey; Mathew and Samuel Taylor and families from Nova Scotia; John Guffy from Kentucky and others. From 1805 to 1810 many from the eastern states as well as the adjoining counties of Ross and Fairfield located in the township. Among them were Lewis (Ludwig), Phillip, George, John, Michael, Adam and Jacob Kramer, all brothers, and their families from Pennsylvania; John Schoonover and family, Ralph and Elijah Austin, John Decker, John Craun, Jonathan Lee and wife, Thos. Gray, Geo. Smith, Jacob Weaver, John Tallman, John Sharp and wife, Samuel Brown, Samuel Bishop, John Swisher, Fredrick Peterson, Phillip Pontius, Alex. Mooberry and family, Abednego Davis, Matthias Wolf, John and Jacob Gander, Emmer Cox, Wm. Elder, Billingsly Bull, Daniel Kramer, Abraham Harris, Geo. Rohr and sons, Cubbage Needels and wife, Henry Whetzel and family, David Wright, John Wright, Joseph Wright, James McClish, John Kile and family, and a few years later, but early enough to help bear the burdens and hardships incident to a pioneer's life in those days were Henry, Harmon, Andrew, Daniel and John Dildine, Jacob Rhoads, Henry and Fredrick Bunn. Michael Rohr, Adam Havely, Christian and Adam Sarber, the Daylongs, John Rager, Zebulon and Elias Leigh, George Seymore, Samuel Murphy, Peter Long, Wm. Patterson, Wesley Toy, Phillip King, Thomas Needels, John, Philomen and Andrew Needels, __Farley, Edward Hathaway, Greazy Harrison, __Hoshor, Wm. Fleming, Jacob Powell, __Francisco, Wm. Perrin, Dr. Wm. Riley, and others whose names cannot be recalled.

Few colored persons have ever lived in the township, in fact so few that they have always attracted the attention especially of the children.

Among the first and best known was Black Charlie (Chas. Hatten) who when a boy was brought here by Wm. Stevenson. After Mr. Stevenson's death he lived with Anna B. Stevenson, a daughter, until he died. He was good-natured, polite, a friend of the children, and always had a bright new penny for them. He could speak "Pennsylvania Dutch." Thomas Gray brought a colored man with him from Maryland in about 1810, who was known as Black Sam. Others, known to persons about Winchester, were Yellow Nick (Nicholas Gossage), Reuben and Samuel Gloyd.

John Kramer
"Uncle Johnnie"
1808 - 1891

John Helpman
1813 - 1883

CHAPTER V
EARLY ENTERPRISES

"The eternal master found his single talent well employed."

—Samuel Johnson

Kramer Mill
(Fisher Mill)
Built by Lewis Kramer around 1808
This picture is from a photo taken in 1888

The first grist and saw-mill is said to have been erected by Mathew Taylor near the mouth of Alum Creek, in 1807 or 1808, and was later destroyed by fire. About the same time Lewis (Ludwig) Kramer built a grist and saw-mill on Little Walnut Creek about one mile southwest of Winchester. In 1852 it was operated by Henry Fictone, then by Geo. Fisher, in 1858 by Fisher & (Geo.) Markley, in 1859 by Fisher & (Ervin) Moore, in 1861 by Moore & (Geo.) Bareis. Soon after this the dam gave way and the mill was abandoned. This building stood until about 1893 when it fell down, and part of the timbers were used in the construction of a stable which stands near its site. George Sparr, father of the late Emanuel Sparr, was a miller at the Kramer mill at an early day, and lived in a log cabin located in what is now Chas. Brun's orchard.

In 1810 or 1811 George Sharp erected a mill on Big Walnut Creek a short distance up the stream from where the Columbus and Groveport

27

Pike now crosses; the only trace left of it is one of the broken burrs lying along the south side of the pike, some two or three hundred yards east of the bridge. These enterprises added much to the convenience of the early settler; as before the mills were built, and sometimes after, when the water would get too low to grind, persons were compelled to go to Springfield. Zanesville or Chillicothe.

For many years after these improvements were made there was no other road than a bridle path, marked by blazed trees, leading to them; persons would come from great distances, and had to wait their turn, consequently many would try to reach the mill in the evening so as to be among the first on the following morning. The writer remembers quite well that this custom continued in practice by many, even until in the fifties while his father was the miller at the Empire Mills.

Soon after the canal was constructed, Wm. H. Richardson built a mill about two hundred yards east of the Groveport Lock on the north side of the canal; it was built for a grist and saw-mill, and was about the size of Chaney's mill. For some reason the machinery for grinding was never put in, so it was used only as a saw-mill. It soon went to decay, and every trace of it is long since gone.

In 1851-52 John Chaney and son (Oliver P) erected a mill one mile west of Winchester, and named it the Empire Mills. It was 35 by 70 feet in size. This was one of the best mills in Central Ohio, and did a thriving business for many years. Sprague, George Bareis, 1854-1861, John F. Bauers, Wm. Evans, Joseph Ashe and John C. Speaks were the successive millers. In 1863 Joseph Rodenfels became proprietor, then Rodenfels. Seymour (Moses) & Co. (Peter Brown) operated it a few years, when Samuel Bartlit purchased it at assignee's sale. In 1884 C. B. and D. H. Cowan put in a "Gradual Reduction Roller system" consisting of an entirely new outfit of machinery, engine, etc. Ebenezer, Jones & Co. (Wm. T. Lewis) purchased it in August, 1894, and built a spur track from the Hocking Valley R. R. to the mill.

On August 23, 1895, at about midnight it was discovered on fire, and with the covered lattice bridge and a frame residence was totally destroyed. A. B. Gillett put up the mill building and Hoosac did the millwright work. Chas. W. Speaks built the mill-race.

While the tail-race was being built, two of the Irish workmen, who had been to Winchester in the evening, on returning were drowned just below the lock.

While Wm. Wilson and Leo Carson were fishing the following day, Mr. Carson's hook got fast to some object, when he got down near the edge of the bank and took the line in his hands, pulling it steadily, when suddenly the stiff corpse with extended arms of one of the drowned men came to the surface very near him.

O. P. Chaney purchased the first wheat run through the mill of Jonathan Boyer, grandfather of "Jim" Jeffries, in November, 1852. Mr. Chaney was first to adopt the use of other than barrels as packages, in which to sell flour. On his trip to the California gold fields in 1849 he observed the canvass sacks in which the flour from Chili was put up for transportation up the mountains. Soon after starting the Empire Mills he noticed the disadvantage of the small buyer who had to pay three cents per pound for his flour while those who could afford to buy it by the barrel paid only two cents. Remembering the canvass sacks, he purchased muslin and employed women to sew them. At first only half-barrel sacks were used, which required one square yard of muslin. Later the quarter-barrel size was also used. For the first two or three years the sacks were not branded, and later by a hand stencil plate.

The Winchester Mills now operated by The Winchester Milling Company — Chas. P. Bauman, Manager — was built by Jacob Carty, M. C. Whitehurst, John Gehm and Abraham Lehman in 1868. The foundation was first started along the north side of the canal, opposite the Yellow-Warehouse basin, but before much progress was made it was decided to build on the present site near the railroad which was then building. John Miller laid the brick and Wm. P. Miller did the carpenter work of the building. The Roller Process was installed in 1884.

The consecutive millers have been George Bareis, John F. Bauers, Jacob Enderly, Joseph Stemler in 1884, since which John Davis has been the miller. Other well known employees are: Wm. D. Beeks, book-keeper; Wm. L. Watters, assistant miller; Walter Mundell, M. Lecrone and Joshua A. Mathias, engineers.

Among the early saw-mills, besides those mentioned in connection with the grist-mills, was one on the John Rager farm, one on the David Martin farm, one on the C. R. McGuffey farm, another on the southeast one quarter of the school section built by John Swisher in 1832. John Rhoads built one on the Hempy farm at an early day and later Samuel Hempy operated it for many years.

John Thompson and George and Isaac Cowden built a woolen mill at Lock No. 19, about one mile west of Winchester in 1832 or 1833. It had two carding and one fulling machines. While Benjamin Kanode, a fuller, worked here one of his children fell into the lock and drowned. In 1843 Judge John Chaney purchased the interest of the Cowdens, and John M. Schoch bought out Thompson; they operated it until 1850, when Mr. Schoch sold his interest to Mr. Chaney, who then erected a new building at Lock No. 21, to which place he removed most of the old machinery, adding new machines and improvements from time to time until 1865 or 1870, when it was abandoned. The old frame is now a part of the barn at O. P. Chaney *s track. One of the machines, used to raise the knap on woolen cloth, had a large cylinder covered with the seed pod of the Teasel. The use of the Teasel for this purpose perhaps explains why there are yet so many of these weeds along the canal banks in the neighborhood of the woolen mill. Next in importance, after the flour and saw-mill, to the settler, was the tannery. Quite a number of these were operated in this township, among which was one located in what is now the southwest corner of the garden on the Amos Bush farm; another was operated by Samuel Hooper about two or three hundred yards northwest of Daniel Wright's residence; Wm. Riley operated one in Winchester located at the northwest corner of Waterloo and Trine Streets. Mr. Riley sold to John Thompson, and the latter sold to Reuben Trine, who operated it extensively for many years and finally removed it due south to the north side of the canal. While operated by J. W. Young in 1884 it was destroyed by fire.

The only market for the surplus live stock raised was in the eastern cities, and to buy up a drove of cattle and hogs and drive them to Philadelphia, Baltimore or other eastern markets often realized those, venturesome enough to undertake the risk of a broken market, large profits. It seems, however, but a question of time until disaster overtook those who engaged in this early enterprise: few succeeded, while many who had accumulated handsome estates lost all in these speculations. A large amount of money was required to buy up a drove, which usually consisted of from 110 to 125 head of cattle and from 150 to 160 head of hogs. Three men were required to drive: one to lead an ox, the "boss," six to ten cattle from the front, and the other in the rear. The cattle went single file about eight to ten feet apart. It required from sixty to seventy-five days to make a trip, and the cost for feed and other expenses was from twelve to fifteen hundred dollars. Farmers along the route prepared feed lots and other conveniences, and often met the drovers several miles out soliciting their patronage. The drovers usually sold their horses at the end of the trip and returned on the stage coaches. The above items, relating to an industry that passed with the introduction of the railway, were received from the late William Black, of Circleville, who was an early resident of Madison Township, being related to the Rareys and a pupil of Thomas Hughes at the Rarey Academy. Mr. Black was engaged in buying and driving stock for the past sixty years. He relates that in the early days all the hogs were weighed one at a time on steel-yards. The first cattle he ever shipped by rail he drove as far as Harrisburg, Pa., where he loaded them on cars; five car loads (75 head) went to Philadelphia, and 17 car loads (256 head) to New York. It was then thought necessary that each of the fifteen cattle in a car should be tied with from 8 to 10 feet of rope. He also observed that *"the offal that the early slaughter house proprietors threw into the streams now make millionaires."*

In the winter of 1834-1835 Jacob B. Wert engaged in pork-packing near where Wm. Mason's tile yard is now located. Beginning November 13, he slaughtered about five hundred head of hogs per day — a total of 35,000 during the season. Hogs were brought from the adjoining counties — Pickaway, Fairfield and Licking — many of them a distance of from twenty-five to thirty-five miles. The offal was sold by the wagon loads to persons who peddled them over the country, This enterprise furnished employment to quite a number of persons, as, besides the large number required in slaughtering and packing, many others found employment in making the pork barrels, etc. The storeroom and warehouse built by Mr. Wert, opposite the Town Hall in 1832, was later occupied by Wm. H. Rarey and James Cooken, and after a few years John Courtright became a member of the firm, which then went under the name of Rarey, Courtright & Co. In the fall of 1846 Joseph Sharp was a member of this firm in place of Mr. Cooken, and some of the entries in an account book show that they received the following hogs from George Rarey, viz: "200 choice hogs at $2,000, 17 hogs same lot $101.43, 55 hogs last lot $323.17," a total of 272 hogs at $2,424.60. Their books show that they slaughtered 833 hogs amounting to $18,351. It required 1,866 pork barrels, and they employed a total of 87 persons. It seems that they simply slaughtered and packed the pork ready for market at so much per head, only buying now and then a small lot of hogs.

In 1836 John Thompson, Wm. Seymour, Jacob Swisher, Wm. Curtis, Abe Harrison, Adam Kramer, John Solomon, George Rarey, Joseph Wright and others built the slaughter house in Winchester now used by Mrs. C. Gayman as a barn, and operated it extensively for a short time, when the venture proved a failure and was discontinued; not, however, until several of those interested had lost all their means.

Wm. Black says; "During one season in the early forties some nine thousand head of sheep were slaughtered at Groveport by Jennings & Son; the pelts were tanned and sold to the Land Office for parchments and the carcasses were 'tanked' (steamed) for the tallow. Comparatively few sheep have been raised in the township, at an early day, on account of wolves and other wild animals, and later because of the ravages of dogs. Stock raising and shipping has always been one of the leading industries of the township.

The Tavern exerted its full share of influence among the early institutions. It not only furnished solid but liquid refreshments as well, and afforded under one roof all that was required in the way of store and gathering place for the neighborhood. One of the first taverns in the township was kept by Adam Rarey in a log house on section No. 28; later (in 1836) he built a brick one on the same site, some of the walls of which were used in the construction of the Rarey mansion. Isaac Decker kept one in a log house that stood on the present site of George Williams' residence in Middletown. Another known as Cedar Grove was kept by Wm. D. Needels, just west of where the Columbus and Winchester Pike crosses Big Walnut Creek. A Mr. Blair kept one in a hewed log house, which then stood on the Columbus and Groveport Pike opposite C. F. Needels' residence. Another called "Cross Keys" was kept at the cross-roads west of Swartz's tile yard on the Columbus and Winchester Pike. Still another known as the "Obetz" was kept near where the Norfolk& Western R. R. crosses the Groveport and Columbus pike; these two latter buildings are still standing, although for many years abandoned as taverns.

Persons wishing to open a tavern in the earliest times were required to file an application with the county officials and when granted were assessed a license fee of one dollar.

Soon after the pioneers came, orchards were set out; this is especially true of peach trees, which grew quickly; large crops were produced, the surplus being converted into peach brandy. As far as the writer could learn few distilleries were operated in this township. Among those within convenient distance were the following: One along the run on Section No. 31, just south of Winchester; one operated by Samuel Loucks in connection with his mill; others were located along the Winchester and Carroll Road, at Kinney's Run, Fisher's Run, Dowdall's Run, Hoshor's Run (Jefferson), Alspach's Run and Chaney's Run. It is said that some persons made as much as six barrels of peach brandy in one season. A powder factory was operated at Waterloo by Judge John Chaney and Esq. John Donaldson at an early day.

Perhaps the first brick house in the township was built by Smith in 1819 on the farm now owned by Jerry Alspach. One of the bricks in the wall bears the following inscription: "Jonathan French, his hand write, June 18th, 1819."

Empire Mill
Built by John Chaney & Son in 1852
Destroyed by fire in 1895

CHAPTER VI
1815-1825

Not many persons settled in this township between 1815 and 1825. Several causes might be mentioned why so few came. The principal one was the lack of a profitable market for the surplus produce; the streams furnished the only available means of transportation. Only one attempt was made to reach New Orleans from this township, when in 1824 or 1825 George H. Stevenson built a flatboat and loaded it at Sharp's Mill, on Big Walnut Creek, with flour, meal and pork. Daniel Ross took the cargo down, arriving safely, but took the yellow fever and died there. Judge John Chaney assisted in loading this boat. During the War of 1812 prices had run up and times were good, but after peace had been declared and the government's purchases ceased, prices soon declined and no market could be found even at the extremely low prices which prevailed. Corn was 10 to 12 cents per bushel, wheat 20 to 25 cents, pork $1.50 per hundred. Many who had gone in debt could not meet back payments, so forced sales were the order of the day. Often not enough cash could be obtained to pay the taxes. Then a great deal of sickness prevailed, especially in 1823 and 1824, when a terrible epidemic of fevers and ague and chills raged. Nearly everybody was sick; often not enough well persons could be found in a neighborhood to care for the sick and bury the dead. The pioneers of those days referred especially to the summer and fall of 1823 as a most discouraging one. Among those who died in the township during these two seasons were: Billingsly Bull (a prominent citizen), Wm. Wright, Nicholas Hopkins, Edward Hathaway, John Todd, Henry Longwell, Elizabeth Bowman, Mrs. Adam Kramer, Greazy Harrison, Mrs. Thomas Featheringgill, Aaron Michael, Mrs. Wm. Seymour, Mrs. Elias Decker. Thomas Blakely, Mrs. Morgan Belford, Mrs. John Moore, Mrs. Daniel Rainier, Mrs. Isaac Lanning, Mrs. Isaac Decker, George A. Kelly, Mrs. John M. Thompson, Rebecca Rainier, and many others.

Capt. A. E. Lee, in his History of Columbus, quotes from Mrs. D. W. Deshler's letters to friends in Pennsylvania as follows:

"October 4, 1823.—The sickness of this county does not abate. The distress that the citizens of this State and of this western country, and

particularly this section of the State, labor under is unparalleled by anything I ever witnessed. This town (Columbus), and towns generally, have been awfully visited, and with such distress as I never wish to behold again, but at the same time nothing to compare with what has been endured in the thinly settled parts of the country. I could relate cases that would appear incredible and impossible, some of which are these: In one instance a mother was compelled to dig a grave and bury her own child in a box that was nailed up by herself, without one soul to assist her. Only think of it! Another case was that of a man, his wife and four children, who had settled three miles from any other house. The father, mother and all took sick, and not one was able to hand another a drink of water or make their situation known. At length a man in search of his horse happened at the house to inquire, and found a dead babe four days gone, in the cradle, the other children dying, the father insensible, and the mother unable to raise her head from the pillow.

In another family, ten in number, only a few miles from town, all were sick except two small children, who actually starved to death, being too small to go to a neighbor's, or prepare anything for themselves. In numbers of families all have died, not one member remaining.

A person a few days ago passed a house, a short distance from town, out of which they were just taking a corpse. One of the men told him there were three more to be buried the next morning, and a number sick in the same house. Such is the distress of our country that the farmers can do no plowing, nor gather their corn, potatoes, or anything else. You would be astonished to behold the faces of our citizens. There is not one, young or old, but that is of a dead yellow color. No kind of business is going on except making coffins and digging graves."

CHAPTER VII
TAX-PAYERS — 1825 - 1855 - 1872

"Who thinks that fortune cannot change her mind
Prepares a dreadful jest for all mankind."

— Pope

The following lists of the property owners in Madison Township reveals the names of many former residents that would not otherwise appear in this book. Besides a comparison of these lists with the present map of the township will furnish a fertile field for the sociological student on the fickleness of fortune.

Even the casual reader must notice how that one generation by a *"strenuous life"* accumulates a competence, only too often to be dissipated by the next.

While it is a lamentable fact that *"poverty often treads on the heels of riches."* there is also a brighter side to the picture — in the fact that an opportunity is thus afforded to the less fortunate, so that every young man or young woman who chooses may secure an estate.

The Spangler Homestead
Built by David Spangler in 1815

List of Chattel Tax Payers in 1825
Isaac Baker, John Baughman, Mary Bennett, Nathan Bennett, Jesse Blair, Samuel Blakely, Henry Bunn, James Barker, John Beard, Joshua

37

Burton, Samuel Bishop, Katherine Bull, R. Blakely, Geo. Bishop, John Blair, John Baker.

Thos. Caventer, Wm. Crossley, Anthony Crum, Wm. Clevenger, Abraham Craun, Peter Cupp, Isaac Craun, Oliver Codner, Emmer Cox, Chas. Chainey, Samuel Codner, John Craun, Chas. Cannon, Jacob Coble, Daniel Cams, Benj. Clevenger, Leven Culom, Jacob Chandler, Jacob Cazey, Joseph Cazey, Jasper Campbell, James Carson, John Chiles, Stewart Corner.

Harmon Dildine, Joseph Decker, Thos. Deacon, Elias Decker, Andrew Decker, James Daugherty, Isaac Decker, Mary Decker, Andrew Dildine, Henry Dildine, Elisha Decker, Ephraim Davidson, Jane Delong, James Decker, Geo. Dowing, Isaac Davis.

Thos. Elder, Wm. Elder, John Enslin, John English.

Thos. Featheringale, Nicholas Foor, Joseph Foor,. Henry Fouse, Jacob Feasel, Frederick Frutchey.

Zebulon Gibeson, Wm. Groom, John Groom, Thos. Groom, Ezekiel Groom, Wm. Goodman, Jacob Gander, John Gander, Daniel Gybby, Thos. Gray, John Guffy.

Adam Havely, Ann Hopkins, Jonathan Hertly, Mary Hughs, Walter Hughes, Philip Hooper, Samuel Hooper, Daniel Hetzell, John Hetzell, Philip Hetzell, John Huiston, Wm. D. Hendren.

John Kooper, John Kile, Wm. Kile, Daniel Kramer, Geo. Kramer, John Kramer, Wm. King, Philip King, David King, Truman King, Sarah King, Jacob Kesler, Geo. Kalb, Thos. Kilpatrick, Geo. Kalb, Jr., John Kalb.

Thos. Long, Peter Line, Zebulon Lee, Sarah Lee, Solomon Lee, Peter Long, Geo. Long, Peter Lirk (or Link), Zebulon Lee, Jr.

Chas. Medford, Daniel Miller, David McCracken, Robt. Mossman, Ebenezer Mitchell, Jacob McClain, Benj. Mullin.

John Needels, Thos. D. Needels, Philoman Needels, Uzzi Neckerson.

Fred Osstott, Thos. Pattrick, James Peter, Wm. Patterson, John Patterson, Sylvanus Parker, James Pearcy, Philip Pontius.

Jacob Ruse, Owen Roberts, Wm. Ramsey, Jacob Rind, Jr., Wm. Richardson, Fred Rower, Adam Rarey. Parker Rarey, Chas. Rarey, Jr., James Ramsey, James Ramsey, Jr., Samuel Ramsey, Jete Roads, Thos. Rathmell, Geo. Rohr, Benj. Rarey, Jacob Rind, Geo. Rarey, John Roads, Jacob Rush, John Rager, Wm. Ross, Chas. Rarey.

Home of John Rager

Jesse Seymour, Geo. Seymour, Abraham Shoemaker, Samuel Stroud, John B. Solomon, John L. Solomon, John Sharp, Adam Sarber, Mary Smith, Archibald Smith, David Smith, Ebenezer Smith, Wm. Smith, Elizabeth Smith, Christian Sarber, Richard Stephenson, John Swisher, John Stephenson, Zachariah Stephenson, Geo. Stephenson, John Schoonover, Henry Schoonover, Abraham Schoonover, Richard Suddick.

Isaac Tilburg (or Tilberry), A. C. Taber, Geo. Titler, Peter Titler, Wm. Toll, Deake Taylor, David Taylor, John Trump, Nicholas Tussing, John Taylor, Matthew Taylor, Benj. Todd, Katherine Todd.

Robt. Woolcoat, John Wright, Geo. Wood, John Wood, Geo. Wheeler, Thos. Wood, Robt. Wilson, Henry Whitzel, Joseph Whitzel, Samuel Whitman, Chas. Wood, Daniel Whitman, John Welton, Wm. Watson, Jacob Wender, John Winterstein, John A. White, Abraham Vorhis, John Vanoay, John Young.

Horses were taxed at $3.00 each, and cattle at $1.00 each. Houses were counted as chattel property and were taxed at the rate of $5.00 on the one hundred dollars valuation. The largest taxpayers were: Wm. Smith, $39.50; Wm. Elder, $36.50; Thos. Gray, $33.00; Wm. Richardson, $32.25; Emmer Cox, $30.75; John Kile, $30.00; Jacob Ruse, $28.00; Philomen Needels, $27.00; Chas. Rarey, Jr., $25.75.

The following houses with their value appear on the Franklin County auditor's books: Wm. Elder, $550; Wm. Smith, $450; Jacob Ruse, $220; Thos. Gray, $220; Henry Bunn, $175; Emmer Cox, $175; Katherine Bull, $150; R. Blakely, $150; Philip Pontius, $150; Henry Schoonover, $150; John Kile, $140; Philomen Needels, $140; Geo. Bishop, $125; Henry Dildine, $125; John Gander, $125; Wm. Richardson, $125; Daniel Cams, $112.50; Chas. Rarey, Jr., $115; Jesse Blair, $110; Harmon Dildine, $110; John and Geo. Wood, $110; and the following were lot owners in Oregon: John Blair, lots Nos. 28, 29, 30, 14 and east half of 13, valued at $112; Wm. Crossley, lots Nos. 47, 67, valued at $140; Isaac Decker, lots Nos. 1, 2, 3, 4, 5, 6, 7, 20, 26, 33, 46, 56, 60, 68, 71, valued at $650; Mary Decker lot No. 52, valued at $25; Joseph Foor, lot Nos. 51 and 65, valued at $150; A. C. Titler, lot Nos. 25, 54, 72, 81, valued at $275; Geo. Titler, lot Nos. 27, 31, 32, west 1/2 of 13, valued at $150; Peter Titler, lot No. 33, valued at $25; Wm. Foll, lot Nos. 53 and 63, valued at $100; Deake Decker, lot No. 55, valued at $25.

The Needels Homestead
From 1802 to 1812 five Needels brothers from Delaware settled in Madison Township. They were John, George, Philemon, Andrew and Cubbage.

The following eight persons owned ten or more horses and cattle:

Wm. Richardson, 5 horses and 11 cattle; John Kile, 5 horses and 8 cattle; Emmer Cox, 5 horses and 7 cattle; Philomen Needels, 4 horses and 8 cattle; Geo. Kalb, 3 horses and 9 cattle; Fred Rower, 4 horses and 7 cattle; Chas. Rarey, 4 horses and 7 cattle; Chas. Rarey, Jr., 5 horses and 5 cattle.

The following tax-payers lived in Fairfield County in territory now in Franklin County:

John Algire, Jacob Algire, Greenburg Ashley, Chas. Bowen, Thos. Bowen, Robt. Bowen, John Bannister, Ammon Butler, Francis Byerly, John Cramer, Philip Cramer, Adam Cramer, Michael Cramer, Jacob Coffield, James Cannon, John Coleman, Jr., Amos Davis, Henry Dove, Geo. Dove, Reuben Dove, Elisha Decker, Henry Fry, Stephen Glanville, Elizabeth Hathaway, Nancy Hathaway, Simon Helpman, Simon Hittman, Abraham Harris, John Hoff, Evan Hughes, Edward Hathaway, Barnibas Johnson, Ludwig Kramer, Andrew Love, Gersham Lee, Elisha McCracken, James Needels, Wm. Perrin, David Painter, Abraham Plummer, Peter Robinold, Wm. Stevenson, Geo. K. Stevenson, Moses Starr, Jacob Shoemaker, Henry Slife, John Slife, Ulrick Slife, Daniel Slife, John Swayzy, Sr., John Swayzy, Jr., John Tallman, Philip Zimmer and John Wolf.

Nathaniel Tallman
1810 - 1888

Dr. G. W. Blake, MD
1823 - 1877

LAND OWNERS 1855

**Home of William Whims
Built in 1849**

"List of the land owners in 1855" by sections, beginning at the northeast corner of the township:

Section **No. 6**, B. F. Mumach, Joseph Vandemark, John Wright, E. McCracken; **No. 1,** S. Hempy, M. Brown, J. N. Peters, Jonathan Ruse, Emanuel Ruse, George Needels, school house; **No. 2,** John Wright (occupied by H. Geese), George Needels (occupied by J. Swanger), John Wright (occupied by J. Docterman), H. Miller, J. A. Kile's heirs; **No. 3**, Jared Forsman, Truro Presbyterian Church, Dr. A. A. Shortt. Abraham Swisher's heirs, Mrs. M. Patterson, P. Shoemaker; **No. 4,** James Carson heirs. Alfred Gray (occupied by J. D. Goss, Matthew Brown, John McGuffey; **No. 5,** Thos. Gray, W. D. Needels (Cedar Grove Tavern). Philip Swartz (Cross Keys Tavern), M. Stack (shoeshop), J. Burkey; **No. 6.** J. A. Suddick, John Heil (school house). A. Magles, J. Clickenger's heirs, J. and W. E. Carson, J. Spangler (saw mill), Wm. Stout heirs, W. H. Chain, Geo. Moore; **No. 7**, Philip Helsel, Daniel Helsel heirs, Jacob Rohr, John Behm, Wm. Helsel heirs; **No. 8**, Wm. D. Needels, James Needels, John A. Needels, John Helsel, Wm. H. Helsel, Jacob Rohr, Joseph Burkey's heirs; **No. 9**, Thos. Needels (White Chapel Church), J. A. Kiles heirs, Widow Winterstein, Wm. D. Needles, John M. McGuffey, Joseph Needels; **No. 10**, Rev. Jacob Bowman, John McGuffey, Wm. Whims, J. L.

42

Stevenson, Thos. Needels; **No. 11,** Wm. Leidey, Jacob Bowman, Isaac Kalb, Jerry Kalb, J. A. Kiles heirs. Wm. Whims, N. A. Stevenson; **No. 12,** Wm. Wildermuth, N. Algire, John Wright (Res.), Samuel Detwiler, Isaac Kalb; **No. 7,** W. K. Algire, M. J. Stevenson, S. Algire, J. Algire, Wm. Perrin, A. B. Stevenson; **No. 18,** A. B. Stevenson, J. E. Stevenson (grave yard, removed to Union Grove), Daniel Bush, M. G. Stevenson, John Good, G. Harpst; **No. 13,** John Wright, Joshua Stevenson, Peter Bott, Andrew Whims, John Alspach, Pitts Brown heirs; **No. 14,** Geo. W. Kalb, Huffman and Ferguson (school house), N. A. Stevenson, J. S. Stevenson, Jeremiah Kissel, John Kelchner, James Needels; **No. 15,** J. L. Stevenson, A. Whims, W. S. Hopkins, T. Needels, John Cable, Thos. Patterson, Oliver Codner, J. A. Kiles heirs, Fred Swisher; **No. 16,** owned by township school board (occupied, northeast quarter by_____; southeast quarter by S. Jobs, northeast quarter by J. Arnold, southwest quarter by Augustus Sallee; **No. 17,** Frederick Rarey, T. J. Bennett, A. and J. Swisher, J. W. Kile's heirs; David Sarber, J. G. Edwards; **No. 18,** Geo. Fisher, John G. Edwards, J. Spangler, Dr. J. P. Bywaters, John Swisher: **No. 19,** Geo. H. Earhart, R. A. Kile's heirs. John Sharp heirs, S. E. H. Kile, Henry Whetzel heirs; **No. 20,** T. C. Hendren (school house), Robert Hendren, Kalita Sallee, D. Wagner, W. Wildermuth, H. Whetzel. Jr. (school house); **No. 21,** Fred Swisher (saw mill), David Whetzel, C. W. Rarey, W. H. Rarey, Wm. McCormick, Jacob H. Rees; **No. 22,** Henry Kramer, Jesse Dildine, O. Codner, Jr., Thos. C. Hendren, Joseph Dildine; **No. 23,** Pitts Brown heirs, P. Tussing, James T. Peircy's heirs, James Needels, L. C. Henderson, Jacob Hornung, Moses Seymour; **No. 24,** John R. Wright, Nathaniel Tallman, Abraham Lehman, Geo. Hoffman (Mennonite Church), Geo. T. Wheeler, Samuel Wheeler; **No. 19,** David Kramer, Emanuel Sparr, Chas. Brown, N. Tallman; **No. 30,** John Kramer, town of Winchester, A. Lehman, Samuel Bartlitt, Samuel Deitz (graveyard), C. Dellinger, Abe Hunsicker; **No. 25,** A. Lehman, Peter Bott, John Chaney and son (Empire Mills), E. B. Decker, Jacob Sarber, John Chaney (school house, woolen mill and lock house), Rev. H. Hendren, W. Mason heirs, Abe Harris, Wm. Smith heirs, Jane Smith; **No. 26,** John Rager (saw mill), John Seymour, Moses Seymour, Jesse Seymour (school house); **No. 27,** Jesse Dildine, T. D. Dildine, Babcock & Co., Wm. Seymour, Jacob Dildine, Frederick Heffinger, H. Dildine, Wm. T. Decker; **No. 28,** town of Groveport, W. H. Rarey, W. T. Decker (graveyard), Abraham Sharp (Baptist Church, toll gate), Samuel Sharp, Lewis Shirey; **No. 29,** James

Needles, Thos. Blakely, A. Sharp, Samuel Sharp, Joseph Sharp heirs; **No. 30,** Jacob Arnold, Wesley Toy, John Cox (surveyor), Henry Whetzel heirs; **No. 31,** Wesley Toy, L. Rarey, Wm. Neil & Co., John Cox (occupied by H. J. Cox), M. Groom, Frederick Bunn (occupied by Cook), McBride, Sheldon & Co., Wm. Rohr; **No. 32**, Samuel Sharp, Parker Rarey, Moses Seymour, A. Sharp; **No. 33,** Wm. T. Decker, Joseph Sharp heirs, L. Rarey, Parker Rarey; **No. 34,** Wm. Seymour, Wm. T. Decker, Solomon Woodring, Samuel Leigh (school house); **No. 35**, John Seymour, Samuel O. Hendren, Wm. Seymour, Solomon Woodring, H. Dildine; **No. 36,** John Deitz, H. Dellinger heirs, Abraham Harris, G. Ordell heirs, J. Seymour, S. O. Hendren (graveyard); **No. 31,** John Colman, John Schrock, Philip Zimmer, Lewis Kramer (graveyard), Samuel Deitz, John Deitz, Geo. Fisher (grist and saw mill), Geo. Kramer; **No. 1,** Daniel Crouse, A. Johns, Wm. Peer, J. Bishop, town of Oregon, (school house), C. P. Dildine, H. Strode heirs, Solomon and Geo. S. Dildine; **No. 2,** Henry Dildine, C. P. Dildine, M. Welton (graveyard); **No. 3,** Daniel Leigh, Morgan Sorrel, Jesse Welton heirs,. Cornelius Black, Thomas Black, Adam Havely; **No. 4,** V. E. Vogle, A. Rarey, Parker Rarey, Edward Gares (graveyard), Charles Pontius, Adam Havely; **No. 5,** W. H. Bishop (wagon shop), Ed. Gares, Casper Limpert, Dr. G. L. Smith, Charles Pontius, W. H. Pyle (school house), Frederick Bunns (blacksmith shop); **No. 6,** Chas. Rohr, Geo. Rohr, Milton Fink's heirs; **No. 7,** E. E. Groom, Fred Bunn, W. H. Harrison, Elias Shook, Joseph Wright; **No. 8,** Fred Bunn, Charles Pontius, Henry Long, Moses Groom, J. Miller, Samuel Murphy, A. L. Perrill; **No. 9,** Thos. Groom (Hopewell Church and graveyard), J. Sawyer, Chas. Pontius, Mrs. Groom's heirs; **No. 10,** S. M. C. Gibby, John Seymour, Harmon Dildine,. L. Ramsey heirs; **No. 11,** S. M. C. Gibby, Rev. Samuel Wilson, Joseph Decker, J. Welton; **No. 12,** John Bacher, John Blackwood, George Long (school house).

The following is a list of persons owning two hundred or more acres of land in Madison Township in 1855. The figures give the number of acres:

Samuel Sharp, 700; John Wright, 680; Wm. T. Decker, 602: Joseph Burkey, 552; Frederick Bunn, 548; Chas. Pontius, 536: John Seymour, 496; Henry Dildine, 420; Thos. Groom, 375; Samuel O. Hendren,. 356; Jared Forsman, 350; Harmon Dildine, 340; Nathaniel Tallman, 337; John M. McGuffey, 334: George Long, 320: Milton Fink heirs, 316; Wm. Seymour, 312; Parker Rarey, 312; Moses Seymour, 296; C. P. Dildine,

289; Joseph Sharp heirs, 278; W. D. Needels, 276 1/2; Geo. Needels, 273; Wm. Whims, 269; John G. Edwards, 262; Abraham Swisher heirs, 260; Adam Havely, 254; Philip Helsel, 243; Thos. Needels, 240: Abraham Lehman, 238; S. M. C. Gibby, 226; John Sharp heirs, 225; John Bacher, 220; Samuel Leigh, 220: L. Rarey, 220; Thos. Gray, 217; J. A. Kile heirs, 216; Solomon Woodring, 210; Jesse Dildine, 208; Joseph Dildine, 207; Samuel Detwiler, 200; Elihu McCracken, 194: Abraham Sharp, 191.

Land owners in 1872

Beginning at the northeast corner of the township:

Section **No. 6**, S. Hempy, G. French, J. Dovel, A. French, A. M. Selby, J. W. Wingert, John Wright, J. R. Vandemark, H. Algire, Mrs. R. Holbert and E. McCracken; section **No. 1,** S. Hempy, J. O'Roark, D. Motts, Geo. King, G. W. Groves, J. W. Peters, E. Ruse, G. W. Ruse, and Geo. Needels; section **No. 2,** John Wright, J. M. Montgomery, H. Miller, and Geo. Needels; section **No. 3,** Zadok Vesey, Truro Presbyterian church, S. A. Needels and Wm. Purely; section **No. 4,** R. E. & S. Brown, J. S. Carson, Mrs. M. E. Whetzel, M. Brown, Alfred Gray, John McGuffey, L. Spencer and Wm. Baird; section **No. 5,** C. H. Gray, R. S. Gray, M. A. Gray, S. H. Whims, Philip Swartz, Lewis Schleppi, M. Barrett, V. Zimmer, F. Spangler, J. R. Leasure, Wm. Baird and Peter E. Swartz; section **No. 6,** Lewis Schleppi, Philip Swartz, John Heil, C. Maley, Alex. Clickenger, Robert Scott, J. Burkey, Peter E. Swartz, H. J. Schleppi, D. Spangler, J. Spangler and Geo. Moore; section **No. 7,** Joseph Behm, G. W. Helsel, John Behm, Adam Helsel, M. V. Weber, I. Worthington, T. Helsel, A. Rohr, and Elias Johnson; section **No. 8,** A. J. Taylor, Behm heirs, M. A. Needels, S. R. Helsel, Jacob Rohr, guardian, J. A. Needels, Jacob Rohr, and M. Rohr heirs; section **No. 9,** Geo. W. Needels, R. J. Needels, Asbury Church, John McGuffey, Mrs. S. A. Kile, J. W. Kile, Mrs. S. A. Needels, A. T. Brown, and L. J. Needels; section **No. 10,** Jacob Bowman, Wm. Whims, Almira Needels, Sarah Ann Needels, and Mrs. M. B. Stevenson; section **No. 11,** Wm. Leidy, Jacob L. Bowman, J. Leidy, Geo. Needels, H. Miller, Jacob Bowman, I. Kalb's heirs, Jerry Kalb, Wm. Whims and N. A. Stevenson; section **No. 12,** A. K. Whims, Samuel Detwiler, John Wright and I. Kalb's heirs; section **No. 7**, W. K. Alkire, S. H. Whims, James Pickering, James Lawrence, and A. Bowman; section **No. 18,** James Lawrence, I. E.

Stevenson, Jacob Bowman, Chas. and Amos Bush and Noah Lehman; section **No. 13,** John Wright, S. Kramer, A. Alspaugh, John Alspaugh, A. B. Stevenson, Sam and Joe Lehman, John S. Lehman, and Samuel Shoemaker; section **No. 14,** Geo. W. Kalb, N. A. Stevenson, J. S. Stevenson, John Courtright, Chaney & Decker, Jacob Bachman, and Chas. Weber; section **No. 15,** Wm. Kramer, Mrs. M. B. Stevenson, Thomas Patterson, O. Codner heirs, Jacob Coble, Mrs. A. Codner, Israel Swisher and Fred Swisher; section **No. 16,** school section, occupied by Sylvester Carruthers, H. C. Swisher, Albert Young and J. W. Cromwell; section **No. 17,** F. Rarey, R. Hendren, G. H. Kalies, John G. Edwards, Mrs. M. Kile, Wm. Wildermuth and B. Hendren; section **No. 18,** John G. Edwards, C. L. Emde, L. Emde, Edwards Station, L. Merle, and Geo. L. Converse; section **No. 19,** W. K. Cox, S. E. H. Kile, W. P. Sharp, John Nau, Mrs. T. S. Doherty, John F. Kile, Robt. A. Kile, and Henry Obetz; section **No. 20,** T. C. Hendren heirs, A. T. Hendren, R. A. Kile, Wm. Wildermuth, Kalita Sallee and Jacob Stoutzenbarger; section **No. 21.** Frederick Swisher, H. C. Swisher, W. H. Rarey, Frederick Rarey, D. Whetzel and Wm. Vance; section No. 22, Eliza McGuffey, B. C. Sims, J. T. Simms, Oliver Codner heirs, A. T. Hendren, S. E. Hendren, Thos. Fagan, J. W. Simms, P. W. Simms, Robt. F. Dildine, Frederick Swisher, Belinda Simms, W. H. Rager, and Mrs. C. Zinn; section **No. 23,** David Martin, Jacob Bachman, Jeff Mosier, John Wright, Philip C. Tussing, and Wm. M. Simms; section **No. 24,** Isaac Lehman, Mennonite Church, L. Shoemaker, David Martin, P. Bond, toll gate, Geo. T. Wheeler, John Rohr, Jr., and Samuel Wheeler; section **No. 19,** Henry W. Shaffer, Mrs. T. Sparr, Mrs. C. Warner, Adam Warner, Lovina Brown, Mrs. Mary Brown, John Brown, Wm. Brown and Nathaniel Tallman; section **No. 30,** Jacob Moore, John Kramer, Abraham Lehman, Canal Winchester, E. B. Decker, Samuel Bartlitt and Samuel Deitz; section **No. 25,** Samuel Wheeler, Simon Alspach, O. P. Chaney, Joseph Burgoon, J. and J. Rodenfels Empire Mills, C. Doss, John Chaney Woolen Factory, John Rager, Robert Thrush, Peter Brown and Chaney, Decker & Co.; section No. 26, John Rager, Mrs. F. L. Wilson, Moses Seymour and Wm. and M. Seymour; section **No. 27,** R. F. Dildine, A. McCoy, Madison Township fair grounds, M. Corbett, M. Zinn, G. L. Smith, W. P. Seymour, Mrs. R. Seymour, Mrs. M. Jones and Wm. T. Decker; section **No. 28,** M. Corbett, Groveport, A. S. and N. S. McCormick, A. Sharp, S. Alspach, Z. C. Payne, Mrs. M. Jones, Wm. T. Decker, Joseph Smith and Wm. H. Rarey; section

No. 29, J. Watson, G. Kentz, Thos. Blakely, C. F. Needels, J. Nau, Adaline Woods, D. C. Weaver, Joseph Smith, Wm. Hanstine, W. Salzgaber, C. Salzgaber, and A. Sharp; section No. 30, T. P. Arnold, John Cox, Wesley Toy's heirs, J. E. Swisher and Wm. McClish; section No. 31, Wesley Toy's heirs, Stephen Smith, Sarah E. Harris, Thos. Fagan, Absalom Rohr and Lewis Bunn; section No. 32, A. Sharp, Joe Smith, J. G. Sharp, Thos. Fagan, G. Rarey, H. Rarey, Smith & Gould, Mrs. S. Rarey, J. Cheeseman and Wm. H. McCarty; section No. 33, Wm. T. Decker, Joseph Smith, Rarey heirs, G. Rarey and Hunter Rarey; section No. 34, W. Seymour, J. Anderix, Wm. T. Decker, Fred Klamforth, and Samuel Leigh; section No. 35, Andrew Wilson, Samuel O. Hendren, Mrs. E. Seymour, Thos. Seymour, R. Seymour, W. Seymour, Jas. D. and P. Decker and Samuel S. Christ; section No. 36, Elisha B. Decker, Chaney, Decker & Co., Phil. C. Harris, L. Alspach, M. Beglin, P. J. Dill and Elias Decker; section No. 31, John R. Wright, M. E. Schrock, Samuel Deitz, E. J. Davidson, Jacob Sarber, Henry Arnold, Daniel Bergstresser, B. F. Ashbrook and A. Bruns; section No. 1, David Crouse, P. J. Dill, Aug. Sallee, Oregon, Elias Decker, P. & E. McCarty, Milton Cummins, Jacob Bishop, Geo. W. Lisle and E. Smith; section No. 2, Elias Decker, F. Dildine, C. P. Dildine, G. W. Lisle, M. F. Sites and Josiah Flattery; section No. 3, Daniel Leigh, A. B. Rarey, C. Black, Thomas Black, Adam Havely, G. S. Dildine, J. A. Bigelow and Wm. Peer; section No. 4, S. Sharp, M. A. Kelley, Hunter Rarey, C. L. Pontius, Chas. Pontius, and H. R. Rarey; section No. 5, W. H. Bishop, G. L. Smith, R. Rarey, F. G. Pontius, and Phil. Pontius; section No. 6, Chas. Rohr, John Rohr, John Lincoln, I. Huddle, Hannah Wolf, Wm. H. McCarty, and A. Sawyers; section No. 7, J. L. Bunn, E. Groome, Samuel Stewart, T. M. Murphy, W. H. Harrison, and J. Wright's heirs; section No. 8, Chas. Pontius, J. L. Bunn, N. H. Bunn, Phil. Pontius, M. H. Kelly, H. Long, S. Murphy, F. Miller and A. L. Perrell; section No. 9, Thomas Groom, Chas. Pontius, Mrs. C. Sawyer, Hopewell M. E. Church and Philip Pontius; section No. 10, Geo. Seymour, Chaney Decker & Co., Daniel Leigh and A. B. Rarey; section No. 11, Wm. Whaley, Miss J. Welton, Geo. Long, P. S. Long, Nathan Whaley, and Chaney, Decker & Co.; section No. 12. Jeremiah Runkle, Samuel Runkle, Geo. Long, and John Blackwood.

John M. Blackwood
1815 - 1881
Invented a cornplanter in 1855 and
manufactured them in Lithopolis.

The following owned a quarter section or more in 1872:

John Wright, 819 acres; Chaney, Decker & Co., 640; E. B. Decker, 160; Madison Township school section, 640; Zadok Vessy, 572; Wm. T. Decker, 530; John G. Edwards, 522; Wm. Whims, 448; A. B. Rarey, 411; Thomas Groome, 374; George Needels, 367; Joseph Smith, 353; Abram Sharp, 332; Geo. L. Converse, 334; N. Tallman, 328; Elias Decker, 323; George Long, 320; James Lawrence, 300; Jacob Bowman, 297; Samuel O. Hendren, 280; John McGuffey, 261; Mrs. M. B. Stevenson, 256; Wm. Wildermuth, 251; Peter E. Swartz, 246; Chas. Rohr, 245; David Martin, 231; G. L. Smith, 219; Samuel Leigh, 220; John Rager, 210; Samuel Deitz, 209; Jacob Rohr, 209; Wesley Toy heirs, 205; Mr. and Mrs. Andrew Wilson, 201; Frederick Swisher, 200; Moses Seymour, 200; William Peer, 200; S. R. Helsel, 200; Jacob Coble, 200; Chas. Pontius, 193; Wm. H. Rarey, 192; Samuel Detwiler, 190; F. G. Pontius, 190; Philip Pontius, 192: Elihu McCracken, 189; S. H. Whims, 187; John Behm, 182; Jacob Bishop, 182; J. P. Arnold, 180; Geo. W. Lisle, 176; A. K. Whims, 171; Abraham Lehman heirs, 170; Thos. Fagan, 168; W. K.

Algire, 165; W. H. McCarty, 164; J. L. Bunn, 167; Samuel Wheeler, 160; John Courtright, 160; and Mrs. M. Jones, 160.

John Courtright
1838 - 1917

CHAPTER VIII
BRIGHTER DAYS
OHIO AND ERIE CANAL

"Life on the Erie canal
A home on the tow path side.
Where the boats go up and down
Sailing against the tide,
Our boat's an hundred feet long,
With the rudder hitched on behind,
Our crew consists of a man
And a mule that's almost blind.
And when we want to stop
I'll tell you how we do —
We all catch hold of the hinder rope
And call out Whoa! ho! ho!
And call out Whoa! ho! ho!"

— From an old song.

Ice Skating on the canal at Canal Winchester

The legislation regarding the Ohio and Erie Canal is entirely too voluminous to find a place in this volume; we could not, however, resist giving space to some extracts which in a measure reveal some of the advantages sought and some of the difficulties to be overcome.

Governor Ethan A. Brown said in his inaugural address, December 14, 1818; *"If we would raise the character of our state by increasing industry and our resources it seems necessary to improve the internal communications, and to open a cheaper way to market for the surplus produce of a large portion of our fertile country."*

On January 7, 1819, the following resolution was introduced in the Ohio legislature: *"That a committee be appointed to take into consideration the construction of a canal connecting the waters that flow into Lake Erie with those that flow into the Ohio River; that said committee be instructed to inquire into the expediency of authorizing the governor to procure one or more skillful engineers for the purpose of exploring and ascertaining the most eligible route for the foundation of said canal."*

In his message January 8, 1819, Governor Brown said: *"You will bear in mind that our productions which form our only great resources are generally of that bulky and ponderous description, as to need every easement in conveyance that we can afford. I have already evinced an anxiety on this subject, excited by a strong sense of its vital importance. Roads and canals are veins and arteries to the body politic. that diffuse supplies, health, vigor and animation to the whole system. Nature strongly invites us; the aspect of the face of this state announces capabilities for the grand object in question, exceeded. I presume, by few regions of the same extent."*

Again, in his message of December 7, 1819, he says; *"I hope for your indulgence, in pressing upon you a subject of so great and general interest to the state. Your observation must have perceived that our principal obstruction to the removal of the commercial distress consists in the cost and difficulty of transporting to market those productions which constitute our great and almost only resource, for regaining and preserving the balance of trade. My conviction of the usefulness of obtaining the information and estimates, which skill and experience can impart induces me to request that the measure recommended last season, of appointing a civil engineer, may again be considered."*

Under date of January 20. 1820, according to a resolution of the House passed on January 14, Governor Brown submitted a very comprehensive document to the legislature, embodying a description of the general features of the territory lying between Lake Erie and the Ohio River, an estimate of the cost of construction and maintenance, and a plan by which the expense could be met: this later proposition provided that either the State of Ohio should purchase from Congress four million acres of land at $1.50 per acre adjoining the route of the proposed canal which it was thought could be readily sold for $3.00 or more per acre after the canal was once in operation, or, second, that Congress should be asked *"to cede two sections to the state, retaining every third section, with the understanding that the state complete the canals, when Congress would be reimbursed by the advanced price which would be obtained for the sections retained."*

January 31, 1822, "an act" was passed, authorizing the governor to appoint an engineer to make surveys of the county between Lake Erie and the Ohio River, and a canal commission was appointed.

Almost every section of the state was anxious that the canal should be located for its convenience, and this condition made the choice of an engineer — who was expected to have considerable influence in locating the route — an important matter; James Geddes of New York State was appointed and made a preliminary survey during the summer of 1822 and reported the result to the Legislature under date of January 4, 1823. The Canal Commissioners were then authorized to secure "rights of way," grants of land, and subscriptions in aid of the canals, and to ascertain whether loans of money could be made. Little progress was made by the surveyors during the season of 1823 on account of the prevailing sickness, mention of which is made elsewhere in this volume.

Under the date of January 24, 1824, the commissioners say: *"It was found impossible to keep an engineer's party together for active service, on account of the sickliness of the season,"* and *"Few of the surveying parties were able to preserve their health or continue their services for more than a week at a time."*

February 24, 1825, "An Act" passed the Legislature authorizing the Canal Commissioners to *"Commence and prosecute the making of a navigable canal on the Muskingum and Scioto route, so called, from the Ohio River at or near the mouth of the Scioto River, by the way of the*

Licking Summit and the Muskingum River to Lake Erie, commencing at the Licking Summit."

Thirty-four members of the Senate voted yea, and only two voted nay; fifty-eight members of the House voted yea, and 13 voted nay. The first shovel full of earth was dug up by Governor DeWitt Clinton of New York on July 4, 1825, at the place designated — Licking Summit.

The following advertisement, which explains itself, appeared in the *Civil Engineer and Herald of Internal Improvement,* a weekly published by John Kilbourne at Columbus, October 11, 1828: *"Ohio Canal proposals will be received on the 14th day of November next, at Lancaster, for the construction of forty-three miles of canal, lying between the Licking Summit and Circleville. Twenty-eight to thirty locks, with two aqueducts and a dam across Walnut Creek are included in the work to be let. Bidders, who are unknown as contractors to the acting commissioner, will be expected to accompany their propositions with recommendations of a substantial and unquestionable character. Plans and specifications of the work may be seen at the office in Lancaster at any time after the 10th of November.*

M. T. Williams, Acting Commissioner, October 10, 1828."

The following are among the most interesting local proposals: *"Section No. 54 is on my enclosed field, therefore I claim the right to it if I think proper at such bid lower than my own. — Adam Rarey."*

"Section No. 52 being mostly on my land, I claim my proprietary right of taking it at the lowest responsible bid, if I should wish to do so.—W. H. Richardson."

"Section No. 43 being on my own land, I will undertake it at the lowest responsible bid, and will be gratified if the job shall be awarded to me at a fair price, as it would be pleasanter to me on my account.— Abraham Harrison."

The above proposition was accompanied by a letter of recommendation from Jacob Claypole,

"Micagal T. Williams, Esq.—Sir: A good part of section No. 42 being on my land, it would be desirable for me to have the job. I therefore offer to complete said section including all the work thereon at the lowest responsible bid. Given under my hand, this 14th day of November, 1828.—Reuben Dove."

"Section No. 36, I want to take through my own land at a responsible bid, but not bound.—Samuel Loucks."

The sections varied in length according to the amount of labor required. The contracts contained a description of the various kinds of work to be done and the stipulated price of each item. For instance, the bid of W. H. Richardson on section No. 52. Grubbing, $3.00 per chain: excavation, 8c per yard; solid rock, 75c; detached rock, 25c; embankment, 10c; excavation for lock and culvert, 20c; stone work, per perch, $4.00; puddling culvert, 20c. We were unable to find a bid, or contract, other than that of Mr. Dove's, on section No. 42, but according to common report J. L. Vance had the contract. Abbott, Abbott & Sherlock had Nos. 43, 45, 58, 62 and 63, for which they received $8,921.82; Samuel, James G. Samuel, Jr., and Wm. G. Hand had sections Nos. 44, 47 and 48 for $17,490.67; Daniel B. McConnell, Elias S. Cunningham, Edward Lewis and Edward Byers had section No. 46 at $5,477.34; Jacob L. Vance had section No. 49 for $3,005.27. The proposition for section No. 49 was written in Egyptian characters. W. H. Richardson had sections Nos. 51 and 52 for $2,937.83 ; Wm. Love & Loy had sections Nos. 53, 71 and 74; they got $2,920.99 for section No. 53; F. Cunningham, Wm. Bland, Thos. Perkins and Andrew Green had section No. 54—through Groveport—for $1,595.77. Adam Rarey's bid for the bridge across the canal on Main Street, Groveport, was $200.00. This bridge was exactly 214 miles from Cleveland. Wm. Butt had sections Nos. 55 and 56 for $3,869.33. Jacob L. Vance and Thomas Gray had section No. 57 for $1,867.71. Thaddeus Williams, Mathew Clark, Aaron Clark and Jonathan Foster had sections Nos. 59 and 60. Joseph Fassett and Lucius Mower had sections Nos. 64, 65, 67, 68 and 69 for $47,015.90. A. Smith and John Patterson had section No. 66. Sections Nos. 44, 46, 47 and 48 had locks; these were first built of stone quarried in the neighborhood of Lithopolis, and were rebuilt in 1846 to 1852 with stone brought from the Hocking Valley. The locks are numbered—beginning west of Winchester (Chaney's Mill), Nos. 19, 20 (Woolen Factory) No. 21, and east of Groveport No. 22. Nos. 19 and 22 were rebuilt in 1845-46.

Lock No. 20
About 1 mile west of Winchester in 1896

The Canal Commissioners in their annual report, under date of January 11, 1832, after referring to the State Dam across Little Walnut Creek, say:

"About five miles below this point the canal receives water from Rager's Run feeder three-fourth of a mile in length; and through the same feeder from Blacklick, a branch of Big Belly Creek, the waters of which are thrown into Rager's Run by a cheap and shallow cut. This feeder is a valuable acquisition to the canal." Nathaniel Bray built this feeder in the summer of 1832 for $735.30. It was only used a few years when it was abandoned.

Traces of a trench dug through a portion of the farm now occupied by Thomas Lowe—being the northwest quarter of section No. 26 —are still plainly visible. It was the intention to follow the bank along the south side of the Winchester and Groveport Road. After the work was begun a change was made and the canal bed located farther north.

The following extracts from *Form of Agreement* set forth the essential features of the specifications for the building of the canals:

"First, in all places where the natural surface of the earth is above the bottom of the canal, and where the line requires excavation, all the trees, saplings, bushes, stumps and roots shall be grubbed and dug up at

56

least sixty feet wide; that is thirty-three feet on the towing path side of the center, and twenty-seven feet wide on the opposite side of the center of the canal, and together with logs, brush and wood of every description shall be removed at least fifteen feet beyond the outward line of the said grubbing on each side; and on said space of fifteen feet on each side of said grubbing, all trees, saplings, bushes and stumps shall be cut down close to the ground, so that no part of any of them shall be left more than one foot in height above the natural surface of the earth, and shall also, together with all logs, brush and wood of every kind, be removed entirely from said space.

Second: The canal and banks shall be so constructed and formed, by excavation and embankment, as either or both shall be necessary, in order to bring the same to the proper level, so that the water may in all places be at least forty feet wide in the canal at the surface, twenty-six feet wide at the bottom, and four feet deep; each of the banks shall be at least two feet, perpendicular measurement, above the top water line; and such a slope shall be preserved on the inner side of the banks, both above and below the top water line, that every foot perpendicular rise in said bank shall give a horizontal base of one foot nine inches; the towing path shall be at least ten feet wide at its surface, and not more than five feet in any place above the top water line; and whenever a difference in the elevation of the towing path shall occur, the ascent or descent shall not be greater than one foot rise or fall in sixty feet in length, and shall be gradual; the towing path shall be smooth and even and shall be so constructed that the side next to the canal will be six inches higher than the opposite side, at the surface, with an uniform and regular slope, so that the water may run off from said path; the bank opposite the towing bank shall in no place be less than five feet wide at the surface; and neither of said banks shall have a slope of lesser base in proportion to its height on the outer than on the inner side, except where there is a redundance of stuff increasing the width of the bank beyond the requisition aforesaid.

Third: In all cases of embankment, where the bottom line of canal is above the natural surface of the earth, all the trees, bushes, saplings and stumps, on the space occupied by the canal and its banks, shall be cut close to the ground, and, together with all logs, brush and wood of every description, shall be removed from a space of at least forty-five feet wide on each side of the center of the canal; and from a strip fifteen feet wide

57

under each bank to be so situated that the inner side of said strip shall be perpendicularly under the outer extremity of the top water line, all the trees, bushes, stumps and roots shall be thoroughly grubbed, and, together with all logs, brush, roots, grass, herbage, vegetable and porous earth, shall be removed entirely without said banks, so that the banks may unite securely with the solid earth beneath.

Fourth: The locks shall be constructed so that the chamber will be 90 feet in length and 15 feet in breadth in the clear. The walls of the lock shall be of solid masonry laid in water cement, and well grouted with water cement. The walls shall be five feet in thickness at the bottom of the lock and four feet at the top water line of the upper canal. Buttresses shall be so built that 20 feet in length of the walls opposite the upper gates, and 17 feet in length opposite the lower lock gates shall be 9 feet thick at the bottom and 8 feet at the top water line. The foundation of the lock, unless a smooth and firm rock foundation can be obtained, shall be composed of solid white oak timber, hewed square, and one foot in thickness, to be laid horizontally across the foundation, level and even, and covered with three inch white oak or pine plank, free from knots, rots or shakes, well jointed and firmly trunneled or spiked to the timber beneath; a flooring composed of two-inch white oak or pine plank, free from knots, rot or shakes, well jointed and securely spiked with spikes ten inches in length, shall be laid throughout the whole chamber of the lock."

When active work began on the construction of the Ohio and Erie Canal in 1829, times at once began to get better; many of the settlers worked on the excavations and thus secured ready cash with which to pay their taxes and other necessary expenses. Wages were $8.00 per month, or 30 3/4 cents and two jiggers* of whiskey per day; a day was from sun to sun. The immediate demand and the prospect of an early outlet for the surplus produce attracted many settlers. Wheat advanced from 25 cents to $1.00 per bushel, and other produce in like ratio. From this time on the township has made a steady and prosperous growth. The Canal Commissioners announced that the canal from Newark to Columbus and Circleville was opened for navigation on September 25, 1831. The first canal boat passed through on a Saturday night, and the next two on the following Sunday forenoon. People come from ten to fifteen miles to see the first boats pass, and gathered in large crowds along the banks; especially is this true of a point where the Middletown road crosses the canal, just east of lock No. 20. Early in the morning they began to gather; the scene is described by the late John R. Wright as resembling a camp-meeting in the size of the crowd in their holiday attire. A brass band of music from Lancaster accompanied the second boat, and it is related by the late Geo. P. Champe that when the first sounds of the music was heard the crowds would shout, "The boat is coming!" and then the words would be taken up by other crowds further down, all followed by a general movement towards the east to meet the boat. Happy the man or woman who was fortunate enough to get passage on this swift-flying (?) craft.

* A Jigger was approximately 1.5 oz. BPC

A party of workmen wintered some sixty head of oxen on the farm now occupied by David Martin, having purchased the corn crop in the shock. They slept in a log-cabin nearby and boarded with Joseph Wright, who lived in a log house that stood where Isaac Lehman's substantial residence now stands. These workmen are spoken of as a jolly set of Irishmen, when sober.

"'An Act" to regulate the navigation and collection of tolls on the canals" was passed February 23, 1830, and contained 78 sections. We quote a few of the regulations:

"No float shall move faster than four miles an hour."

"When a boat or other float shall overtake any other boat or float, it shall be the duty of the master of the latter to turn from the towing path, and give the former every facility for passing."

"When any float shall meet any other float, passing in an opposite direction, it shall be the duty of each to turn to the right side of the center of the canal, and the moving power of the boat which shall turn from the towing path shall be stopped so as to allow the moving power of the other float to pass freely over the towing rope."

"If, on the arrival of any two or more floats, at any lock, a question shall arise as to which shall be first entitled to pass, such question shall be determined by the lock-keeper."

"The owner of every boat shall subscribe and deliver to the collector of whom the first clearance shall be demanded a certificate to be entitled

a 'Certificate of Registry,' containing the name and place of abode of such owner."

"Every owner of a boat who shall change its name from that stated in the certificate of registry, without the written consent of the collector shall, for every such offence, forfeit the sum of twenty dollars."

"No boat shall receive a clearance, or be permitted to pass on either of the canals, unless such boat shall have the name thereof and place where it is owned, painted in some conspicuous part of the outside of the boat, in letters of at least four inches in height."

Rates of toll per ton per mile of various articles: "Flour, wheat, etc., 1 1/2 c; corn, oats, rye, etc., whether ground or unground, 1c; mineral, coal and iron ore, 1/2 c; boards, planks, timbers, etc., per 1,000 feet per mile, 1c; posts, rails, etc., per 1,000 per mile, 2c; boats used chiefly for freight per mile 2c; each passenger, conveyed in any boat, per mile, 1/2 c."

All the boats at first carried passengers. The following is a list of some of the more familiar names of canal boats:

Cincinnati, Red Rover, Lady Jane (these were the first three to pass through this township, and arrived in Columbus on September 25, 1831), *Rockingham, Iola, Searcher, Storm, Eureka, Robin, Chute, Crescent, Danube, Hurricane, Akron, Miami, Boone, Express, Mendon, Josephine, Carlisle, Washington, Henrietta, Antelope, Buckeye, Pirate, Superior, Laurel, Ben Bolt, Ellen, Empire Mills, St. Paul, Embassy, Gallant, St. Louis, L. B. Curtis, Emigrant, Indiana, David Dixon, T. A. Walton, M. M. Greene, Viola, Dick Gorham, Arrow* (this was the name of one of the packet boats). The *U. S. Grant* was the last boat built at the Groveport dry docks. Many of the boat captains would take a load of wheat or corn to Cleveland or Portsmouth and then purchase a boat load of staple merchandise, which they sold to the merchants along the canal on the return trip.

The boat trade was much sought after in the palmy days of the canal. Business houses usually fronted the canal on the tow-path side, and attracted trade by extensive wharves and hitching rings, signs, enumerating the leading articles kept, such as corn, oats, hay, wood, groceries, etc., and a conveniently located well. In the forties Samuel Bartlett, who then kept a store in a frame building where Gayman's store now stands, displayed a muslin sign that extended the whole length of the canal side of the building, and read: *"Boats Loaded to the Water's Edge for Long Sam."*

The "laying up" of from five to ten boats with their crews, in a small town, during the winter furnished plenty diversion and excitement for the natives. One of the events of the season was "a thaw." They would then hitch all their teams to a heavy plank icebreaker that they had built during the winter. Enough stones were put into the stern of the breaker to bring the bow to the surface, when three or four of the most venturesome, whose duty it was to rock it from side to side with all their might, would enter it. When, amid the vociferous swearing of the drivers — for most boat drivers would swear — the great wave which swept the banks on either side and the crashing of the ice as the horses and mules were urged to their utmost speed, occurred one of the exciting episodes in a boatman's life.

Chas. W. Speaks and Henry J. Epply served as Superintendents (State Boss) of this division of the canal. Samuel Loucks and Lewis Kramer petitioned the State for damages to their water powers soon after the canal was built.

The canal at Groveport

Mules were the primary source of power to pull the canal boats. Sometimes the driver, wanting to take a break, would tie a stick so that it protruded over the mules head to which a string and a carrot were tied so that the carrot dangled in front of the mule's face...just out of reach. Of course the mule never got to the carrot, but his constant efforts to reach it kept the boat moving.

Old timers called these mules "bank mules" and when describing certain slow witted individuals would say, "*He's dumber than a bank mule!*"

Fishing in the canal at Groveport
Circa 1908

CHAPTER IX
CHOLERA IN 1833

In the latter part of June, 1833, a man traveling by canal boat from Cleveland, stopped off at the road crossing the canal about a mile and one-half west of Winchester, and went to the residence of a Mr. Woodcock — who lived near where the toll gate used to be kept on the Columbus and Winchester Pike, now owned by Mr. Judy — and at his request Mrs. Woodcock did some washing for him, and it is supposed that the clothes were infected with Cholera. Mr. Woodcock went to George's Creek to fish while his wife did the washing; he soon after returned and drank freely of buttermilk. In a very short time afterwards he took violently sick, his family and near neighbors thinking from the effect of the buttermilk. At that time this was one of the most thickly settled neighborhoods in the township, and of course everybody was always ready to lend a helping hand when they had to depend on each other. It was .not long until nearly the whole neighborhood had gathered to lend what assistance they might, none dreaming of the dread pestilence so soon to enter their homes. Mr. Woodcock soon died, and only a few hours afterwards his wife died also.

Dr. Wiley, who lived in the Wheeler house, now owned by J. M. Lehman, expressed the opinion that they had died of cholera. Nearly all present thought it precautionary to leave at once, and suited their actions to their feelings. But it was too late. Within the next few weeks some 30 or more persons died in this neighborhood alone. Nearly all died in a few hours after being attacked. Among those who died are the following: Wm. Woodcock, a cooper by trade, and his wife; Walter Hughes, and his son Walter, who lived in a log house just south of the road and opposite the residence of Geo. Keichle; Henry Schoonover and son Perry aged 7 years, who lived in a log house on the bank of Walnut Creek, just back of Chaney's track, now occupied by Mr. Bitler; John Schoonover, who lived 200 or 300 yards south of his brother Henry; Wm. Davis and wife, Geo. W. Drain, Benj. Boyd and his wife Polly and two children, Isaac and Sarah; they lived in a log house just north of Union Grove Cemetery, which house was afterwards removed to the first lock west of Winchester, where it stood many years and was finally consumed by fire. Mrs. Isaac McCormack, Evans McCormack, Thompson Cross, wife and son, who lived in a log cabin that stood near where D. H. Tallman now lives; a Mr. Cox, who lived in a log house on the Amos Painter farm: a Mr. Gale, who lived about one hundred yards south of the canal, on the east side of the Oregon Road, and Mrs. Wm. Smith, who lived in the old brick house on the Jerry Alspach farm. She was the last victim. Mr. Martin, in his history referring to this epidemic. writes; *"In the summer of 1833 the cholera made its first appearance in Franklin County. It first broke out in the early part of the summer, in a neighborhood on the canal, in Madison Township, where it proved very fatal, but was confined to the space of a few miles only. On the 14th of July it made its first appearance in Columbus, and continued until about October. During its prevalence there were about two hundred deaths in Columbus, notwithstanding the whole population of the town was not much, if any, over three thousand, and it was supposed that one-third had fled to the country. The mortality and terrors of this season far surpassed any pestilence that ever afflicted Columbus before or since."*

In the latter part of August, 1854, there were three deaths in Winchester supposed to have been by cholera. Two strangers came on a boat; one of them died the next morning and the other soon after; the third one was Dutch Philip (Philip Bourne); he lived in the house now occupied by Mrs. McFadden; it was then plastered on the outside and painted to represent variegated marble, and in consequence was called the "Calico House." The two strangers died in the old Bartlit Store building near the canal bridge, in which Jacob Direling then kept a tavern.

CHAPTER X
OFFICERS OF MADISON TOWNSHIP

"Statesman, yet friend to truth, of soul sincere,
In action faithful, and in honor clear;
Who broke no promise, served no private end,
Who gained no title, and who lost no friend."

—Pope

We will supplement the list of township officers with a list of Madison Township citizens who have held county, state and other honorary positions.

In October of 1827 John Swisher succeeded James Kilbourne as County Assessor, and served until 1835. The office of County Assessor was abolished in 1841, when the office of Township Assessor was created.

Wm. W. Kyle was elected County Commissioner in 1840, and re-elected in 1843, serving six years. Chas. W. Speaks was elected County Commissioner in 1852, serving three years. John G. Edwards was elected County Commissioner in 1866, serving three years.

Samuel Kile, a former resident of this township, served as County Auditor from October, 1867 to 1874.

Aaron C. Headley, a former merchant of Groveport, was elected County Treasurer in 1867, and served two years.

F. M. Senter was elected County Recorder, and served two terms, from October, 1879, to October, 1885. Chas. D. Rarey has served as deputy under Neville Williams, County Recorder, since September, 1898, three years. Chas. C. Swisher is serving a term of three years as deputy (issuing clerk) under John W. McCafferty, County Clerk, beginning August, 1900.

In 1837 John R. Wright was appointed Farm Superintendent of the County Poor Farm, then located about three miles north of Columbus, and served until 1840, when the location was changed and the farm sold.

In 1851 Dr. A. A. Short was appointed Physician of the County Infirmary and served to March, 1857

McConnell Seymour has been a member of the County Board of Elections since 1899.

Samuel Bartlit was elected State Senator in 1853, serving two years.

The following have served as representatives of Franklin County in the State Legislature: Edward Courtright 1851-53. Hiram Hendron 1853-55. Dr. Hugh L. Chaney 1857-59, 1886-88; Ben L. Reese 1860-62, John G. Edwards 1864-66, Benjamin F. Gayman 1892-94, 1896-98.

Jesse Courtright, a son of Richard Courtright, who lived on the John McGuffy farm, was Surveyor of Franklin County for six years, 1848 to 1854.

O. P. Chaney served as a member of the Ohio State Board of Agriculture, 1880 to 1882. James C. Bowers, now a resident of this township, was also a member of this board from 1890 to 1898, serving one year as President and two years as Treasurer.

George F. Bareis was elected a Trustee of the Ohio State Archaeological and Historical Society, of which he is a life member, in 1891, and has been re-elected at the expiration of each term since; was elected a member of the Executive Committee at each of the annual elections since 1895, and was elected second vice president in 1900 and 1901.

John C. Speaks entered the National Guard as a private March 2, 1878, becoming a member of Co. H, 14th Regiment, O. N. G.; First Lieutenant, March 5, 1880; Captain, March 20, 1883; Major, November 8, 1889; Colonel, July 28, 1899; Brigadier-General, December 5, 1899. Mustered into the United States service (Spanish-American War) as Major of the 4th Regiment, O. V. I., May 9, 1898; participated in the Porto Rican expedition, and was mustered out with the regiment January 20, 1899.

Edward Merritt Hughes, son of Abram A. Hughes (a merchant who settled in Groveport in May, 1860;, was born at Lockbourne, Ohio, on July 26, 1866. He was appointed a cadet at large to the United States Naval Academy at Annapolis, Md., graduating on June 7, 1870. He passed through the grades of Ensign, Master, Lieutenant, Lieutenant Commander, and on March 3, 1901, was commissioned Commander in the United States Navy. He was with Commodore George Dewey at the Battle of Manila Bay May 1, 1898, as Executive Officer of the U. S. S. Petrel, and personally burned the five following Spanish War vessels: "Isla de Cuba," "Isla de Lwyow," "Don Juan de Austria," "Marquis del Duero," and the "Don Antonio d'Ulloa."

In a letter written by Commander Wood, of the Petrel, October 1, 1898, to Col. George A. Loud, and published in The Century Magazine, the following reference to Lieut. Hughes is made:

"When the Spanish flag was hauled down at the arsenal the Petrel was within three hundred yards of the arsenal dock and anchored. There she remained until 5:20 p. m., and with one boat's crew burned seven vessels of war in the face of the military garrison in Cavite and the remnants of the crews that had been forced into infantry companies, armed with Mauser rifles. Had they chosen to resist they could have supported their infantry fire with artillery, as the smooth-bore guns mounted at the arsenal were loaded and would have done damage to the ships at the short range. The only boat immediately available to burn and destroy the enemy's ships was a small whaleboat carrying an officer and seven men. With this boat Lieutenant Hughes, the Executive Officer, landed at the arsenal to place a Signalman, and proceeded to burn five of the seven ships. The two remaining were burned later by Ensign Fermier.

The action of Lieutenant Hughes in setting fire to the enemy's sunken ships in the face of a well armed superior, but demoralized force, was the one act of conspicuous gallantry which the battle that day afforded."

We must also include Judge John Chaney, who was a citizen of Madison Township for many years prior to his death, although his official career was in Bloom Township, Fairfield County. The following statement of his public services was made by Mr. Chaney for Dr. Scott's History of Fairfield County, and is unique:

"I was elected Justice of the Peace in 1821, 1824, and in 1827, serving in all three terms, or nine years. I served as Township Trustee twenty-three years. In the Ohio militia, old system, I served at various times as Major, Colonel and Paymaster.

In the years 1828, 1829 and 1830 I was elected to the Legislature as Representative of Fairfield County. In the spring of 1831 the Legislature elected me as one of the Associate Judges of Fairfield County.

In the fall of 1832 I was elected to the Lower House of Congress, from the district composed of Fairfield, Perry and Morgan counties. Was reelected from the same district in 1834 and in 1836. In 1842 I was again returned to the Ohio Legislature, Lower House, and at that session elected Speaker. In 1844 I was elected to the Ohio Senate, the term being two years; and again in 1855 returned to the Lower House. In 1832 my friends placed my name on the Presidential electoral ticket, and I had the honor of helping to make Andrew Jackson President of the United States. In 1851 I was a member of the constitutional convention that framed the present constitution of the State of Ohio. I am now within a few days of the close of my eighty-eighth year, and in the enjoyment of good health." Dr. Scott adds: *"From the friends and long acquaintance of Judge Chaney, I have received the information that never once during his public life did he solicit office."*

Justices of the Peace

The year indicates the date of election: Ebenezer Richards, 1810; George Hays, 1810; Billingsly Bull, 1810, 1817, 1870, 1823; Wm. D. Hendren, 1811, 1824; Elijah Austin, 1811; Elisha Decker, 1815; Emmel Cox, 1817: James McLish, 1817; Nicholas Goeches, 1820, 1823; Wm. Godman, 1820, 1823; Jacob Gander, 1825, 1828; John Swisher, 1826, 1835; Wm. Patterson, 1826, 1829, 1832; A. Shoemaker, 1829, 1832, 1841; Alexander Cameron, 1831, 1834. 1837, 1840, 1843; Isaac Decker, 1835; W. W. Kile, 1838, 1847, 1850 (resigned in March, 1852), 1860, 1864, 1867: James Pearcy, 1838; John Courtright, 1841; John Cox, 1844, 1870; Wm. Mason, 1844; Joshua Glanville, 1846 (resigned September, 1847); Moses Seymour, 1847, 1850; Jeremiah White, 1852; Henry Nicodemus, 1852; M. K. Earhart, 1853, 1863; Joshua Stevenson, 1855; Z. P. Thompson, 1855, 1858; John Helpman, 1856, 1859, 1862, 1865; James B. Evans, 1868, 1871, 1874, 1877, 1880, 1883; Fernando M. Senter, 1873, 1876, 1878 (resigned September 12, 1878); Lemuel Sarber, 1878 (resigned March 8, 1880); Milton Cummins, 1880, 1883, 1889; B. F. Gayman, 1886, 1889 (resigned July, 1890). At a special election July 19, 1890, W. Scott Alspach was elected, re-elected 1893-1896, and served until his death, December 9, 1897; Cornelius Black, Jr., 1892; O. P. Crist, 1898, 1901; Edward V. Bush, special election January 12, 1898, 1901.

John Chaney
1790 - 1881

Dr. Hugh L. Chaney, MD
1820 - 1902

Trustees

The following is a list of the Township Trustees, beginning with 1849:

Jesse Seymour, 1849-1862; Edward Courtright, 1849; Wm. T. Decker, 1849-1850, Joshua Glanville, 1851; John Helpman, 1852-1860, 1863-1865; John Cox, 1852-1862; Moses Seymour, 1861-1868, 1875, 1877-1879; Mr. Seymour died October 1. 1879; Kalite Sallee, 1863-1873, 1875-1876, 1886; Elias Decker, 1866-1874, 1878-1881; O. Codner, 1869-1870; Phillip C. Tussing, 1871-1872; Jacob Rohr, 1873-1874; S. H. Whims, 1874: John S. Lehman, 1875-1876; Charles Rohr, 1876-1877; Wm. Sims, 1877-1879, 1893-1895; Andrew Wilson, 1880-1882; Absalom Rohr, 1880, 1883-1884; John F. Kile, 1881-1884; Geo. W. Lisle, 1882-1885; Andrew D. Kraner, 1885-1890; Benj. C. Sims, 1885, 1888-1891; Edward A. Peters, 1886-1891; M. C. Seymour, 1887-1901; George Sallee, 1889-1891; Daniel Detwiler, 1891 (resigned March 6, 1893); Jeremiah Kramer, 1892-1900; Goodlove Dorrer, 1895 (resigned March 1, 1897); John F. Bachman, 1897; Wm. M. Long, 1897-1900; John G. Rohr, 1898-1901; Albert Bachman, 1900-1901.

Township Clerks

Jacob A. Taylor, 1849-1851; Lemuel Sarber, 1852; Jeremiah White, 1853-1854; Robert F. Dildine, 1855-1859, 1861-1867, 1871, 1881-1883; J. H. Fearn, 1860; Fernando M. Senter, 1868-1870; C. Black, Jr.,

1872-1880; A. M. Senter, 1884-1889; Charles D. Rarey, 1890-1897; Phillip C. Tussing, 1898-1901.

Township Treasurers

Jacob Weaver, 1849-1850; Samuel Sharp, 1851-1854; Geo. McCormick, 1855; Dr. G. L. Smith, 1856-1859; Samuel Sharp, 1860-1863; H. W. Dunn, 1864-1865; (Mr. Dunn died in the spring of 1866); Wm. W. Kile, 1866-1869; S. Allen Peters, 1870-1873; John F. Kile, 1874-1879; John F. Wildermuth, 1880-1884; John L. Chaney, 1885-1893; Wm. R. Smith, 1893-1901.

Constables

Jacob Weaver, 1849; G. W. Myers, 1849; J. J. Needels, 1850; G. Nafzger, 1850; E. B. Decker, 1851-1854; John H. Heston, 1851-1852; Lemuel Sarber, 1853; Jacob Stimmel, 1854-1856; Elias Decker, 1855-1862; John Gehm, 1857-1859; Rufus W. Bailey, 1860; Jonathan Watson, 1861-1862; G. S. Dildine, 1863, 1867-1868, 1873-1875, 1877-1878, 1880-1881; S. W. Dildine, 1863; John A. Kile, 1864-1867, 1882-1885; John Colman, 1884; E. M. Strode, 1865-1866, 1886-1889; James McKelvey, 1868-1869; G. W. Rowland, 1869-1870; Levi Kramer, 1870-1872, 1875-1876; B. C. Sims, 1871-1874, 1879; W. R. Kauffman, 1876-1877; Wm. Schrock, 1878-1880, 1882-1883; B. F. Trine, 1881; C. L. Kraner, 1882; M. E. Schrock, 1884; James Palsgrove, 1885-1889, 1890-1893; Chas. D. Rarey, 1888-1889; J. V. Conklin, 1890-1891, 1894-1900; Joseph P. Rager, 1891-1893; Edward V. Bush, 1894-1896; Sylvester Carruthers, 1897-1901; Samuel Rush, 1900-1901.

Assessors

Jacob Weaver, 1849-1850; Moses Seymour, 1851, 1852, 1856; Elisha B. Decker, 1853, 1854; Henry Long, 1855, 1858-1862; John G. Edwards, 1857; Jacob Bishop, 1863-1867; Milton Cummins, 1868, 1869; M. K. Earhart, 1870-1877; G. S. Dildine, 1878, 1879. Since 1880 there have been two Assessors.

For Groveport Precinct: G. S. Dildine, 1880, 1881; M. K. Earhart, 1882-1884: Chas. P. Long, 1885, 1886, 1888; John A. Kile, 1887; I. R. Earhart, 1889-1891; Samuel Stukey, 1891-1896, 1898-1901; Richard Copeland, 1897.

Winchester Precinct: Phil C. Tussing, 1880-1882; Jacob Bishop, 1883; R. J. Tussing, 1884; P. C. Tussing, 1885; John Chaney. Jr., 1886;

Milton Cummins, 1887-1888; John D. Bishop, 1889, 1893-1895, 1897-1901; David Boyer, 1890; James P. Kalb, 1891-1892; Amor R. Smith, 1896.

The office of *Township Ditch Supervision* was created by the Legislature of 1899-1900, and on September 3, 1900, the Trustees of Madison Township appointed Edward A. Peters to fill the office. Mr. Peters was then elected in April, 1901, and resigned on July 26, 1901. Madison Township was the first in the State to have a Township Ditch Supervisor. Clint A. Stevenson was appointed to fill the vacancy, and assumed the duties of the office on August 11, 1901.

The Decennial Land Appraisers have been:

Thomas Patterson, 1870 and 1880; Edward A. Peters, 1890; James P. Kalb, 1900.

CHAPTER XI
SCHOOLS OF MADISON TOWNSHIP

"Time comes not yet to mow you down.
He points to wisdom's lofty fane,
He bids youth win the golden crown,

Which patient, earnest toil may gain.
He lends the precious hours, and cries
Seize every moment as it flies."

—Cutter *in U. S. School Primer, Edition of* 1846

The early settlers of this township were in hearty sympathy with the ordinance of 1787, which proclaimed that *"Religion, morality, and knowledge being the essentials of good government, schools and the means of education should be forever encouraged;"* and also with the State constitution of 1802, which declared *"that schools and the means of instruction should be encouraged by legislative provision, not inconsistent with the rights of conscience."*

Congress by an "Act," or several "Acts," called "The Compact," passed April 30, 1802, made the following provision: *"That the following propositions be and the same are hereby offered to the conventions of the Eastern States of said territory (Northwest); that the section No. 16 in every township, and where such section has been sold, granted, or disposed of, other lands equivalent thereto, the most contiguous to the same, shall be granted to the inhabitants of such township for the maintenance of the schools within said township."*

In 1803 it was enacted that the sections 16 should be leased for a term not exceeding fifteen years. The rent for every quarter section of one hundred and sixty acres was to consist in making the following improvements: *"Fifteen acres cleared of all timber and other wood and fenced in separate fields, one field of five acres to be sowed in grass, one of three acres to be planted with 100 thrifty and growing apple trees and the remaining seven acres to be arable land. These improvements to be made within the first five years of the lease."* These leases were made by agents appointed by the Governor, who were to give public notice and were to receive bids and execute the leases to those who would agree to make the improvements required, for the shortest term of lease. Two years later, in 1805, this law was amended so that the Township Trustees were authorized to grant these leases for terms not exceeding 15 years. It was made the duty of the Trustees *"to see that the proceeds arising from the lease be duly and impartially applied to the education of youths, within the particular surveyed township, in such a manner that all the citizens resident therein may be equal partakers of the benefits thereof."*

In 1806 the law of 1805 was amended, incorporating every original surveyed township, and provided for the election of a board of three Trustees and a Treasurer, and the power to grant leases was also transferred to these boards.

For many years nothing, or comparatively little was realized from these leases towards the support of the schools, so in 1824 the General Assembly of Ohio sent a "memorial" to Congress, asking the consent of Congress to sell the sections sixteen. Among the reasons cited were: *"That persons renting lands were usually in destitute circumstances which made the collection of the rent uncertain; the tenants were of the lowest class of the community, having no permanent interest in the soil; such persons wasted the timber, so that the loss was equal to or greater than the revenue; Such persons, by the right of franchise exert a pernicious influence on the neighborhood."*

In 1827 the Legislature passed an "Act" which provided for the sale of section No. 16. It was made the duty of the County Assessor to take the vote of all white male inhabitants over twenty-one years of age and report the result to the General Assembly. When no vote was taken or when a majority voted against a sale, another vote might be taken in any subsequent year. These provisions for the sale of section 16 applied to the leased as well as to the unleased lands. Every owner of a lease might surrender his lease and then purchase the land at the last appraisement. In this way many of these sections were sold for much less than their value. It will be noticed that it was immediately after this law was passed that Montgomery, Truro, Hamilton and Violet Townships sold their school lands. Since 1852 the sale of these lands is under the control of the School Trustees and the Probate Court. The greater part have been sold—less than one-eighth of the original surveyed townships now own any school lands. Fortunately Madison retained her section, being one among the very few townships who still own a whole section. In connection with the provisions for the sale of the school lands it was the duty of the Auditor of State to keep a separate account of all monies paid into the State Treasury from the sale of these lands, crediting each sum to the proper original surveyed township; the money so collected is to constitute an "irreducible fund" for the support of the common schools within said township. *"All monies so paid into the State Treasury shall bear an annual interest of 6 per cent, payable on the first day of January of each year; and the faith of the State of Ohio is hereby pledged for the annual payment."* For some reason the school lands of Hamilton, Montgomery and Truro Townships, as well as Madison, were all located in this township.

Hamilton Township was granted section No. *22*, being Range 21, Township 11; the sale of this section aggregated $3,026. Montgomery Township was granted section No. 21, Range 21, Township 11; the proceeds of the sale aggregated $2,716. Truro Township was granted section No. 15, Range 21, Township 11; the sale of this section amounted to $1,810. Violet Township, Fairfield County, was granted section No. 15, in lieu of section 16, Range 20, Township 15, being located in Violet Township; this sale aggregated $1,217.36.

In 1900 Hamilton Township received from this source $180.33; Montgomery, $161.33; Truro, $107.52, and Violet $999.89. Section No. 16, Madison Township, rented for a term of three years—1897-1899 — for $10,357.50, or an average of $3,452.50 per year; $1,422.75 was expended in improvements repairs and other expenses — an average of $474.25 per year—leaving $8,934.75, which was applied to defray the expenses of maintaining the schools, being an average of $2,978.25 per year, or of $4.65 net per acre per year. On the above basis of the net income for the past term of three years, the average value of this land is fixed at an equivalent of $78.00 per acre. Could this land be sold for an average price of $100.00 per acre, as some claim, then the net income would be $6.00 per acre, or an aggregate of $3,840 per year.

Scholars living in the territory that formerly belonged to Violet Township, Fairfield County, or to the two southern tiers of sections, which formerly belonged to Ross County, do not participate in Madison Township's funds — although they are now, for civil purposes, part of Madison — but in the income from the proceeds of their respective school lands.

The following table gives the details of the sale of the several township's lands, as the same appears upon the Auditor of State's records:

HAMILTON TOWNSHIP, RANGE 21, TOWNSHIP 11, SECTION 22.

Date of Sale.	Purchaser.	Part Sold.	No. Acres.	Appraised Value.	Sale Price.
Dec. 20, 1830	Joseph Decker	W. ½ S. W	80	$270 00	$505 00
" 20, 1830	Harmon Dildine	E. ½ S. W	80	270 00	560 00
" 20, 1830	" "	W. ½ S. E	80	300 00	560 00
" 20, 1830	W. H. Richardson	E. ½ S. E	80	140 00	165 00
" 15, 1834	Harmon Dildine	E. ½ N. E	80	270 00	460 00
" 15, 1834	James Swisher	W. ½ N. E	80	270 00	420 00
" 15, 1828	John Mossman	E. ½ N. W	80	200 00	200 00
" 15, 1828	John Mossman and T. C. Hendren	W. ½ N. W	80	160 00	166 00

MONTGOMERY TOWNSHIP, RANGE 21, TOWNSHIP 11 SECTION 21.

Date of Sale.	Purchaser.	Part Sold.	No. Acres.	Appraised Value.	Sale Price.
Dec. 15, 1828	Adam Sarber	W. ½ N. W	80	340 00	413 00
" 15, 1828	John Swisher	E. ½ N. W	80	380 00	458 00
" 15, 1828	" "	W. ½ N. E	80	250 00	456 00
" 15, 1828	" "	E. ½ N. E	80	200 00	402 00
" 15, 1828	Adam Rarey	W. ½ S. W	80	240 00	426 00
" 15, 1828	" "	E. ½ S. W	80	180 00	301 00
" 15, 1828	Benj. Clevinger	W. ½ S. E	80	150 00	160 00
" 15, 1828	Adam Rarey	E. ½ S. E	80	100 00	100 00

TRURO TOWNSHIP, RANGE 21, TOWNSHIP 11, SECTION 15.

Date of Sale.	Purchaser.	Part Sold.	No. Acres.	Appraised Value.	Sale Price.
Dec. 15, 1828	John Kile	W. ½ S. W	80	$160 00	$240 00
" 15, 1828	" "	E. ½ S. W	80	160 00	206 00
" 15, 1828	Jacob Coble	W. ½ S. E	80	160 00	231 00
" 15, 1828	" "	E. ½ S. E	80	160 00	187 00
" 15, 1828	Richard House	E. ½ N. W	80	160 00	235 00
" 15, 1828	" "	W. ½ N. W	80	160 00	351 00
Jan. 19, 1829	Abraham Shoemaker	E. ½ N. E	80	160 00	160 00
Sept. 6, 1829	John Todd	W. ½ N. E	80	160 00	200 00

VIOLET TOWNSHIP, RANGE 20, TOWNSHIP 15, SECTION 15.

Date of Sale.	Purchaser.	Part Sold.	No. Acres.	Appraised Value.	Sale Price.
Feb. 19, 1831	Abraham Pickering	E. ½ N. E			$120 00
May 14, 1831	" "	W. ½ N. E			125 47
" 14, 1831	" "	E. ½ N. W			129 69
" 14, 1831	" "	W. ½ N. W			123 72
March 3, 1832	Chancy Ricketts	N. ½ S. W			228 05
Aug. 3, 1833	J. W. Fisher	S. ½ S. W			313 48
Dec. 11, 1833	Chancy Ricketts	N. ½ S. E			131 42

Up to 1825 the schools received no State aid, and their efficiency depended largely upon the estimation of an education held by the local community, consequently some neighborhoods had much better school facilities than others. In January, 1825, a law was enacted establishing a uniform system for the common schools of the State, and at each successive meeting of the Legislature amendments and improvements were enacted until on February 10, 1829, a new "Bill" embodying in the main the best features of former "Acts" and adding some entirely new provisions, was enacted. This law embodies the leading features by which the public school system of the State has ever since been executed. According to its provision the Trustees of each and every incorporated township are required to divide it into a suitable number of districts, in each of which, annually the householders shall choose three School Directors whose duty it shall be to employ teachers, levy local taxes, etc. Another feature was the levying of a tax of three-fourths of a mill on each dollar of the valuation by the State for the support of the school. The schools at once began to improve. The management being left entirely in the keeping of the local directors, different methods were adopted in different districts; in some schools were held eight or nine months in the year; in others only during the winter months. Usually a male teacher was employed for the winter months, and a female during the summer term, while the larger scholars were otherwise employed. In some districts the tuition was all raised by levy, in others one-half by taxation and the balance by subscription.

James B. Evans
1810 - 19??

Rev. James Heffley
1837 - 1923

In 1853 an entire reorganization of the school district system was enacted. Each township was made a school district, and the districts previously established became sub-districts, and the management of the schools and the power of taxation passed to the Township Board of Education then created. This board consists of one member from each sub-district.

At first there was no one to judge of a teacher's fitness and qualification but the parents. The law of 1825 provided that the Court of Common Pleas annually appoint three suitable persons whose duty it was to examine every person wishing to teach. Since 1853 the Probate Court appoints the examiners. No person, since 1825, could receive any money from the public treasury, as wages for teaching, without a certificate.

Very little information can now be obtained about the teachers for the first twenty-five or thirty years, only that they went from house to house soliciting scholars for "subscription schools;" the price of tuition per scholar depending upon the number that could be secured. The cash required was a small sum, as a large part of the tuition was paid in board and lodging; each scholar was required to furnish entertainment their share of the time. Many of these early teachers left the impress of their morals, patriotism and devotion for the higher attainments of life indelibly stamped upon those who came under their molding influence. Scholars had few books, often only a leaf of a Bible or other book pasted on a thin board. Frequently little or no attention was paid to the education of the girls. There were no "sweet girl graduates" in those days, with costly outfits, extravagance of flowers, etc., which sometimes in these days makes a parent question if free education is not a contradiction.

Nevertheless, some girls were ambitious to acquire the best education possible, so sometimes they had to study clandestinely. The late Mrs. N. Tallman related to the writer her experience; her parents were willing that she should learn to "spell, read and cipher," but were opposed to her learning to write, and forbade the teacher instructing her in the art. This made her all the more anxious and determined to learn, and the teacher was willing to instruct her. Some time afterwards her father called at the school house and found her in the act of writing. When he began to take the teacher to task for disregarding his wish, he only replied: *"Yes, I have taught your daughter to write, and you can't take it away from her."*

For some years, there being no school houses, the schools were held in vacant cabins, usually in the round-log cabin that the pioneer erected on his first arrival, and which became vacant after a few years when he could erect a hewed-log house. Among the first school houses were the following, viz: One on the northeast quarter of section No. 30, then in Violet Township, about fifty paces north of Jacob Moore's residence, and on the east side of the road, on land now owned by Mr. Doval. The depression left by the well is still visible just north of the fence along Jacob Bott's lane. Miss Nancy Hathaway (Mrs. J. B. Evans) and Miss Susan Bowen (Mrs. Bolenbaugh) taught here. One near the center of section No. 14, on land then owned by George Kalb, now owned by T. D. Kalb; a Mr. Calhoun was an early teacher here. One on section No. 16 (school section); Wm. Arnold, Wm. Purdy and Wm. W. Kile taught. A school was taught by a Mr. Fletcher in a log cabin on the farm of John Seymour; another just north of the present residence of Geo. Francisco, taught by Geo. K. Stevenson. Noah Bishop taught a school in a log cabin on the McClish farm on section No. 30. Dr. Wiley, 1817 or 1818; John Colman, 1829 or 1830; Moses Cross, Owen Roberts, Mr. Jones, Mr. Gale and Mr. Cox taught in a log house that stood near the present residence of D. H. Tallman on section No. 25. There was a log school house in Middletown, just east of the present residence of Geo. Williams; later this school was taught in the Middletown Church building by James O'Kane; another one stood on the farm of Chas. Pontius. Another on the Gander Hill on section No. 29. These were all of log, open fire place, chimney of sticks and clay, puncheon floors, slab seats without backs — the choice seats were along the sides, the walls affording backs — clapboard roofs held on by poles and wooden pins, wooden hinges and latch to the door. Some of these had no windows of any kind, unless the cracks and openings in the roof and between the logs and the big opening in the chimney could be called such, as they admitted what light was needed. Others had a small hole cut through a log and a greased paper pasted over. Later improvements consisted in the cutting out of one log four to eight feet long on one or usually on both sides of the building, high enough to admit a row of eight by ten glass, and later the twelve light 8 x 10 windows was considered about the acme in the way of a window. The adoption of the school system in the spring of 1829 soon stimulated the interest in the schools to such a degree that a laudable rivalry sprung up between the districts of the township. The most intelligent and progressive citizens were elected directors. Plain brick school houses were erected, with comfortable seats and double desks made of wide boards (these double desks gave to the boys, by making them sit with a girl), ten-plate stoves, etc. As the population increased larger brick buildings were erected, and in most of the districts, these have been replaced by the modern brick with stone trimmings, slate roofs, slate blackboard, latest improved furniture and appliances, heated with furnaces — models, with possibly one exception; that is there seems to be little regard paid to the effect of the light on the pupil's eyes.

John Gill Edwards
1815 - 1894

Dr. John H. Saylor, M.D.
1836 - 1918

The earliest records of any of the township schools that we were able to find are of district No. 14, afterwards consolidated with No. 1. It is interesting to note that in all the various changes in the numbering and renumbering of the districts that the Pontius district has always been known as No. 1. This record begins September 20, 1839, with an election held in the "old school house on John Solomon's farm." John G. Bennett, Geo. W. Sims and Wesley Bishop were elected directors. Under date of October 12, 1839, Jeremiah White was elected to teach reading, writing and arithmetic, at $16.00 per month of twenty-four days, with the following proviso: *"If it should be ascertained that there is a deficiency in the public funds to defray the expenses, that the school should be discontinued at the expiration of three months."* And finding this to be the case he taught only three months. The following is a list of the names of the scholars with their ages in district No. 14, under date of November 11, 1839, viz: Christena Groom 12, Rebecca Groom 8, Elizabeth Bunn 10, Joseph Burton 5, Juliet A. Sims 10, Geo. A. Sims 8, Joseph E. Sims 6, Samuel Bishop 12, Joseph W. Bennett 5, John Young 6, Wm. Young 5, Thornton Burton 13, Clarinda Rarey 8, Gamaliel Rarey 11, Nicholas Rarey 15, Henry Bunn 12, David Groom 19, Hosea Groom 15, Minerva Johnson 13, Caleb Giberson 19. Mathias W. Bishop 18, James L. Sims 17, Hezekiah Giberson 14, Melissa Young 8, Sarah Bishop 15.

Names and ages of scholars in district No. 1, October 22, 1839: Lafayette Rarey 7, Washington Rarey 5, Daniel Groom 12, John F. Groom 11, Adam Bishop 10, John Bishop 5, Wm. Ranier 7, Franklin G. Pontius 3, Augustus Groom 6, John S. Nevons 12, Miner Groom 5, James Lyons 17, Wm. Bowman 13, Amos Bowman 8, Henry Bowman 5, Benjamin Rarey 12, Alfred Rarey 3, David Rarey 18, Parker Rarey 20, Nancy Rarey 10, Elizabeth Rarey 9, Mary A. Rarey 7, Margaret Rarey 5, Christina Groom 9, Rhoda Groom 7, Nancy Groom 5, Mary A. Rarey 11, Amanda Rarey 7, Louisa Noderer 12, Hester A. Ranier 9, Isabelle Berk 7, Susanna Laufer 17, Mary Bowman 10.

Under date of December 17, 1839, the teacher makes the following note: *"Barred out, but charged the district with the day."* This occurrence recalls the prevalent custom of "barring the teacher out" until he would "treat." The writer remembers an occasion when Zach Seymour, Wm. Decker, Lewis and David Sarber and others piled all the benches and desks against the doors and fastened down the windows, at old No. 4, refusing to admit Israel Gayman, who was then the teacher, until he "treated" the scholars. The directors, E. B. Decker, Philip C. Tussing and Jacob Sarber, were sent for, but the room was kept barricaded until Mr. Gayman went to town and purchased a "treat," which on this occasion was a stick of candy to each girl and a set of "groundy" marbles to each boy. Under date of January 2, 1841, the teacher notes: *"No scholars come out, but I came and charged the district for the day,"* and under dates of February 11, 12, 13, 1841, *"No wood, but charged the district for the day."*

While the early schools taught only the three R's, we note that A. Stuart, teacher in 1847, taught "Reading, Writing, Spelling, Arithmetic.

English Grammar, Geography, Elementary Principals of Algebra, Natural Philosophy, Civil Government, Composition, Declamations, Astronomy and *Electricity.*"

May 1, 1847, a special meeting of the voters was held at the "old school house." Moses Groom was elected chairman and Jeremiah White secretary.

"Thomas Groom moved to build 30 feet by 18 feet; carried by unanimous vote."

"Wm. Rarey moved walls be 18 inches thick up to joists and 13 inches above; carried by unanimous vote."

"Wm. Rarey moved $350.00 be assessed for the purpose of building and completing said house, and if all said $350.00 be not required, the district clerk is authorized to strike from each man's tax on the duplicate an equal ratio, so that no more be collected than will be required to pay the costs and expense of the same; carried by unanimous vote."

Wm. Rarey was appointed, with the Directors — Fred Bunn, Chas. Pontius and Jeremiah White — a building committee. In the spring of 1844 the teacher's register gives an interesting statement of his pay. He taught six months at twelve and one-half dollars per month; he collected $30.90 from the public funds and $44.10 from subscriptions, as follows; Wm. Rarey sent 402 1/2 days, $8.60.3; Chas. Pontius sent 308 days, $8.02.2; Thomas Groom sent 476 1/2 days, $10.05.9; Mary Groom sent 541 1/2 days, $11.43.2; Moses Groom sent 77 days, $1.62.5; Josiah Hulva sent 105 1/2 days, $3.95.5; Frederick Bunn sent 12 days, $0.40.0.

District No. 13 (now No. 10): At an early day the Hendrens, Clevengers, Coxs, Kiles, Ensleys, Haineses, Flemings and others in this neighborhood attended school at either a school house which stood on the "Gander Hill" or at one that stood just east of Big Walnut, along the north side of the Groveport Pike, or, at other times, at the one that stood on the school section. These were all log buildings; the one on Gander Hill was built about 1815, and stood about where Wm. Hanstein's barn now stands. John and Jacob Gander's residence stood on the exact spot where Mr. Hanstein's house now stands. This old log school house stood until about 1850. There was great difficulty in getting to and from school in those days; besides the distance — in some instances two or three miles — there were no roads, only the blazed trees; no bridges across the streams, besides the swamps to avoid. The text books used here at an early day were the *Bible,* English Reader and the original Adam's Arithmetic. The records of this district reveal some interesting methods in vogue in those days. Under the date of June 2, 1838:

"The householders met at house of Wm. Wildermuth; John Kile, Sr., was elected chairman, and Wm. W. Kile secretary."

The result of this election was that Jacob Swisher, Thomas C. Hendren and Wm. W. Kile were elected directors.

"And then proceeded to select a site for a school house, which was decided by vote, and resulted as follows: "At the raise on the south side of the Berkshire road on Wm. Wildermuth's land, opposite to where the wheat stack now stands."

It seems that the proposed building was delayed, for on March 9, 1839, the minutes say: *"Meeting at the house of Wm. Wildermuth for the purpose of taking a vote for the building of a school house by the assessing of a tax, and of choosing a site. The directors having failed to obtain the site that was agreed upon at a previous meeting."*

Those present at this meeting were Thomas C. Hendren, Wm, Wildermuth, John W. Kile, Frederick Swisher, Robert A. Kile, Jacob Swisher, Wm. W. Kile and George Miller.

"The site offered by the widow and Thos. C. Hendren was considered and selected, and it was decided to build the school house by a tax. A levy was made amounting to $225.00 to build the school house."

"May 17, 1839, the Directors contracted with Cullison & Zuck to build the school house in district No. 13, for the sum of $240.00, to be finished by the first of September next."

The following is a list of the valuation of the taxable property in district No. 13, on which a tax of sixteen and one-half mills on the dollar was levied: Wm. W. Kile, $1,507; Robt. A. Kile, $649; John Kile, $2,004; John Kile, $144; Jacob Swisher, $1,702; Wm. Wildermuth, $1,244; Thos. C. Hendren, $240; Nancy Hendren, $144; Wm. Hendren, $40; Samuel Hendren, $40; Hendren's heirs, $1,510; Elk Sims, $144; Jacob Fout, $128; John Miller, $44; Philip Shoemaker, $96; John Shoemaker, $40; Henry Carder, $264; Peter Brown, $96; Fred Swisher, $2,182; Wood's heirs, $472; David Taylor, $144; Peter Stepem, $189;

Benjamin Rarey, $1,180; Phil Needels, $1,316; Adam Rarey's heirs, $1,133.

The following enrollment of the pupils with their age is given under date October 24, 1842:

Polly Husting, Franklin Michel, John S. Rarey, Chas. W. Farrington, Emily Updegraff, Joseph Spangler, Samuel L. Swisher 9, Wm. T. Hendren 8, Mordicai C. Hendren 11, Sarah E. Hendren 9, Geo. L. Hendren 5, Wm. Race 9, John Carder 10, Mary Jane Kile 10, Job Race 10, John A. Kile 7, Sarah J. Kile 6, Joshua Algire 15, John E. Kile 15, Caleb E. Kile 14, Samuel E. Kile 12, James E. Kile 10, Betsy A. Kile 7, Sarah A. Kile 6, Mary J. Kile 5, Henry Algire 8, Samuel E. Kile 17, Geo. Kinsel 16, Jonathan Lee 15, E. Ann Needels 17, Wm. E. Kile 5, Rachel Kile 5, John Swisher 5, Quincy A. Fisk 15, Jesse Sherden 5, John Race 14, Henry Carder 17, Geo. Carder 19, Austin Miller 8. Levi Miller 6, and in the spring of 1844 the following other names appear: Eliza Goodman 27,. Ruth Evans 19, Peter Stimmel 11, Elizabeth Kile 9, James A. Kile 12, Wm. Hendren 9, Israel Kile 5, Wm. Cherry 18, Alpheus Algire 8, Geo. Whitesell 8, John Sourden 12.

Wm. T. Linn, who taught a term of twenty-four days, ending March 24, 1843, recorded what was no doubt an address delivered at his school closing, and is unique:

"This school is very deficient in many respects; there remains much to be done by the Directors and the people before all is as it should be; which operates as an obstacle on the operations of the teacher and the rapid progress of the pupils. Much expense might be obviated and greater proficiency of our pupils secured by proper attention to these matters. The furniture of the school room is faulty; the building should be underpinned, the stove lowered, an outside room attached to the main building and a well dug and securely curbed. No apparatus: The school room should be furnished with two blackboards, Arithmetician and various Geometrician, Triginomical and Arithmetician Figures, which would astonishingly advance the pupils in the acquisition of useful and general knowledge, when used as they would be by the intelligent teacher. The pupils should be furnished with proper and sufficient studies to keep them properly employed; they should be so furnished as to admit of proper classification.

"There is no sense or propriety in keeping pupils spelling and reading when they should be attending to other studies. Scholars should be made to obey the teacher, and never indulge in school tales. Directors and parents should visit the school frequently, not for the purpose of picking flaws and fault-finding, but to see how things are going on, as well as to encourage the teacher and pupils in their arderous avocation; their simple presence will do much, if nothing more is attempted. Friends, do attend to your duties for your children's sake if for nobody's else. Why is it that people expend so much money to so little purpose? No other reason than a want of discharge of duty. Then, why not do it? I do solemnly aver that this district school will never flourish as it should under present circumstances and state of affairs. There are many things of superlative importance to the wellfare of this district, which I cannot enumerate on this occasion, with the exception, that the district should be furnished with a common school Library, and much more apparatus than I have mentioned. With the sincere desire for the wellfare of the youth of this district and the rising generation elsewhere, I subscribe myself,

Wm. T. Linn.

"P. S.—The old and long since exploded system of teaching and governing should not be encouraged in this enlightened age. 'Morality and intelligence are the sheet anchors of a republican people,' 'knowledge is power and ignorance and slavery go hand in hand.' See to it, my friends. W. T. L."

An intimate acquaintance with the leading families of this township for many years leads me to observe the very noticeable fact that in almost every instance the intelligent, substantial and prosperous citizens' names are found connected in an active way with the development of the schools; this is also true in a "very marked way in the church life of the different communities. It is but just to note that in every school district the intelligent, even-tempered, sturdy and self-sacrificing devotion to the present and future best interests of the community can be readily traced to the pioneer families who maintained the church and school, and whose descendants in many cases are even yet the safe-guards of their neighborhoods.

The fact that we are not able to secure a list of the directors and teachers in each of the districts previous to 1853 shall not prevent us from giving such a list in the two districts we were fortunate enough to secure.

The Directors in No. 14 and No. 1 (these two being after a few years consolidated) were:

John G. Bennett, 1839-1841; Geo. W. Sims, 1839; Jeremiah White, 1840-1851, when he removed; Wesley Bishop, 1839-1841; Casper Limpert, 1844; Henry Bunn, 1844-1851, appointed November 2, 1844 in place of Mr. Limpert, who moved away; Joshua Burton, 1844-1845; Chas. Pontius, 1847-1853; Geo. Evans, 1852, appointed in place of Jeremiah White, who moved away.

In district No. 13:

Jacob Swisher, 1838; Thos. C. Hendren, 1838-1841, 1846-1848, 1851-1853; W. W. Kile, 1838-1841, 1843-1846, 1849-1851; John Kile, 1839-1841. The election held on September 17, 1841, was attended by the following four voters: Thos. C. Hendren, John Updegraff, Fred. Swisher and Ebenezer Mitchell and Thos. C. Hendren, John Kile and Fred Swisher each received four votes. Fred Swisher, 1841-1842, 1849; John White, 1842; Daniel Wagner, 1846-1850; Jacob Weaver, 1848-1851. In 1850 the Treasurer reported that he had sold $28.00 in Granville bank paper for $17.50. Kalita Sallee, 1851-1857; Caleb E. Kile, 1852; Wm. Wildermuth, 1853.

District No. 8, now No. 13: In about 1817 a log school house was erected in the woods near the north line of section No. 16, on the southeast side of the Big Belly Road, which then continued in a southwesterly direction from the Thos. Needels house north of Asbury Church through Axley Kile's farm, John Winterstine's farm and intersecting the Groveport Road on the school section.

This building was most likely put up by volunteer labor. John G. McGuffey, Esq., of Columbus, Ohio, says; *"I, in company with my father, saw it in 1837; it was then out of use and repair."* Mr. McGuffey is also authority for the statement that *"My grandfather, John McGuffey, and Richard Courtright helped to erect this building in about 1817,"* and that *"the land was cleared and the house taken down in about 1840."*

Augustus Willie
1816 - 1889

Casper Limpert
1806-1879

Teachers

The following is as complete a list of the teachers who have taught in the township as we were able to secure. Some are from memory, others — the largest number—from teachers' registers. After 1876 the list is taken from the records of Township Clerk. What is now district No. 1, beginning September 20, 1839:

Jeremiah White, 1839; Geo. H. Crookshank, 1839; Miss Pauline Whitehead, 1839; Anson Sprague, Casper Limpert, Dixon A. Harrison, 1842; W. H. Pyle, 1843, 1844, 1846, 1847; Adam Havely, 1840; T. E. W. Fenton, 1841, 1842; Philip F. Milnor, 1844; Margaret Chandler, 1840-1842; Amassa Stuart, 1847; Geo. Adel, _____ Boyd, Oscar Whims, Mary Robinson, N. Z. Moore, 1869; Henry M. Williams, 1870; R. J. Wox, 1872-1874; Amy E. English, 1875.

District No. 13: S. L. Fisher, 1839; Elvina McComb, of Truro, 1840; James I. Conway, 1840; D. L. Eaton, 1840; James Jamison, 1841; Mary A. Jamison, 1841; Philip Myer, 1842, 1843; W. T. Linn, 1843; M. Cambridge, 1843; David Wagner (or Waggoner), 1843, 1844; Miss Letitia Smith, 1844-1846; Eber Smith, 1846; Mr. Martin, 1847 (taught only two days); John Wagner, 1849-1851; Parmdia Parks, 1849; J. B. Gates, 1850; Jeremiah O'Harra, 1850; Martha Smith, 1850; Jane Cross, 1853; Hiram Parker, 1853; Miss Francis Gildersleeve, 1854, 1855;

Isaac Stambaugh, 1854; Isaac Segner, 1855; Jane Sallee, 1856, 1857; Frank Hall, 1856; Miss ____ Gay, 1857; Cicero Campbell, 1857; Nancy M. Hendren, 1858; M. B. Karns, 1858; Hannah Wiris, 1859; John McLead, 1860; Miss Nancy Fulton, 1860 (now Mrs. Geo. L. Hendren) ; Burton Condit, 1860; Joseph Gage, 1861; Kate Sharp, 1865; Ezra McCleary, 1865; Mrs._____ Young, 1866; D. C. Wox, 1867; R. J. Wox, 1867; Miss Jennie Fearn, 1868; George Dildine, 1868; Geo. L. Hendren, 1869; Miss B. Johnson, Miss S. Stevenson, Lida Algire, 1873; Miss Mary Algire, 1873; Mary Wharton, 1874; Samuel Dysart, 1874.

The first school house in district No. 21 (present No. 15) was built in about 1851, on the site of the present building. Among the first teachers here was Jane Sallee (Miss Sallee was the first), David Strang, Rhoda Carson, Rhoda Needels, Melville Karns, Anna Boyd, Elizabeth Stevenson, G. W. Groves, Miss____ Northup, E. P. Holbert, Wm. Hempy, Mary Kissinger, Albert Taggart, A. K. Whims, Lida Algire, Wm. Middleton, Wm. Ricketts, James Cannon, Henry Motz.

Among the teachers in old No. 8 — the Asbury District— were James Conway, an educated Irishman, who taught first in about 1825, and from time to time until 1844 or 1845. A one-legged man by the name of Mason taught in 1837. A Mr. Prentiss and a Mr. Clapham taught in 1842 and 1843; John McGuffey taught in 1829-1830, and his son, Richard C., in 1852-1853, and Frank H. McGuffey, a son of C. R., and a grandson of John McGuffey, taught in 1891, representing three generations in the same district; Elizabeth Wilson, afterwards Mrs. Edward Livingston, in 1840; Judge John M. Pugh in 1846; Houghton Brown, a Mr. Martindale, David Shields, 1856-1857; Henry Motts and others.

Allen Brown taught in the log house opposite old No. 11 in 1852.

District No. 9, now No. 14: Israel Gayman, 1854; Wesley Todd, Maria Painter, John Bosworth, Mr. ____ Webster, Miss Rachel M. Gehm, Henry Motts, who has taught in Madison and adjoining townships for over forty years, says; "*I taught in old No. 9 in the winter of 1859-1860, also three or four years in the early seventies; in old No. 11 winters of 1860-1861 and 1869-1870; in old No. 22 winter of 1868-1869; also one or two terms of which I do not remember date in Zimmer (old No. 7) one term; in Asbury (old No. 8) one term of nine months; in old No. 21 from the fall of 1864 till the spring of 1869 and the summer of 1876.*"

Edward Beard taught in No. 11 in winter of 1858-1859; Grove Karns, 1855-1856; David Gayman taught in the Bush (Nos. 3 and 19) District in 1846, Middletown 1847, and in old No. 4 in 1849; Susan Bowen (Mrs. Daniel Bolenbaugh), Jack Dildine and Milton Stevenson also taught in Nos. 3 and 19 when the school house was of log and stood in Bush's orchard. Among those who taught in old No. 4 were Mary Collins, Christian Gayman, 1854; Lizzie Condit, Grove Karns, Thomas Killin, Mr. ____ Johnson, Miss ____Young, "Puss" Hendren and Israel Gayman, 1860. The old log school house in No. 4 stood about on the site of the present building.

The teachers in the township in 1855 to 1856 were: No. 1, W. H. Pyle; No. 2, L. C. Hendren; No. 3, S. M. Shockly; No. 4, Grove G. Carnes; No. 6, C. Smith and S. D. Sodel; No. 7. R. L. Gay; No. 8, J. T. Young and F. Reed; No. 9, Elizabeth Stevenson, and Christian Gayman; No. 10, M. J. Sallee and T. J. Hawood; No. 11, Rhoda Needels and A. Jackson; No. 12, L. J. Spencer and N. C. Meason; No. 13, Francis Gildersleeve and I. F. Segner; No. 14, E. S. Olmstead and A. J. Taylor; No. 17, H. McArthur and H. McCathen; No. 18, Wm. Hasting, H. Houser and M. G. Stevenson; No. 19, L. J. Spencer and M. G. Stevenson; No. 21, Rhoda Carson and D. Strayer.

This is the only record of the teachers we were able to find until 1876, when they were as follows (the districts in which they taught were not given):

Morris Evans, Carrie Bowman, James A. Hart, W. Ricketts, A. B. Durr, F. M. Senter, A. C. Trone, C. E. Arnold, J. P. Arnold, G. H. Dildine, Wm. M. Groves, Sallie J. Settle, Henry Motz, G. W. Preston, Amy English, Scott Hutson, Emma Marshall, Orpha E. Baugher, Minnie Hendren, Alda Pyle, Mary M. Huddle, W.H. Wills, Anna M. Yantis, Carrie Ewers, D. R. Champe.

From 1877 to 1900 the following were the teachers, by sub-districts, and date of election, viz:

No. 1, Alda Pyle, 1877; A. C. Trone, 1877; H. C. Baily, 1878-1882; A. C. Finks, 1883; E. M. Sims, 1884-1886; D. F. Karnes, 1887-1888; I. L. Earhart, 1889-1890; Cora L. Tussing, 1891; O. V. Earhart, 1891; O. P. Crist, 1892; Chas. C. Swisher, 1893, 1894; W. H. Ellinger, 1895, 1897-1899, resigned in summer of 1899, and Minnie Murphy elected 1899; C. M. Earhart, 1895; Henry Rostover, 1900.

No. 2: D. R. Champe, 1877; J. B. Kramer, 1878, 1880; Della Wilson, 1879; Geo. E. Owen, 1879; M. A. Newberry, 1881; D. F. Karnes, 1882, 1883; Geo. W. Robb, 1884, 1885; M. E. Osbourne, 1886-1888.

New No. 5: M. E. Osborne, 1889, 1890; John D. Miller, 1891, 1893; Jess A. Gayman, 1892-1896; Carrie A. Gayman, 1897-1899; Edith Decker, 1900.

No. 3: W. H. Evans, 1882, 1883; Frank Miller, 1884; Bell C. Hines, 1885; Alonzo W. Strode, 1886-1887; Perry Needels, 1886; A. S. Snyder, 1888.

New No. 2: A. S. Snyder, 1889: T. L. Peters, 1890; Chas. W. Gayman, 1891-1893; J. C. Fickel, 1894, resigned after teaching one week and M. C. Ranier appointed 1894-1895; Alvah L. Peters, 1896, 1897; Harry B. Dolby, 1898, 1899; Henry Notstine, 1900.

No. 4: Amanda J. Schoch, 1873; John G. Beggs, 1874; Orpha E. Baugher, 1877; D. F. Karnes, 1878; Henry H. Dibble, 1879; Etta Rohr, 1879; A. C. Finks. 1880-1881; Della Wilson, 1882; Della Tussing, 1883-1885; A. C. Sims, 1884, 1886, 1887; Mollie Gayman, 1885; Ola D. Fry, 1887; Oliver A. Wright, 1888.

New No. 5: Oliver A. Wright, 1889, 1890; Robt. L. McFarland, 1891; J. K. Bowman, 1892; Carrie A. Gayman, 1893-1896; Josie Crist, 1897, 1898, resigned March 25, 1899; Arthur Henderson, 1899; Grace Colman, 1900.

No. 6: John G. Beggs, 1873; Amanda J. Schoch, 1874; Samantha Stevenson, 1875; Z. C. Payne, 1877; Amy E. English, 1877; F. L. Owen, 1878; W. H. Preston, 1879; Adaline Woods, 1879; Alda Pyle, 1879; L. T. Fisher, 1880; Robt. Samuels, 1881; Adda Needels, 1881,.1883, 1885; E. L. Daymunde, 1882, 1883; Jess A. Keller, 1884; Mary Hendren, 1884; E. E. Toy, 1886, 1887; T. L. Rees, 1888.

New No. 7: T. L. Rees, 1889; U. G. McCarty, 1890; Carrie A. Gayman, 1891, 1892; Nellie Decker, 1893, 1894; J. K. Condon, 1895-1898; O. P. Crist, 1899-1900. No. 7: Wm. M. Groves, 1877; V. R. Livingston, 1877, 1878; J. H. Snyder, 1878; Lizzie Tussing, 1878, 1879; W. H. Pyle, 1879; J. F. Stimmel, 1880; E. M. Mills, 1881-1883; Della Wilson, 1881: N. B. Mills, 1883-1887; O. P. Crist, 1888.

New No. 12: Minnie Whims, 1889-1893; E. A. Swisher, 1890; John K. Bowman, 1891; W. H. Ellinger, 1894; W. E. Sims, 1895, 1896, 1898, 1899; R. K. Carruthers, 1897; Elizabeth Kuhn, 1898; Nettie Dill, 1900.

No. 8: Sallie T. Settle, 1877; C. W. Dickey, 1878; Alda Pyle, 1878; D. F. Karnes, 1879; E. J. Pattrick, 1879; Joseph Mundy, 1880; W. H. Miller, 1881; Henry Motz, 1882; Anna Sniffin, 1883; A. C. Sims, 1883; D. A. Clark, 1884; E. M. Osborne, 1885-1888; Almira Needels, 1886.

New No. 13: J. A. Wright, 1889, 1890; F. H. McGuffey, 1891; Earl S. Barr, 1892; G. A. Wright, 1893; E. M. Fickel, 1894-1896; H. E. Kile, 1897, 1898; H. E. Notstine, 1899; W. E. Sims, 1900.

No. 9; Henry Motz, 1877, 1878; Effie Robertson, 1878; James A. Parkinson, 1879, 1880; E. A. Brobst, 1879; Emma Marshall, 1880, 1881; G. H. Parkinson, 1881; James Shaner, 1882, 1883; Jacob Bachman, 1884; Clinton Alspach, 1885; Ardella Tussing, 1885; S. A. Gillett, 1886, 1888; J. A. Wright, 1887; Oliver A. Wright, 1888.

New No. 14: A. C. Ricketts, 1889; Wm. Bennett, 1890; H. G. Taylor, 1891-1897; Edwin M. Fickel, 1898, 1899, 1900.

No. 10: A. E. Bennett, 1877; T. R. Pyle, 1878-1880; C. B. Coon, 1881; Lottie Guerin, 1881; W. H. Seville, 1882, 1885; R. W. Gardner, 1883; Mettie Helsel, 1883; H. H. Neville, 1884; W. H. Bunton, 1886; W. W. Martin, 1887; J. E. Helsel, 1888.

New No. 11: J. E. Helsel, 1889, 1890; T. L. Peters, 1891; Rose Gayman, 1891-1894; Heber Kile, 1895; Morris Peters, 1896; O. V. Earhart, 1897, 1898; W. S. Dildine, 1899, 1900.

No. 11: Samuel Dysart, 1877; F. P. Newberry, 1877, 1878; Miss L. E. Tussing, 1877; F. A. Owen, 1879; G. H. Thrailkill, 1880; Marshall E. Thrailkill, 1880, 1881; Julia A. Young, 1881; James H. Shaner, 1881; Joseph Mundy, 1882; Della Tussing, 1882; Carrie A. Rader, 1883; G. H. Lighty, 1884; A. C. Sims, 1885: C. L. Hoover, 1886; Geo. W. Robb, 1887; Abe S. Good, 1888.

New No. 9: O. P. Crist, 1889-1891; Bertha Heffly, 1892, 1893; Kirk Carruthers, 1894-1896; A. Francisco, 1897-1899; John K. Condon, 1900.

No. 12: W. J. Dunn, 1877; Lizzie McCray, 1877; Lou D. Bonebrake, 1878; O. G. Welsh, 1879; D. F. Karnes, 1880, 1881; Jess A. Keller, 1882; Jacob Bachman, 1883; A. C. Finks, 1884-1886; E. H. Miller, 1887, 1888.

New No. 6: D. F. Karnes, 1889; B. F. Dildine, 1890-1894; G. W. Strickler, 1895-1897; Carrie Maish, 1898, 1899; Alice Swisher, 1900.

No. 13: J. P. Arnold, 1877; D. M. Spencer, 1877; W. H. Pyle, 1878; Orpha E. Baugher, 1878, 1879; Jess A. Keller, 1880, 1881, 1883, 1887; Mary E. Hendren, 1881; N. H. Tanner, 1882; L. M. Carson, 1882; Hattie

L. Hendren, 1883; E. M. McKinley, 1884; Sophia Whitmore, 1885; J. W. McKinley, 1885; T. L. Peters, 1886; Sadie Stimmel, 1886, 1888; Hattie Seymour, 1887; A. W. Strode, 1888.

New No. 10: A. W. Strode, 1889; Anna Nau, 1889, 1892; W. E. Sims, 1890, 1893, 1894; Mollie Gayman, 1890, 1891; Glenna Carruthers, 1895; Alice Swisher, 1896-1898, resigned March 25, 1899; Sturgis Davis, 1899; Walter Zimmer, 1900.

No. 17: Minnie Flattery, 1877; Mary Huddle, 1877: Maggie Taggart, 1877; M. A. Newberry, 1878; E. H. Owen, 1879; Emma Deterly, 1880-1882; Joseph Mundy, 1883; Ottie Mahlman, 1883; D. F. Karnes, 1884-1886; Mollie Gayman, 1887, 1888.

New No. 4: Carrie Gayman, 1889; Mollie Gayman, 1889; Ora E. Rarey, 1890; D. D. Mosier, 1891, 1892; Anna Crist, 1891; Jessie L. Kile, 1892-1900.

No. 21: James Parkinson, 1877; Eunice Parkinson, 1877; P. D. Snyder, 1878; Geo. W. Eversole, 1879; Carrie Graham, 1879; E. A. Brobst, 1880, 1881; G. W. Lighty, 1882; Sheldon Joseph, 1883; A. Francisco, 1884-1888; C. B. Parkinson, 1885; R. H. McElwee, 1887.

New No. 15: A. Francisco, 1889-1891; Alvin C. Ricketts, 1892; C. G. Smith, 1892; E. M. Fickel, 1893; G. A. Wright, 1894. resigned and W. G. Strickler, 1894: T. S. Sims, 1895, resigned January 20, 1896, and A. S. Snyder, 1896; Frank Wright, 1896-1900.

No. 22: Susie E. Filler, 1877; H. H. Dibble, 1878; Della Wilson, 1878; W. A. Cromley, 1879, 1880; J. F. Given, 1881; C. H. Emswiler, 1882, 1883; W. S. Dildine, 1883; C. M. Robb, 1884; Irene Bishop, 1885; Geo. W. Robb, 1885; J. M. Kelley, 1886-1888; Ottie Mahlman, 1888.

New No. 3: Ottie Mahlman, 1889; A. W. Strode, 1890-1892; W. S. Zaayer, 1893; E. L. Beck, 1894; H. E. Notstine, 1895-1898; Anna Ashbrook, 1899; Harry Dolby, 1900.

Township Superintendents

Rev. James Hefley, 1891-1892; H. H. Shipton, 1893-1895. There has been no township supervision since the summer of 1896.

The following persons have served as members of the Township Board of Education from the various sub-districts, dating from 1853. The sub-districts were renumbered in 1889:

No. 1: Frederick Bunn, Henry Long, Casper Limpert, M. K. Earhart, W. H. Pyle. M. H. Kelley, Absalom Rohr, F. G. Pontius, E. H. Miller; New No. 1, F. G. Pontius, 1889-1892; H. W. Lincoln, 1893-1900.

No. 2: C. Black, Samuel Leigh, Solomon Woodring, Adam Havely, John Begg, L. Rarey, Daniel Leigh, Wm. Peer, J. H. Evans, S. S. Crist, Edward Gares, E. A. Peters, E. D. Kraner, Sylvester Black; New No. 5, Daniel Leigh, 1889; Wesley Black, 1890-1897; John Decker, 1891-1894; Joseph A. Peters, 1898-1900.

Joseph A. Peters
1845 - 1924

No. 3: John Blackwood, George Long, C. P. Dildine, Joseph Burkey, E. A. Peters; new No. 2: E. A. Peters, 1889-1893; Abe Storts, 1894-1896; Geo. Koebel, 1897; M. J. Newberry, 1898-1900.

No. 4: Cyrus Hendren, John Rager, Jacob Sarber, Elisha B. Decker, Philip C. Tussing, S. O. Hendren, Jr., John Rodenfels, Peter Brown, Samuel Wheeler, Geo. T. Wheeler, Herk C. Courtright, Solomon Rager, Jerry Alspach, Wm. Goodwin; New No. 8: D. H. Tallman, 1899-1896; Morgan Thrush, 18971899; John M. Lehman, 1900.

No. 5: Wm. Peer, Elias Decker. Jacob Bishop, Daniel Crouse.

No. 6: Wesley Toy, John Cox, Jacob Swisher, G. H. Earhart, S. E. H. Kile, W. P. Sharp, Jacob Nau, J. F. Kile, John P. Sharp, Chas. Toy, J. P. Arnold, C. F. Needels, Abner Behm, Francis Pettit, John Behm, Wm. Koebel; New No. 7: Chas. Toy, 1889-1892; Morris Kile, 1893, 1894; Jess. A. Keller, 1895; John H. Behm, 1896-1901.

No. 7: J. A. Suddick, W. D. Needels, Joseph Coffman, W. L. Carson, Abel Baldwin, John Heil, Peter Swartz, M. Heil, Philip Swartz. Valentine Zimmer, S. R. Helsel, W. Beard, Joseph Behm, Seymour H. Whims, Peter Spangler; New No. 12: Wm. Zaayer, 1889; L. Reutsch, 1890. 1891; J. M. Suddick, 1892; Peter Zimmer, 1893-1896; John G. Schleppi, 1897-1899; Samuel Swartz, 1900.

No. 8; Thos. Patterson, Abram Swisher, James Needels, J. S. Stevenson, G. W. Needels, Alfred Gray, Jacob Rohr, Oliver Codner, John McGuffey, Wm. Whims, T. E. Linn, H. C. Swisher, Sylvester Carruthers, Wm. Purdy, C. R. McGuffey, Theo. D. Kalb, Joel Needels; New No. 13: T. D. Kalb, 1889-1892, 1900; J. G. Rohr, 1893; John Schleppi, 1894, 1895; Calvin J. Forsman, 1896, 1899; Stanton T. Needels, 1897, 1898, resigned February 20, 1899; J. C. Fickel, 1899, resigned January 1, 1900; John Schleppi, 1900.

No. 9: Jacob L. Bowman, Samuel Detwiler, John Miller, Isaac Kalb, John W. Needels, Jacob Bachman, Henderson Miller, Geo. W. Ruse, Daniel Wright, James P. Kalb, David Wright, Daniel Detwiler; New No. 14: James P. Kalb, 1899-1901.

No. 10: Edward Behm, John G. Edwards, Frederick Anderick, Philip Helsel, Levi S. Johnson, Geo. Hensel; New No. 11: Levi S. Johnson, 1889-1891, 1893-1897; J. W. Edwards, 1892; Daniel Schleppi, 1898-1901.

No. 11: Jeremiah Kissel, J. J. Tussing, Henry Steman, G. W. Kalb, Joshua S. Stevenson, W. S. Hopkins, John Kelkner, N. A. Stevenson, John S. Lehman, S. Shoemaker, J. M. Bennett, M. E. Kalb, Wm. Sims, Benj. Alspach, Wm. Sims; New No. 9: Wm. Sims, 1889, 1893-1895; David Mosier, 1890, 1891; Geo. Holsappel, 1892; Jonas Alspach, 1895-1900.

(In April, 1874, Districts Nos. 1 and 6 were consolidated and No. 12 formed.

No. 12: Absalom Rohr, John Lincoln, J. J. Rohr, O. D. Harris; New No. 6: O. D. Harris, 1889-1892, 1894-1901; L. F. Powell, 1893.

No. 13: Wm. Wildermuth, Kalita Sallee, T. C. Hendren, T. J. Bennett, F. Swisher, W. W. Kile, J. E. Whitmaier, G. L. Hendren, J. P. Wharton, Chas. C. Cromwell, G. W. Preston, M. L. Wildermuth; New No. 10: H. Clay Swisher, 1889-1891; G. W. Preston, 1892; A. M. Brown, 1893-1901.

No. 14: S. S. Edwards, S. O. Eberly.

No. 16: L. Kraner.

No. 17: Samuel O. Hendren, John Seymour, Moses Seymour, Jesse Seymour, W. H. Pyle, Andrew Wilson, George Long, Welton Seymour, E. M. Strode, Thomas Lowe, Thos. L. Peer; New No. 4: Welton Seymour, 1889-1900.

No. 18: James H. Sommerville, Peter T. Krag, Chas. W. Speaks. Martin C. Whitehurst, Philip Price, M. S. Stevenson, E. B. Decker, Wm. Stevenson, John Chaney, Sr., John Helpman, James B. Evans.

No. 19: Isaac Ebright, Thos. G. Bowen.

No. 21: Elihu McCracken, W. H. Algire, Michael Leidy, W. R. Algire, W. Perrin, George Claypole, W. K. Algire, Henry Algire, Amon Algire, Absalom Bowman, George King, G. S. Algire, George D. French, James K. Dill; New No. 15: George King, 1889; Jonathan Ruse, 1890, 1892; Amos Medford, 1891; John Wingert, 1893-1895; James K. Dill, 1896-1898; Frank E. Hempy, 1899-1900.

No. 22: Jacob Bishop, Wm. Peer, Geo. Kramer, Milton Cummins, Geo. Seymour, Geo. Long, Josiah Flattery, Geo. W. Lisle, Geo. Williams, Samuel Runkle, Lewis W. Berger, Wm. M. Long; New No. 3: Jesse Crouse, 1889-1893; Wm. M. Long, 1894; James D. Decker, 1895-1900.

Presidents of Township Board of Education

Since 1853, when the Board was created:

John Cox, 1853; Moses Seymour, 1854; Henry Long, T. C. Hendren, G. W. Kalb, John G. Edwards, 1856, with some intervals to 1878; John Helpman, G. H. Earhart, W. W. Kile, M. H. Kelly, Jacob Bishop, 1879; Milton Cummins, 1880; James P. Kalb, 1881-1889, 1894-1901; E. A. Peters, 1890-1893.

The Franklin County Teachers' Institute was organized at Groveport on February 9, 1867.

Trustees of School Section No. 20

The following named persons served as trustees; the date of service, neither a complete list of names can be given since no records previous to 1882 could be found: John Cox, Wm. Kile, Jacob Reese, Samuel Detwiler, Jacob Bowman, Thomas Hendren, John G. Edwards, Oliver Codner, Kalita Sallee, Samuel E. Kile, Turner Hendren, Jacob Rohr, Clay Swisher and others.

Since 1882 the trustees have been: Jacob Rohr, 1882-1888: Kalita Sallee, 1882-1886; John W. Kile, 1882-1883; John F. Wildermuth,

1884-1886; Joel Needels, 1887-1899; John Mau, 1887-1891; Theo. D. Kalb, 1888 to 1901; Sylvester Carruthers, 1892 to 1901 (since 1893 the term of office has been three years instead of one year, as previously); Robt A. Kile, 1896; Mr. Kile moved out of the township in the spring of 1897 and the Trustees appointed Welton Seymour and who has since continued in office.

The Treasurers of the school funds have been, previous to 1882, Thomas Hendren and Wm. Kile; each served for many years; John F. Kile, 1882-1884; Martin Wildermuth, 1885-1886; Wm. Mason, 1887; in 1888 John G. Rohr and Wm. Mason each received 161 votes; lots were cast and Mr. Rohr declared elected; in 1889 Mr. Rohr and Mr. Mason again received a tie vote, each having 175 votes. This time in casting lots Mr. Mason won. Wm. Mason, 1890-1891, 1896, to date; John L. Chaney, 1892-1895.

The Schools of Winchester

The first school house in what is now the Winchester special school district stood just north of Jacob Bott's lane on the east side of the road, about opposite Geo. W. Lehman's house. It was known as district No. 2, Violet Township, and later became district No. 18. Madison Township. In about 1834 a frame school house was built either on the north side of the lot now occupied by Rev. James Heffly or on the south side of the adjoining lot now occupied by J. K. Miller. Among those who taught here were a Mr. Cruikshank, T. D. Martindale, Aaron Bennedum, T. C. O'Kane, Levi Moore, and others. This building was used as a school house until 1848, when it was sold at public auction for $29.50; it was then removed across the canal on the ice, to the rear of Samuel Bartlitt's store building and occupied as a butcher shop by Geo. Fosket; it was afterwards removed to Dr. Short's vacant lot on Columbus Street, and Noah Bannister used it for a blacksmith shop; later George Derr occupied it, and finally he removed it to the east end of Columbus Street, where it forms the west end of the old blacksmith shop, and now rests in desuetude.

Some idea of the number of scholars, the wages received, the time school was kept, and the branches taught can be obtained from a report made to the directors by Levi Moore and Mrs. Nancy Johnson, who were the teachers in 1845-1846. Mr. Moore had an enrollment of

104 — 66 male and 38 female. He taught in the frame school house, and received $18.00 per month for six months. He taught Reading, Writing, Arithmetic, English Grammar, Geography, Algebra, Geometry and Philosophy. Mrs. Johnson taught in a room rented from Mr. Krag, in the log house then on the Bareis lot. She had an enrollment of 47— 14 male and 33 female, and received $12.00 per month for four months. She taught Reading, Writing, Grammar and Geography. Mrs. Johnson also taught a school — soon after her husband died (he had a cabinet shop in the Shortt stable)—in the old Shortt and Potter office. Some of her scholars tell of her "setting her bread to raise," and giving it other attention in the school room. When the Philip Price house burned—Peter Zarbaugh owned it then—he purchased this office building and Uncle Johnnie Kramer removed it to its present location, where it is now occupied by Mrs. Kildow.

On June 6, 1846, a meeting of the voters was held, when it was decided to levy a tax of $500.00 to purchase a lot and build a brick school house. The selection of a site was left to the directors, and on the 26th of June the directors met and decided to purchase a lot of John Colman; for some reason this site did not please the citizens. July 27, at a meeting of the citizens, a resolution to levy an additional tax of $300.00 was lost; after a great deal of discussion the matter of building was indefinitely postponed.

On September 17, 1847, Daniel Lecrone, John Sargent and J. B. Evans were elected directors. They called a meeting of the citizens *"to vote on a proposition to levy a tax to build."* This meeting was held on November 12, 1847. Reuben Dove had donated a lot just east of the United Brethren Church, and on Samuel Bartlitt's motion a committee of three, viz: Jacob Carty, Almanzer Hathaway and Wm. Fry, was appointed to examine this lot and report at once.

The committee returned in a short time and reported favorably; then a motion to build a brick school house was carried and a tax of $600.00 was levied. At this meeting the directors were authorized to sell the frame school building.

Still the site chosen did not seem to give satisfaction, and at a special meeting it was decided to build on a lot offered by John Kramer, Sr. The building was erected in 1848 on the lot donated by Mr. Kramer; H. J. Epley had the contract for the brick and plaster work at $343.00; and Bennedum and Kissel the carpenter work at $311.00. At a meeting in 1849 a tax of $750.00 was levied to build another school house; nothing was done, however, until April 14, 1851, when another favorable vote was taken, and on motion of Wm. Fry $800.00 was levied. This building was erected on the lot donated by Reuben Dove, which is located just east of the United Brethren Church. J. and J. S. Crites did the brick, stone and plaster work for $303.00, Bennadum and Kissel the carpenter work at $280.00.

September 17, 1860, a committee was appointed by the Board of Education of Madison Township consisting of Jacob Sarber, Wm. Perrin and Henry Long *"for the purpose of visiting the school houses in sub-district No. 18 to ascertain whether they have school room enough, and to report at the April meeting."* On April 15, 1861, this committee submitted a report which *'"was received and the committee discharged,"* and on motion of W. H. Pyle a committee of two—Moses Seymour and W. H. Pyle — was appointed to act in conjunction with the directors of sub-district No. 18 — John Chaney, Sr., J. H. Sommerville, and W. L. Stevenson — to consult the propriety of building a school house and to estimate the probable cost. April 27, 1861, the following resolution was adopted, on motion of W. H. Pyle: *"This (the Madison Township) Board allow the Directors of sub-district No. 18 to contract to build a school house in said district not to cost over $2,600.00."* There was a marked division in nearly every vote taken affecting the building of this school building. John Chaney then moved *"that this Board levy a tax of $1,500.00 on the township to build a school house in sub-district No. 18."* Motion lost. J. L. Stevenson then moved that a tax of $1,200.00 be levied. John Chaney moved to strike out $1,200.00 and insert $1,450.00, and Moses Seymour moved to insert $1,300.00, which latter motion carried. *"May 25, 1861, John Chaney presented from H. J. Epley and wife, a deed, to the Board of Education for "4 or 5" lots in the town of Canal Winchester, for the use of school purposes." and thereupon W. H. Pyle moved to accept the deed, and an order was drawn for $419.33 to pay for same."*

The contract for the building of a school house in sub-district No. 18 was presented and read by the clerk, and on motion received, and a special tax of $1,050 was levied on sub-district No. 18. A motion then prevailed *"that the local directors of sub-district No. 18 be authorized to sell the old school houses and school house lots in said district, to be sold at public or private sale; and time and condition of sale to be left to the judgment of said Directors."* On April 10, 1862. Daniel Hush paid the Board $261.00 for the north lot and building, which was later remodeled and is occupied as a residence by Joshua S. Stevenson. On the same date John Helpman paid the Board $225.50 for the south lot, and Jonathan Vought has occupied it as a residence. A committee of three — Jacob Sarber, John G. Edwards and W. K. Algire — were appointed *"to confer with the local directors in superintending the structure of the school house."*

Wm. P. Miller did the woodwork, and John Miller the brick work, together receiving $2,360.00. The building was erected and enclosed in the summer and fall of 1861, and completed in 1862. This building contained four (4) rooms, and was first occupied in September, 1862.

James H. Sommerville
1819 - 1879

Sarah Jane Sommerville
1845 - 1891

In the spring of 1868 Mr. J. B. Evans, having brought a copy of the Rules and Regulations of the Circleville schools with him, circulated a petition to organize as a special district. On April 1, 1868 notices signed by Geo. W. Blake, Wm. Cater, John M. Schoch, C. Gayman, Jacob Dauterman, Jacob Carty, J. B. Evans and others, were posted, calling a meeting of the voters in district No. 18, to vote on a proposition to organize as a special district, under Act of the Legislature of February 21, 1849. This election was held on April 11, when twenty-nine votes were cast for, and none against, and on April 30, 1868, the following Board of Education was elected: Jas. H. Sommerville, Jas. B. Evans, Dr. A. A. Shorn, C. Gayman, Chas. P. Rees and Mitchell Allen. On May 6 the Board organized by electing Jas. H. Sommerville President, J. B. Evans Clerk, and C. Gayman Treasurer. Rules and regulations were also adopted.

April 25, 1873. John Helpman's motion to build an addition to school building was laid on the table. At this meeting rules and regulations were ordered printed for the first time. The year 1873 was spoken of as a "stormy" year in the Board.

May 6, 1874. A motion to build an addition to school building prevailed, all members voting in favor. On May 18th plans were adopted, and on June 19th bids were opened; a few days later, June 22, all bids were rejected and the building put off indefinitely.

On April 19, 1875, Jas. H. Sommerville, James Heffly and Philip Game were appointed a building committee and instructed to prepare plans, which were submitted and adopted on May 5. The contract for the two rooms in the south wing and the two vestibules was awarded as follows; Wolfe & Zackero, brick work, $2,135.00;O. L. Dibble, plastering. $539.00; Chas. F. Yost, wood work, $2,630.00; E. B. Armstrong, furnace, $390.00 and $900.00 was expended in new furniture. School opened in the remodeled building on Wednesday, September 22, 1875.

In the spring of 1871 twenty evergreen and twenty maple trees were set out. The well on the school grounds was dug in the summer of 1877.

In the spring of 1877, 55 trees were planted on the school grounds. In 1876 there were three superintendents, viz: J. F. Maxwell, one week; C. W. Campbell, September 16 to March 8, 1877, and David O'Brien, March 12 to end of school year.

On June 4, 1877, soon after the election of teachers, a largely attended "indignation meeting" was held in Game's Hall. Jas. P. Kramer was chosen chairman and H. H. Dibble secretary. A set of six resolutions was passed, the following two embodying the complaint: *"Resolved, that a majority of our present school board, namely: four members, did violate and disregard our expressed will, in the election of a Principal for our schools for the coming term, in that they refused to elect a well tried one, who was not only the unanimous choice of ourselves, but also of the pupils in the different departments of our schools."*

"Resolved, that the Board did elect as subordinate teachers, persons known to be objectionable to a majority of our citizens."

The following were the Directors from 1845. The date indicates year of election:

J. B. Schrock 1845, James Clendening 1845, Wm. Harbaugh 1846, Hinton Tallman 1846, 1854-1856, Daniel Leckrone 1846-1847, J. B. Evans 1847, 1866, 1867, John Sargent 1847, Paul Samsel 1848, David Tallman 1848, John Helpman 1849, 1854-1857, 1863-1865, Wm. Fry 1849, James Cannon 1849 (there are no records of 1850), Samuel Bartlitt 1851, H. Nicodemus 1851-1852, Jas. H. Sommerville 1851-1855, 1858, 1860, Peter T. Krag 1852-1854, Chas. W. Speaks 1853, Martin C. Whitehurst 1856, 1857, Philip Price 1857-1859, W. L. Stevenson 1858-1860, Elisha B. Decker 1860-1862, John Chaney, Sr., 1861-1863, A. Hathaway 1861, Mich Allen 1862-1864; John Boyd 1864-1866, Dr. A. A. Shortt 1866-1867, Oliver P. Chaney 1867.

The following have been the officers and members of the Board of Education since this has been made a special district:

Presidents

Jas. H. Sommerville, 1868; M. C. Whitehurst, 1869-1871; John Helpman, 1872, 1876-1881; John H. Speilman, 1873-1875; Rev. James Heffly, 1882; A. L. Shride, 1883-1884; W. H. Lane, 1885-1888, resigned October 29, 1888; Geo. F. Bareis, 1888-1895, resigned May 13, 1895; Robert W. Bolenbaugh, 1895, 1900-1901; Joe C. Shaffer, 1896; Ed. S. Tussing, 1897-1899.

Clerks

J. B. Evans, 1868, 1869; Chas. F. Yost, 1870, resigned July 20, 1870; C. Gayman, 1870; Rev. James Heffly, 1871; W. R. Miller, 1872; Jas. H. Sommerville, 1873-1877; J. P. Wiseman, 1878, resigned January 27, 1879; Dr. A. Starr, 1879-1884; R. W. Bolenbaugh, 1885-1893; P. M. Teegardin, 1894-1896; J. C. Shaffer, 1897; Wm. D. Boyer, 1897-1899; Wm. M. Codner, 1900-1901.

Treasurers

C. Gayman, 1868-1870; J. B. Evans, 1870-1872; W. R. Miller, 1873-1874; Rev. James Heffly, 1875-1877, 1884-1886; Wm. T. Conklin, 1878-1879, resigned October 30, 1879; J. K. Miller, 1879-1882; Geo. F. Bareis, 1887, 1888, 1894 (term of Treasurer was changed to be September 1st in 1888 instead of in April); Philip Caine, 1888-1892: Cary D. Whitehurst, 1893-1894, resigned October 29, 1894; Miss Josephine Chaney, 1895. resigned June 24, 1895; Albert Bachman, 1895-1899; Wm. L. Watters, 1900-1901.

Members

Jas. H. Sommerville, 1868-1870, 1872-1877; Jas. B. Evans, 1868-1874; Mr. Evans resigned June 22, 1874, and Rev. James Heffly appointed; C. Gayman, 1868. 1870; Dr. A. A. Shortt. 1868, 1869, 1873-1875, 1877-1879; Chas. P. Rees. 1868, 1870-1872; Mich Allen, 1868, died May 17, 1868, and Rev. David Shrader, 1868. appointed; M. C. Whitehurst. 1869-1871; Chas. W. Speaks, 1869-1871; Chas. F. Yost, 1870, resigned July 20, 1870, and C. Gayman appointed; O. P. Chaney, 1871, 1872, 1878-1880, 1882-1884; John Helpman, 1872-1874, 1876-1881; W. R. Miller, 1871-1876; Rev. James Heffly, 1871 (resigned July 17, 1871, and W. R. Miller appointed), 1875-1877, 1880-1888; John H. Speilman, 1873-1875; Philip Game, 1875, 1876, 1887-1892: Dr. A. Starr, 1876-1884: J. P. Wisenjan, 1877-1878; resigned January 27, 1879, and Philip Game appointed, but declined to serve, so on February 24, J. K. Miller was appointed; W. T. Conklin, 1878, 1879, resigned October 30, 1879, and S. Harrison Tallman appointed (J. K. Miller elected Treasurer); J. K. Miller, 1878-1882; S. H. Tallman, 1879; Jacob Bott, 1880; John L. Chaney, 1881-1882; Samuel C. Dressler, 1881, 1882; A. L. Shride, 1883-1885, resigned April 20, 1885, and Geo. F. Bareis appointed; Jerry Kramer, 1884-1900; John S. Lehman, 1884-1886; Wm. H. Lane, 1885-1888, resigned October 29, 1888. and George Powell appointed; Robt. W. Bolenbaugh, 1885-1893, 1895-1901; Geo. F. Bareis, 1885-1895, resigned May 13, 1895, and R. W. Bolenbaugh appointed; George Powell, 1888-1894; Dr. L. W. Berry, 1889-1894, 1897; C. D. Whitehurst, 1893-1895; P. M. Teegardin, 1894-1896; Albert Bachman, 1895-1900; Miss Josephine Chaney, 1895, resigned May 13, and Zack E. England appointed; Z. E. England, 1895-1896, resigned August 3, 1896, and Wm. M. Codner appointed; Joe C.

Shaffer, 1896-1897, resigned December 27, 1897, and Dr. L. W. Berry appointed; Wm. D. Boyer, 1896-1899; Wm. M. Codner, 1896, 1899-1900; Ed. S. Tussing, 1897-1899, 1901; James Palsgrove, 1897; John H. Deitz, 1898; Wm. L. Walters, 1898-1901; Rev. T. H. E. Eich, 1901.

Teachers in Winchester

Mr. ____ Cruikshank, about 1840; Aaron Bennedum, early forties; T. D. Martindale, 1844; Levi Moore, 1846; Mrs. Nancy Johnson, 1846; T. C. O'Kane, 1847; Elizabeth McBride, 1848-1849; James Seeds, 1848. 1849; Aaron Shisler, 1850; Mary Hempted, 1850; Geo. M. B. Dove assisted Mr. Shisler for a few months; J. H. Doan, 1851; Mr. Doan also taught a private school in the old frame United Brethren Church in 1851 ; Miss Rhoda Carson, 1851; Mr. Seeds was the first to teach in the north brick building, and Miss Carson the first in the south brick building; William Hasting, 1852-1856; Mrs. Elizabeth Pollay, 1852-1858; ____ Tallman, 1851; H. Houser, 1855; Milton G. Stevenson, 1855; W. R. Eggleson, 1857; Burton Condit, 1857, south building; Tallman Slough and Rachel M. Gehm, north building, 1858; Rhoda M. Needels, 1858.

For several years during the winter term there would be an assistant teacher in the north building, and for several years previous to 1855 all the male scholars attended the north building, and all the female the south. In 1855 the schools were graded when the advanced scholars of both sexes attended the north building, and all the younger ones the south building. J. P. Campbell, 1859; J. C. Forbes, 1859-1860; E. H. Walden, 1860, 1862; G. W. Bethel, 1861.

Since September, 1862, the Principals or Superintendents have been:

A. C. Moon, 1862; Isaac R. Stambaugh, 1863, died after teaching one or two weeks; he lived in the Mrs. Welsch residence on Columbus Street: Milton L. Stevenson, 1863; W. R. Pugh, 1864: Wm. H. Pyle, 1865; G. S. Stevens, 1866, 1867, resigned February 27, 1868, when D. T. Clover, who was then teaching the grammar department, was appointed; G. W. Buck, 1869; J. W. Rutledge, 1870, James Heffley, 1871, 1872; Frank M. Kumler, 1873, 1874; L. K. Powell, 1875; J. F. Maxwell, 1876, one week; C. W. Campbell, September 16, 1876, to March 8, 1877; David O'Brien, March 12, 1877; P. M. Mills, 1877-1880, resigned October 15, 1880; M. E. Thrailkill, November 1, 1880; Chas. A. Harris,

1881-1882, resigned July 5, 1882; L. L. Rankin, 1882-1883; W. H. Hartsough, 1884-1888; Thos. J. Fitzgerald, 1889-1892, resigned August 15, 1892; Thomas M. Fouts, 1892-1894; U. S. Brandt, 1895-1898; W. T. Heilman, 1899-1901.

Other Teachers since September, 1862

E. H. Walden, 1862; Mr. _____ McEntire, 1863; James H. Cannon, 1863; Groves G. Carnes, 1862; Anna Foos, 1864; Luda Fry, 1864-1866; Mollie Thompson, 1865; Clara Leib, 1865; Rachel M. Gehm, 1865; Jennie Hanby, 1866; D. T. Clover, 1867; Jennie Sommerville, 1867-1870, 1875-1885; Sat. A. Wilson, 1867-1871; Lide Algire, from January 1, 1870 (this is the first year of four teachers); Miss M. S. Ebright, 1870; Tilla Raymond, 1871, resigned February 26, 1872, and Miss J. Caly was elected; Mary Tallman, 1871-1872, 1875-1876; Mary Bishop, 1872; Miss S. E. Filler, 1872-1874 (February 3, 1873, schools were dismissed for two weeks on account of measles); Carrie Bowman, 1873-1875, 1877; Laura Schoch, 1873-1875, 1878-1880 (September 25, 1875, school was opened in the remodeled building, and five teachers were employed); Mary E. Gayman, 1876-1885, died August 17, 1885; Lizzie Miller, 1876; Mr. A. Ricketts, 1877-1878; Susie Leckrone, 1878, 1879 (September, 1878, a Mr. Richards was given permission to use Miss Leckrone's room in which to teach drawing, one hour before and one hour after school hours); Mr. A. F. Rohr, 1879; H. H. Dibble, 1880-1894; Iola Wickham, 1880-1884; Rose Zartman, 1881, 1882; W. Scott Alspach, 1885-1896, died February 27, 1897; Mrs. Alice Sibley, 1885; Katie Gayman, 1885; Etta Pickering, 1886; Kate Dowdall, 1886-1889, died February 27, 1890; Lila Starr, 1886-1892; Carrie Gayman, 1887-1888; Minnie McFadden, 1889-1901; Rose Gayman, 1889-1890; Cora Frazier, 1893-1896; Josephine Chaney, 1895-1897, 1899-1901; Robert McFarland, 1897-1898; Minnie Murphy, 1897, 1898; Clinton Alspach, 1897, 1898; Mr. E. S. Heller, 1898, 1901; Harriet Burr, 1899; Edna Perrill, 1899, 1900; Helen P. Bareis, 1900-1901; Madge Kanode, 1901.

Vocal music was introduced in February, 1889. and the following have been the teachers: Mr. H. M. McKee, 1889; Mr. J. D. Luce, 1890; Minnie Luce, 1891, 1892; Mr. S. A. Brobst, 1893, 1895, 1896; Gertrude Bailey, 1894; Rev. J. P. Stahl, 1897-1901.

James Palsgrove has served as Truant Officer since the creation of that office in 1893, with the exception of one year, during which he served as a member of the Board, when Samuel Rush was elected Truant Officer.

Michael Dowdall has served as janitor continuously since 1886.

In 1870 there were four departments, in 1875 changed to five and again increased to six in 1898.

Graduates from the Winchester High School

Class of 1886: Clement V. Moore, Benjamin F. Lehman, John F. Lecrone, Samuel E. Bunn, Kate Dowdall, Carrie A. Gayman and Rose Gayman.

Class of 1887: Luda E. Chaney, Mayme Bartlitt, S. Arville Yost, Bertha B. Heffly, Charles B. Lecrone and Henry W. Lehman.

Class of 1888: Daniel G. Boyer, Laura A. Zerkle, Minnie M. Heffley, Edwin C. Gayman, Frances H. Game, Charles F. Wollenzein, M. Blanche Dibble, Edward J. Bennett, Samuel H. Martin, Harry A. Miller, Gertrude A. Bailey, Francis H. Smith, Minnie McFadden, Amor A. Tussing and Josephine Chaney.

Class of 1889: Charles W. Gayman, Robert L. McFarland and Harlan E. Rainier.

There was no class in 1890.

Class of 1891, Reed H. Game, Edward S. McFadden, Cora Kramer, William D. Boyer and Horace R. Bailey.

Class of 1892: Jess. A. Gayman, Harley J. Zarbaugh, George C. Starr, Lulu M. Shaffer and Effie M. Yost.

Class of 1893: Nannie M. Boyer, Mary E. Powell, Fannie M. Lehman, W. Benton Boyd and Harry B. Caslow.

Class of 1894: Quintin R. Lane, John F. Bartlitt and Laura Smith.

Class of 1895: Jonn C. Gayman, Ona Kramer, John W. Lehman, Frances McVey, Clara Reiner, Jemima Sarber and Clinton W. Yost.

Class of 1896: Homer Z. Bostwick, Lizzie Deitz, Mary Dibble, John King, Edwin D. Lehman, John Palsgrove and Mae B. Schaff.

Class of 1897: Jesse G. Dauterman and Laura R. Kramer.

Class of 1898: Harry E. Bowman, Francis H. Game, Edward O. Herbst, Della Loucks, Bertha Meier, Clyde L. Miller, Ethel Seymour an<l Mary Yost.

Class of 1899: Wilmot Bolenbaugh, Harry Beery, Helen Bartlitt, Grace Colman, Ray Hummel and Chester Seymour.

Class of 1900: Maud Bishop, Jennie Dowler, Mallie Kramer, Mabel Tussing, Edgar Leidy, Charles Long, John Wright and Chauncey Shaffer.

Class of 1901: Albert Bolenbaugh, Minnie Bailey, Mattie Boyd, Madge Chaney, Silas Diley, Edward Judy, Stephen Haffey, Roxie Kalb and John H. Cooper.

Schools of Groveport

The first schools were kept in dwelling houses. Among these was one in a log house which stood where M. Corbett's brick house now stands, about three fourths of a mile east of town. Another was kept in a log house on the Robt. F. Dildine farm.

In 1834 Wm. Richardson erected a frame building directly opposite the residence of Wm. Corbett, and just back of the evergreen trees still standing. His father had sent him the money to build a church, but it was seldom used for religious services. Select schools were held here for some years, when it took the name of Richardson's Academy. The old building stood until a few years ago.

Chas. Rarey and Thos. Hughes, his son-in-law, built a one-story frame school house about one-half mile southwest of town, in about 1841 or 1842, and Thos. Hughes taught a school here. It took the name of Rarey's Academy.

A log school house on the lot occupied by Lottie Sandy, and known as the Margaret Chandler School House, was sometimes referred to as The Seminary.

November 10, 1847, the Directors of District No. 20 met at C. T. Stevenson's shop — Wm. James being Chairman, Dr. Abel Clark Clerk, and A. Shoemaker Treasurer — and rented the Rarey Academy for six months at $3.00 per month (referred to in their records as the Laypole Rarey School House), and also The Seminary for three months at $2.50 per month (referred to in their records as the Margaret Chandler School House); it stood on the lot where J. E. Stewart now lives. J. C. Brown was employed to teach in the former at $25.00 per month, and Margaret Dutton in the latter at $2.00 per week.

On March 28, 1848, the voters met at the Chandler School House for the purpose of selecting a site for a new school house. After lengthy discussion the Directors were instructed to buy lot No. 54, on Walnut

Street (20 voted for it and 1 against). On motion of Dr. Abel Clark *"the Directors were further instructed to levy a tax of $1,200.00 for the purpose of building a brick school house 40 by 50 feet, and should good and sufficient subscriptions be put into the hands of the Directors previous to their contracting the building, then they are instructed to build 40 by 60 feet: in either case, the house is to be two stories high."* This motion was carried by a unanimous vote. The lot was purchased of W. H. Rarey for $100.00.

On April 29, 1848, the Directors (Wm. R. Darnell was appointed a Director in place of Wm. James, who resigned on April 12) met at Darnell & Co.'s store, and contracted with Wm. R. Darnell to furnish material and do the brick work for $700.00, and with D. C. Shockley to do the carpenter work and furnish material for doors, windows, frames and ceiling for $220.00, and with A. Willie to do work and furnish material of the roof, floor and stairs for (amount omitted), and with Thos. Ward to do the plastering for $70.00. The building was erected in the summer of 1848, and cost about $1,650.00. The following notice which was posted in three public places, indicates that it did not take long in those days, after the levy was made, until the money was in hand:

"Notice.—Taxpayers in sub-district No. 20, Groveport, will take notice that at a special meeting of the voters held March 28, 1848, a tax of $1,200.00 was levied. The above tax will be due and payable as follows: One-half the 5th day of June next, and the balance on August 1, 1848.

"By order of the Directors,

May 5th, 1848.   *Ed. Gares, Clerk."*

A school election was held on September 16, 1848, at which only fourteen persons voted. Wm. R. Darnell, Samuel Sharp and A. Willie were elected Directors. On April 9, 1849, another election was held at which the following persons voted: Samuel Sharp, Salem A. Darnell, W. H. Rarey, M. Shaffer, Wm. R. Darnell, M. W. Bishop, J. A. Taylor, K. Tenner, J. Cherry, A. Clark, A. Willi, D. Sarber, J. Anderick, W. Cameron, J. Snyder, F. Taylor, L. Sarber, C. J. Stevenson, H. Long, Peter Long, Jonathan Watson, Isaiah Brown, and R. Shockley.

On February 2, 1850, an election was held to organize under the law of 1849. Thirty-one voted for, and fifteen against. On February 16 the following Board of Education was elected: Wm. R. Darnell and C. J. Stevenson for three years, Thos. Hughes and A. Willi for two years, and Jacob Andericks and Jesse Dildine for one year.

On November 23, 1855, the Board paid G. P. Champe eight dollars for the school house bell.

In April, 1883, F. S. Rarey, President, and G. Adell, Clerk of the Board, were appointed a committee to estimate the probable expense of a new school house, and on June 2, 1883, the following notice was posted: *"Notice is hereby given by the Board of Education of Groveport village school district, that there will be a special meeting of the qualified voters of said district on Thursday, the 14th day of June, 1883, from 1 o'clock to 6 o'clock p. m., to consider the question of levying a tax upon the taxable property of said district to build and furnish a school house, the probable cost of which is estimated at $12,000.00; and if said tax is levied, the further questions whether the levy shall be made from year to year thereafter and what amount shall be levied each year until the actual cost of building and furnishing said house is raised?"*

The result of this election was as follows: Tax, Yes; 87 votes. Tax, No; 33. Yearly, yes; 88. Yearly, no; 26. Amount each year, one-tenth. Terrill & Morris, of Columbus, Ohio, submitted a plan (called the Johnstown plan), which was adopted. Four and one-third (4 1/3) acres of land was purchased of John F. Wildermuth for $721.00, and a lot was purchased of Mrs. Samuel Bechtel for $225.00, and another one at the same price of Chas. Stewart.

August 21, 1883, bids were opened as follows; E. W. Blair, entire building, without blackboards, $10,634.64; C. Zebold, entire building, $12,368.00; E. P. Jackson and M. King, entire building, $13,175.20; John A. Grabowsky, entire building, $16,000.00. There were a number of other bids, but only on parts of the work. On August 24 the bid of E. W. Blair was accepted and changes made in the plans reducing the bid by $634.00, after adding blackboards. On August 27, 1884, the building was taken off contractor's hands. The building was occupied first in September, 1884.

On August 29, 1883, the vacant lot north of the old school house was sold at public auction to F. M. Senter for $320.00, but the Board would not confirm the sale, and on October 6, 1883, it was sold again for $400.00, F. M. Senter being the purchaser.

The sale of the old school building to Deaver & Pettit was confirmed on April 20, 1885, and on December 11, 1886, the purchasers deeded it back to the Board for $600.00 and the Board then sold it to Henry Smith.

Teachers

In 1848-1849, J. C. Brown and D. R. Solomon; 1849-1850, E. G. Chambers, Margaret Rarey and E. Meason.

In 1850 the schools were organized under the law of 1849, and the following have been the teachers, the date indicates the year appointed:

Principals or Superintendents

E. G. Chambers, 1850-1851; J. B. Campbell, 1852; Wm. H. Pyle, 1853; Mrs. D. R. Champe, 1854; S. P. Adams, 1855-1857; G. C. Smith, 1858-1860; John P. Patterson, 1861; T. F. Harwood, 1862-1863: W. R. Pugh, 1864-1865; Z. C. Payne, 1866-1867; G. H. Tracy, 1868; G. C. Dasher, 1869-1870; R. M. Boggs, 1871-1874: N. H. Garner, 1875; A. L. Brooke, 1876-1885; James H. Brown, 1886-1887; J. B. Duzan, 1888-1889; J. A. Wilcox, 1890-1895, resigned November 30, 1895, and J. B. Fairchilds elected December 14, 1895; H. H. Shipton, 1896; Mr. Shipton died August, 1896 and on August 28, 1896, the Board elected Wm. H. McFarland, 1896-1897; Geo. C. Deatrich, 1898-1901.

The teachers in the other departments were:

Miss Lucy Johnson, 1850-1851; Miss Fisk, 1850; Miss Marilla Johnson, 1851; Mrs. A. A. Kidd, 1851; Miss Martha McClandish, 1852; Mrs. A. A. Kidd, 1852; Miss Mary McLain, 1852; Miss ____ Wagner, 1853; Mary E. Dutton, 1853; Miss ____ Needels, 1853; Miss A. M. Havens, 1854; Miss Adda Barrett, 1854; Miss ____ Hamilton, 1854; H. McArthur, 1855; Miss E. Pattrick, 1855; Miss E. N. Barr, 1856-1857; Miss Rebecca McArthur, 1856; A. W. Paul, 1856: Mrs. Adda L. Adams, 1857; Miss S. J. McMahon, 1857; Mrs. D. R. Champe, 1858; Miss Mell E. Sharp, 1858; A. G. Zinn, 1858; Miss Eliza McCoy, 1859-1860; Miss Julia A. Clark, 1859-1860; Miss S. C. Hopkins, 1860; Miss Emma Belt, 1861; Miss Ella O'Harra, 1861-1862; Carrie L. Clark, 1862; Cary L. Hopkins, 1863; Hester A. Havely, 1863; Miss Kate (Cox) Seymour, 1864; Mrs. G.

P. Champe, 1865-1869; Miss ____ Young, 1866; Lizzie Howell, 1866-1867, 1869-1875; Miss Bennett, 1867; O. S. Warner, 1867; Hattie Rees, 1868; R. F. Dildine, 1868; John D. Lamb, 1869; Geo. S. Peters, 1870; Miss Mary Young, 1870-1896 — 27 years; Lide Algire, 1871; Miss ____ Shrigly, Lida O'Hara, Mattie Long, 1874; Miss ____ Yantis, Rachel McCullough, 1872-1873; Henrietta Guerin, 1875-1876; Jennie Guerin, 1875-1876; Alice Spencer, 1877-1879; Ola Spencer, 1877-1878. resigned October 11, 1878, and E. V. Adell elected: Deaza B. Senter, 1879-1885; Della Wilson, 1880; Jennie Lawson, 1881; Rhoda E. Sigler, 1882, resigned November 11, 1882, and Luella Cook elected; Lovett T. Fisher, 1883; Joseph A. Kitzmiller, 1884, 1885; Geo. W. Robb, 1886; Della M. Kile, 1886-1901; S. A. Gillet, 1887; N. B. Mills, 1888, 1889; D. F. Karnes, 1890-1894, 1896-1901; B. F. Dildine, 1895-1901; Alfratta Champe, assistant High School teacher 1891-1892; Mana Clark, 1896; Ola G. Mansfield, 1897-1901.

December 31, 1892, Mrs. Della Peterman was employed at $20 per month to teach vocal music, and she was re-employed from year to year until June, 1896, when the study of music under a special teacher was discontinued.

Directors Sub-district No. 20

A. Shoemaker, Treasurer, 1847; Dr. Abel Clark, Clerk, 1847; Wm. James, 1847, resigned, and on February 12, 1848, the Clerk appointed Wm. R. Darnell, 1848, 1849; Edward Gares, Clerk 1848; Samuel Sharp. 1848; Thomas Hughes, Clerk 1849; C. J. Stevenson, 1849.

February 2, 1850, organized under an "Act" passed in 1849. Thomas Hughes, 1850, 1851; A. Willie, 1850, 1851; C. J. Stevenson, 1850, 1851; Wm. R. Darnell, 1850, 1851; J. Anderick, 1850; Jesse Dildine, 1850.

In 1850 Thomas Hughes was President, A. Willie Clerk, and C. J. Stevenson Treasurer. No further records could be found of the membership of the Board until 1878, since which the following have served:

Presidents

Wm. Chandler, 1878, moved away and W. L. Powell elected June 14, 1878 — December 13, 1879; Mr. Powell having moved away, the Board elected J. S. Pattrick, 1879, 1882; Morris Kile, 1880, 1881; F. S.

Rarey, 1883, 1884; John F. Wildermuth, 1885; Jethro Denton, 1886-1888, 1890-1895; Robt. A. Shaw, 1889; Frank E. Williams, 1896; Edward Gares, 1897-1901.

Treasurers

A. Shoemaker, 1847; A. Willie, 1848; C. J. Stevenson, 1850, 1854, 1855; Geo. McCormick, 1851; Dr. G. L. Smith. 1852, 1856, 1858; J. Weaver, 1857: J. H. Fearn, 1859-1861; Casper Limpert, 1862-1867 (to April 30, 1868); S. Allen Peters, 1869-1878, died, and Dr. G. L. Smith appointed 1878-1883; Dr. Smith resigned August, 1883 and Wm. Mason appointed 1883-1887, 1890, 1891; Dr. J. H. Saylor, 1888, 1889; J. L. Chaney, 1892-1896; Wm. R. Smith, 1897-1901.

Clerks

G. Adel, 1878-1883; moved away and on December 27, 1883, the Board appointed C. P. Long, 1883, 1884, 1890; Dr. J. H. Saylor, 1885: J. L. Chaney, 1886, 1887; Edward Gares, 1888, 1889; Wm. R. Smith, 1891-1895, resigned, and on May 16, 1895, the Board elected J. O. Rarey, 1895; Chas. D. Rarey, 1896-1898, resigned August 26, 1898. having been appointed Deputy Recorder of Franklin County, and the Board elected Philip C. Tussing, 1898-1901.

Members

S. Allen Peters, 1877, 1878, died, and in May, 1878 the Board appointed J. S. Pattrick, 1878, 1882; died December, 1882; W. L. Powell, 1878-1879; Chas. Campbell, 1878-1882, 1884-1886; G. S. Dildine, 1878-1881, moved away and on October 28, 1881, the Board appointed John F. Wildermuth, 1881-1887; on December 13, 1879, Morris Kile, 1879-1882, was appointed in place of Wm. L. Powell, who moved away; Mr. Kile moved out of the district on April 12, 1882; the Board appointed Wm. Mason, 1882-1891, 1895; John A. Kile was appointed December 27, 1883, in place of G. Adel, who moved away, 1883-1885; Dr. J. H. Saylor, 1883-1890; F. S. Rarey, 1883-1885, moved away, and on June 3, 1885, the Board appointed J. L. Chaney, 1885-1889, 1892-1897; Jethro Denton, 1886-1888, 1890-1895; Robt. Kile, 1887.

September, 29, 1887, Jas. K. Rarey was appointed in place of J. F. Wildermuth, who moved away; Edward Gares, 1888-1890, 1896-1901; Robt. A. Shaw, 1888, 1889, 1896-1901; Wm. R. Smith, 1889-1901;

Chas. P. Long, 1884, 1890-1895; John O. Rarey, 1891-1895; Frank E. Williams, 1891-1896; Chas. D. Rarey, 1896-1898 (resigned August 26, 1898, and W. R. Smith appointed); Dr. C. R. Clement, 1895-1901; Philip C. Tussing, 1897-1901; L. B. Carruthers, 1898-1901.

Janitors

J. Cunningham, 1877-1882, 1886-1887; Mr. Cunningham resigned September 29, 1882 and the Board elected Reuben Abbott, 1882, 1883, 1885; E. Childs, 1884; Mark Codner, 1888-1891; Silas Montgomery, 1892-1895; Albert Sandy, 1896-1901.

Truant Officers

John A. Kile, 1890-1892; Elder Thompson, 1893; O. R. Mansfield, 1894, declined to serve and Silas Montgomery elected, 1894, 1895; Albert Sandy, 1896-1901.

Damris R. Champe
1828 - 1908

Mary Young
1837 - 19??

The following is a list of the graduates of the Groveport High School:

Class of 1871: Flora Rarey, Ida L. Smith and Mattie L. Long.

There were no graduates in 1872 or in 1873.

Class of 1874: Ida S. Seymour.

Class of 1875: Emma Rarey

No class in 1876.

Class of 1877: Lizzie L. Long.

Class of 1878: Della M. Champ.

There were no graduates for the next seven years.

Class of 1886: Della M. Kile, Maxa E. Swisher, Katharine A. Corbett, Katharine T. Corbett, Lillie Montgomery, Leota I. Saylor and Thornton L. Peters.

No class in 1887.

Class of 1888: Lizzie Z Zinn, Lena M. Mason, Etoile Montgomery, Sadie Stimmel, Hattie Saylor, Charles C. Swisher, Frank M. McCartney and Frank Mann.

Class of 1889: Cora Tussing, _____ Swisher, Nellie Decker, Kate Denton, Ada Earhart, W. E. Simms, Frank Dildine and M. Leo Corbett.

No classes in 1890 or 1891.

Class of 1892: Jesse L. Kile, Alice Swisher, Nellie Decker, Kate Denton, Ada Earhart, Mary Wildermuth, Chas. H. Lott, Heber E. Kile, Frank Dill, Florence Gares, Ray Herr and Albert Herr.

Class of 1893: Jennie Saylor, Nora Corbett, Grace Cromwell, Lizzie McGuffey, Claude Cromwell, Nora Weatherington, Mary Denton, Alma Montgomery, Alice Rarey, Lula Toy, E. Todd Rohr, Geo. C. Lincoln, George Needels and Arthur Hendren.

Class of 1894: Anna E. Carder, Kirk R. Carruthers, Glenna Carruthers, Frank P. Corbett, J. Collins Fickel, G. Raymond Kile, Nettie D. Weatherington, Minnie L. Murphy, Ola G. Mansfield, Matilda E. Peterson, M. Clark Rainier, Lizzie Saylor, and W. Grant Strickler.

Class of 1895: Bessie Kile, Alva Peters, Alice M. Fickel, Maurice M. Peters, Della Simms, F. Scott Simms and Henry Notstine.

Class of 1896: Florence Swisher, Tessa Stukey, Elsie Swisher, Hattie O. Arnold, Mamie J. Gates, Sarah C. Moore, R. Ross Shaw, Will L. Powell, John H. Montgomery, Harley B. Dolby, LeRoy M. Willie, Edson F. Rainier, Chas. F. Dolby, Chas. C. Plum and J. Russel Strickler.

Class of 1897: Maggie Arnold, Blanche Needels, Florence Seymour, James Simms, Bertie Toy, Martha Walton, Howard Rarey and Laura Schlosser.

Class of 1898: Sadie Copeland, Edith Decker, Nellie Larrison, Alice Paxton, Grade Preston, Josie Schlosser, Bess Seymour, Maud Seymour, Grace Seymour, Louie Stansberry, Amy Swisher, Alva Kile, Bert Peer, Will Peters.

There was no graduating class in 1899.

Class of 1900: Harley E. Peters, Walter Zimmer, Anna Rarey, Lucius Davis.

Class of 1901: Maude Chaney, Ray Decker, Mabel Long, Charles Lincoln, Kathryn Saylor, Nannie Simms, Joseph Rohr, Ray Teegardin and Pearl Tussing.

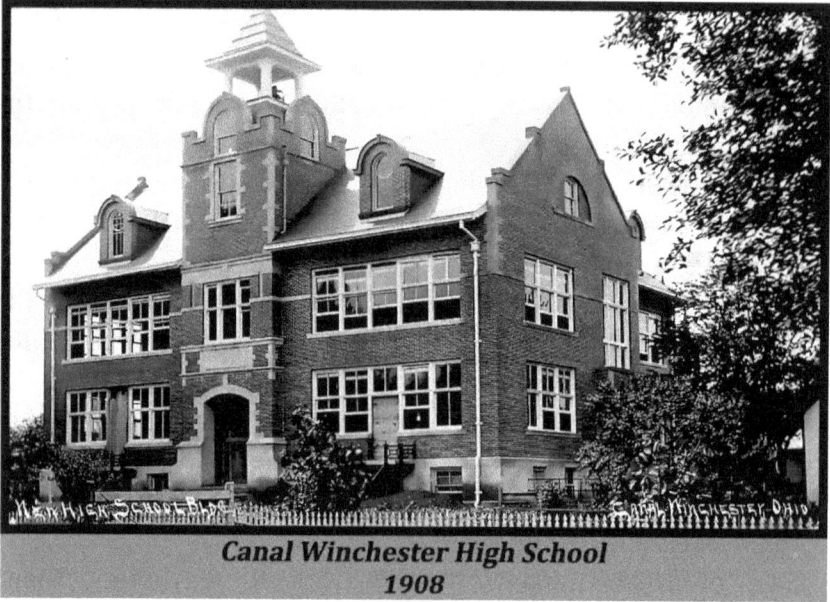

Canal Winchester High School
1908

CHAPTER XII
LITERARY ENTERTAINMENTS

"Discretion of speech is more than eloquence; and to speak agreeably to him with whom we deal is more than to speak in good words, or in good order."

—Bacon

The old-fashioned Spelling School furnished the principal literary entertainment, especially for the young people. The Spelling School became popular with the erection of buildings intended for school houses, and continued in favor well into the sixties. Many became so proficient in the art of spelling that it was nothing unusual to spend a whole evening in pronouncing words — at the beginning from the spelling book, and later from the pronouncing dictionary — and then only "seat" the last few spellers by resorting to "cratch" words. The announcement of a Spelling School was soon heralded over the neighborhood and usually brought together the champion spellers and their friends from the adjoining districts; the spelling began at candle-lighting, and each person was expected to bring a candle. "Pronouncing" was an important factor, and usually two or more persons — in most instances the school teachers — were chosen, who relieved each other in turns.

The Debating Society took the place of the Spelling School for those past school age, especially in the more intelligent neighborhoods. It is the Debating Society which instilled that thirst for knowledge, and whose forum called out and developed that power of *"thinking on one's feet"* and which reveals the secret of the dignified, graceful and attractive force which was so marked in many of our business and professional men of a few decades ago.

On January 25, 1840, a Literary Society was organized in Winchester, and named "The Winchester Institute." The record book containing its constitution, membership roll and the secretary's minutes from its organization to January 11, 1847 inclusive, is before the writer. The following extracts from its constitution will give some idea of its object and method of work. "*The object of this society shall be intellectual and colloquial improvement by the candid investigation and free, polite and manly discussion of such questions as the society from time to time may deem proper."*

"The officers shall be a President, two Vice-Presidents, a Secretary and two Curators."

"It shall be the duty of the President and two Vice-Presidents to sit in hearing questions discussed and then give their decision according to the weight of the arguments."

"The Curators shall collect all monies, furnish lights and fuel, submit questions for discussion and select persons to write essays or to declaim."

"Any respectable male person may become a member by paying to the Curators the sum of 12 1/2c and signing the constitution, providing two-thirds of the members vote for his reception."

"Members' names; F. C. King, A. Hathaway, Henry Eichelberger, D. C. Atwater, W. H. Edmundson, W. B. Waters, (Dr.) Stephen H. Potter, Wm. Fry, (Dr.) Joseph B. Potter, John Helpman, Peter Miller, Samuel Bartlit, D. S. Morrow, Wm. Curtis, Jacob Schrock, Samuel Burkholder, John M. Kramer, Jacob Rone, Robert Cowen, Nathaniel Tallman, John F. Bartlit, Wm. Overholtzer, Peter Kramer, Thomas Kemp, J. J. Needels, (Rev.) W. R. Letzinger, Adam Kramer, John Teems, John Colman, Nathaniel Bray, Abner Ebright, Geo. Ebright, A. Bruner, David Kramer, Andrew Helpman, R. I. Mason, Samuel Morris, John T. Ford, (Rev.) Elias Vandermark."

And later the following others became members:

Z. Collins, C. C. Holmes, (Dr.) C. Langworthy, Peter Kinsler, Wm. L. Stevenson, Levi Moore, Wm. Line, Hinton Tallman, Wash Hendricks, H. W. Rowland, (Rev.) M. Biddler, H. Bresler, (Dr.) G. W. Blake, Wm. Prentiss, James Clendening, Wm. Helpman, Joshua Glanville, Jacob Jacobs, Esq., Jacob Dravenstott, A. Lafabirse, John Farsee, J. B. Evans, T. B. Johnson, (Rev.) Wm. Wilson, Eli Moore, _____ Scunnell, Wm. Hubbard, David Dixon, Philip Price, J. Jeffers, ____ Chever, Wm. Morton, J. N. Slife, A. P. Morton, R. Tallman, G. S. Stevenson, Solomon Gayman, Nathaniel Sprague, W. Decker, Francis Cunningham and Wm. Harbaugh. Meetings were held in the school house, Dr. Stephen H. Potter's office and other places, and begun at candle lighting; sessions were held only during the winter months.

We record rather a long list of the questions discussed, since they reveal the subject matter of some of the leading problems in the public mind half a century or more ago:

118

"Has the African more reason to complain than the Indian?"

"Does the newspaper press produce a salutary influence?"

"Has the brute creation been of more benefit to the community at large than the vegetable production?"

"Which is the strongest passion, Love or Anger?"

"Is there more pleasure in Anticipation than Participation?"

"Is Climate the cause of the Different Varieties in the Human Species?"

"Ought Females to be Equally Educated with Males?"

"Is Conscience Innate or Acquired?"

"Would it be Policy for the State of Ohio to Pass a General Nanking Law?"

"Does the Physician Produce more Benefit than the Preacher (or Divine)?"

"Which Produces the Greatest Influence — the Male or the Female?"

"Has Pride and Ambition had a Worse Influence than Ignorance and Superstition?"

"Has Money done more Injury than Ardent Spirits?"

"Has Wealth greater Influence than Talent?"

"Ought Bank Notes under the Denomination of Fifty (50) Dollars be in Circulation?"

"Does the Present State of Things Indicate Universal Civilization?"

"Ought Capital Punishment be Abolished?"

"Is Ambition a Stronger Passion than Pride?"

"Has the Discovery of the Magnet been of more Benefit to Mankind than the Art of Printing?"

"Has Slavery in the United States Injured the Condition of the Negro?"

"Has the Male more Influence in Court than the Female?"

"Resolved, That Murder is Worse than Seduction,"

"Resolved, That all Laws Making Distinction on Account of Color Should be Repealed,"

"Resolved, That all Banks of Paper Issue should be Repealed."

"Resolved, That Foreign Immigration Should be Prohibited."

In the latter part of the sixties and early in the seventies, the Amateur Dramatic Society was introduced, and many an evening was spent in rehearsals and drills. It is interesting to note that the amateur theatricals began and also stopped at about the same time at both Winchester and Groveport, so the question naturally arises as we observe the passing of these various forms of entertainment as to what will take the place of the present popular lecture course.

July 18 and 19, 1867, G. S. Stevens, who was then Superintendent of the Winchester schools, assisted by others, gave an exhibition under a tent just west of the school house. The program was of a miscellaneous character, only part of which can now be recalled. John Shoemaker acted "Toodles," and Jennie Somerville "Mrs. Toodles;" Lide Algire recited "*The Maniac.*" In "Josephine," a pantomime, Luda Fry acted Josephine, Katie Shortt acted Hortense and David Fry was Eugene; Mr. Stephens and Emma Haskell acted the parts of "Moses and his wife" when Miss Haskell (Mrs. Philip Game) sang the familiar song, the chorus of which is:

> *"Now, Moses, you'll catch it,*
> *Now, Moses, don't touch it,*
> *Now, Moses, you hear what I say;*
> *Tis thus without stopping,*
> *The music keeps dropping,*
> *From night after night*
> *And from day after day."*

Another pantomime was entitled, "*Marriage in War Times;*" "*Fair Bingen on the Rhine*" was recited by Laura Schoch, Katie Stevenson and Nan Evans; *Poe's Raven* was sung by Emma Haskell and Wm. M. Game. Among others who sang were Mame Hische, Ellen Rees, Katie Short, Katie Stevenson, Blanch Bergstresser and Alice Stevenson. A festival was held upstairs in the school house in connection with this exhibition.

In the winter 1869-1870 a Mr. Harry A. Davis, alias Howard, alias Mortimer, and wife(?) came to Winchester. He had considerable ability as an actor, and through his efforts the first amateur theatrical society in Winchester was organized. On Wednesday evening, February 16, 1870, the drama, "*Ten Nights in a Bar Room*" was rendered with the following "cast": *Sample Switchell,* Harry A. Davis; *Romaine,* Joe E. Evans; *Joe Morgan*, H. A. Davis; *Simon Slade,* Levi Kramer; *Frank Slade,* Wm. Trine; *Harvey Green,* Wm. Game; *Willie Hammond,* P. M. Caslow; *Mrs. Morgan,* Mary Speaks; *Mary Morgan,* Ella Blake; *Benny Morgan,* Albert Speaks; *Mrs. Slade,* Ollie Hesser; *Mehitable Cartwright,* Mrs. H. A.

Davis. And on the same evening the farce, *"Paddy Miles' Boy,"* was given. The "cast" was: *Paddy Miles,* H. A. Davis; *Dr. Coates,* Chas. B. Cowen; *Harry Coates*, W. M. Game; *J*ob, Geo. F. Bareis; *Mrs. Fidgett,* Mary Speaks, *Jane Fidgett*, M. Algire; *Reuben,* Pete M. Caslow.

On the following evening the drama, *"Ireland As It Is"* was produced; the "cast" was; *Dan O'Carolan,* Chas. B. Cowan; *Ragged Pat,* H. A. Davis; *Neil O'Carolan*, W. P. Caslow; *Lord Squander*, Wm. M. Game; *Old Stone,* A. B. Lucas; *Connor O'Flaherty,* Geo. F. Bareis: *Slang,* Wm. Trine, *Purdy Magee,* P. M. Caslow; *Judy O'Trot*, Mrs. Davis; *Honor O'Carolen*, Mary Speaks; *Florence O'Carolen,* Ella Blake; and the farce, *"To Oblige Benson,"* with the following "cast": *Mr. Benson*, W. D. Caslow; *Mrs. Benson,* Ollie Hesser; *Mr. Southdown,* H. A. Davis; *Mrs. Southdown,* Mrs. Davis; *Mr. Meredith*, A. B. Lucas. The entertainments were given in the "Rink." It then stood on High Street, just south of the railroad tracks. This building was torn down in 1901. The building was filled to its utmost capacity; every available space was occupied, even on top of the little office in the northwest corner and along the nailing ties. To those on the stage it appeared to be one solid mass of humanity, not only on the floor, but also up the side walls. The scenery was painted by Mr. Davis expressly for this occasion. The "Bills" were printed by Wm. D. Caslow, who operated a small job press for Dr. A. Starr. A foot note on the Bills said: *"Persons holding 50-cent tickets can secure a good seat at any hour they may arrive, as there will be as many of the best seats reserved as there are 50-cent tickets sold."* The music was furnished by the Lithopolis Cornet Band.

In the spring of 1875 the Winchester Dramatic Club was organized, with the following members, viz: W. J. Dixon, of Reynoldsburg, Ohio, manager; Fred. F. Ungemach, Chas. Epply, Wm. M. Game, Chas. Allen, Edward Evans, Wm. H. McClintock, Allie E. Gayman, Geo. W. Miller, Lee Kramer, Wm. D. Beeks, Misses Mary Speaks, Nan Evans, Ella Blake, Lide Leckrone, Kate Allen, Ollie Hesser and Ida E. Speaks, Chas. B. Cowen, prompter. On April 1, 1875, they rendered *"Ten Nights in a Bar Room,"* and on April 2, *"The Coacher's Doom."* After the entertainment Mr. and Mrs. Philip Game tendered the club a reception at their home, and on the following Saturday evening John and Rachel Gehm entertained them at their home on Waterloo Street. On September 24, 1875, *"Uncle Tom's Cabin,"* and on September 25 *"The Octoroon"*; the farces, *"The Specter Bridegroom"* and *"Getting into Trouble"* were also

121

given. Miss Mary Speaks, John Selby, Tall Hite and a Mr. Edwards furnished the music. October 9, 1875, *"The Octoroon"* and *"Getting into Trouble"* was repeated as a benefit. December 10, 1875, a benefit was tendered Mr. Fred T. Ungemach, when the *"Streets of New York"* was rendered, and the following evening *"Nick of the Woods,"* and the farce, *"That Nose of Mine,"* was rendered. February 22, 1876, *"Kathleen Mavoureen"* and the farce, *"My Wife is Out."* On May 6, 1876, they went to Groveport via Capt. James Fay's boat. The Winchester Cornet Band accompanied them. On July 4, 1876, *"The Poacher's Doom"* and *"Take Care of Charlie"* were rendered. In 1878 the club was reorganized, with the following members: Alf. Fairbanks, R. W. Bolenbaugh, Fred Ungemach, Wm. M. Game, Chas. Shoemaker, W. D. Beeks, A. E. Gayman, John Helpman, Jr., John C. Speaks, Albert Speaks, E. C. Chaney, Chas. W. Miller, Hal. V. Chaney, and Misses Ella Vought, Ollie Hesser and Blanch Bergstresser, and on June 13 they rendered *"Daniel Boone,"* and on June 15, *"The Ticket of Leave."*

In the early spring of 1886 the following young people organized a literary society and called it the Y. P. L. S. Misses Rose Gayman, Zell Billingsly, Seppie Yost, Sarah Gayman, Mollie Gayman, Callie Dunlap, Jessie Leoffler, Blanche Dibble, Effie Leonard, Carrie Rees, Lizzie Moore, Recy Sarber, and Henry Lehman, B. F. Lehman, C. V. Moore, O. P. Gayman, Phil C. Tussing, G. W. Tooill, Chas. W. Gayman, John Pickering, Will S. Tussing, Joe Starr, Anexy Ringer, O. P. Dunlop and W. A. Delong. On Saturday evening, May 8, 1886, they rendered a program in Ghem's Hall consisting of dialogues, etc., *"A Natural Spell," "The Train Tomorrow," "Out All Around," "The Masterpiece," "The Wrong Man,"* and *"An Unhappy Pair."*

On December 11, 1886, the Sons of Veterans gave an entertainment in Gehm's Hall consisting of recitations and the following dialogues; *"The Wrong Man," "Saved by a Dream," "Advertising for a Husband,"* and *"From Punkin Ridge."* Those taking part were: W. S. Tussing, Laura Zerkle, Chas. W. Gayman, Carrie Rees, Minnie McFadden, Recy Sarber, Edna Lawyer, Gertie Bailey, Blanch Dibble, Effie Leonard, Fannie Game, Zell Billingsly, Joe Starr, Will S. Tussing, Oliver P. Dunlop, Chas. Alstadt, Henry Lehman, Anexy Ringer, Phil C. Tussing, Geo. W. Tooill, James Adams and Clem V. Moore.

On September 20 and 24, 1886, the drama, *"Enlisted for the War"* was rendered by E. E. Arnold, Harry Miller, Benj. F. Lehman, A. Ringer,

J. B. Outland, Ella Helpman, S. Arvilla Yost, Nellie Schrock and others, the proceeds to be used for the purpose of organizing a drum corps for the Sons of Veterans.

On Wednesday evening, February 16, 1887, the Irish drama, *"More Sinned Against than Sinning,"* was given at Gehm's Opera House by J. W. Shook, B. F. Gayman, G. W. Miller, Joe S. Ashe, C. B. Tuttle, G. W. Sponsler, W. L. Walters, T. A. Arnold, W. C. Bailey, O. L. Dibble and others. On the same evening C. B. Tuttle recited *"Shamas O'Brine."*

December 10, 1887, the Potter Light Guards tendered a benefit entertainment to Amos Walters. The program consisted of a solo by Alice Speaks, a farce, *"Wooing Under Difficulties"*; a drama, *"Tempter, or the Sailor's Return"*; a solo by Capt. John C. Speaks, and a farce, *"Brother Bill and Me."* This entertainment marked the passing of the amateur dramatics in Winchester.

Mozart Club

Among the most notable musical organizations was the Mozart Club, which was organized in the fall of 1874, with the following members: John H. Speilman, Director; Wm. C. Speilman, Ed. C. Speilman, J. Peter Weisman, Wes. H. McClintock, Mary Speaks, Ida Speaks, Carrie Bowman and Ollie Hesser, with Blanch Bergstresser and Katie Short, pianists. The first concert was given on February 18, 1875; at the close of the entertainment the club was invited to a banquet at the residence of Mr. and Mrs. Weisman. Other concerts were rendered during the season of 1875-1876. On March 10, 1876, at their fifth concert, Mr. Meise, of Lancaster, assisted. The sixth concert was given on March 2, 1877, when they rendered *"Pauline, or the Belle of Saratoga,"* and on March 16 they repeated this program at Lancaster, having a special coach attached to the afternoon passenger train, and returning on a special about midnight. On March 28 they repeated it at Groveport, making the trip on a canal boat. Prior to the visit of the Mozart Club to Groveport, some of the young people of the latter place had advertised an entertainment in Winchester to which only about half a dozen tickets were sold. There was quite a rivalry and considerable feeling between the two neighboring towns in those days. With all the advertisement and the attractions incident to the Mozart Club's advent, with quite a company of their friends and a brass band, there were only four or five Groveport persons in their audience. One

123

or two numbers were sung, when it was announced that the concert would be declared off and the money refunded at the door.

In the fall of 1877 the club was reorganized, with the following members: J. H. Speilman, Director; W. C. and Ed. C. Speilman, T. F. Ungemach, J. P. Weisman, Warren Somerville, Wm. D. Beeks, John C. Speaks, B. F. Gayman, Robt. W. Bolenbaugh, Alf. Fairbanks, R. C. Caslow, Mary, Ida and Alice Speaks, Ollie Hesser, Carrie Bowman, Lynn and Jessie Somerville, Sarah C. Schoch, Ida Gayman, Ollie McKelvey and Ella Vought, with Blanch Bergstresser, pianist. On Thursday and Saturday evenings, May 9 and 11, 1878, they rendered the opera, *"Bohemian Girl,"* and repeated it as benefit for Miss Ida Speaks on May 22, 1878. The Mozart Club possessed musical ability far above that usually found in a village, and rendered a high class of music in an artistic way.

Winchester Vocal Society

Another notable musical society was organized in the fall of 1885, and named the Winchester Vocal Society. The members were: Joe S. Ashe, John C. Speaks, Dr. J. W. Shook, B. F. Gayman, Chas. L. Bover, J. M. Armpreister, G. M. Harpst, O. P. Gayman, Will Speaks, M. M. Warner, Alice Speaks, Mrs. Ida Chaney, Kate Weber, Ella Vought, Cad. Watson, Mary Harpst, Edith and Ollie Ashe, Gertie Baily, Fannie Game, Minnie McFadden, Laura Zirkle and Sarah Schoch, with Edna Lawyer, pianist. On April 2 and 3, 1886, they rendered the operetta, *"H. M. S. Pinafore."* On May 1 they repeated it at Groveport. The Winchester Brass Band went with them on Capt. Webb Clellan's canal boat.

Winchester Lecture Course

The first attempt towards furnishing a course of entertainments was by a local committee in the winter of 1885-1886. Rev. Austin Henry, then pastor of the Reformed Church, being among the most active advocates, and the following four entertainments were given: January 28, 1886, G. Paul Smith, Impersonator, and the Forbes family, Musicians. February 11 and 12 Tank-Kee, *Lectures on China* (Tank-Kee also gave a benefit lecture for the Ohio River flood sufferers), and Julia Lee, Reader.

In January, 1888, another course of four lectures was arranged, as follows: Rev. F. E. Marsten, D. D., *"Balky People,"* January 27; Dr. W. H.

Scott, President O. S. U., *"The Use of Books."* February 21; Francis C. Sessions, *"From Yellowstone Park to Alaska,"* February 28; and Dr. N. S. Townsend, *"Great People that I Have Seen,"* March 20. The net proceeds to be used in purchasing books for the Public Library. In the fall of 1888 a committee composed of the pastors of the local churches, arranged the following course of entertainments: December 10, 1888, Anna Vickers (Elocutionist); December 28, General Joseph H. Geiger; January 11, 1889, F. C. Sessions; January 25, Professor Perkins of O. W. U.; February 4, Professor J. R. Smith of O. S. U., and February 22, Professor C. H. Workman. The receipts were $57 and the expenses $70. In the fall of 1889 the prevailing opinion — based on the experience of the season before — seemed to be that a lecture course could not be maintained except at a loss. Mr. A. A. Graham was then managing a lecture course in Columbus and through his solicitations a party of about thirty was made up, and a special train service secured. A coach was attached to a coal train leaving Winchester at about 6 o'clock p. m., and returning on a "light extra" after the entertainment. A similar arrangement was made in the fall of 1890, when the following persons held season tickets: Geo. F. Bareis, S. T. Needels, C. D. Whitehurst, Laura and Ella Whitehurst, O. P. Gayman, Philip Game, Edwin S. Gayman, H. H. Dibble, Professor Thomas Fitzgerald, Kate and Emma Weber, C. V. Moore, Gertie Bailey, S. E. Bailey, Lila Starr, R. J. Tussing, Mrs. J. B. Potter, Mrs. Rachel Griffith, Rev. C. W. Bostwick, Rev. A. Snider, Oliver A. Wright, Ed. Crayton, E. C. Chaney, Sam H. Martin, Ben F. Bowman, Daniel Detwiler, Dr. L. W. Beery, Win. Schrock, Pet. Schoch, O. P. Bowman, and Mrs. McFadden, from Winchester; O. E. D. Baugher, Stella Crumley and Dr. G. S. Courtright, from Lithopolis, and J. L. Chaney, J. K. Chaney, W. H. Zinn, Ed. Denton, Chas. Swisher, J. M. Kelley, Welton Seymour, F. G. Pontius, A. M. Rarey, J. D. Rarey, John O. Rarey, C. P. Long, Rev. G. W. Lott, Professor J. A. Wilcox and Dr. C. R. Clement, of Groveport. On the evening of April 23, 1891, just before the train left the depot at Winchester, John L. Chaney, of Groveport, on behalf of the patrons of this lecture course, presented Geo. F. Bareis with a handsome antique oak rocking chair *"in appreciation of the time he has given and the personal expense he has been at in making the arrangement for so profitable a season of entertainments."*

On November 6, 1891, at a meeting held at the residence of Geo. F. Bareis a committee was appointed to manage a Citizens' Lecture

Course, and the following courses have been given: Season of 1891-1892. "Spedon," "Imperial Quartette," "Col. L. F. Copeland," "Eli Perkins," "Dr. A. A. Wittetts".

1892-1893, Major H. C. Dane, Fisk Jubilee Singers, Leland Powers, Lotus Glee Club, Geo. R. Wendling, Col. Sandford, Col. L. F. Copeland.

1893-1894, Ariel Ladies, Morgan Wood, Bob Burdette, John Thomas Concert Co., John Temple Graves, Byron King.

1894-1895, Smith Sisters, Prof. J. B. DeMotte, Hon. L. I. Handy. Shubert Male Quartette, Brooks-Macy Combination.

1895-1896, Swedish Quartette, Prof. J. B. DeMotte, Franz Wilzek Concert Co., Henry Hall, Henry Watterson.

1896-1897, Col. Geo. W. Bain, Robt. Nourse, Dr. Eugene May, Nashville Students Concert Co., Harvard Quartette.

1897-1898, Ladies Symphony Orchestra (at 1 o'clock p. m., December 20, 1897), Dr. A. A. Willetts, Vandalia Varnum, Arion Cooke Combination. The price of season tickets for these four entertainments was $1.25. Each of the above courses of entertainments was managed by a citizens' committee. No "course" was undertaken during the season of 1898-1899. The lecture course entertainments for the following three seasons have been given under the auspices of the Knights of Pythias Lodge, No. 125.

1899-1900, Ariel Ladies Quartette, Spillman Riggs, DeWitt Miller, Uncle Josh Picture Play Company and Dr. Eugene May.

1900-1901, John Thomas Concert Co., Samuel Phelps Leland, W. H. J. Ham, W. Hinton White and Slayton's Jubilee Singers.

1901-1902, The Rogers-Grilly Recitals, Slayton's Jubilee Singers, Homer T. Wilson, Edward T. Hagerman and Lovett's Boston Stars.

The following interesting history of some of the entertainments of Groveport was gathered up by Mr. A. M. Senter. Back in the sixties some of the young men organized a reading club, rented a room upstairs in the old frame building that burned down about where Vogle's Grocery now stands. The members were: John Wallace, Chas. Wallace, John Byrne, Luke G. Byrne, F. M. Senter, A. M. Senter, W. C. Gill, Wm. Schockley and Geo. Rowland. They gave a series of theatrical entertainments each winter for two or three years. The proceeds were used to furnish the reading room with furniture, carpet, books, etc. The reading room was nick-named "The Loafers' Lodge." These entertainments were the first in the way of amateur theatricals that were given in Groveport. John Wallace did Irish comedy, A. M. Senter Dutch comedy, Wm. Shockley took the "heavy" parts. The boys dramatized a novel and produced a play called *"Villainy Foiled."* At one time the rehearsals were held in the reading room. "Mrs. Grundy" had too much to say about the ladies who were to assist meeting there for rehearsals, and the consequence was that a short time before the date given out for the play the ladies left. But the boys were not to be balked, so rewrote the play, cut out some characters, dressed Shockley and Gill in women's attire and gave the show.

In March, 1873, another company was organized with the following persons as members: B. Frank Winzell, James Corbett, Frank Champe, Elliot Adel, John Wallace, Chas. Wallace, Thomas Byrne, Wm. R. Smith, Wm. Bright, Chas. Williams, Oscar Kramer, Jas. K. Trice, Wm. Gares, and Misses Vic. Campbell, Ella Wallace, Mell Dildine and Georgia Campbell. On March 25, 1873, they played *"Nick of the Woods"* and *"The Irish Tiger"*; March 26, *"The Last Loaf"* and *"Do You Know Me?"* March 27, *"The Irish Yankee"* and *"No one Round the Corner"*; and on March 28, *"Nick of the Woods"* and *"The Last Loaf."* The receipts were $115. These entertainments were given in the Baptist Church. April, 1876, two amateur theatrical companies were organized, The Excelsiors and The Thespians; the members of the Excelsiors were: Misses Vic. Campbell, Georgia Campbell, Ella Wallace, Deaze Senter and Mrs. F. M. Senter, and John Wallace, Chas. Wallace, Chas. Williams, E. E. Williams, Frank Champe, D. Fisher Karnes, A. M. Senter, James Corbett and F. M. Senter. April 15, 1876, they gave the first entertainment ever given in the Town Hall. Entertainments were given July 14, 1876; August 28, 29 and 30, 1877; and August 3, 1878. Assisted by W. N. Compton, of Columbus, Ohio, they again appeared at the Town Hall, and also one night at Canal Winchester, and one night at Lithopolis. Some of the plays rendered were *"The Dutchman's Ghost,"* *"Idiot Witness,"* *"The Persecuted Dutchman,"* *"Ten Nights in a Bar Room,"* *"Toodles,"* *"The Limerick Boy,"* *"Bread on the Waters,"* *"The Irish Broom Maker,"* *"Rum, or the First Glass,"* and *"The May Pole Dance."*

The "Thespians" was organized by Prof. N. H. Garner, then principal of the schools, and assisted by W. N. Compton, of Columbus, they played *"Black Eyed Susan,"* which was Mr. Compton's favorite. On April 26, 1876, the members of the company were N. H. Garner, W. N.

Compton, Wm. R. Smith, John Decker, Chas. P. Long, Geo. Smith, E. V. Adell, Will Weaver, Misses Addie Clelland, Myrtle Kelly, Ida Smith, Ella Coble, Jennie Guerin and others.

Hodge and Williams Minstrels was organized in the fall of 1876 and appeared November 15, 1876, and quite a number of times thereafter; their last appearance being on November 11, 1879. The company was composed of Thomas and Geo. Hodge, E. E. Williams, Chas. Hunter, B. F. Angle and others. Some of the leading features were Thos. Hodge and Williams' double clog, B. F. Angle's song and dance, Thos. Hodge's essence, E. E. Williams, female impersonator, Chas. Hunter, vocalist; Ned Williams, great burlesque orator; G. M. Hodge, negro comedian; M. P. Sandy, negro impersonator. It is said of them that they were always sure of a full house, and that they sent their patrons away well pleased.

Shortie's Minstrels was the Hodge and Williams Company, with a few additions, under the management of Marion Corwin, alias "Shortie" Corwin. They gave entertainments on December 30, 1878, and February 26, 1880.

After a lapse of some years, "Shortie" concluded to arrange for an entertainment, which at the same time should be a reunion; so written invitations were sent to each of the former members to be present on January 1, 1886. He engaged the Lithopolis Glee Club and the Madison Brass Band, and before the doors opened a grand street parade was given, led by "Shortie" himself. Immediately after the entertainment a banquet and reunion was held at M. Corbett's.

The Juvenile Minstrels were organized by Pat. Cavanaugh, El Hunter and others, and were pupils of Hodge & Williams; they were boys from 14 to 16 years of age, and appeared March 23, 1878, and March 19, 1881, to full houses. February 28, 1886, *"The Social Glass"* was rendered by G. Mac. Rarey, E. P. Dildine, Chas. Pattrick, E. G. Peters, C. D. Rarey, T. L. Peters, Minnie Parker, Nettie Rarey and Zoa Mansfield. On January 17, 1891, *"The Border Land"* was given by Chas. D. Rarey, O. P. Crist, Phil C. Tussing, B. F. Dildine, T. L. Peters, Geo. Willie, E. A. Swisher, Cora Tussing, Alice Swisher, Eva Pontius and Florence Gares, and on February 21, 1891, *"From Sumpter to Appomattox"* was played by C. D. Rarey, P. C. Tussing, O. P. Crist, B. F. Dildine, E. G. Peters, T. L. Peters, Cora Tussing and Florence Gares, and was repeated at Ashville, Ohio. This was the last of the amateur theatricals in Groveport.

In the spring of 1889 the members of the W. R. C. of Groveport concluded to render a play entitled, *"The Crowning of the Queen of Fame,"* and they appeared in the Town Hall February 23, 1889, and repeated it on March 28 at Winchester; the trip was made on a canal boat. The group picture is made up of such of the individual photographs in costume as we were able to secure. Several of those taking part did not have pictures taken at the time. The "cast" was as follows, viz: *Goddess of Fame*, Miss Lena Rarey; *Page,* Master Fred Rarey; *Queen Isabella of Spain,* Mrs. James K. Chaney; *Caroline Hershel,* Mrs. O. R. Mansfield; *Pocahontas,* Mrs. T. C. Thompson; *Martha Washington,* Mrs. Peter Reeves; *Jeanne de Arc*, Mrs. M. W. Darst; *Ruth,* Miss Lizzie Long; *Martha Goose,* Mrs. W. P. Seymour; *Xantippe*, Mrs. L. F. Powell; *Mary Queen of Scots*, Mrs. W. H. Hutson; *Mrs. Browning,* Mrs. Rachel Huffman; *Mrs. Partington,* Mrs. W. H. Zinn; *Ike Partington,* Mr. C. D. Rarey; *Sister of Charity,* Mrs. R. A. Shaw; *Miriam, Moses' Sister,* Mrs. J. L. Chaney; *Elisabeth Fry, the Quakeress,* Mrs. J. D. Reed; *Sappho, the Greek Poet,* Mrs. C. A. Williams; *Queen Elisabeth,* Mrs. J. B. Duzan; *Jennie Lind,* Mrs. J. O. Rarey; *Fanny Fern,* Mrs. J. D. Rarey; *Rosa Bonheim,* Miss Florence Gares; *Madam Sontag,* Miss Jennie Denton; *Miss Francis Willard,* Mrs. D. M. Willie; *Harriet Hasmer,* Mrs. C. Black, Jr.; *Florence Nightingale,* Mrs. A. M. Rarey; *Hypatia,* Mrs. Ed. Gares; *Tabitha Primrose,* Mrs. C. L. Pontius.

"QUEEN OF FAME" GROUP

Rear Row — C. D. Rarey, Mrs. Jane Reeves, Master Fred Rarey, Mrs. Jennie Black. Mrs. Ida Chancy, Mrs. Kate Seymour, Mrs. Anna Mansfield, Mrs. Rachel Huffman, Mrs. J. B. Duzan, Mrs. A. M. Rarey, Mrs. Alice Chaney.

Middle Row —Mrs. D. M. Willie, Mrs. Wm. Mason, Miss Lizzie Long, Mrs. Henry Zinn, Mrs. Emma Rarey, Miss Minnie Denton, Mrs. Lida Thompson, Mrs. Ella Powell, Mrs. F. Gares, Mrs. May Hutson.

Front Row—Mrs. C. A. Williams, Mrs. Fannie Pontius, Miss Florence Gares, Miss Lena Rarey (Queen), Mrs. Hannah Shuw, Mrs. Helen Darst.

Groveport Lecture Course

1894-1895, *"Chas. T. Grilley Concert Co.," "The Harvards," "Col. L. F. Copeland," "Smith Sisters," "'Howard Saxby," "Jules Levy Grand Concert Co," "Dr. A. A. Willetts," "F. D. Losey"*.

1895-1896, *"Lovett's Boston Stars," "Major H. C. Dane," "Col. L. F. Copeland," "English Hand Bell Ringers," "Dr. A. A. Willetts," "John B. Koehne"*.

1896-1897, *"Nashville Students Concert Co.," "H. H. Barbour," "John Thomas Concert Co,"" Weaver," "A. W. Lamar"*.

1899-1900, *"Chas. H. Frazier," "Spellman Riggs," "Uncle Josh Picture Play Co," "W. T. S. Culp," "Apollo Quartette"*.

1900-1901, *"Parker Concert Company,"* Dr. J. T. Hedley, DeWitt Miller, Dr. H. C. McGowan and Oxford Music Club; 1901-1902, Melvin Robinson, Richie Novelty Co., The Swiss Bell Ringers, Leonard Garber and Hungarian Orchestra.

130

CHAPTER XIII
MIDDLETOWN

In 1817 Isaac D. Decker laid out a town on the northwest quarter of section No. 1 (formerly in Ross County), and named it Middletown, perhaps from the fact that it is located about halfway between Lancaster and Columbus. What is now the Columbus & Lancaster Pike was then the only road through this section of country, and the travel following along its route invited Mr. Frederick Baugher to lay out a town in about 1815, some two miles further east, which he named Centerville, the name no doubt being adopted for the same reason that Mr. Decker's town was named Middletown, the object of each being to establish a halfway station or stopping place. Some few years later the name of Centerville was changed to Lithopolis. It is supposed that Dr. W. W. Talbott, of Jefferson, who was a Greek scholar, suggested or coined the name, which literally translated is Stoney-city. The name of Middletown was also changed in 1830 to Oregon. About the same time guide boards were put up at different cross roads directing the travel toward it. Whoever put them up seems to have had an idea that in order to indicate the direction of the town the name on the guide-board should spell towards it. One of these boards on the west side of the Oregon Road, at a point near where the Columbus and Winchester Pike now intersects it, read Nogero; the supposition being that whoever read it would understand that in order to reach Oregon he must travel in the direction of the spelling. The first post office in the township was established here in 1829, and Dr. Hersey appointed postmaster. In 1833 Dr. Hersey resigned and Isaac D. Decker was appointed. The post office was discontinued about 1842. Only two or three buildings remain on the site of the town, although the place is still known by its original name, Middletown. Mr. Decker, who laid out the town, built a tavern on the lot now occupied by Geo. Williams.

CHAPTER XIV
WINCHESTER

Henry Dove entered the quarter section on which the village is located, in about 1802 or 1803; prior to his death he divided it and gave his son Reuben the east half and his son Jacob the west half, the center of High Street being the dividing line. Jacob afterward sold his land to John Colman.

The first tree cut on the site of Winchester was a walnut directly in front of the residence of M. C. Whitehurst — now owned by Wm. H. Lane, Esq.— where the Reuben Dove homestead was located (Mrs. M. C. Whitehurst was a daughter of Reuben Dove). The first log cabin was built of poles, on the same site, in primitive fashion, without the use of nails, iron, or glass. Some years later a two-story hewed log house was erected which stood until the present brick house was built in 1865.

When the canal was begun in 1827, Mr. Dove had the field, through which the canal was to be dug, in wheat, and objected to having it destroyed, but to no avail. Finally he threatened to bring suit against the state for damages to his crop. Some of the workmen suggested to him that here would be a good site for a town; being about half way between Lancaster and Columbus, and said: *"We believe there will be more money in laying out a town than in trying to collect damages from the state."* Acting on this suggestion, in company with John Colman, they employed James O'Kane to survey and plat a town, which was named Winchester, from the fact that Mr. Dove's father formerly lived at Winchester, Va., and accordingly on November 5, 1828, the following description, accompanied by a plat, was recorded at Lancaster, in Fairfield County:

"The within is a plan or plat of the town of Winchester, laid off in the southeast quarter of Section 30, Township 15, Range 20, of the land directed to be sold, by an 'Act' of Congress, at Chillicothe; the lots are four (4) perches in front and ten (10) perches deep, and contain one-fourth acre each, except the lots Nos. 9, 10, 17 and 18, they being of a triangular form, as marked on the within plat. The streets are four (4) perches in width; High Street runs north and south; Columbus Street runs with the bearings of the canal, which is west, 25° north; both are given for public use. The lots are numbered, beginning at the northeast

corner, then west and east until the same are numbered to twenty-five (25). Given under my hand and seal, this 4th day of November, 1828.

"James O'Kane, Surveyor
(Signed) Reuben Dove (Seal)
John Colman" (Seal)

On March 30, 1829, Mr. Dove recorded an addition to the original plot, being the lots on both sides of Columbus Street, to the east section line and on both sides of Waterloo Street, beginning at High Street and continuing to the east section line; they each contain one-fourth (1/4) acre, and are numbered from one to fifty. Lot No. 17 (Arendt's Shoe Shop) is given for a basin, lot No. 44 (Vought's) for school purposes and lot No. 2 (Binkley's) for public use.

May 3, 1836, David Dixon laid out an addition, being the lots between the canal and West Street, and between Washington Street, and the alley just west of High Street, and the lots on the south side of West Street and east of Liberty Street.

On April 25, 1839 John Colman laid out an addition of 22 lots lying west of Liberty Street, and between West Street and Franklin Alley.

On November 9, 1839, David Dixon laid out his second addition, consisting of 53 lots west of Washington Street, and between West Street and the canal. Clinton Street then extended to the canal.

On November 10, 1869, Wm. P. Miller laid out his first addition, containing nine lots, bounded by High, Friend and Mound Streets and Cherry Alley.

July 19, 1870, Wm. P. Miller's second addition was laid out. It consists of 22 lots on the east side of High Street, between Railroad Street and the alley just north of Waterloo Street.

July 21, 1871, Wm. P. Miller laid out an amended addition containing 38 lots and bounded by High Street on the west, Town Alley on the east, Railroad Street on the north and the alley north of Waterloo Street on the south, reserving a two-acre lot between Cherry, Town and ____ alleys.

December 16, 1870, John Kramer laid out an addition consisting of 10 lots, and bounded by Mound, Oak and Elm Streets and Mill Alley, and on February 2, 1874, he filed an amended plat, bounded as following: High, Elm, Mound and Oak Streets.

May 27, 1871, Henry Will laid out an addition consisting of 5 lots, bounded by Friend (now Elm) Street on the east, Union Alley on the north, and the Columbus and Winchester Pike on the south and west.

August 31, 1871, Reuben Trine laid out an addition consisting of 27 lots on the west side of Trine Street, and between Waterloo Street and Railroad Street.

March 8, 1876, John Kramer laid out his second addition consisting of 8 lots, bounded by High, Oak and Mound Streets and Mill Alley.

On November 10, 1882, the corporation line was extended north of the railroad, taking in the mill and the beer garden.

January 20, 1883, Washington Street was extended north, across the canal to the Columbus and Winchester Pike, and on November 9, 1885, Solomon S. Lehman platted an addition of 4 lots on the south side of West Waterloo Street, near High Street. That part of Winchester between High Street, Cherry Alley and West Waterloo Street containing two acres, purchased by Daniel Bergstresser from John Kramer, has never been laid out into lots.

John Graham's map of Franklin County, published in 1856, in its plat of Winchester shows a street sixty feet wide, named North Street, running parallel with Waterloo Street, its center intersecting High Street just opposite the alley, between J. S. Stevenson's and J. K. Miller's lots. Lots Nos. 1 and 2 fronted on High Street, and Nos. 3 to 19 fronted north on North Street. This map also shows a street sixty feet wide at the east side of town called County Line Street. No plat of this addition could be found. No alley is shown on this map in the rear of the lots on the south side of Columbus Street.

In 1832, when Esq. James B. Evans came to Winchester buildings had been erected on the following lots: A two-story hewed log house on lot No. 2, occupied by John Boyer, a cooper and basket maker; Mr. Boyer had a family of 17 children, but this was not an unusual number for those days; a two-story hewed log house on lot No. 8. J. L. Vance then kept a store here; later it was occupied as a dwelling, schoolroom, and when Peter E. Ehernhart came here he occupied it as a residence, and set up his coverlet weaving loom in one of the rooms. In about 1860 John M. Schoch removed it to lot No. 6, and some years later he removed it to lot No. 9, where it was used as a pig-pen until the summer of 1896, when it was torn down. The old logs are now doing service as ground-logs at the lumber yard.

135

Another hewed log house then stood on lot No. 22, and was occupied for many years by Nancy and Sally Hathaway; the latter was an invalid for 30 or 35 years.

There was a hewed log house on lot No. 13 (Dr. Blake's corner); also a log house on lot No. 17, at the south end of High Street: a blacksmith shop was also located here, and a road led round to Epply's Spring (now Mrs. Hunsicker's). A two-story log house on the town lot. This was then occupied as a store by Carty & Julian, later by Daniel Lecrone as a shoe shop, then for several years as a residence by Jacob Zarbaugh, who had a blacksmith shop just north of this house, but on the same lot. The old town pump just in front of this house "served its day and generation."

In 1870 Austin Decker took the house on the town lot down and removed it to lot No. 4 on Oak Street, where it is now occupied by Henry Lechliter as a residence.

A one and a half story log house stood on lot No. 16, then occupied by James McKelvey's father. Dr. J. W. Shock tore it down in the summer of 1900; a two-story house then stood on lot No. 6, Columbus Street, and was occupied by Widow Todd; a log house on the southwest corner of High and West Streets; another, the Coleman homestead, then stood just south of the present residence of Mrs. Margaret Seymour; a one-story log house stood next to the canal, on lot No. 7; Fred Walters kept a saddler and bakeshop and a grocery here.

A log house stood on the site of Gayman's Store; it was then used as a boarding house by J. L. Vance, who was the contractor for this section of the canal; it consisted of two rooms; the front was one and one-half stories high and was connected by a passageway some eight or ten feet wide, across which the roof from the one-story room in the rear extended.

There were only two frame buildings in town then. The first one was erected by Peter Bennadum on lot No. 20, now occupied by the residence of O. P. Chaney. Mr. Bennadum kept a tavern and had sixteen boarders. In 1832 Paul Samsel had built another frame house in which he lived and kept a tailor shop. It was located on lot No. 34, and stood out to the street on a wall some six or seven feet high. It has been remodeled, and is now the residence of Mrs. Sarber. These buildings stood out to the street, as was the custom for many years after. A few years later a part log and part frame was built on the site of Samuel

Bartlitt's Store building; Samuel Taylor kept a tavern in one part and his son-in-law, Mr. ____Sheldon, a grocery in the other part; the frame part still stands in the rear of the same lot, and was Cowen's Cooper Shop.

In 1833 or 1834 a part log and part frame warehouse — as buildings for the storage of grain were then called — was built on the north side of the basin by Joseph Wright, and in 1836 he moved to town and built the frame house that stood on the site of Peter Weber's brick house. Mr. Wright owned and had lived on the farm now owned by Isaac Lehman.

Isaac Lehman
1834 -1915

In 1837 Almanzar Hathaway and James Clendening built the frame warehouse on the east side of the Basin. They erected a tramway from Waterloo Street to the top of this warehouse. The corn was then drawn up in a small car with a rope which was wound around a big drum, by horse power.

In 1847 or 1848 the Wright Warehouse was removed (part of it is the frame of P. M. Teegarden's stable), and Samuel Bartlit built the large frame building which stood on the north side of the Basin.

In 1834 or 1835 Carty & Rodgers built a frame warehouse on the west side of High Street and north of the canal. In 1843 this building, known as the *red* warehouse, was moved further west and the large frame warehouse, that is now being torn down, was put up. Michael Ebright did the carpenter work.

About 1840 Eichelberger and Loucks built a warehouse on the south side of the canal, on Liberty Street; this building was afterwards converted into a tannery by James H. Sommerville, and was torn down a few years since.

The yellow warehouse was built in 1842 by Heil Brockway; Johnson and Mathews did the carpenter work; later he sold to Samuel Bartlitt.

David Dixon (an uncle of Wm. and John Fry), built a frame store room on the site of the Commercial Hotel in 1832 or 1833. John F. and Samuel Bartlitt afterwards occupied it. Moses Levy also kept a store here. When the hotel was erected in 1860 this building, known as the *red* store, was moved to where Schoch's barn now stands and was used for a stable.

In 1837 Fred Slough, father of the late Judge Tallman Slough, of Lancaster, Ohio, a cabinetmaker by trade, built a two-story frame house on the south end of lot 7, now owned by Ellen Alspach, and later sold it to Fred Walters, who removed it to the north end of the adjoining lot on the west. Peter Krag purchased it and built a large addition to it, including a ball room, and kept a tavern; in 1852 Mr. Krag sold it to John M. Schoch, who continued it under the name of *Commercial Hotel,* until 1860, when David Sarber, John Kissel and others successively occupied it. After changing owners several times, John Helpman purchased it and rented it; at one time 8 different families occupied it, from which it got the name "Poor House"; it was purchased by Geo. F. Bareis in 1876, occupied as a residence for 10 years and torn down in 1898.

In 1852 Peter Krag built the Commercial Hotel, and in 1860 sold it to John M. Schoch. The Hawkstage Coach Line established a station here from 1860 to 1869; while horses were changed each passenger's "way-bill" was examined and registered. Then, being located half way between Lancaster and Columbus, made it a stopping place for all the travel between these points.

The Merchants' Hotel was built in 1871 by Isaac Ebright, who kept it some three years when he sold to Jonathan Boyer. Aaron Fenstermaker leased it of Mr. Boyer and kept it until April, 1877, when Louis W. Bover purchased and operated it until in 1884. Al. C. Conn then bought it at assignee's sale and in the spring of 1896 sold it to Noah Cherry, who still operates it.

In 1879 Ferd Leonard opened a hotel at the northeast corner of High and Mound Streets under the name of "Leonard House," but soon discontinued it. In the fall of 1891 Mrs. C. W. Bostwick rented this same building and kept a boarding house until the fall of 1896, when she moved to Columbus.

A. C. Conn built the "Conn House" in 1884, and operated it as a hotel until he purchased the Merchants' Hotel; this building was destroyed by fire on December 1, 1896.

About 1845 Wm. Harbaugh built an oil mill on lot No. 76, Liberty Street; he operated it for a few years when he sold to Frederick Yockey (or Eauca) and in about 1850 it was abandoned. The mill stones were peculiarly arranged; the lower stone lay flat, and the upper one was on edge, with a pole through its center; a horse was hitched to one end of this pole and in his walk around in a circle revolved the top stone which mashed the flax-seed. These stone were afterwards cut into halves and used as door steps at the McFadden residence, on the corner of West and Washington Streets, where Mr. Yockey then lived.

In 1837 Reuben Dove built the west end of the Dauterman Building at the southeast corner of High and Columbus Streets, and a few years later Dr. Stephen Potter built the east end. When Mr. Dove built he followed the acute angle of the street — being the first building to follow the oblique angles. Some of the citizens in a jocular way suggested that he secure the services of Rev. George Hathaway, who was also a blacksmith, to make a handle for the building when it could be used as a flat iron.

In 1850, after Dr. J. B. Potter was elected and appointed postmaster he kept the post and telegraph office here. This building has been occupied by James B. Evans, tailor shop, and by E. D. Orwig, Hart & Armpreister, Geo. E. Becker, John Chaney, Jr., Jacob Dauterman and others as a grocery store. Jacob Dauterman also kept a barber shop in this building for many years. In about 1840 John Pry did the carpenter work on the Carty residence on the southwest corner of High and Waterloo Streets; it was occupied by Jacob Carty as a residence until 1874 when he built the brick residence now occupied by R. J. Tussing. After this it was tenanted by different persons, among them Dr. F. L. Gilbert, dentist; W. R. Miller, hardware; M. Winder, bakery; Edward

Winders, grocery and restaurant, and others. After C. Kuqua purchased it he erected a one-story building directly on the corner of the streets in which to display buggies; later this room was occupied successively by Oliver L. Bott, Willis Houser and Jacob Kumler with a drug store. In 1884 Solomon S. Lehman purchased it and sold the buildings to make room for the business block which was erected that year. One part of the Carty house was removed to lot No. 20, just west of John Helpman's lumber yard office, where it was consumed by fire the next night after it was rolled onto the lot. The other part of the old house was removed to lot No. 17, Trine Street, by Wm. Cater, where it still stands. One of the shop buildings which stood on the Carty lot, facing High Street, was removed to East Waterloo Street, and was occupied by John A. Wilson with a restaurant, and is familiarly known as the "Great Eastern." L. L. Poor removed the remaining shop building to West Waterloo Street, just outside the corporation line, where during the time local option prevailed in Winchester it became well known as the "Blue Goose." It now forms part of Charles Hoffman's residence.

John F. and Samuel Bartlit came to Winchester in 1839, and conducted a store in a frame building that stood on the site of Gayman's Store. After a few years they moved to the south side of the canal and occupied the "red" store building. They only remained here a short time, when they removed to their former location. In 1844 John F. sold his interest and went to Waterloo and later to Columbus (John F. Bartlit built the Reformed Parsonage; it was plastered on the outside, as were also Mrs. McFadden's, Mrs. McKelvey's and Wm. Schrock's; the latter stood on the site of the present Reformed church).

In 1847 or 1848 Samuel Bartlit built the warehouse mentioned on another page, and about this time Wm. Fry secured an interest in the business, and this poetic sign was painted on the west end of the warehouse:

"Bartlitt and Fry,
Cash for
Wheat, Corn and Rye."

William Fry
1815 - 1854

Samuel Bartlit
1811 - 1880

This sign, although painted over by the sign of Tallman, Stevenson & Co., could still be dimly seen when the building was destroyed by fire. In 1851 Samuel Bartlit erected the brick store room (Gayman's); Jacob Dellinger did the brick work and John Fry the carpenter work. This firm continued until 1854, when Mr. Fry died in Cleveland, on his way home from New York, where he had gone to buy goods. Samuel Bartlit and his nephew, Samuel Pond, continued the business until September, 1856, when Mr., Pond bought the dry goods department and Mr. Bartlit continued the grain department. In the fall of 1857 Mr. Pond died and David and Christian Gayman bought the stock and continued the business until 1891, when David retired and the firm name became C. Gayman & Son. In 1877 the store room was remodeled and in 1880 an addition added, and in 1899 the roof of the old part of the building was changed to correspond with the new part. After Mr. Pond's death Mr. Bartlit sold the grain business to (Nathaniel) Tallman, (Wm. L.) Stevenson and (Hinton Tallman) Co., agreeing not to go into the grain business for four years. At the expiration of this term in 1861 he again went into business on the south side of the canal, occupying the yellow warehouse and the adjoining store room; he associated John Gehm and L. C. Bartlit (a nephew) with himself, each to receive one-third the profits. In 1864 they dissolved partnership, John Gehm retiring from the firm and L. C.

141

Bartlit continuing the general store department, which he sold to Aaron Fenstermaker about 1870. In 1865 Chas. W. Speaks* became a partner in the grain business, and the firm continued under the title of Bartlit & Speaks until 1879, when Mr. Bartlit retired.

*Father of Oley Speaks, see photo

Oley Speaks
1874 - 1948
Son of Charles W. Speaks
Oley was a famous baritone singer and
composer of over 250 songs. Including
"The Road to Mandalay"

John Helpman and Henry W. Shaffer built the old planing mill in the spring of 1857. The familiar tones of the bell in the old "factory" belfry was the time regulation for many years. Another familiar bell was the one on the Commercial Hotel, and which was for many years rung at meal time.

The first bridge across the canal in Winchester was built on wooden abutments with trestle approaches, and was located on High Street, and about the same time another one of similar construction was built at the east line of town, but being little used was never rebuilt. In about 1840 stone abutments with earth approaches were constructed, and a covered bridge with double driveways was erected; this bridge stood until the winter of 1869-1870, when, during a certain night it fell into the canal. In the spring of 1870 the iron structure that now spans the canal at East Street, Groveport, was erected at High Street, in Winchester, and served until 1883, when the present turn bridge was built. The surplus stone and earth in the High Street abutments were used in the construction of the Washington Street bridge, which was completed in the fall of 1883. The first team crossed the High Street turn bridge on February 1, 1884. The old mile stone "210" (miles from Cleveland) stood directly under the High Street bridge, and when the stone abutments were built it formed part of the wall and later was built into the present abutments.

Canal Bridge on High Street, Winchester
Taken down in 1883 and moved to East Street, Groveport

When the post office was established at Waterloo in 1839 — with Abner Clough postmaster — an effort was made to have it located at Winchester; when this effort failed the citizens arranged to have their mail sent to Lithopolis. In 1841, when the post office was finally removed from Waterloo and established at Winchester, considerable ill-feeling existed, due to the rivalry between the towns. Mr. Evans relates that when he was returning from Waterloo with his commission as postmaster, the women and children came out and hissed at him as he went along the street. A controversy arose about the post office sign, when Esq. John Donaldson secured it and brought it to Winchester, saying: *"Since you have the post office you shall also*

143

have the sign." At a meeting of the citizens to select a name for the office — since there were then five other Winchesters in Ohio — Carlisle and Pekin were among the names proposed; no definite conclusion was reached, when the post office department added the prefix "Canal." The same office case that Mr. Evans had made was in constant use for some fifty years, when during the administration of Mr. Bailey the present case was purchased.

The successive postmasters have been: James B. Evans, 1841-1850, when Mr. Evans resigned and moved to Circleville. Mr. Evans kept the office in a two-story house that stood on lot No. 13, Waterloo Street. This building was destroyed by fire on January 21, 1891; Dr. Joseph B. Potter, 1850-1853; the citizens chose Dr. Potter at a special election; he kept the office in the Dauterman Building corner of High and Columbus Streets; Peter Krag, 1853-1857, office in the Commercial Hotel; David Gayman, 1857-1870, office in Gayman's Store; Josiah K. Miller, June 1, 1870, November 16, 1885, office in Bergstresser Building, until Mr. Miller's business block was completed in 1880, when the office was kept there; Robt. W. Bolenbaugh and Johnnie (Burnie) Southward were clerks; James B. Evans, November 16, 1885 — May 17, 1889, the present quarters were built in November, 1885, and occupied first by Mr. Evans. The clerks were Nan Evans and Lil Alstadt; Rev. J. W. Sleeper, May 17, 1889, to March 2, 1890, when Mr. Sleeper died; Lil Alstadt and Abe Good were clerks. After Mr. Sleeper's death his bondsmen selected Abe Good to serve as postmaster until a regular appointment would be made; S. E. Bailey, April 1, 1890 — June 3, 1893; Horace and Gertrude Bailey were clerks. In May, 1890 Mr. Bailey purchased the present office case, the old one having been used continuously since the establishment of the office; James Palsgrove, June 3, 1893 — July 1, 1897; Zack E. England and John Palsgrove, clerks; Henry H. Dibble, the present incumbent, has served since July 1, 1897; Mary Dibble is clerk.

In order to test the Morse system of telegraphy a line was erected between Baltimore and Washington and on May 27, 1844, the first message was successfully transmitted. Five years later, in 1849, a telegraph line, connecting Columbus and Lancaster, and later farther down the Hocking Valley, was established. James B. Evans went to Zanesville to learn and became the first operator in Winchester. Capt. Philip Game, who then lived with Mr. Evans, also learned to operate.

The messages were then received on a ribbon of paper. In 1850 when Dr. Potter conducted the office, Edward Potter became the operator, and received by sound. When the line was extended farther down the Hocking Valley, Edward Potter went to Logan and Peter Krag became the operator. Messages of 10 words cost 25c and of 5 words half that price.

Winchester has always been a good grain market and drew trade from many miles. Before the introduction of the modern unloading devices, the corn had to be shoveled off by hand and the wheat elevated by horse power. This slow process often congested the movement of grain until almost every street in town was filled with teams waiting their turn. By the time navigation opened up in the spring, the large cribs and bins would be filled and loading boats would be the "order of the day," employing many men, carrying ear corn onto the boats in one-bushel baskets. What corn was shelled was run through a "pot-lid" sheller and fed in by hand one ear at a time.

Although the territory from which grain is hauled to this market has become greatly reduced by the building of the Norfolk & Western and the Ohio Central Railways, still the fact remains that now farms on which then only three to five hundred bushels were grown, now yield as many thousand bushels. The following item which appeared in the *"Winchester Times"* of April 18, 1877, incidentally illustrates the multiplied ability to handle grain over the old methods; *"Our grain dealers shelled eighty car loads of corn last week, and O. P. Chaney shipped 52 cars, Bartlit & Speaks 32 cars and Whitehurst, Lehman & Carty 25 cars — a total of 109 cars shipped out in one week."*

Philip Game was the first business man in Winchester to advocate and inaugurate a store for separate lines of goods when in 1868 he in company with Chas. P. Rees, under the firm name of Rees & Game, put a stock of hardware and stoves in the room then just completed by Mr. Rees. They continued until 1871 when Mr. Game sold his interest to John Chaney, Jr., and the firm name became Rees & Chaney.

Philip Game and his brother John Gehm then concluded to build the opera house block, when Philip formed a partnership with his brother, Wm. M. Game, and arranged to occupy the south room with a stock of family groceries, under the firm name of Game Brothers. They continued until 1878 when Philip sold his interest to his brother John, and the firm name was changed to John Gehm & Brother.

In March, 1880, Philip Game concluded to put a stock of boots and shoes in the room formerly occupied and built by J. W. Hische, being the north room in the opera house block. Mr. Game conducted this store until January 22, 1885, when he sold to Adam Weber.

It was prophesied of each of these ventures that they would fail; the general opinion then prevailing that only a general store could succeed, but the uniform success attained showed the soundness of his judgment.

Canal boat passing through High Street Bridge, Winchester, 1881. Also showing the Whitehurst and Carty Warehouse, built in 1843 and torn down in 1901.

The Winchester Times

Horace Mann said, *"There are no tools more ingeniously, wrought, or more potent than those which belong to the art of the printer."* The local newspaper, which prepares in readable form the neighborhood happenings, eliminating everything that tends to lower and debase, and which publishes from week to week notices of births, marriages, anniversaries, deaths, and which makes note of the various religious, educational, political and social events of the vicinity, is an influential factor in all that contributes to lift up a community to a high standard of American citizenship.

The tone of the *Times* has been in the main one of dignity and impartiality, avoiding sensationalism and other characteristics of "yellow journalism." Since its establishment the consecutive issues at once make up a history of Madison and adjoining townships.

The Canal Winchester Times was established by Major J. W. Stinchcomb, and the first issue appeared under date of March 16, 1871.

In 1874 Charles M. Gould, of Logan, Ohio, purchased the plant, which was then located in the second story of the building now occupied by Charles Painter, and continued the publication of the paper as a Democratic organ until November 9, 1876, when Rev. James Heffly and Oliver L. Bott became proprietors and conducted *The Times* as an independent paper in the Bergstresser Building. On April 12, 1875, while the paper was under the management of Mr. Gould, Benj. F. Gayman became an apprentice in the office.

Oliver P. Gayman
1859 - 1942

The firm of Heffley & Bott continued but a short time, when the latter retired. In the autumn of 1877 Oliver P. Gayman entered the office as an apprentice. Mr. Heffley remained the sole owner until May 1, 1879, when B. F. Gayman, shortly after reaching his majority, purchased a half interest. The firm of Heffley & Gayman continued until September 8, 1881, when the latter purchased Mr. Heffley's interest and continued the sole proprietor for five years. September 2, 1886, his brother, O. P. Gayman, purchased a half interest, and they still continue in joint partnership. On January 11, 1901, they also purchased *The Buckeye News* of Lithopolis, Ohio, and both papers are now issued from *The Times* office.

The *Canal Winchester Bank* was opened for business on February 23, 1887, in a building erected especially for it. The stockholders were Gilbert Shaffer, President; Stanton T. Needels, Cashier; B. D. Gehm and Wm. F. Zigler. On March 22, 1888, Mr. Shaffer retired and Mr. Needels became President and C. V. Moore Cashier. The present owners are Wm. M. Game, President; C. V. Moore, Cashier, and Ervin Moore, with E. C. Chaney as bookkeeper. Previous to the starting of this bank the grain dealers did the banking business, often holding large amounts on deposit, and frequently advancing considerable sums on grain or growing crops, all usually without interest.

In February, 1887, Sol. S. Lehman and others agitated the idea of drilling for gas. A preliminary meeting was called and a committee appointed to solicit subscriptions. This committee secured subscriptions for two hundred shares of $25.00 each, aggregating $5,000.00, within four days. O. P. Chaney, M. C. Whitehurst, Dr. J. B. Potter, Sol. S. Lehman, B. D. Gehm, S. T. Needels and Jacob Bott, being the seven persons subscribing the largest amounts, were authorized to incorporate under the name "*Canal Winchester Natural Gas and Oil Company.*" A committee consisting of O. P. Chaney, Ervin Moore and Prof. W. H. Hartsaugh, was sent to Findlay, Lima and Bowling Green to make investigations. M. C. Whitehurst, Ervin Moore, George Powell, O. P. Chaney, Sol. S. Lehman, Prof. W. H. Hartsaugh and Philip Game were elected Directors. Philip Game was elected President, W. H. Hartsough Secretary and C. D. Whitehurst, Treasurer. Some $4,000.00 was expended in sinking a well on West Waterloo Street to a depth of (?) about 2,500 feet.

On the morning of July 4, 1887, some boys touched a lighted match to the pipe, when a flame some ten or twelve feet high shot up. Although the drillers had intended to observe the *"fourth,"* it is said *"they at once began to drill again,"* thus arousing a general suspicion that for some reason they were not anxious to find gas.

As no record was kept nor made of the quantity, quality or depth at which gas was found, the question of the amount of gas that might be found here is still an open one.

In the spring of 1900 the *Federal Gas and Fuel Co.* of Columbus, under the local name of the *Consumers' Gas Company of Canal Winchester*, laid a 6-inch main down High Street, with laterals of smaller sizes through all parts of the village, and on April 6 the natural gas was turned on. A. S. Lehman's drug store was the first room lighted, and later in the same evening C. Gayman & Son's store.

The telephone line from Columbus via Groveport and Winchester was put up in the summer of 1882. About the first of November, 1881, Geo. H. Twiss, of Columbus, canvassed the towns of Groveport and Winchester in the interest of a *Columbus Telephone Company*. A meeting of those interested was held at Cowan's office. The conditions of the telephone company were stated to be as follows: *"In order to secure the construction of a line to Columbus it is necessary to sell six thousand tickets in advance, each ticket to cost fifteen cents, which will entitle the holder to a five minute talk over the line; the sale of the tickets to be divided between Groveport and Winchester."*

About 4 o'clock p. m. on July 6, 1882, the connections were made to Columbus, and the citizens invited to a free use of the line. Within a day or two the branch line to Lithopolis was connected with the main line, Lithopolis purchasing two hundred and fifty dollars worth of tickets.

The Winchester Times of July 13, 1882 recounts some amusing incidents that took place on the afternoon when the line was connected up. *"One of our oldest citizens, who is considerably deaf, was curious to know whether he could hear through the telephone. Mr. Ross (the Superintendent from Columbus), asked him who he wanted to speak to. The citizen not being particular on that point, Mr. Ross called up the central office and informed the lady attendant that a gentleman in Canal Winchester wanted to talk to her. The citizen took hold of the telephone and for some moments said not a word. In the meantime the patient lady at the other end of the line continued to call out: 'Hello! What is it? Well?' and other interrogations of similar import. The citizen after satisfying himself that his deafness did not prevent him from hearing through the telephone, turned a countenance, lighted by a benign smile on the crowd and said: 'She just keeps on hollering 'hello!'*

Other of our citizens, supposing that ordinary conversation could not be carried on between Winchester and Columbus, yelled at the top of their voices. Others would hold the receiver to their ears, and when the first message came over the line would dodge like amateur base ballists."

At first the office was located in Heffley's Drug Store, in the Bergstresser Building, but it now is in Lehman's Drug Store.

The Franklin Telephone Co. established the telephone exchange in Winchester on February 8, 1901, and extended it to Reynoldsburg, Brice, Groveport and Lithopolis in the fall of the same year, connecting the above towns with the Winchester exchange. The price of the service, including the above mentioned towns, is; for office $24.00, and for residences $12.00 per year. A "flat rate" to Columbus, giving the free use of the Columbus exchange, is furnished for $12.00 per year extra. There are one hundred and twelve subscribers in the Winchester exchange, and thirty-two in the Groveport exchange.

The following extracts are taken from the records of the proceedings of the Franklin County Commissioners:

"January 19, 1866, a petition from John Helpman and others, accompanied by a plat, was received, and March 13 set for its hearing." Under date of March 13, 1866, *"This day being set for the hearing of the petition for the incorporation of Canal Winchester in Madison Township. After the examination of the proceedings, it was found that the petitioners had failed to notify according to law, and the proceedings in said matter were all annulled, consequently a new petition was presented, and was placed on file, and Thursday, May 24, 1866, set for the first hearing."* Then under date of May 24, *"First hearing, continued until May 31,"* and under date of May 31, 1866, *"After examining the petition and plat and hearing the evidence of John Helpman that due notice had been given, the Commissioners being satisfied that the proceedings were all in accordance to law, it is hereby ordered that the incorporation be granted; same to be indorsed on the petition and passed over to the County Auditor."*

The first election was held in the fall of 1866, when the following officers were elected: James B. Evans, Mayor; Charles W. Speaks,

Recorder; Christian Gayman, Treasurer, and John Chaney, Reuben Trine, John Helpman, Elisha B. Decker and Martin C. Whitehurst, Councilmen.

On April 8, 1867, Christian Gayman was elected a Councilman, and John Gehm was elected Treasurer. The records of the first six years have been lost or destroyed, hence the names of the Councilmen can be given only since 1873. It was during these years that the streets were graded and most of the sidewalks and gutters put down and the sewers constructed. The following have been the officers:

Mayors: James B. Evans, 1866-1868, 1871-1873, 1876-1885; John Helpman, 1896; Joshua S. Stevenson, 1870; Charles B. Cowan, 1874-1875; B. F. Gayman, 1886-1890, resigned July 7, 1890, being temporarily located at Owensboro, Ky., and Wm. H. Lane appointed. In April, 1891, Mr. Gayman was again elected, and on October 19, 1891, resigned, having been elected a member of the Ohio House of Representatives, and W. S. Alspach appointed, 1891 — until December 9, 1897, when he died and Oliver P. Gayman was appointed and elected, 1898-1901.

Clerks: Chas. W. Speaks, 1866; M. C. Whitehurst, 1867; A. Starr, 1868; James B. Evans, 1869-1870, 1874; Chas. B. Cowan, 1871-1873; Joe Edw. Evans, 1875, resigned September 7, 1875, and Charles. Epply appointed; Chas. Epply, 1876, resigned August 17, 1876, and J. E. Evans appointed, and on March 30, 1877, T. F. Ungemach was appointed in place of Mr., Evans, deceased; T. F. Ungemach, 1877-1879; Henry H. Dibble, 1880-1892; Wm. D. Beeks, 1893-1901.

Treasurers: Christian Gayman, 1866; John Gehm, 1867- to September 30, 1885, when he died and Philip Game was appointed; Philip Game, 1886-1891; C. V. Moore, 1892-1897; Edw. C. Chaney, 1898-1901.

Marshals: John Kile, 1867; James McKelvey. 1868-1870; Lee Kramer, 1871-1872; Adam Shaner, 1873-1875; J. W. Bowen, 1876-1877; Henry S. Binkly, 1878-1881, 1888-1891, resigned July 6, 1891, and Wm. Schrock appointed; Wm. Schrock 1882-1885; Samuel Anderson, 1886-1887; Andy Burnsides, 1892, resigned July 27, 1892; Jesse Shaffer, 1893; Edw. V. Busch, 1894, resigned November 4, 1895, and Samuel Travis appointed; Geo. C. Ford, 1896, resigned June 13, 1896, and Wm. Pearsol appointed; Wm. Pearsol, 1897; John Zwayer, 1898-1901.

The Village Marshals have always been appointed to serve as sanitary police officers.

Councilmen: John Chaney, Sr., 1873-1874; Rev. James Heffly, 1873, 1877-1882; A. Hathaway, 1873; John H. Speilman, 1873. resigned September 29, 1874, and M. C. Whitehurst appointed; James H. Sommerville, 1873, 1874, resigned January 4, 1875, and J. B. Evans appointed; John Deitz, 1873, 1874; Chas. F. Yost, 1874, 1875; James P. Kramer, 1874, 1875, 1882; M. C. Whitehurst, 1875-1878; Wm. P. Miller, 1875, C. Kuqua, 1875-1876, resigned June 2, 1876, and John Chaney appointed; T. F. Ungemach, 1875-1876, resigned March 30, 1877; John F. Bauer, 1876, resigned July 21, 1876, and John R. Clement appointed; Mr. Clement declined to serve, when Rev. James Heffly was appointed; H. H. Dibble, 1876-1879; Noah H. Hummel, 1876-1877; I. L. Decker, 1877-1884; Wm. T. Conklin, 1878-1879; John W. Griffith, 1878-1879; Wm. M. Game, 1879-1880, 1897-1898; Samuel Travis, 1883-1884; Sol. S. Lehman, 1883-1884; B. F. Gayman, 1884-1885; J. E. Billingsly, 1884-1885; Rev. A.C. Kelley, 1884-1885; W. Scott Alspach, 1885-1886, 1889-1890; S. E. Bailey, 1885; Edw. C. Chaney, 1885-1886; John A. Whitzel, 1886-1887; Cary D. Whitehurst, 1886-1891; Church B. Tuttle, 1886-1889; Joe S. Ashe, 1887-1888: Dr. J. W. Shook, 1887-1888; Wm. L. Walters, 1887-1888, 1892-1897; Wm. H. Harpst, 1888-1889: Ervin Moore, 1889-1896; Peter S. Long, 1889-1893, resigned March 5, 1894; B. D. Gehm, 1890-1891, 1896, resigned June 1, 1897; E. C. Chaney, 1890, to July 3, 1893, when he resigned; Geo. W. Sponsler, 1891-1900; C. Gayman, 1892, March 23, 1896, when he died; Lee Kramer, 1894-1896: Henry Rush, 1894-1895; Joe C. Shaffer, 1896-1897; Dr. G. F. Owen, 1897-1898; David Boyer, appointed July 5, 1897, May, 1900; J. A. Mathias, 1898-1899, appointed in place of David Bover on May 14, 1900; Phil Weber, 1898-1901; Jacob E. Zarbaugh, 1898, died May 28, 1899; Levi Teegardin, appointed June 11, 1898; Wm. E. Sims, 1900-1902; Geo. W. Smith, 1899-1900; Stephen Boyd, appointed June 5, 1899-1900; Samuel Savior, 1901; Arth. Chaney, 1901; Geo. F. Bareis, 1901; Lewis Sarber, appointed July 2, 1902, in place of Wm. E. Sims, who moved away.

City Solicitor: Wm. H. Lane, 1887-1888, 1890-1898; Charles Pickering, 1889.

Board of Health: The Board of Health was established in 1888. The following have been the members; the date indicates time of appointment:

Rev. James Heffly. 1888; Dr. J. W. Shook, 1888; Dr. A. A. Short, 1888; Geo. F. Bareis, 1888-1800; Philip Game, 1888-1890; H. H. Dibble, 1890-1896; Al. Lane, 1890; Dr. L. W. Beery, 1891-1893; Lee Kramer, 1892; David Boyer, 1892-1895; C. D. Whitehurst, 1892-1894; Sol. S. Lehman, 1892; R. C. Caslow, 1892-1893; J. K. Miller, 1893; Ezra H. Tobias, 1893-1895; D. H. Cowen, 1893-1896; Adam Weber 1894-1896; S. E. Bailey, 1895-1896; J. E. Hedges, 1895, resigned March 7, 1897; Chas. W. Miller, 1896-1899, resigned October 2, 1899, and Frank Glatfetter appointed 1899-1901; Wesley Davis, 1896-1901, resigned December, 1901, and Don Young appointed; Milt Armpreister, 1897-1899. resigned October, 1899, and G. M. Herbst appointed 1899-1901; Sam Savior, 1897-1899; Wiley Brown, 1898-1901; Wm. M. Codner, 1898, resigned May 1, 1899, and on June 15, Wm. Pearsol appointed; George Rush, 1901, moved from village and Dr. E. L. Carlton appointed.

The **Clerks** have been: Geo. F. Bareis, November 12, 1888 to September 9, 1892; Henry H. Dibble, September, 1892 to October 17, 1898; J. M. Armpreister, October, 1898 to October 16, 1899; G. M. Herbst, October 1899, to present time.

The **Health Officers** have been: Dr. J. W. Shook, November 12, 1888 to February, 1891; Dr. L. W. Beery, February, 1891, to September, 1895. Since September 16, 1895, Dr. W. S. Gayman has served.

The Village Marshals have always been appointed to serve as sanitary police officers.

Street Commissioners: John Schrock, 1873; Lee Kramer, on south side, 1874; John Kissel, on north side, 1874; Mr. Kramer declined to serve then John R. Wright appointed; Mr. Wright resigned, then John Karns was appointed; as it was found that Mr. Karns lived outside the corporation, George Powell was appointed; John R. Wright, 1875-1876; Joshua Shaner, 1877, resigned and H. S. Binkly appointed; Adam Shaner, 1879; Isaac Wright, 1880; John Colman, 1881; Joshua Shaner, 1882-1883. moved away and Wm. R. Miller appointed: Jonathan Vought, 1884-1885; Samuel S. Anderson, 1886-1887; Wm. Boyd, 1888-1889, resigned January 6, 1890, and John McFarland appointed; Mr. Boyd served again, 1892-1894; Edw. V. Bush, 1895, resigned and John

McFarland appointed; Mr. McFarland resigned December 24, 1895, and Wesley Davis appointed. The office of Street Commissioner has been abolished.

September 28, 1875. the Town Hall building was purchased from L. C. Bartlit and the addition was added in 1877.

Jennie Sommerville served as Librarian in 1880, 1881, 1882, and perhaps on up to 1889, when Mina Kissel was appointed. The latter served until November, 1895, when she resigned. Lydia Alspach was appointed January 6, 1896, and resigned June 6, 18980 since which date Grace Colman has occupied the position.

The iron prison cages were purchased in the spring of 1890.

The engine house was moved to the front of the town lot in August, 1898.

Fires: The first building in Winchester that was consumed by fire was a frame house that stood just east of Mrs. Poor's residence on Waterloo Street, and belonged to Nathaniel Tallman. It burned on a Sunday morning in 1838 or 1839, and was occupied by a family named Birely. Perhaps the next fire was that of the Plott residence which stood on the lot now occupied by Mrs. W. S. Alspach in about 1852 or 1853. One of the rooms was filled with corn at the time, thus causing quite a hot fire. Dr. Geo. W. Blake's residence at the northeast corner of High and Columbus Street burned at about 3 o'clock a. m. in October or November, 1860. E. B. Decker's saw mill, adjoining the foundry building on the west, burned about midnight December 10, 1876. An epidemic of fires began with the burning of O. P. Chaney's warehouse on June 2, 1878. This fire was discovered about 8;30 on a Sunday morning, in the cupola on the large building running north and south along the east side of the basin, and spread very rapidly to the long cribs towards the east along the north side of the canal, and also to the large building to the west. This latter building stood along the north side of the basin and was of about the size and general appearance of the Whitehurst and Carty Warehouse. The buildings contained many bushels of grain at the time. The water had been drawn from the canal, and the corn when released rolled into the canal bed, where it continued to burn for a week or ten days. Help was telegraphed for from Columbus, but by the time the special train brought a fire engine down, the citizens had the fire under control. For a time it seemed as if the village was doomed. Many of the citizens removed their valuables out of town, fearing its total destruction. Later in the same year Mr. Chaney built an elevator near the railroad, on the site of the present one which was also consumed by fire on September 29, 1880. The fire was first discovered about 5 o'clock a. m. When discovered it had gained such headway that no attempt was made to save it. Mr. Chaney at once began the erection of the present building; the east part of this building was formerly the Loucks Mill. On Saturday evening, September 15, 1883, C. P. Rees' hardware store on High Street caught fire at lamp lighting time, it is supposed, from the fumes of gasoline used in polishing stoves. It was a furious fire, and both stock and building was soon totally consumed. Lee Lodge No. 384, I. O. O. F., owned and occupied the upper story, and lost all their furnishings and records. On the morning of September 29, 1883, three stables along the alley, between Liberty and Washington Streets, belonging to Mrs. Mary Wilson, Michael Lecrone and Henry Herbst, were burned. On October 30, 1883, at about 1 o'clock a. m., a cry of "Fire, fire!" called the citizens to the carriage works of C. Kuqua, on West Waterloo Street. No other buildings were nearby, and this one too nearly consumed to be saved. Simon Brown had erected this building a few years previous.

About this time a report was circulated that some "tramps" had felt offended at the treatment received by the town officials and had therefore sworn vengeance. Most of the citizens became very uneasy, when the village council concluded to purchase a hook and ladder truck, which arrived on June 2, 1884.

A fire company with thirty-five members was organized on November 27, 1883, called the *"Winchester Protectors."* Rev. J. W. Davis was elected captain in recognition of the active part he had taken at the C. P. Rees fire. This company was kept up, with J. W. Young, Wm. G. Ochs and Chas. W. Miller as successive captains, until the spring of 1888, when on account of the council authorizing the marshal to ring the fire bell as a signal for the saloons to close they disbanded. They held their last meeting on April 26, 1888, when they voted the balance of the funds in their treasury to the base ball club. The fire bell was put on the Town Hall in April, 1885.

On Tuesday evening, February 19, 1884, the hook and ladder truck was used for the first time at the burning of "Uncle Johnnie" Kramer's stable on Mound Street. This was the fourth fire within a few months.

At the April election a proposition to purchase a hand fire engine was submitted to the voters; 99 voted for and 53 against, and on June 2, 1884, it arrived. On April 14, 1884, at about 10 o'clock in the evening, the planing mill on East Waterloo Street and the canal was discovered on fire. Although the citizens made a heroic effort to save it, by the next morning only the brick stack and the warped machinery was left to mark the remains of the buildings and lumber. On the evening of the fire one of the buildings from the Carty Corner was moved onto the lot adjoining the lumber yard office, and was also consumed. It was with great difficulty that the buildings on the opposite side of the street were saved. John Helpman and Henry Shaffer had erected this mill in the spring of 1857. It had been operated by Mr. Helpman until about six months previous to the fire, when George F. Bareis had purchased it. The present planing mill was built and equipped the same season.

Early on February 5, 1885, fire was discovered in the store room on the northeast corner of High and Waterloo Streets, occupied by James A. Billingsly with a dry goods store. The fire had gained so much headway before discovered that it soon communicated to the drug store of R. C. Caslow adjoining on the north, which had, during the proprietorship of Weisman & Speilman, been connected by an open archway. Both buildings were completely destroyed.

The storage shed of the Central Ohio Baling Company burned on Friday, July 28, 1893. On October 11, 1894, at about 4 o'clock p. m., the Hocking Valley Depot was discovered to be on fire, and was totally destroyed. The present depot was occupied first on December 3 of the same year. The Empire Mills, with the adjoining covered bridge and residence, were totally destroyed by fire on Friday night, August 21, 1895. David Dover's stable was entirely consumed by fire on April 8, 1898. The records of W. D. Beeks, the village clerk, referring to this fire, says: "At this juncture the fire alarm sounded, and fire found to be on the premises of one of our fellow councilmen — Mr. David Boyer. The council chamber was soon empty, and business only partially transacted."

While these fires were misfortunes and much regretted at the time, the village has gained new and modern buildings in the stead of the old ones destroyed. The business rooms in Winchester (as well as the sidewalks) are much above the ordinary for a place of its size, and traveling men often remark that *"there are more plate glass stone fronts here than in most towns of the size of Winchester."*

Business Enterprises in Winchester
1830-1840

J. L. Vance, store on lot No. 8; David Dixon, store lot No. 9; Peter Bennedum, tavern, lot No. 20; Paul Samsel, tailor lot No. 32; Samuel Taylor, tavern, on Samuel Bartlit store lot; Stephen Potter, physician; J. B. Potter, came in 1838, physician; Joseph Wright, grain, lots Nos. 19 and 20, Waterloo Street (A.) Hathaway & (James) Clendening, grain, lots Nos. 19 and 20; Carty & Julian, store on town lot; Carty & Rogers, store and grain, north side of canal; Eichelberger & Loucks, slaughter house (Somerville's tannery); Fred Slough & Co., cabinet shop, on lot No. 7; Ira Mason, tavern, town lot: Henry Eichelberger and Henry J. Epply, brick yard and brick masons; J. B. Evans, located 1832, tailor; Daniel Lecrone, shoe shop, town lot; Wm. Fry, tailor, 1838.

1840 -1850

A Mr. Pratt, of Zanesville, built and operated a general store on lot 13; Samuel Dressbach and Chas. D. Corner managed it. Peter T. Krag, tavern, lot No. 8; Bartlit Bros. (Jno. F. and Samuel), general store, where Gayman's store; Whitehurst & Carty, store and grain; Moses Levy, clothing, lot No. 9; Isaac Shoemaker, harness, where J. K. Miller's residence; Henry Nicodemus, wagon shop, in Flinchbaugh Shop (Uncle Johnnie Kramer moved it from Waterloo on a sled); Jacob Schrock, wagon maker, lot No. 3, West Street; Wm. Hendricks and John Moore, wagon maker, shop rear of lot No. 1, West Street; Jacob Dravenstatt, wagon maker; Daniel Rocky, pump maker, also occupied the shop on the lot No. 1 (Drs. J. B.) Potter & Langworthy, until 1843, then Potter & (Isaac) Titus, then Potter & (Robt.) McLane; Dr. G. W. Blake, located 1843, office on lot No. 20, Columbus Street; Elizabeth Lee, milliner in the Mrs. Welsh House, Columbus Street; ____ Eversole, coverlet weaver, on lot No. 8, Columbus Street; Peter E. Ehrenhart, a weaver, succeeded; Lewis Stands, a cabinet shop, lot No. 7; Paul Samsel, tailor; Elias Lines, blacksmith shop, south end of High Street; Wm. Overholser, tin shop; Henry Epply and Henry Eichelberger, brick yard and brick masons; James Cannon, blacksmith shop, Waterloo Street; James H. Somerville, tanyard, Liberty Street; George Lehman, shoe shop, lot 5, West Street; he also sold soft drinks — Honey Mead, Metheglin and Silver-Top; Andrew Boyer, cooper, lot No. 2. Columbus Street; Joseph Johnson, cabinet shop, lot No. 5, Columbus Street (rear end); Daniel Bergstresser, harness shop, High and Waterloo Street; Wm. Curtis, slaughter house, lot No. 23, Columbus Street; Ira and Geo. Mason, tavern, south side of canal, on High Street; Wm. Riley, tannery, corner Waterloo and Trine Streets; Wm. Harbaugh, linseed oil mill, Liberty Street; Bennedum & Mathews, cabinet shop, rear end lot No. 5, Columbus Street; Wm. and Lafayette Tallman, store, lot No. 9, High Street; Bartlit & Fry, grain; Robt. McCurdy, store; John Wolf, blacksmith at Line's shop; James McKelvey, tailor; J. W. Hische, 1847, harness; Kelley, tailor; Heil Brockway, packet line; Jacob Direling, grocery, Bartlit store building; Gus Finnefrock, shoe maker; Peter Bolenbaugh, shoe maker; Geo. McCombs, teamster; Daniel Leckrone, shoe shop; Daniel Boyer, basket maker; Wright & Tallman, grain; Tallman, Helpman & Allen, store and lumber yard; in 1849 the firm dissolved, Mr. Helpman continuing the lumber yard on lots Nos. 1 and 2, Columbus Street, and Tallman, Allen & Co. continuing the store on the corner of High and West Streets; J. B. Evans, tailor and post office, on Waterloo Street, lot No. 13; Joseph Bennedum, cabinet maker and undertaker; John Fry, carpenter; Whitehurst & Carty, grain; John Thompson, tannery, Waterloo Street; Wm. Fry, tailor; Jacob Carty & Son, store; Amanda Schrock (daughter of Jacob), milliner; Eliza Bishop, milliner and dressmaker; Wm. Jacobs, tavern, 1843, where Town Hall; Geo. Fosket. butcher shop and grocery, rear of Bartlit store building; J. B. Ford, butcher; John Gehm. Dick Jeffres, Chas. D. Comer, Clint Atwaters and Herod Cater were clerks.

1850-1860

Samuel Bartlit, store and grain; Bartlit & Fry, store and grain: Samuel Pond, store; D. and C. Gayman, store; Tallman, Speaks & Co., store; Amon Algire, store; Whitehurst & Carty, store and grain, Philip King, gunsmith; Rufus W. Bailey, butcher shop; Leo Carson, carpenter; Potter & Shortt, physicians, 1856-1861, 1865-1874; Tallman, Stevenson & Co., grain; C. P. Rees, 1859, tin shop; Jacob Dauterman, 1855, barber shop; Empire Mills, John Chaney & Son, George Bareis miller; Amaziah Wise, son of Rev. Geo. Wise, store; Levi Brown, grocery; Wm. Overholser, tin shop; Hiram Siball, tailor; James

McKelvey, tailor; Wm. Cater, tailor; Dr. G. W. Blake; John Helpman & Son, lumber; Helpman & Shaffer, planing mill, 1857, and lumber; Geo. Gregg, store; August Groff, cabinet shop; Aaron Fellers, picture gallery; Isaac Shoemaker, harness; Daniel Bergstresser, harness; J. W. Hische, harness; Nicholas Gettel, shoe maker; Chas. Dagon, tailor; Peter Weber, shoemaker; Peter Bolenbaugh, shoemaker; Joseph Miller, tailor; James Cannon, blacksmith; Wm. Riley, tanner; Reuben Trine, tanner; James H. Somerville, tanner; Jacob Dellinger, brick maker; John Fry, carpenter; John Kissell, carpenter; Noah Banister, blacksmith; Geo. Derr, blacksmith; Daniel Lethers, stage coach line (drowned November, 1857, at lock west of town); Wm. Wilson, stage driver; Riley Rhodes, picture gallery; David Shrader, picture gallery; Henry S. Binkley, picture gallery; Jacob Rawn, Grocery; Geo. Lehman, drug store; Al. Chandler, grocery; John Kissell, grocery; Sol. Dildine, grocery; Wm. L. Stevenson, grain; Tallman, Hathaway & Co., grain; Frederick Eauca, oil mill; Jacob Harbaugh, cabinet maker and undertaker; John Miller, brick mason; Wm. P. Miller, carpenter. Clerks: Geo. M. B. Dove, August Korn, Dick Jeffres, John Gehm, Wm. Thompson, Wm. Tallman, Phil Game, Lew Dellinger, David Gayman, Mal B. Karnes, John M. Schoch, hotel; Wm. Harbaugh, cabinet maker; Schrock & Flinchbaugh, wagon maker; Henry Will, carpenter; Henry Harpst, carpenter; Abraham Hunsicker, carpenter; Daniel Gayman, carpenter; H. J. Epply, brick mason; Fisher & Markley, then Fisher & Moore, Kramer Mill; Philip Price, sexton at graveyard; Samuel Taylor, tavern, and his son-in-law, Sheldon, a grocery in the Samuel Bartlit building; Wm. Lines, Mitchell Allen, John McCombs, Joseph and Silas McClellan and Isaac Kramer, were plasterers.

1860-1870

General Stores: D. and C. Gayman, Amon Algire, John and Philip Game, Shrader, Rightly & Miller, Samuel Bartlit & Co. (L. C. Bartlit and John Gehm), L. C. Bartlit.

Grain: Samuel Bartlit & Co., Bartlit & Speaks, O. P. Chaney & Bro., Chaney, Decker & Co. (E. K. Chaney), Whitehurst & Carty, Whitehurst, Gehm & Co. (Jacob Carty and Solomon Lehman).

Other Stores: David Lehman, drugs; Dr. A. Starr, drugs and printing office; Daniel Bergstresser, groceries, etc.; George King, groceries, etc.; John Kissel, grocery; Peter Caslow, grocery; C. P. Rees, tin shop; Rees &

Game, hardware, 1868; Mrs. Fay Decker, milliner; Mrs. C. Ehrenhart, milliner.

Physicians: Dr. J. B. Potter, Dr. A. A. Shortt, Dr. G. W. Blake, Dr. J. J. McConkly, Dr. Geo. Hendren.

Tanneries: Reuben Trine and James H. Somerville.

Shoe Shops: Peter Weber, Reuben Trine, Elisha Himrod & Son, Martin Zahn.

Tailor Shops: James B. Evans, Wm. Cater, James McKelvey, Chas. Dagon.

Blacksmith Shops: Peter and Jacob Zarbaugh, George Derr, Chas. B. Cannon.

Jacob Dauterman, barber; David Shrader, picture gallery; Thos. Pinney, saloon; J. W. Hische, harness; Daniel Bergstresser, harness.

Brickmasons: John Miller, Henry Epply, Jacob Dellinger, Chas. Zarbaugh, Wm. Boyd, Geo. Powell.

Carpenters: Daniel Gayman, Israel Gayman, Abraham Hunsicker, I. L. Decker, Henry Will, Henry Herbst, Jacob Comp, Hiram Shaffer, Leonard & Leighner, Wm. P. Miller, Chas. F. Yost, L. S. Shoemaker, Armpreister & Brown, Leo. F. Carson, Chas. W. Ramsey, D. B. Washburn.

Hotels: John M. Schoch, Commercial Hotel; David Sarber, in "Poor House" building; John Asbell, 1867, Epply Corner, West and High Streets.

Helpman & Shaffer, lumber yard; Jacob Harbaugh, cabinet maker and undertaker; Peter Ehrenhart, weaver, ____Hale, house painter; George Bush, cooper; S. B. Phipps, singing school; Wm. Cater, Jr., saloon; Rufus W. Bailey, butcher shop; Rodenfels, Seymour & Co. (Peter Brown), Empire Mills; Wm. Houck, butcher shop; John T. Flinchbaugh, wagon shop; Chaney & Stevenson, woolen factory; ____ Lowery, woolen factory; Schrock & Algire, agricultural implements; James Griffith, brick yard; Wm. Brown, cider press; Armpreister & Brown, undertakers; Jacob Moore and O. L. Dibble, plasterers.

1870-1880

Stores: D. & C. Gayman, dry goods; Spielman Bros. & Weisman, dry goods; Rees & Game, then Rees & Chaney, then Chas. P. Rees, hardware; Game Bros., then John Gehm & Bro., groceries; L. C. Bartlit, clothing; John R. Clement & Co., clothing; B. S. Hewitt, clothing; Focht Bros. (Ezra & Sam), groceries; W. R. Miller & Co., hardware (Kuqua building); Theo. Hod Learn, tinner; J. H. Shoemaker, groceries, Bergstresser building; W. R. Miller & Son, then J. K. Miller, groceries; E. D. Orwig, then Foor Bros. (Wes. and Minor), then Hart & Armpreister, then Jacob Dauterman, groceries; John Chaney, groceries; Speilman Bros., drugs; A. Starr, drugs; W. P. Miller, furniture and undertaking; O. L. Bott, drugs; Willis Houser, drugs; E. K. Stentz, jewelry store; Joe E. Evans, cigars and news; Peter Caslow, grocery; A. A. Delong, boots and shoes, north room of Game building.

Major J. W. Stinchcomb, then Chas. M. Gould, then Bott (O. L.) & Heffly (Rev. James), "Winchester Times;" printers, Wes. H. McClintock, W. D. Caslow, Geo. W. Miller, Joe E. Evans, Geo. and Will Stinchcomb, Geo. Hische, D. W. Clelland, coal; Wm. Brown, cider press; Adam Shaner, repair shop; Geo. Leighner, lumber (at R. R.) ; John Helpman. lumber and planing mill; E. B. and I. L. Decker, saw mill; M. Leckrone, saw mill; Simon Brown, carriage manufacturer; C. Kuqua, carriage manufacturer; Fred Ungemach, jeweler; Al. Leckrone, engineer at mill; Walter Mundell, engineer at mill; Simon Shaffer, engineer at planing mill; Simon Helpman, engineer at planing mill; J. Wes. Bowen, stonecutter; George Powell, tile yard, east end of Columbus Street; Israel Gayman, wash machines and churns; Moses Gayman, wash machines and pumps; James McKelvey, auctioneer; J. T. Flinchbaugh, wagon maker; Bott & Epply, insurance; Daniel Holland, then Wm. Dressback, milk wagon; James Griffith, brick yard; Powell & Miller, brick yard; Jas. R. Algire, machine shop, near R. R.; Peter Ehrenhart, weaver; Shaffer & Boyd, broom manufacturers; Miller (G. W.) & Detwiler, bed springs; Leoffler (M.) & Dibble (O. L.), bed springs; Kissel & Brown, agricultural implements, Old Rink; Speaks (C. W.) & Cowan (C. B.), walnut logs; John Kissel, saloon (Hole in the Wall), near R. R.; Kester & Dibble, cooper shop; A. B. Stevenson, woolen mills (2 miles west of town); Harpst & Prentiss, restaurant (over S. Bartlit's store).

Grain: Chaney, Decker & Co., after 1874 O. P. Chaney; Bartlit & Speaks; Whitehurst, Lehman & Carty.

Meat Markets: Stephen Boyd, Sylvester Foor, Ford Bros., Bailey & Zirkle, M. L. Foor, Lynch Bros., Kramer & Fenstermaker.

Tailor Shops: J. B. Evans, Frank Arnold, Wm. Arnold, Henry Plekenpol, Miss Julia Dixon, tailoress.

Carpenters: Geo. W. Leighner, Ferd Leonard, Geo. Shuman, Frank Shaffer, Hiram Shaffer, Daniel Gayman, Abraham Hunsicker, Benj. F.

Hatfield, Daniel Benson, I. L. and Austin Decker, Henry Herbst, Henry Will, Geo. F. Bareis, Chas. F. Yost, James P. Kramer, Chas. W. Ramsey, Jacob Comp, Jacob Harbaugh.

Brick Masons: N. J. Wolfe, Geo. Powell, N. O. Selby, H. J. Epply, John Miller, Wm. H. Hische, Geo. Allely, Wm. Boyd, Chas. Zarbaugh, Chas. Zachero.

Tallman Bros. (Wm. and Harrison), agricultural implements; M. Winders, bakery, Waterloo Street; Chas. Guy, billiard hall.

Barbers: Jacob Dauterman, Frank A. Buechler, John Finkbone.

Picture Galleries: J. T. Trimmer (where post office), J. W. Rusk (Leonard gallery), C. Hempstead (Miller gallery), Glatfetter & Beeks (where Phil Game's residence).

Dressmakers: Miss Harriet Cater, West Street; Mrs. Lena McKelvey, Columbus Street; Mrs. F. Leonard, Waterloo Street; Mrs. L. Fenstermaker, Mound Street.

Livery Stables: Simon Brown, Glatfetter (N.) & Good (Absalom), Nathaniel Glatfetter, J. Miner Foor.

Shoe Shops: R. Trine, Peter Weber, Martin Zahn, Jas. H. Somerville, Arendt & Dibble, shoe store.

Harness Shops: J. W. Hische, Wm. H. Wright, W. L. Arendt, George Arnold, Daniel Bergstresser.

Blacksmith Shops: Thomas Martin, L. L. Foor, James Rawlins, Geo. Derr, Henry Weber, rear of Rees' store; R. M. Cole, Chas. B. Cannon, Chas. Feistkorn, Peter Zarbaugh.

Plasterers: Jacob Moore, O. L. Dibble, Henry H. Dibble.

Painters: (Jacob and Will), Schott Bros., O. J. Lawyer, Jacob Zarbaugh, Henry Zarbaugh, W. Lea Berian, James Walker, carriage painter.

Physicians: Dr. J. B. Potter, Dr. A. A. Short, Dr. G. W. Blake, Dr. ____ Nash, Dr. ____ Bright, Dr. M. Valentine, Dr. V. A. Valentine, Dr. F. L. Gilbert, dentist, Carty Building.

Hotels: John M. Schoch, Commercial; Isaac Ebright.

Millinery: Mrs. C. Ehrenhart, Mrs. F. Leonard, Mrs. Sarah D. Evans.

Music Teachers: Miss Laura Partridge, Mr. C. B. Hunt, Mr. ____Brown, Mr. ____ Suter, Mrs. Anderson.

Writing Teachers: J. H. Perkins, M. D. L. Schoch, T. F. Ungemach, watchmaking.

Clerks: Chas. Epply (drug store), Wm. (Bricky) Helpman (lumber yard), Callie Turner (at Mrs. Ehrenhart's), Ray Miller, Geo. W. Himrod, Chas. Kuqua, Arthur Pratt, Chas. W. Miller, Wm. Fenstermaker, Samuel Kuqua, Louis H. Shuh (dry goods); Wiseman & Speilman had Tom Levitt, Dick Caslow and Harry Saunders, Wm. Schrock, E. E. Geisy, John (Burnie) Southworth, Robt. W. Bolenbaugh, W. D. Beeks, Wm. M. Game, Homer Bailey, John Harpst, Wm. H. Harpst, B. F. Gayman, Clark Lechliter, A. E. Gayman, Edwin S. Gayman, J. K. Miller, Henry Pflenger, Geo. E. Becker, Herb. E. Bradley.

1880-1890

Stores: D. & C. Gayman, J. E. Billingsly, 1882, L. Stecker (Town Hall), J. R. Malone & Co. (Grange building), John A. Whitzel, then Whitzel & Gehm (B. D.), High and Waterloo; John Gehm & Bro., groceries; Geo. E. Becker, groceries, Dauterman corner; Jacob Dauterman, groceries; John Chaney, Jr., groceries; M. Winders, groceries (Carty Building); Lane & Smith, groceries, Waterloo Street; Al. Lane, groceries, Waterloo Street; Wm. M. Game, groceries; Alspach & Sponsler, groceries; Philip Game, boots and shoes; Adam Weber, boots and shoes; W. H. Trine, boots and shoes; S. H. Arendt, boots and shoes; M. Zahn, boots and shoes; Geo. W. Hinrods, groceries.

Grain: O. P. Chaney & Son, M. C. Whitehurst & Co., also operated mill; C. B. and D. H. Cowen, Empire Mills (Joe S. Ashe, miller); Evans & Speaks (John C.), Empire Mills.

Lumber: John Helpman, Geo. F. Bareis.

Hotels: John M. Schoch, Commercial; L. W. Boyer, Merchants.

Drugs: R. C. Caslow, Willis Houser, Carty Corner; Jacob A. Kumler, Carty Corner; James Henley, Bergstresser Corner; Crayton Bros., Lehman Block; E. H. Tobias.

Physicians: Dr. J. B. Potter, Dr. A. A. Short, Dr. V. A. Valentine, Dr. M. Valentine, Dr. C. R. Clement, Dr. J. W. Shook, Dr. L. W. Beery, Dr. S. W. Walters.

Dentists: Dr. F. H. Houghton, Dr. N. B. Sibley, Drs. Latham & Eckert, Drs. Graham & Eckert, Dr. H. L. Crider.

Jewelers: W. H. Kirk, Leonard Building; T. F. Ungemaugh, Geo. Reber, Chas. C. Reibe.

Tailors: J. B. Evans, Frank Arnold, Henry Arnold, Henry Plekenpol, John A. Whitzel, merchant tailor store; John Stukey.

Dressmakers: Mrs. Lena McKelvey, Miss Harriet Cater, Mrs. Louise Fenstermaker, Mame Hische, Mrs. F. Leonard, Shride & Weber, Alice Dowdall.

Barbers: Jacob Dauterman, Chas. Dauterman, Miller Block; Frank A. Buechler, Miller Block; John Finkbone, Isaac Finkbone, James Allen, Harry Speaks (apprentice).

Blacksmiths: L. L. Foor, R. M. Cole, Derr (Albert) & Cole (Wm. M.), Derr & Fulton.

Harness: J. W. Hische, Wm. H. Wright, Wright & McKinley, Geo. Arnold (Waterloo Street).

Jacob Carty
1805 - 1897

Martin C. Whitehurst
1820 - 1893

Hardware: Chas. P. Rees, Kramer Bros., Ochs & King, J. B. Outland, tinner; W. R. Miller & Son.

Bakers: M. Winders, Ed. Winders, A. P. Avery, Frank Strong, M. Murdock.

Painters: O. J. Lawyer, Ed. V. Bush, Jacob Zarbaugh, Henry Zarbaugh.

Picture Galleries: J. T. Trimmer, James Hood, L. M. Baker, Mulligan Bros., C. Hempstead.

Milliners: Mrs. C. Ehrenhart, Shride (Mrs. Bettie) & Weber (Emma), Mrs. E. Leonard.

Meat Markets: S. E. Bailey, M. L. Foor, Decker & Bailey.

Coal: John Helpman, D. W. Clelland, Jerry Alspach.

Farm Implements: Tallman Bros., C. Al. Conn, Diley & Delong, John P. Diley, W. H. Tallman, Long & Bishop.

Brick Yards: James Griffith, Wolf (N. G.) & Hische (W. H.), Brice Taylor & Co., W. R. Miller.

Carpenters: Daniel Gayman, Abraham Hunsicker, Ferd Leonard, Sam C. Swonger, Henry Will, Henry Herbst, Jacob Komp, I. L. Decker, Austin Decker, Chas. F. Yost, Chas. Brown, Hiram Shaffer, Simon Shaffer, Frank Shaffer, M. J. Leoffler (cabinet maker).

Brick Masons: N. J. Wolf, Wm. Boyd, Wm. H. Hische, Chas. Zarbaugh.

Millers: Joe S. Ashe (Cowans), A. J. Adams, Evan Owen.

Attorneys: W. H. Lane, Chas. C. Pickering.

Furniture and Undertaking: W. P. Miller, Chaney (W. E.) & Leoffler (M. G.).

Music Teachers: Sarah M. Keane, Mary Speaks.

M. Leckrone, saw mill, Moses Gayman, pumps; John R. Clement & Co., clothing (Town Hall); J. R. Clement & Co., baling shed (Waterloo Street); Miner Foor, livery; Adam Shaner, repair shop; Joseph Angle, weaver; Frank Foor, dray; T. D. Worstall, cigar factory (south of school house); Israel Gayman, churns; Chaney (E. C.) & Whitehurst (Geo. A.), gents' furnishings (Lehman Block); ____ Richards, notions (Town Hall); John Brown, restaurant (Grange Building), and beer garden north of R. R.; Horace I. Pierce, Jersey cows and maple sugar; Lane & Hartsough, life insurance agents; John W. Young, tannery; Henry A. Mason, monuments; James N. Tussing, auctioneer; roller skating rink in foundry building, by Cary D. and Geo. A. Whitehurst and Sol. S. Lehman, later by John C. Speaks and Ed. C. Chaney; A. E. Gayman, penmanship; Chas. Varner, engineer planing mill.

1890-1900

Adam Weber, boots and shoes; Alice Dowdall, dressmaker; H. H. Dibble, notary public and insurance; Wm. M. Game, groceries; Alspach & Sponsler, groceries; Miller & Teegardin, Teegardin Bros., P. M. Teegardin & Co., Teegardin & Rush, groceries; W. P. Miller, furniture and undertaker; H. A. Thompson and Wm. M. Codner, agents C. H. V. & T. R. R.; John A. Wilson, Great Eastern restaurant; Daniel E. Alspach, restaurant and bakery; Noah Cherry, Merchants Hotel; Chas. Painter, saloon; Martin L. Kemp, barber; Smith Bros., barbers; Mulligan Bros., photos; Rhoads & Glatfetter, photos; Fred McVey & Co., meat market; Bailey Bros., meat market; J. B. McVey, stock dealer and auctioneer; Dr. G. J. Gray, Dr. L. W. Beery, Dr. W. S. Gayman, Dr. G. F. Owen, Dr. J. W. Shook, Dr. A. A. Shortt; Dora O. Sando, instructor in elocution; J. K. Bowman, bicycles; H. T. Noecker, farm implements; Phil Weber, boots and shoes; C. Gayman & Son, dry goods; B. D. Gehm, dry goods; T. J. Boyd & Co., dry goods (I. O. O. F.), Frank Hendersheit manager; Geo. Powell, tile; Boyer & Powell, tile; L. C. Bartlit, lamp lighter; Geo. E. Smith, huckster; O. P. Chaney & Son, grain; M. C. Whitehurst & Sons, mill and grain; G. W. Lamb, receiver, mill, Winchester Milling Co., C. P. Bauman, manager, mill and elevator; W. H. Lane, attorney; Aaron Smith, shoe shop; Dunlop & Deitz, Chas. F. Dunlap, coal and farm implements; Wm. Pearsall, dray; Dr. A. Starr; E. V. Bush, painter; O. J. Lawyer, painter; Brown Bros., painters; John Brown,. painter; Levi Teegardin, saw mill (west of foundry); Hempy Bros., saw mill, 1898-1899, north of R. R.; Chas. Zarbaugh and Wm. Boyd, brickmasons; Henry Will, Jacob Komp, Jonathan Rinehard, Wm. Burnett, Chas. Hoffman, Chas. Brown, Austin Decker, Chas. F. Yost, George Yost, Geo. Krepps and Israel Gayman, carpenters; J. F. Flinchbaugh, wagon maker; Albert Derr and John Peirson, blacksmith shop; Wm. Cole, blacksmith shop; J. W. Eastman, blacksmith shop; Chas. Hall, blacksmith shop; Lill Caslow, dressmaker; R. C. Caslow, drugs; John S. Lehman, milk; Samuel Saylor, livery; W. L. Arendt, harness; Mrs. Lena McKelvey, dressmaker; Mary Arnold, dressmaker, Mame Hische, seamstress; Hattie Shaner, seamstress;. Mrs. Avery, milliner; Miss Ellis, milliner; Guthrie Sisters, milliners; O. L. Dibble, plasterer; R. J. Tussing, green houses; Central Ohio Baling Co., Jas. P. Kalb, S. T. Needels, Sol. S. Lehman, C. D. Whitehurst and others, Joe C. Shaffer, manager; Frank Arnold, tailor; Dr. S. H. B. Cochrane, dentist; Mrs. Laura Blackwood, music teacher; Miss Jesse Chaney, music teacher; Miss Lynn Sommerville, music teacher; Geo. and Daniel Kramer, pumps; Moses Gayman, pump manufacturer; John Davis, miller; Joshua A. Mathias, engineers; W. L. Walters, miller; J. B. Evans, tailor; E. H. Tobias & Co., drugs; Al. Lane, groceries; Canal Winchester Bank, S. T. Needels, president, C. V. Moore, cashier, Wm. Game, president, C. V. Moore, cashier; W. H. Lane, Quinton Lane and Ervin Moore; G. F. Bareis, lumber; A. S. Lehman (Ed. D. Lehman, manager), drugs; Winchester Times, B. F. Gayman proprietor, O. P. Gayman editor; Long & Bishop, farm implements; J.

McFarland & Co., farm implements; Geo. Delong, coal and farm implements; John M. Schoch, Commercial Hotel; Chas. Varner, engineer; Mrs. S. E. Bailey, boarding house; Mrs. Rev. Bostwick, boarding house; Chas. Evans, tailor; N. Barclow, logs and lumber; John Zahn, shoemaker; Chas. W. Gayman, clothing; James E. Lane, groceries; Mrs. C. Ehrenhart, Sallie Rousch, milliner; Ethel Ebright, milliner; Dibble & Wilson, bakery and restaurant; Alspach & Foor, bakery and restaurant; Homer Dibble, bakery; Adam Spousler, dray; Reuben Martin, baker; J. E. Hedges, repair .shop; C. P. Rees, hardware; Marion Corwin, groceries and buggies; Kramer & Bolenbaugh, hardware; Jas. McKelvey, tinner; Edw. Colman, tinner; Geo. R. Janeway, tinner; Thos. Morton, cider press; Consumers' Gas Co., Drs. Latham and Eckert, dentists; Beery & Gayman, physicians; John Stukey, merchant tailor; Frank Pannabaker, tailor; A. P. Avery, bakery; J. K. Miller, groceries; Crayton Bros., drugs; Miss A. I. King, milliner; Miss S. L. Guthrie, milliner; Winchester Telephone Exchange; John Palsgrove manager, and Mary Yost and Ethel Seymour operators; Dr. E. L. Carlton, physician.

1890-1898

Clerks: W. D. Beeks, G. M. Herbst, E. C. Chaney, John Bartlit, Geo. E. Fry, Frank Hische, John Sponsler, Chas. Sponsler, Henry Lechliter, Herb Cannon, Wm. Bolenbaugh, Eliza Gayman, Alice Snyder, Ona Kramer, Lou Shaffer, John Gayman, Harry Beery, Herb Tobias, Milt Armpreister, Harry Caslow, Henry W. Lehman, Bert Miller, Geo. W. Hinrod, Frank Dildine, Chas. Miller, Hugh Caslow, Zack England, Harry Miller, Frank Miller, Geo. W. Miller, Jacob Lehman, Jesta Hancock, Noah Beery, A. D. Bolenbaugh.

CHAPTER XV
GROVEPORT

Main Street Groveport
Ca. 1908

Among the earliest enterprises was the Adam Rarey log tavern, built in about 1812, which stood where the John S. Rarey mansion now stands. For many years the township elections were held here. In 1831 or 1832 John Champe ran a harness and shoe shop where Marion Corwin built a residence, now occupied by Wm. Corbett. Mr. Champe had formerly worked at a tannery on the Benjamin Rarey farm, located about two miles south of town, now owned by Michael Corbett.

On September 14, 1832, Love & Loy, who had the contract for constructing section No. 53 of the canal, being about one mile in extent from the lock east of town to near where Rarey's Academy used to stand, completed the excavation. The last earth taken out was at a point where the Lancaster and Columbus Road crosses the canal, and two days later the water was let in, and on the following Tuesday or Wednesday great crowds of people assembled on both sides of the canal, some coming ten or twelve miles to see the first boats pass. George Champe related to the writer that *"when they heard the cheering and the music of the band in the direction of Winchester, all eyes and feet were expectantly turned in that direction. Three boats passed, viz: 'Cincinnati,' 'Red Rover' and the 'Lady Jane.'"*

In 1832 J. D. Cox and Jacob B. Wert leased some land of Adam Rarey at the southwest intersection of the canal and the Lancaster and Columbus Road, just opposite the Town Hall, and erected a warehouse with a store room on the west end. Frederick Fruchey did the carpenter work. In the spring of 1833 Mr. Wert began to buy grain and sell goods. In September, 1843, Mr. Wert employed Wm. Lathrop, then surveyor of Franklin County, to lay out a town just west of the section line (College Street), and on October 9, 1845, Jacob Weaver and J. B. Wert had the plat recorded, naming it Wert's Grove, the latter part of the name being most likely suggested by a large sugar camp nearby. The description adds, *"All lots west of Center Street on the land owned by Jacob Weaver and all east owned by J. B. Wert."*

The "Plat" of Rarey's-port was recorded February 8, 1844, consisting of lots Nos. 1 to 65, bounded by the section line, North Alley (Buckeye), Sugar Alley and the Ohio canal. *"The above plat is situated on the east half of section No. 28, in Madison Township, Franklin County, Ohio, and was surveyed and platted by me for the proprietor, Wm. H. Rarey. W. Lathrop, surveyor."* Seven parcels of land were *"reserved to be disposed of as the proprietor may hereinafter determine."*

The old Main Street Bridge in Groveport
Built around 1848

June 3, 1848, a sub-division of in-lots, Nos. 28, 29 and 30, town of Rarey's-port, now Nos. 1 to 6 inclusive, and an addition to said town represented by lots Nos. 139, 140, 141, 142 and 146, was recorded.

Abram Sharp's addition, consisting of 12 lots, numbered 1 to 12 at the west end of Groveport was recorded March 3, 1852.

August 11, 1870, the following territory was annexed to the corporation: *"Beginning at the intersection of the half-section line, on the north side of the canal, taking in land then owned by Wm. T. Decker, Margaret Jones, Wm. Chandler, Henry Long, Wm. H. Rarey, Michael Corbett, Columbus & Hocking Valley Railroad, C. P. Dildine, D. Westenhaver, Pat. Corbett, John Yourd, Letis Stine, Abram Sharp, Z. C. Payne, G. W. Kalb, D. C. Weaver, Joseph Smith and William Mason."*

A. P. Rarey's sub-division, lots Nos. I to 7, was laid off and platted by Chas. D. Rarey in about 1880. No record of this plat could be found.

On December 31, 1895, Charles Campbell recorded a sub-division consisting of ten lots on the west side of College Street.

February 23, 1897, Patrick Corbett's administratrix's addition was recorded, consisting of 16.54 acres, and divided into 45 lots. *"Lots Nos. 1, 2. 8, 9, 11. 12, 16, 17, 18, 19, 20, 21, 22, 23 and 31, together with parts of lots Nos. 3, 13, 14, 15, 24, 25, 26, 27, 28, 29. and 30, are situated within the corporate limits, balance of tract being and lying in the Groveport School District north of the railroad."*

It has not been definitely ascertained just when the post office was established, but it was at an earlier date than usually reported. The Ohio Gazetteer of 1837 says: *"Wirt's Grove, a post office at the crossing of the Ohio canal and the Columbus and Lancaster Road in Madison Township, Franklin County, 11 miles from Columbus and 17 from Lancaster. Mails daily in stage coaches, from Columbus and Lancaster. This is the place of holding elections for Madison Township."*

This indicates that the post office must have been established as early as 1836. Jacob B. Wert was the first postmaster and served until 1848. He had built a store room and dwelling on the southwest corner of Main and East Streets, in 1834, and here kept the post office. Mr. Wert was a prosperous and enterprising citizen. He died October 11, 1850, and his remains were buried in the Obetz Graveyard. Mr. Wert's widow, Julia A. Wert, married Heath M. Ware, an attorney, on May 24, 1853, and removed to Columbus, where she has since resided.

Mr. Wert was succeeded as postmaster by Edmund Gares, 1848-1851; A. C. Headly, 1851-1853; Samuel Sharp, 1853-1857; John L. Champe, 1857-1864; Henry Long, 1864-1877; Cornelius Black Jr., 1877-1885; A. M. Rarey, 1885-1889; John C. Coon, 1889-1893; Chas. D. Rarey, 1893-1897; John C. Coon, 1897-1901; James K. Rarey, 1901.

After Mr. Rarey laid out Rarey's-port he made every effort to have the whole town known by his name and to have the name of the post office changed. He advised his friends when writing to direct their letters to Rarey's-port, and it is said when letters did come addressed to Rarey's-port Mr. Wert would change them to read Wert's Grove. Each proprietor was anxious to perpetuate his own name, when finally the citizens took the matter in hand and held a public meeting in Wm. James' one-story cooper shop that stood on the west side of Walnut Street south of Main Street, and next to Clippenger's Tannery.

No conclusion was reached, but at another meeting held at the same place, soon after, being in the winter of 1846-1847, a name was agreed upon. Reports of the success of the United States troops in the first battle of the Mexican War suggested the name Palo Alto, and it was proposed. Dr. Abel Clark then proposed to drop the personal names and retain the latter part of each. This suggestion was adopted and hence the name *Grove port.*

The same winter the village was incorporated, and on April 17, 1847, an election was held *"for the purpose of electing one Mayor, one Recorder, and five Trustees."* Jonathan Watson and Wm. James were judges, and Alexander Fleming, clerk of this election. Those voting were: Wm. R. Darnell, John Swisher, Wm. James, H. H. King, Thomas Hughes, John Gamblen, George Champe, C. J. Stevenson, Jacob Anderick, John Yourd, Peter Rawn, R. E. Robinson, Abel Clark, R. Shockley, J. P. Bywaters, V. Matthews, Joseph McFee, Simon Van Horn, Joseph Cherry, Franklin Taylor, Daniel McIntire, Jonathan Lee, Thomas Champe, Wm. W. Mitchell, Salem A. Darnell, B. Callahan, Nathan Champe, H. K. Brotherton, Alex. Fleming, Jonathan Watson, John Champe, Joseph Vance, Bennett Thompson, Thomas Goodman, Henry Long, Moses Shaffer, Wm. Craner, Geo. W. Fearn, Wm. Watson, Geo. C. Darnell, Lewis Shirey, Geo. S. Nigh, Wm. H. Rarey, Barnet Milliser, John H. Reed, Samuel Bateman, Jacob Rawn, John T. Solomon, John A. Taylor, A. Willie, George Carder, Jackson Carder, Edmund Gares, Jephtha King, Z. P. Thompson, John Childs, A. Shoemaker, Jacob

Burgett, George McCombs, John R. Smith and E. M. Dutton — a total of 62. Of these Edmund Gares is still living and in active business. The election resulted as follows; Abraham Shoemaker, Mayor; Dr. Abel Clark, Recorder; Samuel Sharp, E. M. Dutton, Dr. J. P. Bywaters, C. J. Stevenson and Wm. W. Mitchell, Trustees.

The council (Trustees) appointed A. Willie, Treasurer, Wm. James Marshal, and Wm. H. Rarey, Alex. Fleming and Joseph Cherry Street Commissioners. The first ordinance passed made it unlawful to obstruct any street or alley. The second ordinance made it the duty of *"owners of lots fronting on Main Street to make sidewalks by November next,"* and the third ordinance made it *"unlawful to run horses (a common pass-time) on the streets and alleys, or to engage In fighting, brawling, quarreling, shooting of guns or pistols or otherwise unnecessarily disturbing the peace and quietude of the town."*

"The Street Commissioners are authorized to employ from one to three two-horse teams at a price not to exceed one dollar and fifty cents per day for man and team, to grade Main Street, between May 1 and June 15."

The above were all passed on April 29, 1847. On July 26, 1847, the Street Commissioners were instructed to build four bridges across "Joppa" Brook. After reading over the proceedings of the village council for the past half century, the impression is left on one's mind that "Joppa" is a very expensive fixture.

On November 20, 1847, A. Fleming resigned as Street Commissioner, removing from town, and Jacob Anderick was appointed; and E. M. Dutton resigned as Councilman and William Toy was appointed to fill the vacancy. Council meetings were then held at the houses of the Mayor, and of C. J. Stevenson, and the elections were held at C. J. Stevenson's shop.

May 1, 1848, Mr. Gares presented a petition, signed by forty-two citizens, praying that the town council would take into consideration *"the subject of taxing dogs, in any way as they think proper to decrease their number."*

On April 20, 1849, the Marshal was instructed to notify Wm. H. Blair to remove the old slaughter house (formerly owned by J. B. Wert), or so much of it as obstructs East Street.

The beginning of the multiplied legislative efforts to suppress the saloon and the sale of intoxicating drinks dates from May 1, 1849, when an ordinance took effect, *"Making it unlawful for to retail spirituous liquors of any kind within the corporation; anyone offending shall not pay less than ten dollars nor more than one hundred dollars."*

Dr. Abel Clark, Treasurer, appeared and reported the following: *"Groveport, Ohio, April 20, 1840.—: Received nothing; paid out nothing."*

October 31, 1851, Darnell & Co. were given the privilege of building cribs in the street adjoining their store, *"until they shall shell their corn next summer, for which they agree to pay five dollars."*

In 1852 council was petitioned to make it unlawful for swine to run at large on the streets, but council *"considered it imprudent to pass such a law at present."*

Ordinance No. 15, passed May 2, 1854, *"provides seventy-five cents to each councilman, for each meeting of council attended."* It was carried by a unanimous vote. The provisions of this ordinance remained in force and was taken advantage of by each succeeding council, until on April 18, 1867, the new council declared the orders issued by the old council *"as null and void as they are contrary to law."*

The councils of 1869 and 1870, however, again took pay under the ordinance of 1854.

May 22, 1857, *"council resolved that hereafter the ordinances passed shall be published in the "Rose-Bud."*

July 9, 1858, E. W. Edwards *"moved that Joppa be 'trunked' from, northeast corner of Hickory Alley to alley north of Elm Street, with a 'trunk' two feet wide and fourteen inches high."* This motion was laid on the table.

May 2, 1863, only ten votes were cast at the annual village election, viz.; Geo. P. Champe, Dr. J. H. Saylor, H. F. Woodring, Isaac Johnson, G. S. Dildine, Robert F. Dildine, Thomas Champe, Jacob Burgett, R. W. Johnson and D. C. Weaver and, on May 14, in the following year, exactly the same number, ten votes, were cast by the following persons: Geo. P. Champe, H. O. Glick, S. Baughman, S. Van Horn, James Hamler, J. Burgett, J. H. Reed, Wm. Byrne, Wm. Sharp and Casper Limpert.

In 1867 the contract was awarded to Chas. Bowers to build a calaboose at $185.00, and on July 2, 1879, a contract was awarded to Geo. F. Bareis at $374.00 to build the brick prison located along the canal.

Town Hall

At the election held April 5. 1875, the question of building two Town Halls — one at Winchester, the other at Groveport — was submitted to the voters, with the following result: Winchester precinct, 107 votes for and 180 against; Groveport precinct, 211 votes for and 87 against. On May 6 following, a meeting was held *"to make arrangements concerning the erection of a Town Hall in Groveport, in connection with the village council and other parties."* The following persons were present: Kalita Sallee, Moses Seymour and John S. Lehman, Township Trustees; W. L. Powell and Wm. Chandler for council; Wm. Chandler and F. M. Senter for I. O. O. F. Lodge, and Mr. Chandler and J. P. Arnold for the F. & A. M. Lodge. Moses Seymour was chosen chairman and C. Black, Jr., the Township Clerk, acted as Secretary. Wm. Chandler and Kalita Sallee were appointed a committee to employ an architect to make plans and specifications; they employed J. H. Harris of Columbus.

Another meeting was held on May 13, when the following propositions for locations were received: From John F. Wildermuth, proposing to give his corner lot (southeast corner Main and Walnut Streets), for the use of one of the store rooms for a term of ten years; from the I. O. O. F. Lodge, proposing to give deed for corner lot on Main and Front Streets for $450; from J. V. Conklin, proposing to give deed for northwest corner lot, Main and Walnut Streets, for $1,500. These locations were voted on by ballot and the I. O. O. F. lot selected. The following assessment or division of the cost was made, based on the architect's estimate, viz: Madison Township, first story, $9,116; village of Groveport, second story, $650; I. O. O. F., $1,050; F. & A. M., $1,050.

Bids were opened on June 22, 1875, as follows, for the building complete: A. B. Rarey,$9,500; W. W. McCoy, $10,745; Hershiser & Gibson, $10,962; Vory's Bros., $11,545; Kennoder & Denig, $12,831; R. A. Rowland & Co., $12,885; Harris W. Newell, $13,000.

There were also quite a number of bids for separate parts of the work. The contract was awarded to Mr. Rarey, but at a meeting held on June 30 he appeared and *"stated that he could not build said hall at his bid of $9,500, and therefore waived his contract."* The contract was then awarded to Wm. W. McCoy at his bid. In the spring of 1876 H. H. Scofield & Co. occupied the east room with dry goods, and Theo. Faulhaber the west room with a stock of groceries. On November 26,

1881, the township house was sold to Robt. Shaw for $303, being lot No. 13, formerly Wert's Grove.

The following is a list of the officers of the village of Groveport. The date shows year of election. One of the record books, 1870 to 1877, could not be found, hence the omission of some names:

Mayors: A. Shoemaker,1847-1848, Henry Long, 1849, 1866; Z. P. Thompson, 1850, 1851, 1855, 1856, 1859, 1860; E. W. Edwards, 1852; Jeremiah White, 1853-1854; Noah Steele, 1857; Lemuel Sarber, 1858; Jonathan Watson, 1861, 1862; Robt. F. Dildine, 1863, 1865; Z. D. Dildine, 1864; W. W. Kile, 1867 (records of several years lost); F. M. Senter, 1875, 1877; Robt. A. Shaw, 1878. 1891, 1893, 1896-1901; Adam Shaner, 1892 (Robt. A. Shaw and Adam Shaner each had 78 votes in 1892; lots were cast and Mr. Shaner won; March 8, 1893, Mr. Shaner had a stroke of paralysis and Robt. A. Shaw was appointed for the balance of the term); Samuel Stuckey, 1894-1895.

Clerks: Dr. Abel Clark, 1847, 1851, 1853; Edmund Gares,1848, 1849; Dr. H. L. Chaney, 1850, resigned and Abram Sharp appointed, 1852; W. H. Pyle, 1854; A. C. King, 1855; Robt. F. Dildine, 1856, 1860-1862, 1864, 1867-1870; Hiram McArthur, 1857; H. C. Darnell, 1859; B. F. Champe, 1863, 1875, 1876; Z. D. Dildine, 1865, 1866; Moses Welton (records of several years could not be found); Wm. Chandler, 1876-1877; D. F. Karnes, 1878, resigned March 19, 1879, and E. V. Adel appointed, 1879; A. M. Senter, 1882-1887; F. S. Rarey, 1880, 1881; Chas. D. Rarey, 1888-1897; A. H. McBriar, 1898; W. L. Piester, 1899, resigned after about two months' service and W. C. Black appointed, 1899-1900; Phil C. Tussing, 1901.

Treasurers: The Treasurers were appointed by the council until 1868, since which time they are elected. A. Willie. 1847; Dr. Abel Clark, 1848; Jacob Stimmel, 1849, refused to serve and Abraham Sharp appointed, 1849, 1851, 1868; Samuel Sharp, 1850; Jacob Rawn, 1852; A. C. Headly, 1853; J. K. Low, 1854; C. J. Stevenson,1855; Moses Zinn, 1856, 1857; Noah Steele, 1858; Jiles Weaver, 1859-1862: Casper Limpert, 1863-1865; Dr. G. L. Smith, 1866, 1867, 1878-1883. resigned August 31, 1883, and F. S. Rarey appointed; S. Allen Peters, 1869-1878, died April, 1878; F. S. Rarey, 1883-1885; M. H. Kelley, 1887-1895, died February 26, 1896, and A. M. Rarey appointed, 1895, 1897; L. B. Carruthers, 1898-1901.

Marshals: The marshals were appointed by the council previous to 1868, since which they have been elected. Wm. James, 1847; Lemuel Sarber, 1849, 1852, 1857, 1860, 1865, 1867; James Turner, 1850, 1858, 1859; Benjamin Calhoun, 1851; O. F. Connell, 1853; Jacob Stimmel, 1854, 1857; Wm. Watson, 1855, 1856; Joseph Cherry, 1861; G, P. Champe, 1862, 1863; John A. Kile, 1866, 1890, 1891, 1897; Joseph Lytle, 1868, H. O'Harra, 1869; G. W. Bowland, 1869, 1870; F. M. Groom, 1871; T. H. Carder, 1879, resigned September 17, 1879, and E. Cassidy appointed, 1879, 1880; J. W. Click, 1881-1885; J. D. Weakly, 1886, 1887; Isaac Musselman, 1887, resigned September 27, 1887, and J. D. Weakly appointed; John Cramer, 1888, 1889; W. E. Thompson, 1892-1895, 1898; R. R. Paxton, 1896, 1897, 1899, resigned October 14, 1897, and John A. Kile appointed, 1900, 1901.

Street Commissioners: Wm. Sharp, 1877-1880; Martin Shirey, 1881, moved out of corporation, and on September 19, 1881, a special election was held and Stephen A. Lester elected, 1881, 1882; A. M. McCoy, 1883, 1884; J. M. Weakly, 1884, resigned April 30, 1884, and A. M. McCoy appointed; D. C. Weaver, 1885; Charles Pearce, 1886-1889; John A. Kile, 1890-1892, 1899; Thomas Dolby, 1893-1896; Frank Slosser, 1897, 1898, 1900-1901.

Bridge Turner and Lamp Lighter: The old covered bridge was built about 1847 or 48, and was torn down in 1887. In March, 1887, council agreed by resolution to employ a competent person to turn the bridge then to be erected over the canal on Main Street. The following persons have served as bridge turners: John Cramer, 1887, 1888, 1897, 1898; M. Codner was elected in 1889 but refused to sign the contract, when Joe Miller, was elected, 1889; Erasmus Friend, 1890-1892; W. E. Thompson, 1893-1895; A. H. McBriar, 1896.

October 13, 1892, thirty-five street lamps were purchased and Joe Miller employed to light them; on November 5, W. E. Thompson elected, 1892-1896; John Cramer, 1897-1901.

Janitors of the Town Hall: James R. Littleton, 1876-1877; J. W. Glick, 1878; John Black, 1879, 1882, 1883; John S. Patrick, 1880, to July 1, 1882; Silas Montgomery. 1884, 1885; Jacob Reed, 1886, 1887; John Cramer, 1888-1898, 1901; Sylvester Carruthers, *1*899-1900.

John Cox, Surveyor
1804 - 1873

William H. Rarey
1812 - 1877

Councilmen: Council met at various places. We made a note of a few of these, as follows: At A. Shoemaker's house, 1847; Dr. A. Clark's office, 1850-1851; Henry Long's office, 1850; Paul & Fuller's office, 1850; E. W. Edward's office, 1852; Z. P. Thompson's office, 1857. Samuel Sharp, 1847-1848; E. M. Dutton, 1847, resigned November 20. 1847, and Wm. Toy appointed; Dr. J. P. Bywaters, 1847; C. J. Stevenson, 1847; W. W. Mitchell, 1847; Jacob Anderick, 1848, 1849; Joseph Cherry, 1848, 1849; A. Willie, 1848, 1849; Salem A. Darnell, 1849-1851; W. C. Furgeson, 1849-1851; L. Sarber, 1850, 1851; Jonathan Watson, 1850-1852; E. W. Edwards. 1851-1852; J. K. Low, 1852-1853; J. Rawn, 1852-1853; John Todd, 1852-1853; A. C. Headly, 1853-1854; Dr. G. L. Smith, 1853-1854; Wm. Cater, 1853-1854; G. J. Stevenson, 1854-1855; Geo. McCormick, 1854-1855; James Sandy, 1854-1860; Chas. Campbell, 1855; Jeremiah White, 1855-1856; Thos. Champe, 1855-1856; Jiles Weaver, 1856-1861; Lew Shirey, 1856-1875; Moses Zinn, 1856-1857; S. E. Adams, 1857-1858; A. C. Swain, 1857-1858; J. Burgett, 1858-1859; G. C. Smith, 1861-1862; Casper Limpert, 1863-1864; M. Codner, 1865-1866; C. P. Dildine, 1865-1866; Solomon Woodring, 1866-1867; W. H. Pyle, 1866-1867; S. A. Peters, 1866-1878; W. R. Kaufman, 1866-1867; Geo. Welsh, 1868-1869; John Corbett, 1868-1869; Henry Fulton, 1868-1869; John Byrne, 1869-1870; M. K. Earhart, 1869-1870; Wm. Chandler,1869-1878; John F.

Wildermuth,1870-1887; J. Rodenfels, 1871-1872; G. W. Kalb, 1871-1872; W. L. Powell, 1875, 1878, 1879; Morris Kile, 1878-1880; S. Allen Peters, died April, 1878, and Morris Kile appointed; Henry Long,1878-1881, died 1881, and at a special election held May 3, 1881, G. S. Dildine and Geo. Adel each received 54 votes; lots were cast and Mr. Adel won; Geo. Adel, 1881, 1882; W. L. Powell, 1875-1879; Z. C. Payne, 1878-1882; G. S. Dildine, 1879-1880; J. S. Patrick, 1875-1881; Dr. J. H. Saylor, 1875, 1880-1881, 1887-1888, 1896-1899; S. E. H. Kile, 1881-1884; Theo. Faulhaber, 1881-1884, moved away and a special election was held November 15, 1884, and J. O. Rarey elected; Wm. Mason, 1882-1887, 1889-1892, moved away and J. C. Coon appointed; Mr. Coon declined to serve and then Jas. D. Rarey was appointed; Wm. C. Gill, 1882-1887; C. P. Long, 1883-1884; Chas. A. Williams, 1883-1885, resigned March 23, 1885; John O. Rarey, 1884, 1895-1896; Jethro Denton, 1885-1896; Mr. Keller, 1885-1886; James K. Chaney, 1886, 1896-1898, resigned June 13, 1898, and E. P. Dildine appointed; Mr. Dildine declined to serve, then David Downhour was appointed; John L. Chaney, 1887-1889; Adam Shaner, 1887-1888; D. F. Karnes, 1888-1889, 1892-1893; Richard Copeland, 1888-1891; Moses W. Darst, 1889-1890, resigned and R. F. Dildine appointed June 26, 1890; W. H. Zinn, 1890-1891; L. F. Powell, 1890-1891, 1897-1900; A. M. Senter, 1891-1894, 1896-1900; Dr. C. R. Clement, 1892-1895; W. R. Smith, 1892-1895; Jas D. Rarey, 1892-1893; John C. Coon, 1894-1895; Frank E. Williams, 1894-1895, 1901; Chas. R. Behm, 1896-1898, resigned August 29, 1898, and R. F. Dildine appointed, 1899-1900; James Strode, 1897-1898; David P. Downhour, 1898-1901; J. H. Dunkley, 1899-1900; F. M. Strickler, 1900-1901; John Sims, 1900-1901; W. H. Hewetson, 1901; Chas. D. Rarey, 1901.

Business Enterprises

In the following list of the business enterprises of Groveport it has been the object of Mr. A. M. Senter —" who arranged and gathered the items together from many different sources — to take up one line of business and trace it by the successive firms occupying the different buildings. In many cases it was next to impossible to get exact dates, consequently very few are mentioned:

Dry Goods (General Stores):

Warehouse Building—Cox & Wert, 1833; J. B. Wert, Kooken & Rarey; Rarey, Courtright & Co.; Sharp & Ewing; Sharp & Paul; Sharp & Vogel, 1854-1858; Headly & Eberly, 1848-1851; Samuel Sharp & Co., 1852-1854; Long & Ewing, 1851-1852.

Wert's old Building — J. B. Wert; Darnell & Co.

Simms Building — C. W. Furgeson, 1842.

Dildine & Tussing Corner—Gares & Taylor, 1847-1851; Chapman & Smith, 1851-1853; Weaver & Champe, 1853-1865.

Post office Building — Darnell & Co., 1847, failed in 1851; A. C. King, A. Hughes, 1860-1863; Mrs. Hughes & (Harrison) Dunn, 1863-1864; Dunn & Long, 1864; A. J. Vanwormer, Mrs. A. J. Vanwormer, Shed Kramer, Adam Havely.

Campbell Hotel Building—Leonard Sarber, Darnell & Co. had their store in the house now owned by A. M. Senter during the time they were erecting the post office building.

Grain: J. B. Wert, Rarey, Courtright & Co., Sharp & Paul, 1848; Long & Paul, Chas. Campbell, McCormick & Stimmel, John Conn, Samuel Sharp, 1860-1863; Dildine & Peters, A. B. Rarey & Co., A. L. Shride, Henry Long, A. O. Mauck, O. P. Chaney & Co., 1880-1898; C. P. Long, C. S. Herr & Co., 1898-1901.

Flouring Mills: Rodenfels, (Moses) Seymour & Co. (Peter Brown), 1871; Zinn & Kile, Northrop Bros., Burke & Foster, Nitterhouse & Pitzer, A. B. Rarey, Smith, Dildine & Co., Hewit, Decker & Co., A. O. Mauck, 1884.

Hotels:

Campbell House — John Champe, Isaiah Brown, Wolf Bishop, ____ Finks, Chas. Gordon, Jacob Wagner, Daniel McIntire, G. S. Dildine, Woodring & Cherry, G. S. Dildine, Michael Keller, Chas. Campbell, A. H. McBriar, G. W. Shaw, Frank Wise, Mrs. Codner and Arthur Lodge.

Powell's House— (west -end) James Fleming.

Madison House—(now Mrs. Henry Long's residence, then stood on Main Street) Peter Rawn, Jacob Kauffman.

Corbett House—Michael Corbett.

Drugs: A. E. Swaine, John Swaine, John Byrne, Limpert & Byrne, ____ Vance, C. Black, J. O. & F. S. Rarey, L. E. Eyeman, Wm. R. Smith.

Harness: C. J. Stevenson, B. F. Townsend, L. W. Hampson, John Allen, W. L. Powell, John Sidner, Chas. Hunter, W. H. Zinn, C. Black.

Shoemakers: Thomas Champe, George Crooks, George Champe, Jacob Burgett, Jeptha King, Ephraim Edwards, Chaney Himrod, Wm. Durant, W. Horsey, L. Hedrick, H. Fulton, E. Cassidy, John Cassidy,. Frank Slosser.

Tailors: George Fearn, Jacob Rawn, ____ Jewett, Al. Fearn, Wm. Cater, A. Hughes, Jas. Bannum, Jas. Littleton.

Blacksmiths: Jacob Andrie, Wm. Funk, James Dutton, Lewis Shirey, M. Shirey, Isaac Williamson, H. Moore, Israel Swisher, Leonard Sarber, W. R. Kauffman, Wm. Thompson, Eli Remalia, Philo Williams, Wm. Hunter, Samuel Longebach, John Lynch, Michael Kramer, Chas. A. Williams, Thomas Thompson, Frank E. Williams, Joseph Nailer.

Wagon Makers: ____ Dutton, Jacob Jones, James Stevenson, ____ Steele, ____ Smith, Smith Allen, George Rei, N. S. McCormick, L. A. Guerin, John Durritt, Samuel Webster, Orin Mansfield, R. R. Paxton.

Saw-Mill: Moses Zinn, Wm. Chandler, Wm. Mason, W. H. & J. P. Rager, Zinn, Kile & Mason, George Mansfield.

Boat-Dock Proprietors: Jonathan Watson, Wm. Chandler, Wm. Sharp.

Dock-Carpenters: Chas. Washburne, Sylvester Hunter, George Bailey, ____ Bailey, Daniel Washburn, Wesley Sandy, James Sandy, Isaiah Cook, John Fry, Joseph Cherry, Wm. Chandler, Asa Houseman, H. Sanford, Thomas Jones, Jacob Reed, J. Williamson, Benj. Callahan, Z. Eddy.

Coopers: U. Jenkins, O. W. Durant, Kinsey Tanner, Jonathan Jones, Thomas Thompson, Gilbert Thompson, Wm. James, J. R. Smith, George Darnell, ____ Tolbert, Philip Smith, A. Sandy.

Brick Yards: John Champe, Proprietor; ____ Boner and James Synder, Molders; ____ Atchison, Prop.; ____ Temple, Molder; Bywaters & Thompson, Props.; O. Barnhart and John Ell, Molders; Jonathan Watson, Prop.; Wesley Sandy, O. Barnhart, John Paul and Wm. Blakely, Molders; Fearn & Watson, Props.; Wm. Blakely, Molder; Wm. Blakely, Prop. and molder; Wm. Mason, Prop.: John Nichols, O. Barnhart and J. R. Smith, Molders; Mason & Kauffman, Prop.; Noah Hummel, Molder; McCoy & Nichols, Props.; John Nichols, Molder; Wildermuth & Senter, Props.; O. Barnhart and John Nichols, Molders; John F. Wildermuth, Prop.; John Nichols, Molder; J. M. Kelley, Prop.; John Nichols, Molder.

Bricklayers: Wm. Blair, Sr., was the first bricklayer in Groveport and laid the brick in the first buildings; Daniel Campbell, John Wallace, Sr.,

Benj. Gares, John Wallace, Jr., Robt. Campbell, Edw. Campbell, M. F. Sandy.

Tile Yard: Was established by Kile & Mason in 1876; Moses Zinn bought Wm. Mason's interest in 1877; Wm. Mason bought out Zinn & Kile in 1882 and has conducted the business ever since, with the exception of three years, April, 1893-April, 1896, when Marion Corwin had the yard leased.

Saloons: Woodring & Sarber, J. Butler, Robt. Kile, Limpert & Corwin, Moore & Corwin, Marion Corwin, Alva Harris, H. Bornstein, Wm. Harmon, E. Senter, Milt. Miller.

Undertakers and Cabinetmakers: A. Willie, 1842-1855; Moses Zinn, 1855-1864; Black & Black, 1875-1901. (Moses Zinn owned the first hearse.)

Attorneys-at-Law: M. S. Hoit, Z. C. Payne.

Tannery: S. Clippinger, Prop., 1848; C. H. B. Sullivan and Peter Reeves, Tanners.

Tombstones: Geo. Welsh, John M. Strickler.

Groceries:

Warehouse Building: C. Limpert, J. H. Fearn (1860-1862), McCormick & Fearn (1845).

Simms Building, Wash Simms, George Dildine.

Old Limpert Building, McCormick & Stimmel, John Todd.

Miller Saloon Building, C. Limpert (1859), Limpert & Brown (1861), Limpert & Fearn (1865), McCormick & Stimmel.

Post office Building: H. Mansfield, Kelley & Kile, Kelley & Coon, John C. Coon.

Dildine & Tussing Building, Cor. Main and College Streets, John A. & James A. Kile, James Seymour, C. E. Seymour, Jacob Dildine, Kile & Woodring, John F. Wildermuth (1867), Kindler & Williams (1880), Samuel Kindler (1884), Rarey, Adel & Co., Dildine & Tussing.

Building near Township House, near Cor. Main and Center Streets, John Conn, J. H. Fearn, D. C. Weaver.

Falhaber Building (it stood just west of Town Hall), Theo. Falhaber, Gilbert Sims (was moved across the street), then Wm. Kelley, L. Kallies, Joseph Kelly, Kelley & Vogle, W. B. Vogle.

Town Hall, Theo. Falhaber, Falhaber & Black, C. Black, Jr., Black & Rarey Bros., A. M. & J. D. Rarey, Jos. K. Rarey.

J. Nafzger kept a grocery in the basement of A. M. Senter's residence, 1848-1852; A. J. Vanwormer one in the brick residence now owned by Anna Wallace on Blacklick Street. C. C. Weaver kept the first temperance grocery in the east room of the Dildine & Tussing Building, J. K. Rarey in the Powell Building.

Hardware: Bigelow & Powell, Geo. W. Bigelow, L. F. Powell, W. H. Zinn, Caruthers & Dorer, Caruthers Bros.

Tinners: Chas. Campbell, L. F. Powell.

Carpenters: Moses Zinn, Snyder Gares, H. O. Glick, Geo. Rowland, Pierce Shockley, Fred Finkbinder, W. C. Gill, Chas. D. Rarey, George Burgey, Wm. Burgey, Wm. Wildermuth, Frank Kineaster,. Samuel Stucky, David M. Willie.

Painters: G. S. Nigh, John Gamblen, Wm. Ormand, Schott Bros., James Hamler, Frank Strickler.

Barbers: James Howell, Jerry Peister, Wm. Anderson, John Schultz, Samuel Jones, Frank Bowers, J. M. Kelley, Wm. Springer, D. I. Crossen, Frank Powell, Wm. Peister, Wm. Howell, Byron Seymour.

Byron Seymour, Barber
Standing on a foot bridge at Walnut Street

Pork Packers: J. B. Wert, Rarey, Courtright & Co., C. Limpert.

Butchers: Thomas Hughes, Wm. Watson, Thomas Champe, Robt. Burnham, S. S. Senter, (F. M.) Senter & (G. S.) Dildine, A. D. Kraner, Z. D.

Dildine, A. M. & R. L. Senter, Rarey & Dildine, A. N. Perrill, Jacob Dildine, (R. A.) Shaw & (Thos.) Decker, Jethro Denton, Henry Miller, John Lonas, Benj. C. Sims, M. H. Kelly, Cyrus Strader, John C. Coon, Dildine & Tussing, Henry Miller, Jr.

Samuel Socrates Senter
1818 - 1863

Bakers: John Eagle (early date), F. M. Senter (about 1864), J. F. Jones, Mrs. Iva Sharp, George Berger.

Milliners: Mrs. Clarissa Searls, Mrs. Lovina Williams, Mrs. Delilah Wildermuth, Mrs. Mattie Conklin, Misses Spencer & Weatherington, Mrs. Lizzie Piester.

Cigarmakers: Wm. Loudenslager, The Diamond Stogie Co., F. S. Rarey, G. M. Rarey, Chas. P. Long, Wm. R. Smith.

William R. Darnell
1818 - 1874

Salem Darnell
1820 - 1887

Feed Mill: After the flour mills burned. A. O. Mauck started a feed mill in a building opposite the R. R. depot. The successive owners were: Moses Darst, J. P. Rager and W. H. & J. P. Rager, who removed it to the old schoolhouse building. Soon after they burned out and W. H. Rager rebuilt it. Now operated by E. J. Bennett. Wm. Leyshon occupies the building opposite the depot, dealing in coal and grain.

Wm. Blair, Jr., and Fred Finkbinder built many of the post and rail fences in Madison Township.

Plasterers: John Yourd, Samuel Getty, Wm. Funk, Chas. Herrick, John Cunningham, John Cunningham, Jr.

Physicians and Surgeons: Abel Clark, J. B. Bywaters, G. L. Smith, Hugh L. Chaney, ____ Bolen, ____Tipton, J. F. Jones, Thos. Sparrow, R. Morden, Dr. McCollum, ____ Peters, ____ Taylor, C. R. Clement, ____ McNeal, W. Hewetson, ____ Green, ____ Scully, ____ Cullison.

D. Sarber, *Bridge-builder;* Elisha Stine, *Millwright;* Geo. W. Lechner, *Stair-builder;* Weaver & Adel, *Clothing Store,* in Howell's Shop; J. W. Conklin, *Auctioneer;* C. E. McComb, *Grain and Stocks;* S. E. Adams, Editor and Prop, of a *Weekly Newspaper,* called the "Rose Bud," published in 1857.

In 1856 the following enterprises were located along the canal:

At Blacklick Street, Jonathan Watson's boat yard.

At Elm Street, Gurry's Warehouse.

At Hickory Alley, Charles Campbell's warehouse.

Just north of the Main Street bridge, M. Zinn's Cabinet Shop.

South side of Main Street, Samuel Sharp & Co. warehouse.

End of Cherry Street, Mr. Sharp had another warehouse.

South side of Cherry Street, G. McCormick's Warehouse.

Sugar Alley, A. W. Paul's Warehouse.

Walnut Street, W. H. Rarey's warehouse.

Groveport Enterprises — 1900

Edward Gares, Dry Goods, Shoes, etc.

Dildine & Tussing, Groceries, Dry Goods, Shoes. Meat Market.

Caruthers Bros., Hardware, Farm Implements, Harness, Seeds, etc.

J. M. Kelley, Restaurant.

W. R. Smith, Drugs.

W. B. Vogle, Groceries.

Milton Miller, Saloon.

George Berger, Bakery.

Jas. K. Rarey, Groceries.

Frank M. Powell, Barber.

John C. Coon, Postmaster, Groceries, Shoes, Meat Market.

Geo. W. Bigelow, Hardware.

Thomas Thompson, Blacksmith.

Frank E. Williams, Blacksmith.

Joseph Nailer, Blacksmith.

R. R. Paxton, Wagon Maker.

Orin R. Mansfield, Wagon Maker.

John M. Strickler, Monuments.

Geo. W. Shaw, Campbell Hotel.

M. Corbett, Corbett Hotel.

Capt. J. V. Conklin, Livery and Auctioneer.

L. F. Powell, Tinner and Roofer.

Henry Jones, Tinner and Roofer.

Wm. Mason, Tile.

A. P. Brown, Agent H. V. R. R. and Telegraph Operator.

Wm. Leyshon, Coal and Feed.

C. S. Herr & Co., Grain and Coal.

W. H. Rager, Feed Mill.

Geo. Mansfield, Saw Mill and Cider Press.

E. Seufer, Saloon.

Mrs. Lizzie Peister, Milliner.

Miss Mary Kile, Dressmaker.

C. Black,Sr., Harnessmaker.

Frank Slosser, Shoemaker.

Wm. Howell, Barber.

Wm. Peister, Barber.

Chas. R. Clement, Physician.

J. H. Saylor, Physician.

Walter Hewetson, Physician.

Fred Finkbinder, Carpenter.

John Hunter, Carpenter.

George and Wm. Burgey, Carpenters.

Frank Kineaster, Carpenter.

Samuel Stuckey, Carpenter.

Frank Strickler, Painter.

James Hamler. Jr., Painter.

George Washington Bigelow
Groveport Hardware Executive

Groveport Brass Band, organized Sept. 7th, 1898; Wm. Caruthers, R. K. Caruthers, S. B. Davis, C. L. Jordon, J. H. Dunklee, L. C. Davis, C. F. Dolby, A. J. Jordon, L. A. Sims, M. F. Jordon, V. E. Lowery, Ray Teegardin, B. R. Seymour, J. E. Baitson.

The Bell Telephone Line was established by Geo. H. Twiss, who represented Columbus citizens, in the summer of 1882. The office was located in Rarey Brothers' Drug Store. C. Black, Sr.—familiarly known as "Uncle" Black—has been the operator for the past several years, the toll station being located in his harness shop.

The Franklin Telephone Company (Citizens') established a toll station in Carruthers' Store in January, 1901, and on January 4, 1902, they opened the Exchange, with W. C. Black, manager, and Nannie Simms, operator. The "Central" is located in the office building formerly occupied by Dr. Hugh L. Chaney and has thirty-one phones connected.

Board of Health

The Board of Health was established on Nov. 12th, 1889, with the following members: D. F. Karnes, C. Black,Jr., Adam Shaner, W. R. Smith, Richard Copeland and Wm. Mason.

On July 30th, 1891, Dr. Hewetson and Wm. R. Smith were appointed for three years; Mr. Hewetson declined to serve and O. R. Mansfield was appointed; D. F. Karnes and James K. Rarey for two years, Adam Shaner and R. F. Dildine for one year; the latter declined to serve and Dr. C. R. Clement was appointed; Samuel Kindler was appointed in 1892.

The minutes of the Council of July 9th, 1896, furnishes the following explanation: *"The Board of Health of the Village of Groveport, Ohio, having failed to meet in the last three years, has by the statutes of limitation become inoperative and ineffective and of no force."* Mayor Shaw then appointed the following members: Dr. C. R. Clement and Chas. D. Rarey for three years; R. F. Dildine and James Strode for two years and Edmund Gares and Phil C. Tussing for one year.

Jan. 13th, 1898, Frank Slosser was appointed in place of James Strode, who became a member of the Council, and James K. Rarey and Lyon Carruthers were appointed in place of Ed Gares and P. C. Tussing, whose terms had expired. In 1899 the members of the Board were: C.

R. Clement, Frank Schlosser, L. B. Carruthers, C. D. Rarey, R. F. Dildine and J. K. Rarey.

Dr. C. R. Clement has served continuously as Health Officer since 1889.

John A. Kile served as sanitary police 1889-91; W. E. Thompson, 1892-93; R. R. Paxton, 1896-1901.

Fires in Groveport

J. B. Wert's store and residence on the southwest corner of Main and Church streets was destroyed by fire in 1846 or 1847.

Solomon Clippenger's tannery burnt in the spring of 1850. It was located on the west side of Walnut Street, near the canal, and at the time of the fire a harness and saddler shop was connected with it.

The barns of Abram Sharp and Casper Limpert burned in the spring of 1862.

J. P. Arnold's residence, west of Groveport, was destroyed by fire on Saturday morning, Jan. 16, 1875.

The old Laypole Rarey Academy building burned on September 30, 1879.

Rager's Saw Mill—formerly operated by Moses Zinn and later by Wm. Chandler—was consumed on Sunday morning, December 14, 1879.

The Warehouse block, located on the south side of Main Street, near the canal, was destroyed on June 17, 1882. At the time of the fire it was owned by A. B. Rarey and was occupied by Thompson & Williams, blacksmiths, O. R. Mansfield, wagon maker, and Jethro Denton, meat store.

The Eldorado Mills, built by Rodenfels, Seymour & Co., in 1871, on the west side of Front Street and just north of the railroad tracks, was totally destroyed by fire on September 2, 1884. The fire was discovered at about eleven o'clock at night.

On August 13, 1877, while Burk & Foster were operating the Eldorado Mills, the boiler exploded and a boy named ____ Allen, aged eight years, was killed, and Addison McCoy, the engineer, had his legs scalded.

Dr. J. H. Saylor's barn burnt on February 16, 1897. This was a remarkable fire, as the hotel barn, just across the alley, was saved by the bucket brigade, while the pine siding, on the side next to the fire, was half burned through.

A view of the canal at Walnut Street, Groveport
Ca. 1906

CHAPTER XVI
ROADS

"One day, through the primeval wood,
A calf walked home, as good calves should;
But made a trail all bent askew,
A crooked trail, as all calves do.
The trail was taken up next day
By a lone dog that passed that way;
And then a wise bell-wether sheep
Pursued the trail o'er vale and steep,
And drew the flock behind her too,
As good bell-wethers always do.
And from that day o'er hill and glade
Through those old woods a path was made;
And many men wound in and out,
And dodged, and turned, and bent about,
And uttered words of righteous wrath
Because 'twas such a crooked path.
But still they followed — do not laugh —
The first migrations of that calf,
And through this winding woodway stalked,
Because he wabbled when he walked.
This forest path became a lane,
That bent, and turned, and turned again.
This crooked lane became a road
Where many a poor horse, with his load,
Toiled on beneath the burning sun,
And traveled some three miles in one,
And thus a century and a half,
They trod in the footsteps of that calf."

— Sam Walter Foss

The early roads were located without the least regard to straight lines, for there were many swamps which had to be avoided. Consequently, the bridle paths that wound about on the higher ground—marked by blazed trees—through the deep shade of the dense forest became the pioneer roads, and are in many instances even yet followed in their zigzag windings. The first road to be located through this township was what is now called the Columbus and Lancaster Pike, via Groveport and Lithopolis.

"At a session of the associate judges of Franklin County, held on September 8th, 1803, the following action was taken, on the prayer of a petition signed by a number of citizens of this county, praying for a view of a road leading from the public square in Franklinton, out of said town on the Pickaway Road, thence the nearest and best way to Lancaster, in Fairfield County, until it intersects the line between the counties aforesaid. Ordered that the prayer be granted and that John Brickell, Joseph Dickson and Joseph Hunter be appointed viewers of said road. It is further ordered that Joseph Vance be appointed surveyor to attend said viewers, and that he make a survey and report thereof to our next January term." Martin further says: *"This road was made to cross the Scioto at the old ford below the canal dam and pass through the bottom fields (then woods), to intersect what is now the Chillicothe Road (Parsons Avenue) south of Sewart's Grove."*

A number of years later—through the influence of Edward Courtright, John Chaney, Joseph Wright and others—the old State Road from Columbus to Winchester was located. The first bridge across Big Walnut on the line of this road was built of logs in about 1821; the floor "plank" was made of logs 8 inches thick, hewed on top and bottom sides: it stood until about 1829, when the ice broke up on the creek and took it down with a great crash, the noise of which could be heard three or four miles away. The bed of Big Walnut Creek was then along the bank, within one hundred yards of McGuffey's house.

Not much that is complimentary can be said of the first fifty years of road-making in the township. As soon as the rainy weather would set in, the roads would become next to impassable and remain so until late in the following spring; then there were scarcely any bridges, so travel, except on horseback or afoot, was almost entirely suspended. A four or six-horse team and a "prairie schooner", as the old Pennsylvania wagons were often called, stuck in the mud was a familiar sight and caused many a pioneer driver to give vent to expressions not found in his prayer-book. Many different plans and methods were employed, but the limited means at hand prevented anything permanent being accomplished. Often the residents in a neighborhood would turn out and make a corduroy road through a swamp or put up a temporary bridge of logs.

Example of a corduroy road

The writer has before him a four-page pamphlet, entitled *"An Act to Incorporate the Columbus, Winchester, Jefferson and Carroll Road Company,"* and the following quotations will fully explain its object:

"Be it enacted by the General Assembly of the State of Ohio, that (Dr.) M. Z. Kreider (Lancaster), Jacob Claypool, Geo. W. Meason (lived where Dressback Drum now lives), Wm. F. Breck (General Store in Carroll), Oliver Tong (Carroll), John Chaney, (Dr.) Wm. W. Talbott (Jefferson), Barnhart Fellows (tavern in Jefferson), (Dr.) J. B. Potter, Henry Eply, David Dixon, Reuben Dove and Samuel Taylor of Fairfield County and Geo. T. Wheeler, Zenas Collins, Daniel Riskad, James Suddick, Edward Courtright (on McGuffey farm), Daniel Handly, Alex. Mooberry (East Main Street, Columbus), Geo. White (just west of where N. & W. R. R. crosses Livingston avenue), (Dr.) Geo. Frankenberg (on Livingston Avenue), of the county of Franklin and their associates, be and are hereby created a body corporate, by the name of the Columbus, Winchester, Jefferson and Carroll Road Company, for the purpose of constructing a graded road from Columbus via Winchester, Jefferson and Carroll to Tallman's (Hooker's) in Fairfield County.

193

The capital stock shall be $10,000 in shares of $5 each. Said road shall be constructed as nearly on the ground now occupied by the State road leading from Columbus via Winchester to Jefferson as convenience and the nature of the ground will permit; and thence by Carroll to Tallman's, as nearly as possible, upon the ground now occupied by the present roads between these points.

That said company shall not at any time cause tollgates to be erected on said road, nor exact tolls or contributions from travelers thereon.

This act shall not become forfeited for non-user within the space of four years. Passed March 25th, 1841."

On February 28th, 1845, by "act" of the General Assembly, the time of forfeiture was extended four more years. By 1850 this road was graded and bridges with wooden abutments had been erected. The State road was followed from Columbus to a point between Jefferson and Carroll (Alspach's Corner); the State road was then open on past Jesse Brandt's, and at its intersection with the road from Betser's church and from Smaltz's church was called Five Points.

Columbus and Groveport Pike

On March 19, 1849, an "act" was passed incorporating The Columbus and Groveport Turnpike Company, to construct a turnpike road from Columbus to Groveport, with the privilege of extending it. The capital stock was not to exceed $20,000, in shares of $25 each.

The incorporators mentioned in the act are: Wm. Harrison, Nathaniel Marion, Wm. H. Rarey, William Darnell, Edmund Stewart, Wm. W. Kile and their associates.

The organization was effected in April, 1849, when John Sharp was elected President: John Cox, Secretary; Jacob Weaver, Treasurer, and Wm. W. Kile, William Merion, Samuel McClelland, and perhaps others, Directors. John Cox was the surveyor, John Sharp, superintendent, and order number one was for $3 in favor of Moses Seymour for four days' labor as chainman, issued under date of September 15, 1849.

The grading and graveling was divided into sections and the following were among the contractors: Peter Marx, John Swisher, Jr., T. J. Bennett, Patrick McGuire and Luther Stafford. David Sarber repaired the bridge across Big Walnut, and Gideon Vandemark built a toll-house. In January, 1851, Wm. W. Kile was president.

Stock certificates to the amount of $14,400 were issued; it is said that the pike cost somewhat more than was subscribed, but that this amount was soon paid out of the earnings of the road. Stock certificate number one was issued to Wm. W. Kile for four shares, under date of October 9, 1851. Other certificates were issued, on various dates, on up to January 10, 1853, to the following persons: Jacob Weaver, 8 shares; Lewis Hoster, 2; Joseph Schneider, 3; Jacob Strickler, 4; Thomas F. Jones, 2; Peter Shaffer, 1; Jacob Nafzger, 6; John H. Earhart, 4; Edmund Stewart, 4; Amor Rees, 8; John Bachman, 8; Chas. Obetz, 8; Edmonson Earhart, 4; Wm. Merion, 8; John Case, 4; Moses Seymour, 4; Harmon Dildine, 20; Conrad Born, 7; Jacob E. Baylor, 2; James Bayley, 2; Lincoln Goodale, 8; Oliver P. Hines, 3 ; Jacob Hare, 4; Charles Scott, 4; Ridgeway & Co., 12; R. W. McCoy, 10; John Swisher, 8; Abram Sharp, 8; Wesley Toy, 4; Samuel Parsons, 14; Cyrus Fay, 7; Dwight Stone, 7; Lincoln Kilbourne, 6; Jacob Arnold, 8; G. Horiger, 1; Nicholas Maurer, 8; Lewis Shirey, 2; Gares & Taylor, 4; Abram Shoemaker, 4; James D. Osborn, 8; John Sharp, Jr., heirs, 8; Alfred P. Stone, 4; Wm. A. Platt, 4; John Yenner, 2; Wm. Jones, 2; Thomas & Starling, 2; John L. McElvaine, 2; Philip Baker, 2; David Spade, 2; Thomas Moodie, 12; Jacob Anderick, 20; Samuel E. Kile, 4; Samuel Sharp, 26; Wm. Toy, 18; Joseph P. Bywaters, 8; Daniel Eswine, 4; Elias Johnson, 4; Wm. Riley, 4; James R. Paul, 16; Charles Pontius, 32; Benjamin W. Townsend, 8; Jeremiah Clark, 4; John W. Baker, 4; Dwight Stone & Co., 12; Joseph Rodenfels, 2; George Machold, 4; Wm. H. Rarey, 20; Frederick Swisher, 8; George Kanamaker, 2; C. J. Stevenson, 4; Lorenzo Porter, 4; John Stirling, 2; Abram Sharp, 18; Philo B. Watkins, 4; Jacob Stimmel, Jr., 4; John Sharp. *22*; Rollin Moler, 4; Jacob Shultz, 4; Ann Katharine Rarey, 24; John Ostott, 2; Wm. Merion, 2; Lewis Mills, 4, and Eli Gynne, 20.

The stock soon became valuable as an investment and gradually drifted into the hands of Columbus capitalists. Semi-annual dividends at the rate of 6 per cent were paid in May and November on up to 1881; from 1882 to 1885, 4 per cent., and in 1893, 5 1/2 per cent, was paid the stockholders.

The treasurer's statement in 1875 shows the following receipts and expenditures: Receipts, Gate No. 1, $1,166.50; Gate No. 2, $706.30; a total of $1,872.80; paid to stockholders, $864.00; taxes, $68.50; rent to A. Sharp, $6.00; J. Stotzenberger, $128.00; directors' expenses, $25.00; repairs, $246.70; gate-keepers, $432.00; balance in treasury, $50.00.

The gate-keepers were paid $18 per month. Joan Geary kept gate No. 2 for many years—1869 to February, 1887, when she was succeeded by Jack Thompson. D. Palsgrove kept gate No. 1 from 1869 to April 1, 1871, and was succeeded by Josiah Brink, who continued to keep it for many years. The last gate-keepers were Jack Thomas, gate No. 1, James Gisler, gate No. 2, and Henry Batzeson, gate No. 3.

Wm. Merion was treasurer for many years and was succeeded by Washington S. Johnson on Jan. 1, 1887.

On March 23, 1887, the affairs of the stockholders was put into the hands of a receiver and Washington S. Johnson was appointed receiver. In the spring of 1890 a proposition that Franklin County purchase the toll roads in the county was submitted to the voters. The vote on this proposition in Madison Township was: Groveport precinct, yes 6, no 390; Winchester precinct, yes 30, no 242.

Mr. Johnson continued to operate the turnpike as a toll road, expending all the receipts in expenses and improvements until November 2, 1897, when the bridge over Big Walnut was burnt. Sometime after the commissioners of Franklin County paid the stockholders one thousand dollars for the improvement and the stockholders transferred their interests to the county. The substantial new iron bridge was erected in 1898 at a cost of $25,905.00.

Groveport, Winchester and Lancaster Pike

In the spring of 1863 subscription lists were circulated to build this turnpike from Groveport to Hooker's. The following is a list of the subscribers and the numbers of shares, twenty-five dollars constituting a share:

Groveport list: John Rager, 20 shares; Jacob Arnold, 4; Dr. H. L. Chaney, 4; Dr. G. L. Smith, 5; Samuel Sharp, 4; Moses Seymour, 10; Andrew Wilson, 8; B. C. Sims, 2; R. F. Dildine, 1; C. E. Seymour, 8; H. C. Mason, 2; John S. Rarey, 8; Phil C. Tussing, 4; Moses Zinn, 4; Abraham Sharp, 4; Ruth Seymour, 4; Adam Smith, 4; Jackson Smith, 3; H. Hendren, 2; S. O. Hendren, 1; Wm. Mason, 1; John Smith, 2; G. S. Dildine, 1.

Winchester list: John Chaney, 40 shares; John Helpman, 12; Samuel Bartlit, 12; O. P. Chaney & Bro. (E. K.), 24; E. B. Decker, 12; R. Trine, 8; M. Allen, 8; John R. Wright, 8; M. C. Whitehurst, 8; C. W. Speaks, 4;

David Gayman, 4; S. W. Dildine, 4; G. M. B. Dove, 4; J. W. Hische, 2; A. Hathaway, 4; C. Gayman, 6; Daniel Gayman, 4; H. W. Shaffer, 4; Henry Will, 1; L. T. Carson, 1; Henry Harpst, 1; J. T. Flinchbaugh, 1; C. B. Cannon, 1; Wm. P. Miller, 1; Jacob Dauterman, 1; John M. Schoch, 6; Daniel Bergstresser, 2; Elijah Dove, 8; Rev. James Heffly, 2; I. L. Decker, 4; Dr. A. A. Short, 8; James McKelvey, 2; John Miller, 1; Geo. Derr, 2; Jacob Carty, 8; Dr. G. W. Blake, 3; John Kissel, 1; H. J. Epply, 2; A. M. Selby, 1; John Gehm, 3; Jacob Zarbaugh, 2; Jacob Harbaugh, 1; Peter Weber, 1; E. H. Walden, 2; W. J. Meeker, 4; John Kramer, 4; Chas. Brown, Sr., 4; Wm. Cater, 1; Amon Algire, 4; John Schrock, 4; Samuel Deitz, 4; Daniel Foor, 4; Sylvester Foor, 4; M. & C. C. Schrock, 4; Peter E. Ehrenhart, 2; Jacob Bott, 4; Jacob Sarber, 2; Geo. Powell, 2; D. C. Sarber, 2; James H. Somerville, 2; John G. Brunner, 4; M. G. Stevenson, 4; Frank Armpreister, 4; John Robinson, 4; Henry Zarbaugh, 1; Jacob Brenner, 12; John Armpreister, 1; Wm. Leight, 4; Henry Fictore, 4; Geo. Loucks, 16, and Ervin Moore, 4.

There were subscription lists at Jefferson, Carroll, Meason's and Lancaster, in all $17,750.00 was subscribed. The officers were: John Chaney, president; E. E. Meason, secretary; John Helpman, treasurer. After Mr. Meason's death August Shearer was elected secretary. John Robinson was the contractor. A tollgate was established at Winchester, and Jacob Zarbaugh, Sr., appointed gate-keeper. He lived on lot No. 32, where Mrs. Sarber now lives. A building, formerly used as an office by John Helpman, when his lumber yard was still on the south side of the canal, and which stood on lot No. 1, was moved along the pike just in front of Mr. Zarbaugh's house and served as a toll-house. Later this building was removed across the creek; the roof was removed to allow it to go through the bridge; later, Ervin Moore purchased it, together with the toll-house that was erected at the intersection of the pike and the Lithopolis Road and removed them about one-fourth mile further east, where they still remain.

Other gate-keepers were Geo. Hott and Mrs. Red. A gate was established at the Empire Mills and Granville Derr and John A. Wilson were the keepers. Mrs. Frances Sarber served as gate-keeper for many years at the Groveport gate.

The first bridge on this road across Little Walnut Creek had an abutment in the middle of the creek and consisted of only heavy stringers and floor. The present bridge was erected in the early fifties. The levee at the Winchester bridge was built in the spring of 1896 and the stone dressing was put on in the following fall.

Columbus and Winchester Pike

The Columbus and Winchester Turnpike was built in 1865. The following is a list of subscriptions, viz: John Butler, $200; E. Ergdon, $100; A. Gray, $200; Wm. Bulen, $500; John Swisher, $400; Thomas Needels, $500; Wm. Whims, $300; J. S. Stevenson $200; David Martin, $200; Geo. T. Wheeler, $100; Samuel Detwiler, $200; Jacob Bowman, $200; Thomas Gray, $300; Abraham Lehman, $750; J. B. Potter, $300; George Needels, $250; P. Gray, $200; Geo. W. Needels, $250; James H. Marshall, $100; John Heil, $100; Bennett Thompson, $100; Sylvester P. Stevenson, $100; Wm. D. Needles, $100; W. S. Clymer, $100; Samuel G. Carson, $100; James Needles, $100; Henry Wenger, $100; Jacob Bott, $50; Samuel Wheeler, $100; Peter Bott, $100; Samuel Ferguson, $100; J. J. Shearer, $50; John Schrock, $100; Charles Brown, $100; Whitehurst & Carty, $300; Tallman, Stevenson & Co., $300; Anion Allgire, $100; D. & C. Gayman, $50; Daniel Bergstresser, $50; O. J. Brown, $100.

The road was operated as a toll road until 1888, when it was turned over to the county commissioners, and the toll-gates were removed.

The photograph of the wrecked bridge that spanned Big Walnut on the Columbus and Winchester Pike was taken on March 23d, 1898, the next day after it was washed from its abutments. It was built in 1850 or '51 by David Sarber and George Meyers. John G. McGuffey, Esq., says *"Up to 1853 all the water in Big Walnut came along south of the road as now located, up to the foot of the hill on which father's old house stands and then ran south fifty or sixty rods, and then bore west until it passed the west line of my grandfather Courtright's farm; in 1853 or '54 it began to wash a channel where it now runs."*

The present bridge was built in 1899, and cost $28,598.00. For several months, during the spring and summer of 1898 while the bridges on both the Groveport and Winchester Pikes were out, travel was very much inconvenienced, except at such time when the water was at a low stage, when a ford was used near the Groveport Pike bridge and another about half mile north of the Winchester Pike along the road through the land of Samuel Brown.

Big Walnut Bridge on Winchester Pike
Built about 1850, wrecked March 23, 1898 at 11 a.m.
Camera was located 200 yards south of West abutment.

Walnut Creek and Groveport Pike

This road was built as a free pike by taxation—one mile limit. Chas. Pontius Sr., Thomas Fagan and Charles Rohr were the directors; it was built in 1882 at a cost of about $2,100 per mile and extends from Groveport to the south township line a point just west of the Hopewell Church.

Union Grove Cemetery Road

In the spring of 1892, Hon. B. F. Gayman, a member of the Legislature, introduced a "Bill" which became a law March 3d, 1892, authorizing the commissioners of Franklin County, to levy a tax and build a road from Winchester to Union Grove Cemetery, *"at an aggregate sum not to exceed ten thousand ($10,000) dollars."* The contract for its construction was awarded to Michael Corbett, of Groveport. Work on its construction was begun in the following September and it was completed in November of the same year, at a cost slightly exceeding the appropriation. The four-foot brick walk along the stone curb called for in the original specification had to be omitted in order to keep within the limit of the appropriation. Mr. Gayman's bill contains a very wise provision for keeping this road in repair: *"And for keeping said road, side-walk and curbing in good repair, said commissioners shall, when necessary, levy a tax not to exceed one-fortieth of a mill, on said taxable property of said county."*

Within the last few years, through the discussions at Farmers' Institutes, and at the Grange, and the introduction of the bicycle, a new era of road-making has appeared. Now there is a commendable rivalry between road districts and even between townships and counties, to build the most durable and sightly bridges and road beds.

CHAPTER XVII
COACH AND MAIL LINES

"Spinsters fair and forty,
Maids in youthful charms
Suddenly are cast in —
To their neighbor's arms!
Children shoot like squirrels
Darting through a cage;
Isn't it delightful.
Riding in a stage."

— Ohio Statesman

The nearest post-offices for the first few years were Franklinton and New Lancaster. Whoever went to Franklinton—where most of the settlers of this township got their mail—would get the mail for his whole neighborhood. During the winter when the streams were swollen it was often several weeks before anyone could go.

The first post-road through Madison Township was established in 1814. Hon. James Kilbourne, then Congressman from the Fifth Ohio District published a circular under date of September 8, 1814, announcing, among others, the establishment of a post-route *"from Athens, by New Lancaster, to Columbus,"* The circular does not state, but very likely the mail was not carried oftener than once a week. In 1822 the mail was carried three times each week, arriving in Columbus, on every Tuesday, Thursday and Saturday, and leaving every Monday, Wednesday and Friday. These early mails were carried on horseback, the post-boy usually tying his letters up in his handkerchief, and when delivered to the post-master were carried about in his hat to be handed to their owners as he chanced to meet them,—a primitive free delivery as it were.

The post-man — whether a footman, horseman, stage coach driver, and we might include the modern railway conductor, has always attracted a crowd, *"who hungrily devour and retail the budget of gossip brought from the outside world."* The post-man carried a tin horn which he blew on his approach to the post-station; this custom was continued by the coach driver and is continued by the steam whistle of the locomotive. It is said some of the mail carriers could blow very musically sounding tunes on their tin horns; each particular post-man could be distinguished, as the small boy can now tell the number or name of the locomotive, by its whistle.

For many years there was no regularity in the arrival of the mails; they were sometimes, especially in the winter, two or three weeks late. To satisfy a demand for the more certain and speedy transmission of important messages the Express-post was established; this system provided that horses be stationed every ten miles. The post-boy who carried the letters in a bag or valise thrown over his shoulders, was required to make the ten miles in one hour. It took but a moment to dismount and remount at the different stations. Letters carried by Express-post cost from two to four times the usual postage.

Wm. Neil and A. I. McDowell established a tri-weekly stage coach line between Lancaster and Columbus via Courtright (Greencastle), Centerville (Lithopolis), and Middletown (Oregon) in the summer of 1827. It is very probable that coaches ran at irregular intervals as travel demanded some years earlier than the above date. The terrible condition of the roads during the winter season prevented travel except afoot or on horseback.

The following paragraph appeared in the *Ohio State Journal*, Friday, December 11th, 1829 and is quoted in Capt. Lee's *History of Columbus*:

"Unparalleled Expedition. By the extraordinary exertions of the Ohio State Coach Company, the President's message, which was delivered at Washington City, at twelve o'clock, noon, on Tuesday last, was received at our office at fifteen minutes before eleven in the evening of the following Wednesday, having traveled the whole distance between the two places— estimated at about four hundred and twenty miles— over excessively bad roads, in the space of thirty-four hours and forty-five minutes—a performance unparalleled in the annals of traveling in this section of the country.

Another example of rapid travel is quoted from the *Ohio Statesman* of December 11th, 1846:

"Unparalleled Speed. The President's message was received on the western bank of the Ohio River, opposite Wheeling, by the Ohio Stage Company, at thirty-five minutes past one o'clock, P. M., on Thursday, and was delivered at Columbus at ten minutes past eight o'clock the same evening, having been conveyed from Wheeling to Columbus—135

miles—in the unparalleled short space of six hours and a half." This was the last President's message before the establishment of the telegraph.

In 1849, Darius Talmadge, who owned the line between Columbus and Lancaster and H. T. Hoyt, who owned the line between Lancaster, via Logan and Athens to Pomeroy established a daily coach line between Columbus and Pomeroy, via Oregon and Lithopolis.

In 1850 W. B. & J. A. Hawks secured the contract for carrying the mail over this route.

In 1860, McClure & Rice became the mail carriers and run daily coaches via Winchester; after about one year they were succeeded by W. B. & J. A. Hawkes who continued the line up to the time when the Hocking Valley Railroad began running trains.

In April, 1864, just when the passengers got aboard of one of the four horse coaches in front of the Commercial Hotel in Winchester, the horses suddenly started to turn, when the coach was upset. There were twelve passengers on the inside and seven on top, besides the baggage. No one was seriously hurt.

The late Col. Ferdinand F. Rempel of Logan, O., kindly furnished the following very interesting items in regard to the coach line of which he was the proprietor:

"I think it was in 1855 that I first became interested in the line between Lancaster and Logan and soon after in the line between Lancaster and Columbus, and finally in a through line to Pomeroy, purchasing the running stock of the Ohio Stage Co., of which Judge P. Van Trump was the president, and Darias Talmadge was a large stock-holder. In making that purchase, I connected the Columbus-Lancaster line with the Hocking Valley, Athens and Pomeroy line; making it a through route from Pomeroy to Columbus. Part of the time H. T. Hoyt and myself had a joint interest in the same, until sometime in 1865, when I sold to Col. C. H. Grosvenor and Thos. Beaton, that portion from Athens to Pomeroy, and they conducted the same up to the time when the railroad was built.

I had 96 horses on the entire line; 16 between Lancaster and Columbus where we used four-horse Troy coaches. On the line between Lancaster and Logan we ran two dailies in summer, and one daily in winter, using four-horse coaches, fancy platform wagons or omnibuses as roads would warrant. The line between Logan, Athens and Pomeroy was served with two-horse hacks; in the winter season this route was very difficult to serve, owing to the very bad clay hills between Athens and Pomeroy. I employed on the through lines from twelve to sixteen drivers and stable men. The speed was at an average of six miles per hour on fair roads. We had a general agent at Lancaster, John Borland, who served as such for twelve years on my line. The proprietors of the hotels where the stage offices were located received the fare, and settled for it every three months.

Among the best known drivers were Andrew J. Sickles, E. McFarland, Milton Myers, Henry Bimpel, John Plunk, Wm. Kruse, Wm. Bowen, Wm. Blackhaus, Fred Klein, Louis Whetzel and Rufus Snively, (passenger conductor on the Hocking Valley R. R.)

During the time of my running the lines, the coaches carried a substantial iron safe, in which the funds were safely conveyed from station to station, supplying the banks, etc., the Adams Express Co., being in close connection with the lines, myself sharing the express charges. Part of the time the coaches ran via Lithopolis and later by way of Canal Winchester. It was at the time that W. B. & J. A. Hawks owned the Columbus and Lancaster line that the Hon. A. McVeigh and son lost their lives by an upset near Winchester and the damages paid amounted to several thousand dollars. It was during my ownership that driver Stutser lost his life by the running away of a four-horse coach team at Lancaster.

The fares of my lines were very remunerative, and during my fourteen years of ownership without losses or damages to passengers."

The accident to which Col. Rempel refers, happened on Friday evening, September 16th, 1864, at a point east of Peter Brown's barn near the small bridge, Hon. A. M. McVeigh, a prominent attorney and politician of Lancaster, Ohio, who was to make a speech at Lancaster that evening was instantly killed, his son was so badly injured that he died that same evening, and an old lady's injuries proved fatal on the following Monday morning. It is said *"the coach was overloaded and the driver was drunk."*

Col. F. F. Rempel still has one of the old blank way-bills in his possession. The driver carried one of these from the starting point through to the end of the route. At each station he presented it to the agent, who would enter the number of passengers, destination, fare, etc., that started from his office and also noted whether the number of passengers arriving corresponded with the way-bill. The agent also made out a duplicate record on a separate sheet which he deposited into a locked pocket that was permanently fastened at the front end of the coach and only opened at the terminals. From the record of those reports the settlement with the different agents was made every three months. There were nineteen stations on the route from Athens to Columbus. Lithopolis was No. 17, Groveport, No. 18.

Elisha B. Decker
1818 - 1879

John M. Schoch
1812 - 1888

The following extracts from *Rules and Instructions* for agents of *Rempel's Mail Coach Line* from Athens to Lancaster and Columbus, reveals some of the principal features of travel by coach half a century ago.

"Names of passengers, in no instance, are to be entered on the Way-bill, TO PAY, neither FREE."

"Any person traveling by Stage, whose name is not regularly entered on the Bill, is not to be suffered to proceed, unless he exhibits, at the different offices on the route, a written permit, dated at the office from whence he left."

"Passengers having more than 40 pounds of baggage, are liable to be charged at the rate of one seat for every hundred pounds excess, at any office between Columbus, Lancaster and Athens, where it may be ascertained."

"All baggage is at the risk of the owner."

"Agents will pay particular attention to the proper entry and forwarding of express goods, and make charges, discretionary, for the same, on the Waybills, according to the value, size and weight of such goods, and the distance."

The following rules and rates for forwarding money and other valuable packages to be strictly obeyed:

On all sums less than $100-twenty-five cents; on all sums upwards of $100 and less than $1,000-fifty cents; on all sums upwards of $1,000 and less than $3,000-one dollar; on all sums upwards of $3,000 and less than $5,000- one dollar and fifty cents; on all sums above $5,000-at the rate of fifty cents per 1,000."

"Agents must in no instance receive packages without they are properly sealed, and, receipt for them "Said to contain," as the proprietor only agrees to deliver the package as received—seals untouched—either to the parties on Rempel's route, or, if ordered to any other point on any other route, deliver the same to the Adams Express Co. for further forwarding. Agents can, by Rempel's Express, forward packages to any point in the United States, Canada, or Europe; also take for collection money due, which will receive prompt attention."

"Persons desiring their friends or relations from any foreign port brought to the United States, either by steam packet or first-class sailing vessels, or wanting to forward friends to such ports, will please call at Rempel's office in Logan, where arrangements can be made at reasonable rates."

"Agents must receive only par funds for fare and charges—the Proprietor will not be responsible for uncurrent money taken."

"In no instance allow mechanic's bills—for repairs, horseshoeing etc., to be charged in account, but have such charges paid immediately when the work is done."

"All charges between Proprietor and Agents to be made on the Way-Bill, and such to be settled at the expiration of each quarter year."

"The keys belonging to the office and coach safes should be carefully guarded, and only placed to be handled by the Agent, as the loss of such keys would subject us to change the locks."

"Every Way-Bill to be examined carefully on each arrival, in order to ascertain if the number of passengers are entered correctly, and all way-fare entered on the Way-Bill."

206

"No intoxicated passenger to be admitted on the coaches when objections are made by any other passenger."

"Ladies, in every instance, are entitled to a choice of seats."

"Passengers who have paid for their seats on a regular mail coach or hack, should have them reserved, in every instance, without the through-passengers take up all such seats in passing the way-offices."

"Passengers who have paid the fare for their passage, and accidentally be not ready when the conveyance is off, should in no instance have their fare refunded, but courteously be entitled to same passage on some other trip."

"No passengers are entitled to seats in coaches until fare be paid in full."

"Make engagements for extra coaches, carriages, etc., at reasonable rates, and inform the Proprietor as early as convenient what size coach or hack you have agreed to furnish, and the time it is to reach your office, also the number of passengers and the price agreed upon for such extra service. You will be subject to no disappointments in making such arrangements."

"Drivers are not permitted to carry way-passengers past any regular stage office on the route-fare unpaid. Agents will in every instance report such failures. All reports by Agents will be strictly confidential."

"Report to the Logan office the changes that may take place in your Railroad departures and arrivals, in order to connect coaches accordingly."

In about 1850 Abraham Hunsicker was running a daily hack line between Winchester and Columbus, via Groveport. He used a team of dun horses. In 1854 Jacob Direling was running the same line; still later, Daniel Lethers was the proprietor and Wm. Wilson the driver. In the fall of 1857, while the road was very bad, Mr. Lethers would leave the coach at Groveport and transport the passengers and baggage by boat to Winchester. On the evening of November 18, it being a stormy and dark night and the boat being delayed, Mr. Lethers went to the first lock to meet it and get the lock ready, when, in some way, he fell into the canal and was drowned. Mr. Wilson continued as driver until McClure & Rice started their line, when he became one of their drivers.

1850's Hack or Carriage

In the "forties" Heil Brockway operated a daily packet line between Cleveland and Lockbourne, with headquarters in Winchester. The horses went in a trot and were changed at regular stations. The packet boats were built quite narrow for speed and were comfortably fitted up for passengers. During the time this line was in operation Winchester had daily mails. In about 1850 James Cannon, Sr., carried the mail on horseback along the towpath between Winchester and Lockbourne, receiving the mail at Groveport and making three trips a week. Paul Samsel was also a mail carrier over this route. Later, Winchester got its mail from Lithopolis, the government Star Route providing for three mails a week and the citizens providing the means to get it daily.

According to *"Kilbourne's Gazetteer,"* there were post offices at the following neighboring places in 1841: Talbotts (Jefferson), West Carrollton (Carroll), Courtright (Greencastle), Oregon (Middletown), Pickerington—called Jacksonville until 1828, when the name was changed—Wert's Grove (Groveport). The post office at Waterloo was established in 1839 and removed to Winchester in 1841.

The rates of postage were quite different at an early day from those which prevail today. The postage on letters depended on the distance—thus, for a letter fifty miles or less, 6 1/4 cents; over fifty and under one hundred miles, 12 1/2 cents; between one hundred and fifty and three hundred miles, 18 3/4 cents; over three hundred miles to any office in the United States, 25 cents. Two sheets folded together was counted as a double letter and double rates charged. The rates were changed from time to time; for a while the rate for all letters was 10 cents, then 5 cents; then, on March 3rd, 1851, the three-cent stamp was introduced. Prior to this, few persons paid the postage in advance; the price was marked in one corner and paid by the person receiving it. As I write, there lies before me a number of letters received by Nathaniel Tallman during the years 1847-1851 with the price of the postage marked upon them. The uniform postage from Cleveland is 5 cents and on one from Philadelphia, Pa., which contained a canceled note, the postage was 20 cents. Among them is also the first three-cent stamp, received under date of Aug. 12, 1851. No envelopes were used; letters were written on two or three pages of the folded sheet, the fourth or outside page was left blank for the address and then so folded as to allow the blank page to form the whole outside of the letter. Perhaps few persons now living remember how to fold up a letter in this old way. Small thin wafers were sold at all the stores with which the letters were sealed by simply moistening them with the tongue.

Registered letters were authorized March 3, 1855.

Postal cards, costing one cent, were authorized on June 8, 1872, and first issued in May, 1873.

Postal notes were first issued in September, 1883.

A post office and station was established at Edwards soon after the Hocking Valley Railroad was built. John G. Edwards, John W. Edwards and Levi S. Johnson were the successive postmasters. The office was discontinued in the fall of 1895.

A post office was established at Zimmer in March, 1891 and George C. Zimmer was appointed postmaster on March 13 and the office was opened for business on May 1 of the same year. Mr. Zimmer continued as postmaster until February 1, 1901, when the office was discontinued.

In March, 1888, a daily mail route was established between Winchester and Cedar Hill, with two daily trips between Winchester and Lithopolis. G. T. Clover was the first carrier. Later that part of the trip between Lithopolis and Cedar Hill was transferred to the Carroll and Cedar Hill route.

Rural Free Delivery

In 1896 Congress appropriated $10,000.00 to test Rural Free Delivery. On October 6, 1900, Route No. 1 from Groveport was granted and Wm. J. Peters appointed carrier. Service was begun on October 15, and on October 10, 1900, Routes No. 1 and No. 2 from Winchester were granted and put into operation on November 1 with Chas. P. Lecrone as carrier on No. 1 and Geo. E. Smith as carrier on No. 2.

Route No. 2 from Groveport was granted on December 11, 1900, and was put into operation on January 16, 1901, with Geo. W. Preston as carrier.

Route No. 3 from Winchester was granted on November 19, 1900, and John S. Lehman appointed carrier, who made his first trip February 1, 1901.

The following reports of the different routes for the month of March, 1901, may form a basis for comparison in the years to come of this progressive movement, which is so rapidly gaining popular favor:

Route No. 1, Groveport
Delivered:
Registered letters, 2.
letters, 583.
postal cards, 237.
newspapers, 4,155.
circulars, 485.
packages, 60.
Total, 5,520.
Collected:
Registered letters, 2.
letters, 502.
postal cards, 117.
circulars, 23.
packages, 5.
Total, 658.
Delivered and collected, 6,178.

Route No. 2, Groveport

Delivered:

Letters, 756;

postal cards, 269;

newspapers. 3,949;

circulars, 404;

packages, 78;

Total, 5,457.

Collected:

Registered letters, 3.

letters, 531.

postal cards, 97.

newspapers, 11.

packages, 11.

total, 674.

Delivered and collected, 6,131.

Route No. 1, Winchester

Delivered:

Registered letters, 1.

letters, 450.

postal cards, 178.

newspapers, 2,262.

circulars, 417.

packages, 93.

Total, 3,401.

Collected:

Money orders, 5.

letters, 369.

postal cards, 65.

packages, 6.

total, 543.

Delivered and collected, 3,944

Route No. 2, Winchester

Delivered:

Registered letters, 2.

letters, 603.

postal cards, 173.

newspapers, 2,212.

circulars, 127.

total, 3,189.

Collected:

Registered letters, 6;

money orders, 5.

letters, 446.

postal cards, 76.

newspapers, 1.

packages, 14.

Total, 548.

Delivered and collected, 3,737.

Route No. 3. Winchester

Delivered:

Registered letter, 1.

letters, 326.

postal cards, 67.

newspapers, 1,726.

circulars, 208.

packages, 58.

total, 2,386.

Collected:

Letters, 252.

packages, 2.

total, 283.

Delivered and collected, 2,669.

In the above tables the daily newspapers which are received by mail on the Groveport routes are included, while the dailies on the Winchester routes are received by express and are, therefore, not included. Route No. 1 carried 468; Route No. 2, 468; Route No. 3, 208 during the month of March.

CHAPTER XVIII
RAILROADS

"Down aroun' the depo' when the keers come in,
What a hustle an' a bustle an' a clatter and a din,
Engine kinder puffin', an' a blowin' off its steam,
Drayman sorter fussin' an' a cussin' at his team,
Boy a sellin' papers an' a shoutin' out the news,
'Nother one a waitin' fer to blacken up yer shoes,
Ain't like any other place 'at I have bin,
Down aroun' the depo' when the keers come in."

"Down aroun' the depo' when the keers come in,
People there a-meetin' and a greetin' of their kin,
Some are disappointed like an' lookin' kinder glum,
Some a-sorter wishin' their relation hadn't cum,
The joyful, the sorrowful, the sober an' the gay,
Kinder sorter mixi' up in every sorter way;
Lat o' folks 'at's bin away an' gettin' back agin,
Down aroun' the depo' when the keers cum in."

On April 10th, 1834, two years before there was a mile of railway in the state of Ohio, Hon. John Chaney, then a member of Congress from this district, introduced this resolution: *"Resolved, That the committee on roads and canals be instructed to inquire into the expediency of granting to the state of Ohio a quantity of unsettled lands in the counties of Fairfield, Hocking, Athens and Washington for the purpose of aiding the state in the construction of the Hocking Valley Railroad from Lancaster to the Ohio River."* (Congressional Globe, 1834, page 301.)

This resolution was referred to the proper committee, but was left to die in their hands. This was at a day when the canals were more popular than railways, besides it is said that Hon. Thomas Ewing—who was then called the "Salt Boiler"—had interests in the salt wells at Salina and was, therefore, opposed to this railroad.

Dr. Hugh L. Chaney is authority for the further information that his father expected to make provision in a "Bill" to be introduced—providing his resolution should receive favorable consideration—that should there be any surplus funds remaining after the railway was built, the same should be applied towards the erection of a new capitol building at Columbus.

Although the provisions of Mr. Chaney's resolution did not become a law, his foresight was prophetic, and most remarkable, especially when we remember that the first locomotive ever used in Ohio was not until July of 1837, and that there were no railroads into Columbus until February 22, 1850.

On September 25, 1852, a public meeting was held at Nelsonville with a view to building a railroad to Columbus. Other meetings were held later, and considerable interest was stirred up along the proposed line.

At a meeting held at Lancaster in the summer of 1853, subscription books were opened, but for some reasons the enterprise again failed. Thirty-two thousand, four hundred dollars was subscribed at Winchester in the summer of 1853, under the following heading: *"We, the undersigned, hereby subscribe to the capital stock of the Columbus and Hocking Valley Railroad Company the number of shares affixed to our names, respectively; and agree to pay said company the sum of fifty dollars on each of said shares in such installments as may be required by the directors thereof. It is understood that the conditions of this subscription is, that the railroad of said company shall be located within one-fourth of a mile of Winchester, in Franklin County."* Samuel Bartlit, 50 shares; Wm. Fry, 50; J. B. Potter, 60; H. Tallman, 50; D. Bergstresser, 20; Peter T. Krag, 10; John Helpman, 20; C. W. Speaks, 10; John Schrock, 10; M. Allen, 10;. H. J. Epply, 10; Daniel Gayman, 6; Reuben Dove, 20; A. Hathaway, 20; Thomas Patterson, 2; Ira Ricketts,. 2; G. T. Wheeler, 10; A. I. Dildine, 4; A. D. Benedum, 20; J. W. Porter, 4: Aaron Fenstermaker, 4; Elias Kemerer, 20; John Chaney & Son, 20; W. L. Stevenson, 20; M. C. Whitehurst, 10; Abraham Lehman, 20; Samuel Loucks, 40; John Kramer, 20; Nathaniel Tallman, 20; George Faskett, 2; Chas. Brown, 4; Elijah Dove, 4; Isaac Kalb, 4; Abram Harris, 4; Henry Fictore, 2; Eli Zimmer, 10; Pitts Brown, 10; Andrew A. French, 10; David Kramer, 6; Ervin Moore, 6; Wm. H. Tallman, 10; Jacob Powell, 20; George Harmon, 10; John Deitz, 4.

This line was surveyed to enter Columbus from the East—leaving Groveport to the south, and going north of Asbury Church.

More or less interest continued until the spring of 1864, when the Mineral Railroad was incorporated and surveyed. This survey went over two routes; the one north of Asbury and the other by way of Groveport. In the winter of 1865-66 the agitation became active again and Winchester raised a subscription of $30,000.00 and Groveport one of $25,000.00.

The citizens of Groveport, in order to secure the railroad, agreed to furnish the right of way from Big Walnut Creek to Winchester, which they did at a cost to them of $7,500.00.

In May, 1867, the construction of the road was contracted for with Dodge, Case & Co., track laying between Columbus and Winchester began in the following November.

On July 16, 1868, the first engine and car were run from Columbus to within about a mile of Winchester.

On January 13, 1869, the members of the Legislature, state officers and others made a trip from Columbus to Lancaster, and the following day a free ride from Lancaster to Columbus and return was given the public. Free meal tickets were distributed on the train. Eighteen passenger coaches and box cars were completely filled, even standing room on the platforms was at a premium. The track was not well ballasted and the train had to run slowly. It was with great difficulty that the engine moved the train from Winchester and when at a point about opposite Powell & Boyer's tile yard they stalled. Many got off the cars and pushed and then ran along for quite a distance.

Daily trains between Columbus and Lancaster began running on January 18, 1869. Trains began running to Nelsonville on August 17, 1869 and to Athens on July 25, 1870.

June, 1867, the name was changed from the "Mineral" to The Columbus and Hocking Valley. In 1881 the Columbus and Hocking Valley, the Columbus and Toledo, and the Ohio and West Virginia Railroads were consolidated under the title, The Columbus, Hocking Valley and Toledo Railway Company.

The railway conductor, like the coach driver of old, is a very important personage. He is charged with the safety of the traveler; he must furnish every passenger a seat even when there is scarcely standing room; he must listen to the complaints of the patrons, but is helpless to remedy the evils complained of—he must be civil and courteous to the rudest and most offensive or hear the terrible (?) threat, "I'll report you," whatever that means. His knowledge of, and patience in dealing with human nature, and especially his never-failing civility and gallantry to women commands the respect of every sensible observer. Among the passenger conductors well known to the public are: Geo. R. Carr, afterwards superintendent; Rufus J. Snively— who aided in the construction of the road and has been running a passenger train ever since (Mr. Snively died August 10, 1901); W. Shannon Josephs, Henry Kilbourne, Edw. Kilgore, Phil Thompson, Bert Barnes, James Galvin, W. C. Bennett, L. E. Brady and J. R. Smith. Nor must we forget Tommy (Wiley), the brakeman.

The agents at Groveport have been: Samuel McComb, A. Wilson, J. C. Hannum, A. W. Swisher, H. W. Zinn and A. P. Brown. At Winchester: A. B. Lucas, M. C. Whitehurst, November 15, 1876, to December 11, 1877; Cary D. Whitehurst, C. B. Tuttle, H. A. Thompson and Wm. M. Codner.

When the railroad was first built, a switch was run down the west side of High Street; one spur running along Whitehurst & Carty's warehouse to the canal and another crossing High Street and running along the Chaney, Decker & Co.'s warehouse, the track through the basin being laid on trestle work and cars frequently stood on this track along the street. It was torn up in August, 1876.

Electric Lines

1889
Thomas Edison's electric locomotive pulling two passenger cars.

For several years previous to 1899 the building of an electric railway was talked of.

On June 26, 1899, The Columbus, Winchester and Lancaster Traction Company was incorporated by Thos. A. Simons, Richard E. Jones, David C. Beggs, Howard C. Park, F. D. Simons of Columbus, and Franklin Post and Theo. B. Beatty of New York City. On the same date The Columbus and Lancaster Traction Company, which had been incorporated about two months previous and which had secured the right of way along the proposed route, applied to the Commissioners of Fairfield County for a franchise to construct an electric line from Lancaster via Campground, Rock-mill, Greencastle, Lithopolis to Winchester. The latter company was represented by Judge D. Dwyer and Judge O. B. Brown of Dayton, Dr. F. S. Wagenhals of Columbus and others, and was spoken of as the Dwyer Line in distinction from the former company which was known as the Simon's Line. The representatives of both companies made an active effort to secure the franchise through Winchester and Groveport laboring under the impression that such a recognition would be helpful in securing a favorable decision from the county commissioners. A special meeting of the Winchester council was called for July 5, 1899, at which representatives of both companies, as well as many citizens were present. The Columbus and Lancaster Traction Co., presented a resolution establishing a route over Washington, West and Columbus Streets, this the Columbus, Winchester and Lancaster Traction Company zealously opposed. There seemed to be an almost unanimous sentiment in favor of the Dwyer people and the resolution was passed. On the following evening a citizens meeting was held and resolutions passed and a committee consisting of W. H. Lane Esq., James Palsgrove, E. C. Gayman, Dr. L. W. Beery and Dr. G. F. Owen, appointed with a view to *"giving all the assistance possible"* to the Columbus and Lancaster Traction Company.

On July 17, the Fairfield County commissioners in company with Judges Dwyer and Brown and citizens from Greencastle and Lithopolis went over the proposed route coming to Winchester late in the afternoon; stopping at the residence of W. H. Lane where they were met by citizens of Winchester.

On the following Tuesday, the commissioners went over the route by the way of Carroll, this being the one over which a franchise was sought by the Simon's people. On the following Friday the commissioners granted a franchise to the Dwyers.

On August 7, 1899 an ordinance was passed by the council of Winchester granting the Dwyer's a franchise, stipulating that work must begin within four months from the time they obtain a continuous franchise from Columbus to Lancaster, and that cars shall be run at least six times each way daily. The fare was to be, from Winchester to Groveport or Lithopolis 5 cents or 25 tickets for one dollar, fare to Columbus, one way 25 cents or round trip 40 cents; Groveport to Columbus, one way 20 cents, round trip 35 cents.

On August 18, 1899, the Franklin County commissioners granted the same company a franchise; this with the franchise granted by the council of Groveport, over Main Street on August 10, gave them a right of way over the entire route.

Surveying and other work was begun, but by the fall of 1900 many questioned whether the road would be built, notwithstanding the report that some $6,000 or $7,000 had already been spent upon the project. During November and December, 1900, the Simon's Company again made an effort to secure the franchise in Franklin County, setting forth that the former franchise had become void, the road not having been begun by September 1, 1900, as was stipulated in the franchise. Several hearings were had and considerable excitement aroused along the proposed route when finally the Simon's people were granted a franchise; this was followed by the granting of franchises by the council of Groveport, February 28, 1901, and by the council of Winchester, March 4, 1901. These franchises were similar to those granted the Dwyer Company being over the same streets. Work was to be begun by October 1, 1901, and the road completed within one year. The cars were to be propelled by *"electricity or other motive power except steam."*

While all this conjecture as to which company if either would construct and equip this road was holding the attention of the people along the proposed route and of the press, a cloud of hope, at first *"no bigger than a man's hand"* appeared. The Scioto Valley Traction Company was incorporated September 80 1899, for $100,000.00 and sought a franchise from Columbus towards Chillicothe; on December 19, 1900, the capital stock was increased to $1,000,000.00; and on January 7, 1901 a certificate of *Enlargement of Purpose* was filed. This latter contemplated the extension to Lancaster.

Little attention was paid to this venture by the people down the Hocking Valley until it was discovered that they were quietly buying private right of way from the junction of the Groveport Pike and the Norfolk and Western Railway. Although many were skeptical, still the surveying and buying went steadily on during the summer of 1901, until September 5, when the contract for grading the entire line was awarded to W. O. Johnson & Co., of Cedar Rapids, Iowa; the most skeptical now admitted that the prospects for the building of an electric line was now very encouraging. Work was at once begun, Mr. Johnson with his extensive outfit of teams, wagons, scrapers and camp outfits arrived soon after and by January 1, 1902, the grading is well under way along the line.

The council of Groveport granted the Scioto Valley Traction Company a franchise over Blacklick Street on September 12, 1901, stipulating that the road must be completed within eighteen months from September 1, 1901; Fares, through the village, single cash fare, 5 cents, six tickets 25 cents, thirty tickets, one dollar.

Scioto Valley Traction Company

Scioto Valley Traction Company
Note the lead car is the same as pictured in the previous SVTC photo.

Lancaster Traction Company

CHAPTER XIX
WAR TIMES

"Ah, never shall the land forget
How gushed the life blood of the brave,
Gushes warm with hope and courage yet
Upon the soil they fought to save."

Bryant

General John C. Speaks
1859 - 1945
He served as a member of the Ohio National Guard for more than forty years, advancing from Private to Brigadier General. During the Spanish–American War he served as major of the Fourth Regiment, Ohio Volunteer Infantry, participating in the Puerto Rican campaign. He commanded the Second Brigade of the Ohio National Guard on the Mexican Border in 1916. During the First World War he commanded the Seventy-third Brigade.

It is practically impossible to get anything like a complete list of the Revolutionary soldiers buried in this township. This is equally true in regard to the names of those who served in the War of 1812 or in the Mexican War.

The following is a partial list of those who enlisted for service in the Mexican War or who served in that war and were buried in this township: John Ford, John Ell, Harvey Johnson, David Tryne, Samuel Simons, Daniel Swisher, Isaac Tracy, Orange Barnhart, Jacob Mosier, Daniel Rowhan, John Nafzger, John Heston (Sergt.), James McKelvey, Peter Brown and ____ Jobes.

Evidence is not lacking to prove that Madison Township furnished her full quota then as she also did in the War of the Rebellion and the late Spanish War.

Commander Edward M. Huges
1850 - 1903

U.S.S. HUGHES
DESTROYER
NAMED FOR COMDR. EDWARD M. HUGHES, U.S.N.
BUILT AT THE BATH I. W. CORPN., BATH, MAINE

AUTHORIZED	MARCH 27, 1934
KEEL LAID	SEPTEMBER 15, 1937
LAUNCHED	JUNE 17, 1939
FIRST COMMISSIONED	SEPTEMBER 21, 1939

The writer has before him the commission of Wm. T. Decker as Captain of the 4th Cavalry Company, 2d Brigade. 7th Division of the Militia of the State of Ohio, signed by the Governor, Joseph Vance, under date of November 2, 1838. This company was called *"The Light Horse Company."* The following is a partial list of members: Wm. T. Decker, Captain; Moses Groom, Ezekiel Groom, Wm. H. Rarey, Joseph Dildine, Laypole Rarey, Frederick Bunn, Wm. W. Kile, John W. Kile,

John Algire, Charles Pontius, Parker Rarey, Daniel Rarey, Isaac Seymour, Harvey Decker, Jesse Welton, John Seymour, Jacob Lehman, Isaac Welton, Isaac McCormick, Adam Havely, Frederick Rarey, Isaac Hankins, John Hankins, Henry Dildine and Moses Seymour.

At about the same time, another military organization flourished at Groveport, called *"The First Rifle Company,"* or *"The State Rifle Company."* One of the *"events"* in the life of these two companies was a sham battle in Rarey's Grove. The following is a partial list of the members of the *"State Rifle Company"*: Jacob Weaver, Captain; Jacob Andrix, Captain: Adison McCoy, Lieutenant: James Blakely, Drummer; Henry Dildine, Bugler: M. K. Earheart, J. J. Miller, Thos. Champe, Geo. P. Champe, Jeremiah Kalb, Thomas Black, Henry Kraner, John Cox, Wm. Cox, John G. Edwards,Turner C. Hendren, D. C. Hendren, Kalita Sallee, John Clevenger, Wm. Clevenger, John Swisher, John Cross, Isaac Kalb, Amos Bennett, Thomas Blakely, George Blakely, George Miller, Nathaniel Champe, John Kiner, Wm. Nichols, John Swisher, Wm. Swisher, Aaron Kramer, John Hastings, Jacob Miller, C. P. Dildine, Solomon Woodring, Wm. Hopkins, Elias Decker, Wm. Toy, Andrew Whims, Philip Shoemaker, Billingsly Shoemaker, James Sherdon, Wm. Cramer, Albert Oglert, Albert Jenkins, Joseph Dildine, John Todd, Wm. Todd, John Townsend, Wesley Todd, John Allgire, Zacharias Algire, John W. Needels, John Bennett, Frederick Swisher, Geo. Brown, Jackson Carder, John Rathmell, Daniel Crouse, Marcus Richardson, John Rager, John L. Stevenson, James Stevenson and John Shoemaker.

Along in the early "forties" (perhaps 1844 to 1846) a military organization flourished in Canal Winchester, known as:

Violet Guards

Among those most active in its organization was Jacob Schrock, although he was never a member, yet his was the only military funeral conducted by the company. He was buried in the Lutheran and Reformed graveyard. A salute was fired over the grave; quite a number of boys were sitting on the fence nearby, as boys will, and when the guns were discharged they were so taken by surprise that nearly all of them fell off the fence, backwards.

The company met for drill on the last Saturday of each month; at first, a fine of 50 cents was assessed for non-attendance, but as many failed to attend regularly the fine was advanced to $1.50; after this the attendance was always good, as wages were only about 75 cents per day.

On the return from the Pleasant Run encampment of the regiment, held at Lancaster, Ohio, the driver of the artillery crowded the team onto the pony squad several times, to their great annoyance, when Captain Potter gave them orders to use their bayonets at the next offense. This they did as they were crossing a bridge near Lancaster, causing the team, cannon, driver and all to land upside down in the stream below, a distance of some six feet.

A three days' encampment was held in Samuel Deitz's Grove, near Winchester. Their tents were made by the ladies of Winchester. White pants were worn on dress parade; elaborate helmets with bright shields and ostrich plumes, costing seven dollars each, also added to their attractiveness. One of these helmets is in the possession of the writer, through the kindness of Mr. John Brenner.

The following is as complete a list of the officers and members of this company as could be secured from surviving members; no records could be found: Dr. J. B. Potter, Captain; G. A. Finnefrock, First Lieutenant; Mr. Finnefrock moved away and Isaac Titus was elected First Lieutenant; John Hendricks, Second Lieutenant; Hinton Tallman, Color-bearer; Chas. B. Cannon, Joseph Miller, Jacob Harbaugh and

George Moore composed the Pony Squad; John Brenner and John Carnes were the Pioneers; Geo. McComb and John Kissell, Fifers; Jason Herrick and Henry Decker, Snare Drummers; Emanuel Harmon, Bass Drummer, and the following privates: Ervin Moore, James B. Evans, Chas. Lethers, Henry Fictore, John Harris, Geo. Harris, Simon Hansha, Isaac Ebright, Levi Kramer, Geo. Moore, John Deitz, Silas Hirkins, Alex. Dunlap, Wm. Curtis, Joe Bennadum, Eli Boyer, Philo Williams, Henry S. Herrick, Henry Schrock, Henry Zimmer, Peter Bolenbaugh, Levi Moore, John Pearcy, Benj. Shoemaker, Sol. Gayman, Wm. Leight, Julius W. Hische, Simon Matthews, David Garling and Henry Epley, Geo. M. B. Dove and Joe S. Johnson were markers.

Still another early military organization was what is now spoken of as Heston's Independent Company, of which John Heston was Captain; Samuel E. Kile, Lieutenant; Wm. Blair and James Canode, Fifers; James Blakely and Stephen McAdams, Snare Drummers; J. L. Champe and Geo. Champe, Bass Drummers; James Sandy, Benjamin Sims, Orange Barnhart, William Blakely and other members.

During the time of the Mexican War nine different boats were engaged to carry soldiers from Cleveland to Portsmouth. Among them was the *"Scioto"*—afterwards named the *"Ocean Wave"*—then owned and run by Chas. Campbell. The carpenters were just ready to raise the frame of Samuel Sharp's warehouse, south of Main Street along the canal, when Captain Campbell's boat load of soldiers came along. The timbers being very heavy, the soldiers were solicited to assist, which they agreed to do, providing someone could be found to play the snare drum. James Blakely, then being a member of a military company, put on his uniform and, after the raising, accompanied them for some miles.

Capt. Jacob V. Conklin of Groveport
45th Regiment O.V.I.

Pvt. John Walton
95th Ohio Volunteer Infantry

For the purpose of listing every man subject to military duty, the township was in 1863 divided into the following four military districts, viz.:

Military District No. 1

Commencing at the Ohio canal at the east line of the township, then north to northeast corner of Section No. 18; then west to the original county line; then south to the Ohio canal; then down the canal to the section line between Sections No. 25 and No. 26; then south to the Pickaway County line; then east to the Fairfield County line; then north on said line to the southwest corner of Section No. 31; then east to the southeast corner of Section No. 31; then north to the place of beginning.

Etching by Edwin Forbes 1876

Militiamen of District No. 1

J. W. Algire	James R. Algire	M. Allen
Levi Alspach	John Andrews	R. W. Bailey
L. C. Bartlitt	Christian Bickel	J. M. Blackwood
G. W. Blake	John Brixner	Peter Brown
Henry Brown	Charles Brown	Charles Bush
Amos Bush	C. B. Cannon	James Cannon
Leo F. Carson	Samuel Carty	Elijah Cassidy
O. P. Chaney	John Coleman	Gotleib Cook
Daniel Crouse	J. J. Cummins	B. F. Dagon
Jacob Dauterman	E. B. Decker	A. Decker
I. L. Decker	Elias Decker	George Derr
S. W. Dildine	William Dodson	G. M. B. Dove
William Farrand	George Farrand	John T. Flinchbaugh
J. W. Ford	Cyrus Fultz	Irvin Fultz
Moses Gayman	C. Gayman	David C. Gayman
Daniel Gayman	John Gehm	William Gladville
I. Glatfelter	Andrew Good	James Hamlin
Jacob Harbaugh	Geo. M. Harmon	Samuel Harmon
Henry Harpst	P. C. Harris	James Heffly
S. O. Hendren Jr.	Henry Hesser	J. W. Hische
John Karnes	G. G. Karnes	Simon Kissel
John Kissell	Malcolm Koch	George Krabbs
Henry Kramer	Levi Kramer	Elijah Kramer
Jerry Kramer	Jacob Kramer	Andrew Lehman
Solomon Lehman	Benjamin Lehman	Jacob Lehman
Washington Lehman	Abram Lehman Jr.	George Long
Peter S. Long	William Mason	James McKelvey
J. W. Meeker	W. J. Meeker	John Miller
W. P. Miller	A. C. Moon	Robert Moore
Jacob Moyer	J. D. Ordel	William Palsgrove
C. P. Rees	John A. Rhoads	James Robinson
William Root	Samuel Runkle	David C. Sarber
Jacob Sarber	Lew Sarber	M. D. L. Schoch
M. E. Schrock	Collin Schrock	A. Selby
Henry Shaffer	Jacob Shearer	A. A. Shortt
Jas. H. Somerville	Lewis B. Spangler	Emanuel Sparr
C. W. Speaks	George Steman	M. G. Stevenson
A. B. Stevenson	I. E. Stevenson	Harrison Tallman
John Trager	E. H. Walden	Peter Weber
M. C. Whitehurst	H. Will	John Williams Jr.
William L. Wilson	Henry Zarbaugh	Peter Zarbaugh
Charles Zarbaugh	Jacob Zarbaugh	

Military District No. 2

Commencing at the south line of township and the section line between No. 11 and No. 12, thence north on said line to the Ohio canal, thence down the canal to Groveport Bridge, thence across the canal, thence west on the Columbus and Groveport Pike to the west line of the township, thence south on said line to the southwest corner of the township thence east to the place of beginning.

Etching by Edwin Forbes 1876

Militiamen of District No. 2

Jacob Andrix	Thos. Begg	Malon A. Bishop
John Bishop	A. J. Bishop	C. Black
John Black	R. Blackwood	Wm. Blakely
Adam Brinker	Lew Bunn	Jacob Burger
James Burns	Joseph Caldwell	G. W. Canfield
A. T. Carder	Wm. Cawthon	G. P. Champe
H. L. Chaney	W. R. Coffman	A. I. Conn
Pat Corbett	M. Corbett	William Corbett
F. Cornell	John Cox Jr.	S. S. Crist
Joseph Crossley	Darius Cutshall	Daniel Davis
Napoleon Davis	Allen Davis	Geo. Davis
E. J. Decker	Wm. V. Decker	E. P. Decker
A. F. Dildine	C. P. Dildine	Z. D. Dildine
R. F. Dildine	W. H. Dunn	M. K. Earhart
Henry Easterday	Peter Egan	J. H. Evans
Henry Farrand	J. F. Finks	Ed Gares
Gamaliel Giberson	Jacob Glett	H. O. Glock
John Hamilton	Wm. Hanstine	J. R. Harrison
Adam Havely	F. Hefflinger	John Hefflinger
John O. Honoman	W. S. Hopkins	John Hillis
Wm. Keelan	Andy D. Kraner	I. M. Lechner
David Leigh	Ed Lincoln	J. Lincoln
H. Long	Pat. Lyons	Sol. Mason
Wm. McCarty	G. W. Miller	Joe Millizer
Jno. Murphy	Thos. Murphy	Marcus Nelson
Wm. Peer Jr.	Phil Pontius	F. G. Pontius
W. H. Pyle	I. Hunter Rarey	Gamaliel S. Rarey
John S. Rarey	A. B. Rarey	H. W. Rarey
Job Rohr	Chas. Saltzgeber	Lew Saltzgeber
Wm. Saltzgeber	Daniel Sawyer	J. H. Saylor
Wm. Seymour	J. Welt. Seymour	Thos. Seymour
G. L. Seymour	Geo. Seymour	James S. Seymour
C. E. Seymour	J. P. Sharp	Wm. Sharp
Mart. Shiry	B. C. Sims	G. L. Smith
Steve Smith	E. M. Strode	Irwin P. Swisher
H. C. Swisher	I. I. Swisher	Jerome Thompson
Volney Thompson	Robt. Thrush	Nathan Toy
Chas. Toy		David Tussing
Simon Van Home	Wm. Vance	Nathan Vance
Nathan Wahley	Chas. Wallace	Mart. Waltermire
David C. Weaver	Aug. Weiman	David Westenhaver
Chas. Williams	Geo. Williams	Philo Williams
W. R. Williams	Chas. Williams	R. L. Willie
A. Wilson	C. P. Woodring	Jacob Yarger
A. G. Zinn		

Military District No. 3

Commencing on the turnpike bridge in Groveport, thence northwest on said pike to the west line of the township, thence north on said line to the northwest corner of the township, thence east on the north line of the township to the northwest corner of section No. 3, thence south on said line to the Ohio canal, thence down said canal to the place of beginning.

Etching by Edwin Forbes 1876

Militiamen of District No. 3

Geo. S. Algire	John Algire	David Baugher
A. Behm	E. G. Behm	W. D. H. Blair
G. W. Blakely	Wm. Blakely	Henry Brooker
Ed. Brown	Ed. Burden	R. E. Burnham
Joe Callis	Burton Carey	Isaac Carey
Michael Carey	Syl. Carruthers	S. G. Carson
Wm. L. Carson	Thos. Champ	J. L. Champe
W. H. Chandler	Ol. Codner	Ed. Coffman
John Corbett	W. K. Cox	S. A. Darnell
E. P. Decker	John Dellinger	J. W. Dennis
Harrison Dennis	G. S. Dildine	John Dinan
J. M. Diviney	B. J. Dougherty	Geo. Emde
Wm. Ewing	Thos. Fagan	J. H. Fearn
C. W. Ferrington	Fred Finkbinder	I. W. Frey
Wm. C. Gill	J. A. Gray	Isaac Hamler
James Hamler	Isaac Hamler	Ralph Hanner
T. J. Harwood	Robert Hedren	Levi Hedrick
John Heil	Michael Heil	Samuel R. Helsel
Adam Helsel	Nic. Helsel	G. W. Helsel
G. L. Hendren	Wm. Hendren	Alex Hetchins
H. H. Hill	J. G. Howell	Jacob Schleppi
Samuel Jobs	B. H. Karnes	S. E. H. Kile
J. F. Kile	R. A. Kile	John A. Kile
James A. Kile	Eph. Kissel	Frank Kohlstein
Jacob Komp	Wm. Kramer Jr.	Daniel Lones
Adam Malee	David Mann	Noah McCormick
R. C. McGuffey	Clem McGuffey	Jacob Miller
Josiah Naftzger	Christ Naftzger	John Nau
A. P. Needels	G. W. Needels	C. F. Needels
J. H. Needels	John Nichols	Zebidee Parrot
Jerry Patsel	Wm. Peters	A. Minor Rarey
J. H. Reed	J. H. Rees	John Reicelt
John Reiling	Phil Reinhart	John Salee
Peter Sallee	Aug. Sallee	Henry Sanford
Jas. Savely	P. M. Schockley	Phil Schy
F. M. Senter	A. M. Senter	John G. Sharp
Abe Sharp	N. Shepherd	Lew Shirey
Wm. Shockley	A. J. Smith	Simon Smith
David Spangler	Michael Stevens	S. P. Suddick
A. L. Suddick	Richard Suddick	Phil Swartz
P. E. Swartz	Israel Swisher	John Swonger
W. H. Thompson	Wm. Townsen	Geo. W. Townsen
Meloy Townsen	John Townson	C. C. Weaver
H. P. Weaver	E. M. Welsh	Henry Whitzel
J. F. Wildermuth	H. F. Woodring	Al. Young
Val. Zimmer	Moses Zinn	

Military District No. 4

Commencing on the Ohio canal, on the section line between section No. 27 and No. 28, thence north on the said line to the north line of the township, thence east on the said line to the northeast corner of the township, thence south on township line to the section line between No. 7 and No. 18, then west on said line to the original county line, thence south on said line to the Ohio canal, thence down the canal to the place of beginning.

Etching by Edwin Forbes 1876

235

Militiamen of District No. 4

W. K. Algire	Henry Algire	Sol Alspach
Amos Alspach	S. J. Alspach	Jacob Alspach
Jacob Baughman	John Bear	T. B. Bennett
Wm. Bernard	Burr Boham	Geo. Boham
Chas. Bowen	Abs. Bowman	Jacob Bowman
John Brant	John Bricker	Jas. D. Brown
A. T. Brown	O. J. Brown	Geo. Brown
Samuel Brown	N. Champe	John Chaney
E. K. Chaney	Jacob Coble	Robt. Codner
Mark Codner	John Cunningham	Elisha Davis
Lang Decker	Mart Detwiler	G. H. Dildine
Jacob C. Dildine	R. G. Dildine	C. C. Dill
Andrew Dobbie	Levi Dochterman	F. Dochterman
Jas. Fagan	John Feasel	Samuel Ferguson
Adam Frame	Geo. Francisco	W. J. Godlove
John Imbody	Wm. Imbody	Jas. Imbody
M. E. Kalb	Daniel Ketchner	Geo. King
Jonas Kissel	Isaac Kissel	Jerry Kissel
John Kissel Jr.	W. R. Kraner	James Layton
Isaac Lehman	Henry Leidy	Wm. Leidy
G. D. Leidy	Geo. Leidy	David Martin
G. S. McGuffey	Ben Motts	Jacob Motz
Geo. B. Myers	F. F. Myers	John O'Roark
Jas. T. Pearcy	Geo. Perrin	Jas. Pickering
Price Powell	Wm. Purdy	Wm. H. Rager
Adam Rager	Geo. Ruse	Fin Ryan
Jas. Sandy	Samuel Shoemaker	Ed Shumaker
John Shuman	Wm. Sims	J. T. Sims
John Smith	Adam Smith	Jacob Smith
R. S. Stevenson	N. A. Stevenson	C. N. Stevenson
H. M. Swanker	Samuel Swonger	Henry Swonger
A. J. Taylor	G. W. Taylor	P. C. Tussing
Geo. Vandemark	Noah Vandemark	Jacob Vandemark
S. Wheeler	Allen M. Whims	Chas. Whims
S. H. Whims	A. J. Whims	Andrew Whims
Daniel Wright	David Wright	John T. Wright

In the spring of 1861, Dr. J. B. Potter and Philip Game recruited a company of some eighty men, with the understanding that Dr. Potter would be Captain and Mr. Game and J. C. Forbes, Lieutenants. The method pursued was to drive about in a wagon, with a flag, fifer and drummer and the general excitement incident to the war did the rest to fire the patriotism of those solicited. Lithopolis, Pickerington, and other towns were visited in this way. The citizens of Winchester provided meals and lodging for the men for about a week, while Dr. Potter went to see the governor about their enlistment and assignment. When he returned on April 22, 1861, and reported that the quota of men needed was already supplied, they met on High Street in front of Dr. Blake's office and disbanded.

In the summer of 1862, a meeting was held to formulate a plan to raise money to pay those enlisting from the township, a bounty. Under date of August 7, 1862, subscription papers with the following headings were circulated:

"We, the undersigned, each agree to pay the amount set opposite our names, to be equally divided between the volunteers, who have already, or, may hereafter enlist, under recent call of the President, for the first 300,000 men, and who may be enlisted at this place, to be paid to each volunteer as soon as he is accepted in the service, providing, however, that not more than forty dollars shall be paid to each volunteer, but any excess, over and above the said forty dollars, shall be applied to the relief of the families of said volunteers, or otherwise at the pleasure of the donors."

The writer has in his possession three different original copies of these subscription papers. We present the names and the amount subscribed on these papers:

First paper, M. C. Whitehurst, $50; Samuel Bartlitt, $50; Nathaniel Tallman, $50; Jacob Carty, $50; D. & C. Gayman, $100; W. L. Stevenson, $50; John R. Wright, $50; O. P. Chaney & Bro., $50; G. W. Kalb, $20; Jas. H. Somerville, $10; Samuel Hempy, $1 ; Daniel Bergstresser, $10; Wm. Allen, $5; A. Hathaway, $5; A. B. Stevenson, $5; C. W. Speaks, $5; Jeremiah Kissell, $3; Dr. G. W. Blake, $10; E. B. Decker, $25; Michael Schrock, $3; Elihu McCracken, $50; John Helpman, $25; John M.

Schroch, $10; A. C. Moon, $5; Dr. A. A. Short, $20; I. L. Decker, $10; Reuben Trine, $5; John Chaney, $50.

Second paper, Jacob Yarker, $1; Jacob Koble, $10; A. Willi, $5; Moses Seymour, $20; T. C. Hendren, $40; Fred Rarey, $5; F. G. Pontius, $10; W. P. Toy, $5.

Third paper, Jacob Arnold, $25; Moses Zinn, $50; C. P. Dildine, $100; G. W. Needels, $50; Wm. Pyle, $5; Jacob Swisher, $5; Fred Swisher, $25; S. R. Helsel, $5; Jacob Coble, $10.

The whole amount subscribed was $1,229.00. E. B. Decker was elected treasurer and the following twenty-eight men, who had enlisted, were paid forty dollars each: J. B. Evans, G. W. Bethel, Benton Kramer, Henry Game, Lewis Bowen, D. D. Leady, Mart. Kramer, John H. Foor, Joe Miller, Samuel E. Wright, H. H. Kalb, Alfred Cannon, Eli Holbert, Geo. T. Wheeler, Henry S. Binkly, Wm. Dellinger, Israel Gayman, S. E. Bailey, Chas. F. Yost, David Yost, Wm. McCracken, Amos Leady, John W. Kile, John Warner, Enoch Needels, Lincoln Stevenson, John Rager and Jackson Blakely, all these men were from this township.

In February, 1864, an organization was formed, called "*The Madison Township Military Bounty Society for the relief of the township from the Draft.*" Any one paying fifteen dollars, or more, into the treasury became a member, and it was resolved to pay each recruit who would credit himself to this township $100. C. P. Dildine President, A. Sharp Secretary and John Helpman Treasurer, were the officers. Local societies were formed at Groveport and Winchester; the officers of the latter were E. B. Decker President, M. G. Stevenson Secretary, John Helpman Treasurer. A solicitor was appointed for each school district.

The following' is a list of subscribers in February and March, 1864, and the solicitors by school districts:

Fractional district south of Creek. Michael Schrock solicitor, Henry Kramer, Jacob Kramer, Lewis Kramer, John D. Ortel, Carl Schrock.

District No. 19. Emanuel Sparr and Jas. Pickering solicitors, Irvin E. Stevenson, James Pickering, Emanuel Sparr, S. H. Tallman, Lee Kramer, Israel Glatfelter, Absalom Bowman, John R. Wright, Daniel Bush, Elizabeth Good, Elizabeth Kramer, Nathaniel Tallman and Andrew Good.

District No. **21.** J. Vandemark solicitor, Jacob Vandemark, Geo. Vandemark, Joseph Vandemark, Wm. K. Algire, Henry Algire, James Imbody, Geo. King, Jacob Alspach, Elihu McCracken, John Bicker, Wm. Perrin, Geo. Francisco.

District No. **9.** Samuel Detwiler solicitor, Samuel Detwiler, David Lehman, Samuel Detwiler Jr., Henry Leidy, Wm. Leidy, Henderson Miller, T. B. Bennett. Jacob Bowman, James D. Brown, Geo. W. Ruse, Jonathan Ruse, Samuel Swonger, Isaac Kalb, John Wright, Adam Rager.

District No. **22.** Jacob Lehman solicitor, Jacob Bishop, Samuel Runkle, A. F. Dildine, Geo. Long, Jacob Lehman, Andrew Lehman, G. W. Lehman, C. P. Dildine, Daniel Crouse, Simon Kissel, John Cummins, John Blackwood, Wm. Whaley, Elias Decker, Geo. Seymour, John Andrews. Malcolm Koch, Henry Farrand, Wm. Peer, Geo. Williams, A. F. Dildine, Philip Kuhns, Volney Thompson.

District No. **4.** Jacob Sarber and Phil. C. Tussing solicitors, Jacob Sarber, John Chaney Jr., E. K. Chaney, Adam Smith, P. C. Tussing, Wm. Mason, Henry Hesser, John Wood, Samuel O. Hendren, John Shuman, John Rager, P. C. Harris, Emanuel Beamerdife, Geo. Myers, Jackson Smith and Samuel Wheeler.

District No. **11.** Mathew E. Kalb, solicitor. N. A. Stevenson. M. E. Kalb, Joshua S. Stevenson, John Keltchner, G. W. Brown, David Martin, Owen J. Brown, Daniel Keltchner, F. Swonger, Robert Codner, Mark Codner, Jacob Coble, Wm. M. Sims, J. T. Piercy, Jeremiah Kissel, Allen T. Brown, Samuel Furgeson, G. W. Kalb, John T. Sims, Emanuel Bott, Fredrick Myers, John Kissel Jr., Reynolds Kraner, Simon Alspach.

District No. **18.** Jacob Shearer solicitor, Jacob Shearer, Abraham Lehman, A. T. Lehman, S. S. Lehman, Peter Brown, Chas. Brown, Benj. Lehman, J. K. Lehman, Henry Brown, Isaac Lehman. Chas. Bush, John Lehman.

District No. **18.** In Winchester, John Gehm, solicitor. M. C. Whitehurst, J. H. Sommerville, L. C. Bartlitt, O. P. Chaney, E. B. Decker, M. G. Stevenson, John Gehm, John Kissel, Jacob Dauterman, Jacob Zarbaugh, Peter Zarbaugh, John Trager, L. F. Carson, G. M. B. Dove. John Miller, H. W. Shaffer, Dr. G. W. Blake, David Gayman, Daniel Gayman, Henry Herbst, Mich. Allen, Peter Weber, Jacob Harbaugh, John Helpman, Henry Zarbaugh, Chas. Zarbaugh, Samuel Bartlitt, C. W. Speaks, W. P. Miller, C. P. Rees, Jno. T. Flinchbaugh, C. B. Cannon, A. Decker, Wm. Palsgrove, J. R. Algire, C. Gayman, Dr. A. A. Shortt, John

239

Chaney Sr., James McKelvey, J. W. Hische, Samuel Deitz, S. W. Dildine, Amon Algire, Henry Will, Jacob Moore, Christ Bickel, Grove G. Karns, Wm. Barnert, John Coleman, W. J. Meeker, J. W. Meeker, Daniel Bergstresser, Peter Bott, Geo. Derr, D. C. Sarber, Reuben Trine.

The following fifty-three recruits were paid from $90 to $150 each, or a sum total of $6,568.00 on the President's calls of February and March, 1864: Frederick Barbach, James Savely, James Conaway, E. P. Decker, Chas. Wallace, Serg. William Veiler, Robt. A. McGinnity, W. R. Borland, J. D. Woodall, W. J. McCloy, Elisha W. Beedle, Jacob R. Melborn, James Campbell, David McBeth, John Sheabon, Ferdinand L. Groom, Allen S. Felch, Geo. W. Bronton, Oliver C. Jones, Wm. W. Keyser, James Raynor, Jeremiah Hartin, James W. Wilson, John Bradshaw, Aaron Brown, Alonzo Conover, Mark Lane, Elmer P. Shepherd, Wm. Boroughs, James W. McKenzie, Abraham C. McLeod, Curtis B. Hare, John Corothers, Wyatt R. Johns, Patrick McGravan, Henry Archer, Simon McCarty, James Bird, Oliver C. Tarbot, Jerome Emmons, Grafton Pearce, John Newcomer, John Holzapple, Fredrick Stein, Geo. Wm. Lybrand, James T. Lybrand, John Benbow, John W. Bates, Chas. E. Bates, Ransford R. Whitehurst, Jacob E. Benner and James A. D. Smith.

We have before us one of the little books, furnished to each sub-school district solicitor, which contains the articles and rules of the society at Winchester, and these no doubt agree with those adopted by the township organization:

"This society shall be called the Winchester Military Bounty Society in aid of the Madison Township Society for the relief of the township from the draft.

"We hereby adopt the following rules for the government of this society:

"(1) This society shall have a president, a secretary and a treasurer.

"(2) The duties of the president shall be to preside at all the meetings.

"(3) The duties of the secretary shall be to keep the names of all the subscribers and all accounts necessary for the society.

"(4) The duties of the treasurer shall be to receive and pay out all the moneys belonging to said society.

"(5) The president, secretary and treasurer shall form a board to confer with the parent society and see that all moneys are duly expended and accounted for.

"(6) Each subscriber shall become a member of this society by subscribing his name and paying into the treasury not less than fifteen ($15) dollars,.

"(7) There shall be raised seven thousand three hundred ($7,300) dollars, so that each acceptable volunteer shall be paid one hundred ($100) dollars after the new recruit is credited for this township.

"(8) That each person subject to draft shall pay not less than fifteen ($15) dollars, and all other persons be requested to contribute to the same.

"(9) That in case the amount necessary is not all raised to release the township from the draft, the treasurer shall refund the amount subscribed by each person.

"(10) That in case the volunteers cannot all be had and any member of this society should be drafted and accepted, such member shall be paid one hundred ($100) dollars.

"(11) That if there should be any funds in the hands of the treasurer belonging to this society, when the men are all raised, unexpended, it shall be refunded 'pro rata' to each subscriber."

At a meeting held at Canal Winchester, O., March 19, 1864, *"To raise an additional fund to clear Madison Township from a draft on the last call by the President for two hundred thousand (200,000) more men,"* The foregoing Articles and Rules were adopted with two amendments, to-wit: Article (6) six was amended making ten ($10) dollars a membership instead of fifteen ($15) dollars. Article (7) seven was amended to insert three thousand three hundred ($3,300) dollars to be raised in Madison Township instead of seven thousand three hundred ($7,300) dollars on former two calls.

In response to the next "call" (September, '64), the following twenty-eight men were paid $11,270, receiving about $400 each: Geo. W. Williams, Albert R. Harley, Joseph Gibbard, Robt. Turner, Chas. Emrick, Wm. Johnson, Henry Harwood, John Wiles, Wm. Warner, Geo. D. Coe, James W. Combs, D. J. Hussey, James Robinson, Karl Hoffman, John Green, Samuel Campbell, David Wheeler, Geo. W. Alwood, Eli Francis, James W. Hill, William Cutmore, Edward Wilson, Francis M. Stanfield, Jackson Miller, Robt. Davis, James O. Adams, Geo. W. Adams and Chas. E. Harrison.

On the last "call," December 19, 1864, the following persons subscribed the amount indicated by the figures (in dollars) which follows their names:

John O'Roark, 12: Jacob Vandemark, 30; Geo. Vandemark, 30: Noah Vandemark, 20; Geo. Francisco, 35; Jacob Alspach, 15; Elihu McCracken, 55 ; John Wingert, 35; G. H. Dildine, 10; H. Algire, 18; James Imbody, 35; Jacob Farrell, 15; John Ferall, 40; Samuel Hempy, 20; G. W. Burman, 35; John Bricker, 25; Wm. Perrin, 40; Wm. R. Algire, 60; Geo. W. Ruse, 110; Henderson Miller, 50; Jonathan Ruse, 60; Jonathan B. Leasure, 10; John Wright, 128; John T. Wright, 20; Samuel Detwiler, 140; Samuel Detwiler, Jr., 60; Jacob Bowman, 140; Wm. Leidy, 60; Isaac Kalb, 55; Jacob Baughman, 45; Irvin E. Stevenson, 100; Absalom Bowman, 60; Levi Kramer. 30; Amos Bush, 25; Chas. Bush, 25; Daniel Bush, 90; Henry Brown, 10; S. H. Tallman, 70; Israel Glatfelter, 10; Emanuel Sparr, 20; James Pickering, 25; Wm. Ashley, 5; N. Tallman, 30; Jacob Shearer, 75; L. C. Bartlit, 100; C. Gayman, 140; John Miller, 70; J. W. Hische, 50; Henry Zarbaugh, 65; Wm. P. Miller, 100; Peter Weber, 45; David Gayman, 55; James R. Algire, 40; C. P. Rees, 30; J. T. Flinchbaugh, 70; John Trager, 35; Peter Brown, 35; Abraham Lehman, 145; Benj. Lehman, 20; Chas. Brown, Sr., 75; Daniel Bergstresser, 20; Dr. G. W. Blake, 50; Geo. Derr, 15; Wm. Caslow, 35; James Fay, 100; John Kissell, 70; Whitehurst & Carty, 70; Jacob Harbaugh, 40; Amon Algire, 20; Jacob Zarbaugh, 30; Andrew Lemon, 20; Samuel Deitz, 35; Leo F. Carson, 10; Daniel Gayman, 80; John M. Schoch, 15; Wm. Palsgrove, 38; Austin Decker, 35; E. B. Decker, 60; Grove G. Karnes, 25; John Gehm, 75; Henry Herbst, 20; Jerry Kramer, 75; G. W. Lehman, 15; Jacob Moore, 20; Chas. Brown, Jr., 15; Gotleib Cook, 15; Wm. Wilson, 10; Henry Will. 25; John Chaney, 55; P. C. Tussing, 55; Isaac Lehman,

85; L. G. Sarber, 45; Samuel Wheeler, 25; Jacob Sarber, 50; Jackson Smith, 50; David Lehman, 45; John Shuman, 50; Abe S. Lehman, 75; Adam Smith, 35; Robt. Lowry, 30; Joseph Rodenfels, 20; Emanuel Bemisdorfer, 25; George Bareis, 15; John Rodenfels, 3; John H. Tussing, 3; Levi Dauterman, 4; David Sarber, 2; John Wood, 5; Chas. Bower, 25; David Martin, 90; E. Kissell, 60; Joshua S. Stevenson, 20: Solomon Alspach, 50; N. A. Stevenson, 25; Samuel Shoemaker, 70; John Courtright, 25; Jacob Coble, 20; Simon Alspach, 35; Amos Alspach, 40; John Alspach, 75; John Lehman, 35; Oliver Codner, 90; Daniel Kelchner, 75; Fred Myers, 25; O. J. Brown, 70; Jacob Burky, 5; W. R. Kraner, 10; Henry W. Shaffer, 85; C. B. Cowan, 30; Reuben Trine, 5; Jacob Dauterman, 25; James B. Evans, 10; John Karnes, 5; John Schrock, 30; Collen Schrock, 50; John Helpman, 50; Mrs. Elizabeth Good, 10; S. Knepper, 10; Ed K. Chaney, 50; Oliver P. Chaney, 50; John Chaney, Sr., 60; Jacob C. Komp, 10; Dr. A. A. Short, 25; Henry Leidy, 40; Samuel Brown, 50; J. B. Bennett, 30; B. B. Shoemaker, 10; Jerry Kalb, 15; Sam O. Hendren, 30; P. C. Harris, 50; Geo. Myers, 5; Wm. Mason, 15; Daniel Motz, 10; Henry Motz, 5; Joseph Vandemark, 60.

(*Note.—No subscription lists could be found of the local society at Groveport, but the following persons turned money into the treasurer's hands and were perhaps the solicitors for that part of the township, viz.: Moses Zinn, C. P. Dildine, E. Behm, Abraham Sharp, C. P. Woodring and Kalita Sallee.*)

In addition to the above subscription, on February 7, 1865, the Township Trustees levied a tax of $4,000, to relieve the township from this "Draft," and one week later issued forty bonds of $100 each, made payable March 1 and September 1, 1866, and the following persons advanced the money on them, viz: Moses Seymour, 3; Rebecca Ramsey, 2; Augustus Sallee, 5; Mitchell Allen, 6; Chas. W. Speaks, 6; Abraham Lehman, 8; Elihu McCracken, 5; Henry Algire, 1; Elizabeth Good, 4.

With this money the following forty-one recruits were paid $20,695, ranging from $450 to $525 each, viz.: Joshua Miller, Amos G. McCormick, Wallace Bennett, Simeon L. B. McMiller, Wm. H. Liverpool, John Hood, Peter Rivers, Chas. Albright, Peter Becker, Christ Benninghoff, Mathias Blinn, Martin Decker, August Fisher, John A. Geiszler, Henry Hach, Chas. Stark, Jacob Solomon, Genzs Schaf, Christian Weber, Otto Hels, Anion Luft, John L. Stulzig, John King, Geo. W. Foster, Alfred Feringer, Isaac Hemler, Martin S. Seymour, Gottlieb

Lochenmaier, Frank Wehrle, Louis Schmelt, Harvey D. Harris, David D. Crompton, Michael Henry, Fredrick Kemmerle, Ralph Hammer, James Logan, Wm. A. Stipher, James W. Pierce, Wm. R. Ramsey, Chas. B. Cannon and Jacob Dauterman. The three last mentioned enlisted from this township and were paid $525 each, the only ones who were paid so large an amount. In this way the township furnished 150 men to whom they paid bounty to the amount of $39,762.

On June 3, 1865, at a meeting for the settling up of the affairs of the society, the treasurer reported a balance of $132.70, which he was instructed to divide equally among the veteran volunteers of the 46th O. V. I.—who had re-enlisted while in Tennessee—supposed to be eleven in number.

At a called meeting held December 2, 1865, the above action was rescinded; the treasurer reported that $165.60 had been collected, making a total of $298.30 and it was then determined to divide this amount equally among the re-enlisted veterans credited to this township who had not already received local bounty, and $100.67 was accordingly paid to the following ten men: G. F. Thompson, Albert McCarty, Robt. John, N. Evans, J. W. Wallace, A. Mansfield, J. W. Andrews, F. Drum, Peter Miller and S. Mumhal. After these were paid the treasurer, John Helpman, paid the balance, $182.63, into the hands of W. W. Kile, Township Treasurer.

The following list of the wives of soldiers who were entitled to monthly bounty appears on the Township Trustees' records:

Julia Ann Robinson, Eliza Yourd, Rhoda Skinner, Elizabeth Hodge, Jane Gares, Samantha Hamler, Sarah Hampson, Mary Herrick, Permelia Sarber, C. Remaley, Mahala Miller, M. E. Fry, E. M. Stevenson, Rebecca Conaway, Mrs. Van Horne, Amanda Durant, Sarah Williamson, Eliza Blakely, Ann Kraner, Abigail Reeves, Amanda Edwards, M. Himrod, Julia Binkley, Lucinda Wheeler, Mary Dellinger, Mary Yost, Susan Dagon, C. L. Leady, E. J. Hodge, Susan Miller, Jane Gillett, Mrs. G. Rei, M. E. Travis, Kate Adams, H. A. Thompson, Mrs. Gayman, Mary Yarger, Mrs. Burnham, Mrs. Hedrick, E. J. Kraner, Melisa Smith, Mary Hesser, Sarah Moore, Catharine Kramer, L. F. Williams, Mrs. Davis, Mrs. Fink, Mrs. Corbett, Mrs. Milliser, Mrs. Barnhart, D. B. Campbell heirs, C. Lester, Mrs. Coffman, Priscilla Savely, Mrs. Zimmerman, Mrs. Bailey, Mary Holzapple, Mary Cannon, R. L. Stevenson and E. E. Clark.

The following soldiers are buried in Union Grove Cemetery, near Winchester:

Rufus W. Bailey, Co. B, 178th O. V.I.

Lewis W. Bowen, Co. D, 95th O.V.I.

Rev. C. W. Bostwick, 149th O. V. I.

Wm. Badger, Co. C, 95th O. V. I.

Peter Brown, Co.__, 43d O. V. I.

Chas. B. Cannon, Co. C, 191st O.V.I.

Wm. Cater, Co. H, 1st Battery, 15th U. S.I.

R. I. Cromwell, Co. G, 133d O. V. I.

 Co. C, 191st O. V. I.

Leroy Dibble, Co. D, 22d O.V.I., later lieutenant Co. F, 187th O. V. I.

Henry Game, Co. D, 95th O.V.I.

Philip Game, Co. __ , 15th U. S. I.

Wm. Hesser, Co. B, 113th O. V.I.

R. T. Hummell, Co. G, 133d O. V. I.

John W. Kile, Co. B, 113th O. V. I.

A. D. Kraner, 180th O. V. I.

Noah Looker, Co. __, 46th O. V. I.

S. B. McFadden, Co. B, 52d U. S. Colored

H. P. Moore, Co. F, 8th Indiana

Cyrus Miller, Co. B, 113th O. V. I.

Dr. J. B. Potter,, Surgeon 30th O. V. I.

Martin Root, Co. F, 15th U. S. I.

Wm. Stenrock, U.S. Navy (Pa.)

James Sandy, O. V. I.

Lincoln Stevenson, Co. B, 113th O. V. I.

Leonard Sarber, Co. H, 18th U.S. I.

Edward Selby, Co. H. 63d O. V.I.

John Stotts, Co. D, 38th O. V.I.

John Shaffer, Co. D, 13th O. V. I.

Adam Shaner, Co.__, _____

Samuel Travis, Co. A, 160th O. V.I.

B. F. Trine, Co. A, 2d Bat., 15th U. S. I.

Geo. T. Wheeler, Co. B, 113th O. V. I.

In the Mennonite Graveyard:

Isaac Detwiler, Co.__, 1st Bat., 15th U.S.I.

Samuel Hare, Co. __,__

John Leidy, Co. F, 1st O. V. I.

Henry R. Strohn, Co. F. 159th O. V. I.

Theobald Phaler, Co. B, 6th U. S. Cavalry

In the Raver Graveyard:

Adam Raver, Co__, __.

In the Hoshor's Graveyard:

Frank Bland, Co. A, 1st Bat., 15th U. S. I.

In the Job's Graveyard:

Wm. Arnold, Co. F, 95th O. V. I.

John Cherry, Co. __,____;

____ Smith, Co.__, ____.

It has been the custom for many years for the Mayor of Winchester and Alfred Cannon Post to raise a joint committee to arrange for the proper observance of "Decoration Day." The usual custom is to decorate the graves in Raver's, Hoshor's and Job's in the forenoon, something after the following order:

Leaving town at about 7:30 a. m., at each graveyard a short program being observed, consisting of a song, prayer, short address and closing ode, arriving at Winchester at about 11:00 o'clock. Various programs have been arranged for the afternoons, when the graves in the Mennonite and Union Grove are decorated. Some of the programs have provided for very simple and impressive services by Alfred Cannon Post; others have been rendered by local "talent"; still others by foreign speakers. The exercises usually take place surrounding the Gunboat mound erected by the members of Alfred Cannon Post in Union Grove Cemetery, but they have been observed in Tallman's and Lehman's Groves and in Game's Opera House. The following is one of the more elaborate programs observed in 1890: The procession was formed on High Street in the following order:

1st, Drum Corps; 2d, Potter Light Guards; 3d, Company of 24 girls, with flowers, under command of Capt. Philip Game; 4th, Alfred Cannon Post; 5th, ex-soldiers not members of G. A. R.; 6th, Citizens on foot; 7th, school children in wagons; 8th, speakers in carriages; 9th, Citizens in carriages.

Exercises at Cemetery: Decoration of graves by company of girls; song; G. A. R. service; prayer.

Exercises at Lehman's Grove: Two songs, one by school children and one by choir; prayer; two songs; address by Rev. J. C. Jackson, D. D.; two songs and benediction.

At the close of the exercises held in Tallman's grove in 1882—it was estimated that one thousand persons were in attendance—a movement was inaugurated looking towards the erection of a Soldiers' Monument. One hundred and fifty dollars ($150.00) in subscriptions and cash was secured and a meeting called for the purpose of organizing a Monumental Association. This meeting was held in the Town Hall on Friday evening, June 2, 1882. A temporary organization was formed and named *"The Soldiers' Monumental Association of Canal Winchester and Vicinity,"* with John Helpman, President; Geo. F. Bareis, Secretary, and Rev. A. C. Kelly, Treasurer. The object was to secure two thousand ($2.000) dollars with which to erect a Soldiers' Monument in Union Grove Cemetery. A committee, consisting of John Helpman, Henry S. Binkly, Capt. Philip Game, Garrett W. Miller, Jacob L. Bowman, George Loucks and Capt. John W. Kile, was appointed to solicit funds and instructed to call a meeting for permanent organization, when five hundred ($500) dollars was secured. Nothing tangible came from this movement which had so propitious a beginning.

Potter Light Guards

On March 2d, 1878, Co. H. was mustered in by Col. Geo. D. Freeman of the 14th Reg., O. N. G. Philip Game, Captain; Brice Taylor, First Lieutenant; Wm. H. Schrock, Second Lieutenant. There was no change in the commissioned officers during the five years' service except that Brice Taylor resigned and John C. Speaks was commissioned to fill the vacancy.

Co. H was named *"The Winchester Guards,"* but at the annual encampment held at Delaware in 1879 the name was changed to *"The Potter Light Guards,"* in honor of Major Joseph B. Potter, M. D.

When Capt. Game's commission expired on March 2, 1883, Lieutenant John C. Speaks was elected and commissioned Captain and served as such until he was elected Major of the 14th Regiment. Geo. W. Tooil was then elected Captain. His profession, that of teaching school, took him to Tarlton, Ohio, thus depriving the company of the personal oversight of the Commanding Officer. The lack of interest of the members of the company, as well as of the citizens soon manifested itself and continued to wane until on January 4, 1891, the officers and men were honorably discharged and the company transferred to Portsmouth, Ohio, and thus ended an organization that was once the pride of the community.

Company H experienced and performed with credit and honor active service at the Cincinnati riot in 1884. One night at Carthage, Ohio, they rested on their arms, expecting momentarily to be called to the Hocking Valley mines during the strikes. They had a position of honor at the Garfield obsequies in Cleveland, standing guard near the vault in Lakeview Cemetery. Annual encampments were held at the following places during the time Company H belonged to the 14th Regiment, viz.: Marysville, 1878: Delaware, 1879; Niagara Falls, 1880; Lakeside, 1881; Detroit, 1882; Cuyahoga Falls, 1883 ; Franklin Park. Columbus, 1884; brigade encampment, Columbus, 1885; Springfield, 1886; Lancaster, I887: from this encampment they went to Gettysburg, Baltimore, Washington, Columbus, 1888; New York City, 1889; Toledo, Presque Isle, 1890; Marion, 1891.

The following list comprises the names of the original members as well as all those who become members during the first five years of Company H's organization:

Chas. Allen, Robt. Allen, Geo. Arnold, Thomas Arnold, Geo. Bush, Wm. Bush, Homer Binkley, Elmer Binkley, Milton Boyd, Stephen Boyd, Reuben Boyd, Chas. Blake, Ed. C. Brenner, Wm. Bailey, Martin Crook, John Chaney, Ed. C. Chaney, Arthur Chaney, John T. Corbett, Wm. Cutch, B. F. Champe, Wm. Cater, Alf. Carder, R. S. Codner, Alf. Cannon, Granville Derr, W. Dennis, James M. Evans, Chas. Evans, Richard Fulton, Sylvester Foor, Wm. Foor, Darius Fenstermaker, Abe L. Good, Nobel Griffith, Philip Game, D. H. Glick, Chas. Gibson, James Gibson, Isaac Hummel, Fred Henry, Geo. W. Himrod, John Helpman, Jr., Chas. Hische, Frank Harpst, W. Hockinsmith, Harry Hampson, Geo. Hodge, Thos. Hodge, J. W. Hudson, Wm. Hunter, Chas. Kuqua, Sam Kuqua, Aaron Kissel, Geo. Kildow, Seymour Justice, Stephen Lester, John E. Lawyer, Oscar E. Miller, Geo. W. Miller, Chas. W. Miller, Ed. J. Moore, J. S. Mathias, W. L. Ringer, J. P. Rager, Albert Speaks, John C. Speaks, J. W. Shoemaker, Chas. Shoemaker, Geo. Shoemaker, N. O. Selby, Wm. Smith, John Sunday, Warren C. Somerville, S. C. Swonger, Wm. Schock, Robt.

Shaner, John Southworth, Chas. Stewart, Ed. Selby, Geo. Sarber, Brice Taylor, B. F. Trine, D. H. Tallman, L. W. Tisdale, T. F. Ungemaugh, Wm. Wilson, W. L. Walters, Adam Weber, Geo. Will, Isaac Wright, W. S. Weaver, Geo. Yost, John L. Yourd and B. F. Zinn. Arth. A. Chaney was one of the snare drummers, although at the time of the organization not yet fourteen years of age.

After March 2, 1883, the following became members:

James Allen, James S. Adams, Emmet Ashe, Chas. H. Anderson, J. W. Anderson, C. A. Andrews, James Armstrong, Ed. E. Adams, Wm. Bailey, Vet., Geo. Billingsly, Frank Busch, Homer Binkly, Vet., Robt. Boyer, Daniel G. Boyer, Homer Boyd, Ed. J. Bennett, Wiley Brown, John Brown, Wm. F. Bartlitt, Morgan Boyer, Frank W. Boyer, H. J. Bope, H. C. Brogler, Chas. Boyer, John Benedum, Chas. Baughman, Eber L. Boyd, A. Bope, R. C. Broyler, G. W. Boyer, E. Biddle, G. W. Cook, Edward Colman, Henry A. Colman, Wm. Cole, Alfred Cannon, Vet., Wm. Colman, G. C. Courtright, Albert Crebbs, C. W. Campbell, Louis Crogge, John Cunningham, James W. Cunningham, Herb. S. Cannon, Jesse Cannon, Chas. Dauterman, Oliver P. Dunlop, Chas. F. Dunlop, W. A. Delong, D. L. Davis, W. W. Davis, Chas. Evans, Vet., Lestie Fulton, C. W. From, E. C. Fisher, Wm. Fletcher, David H. Glick, Vet., Wm. S. Gayman, Chas. F. Gorman, Frank Grove, Jacob Geishart, Frank Hische, Charles Hische, Vet., John W. Hische, B. B. Holland, Ed. P. Hamler, Chas. Hall, Harry Justice, Henry Johnson, F. L. Johnson, Wm. Komp, Elmer Kramer, Chas. F. Koffits, John Kramer, Bert Kramer, Henry Krohn, Chas. B. LeCrone, Wm. H. Mast, Clement Moore, Riley Marr, James A. McKelvey, Geo. E. McKelvey, Thos. E. Moss, Thad Miller, D. S. Miller, A. G. Miller, Ed. S. McFadden, Henry A. Miller, John Mosier, Milton A. Miller, _____ Outcalt, John Pickering, James P. Roberts, Chas. Raver, L. Rowe, L. C. Raha, Chas. H. Shoemaker, Vet., John C. Speaks, Vet., John Smith, Wm. Speaks, Ed. Selby, Vet., Geo. Shoemaker, Vet., Chas. Slough, Daniel Stack, Chas. E. Shortt, Wm. Swisher, Van A. Snyder, James W. Spencer, Chas. Seibert, K. S. Seibert, Chas. Sunday, G. C. Snyder, Harry Schrock, Samuel Travis, Wm. S. Tussing, Grant Travis, E. J. Travis, L. A. Trine, Geo. W. Tooill, J. E. Tussing, Chas. K. Taylor, Wm. E. Thompson, Wm. Tisdale, Chas. G. Violet, Chas. A. Werner, John Worrell, Marion Washbourne, Amos Watters, W. L. Watters, Vet., Daniel H. Will, Chas. F. Wolenzine, A. M. Washbourne, Alva B. Walters, Finley Walters, J. W. Wildermuth, H. J.

Wildermuth, W. P. Wagoner, E. O. Weist, George Yost, Vet., Frank Young, John Zahn, Edward Zirkle.

The following is a list of the commissioned officers who served with Company H during the period in which the organization was located at Canal Winchester, viz.:

Captains: Philip Game, John C. Speaks and Geo. W. Tooill.

First Lieutenants: Brice Taylor, John C. Speaks, Wm. Schrock, Wm. L. Walters, Charles Slough and F. M. Van Buskirk.

Second Lieutenants: Wm. Schrock, Geo. W. Tooill, Harry A. Miller and Edward O. Weist.

The following men from this township enlisted for service in the Spanish-American War:

Major John C. Speaks, 1st Battalion, 4th Regiment, O. V. I.

Sergeant, Ed. S. McFadden, Co. G, 4th O. V. I.

Corporal, Chas. E. Evans, Co. G, 4th O. V. I.

Eber L. Boyd, Co. B, 4th O. V. I.

C. C. Bennett, Co. B, 4th O. V. I.

Frank C. Dauterman, Co. B, 4th O. V. I.

Charles Sponsler, Co. B, 4th O. V. I.

Ralph W. Taylor, Co. B, 4th O. V. I.

Chas. K. Taylor, Co. C, 4th 6. V. I.

Fred Schrock, Co. F, 4th O. V. I.

Ben Himrod, Battery H, 1st O. V. A.

R. E. Wright, Co. A, 3d O. V. I.

Jess G. Dauterman, Co. I, 12th Minn. V. I.

W. A. Tallman, artificer Co. D, 6th O. V. I.

Nevin Loucks, Hospital Corps.

W. L. Powell, Troop D. 1st O. V. C.

T. Heise, Troop D, 1st O. V. C.

H. Willie, Troop D, 1st O. V. C.

E. E. Add, Troop D, 1st O. V. C.

E. M. Cavinee, Co. A, 4th O. V. I.

Ervin Simms, Co. A, 4th O. V. I.

Edw. Johnson, Co. A, 4th O. V. I.

Turner Carder, Co. A, 4th O. V. I.

Homer Cramer, Co. A, 4th O. V. I.

H. Wallis, Co. A. 4th O. V. I.

S. French, Co. A, 4th O. V. I.

E. A. Cunningham (Angle), Co. B, 4th O. V. I.

Jesse Thrush, Co. B, 4th O. V. I.

Edw. Simms, Co. F, 4th O. V. I.

T. Eberly, Ind.

James F. Roberts, Co. D, 3d O. V. I.

Corporal Claude Stout, Co. B, 4th O. V. I.;

R. R Shaw, 13th Signal Corps

H. R. Rarey, 13th Signal Corps

Sergeant Roy Willie, U. S. Hospital Corps

George Gill, 17th U. S. Inf.

From Lithopolis:

Lieut. F. L. Oyler, Co. B, 4th O. V. I.

F. E. Groves, Co. B., 4th O. V. I.

Thomas Decker, Co. H. 158th Ind.

From Carroll:

L. Herman Wagner, Co. I, 4th O. V. I.

Ben J. England, Co. I, 4th O. V. I.

From Brice

S. England, Co. C, 4th O. V. I.

F. Swanger, Battery H, 1st O. V. A.

From Pickerington:

Edw. Milnor, Co. A. 7th O. V. I.;

Wm. Brenneman, 17th U. S. I.;

Arch. Hummell, 17th U. S. I.

The 14th Regiment, O. N. G., was merged into the 4th Regiment, O. V. I. at the beginning of the Spanish-American war, which explains why so many of the "boys" from Madison Township were members of the 4th Regiment.

On Friday evening, October 26, 1898, a meeting was held at the Town Hall in Winchester of the ex-members of Company H for the purpose of arranging to go to Columbus on the following Sunday to take part in the reception of the 4th Regiment, O. V. I., who were to arrive on that day. Some 40 of the former members of Co. H were in line under the command of Capt. Philip Game. A large number of *"citizens"* also accompanied them to Columbus. A reception was arranged for those who went to the war from Winchester. A committee was appointed consisting of Wm. L. Walters, C. F. Dunlop and Dr. W. S.

Gayman, who were to act with a committee appointed by Mayor O. P. Gayman, viz.: Dr. J. W. Shook and Wm. D. Boyer. This committee arranged the following program, which was carried out on Wednesday evening, November 9, 1898:

Six o'clock dinner at D. E. Alspach's Restaurant; At 7:45, Game's Opera House; Hymn, America. Address of Welcome by Mayor O. P. Gayman: Response by Rev. A. Snyder; Impromptu Speeches by Rev. J. P. Stahl, Geo. F. Bareis, Capt. Philip Game, Rev. W. L. Alexander and Supt. of Schools, U. S. Brandt, and Corporal Ed. S. McFadden spoke for the boys. The musical part of the program consisted of a solo, *"When the Boys Come Home,"* by Mrs. J. L. Chaney; Piano duet, Mrs. J. L. Chaney and Miss Jessie Chaney; Piano solo, by Miss Ruth Stahl, Song; Duet, by Misses Madge Chaney and Kate Shook; and solos were sung by Miss Alice Snyder and Mr. W. D. Beeks. Major John C. Speaks sent the following message: *"It is impossible for me to attend your meeting to-night, but you may say to the audience that no braver soldiers ever entered the field than the boys from your place."*

The following were present and occupied seats on the platform: Edward S. McFadden, E. L. Boyd, C. C. Bennett, Frank C. Dauterman, Chas. Spousler, Ralph W. Taylor, Chas. K. Taylor, Ben. Himrod and George Martin, a former Winchester boy, Co. G, 17th U. S. I.

Irvin E. Simms died August 31, 1898 at Guayama, Porto Rico, and was buried September 1, with military honors. His body was brought back from Porto Rico and reinterred in Union Grove Cemetery on April 30, 1899.

Adrian S. Foor died July 2, 1898 at Santiago de Cuba. He enlisted in Co. A, 17th Reg., U. S. I., and was killed in battle. His remains arrived at Lithopolis, on Sunday April 2, 1899 and the funeral took place on the following Sunday April 9, and was attended by Winchester lodge, Knights of Pythias in a body, His body lies in the Lithopolis Cemetery.

Alfred Cannon Post, G. A. R., No. 261

This post was named after Alfred Cannon, who enlisted July 2, 1862 in Co. D, 95th, O. V. I., *"that his name and the story of his self-sacrifice may ever be remembered."*

While confined in Andersonville prison, an exchange of prisoners was made; lots were cast to determine who should go free. Alfred Cannon drew one of the lucky numbers, but handed it to a comrade who had a family at home, saying *"Go home to your family,"* and he himself staid in prison where he afterwards died. His remains are interred in the National Cemetery at Salisbury, N. C., his grave is numbered 470.

The following sketch was read by Capt. Philip Game at the celebration of the 25th anniversary of the founding of the G. A. R., held in the M. E. Church on Monday evening, April 6, 1891: (The Post occupied seats on the west and Potter Light Guards on the east side of the room.)

"Alfred Cannon Post, No. 261, Department of Ohio, G. A. R., was instituted October 3, 1882, by Dept, Com. Chas. T. Clark assisted by Wm. J. Elliott and others, with the following charter members; Mitchell Allen, S. E. Bailey, Henry S. Binkly, Martin Crooks, Israel Gayman, Wm. Hesser, Wm. Harold, Wm. Helpman, John S. Lehman, Philip Game, Walter Mundell, Jacob Moore, Rev. D. Y. Murdock, Thomas Morton, Major J. B. Potter M. D., Wm. Schrock, N. O. Selby, James Palsgrove, Samuel Travis, Brice Taylor, Geo. T. Wheeler and Chas. F. Yost, 25 in all. The following were the first officers, Dr. J. B. Potter, Com., J. B. Evans, Sen. V. Com., Walter Mundell, Jr. V. Com., D. Y. Murdock, Chap., Philip Game, Officer of the Day, S. E. Bailey, Officer of the Guard, C. F. Yost, Q. M. Total membership to April 1, 1882, 82; loss by card, discharge, removal and death 42. The oldest and youngest members are present tonight. Comrade Evans enlisted at the age of 52 years, his present age is 81. and Rev. C. W. Bostwick enlisted when a boy of 17, his present age is 41 years, difference in their ages is 38 years, present average age of those enlisted 51 years."

The following have been the commanders; J. B. Potter, 1882-1883; Walter Mundel, 1884-1885; Henry H. Dibble, 1886-1887, 1892-1903; Philip Game, 1888-1889, 1894-1897, 1899-01; O. L. Dibble, 1890; J. K. Miller, 1891; S. E. Bailey, 1898.

Besides the charter members the following names have been enrolled: O. L. Dibble, Samuel S. Lehman, John Sunday, John Quick, Eli Lehr, Andrew Burnside, Cheney Buckingham, Dr. Augustine Starr, O. J. Lawyer, Dr. Milton Valentine, Jacob Dauterman, Dr. Geo. S. Courtright, Israel E. Crumley, David Baker, Hiram Shaffer, Jacob Sipe, Martin Flowers, J. K Miller, John Walton, Lewis Junkhurth, John F. Stallsmith, Hiram F. Hays, Joseph Burgoon, John W. Bowen, Sol. S. Lehman, Samuel Armstrong, Henry H. Dibble, George W. Foor, Rev. Ralph Watson,

Samuel S. Strunk, Jacob Kuhn, Wm. H. Cater, Noah Lehman, H. J. Fulton, Aaron S. Smith, Orrin White, Ansel Walters, Stephen A. Lester, Leroy S. Dibble, Robt. H. Lawyer, James N. Tussing, Reuben McThomas, John Shaffer, Jacob Lepps, Michael A. Ebright.

The following are deceased, viz:

Jacob Dauterman, January 3, 1884; Dr. J. B. Potter, March 27, 1887; Reuben McThomas, July 26, 1888; John Shaffer, August 22, 1888; Wm. H. Cater, December 9, 1888, Hiram F. Hays, June 19, 1890; Dr. Milton Valentine, July 2, 1891; Rev. C. W. Bostwick, July 10, 1891; Wm. Hesser, March 7, 1892; M. A. Ebright, June 13, 1892; Orrin White, Nov. 3, 1892; Leroy S. Dibble, July 5, 1900; Henry S. Binkley, July 29, 1899; Wm. Helpman, May 24, 1899; Samuel Travis, July 30, 1900; Geo. T. Wheeler, February 14, 1898; Philip Game, February 15, 1902.

Sons of Veterans

Philip Game Camp, No. 137, Sons of Veterans, was organized and mustered in on September 8, 1886, by E. H. Archer of the Adjutant General's office, Columbus, Ohio. The officers were S. E. Bailey, Capt.; Wm. S. Tussing, 1st Lieut., Anaxy Ringer, 2nd Lieut.; John Adams, Chaplain; Chas. C. Dibble, Orderly Sergt.; Ben. F. Lehman, Quartermaster Sergt.; Samuel Burnsides, P. Gd.; Geo. W. Smith, Capt. of the Guard, Chas. Dauterman, Sergt. of the Guard; Thomas Bailey, Color-bearer; Jesse Cannon, Principal Musician; Jas. Tussing, Camp Guard. This organization was kept up for only about two years when they surrendered their charter. Meetings were held in the G. A. R. hall.

Jonathan Watson Post, G. A. R., No. 464

This Post was chartered June 23, 1884, and instituted July 2, following by Dept. Com. Clark, assisted by comrades C. L. Bancroft, Andrew Swartz, E. W. Blair and ____Groves of Columbus, Geo. Wheeler of Winchester and Jacob Kuhns of Lithopolis. This Post was named after Jonathan Watson who enlisted as a Private in Co. B, 113th O. V. I., he was promoted to Orderly Sergeant, 2d Lieut., and 1st Lieut. He died at London, Ohio in 1868 from the effects of wounds received at Chickamauga and Kennesaw Mountain, one of which cut his nose and put out one of his eyes. He was a boat builder by occupation, and a good soldier.

The first officers and charter members were: John W. Kile, Com.; J. V. Conklin, Sen. V. Com.; A. M. Rarey J . V. Com.; G. W. Biglow, Chap.; A. O. Maught, Officer of the Day; Theo. Falhaber, Ser. Major; Samuel Kimler, Adj.; Frank Slosser, Q. M.; Jacob Cavinee, I. G.: R. Copland, O. G.; A. J. Smith, Q. S.; Wm. M. Sharp, W. C. Gill, W. L. Parker, James Nolan, H. P. Moore, Albert Sandy, D. M. Willie, O. R. Mansfield, John Stott, John Reed, Edward Campbell, Chas. Hattenfels, James Byrne, Peter Reeves, Thomas Athey, Robt. A. Shaw, Thomas Thompson, Orange Barnhart, John Sidener, Thomas Ryan and John Cramer, thirty-two in all.

The following have since been mustered in: O. D. Harris, James Hamler, Isaac Foust, A. D. Kraner, Edward Carder, James F. Gray, Madison Burke, John Warner, James A. Kile, Samuel Bachtel, Wm. Hamler, Jacob Kuhn, Adam S. Shaner, Joseph A Peters, John F. Stallsmith, Thos. Dolby, Henry Miller, Samuel Van Gundy, Bernard Thompson, J. M. Strickler, John Cavinee, George Mansfield, Alonzo Wright, Wm. Townsend, Samuel E. Fort, Perry Robinson, James Fickel, Alfred Gray, Elias Tharp, Geo. Vaughn, Simon Heise.

The following members have died: James Nolan, while in Tennessee; Edmund C. Carter, January 11, 1887; Bernard Thompson, January 19, 1888; Wm. J. Townsend, November 14, 1889; Madison Burk, December 23, 1890; Andrew D. Kraner, September 27, 1893; Haynes P. Moore, May 25, 1894; John W. Kile, November 22, 1894; Alonzo Wright, September 3,1895; John Stott, November 15, 1895; Isaac Hamler, June 19 ,1895; Thomas Ryan, October 26, 1895; Adam Shaner, February 12, 1897; Henry Miller, November 24, 1899; John D. Reed, at Columbus, Ohio; Samuel E. Fort; Edward Campbell; Wm. Hamler.

Other soldiers not members of the G. A. R. from Groveport who have died are Hiram Cramer, at Chattanooga, Tenn.; Peter Miller, at Rasacco, Ga.; Hiram Cross, at Snake Creek, Ga.; Miller Clark, killed in front of Atlanta, Ga.; Jacob Miller; Richard Johnson, Edward Stevenson, Joshua Stevenson, Lewis Hampson, Daniel Campbell, Charles Campbell, February 4, 1892, and others.

The following have been the commanders: John W. Kile, 1884; Robt. A. Shaw, 1885, 1889, 1901; A. O. Mauck, 1886; Samuel Kindler, 1888; Geo. W. Bigelow, 1890, 1893-1895, 1899-1900; Thomas Thompson, 1891; Joseph Peters, 1892; Orin R. Mansfield, 1896; Richard Copeland, 1897.

On December 14, 1900, Jonathan Watson Post voted to disband and at a called meeting held on December 28, 1900, it was decided to sell the Post's property at auction. The proceeds of this sale was divided among the members in good standing at the time:

Thomas Thompson, O. D. Harris, O. R. Mansfield, Wm. L. Parker, Wm. Sharp, Joseph Peters, Orange Barnhart, Geo. W. Bigelow, Thomas Dolby, J. V. Conklin, James Fickel, Alfred Gray, Elias Tharp and G. W. Vaughn.

The charter however was retained and on February 8, 1901, the Post was reorganized with the following officers: Robert A. Shaw, Commander ; John Cavinee, Sen. V. Com., O .R. Barnhart, Jun. V. Com.; J. V. Conklin, Q. M.: H. Smalley, Surgeon; Geo. W. Bigelow, Chaplain; Thomas Thompson, Officer of the Day; R. Copeland, Officer of the Guard; John M. Strickler, Adjutant.

Woman's Relief Corps, No. 165

Jonathan Watson Woman's Relief Corps was chartered November 8, 1886, with the following officers and charter members: Victoria Maught, President; Mary Kindler, S. V. P.; Maggie Rarey, J. V. P.; Nellie Willie, Secretary; Ina Sharp, Treasurer; Mary Sandy, Chaplain; Hannah Shaw, Con.; Lizzie Copeland, Assist. Con.; Anna Mansfield, G.; Lida Thompson, Assist. G.; Kate Gill and Anna Reed.

Meetings were held in the G. A. R. hall. Various means, such as festivals, camp-fires and entertainments were given for the purpose of assisting the Post. Among the most notable of the entertainments undertaken was the rendering of *"The Queen of Fame'* the details of which are given in another chapter.

The organization disbanded in June, 1893. The last officers were: Mrs. Nettie Willie, President; Mrs. Jane Reeves, S. V. P.; Mrs. Mary Sandy, J. V. P.; Mrs. Lida Thompson, Secretary, Mrs. Bettie Dolby, Chap.; Mrs. Anna Mansfield, Con.; Mrs. Kate Seymour, G.

Sons of Veterans, No. 107

The John Wallace Camp, Sons of Veterans was organized at Groveport, December 8, 1886 with the following charter members: George Copeland, Capt.; James Spencer, 1st Lieut.; Harry Kindler, 2d Lieut.; L. B. Wheeler, Chaplain, E. J. Pettit, Q. M. Sergt.; G. F. Sharp, 1st Sergt.; L. H. Hamler, Color Sergt.; W. E. Thompson, Sergt. of G.; E. J.

Spencer, Corp. of G.; L. G. Mansfield, Camp G.: Edward Hamler, Picket; W. E. Smith, C. M.

Additional members mustered in were Thos. Hamler, Isaac Musselman, Jacob Cavinee Jr., Geo. Willie, This camp was instituted by H. F. Guerin and J. M. Walcutt. This charter was surrendered on June 8th, 1887. The meetings were in the G. A. R. hall.

Reunion of the 113th Regt., O. V. I.

In the summer of 1887, a Committee of Arrangements was raised by appointment of Mayor B. F. Gayman and by Alfred Cannon Post, consisting of Capt. Philip Game, S. E. Bailey, Sol. S. Lehman, W. H. Hartsough and Geo. F. Bareis. Great preparations were made in the way of decorations which have never been excelled in Winchester, and especially for the big dinner that was served in the "Rink." The committee on "Dinner and Tables" was organized into companies, each having a captain. Each member of the several companies was designated to prepare some certain hot dish as Baked Beans, Pot-pie, etc.; in this way a warm dinner was served to some 800 or 900 persons.

The reunion took place on September 20, 1887. The procession, which was a large one, formed near the depot on High Street, then marched to Mound; on Mound to Elm, on Elm to Washington, on Washington to West, on West to Columbus, counter-marched on Columbus to High, on High to Waterloo, on Waterloo to Trine, on Trine to Mound, on Mound to High, then to Game's Opera House. A male chorus furnished the music; the chorus consisting of 1st Tenors, Joe S. Ashe and Milt Armpriester; 2d Tenors, J. W. Shook and M. M. Werner; 1st Bass, Frank Brown and B. F. Gayman; 2d Bass, L. H. Schuh and C. L. Boyer, Rev. L. H. Schuh, director and Edna Lawyer, organist. *"The Winchester Times"* of September 28, 1887 says of the reunion, *"It was the grandest and most successful occasion in the history of Winchester. Everything moved like clockwork, and there was not a single mistake."*

CHAPTER XX
MADISON TOWNSHIP AND WINCHESTER FAIRS

"Ho! all ye farmers roundabout, and village people, too.
Don't fail to come to Winchester, whatever you may do;
For 'tis the season of the year—and mark it well with care,
When folks of country and of town conspire to hold a fair.
'Twill be the opportunity to meet your old time friend;
'Twill be the time, young lass or lad, a happy day to spend.
Of all the things to be displayed, of love or beauty rare.
No better place may well be found than C. Winchester Fair."

Rev. J. P. Stahl *in Winchester Times.*

On February 27, 1846, *"A Bill for the Encouragement of Agriculture,"* was passed, creating The Ohio State Board of Agriculture. Out of the fifty-three members, but nine were present—while ten were required to make a quorum. At its first meeting on the first Wednesday of April, 1846, Secretary Miller says, *"We do not find the fact recorded, but according to tradition, a messenger was sent after Mr. Chaney. (Judge John Chaney, who then lived near Carroll), the member whose home was nearest Columbus, where the meeting was held, and by hard riding during a part of a very stormy night, Mr. Chaney reached the city before midnight and a legal organization of the Board was thus secured."*

At the second annual State Fair, held at Columbus, in 1851, two Madison Township farmers secured premiums; W. H. Rarey, 2d best filly, 1 year old, $3.00; and Moses Seymour, 2d best stallion, 4 years old, $10.

On September 6, 1851, the Franklin County Agricultural Society was organized and the following October held its first fair. Among the most active, and one of the first directors was Wm. H. Rarey. In May, 1852, he was re-elected and became one among the first seven Life-members by the payment of twenty dollars towards purchasing the Franklin County Fair Grounds, now Franklin Park. In 1853 Moses Seymour was elected vice president, and Chas. W. Speaks a director. In 1854, Moses Seymour, in 1855, Chas. Pontius and Alexander Mooberry and in 1857, Wm. T. Decker served as directors.

At the county fair held in October, 1851, Madison Township citizens secured eleven of a total of sixty four premiums offered, viz: Moses Seymour, best stallion, $5; Wm. H. Rarey, 2d best stallion, $3; John S. Rarey, best two year old colt, $2; Charles Pontius, best filly, two year old, $3; Wm. Toy, 2d best stud colt, diploma; Wm. Toy, 2d best brood mare and foal, $3; Wm. H. Rarey, best sow, $3; Wm. H. Rarey, best sow and pigs, $1; C. J. Stevenson, best saddle and bridle, $2; W. S. Hopkins, best needle work (quilt), $2; Columbus and Groveport Turnpike Co., best road, two certificates. All the five dollar premiums were paid in silver cups and all the three dollar premiums in silver medals. September 15, 1854, Chas. Pontius was awarded a book *The American Cattle Doctor,"* for the best bull calf.

Charles Pontius
1812 - 1887

In the fall of 1857, the Madison Township Agricultural Society was organized, each of the following persons having subscribed five dollars, which constituted a membership fee, viz: Moses Seymour, Abraham Sharp, Geo. McCormick, Solomon Woodring, C. Rarey, Kalita Sallee, J. H. Fearn, Dr. G. L. Smith. Wm. H. Bishop, Dr. Hugh L. Chaney, C. P. Dildine, Ezekiel Groom, O. P. Chaney, R. Hendren, Jacob Arnold, Moses Zinn, T. C. Hendren, Jacob Rohr, S. Stimmel, Fred Swisher, J. H. Rees, John G. Edwards, Samuel Sharp, Chas. Pontius, James Needels, Henry Long, Fred Bunn, John McGuffy, Wm. T. Decker, John Swisher,

John Cox, Jacob Sarber, Thornton Decker, Z. H. Perrill, A. L. Perrill, Edward Gares, Adam Havely, Elias Helpman, C. F. Needels, Elisha B. Decker and others whose names we could not secure. The above list of names is representative of the most substantial and enterprising citizens of the township of that day.

The first officers were, Moses Seymour, President; C. P. Dildine, Vice President; Edward Gares, Secretary; and Samuel Sharp, Treasurer.

The first fair was held the same fall and annual fairs thereafter until the fall of 1875. October, 1875. the *Columbus Gazette* says *"The Madison Township fair was a failure on account of rain."* March 16, 1876, the following notice appeared in the *Winchester Times: "A meeting of the citizens of Madison Township will be held in the town hall, Groveport, on Saturday, March 25, 1876, for the purpose of nominating candidates for the office of president, vice president, secretary, treasurer and members of the Madison Township Agricultural Society for the ensuing year. By order of J. P. Arnold, President.*

Charles Campbell
1818 - 1902

Edmund Gares
1825 - 1903

Neither any of the records, nor the result of this last election could be found, further than that C. Fay Needels was elected president. In the summer of 1878, the grounds and buildings were sold to M. Corbett under an execution issued in favor of Lee Lodge I. O. O. F. of Winchester. The summons of Sheriff Josiah Kinnear contains the names of the Directors as follows, viz: Moses Seymour, Henry Long, Chas. Pontius, Wm. F. Decker, E. B. Decker and C. P. Dildine.

The fairground was located on the Groveport and Winchester Pike, on the northeast quarter of section No. 27 and contained about seven acres. No details of the receipts, attendance, etc., could be obtained; there is however no question but that the Madison Township Agricultural Society had much to do with the development of the stock and grain industries of the township. We were not able to verify, nor can we deny the common report that more stock was entered for exhibition at this fair during its first years, than at the Franklin County or even at the Ohio State Fairs.

A special stable was erected for John S. Rarey's famous horse. *Cruiser;* it stood on the east side of the grounds near a clump of trees.

Winchester Fair

For several seasons previous to 1898 the members of Madison Grange would bring to their hall, on a stated day, some of the choice products of their farms, for mutual observation and benefit. These displays grew to such proportions that it was proposed to hold a public display; accordingly an agricultural and art fair was held on October 21 and 22, 1898, in the old foundry building, under the auspices of Madison Grange. There were three hundred and sixty-three entries besides those in the Pet Stock show. No entry nor admission fee was charged; the premiums, which consisted of cash and articles of merchandise, were contributed by members of the grange, merchants of Winchester and others.

The second annual fair was held in the Central Ohio Baling Company's shed, on October 6 and 7, 1899. under the same auspices.

The third annual exhibition was held in the baling shed on October 3 and 4, 1900, by the Winchester Fair Association; the active members of this organization consisted of members of the grange and business men of Winchester. The premiums of cash and merchandise amounted to $242.75.

The fourth annual fair was held on October 2 and 3, 1901. The old rink building, on west Waterloo Street, with the addition of three canvas tents furnished the shelter. Heretofore no admission fee was required, this year an admission fee of ten cents, single admission, or 25 cents season ticket was tried with a view to putting the fair on a more nearly self-supporting basis, with the following result: Total expenses, $317.80. The receipts for admissions was $268.70 and the balance to pay for the expenditures was made up by an assessment of 20 per cent on a guarantee fund previously subscribed.

Each succeeding year the attendance has increased and the displays are larger and better than the year before.

CHAPTER XXI
FRANKLIN FARMERS' INSTITUTE

"The first farmer was the first man, and all historic nobility rests on possession and use of land."

Emerson

At the annual meeting of the Ohio State Board of Agriculture in the Fall of 1880, Secretary W. I. Chamberlain *"Asked for authority to co-operate with local or county agricultural societies and Granges in calling and organizing Farmers' Institutes or Agricultural conventions."* Oliver P. Chaney, of Winchester, who was a member of the board, then offered the following motion, which was adopted: *"That the Secretary of this Board be authorized to proceed forthwith to enlarge the work of the Department of Agriculture for the better promotion of the agricultural and stock-breeding interests of the state, and to defray the expense of carrying on the work during the remainder of the fiscal year, he be authorized to expend not to exceed the sum of one thousand dollars."*

The first Autumn meeting of the Central Ohio Farmers' Institute was held in the City Hall, Columbus, on October 20th and 21st, 1887. Absalom Rohr of Madison Township was then elected a member of the executive committee.

The following December a meeting was called at Groveport, at which Edw. A. Peters, Absalom Rohr, Charles Toy, Welton Seymour, O. D. Harris, Miner Seymour, John A. Kile and Franklin C. Pontius were present. The report that they could secure aid from the State Board of Agriculture encouraged them to organize an Institute which they named *"The Franklin Farmers' Institute."* The following officers were then elected: Edw. A. Peters, President; Miner Seymour, Secretary and Absalom Rohr, Treasurer. The first institute was held at Groveport on Friday and Saturday, December 23d and 24th, 1887. The speakers were Rev. A. B. Brice, D. D., Rev. W. R. Parsons, L. W. Bonham, Joseph A. Kitzmiller, A. A. Graham and Professors H. A. Weber, C. N. Brown and W. H. Hartsough.

The second institute was held at Groveport on January 21st and 22d, 1889; the speakers were Rev. A. R. Miller, J. T. Hickman, T. B.

Terry, W. R. Parsons, F. P. Dill and Professors H. A. Weber, W. H. Hartsough and W. R. Lozenby. Music by the Winchester Brass Band.

The third annual institute was held at Winchester on February 10th and 11th, 1890. The speakers were Prof. C. M. Weed, T. B. Terry, S. H. Ellis, F. P. Dill, B. F. Gayman, E. A. Peters. Chas. W. Bachman, Thos. Fitzgerald and Miss M. C. Alspach.

The fourth was held at Groveport on January 26th and 27th, 1891. The speakers were: J. T. Hickman, W. W. Farnsworth, J. L. Shawver, C. P. Aubert, John L. Chaney, Geo. L. Hendren, J. A. Wilcox and Rev. Geo. W. Lott.

The fifth at Winchester February 17th and 18th, 1892. The speakers were T. B. Terry, E. C. Ellis, J. H. Brigham, W. G. Green, Mayor W. S. Alspach, James P. Kalb, Edw. A. Peters, Amor R. Smith, Rev. L. C. Sparks, Geo. L. Hendren and Miss Dora O. Sando.

The sixth at Groveport, December 9th and 10th, 1892. The speakers were J. L. Shawver, A. T. McKelvey, Prof. Wm. R. Lazenby, Wm. Stahl, B. F. Gayman, Geo. L. Hendren, A. R. Smith, John L. Chaney, and E. A. Peters.

The seventh at Winchester February 2d and 3d, 1894. The speakers were J. H. Brigham, Prof. Samuel Johnson, Hon. F. B. McNeal, Mayor W. S. Alspach, John W. Kile, Dr. L. W. Beery, E. M. Mills, John F. Bachman, and Prof. H. H. Shipton.

The eighth at Groveport February 4th and 5th, 1895. The speakers were Dr. W. I. Chamberlain, L N. Bonham, Prof. Thos. F. Hunt, A. R. Smith, Prof. H. H. Shipton and Mrs. W. F. Barr.

The ninth at Groveport, December 17th and 18th, 1895. The speakers were S. H. Todd, F. A. Derthick, Hon. J. B. McNeal, Mrs. Myers, W. T. Betz and G. W. Stockman.

The tenth at Winchester on January 6th and 7th, 1897. The speakers were Hon. J. H. Brigham, General S. H. Hurst, C. W. Burkett, Mrs. M. S. King, Prof. W. A. Kellerman, Prof. U. S. Brandt, C. L. Newberry and Hon. B. F. Gayman.

The eleventh institute was held at Groveport January 16th and 17th, 1898. The speakers were O. E. Bradfute, T. C. Laylin, Prof. Aug. D. Selby, Mrs. M. S. King, N. C. Marion, Samuel Taylor and Geo. F. Bareis.

The twelfth was held at Winchester on December 26th and 27th, 1898. The speakers were W. W. Farnsworth, G. C. Housekeeper, Prof. Thos. F. Hunt, Rev. J. P. Stahl, John F. Bachman, and Hon. B. F. Gayman.

The thirteenth was held at Groveport on January 26th and 27th, 1900. The speakers were S. H. Todd, F. L. Allen and E. M. Fickel.

The fourteenth annual institute was held at Winchester February 15th and 16th, 1901. The speakers were W. N. Cowden, Lowell Roudebush, Prof. J. W. Decker, Herbert Osborn, Dr. J. D. King and A. L. Peters.

The fifteenth annual institute was held at Groveport February 21st and 22d, 1902. The institute speakers were G. C. Housekeeper and W. N. Cowden and the local speakers were Prof. Geo. C. Dietrich, S. B. Davis, Mrs. Hettie Myers, Mrs. Ellen Bowman and Miss Elizabeth King.

The first annual picnic was held in O. P. Chaney's grove on August 13, 1891. The speakers were General S. H. Hurst, Waldo F. Brown, Rev. W. R. Parsons and Rev. James Heffly.

The second annual picnic was held in Franklin Park, Columbus, on August 25, 1892.

The third annual picnic was held in Lehman's Grove on Saturday, August 17th, 1893. The speakers were Hon. A. T. McKelvey, Prof. Thos. F. Hunt, and Hon. B. F. Gayman. The attendance was estimated at between two thousand and three thousand.

The fourth annual picnic was held in Lehman's Grove on August 22, 1894. The speakers were Hon. W. I. Chamberlain and Hon. Alva Agee.

The fifth picnic was held in Lehman's Grove on August 22d, 1895. The speakers were General S. H. Hurst and Hon. A. T. McKelvey.

The sixth picnic was held in Lehman's Grove on August 26th, 1896. The speakers were S. H. Ellis and Geo. E. Scott.

The seventh picnic was held in Lehman's Grove on August 19th, 1897. Speakers, Hon. J. E. Blackburn, Hon. E. E. Elliot and W. T. Betz.

The eighth picnic was held in Lehman's Grove on August 18th, 1898. The speakers were T. C. Laylin, C. M. Freeman and Mrs. M. S. King.

The ninth annual picnic was held in Mrs. Rhoda Rohr's Grove, August 10, 1899. The speakers were Rev. L. H. Schuh and R. H. Wallace.

The tenth annual picnic was held in Lehman's Grove on August 9th, 1900. The speakers were President W. O. Thompson and Warren J. Smith.

No picnic was held in 1901.

The successive officers have been:

267

Presidents — Edw. A. Peters, John W. Kile, John F. Bachman, Edw. A. Peters, Edw. S. Tussing, John F. Bachman and Clint A. Stevenson.

Secretaries — Miner Seymour, died December 28, 1887; R. Judson Tussing, Morris Kile, Theo. D. Kalb, Amor Smith, and A. W. Strode.

Treasurers — Absalom Rohr, Edw. S. Tussing, McC. Seymour, Charles Baird, Theo. D. Kalb.

Madison Grange, No. 194

Was instituted November 4th, 1873, by S. H. Ellis, and worked under a dispensation until March 23d, 1874, when it was chartered.

The charter members were Garrett W. Miller and wife, James P. Kalb and wife, John Beggs, John S. Lehman and wife, John Courtright, Geo. W. Ruse and wife, Benoni Steman, John Bishop, Isaac Lehman, Absalom Bowman and wife, Wesley Lawrence and wife, Andrew French, Miss Jennie French, Joseph Lehman and wife, Samuel Lehman and wife, B. B. Shoemaker, B. F. Leidy and wife, Samuel Bowman and wife, Noah Rinesmith, P. S. Kiner and John Schrock. The first officers were: James P. Kalb, M.; John S. Lehman, O.; John Beggs, L.; John Bishop, Secretary; Isaac Lehman, Treasurer.

The first meetings were held in the Samuel Bartlit Building, just south of the canal bridge. In 1874 they erected the building on North High Street, the upper floor of which has since been occupied as a meeting place. The presiding officers have been: James P. Kalb, 1874, 1877, 1879; Garrett W. Miller, 1875, 1878, 1881, 1883; B. F. Ashbrook, 1876; R. J. Tussing, 1880, 1892; John S. Lehman, 1882; Sam. S. Lehman, 1884, 1887; Ed. S. Tussing, 1885, 1886, 1890, 1891, 1897-1899; John M. Lehman, 1888, 1889, 1893, 1900, 1901; James A. Alspach, 1894; Amor R. Smith, 1895, 1896.

Hamilton Grange, No. 436

Was chartered in the spring of 1874, and instituted with the following officers; Elias Shook, M.; Christian Kartzholtz, O.; T. M. Huddle, C.; A. P. Sawyer, L.; J. C. Platter, Secy., and the following other charter members: A. C. Finks, Rebecca Shook, J. J. Rohr, Job Rohr, Elizabeth Thompson, G. L. Thompson and R. M. Williams.

The organization was effected and the first few meetings were held in the Lockbourne Schoolhouse; then for a short time the meetings were held at the residence of Elias Shook and later in the lower hall of the Masonic Building. In 1879 the membership was reported to be about thirty.

In the spring of 1881 the organization changed its meeting place from Lockbourne to Groveport. The date of the first minutes at Groveport is May 7, 1881, with the following officers; Wm. H. Rohr, M.; Elias Shook, O.; T. M. Huddle, Chap.; Charles Pontius, L.; Absalom Rohr, Secy. Since then the officers have been:

In 1882: Wm. H. Rohr, M.; J. C. Wright, O.; Chas. Pontius, L.; Joseph Brantner, Chap.; Ab. Rohr, Secy.

In 1883: Wm. H. Rohr, M.; J. V. Wright, O.; Rhoda Rohr, L.; Wm. Wright, Chap.; Ab. Rohr, Secy.

In 1884: Wm. Wright, M.; N. P. Vause, O.; J. C. Wright, Chap.; Chas. Pontius, L.; Rhoda Rohr, Secy.

In 1885: Wm. Wright, M.; N. P. Vause, O.; A. C. Finks, L.; I. W. Wright, Chap.; Ab. Rohr, Secy.

In 1886: A. C. Finks, M.; R. M. Williams, 0.; F. G. Pontius, Chap.; W. H. Rohr, L.; Ab. Rohr, Secy.

We could not get the record of officers between 1886 and January 5, 1895, when they were Rhoda Rohr, M.; Ella Baird, O.; McC. Seymour, L.; Theo. D. Kalb, Chap.; Edw. A. Peters, Secy.

In 1896: Rhoda Rohr, M.; Ella Baird, O.; Harley E. Rainer, L.; Chas. Rohr, Chap.; Morris Kile, Secy.

In 1897: Rhoda Rohr, M.; Ella Baird, O.; E. A. Peters, L.; A. W. Strode, Chap.: Morris Kile, Secy.

In 1898: Same as in 1897.

In 1899: Rhoda Rohr, M.; Ella Baird, O.: Geo. L. Hendren, L.; Ida Strode, Chap.; Morris Kile, Secy.

In 1900: Chas. S. Baird, M.; Welton Seymour, O.; A. W. Strode, L.; Ida Strode, Chap.; Morris Kile, Secy. In 1901: Chas. S. Baird, M.; O. D. Harris, O.; Rhoda Rohr, L.; Ida Strode, Chap.; A. W. Strode, Secy.

The following members have died: Joseph Brantner, January 2, 1886; Miner Seymour, December 27, 1887; Absalom Rohr, April 10, 1889; Harry W. Rohr, December 22, 1890; Benjamin C. Simms, January 17, 1891; Wm. Goodwin, September 22, 1892: Mrs. O. D. Harris, December 5, 1892; Mary Johnson, April 23, 1900; S. R. Helsel, January, 1900; E. Tod Rohr, December, 1900; Clara J. Pontius, May 5, 1900; George Seymour, March 9, 1901.

The members of Madison and Hamilton Granges, comprising many of the most progressive and enterprising farmers of Madison and adjoining townships, had very much to do with the organization of *Franklin Farmers Institute* and other movements looking to the general welfare and advantage of the township, and they have always had the hearty sympathy and co-operation of the business men and other citizens. These organizations afford their members a splendid opportunity to discuss the various problems that concern their calling in the regular monthly meetings.

CHAPTER XXII
TEMPERANCE

"There is a little public house
Which every one may close:
It is the little public house,
Just underneath the nose."

What was known as the Washington Temperance movement was started in 1842-1843. This agitation led to organizations both at Groveport and at Winchester; the former held meetings for many years in the school house.

In 1846 Dr. J. B. Thompson of Columbus instituted a "Sons of Temperance" lodge at the M. E. church in Winchester. Meetings were held for a time in the house now occupied by Moses Gayman on lot No. 1, and later in the house now occupied by Mrs. Selby on lot No. 10, then owned by Wm. Curtis. Only a few of the members can be recalled: Dr. J. B. Potter, J. B. Evans, A. Hathaway, Wm. Curtis and Joe Miller.

In the winter of 1871-1872 a lodge of I. O. Good Templars was organized at Winchester. Meetings were held over the Samuel Bartlit store and later in Bergstresser's Hall.

On December 17, 1872, Groveport Lodge No. 400, I. O. G. T., was instituted by Bro. Gill, with the following officers, viz.: M. A. Shaner, Chief Templar; Miss R. McCullough, V. T.; Rev. S. M. Bright, Chap.; Miss Mattie K. Long, R. S.; W. L. Powell, F. S.; Mary Young, Asst. S.; G. S. Dildine, M.; Mrs. A. Chandler, A. M.; Miss Lizzie Howell, I. G.; B. F. Champe, O. G.; Geo. Kalb, Treas.; Mrs. A. T. Hendren, R. H. S.; Mrs. D. R. Champe, L. H. S.; Wm. Chandler, L. Dept. This charter was surrendered in 1875. The meetings were held in Rarey's Hall, which burned June 13, 1882.

On April 7, 1884, another lodge was organized and named Morning Bright Lodge, No. 562. It was instituted by Rev. Milburn with the following officers and members; N. J. Kidwell, C. T.; Miss Mary Mason, V. T.; Miss Maud Champe, R. S.; Wilmer Fisher, F. S.; Wm. H. Bishop. Treas.: Rev. J. B. Bradrick, Chap.; Jacob Reed, M.; Miss Lula Wright, Dept. M.; Ed. Peters, O. G.; Kate Bradfield, I. G., and A. J. Bradfield, C. Black, *Sr.,* Chas. Stewart, Lydia Whims, B. Reed, L. Crosley, C. Patrick, Lydia Black, Eliza Black, Julia Bradfield, Kate Gill, Kate Cutshall, Jennie

Glick, Susan Howell, Ann McCullough, Mrs. A. B. Rarey and Lula Wright. Meetings were held in Biglow's Hall on Main Street.

The Woman's Crusade

Dr. Dio Lewis
1823 -1886

Dr. Dio Lewis, a Boston physician and lecturer, in a lecture at Hillsboro. Ohio, on December 23, 1873, urged the women to go into the saloons and pray. The next morning the women met and while singing the hymn — the first two lines of which became the watchword of the movement —

"Give to the winds thy fears,
Hope and be undismayed,"

formed in line, two by two, and proceeded to visit the saloons and drug stores. In April, 1874, the first meeting was held in Winchester, and the following officers elected: Mrs. J. B. Evans, Pres.; Mrs. C. F. Yost, 1st V. Pres.; Mrs. Jonathan Vaught, 2d V. Pres.; Mrs. J. W. Hische, 3d V. Pres.; Mrs. Prof. Kumler, Secy.; Mrs. Jas. P. Kramer, Asst. Secy., and Mrs. Rev. S. P. Manger, Treas. Enthusiastic meetings were held at the M. E. and U. B. churches alternately. The object of the crusade was the closing of the saloons by moral suasion. The saloons of Elijah D. Orwig, John M. Schoch, John Gehm & Bro. and John Kissell were visited. Prayer, Scripture reading and singing constituted the service. Where admitted the service was conducted in the saloon, at other places on the sidewalk just in front of the doors, the women always kneeling during the prayers.

The daily visits of the crusaders attracted large crowds. Besides the officers mentioned above, the following others joined the crusade: Mrs. David Gayman, Mrs. Geo. Powell, Mrs. W. C. McClintock, Mrs. M. C. Whitehurst, Mrs. A. A. Short, Mrs. J. B. Potter, Mrs. E. B. Polloy, Mrs. Wm. Cater, Mrs. C. P. Rees, Mrs. O. L. Dibble, Mrs. Samuel Deshler, Mrs. Binkly, Mrs. Somerville, Mrs. A. Starr, Mrs. Moore, Mrs. Isaac Ebright, Mrs. L. C. Bartlit, Mrs. John Kramer, Mrs. Sarah Miller, Mrs. Sarah Helpman, Mrs. Martin Kramer, Mrs. Bailey, Mrs. Cater, Mrs. Elisha Himrod, Mrs. Mary Wilson and Misses Kate Moore, Abigail Gayman, Mary Speaks, Laura Whitehurst, Jennie Somerville, Anna Helpman, Sarah Derr and Mary Tallman. Meetings were held at stated times for some three years, until the Murphy Movement was inaugurated.

272

We failed to find the records of the crusade movement at Groveport. The following list of names, not at all complete, is made from memory: Mrs. Geo. W. Kalb, leader; Mrs. G. P. Champe, Mrs. S. M. Bright, Mrs. A. McCoy, Mrs. Wm. Chandler, Mrs. Z. C. Payne, Mrs. J. F. Wildermuth, Mrs. Samuel Leigh, Mrs. G. W. Bigelow, Mrs. Henry Long, Mrs. W. V. Decker and others.

The Murphy Movement

The Murphy movement was inaugurated at M. E. Church in Winchester on Saturday evening, April 21, 1877, Rev. W. C. Holliday, pastor. Rev. Chadwick, Messrs. Kent, Arnold and Barringer, of Columbus, and Dr. Von Bonhorst, of Lancaster, spoke, and remained over Sunday. Eighty signed a pledge card the first evening, and at a meeting held at the U. B. church on Sunday evening about 80 others signed it.

Such excitement on temperance was never known in the township before. At the meeting on Monday night Actor Hall, an ex-saloonist; Dunn, Alger, Greenleaf and Windel — all said to be ex-drunkards — occupied seats on the platform. Pastors of the M. E., U. B. and Reformed churches were active in the movement. *"Blue Ribbon"* is the badge.

On Tuesday evening at U. B. church Mark Wilson, one of Francis Murphy's converts in Pittsburg; Jacob Baugher and Wm. Brown of Lithopolis made speeches, and 50 more signed, and the following committee was appointed to *"keep the ball rolling:"* Revs. Holliday, Johnson, Manger and W. R. Miller, and Messrs. John Helpman, J. B. Evans, David Gayman, Ezra Fought, B. F. Gayman, E. B. Decker and C. W. Speaks.

On Wednesday evening meeting held in Game's Hall (churches too small); speakers Mr. Wilson of Pittsburg, and Mr. Lloyd of Columbus.

Thursday evening hall again filled; meeting conducted by Thomas Arnold of Lithopolis, and Winchester boys followed with speeches.

Friday evening meeting led by Tracy Bros, and Alger of Columbus, said to be converted drunkards. At close of Friday evening's meeting about 400 had signed the pledge.

On Sunday Revs. Holliday and Chadwick, with some Winchester boys, went to Asbury and Powell's and got 70 signers. On Sunday evening many could not get into the hall on account of the large crowds. Rev. Chadwick spoke, followed by 'Bricky' Helpman, Chas. Allen, Al. Decker and Al. Gayman, and another 100 signed."

On Monday evening a permanent organization was effected and a constitution adopted, which had been recommended by a committee consisting of Rev. W. C. Holliday, M. C. Whitehurst and O. P. Chaney. Rev. A. C. Kelley, Pres.; Adam Shaner, 1st Vice Pres.; H. S. Binkley, 2d V. P.; W. D. Beeks, Secy.; B. F. Gayman, Asst. Secy.; J. B. Evans, Treas.

Executive Committee: John Helpman, Wm. Hesser, W. R. Miller, Henry Eply and F. Leonard.

Sunday, April 29, Rev. S. P. Manger and 'Bricky' Helpman held a meeting at Royalton, and Rev. Holliday and Bert Chaney one at Pickerington. Gen. Joe Geiger spoke at U. B. Church May 9, and on same evening about 50 persons went with Adam Shaner to Carroll, where he spoke.

On Thursday evening, May 10, Wm. Helpman, Chas. Allen, Allie Gayman and Tommy Morton conducted a meeting at Pickerington.

A "*Murphy*" picnic was held in John P. Morris' grove on June 17, Adam Shaner, Wm. Helpman and E. B. Dolson speakers.

June 14 an ice cream festival was held for benefit of a public library, and on July 2 at a citizens' meeting at Game's Hall a committee was appointed to have charge of the library and reading room. Many persons donated books, among them Samuel Bartlitt and Mrs. Palloy 100 volumes. Mrs. C. Ehrenhart, donated one-half the profits of two days' sales, amounting to $9.00, etc. Altogether about 300 volumes had been donated. The library and reading room was formally opened December 24, 1877. A brief address was delivered by Rev. A. C. Kelley, one of the Trustees. Regular weekly Murphy meetings were kept up until October 4, 1879, when a Woman's Christian Temperance Union was organized, with the following officers, viz.: John Helpman, Pres.; Aaron Smith, 1st V. P.; David Gayman, 2d V. P.; Chas. Allen, Secy.; Geo. B. Hische, Asst. Secy.; Sarah Miller, Treas.; John Helpman, Chas. Allen, W. R. Miller, H. S. Binkley and Adam Shaner, executive committee.

Miss DeYelling, of Massachusetts, addressed a temperance meeting in Winchester October 18, 1879; Col. Isaac Tucker, November 21, 1879; Mrs. Mary A. Woodbridge, president of the W. C. T. U. of Ohio, December 19, 20 and 21, 1879; George Colderwood, May 6 and 7, 1880; 575 persons signed the temperance pledge from April 21, 1877, to April, 1880. Most of the above information is obtained from the minute books and from the *"Winchester Times."*

Murphy Movement at Groveport

The first meeting was held on Wednesday evening, April 25, 1877. Rev. Chadwick led the meeting and Messrs. Alger, Dunn, Kent and Windle were the speakers; 150 persons went forward to a table and signed the pledge. Thursday and Friday evening 100 more signed. On Sunday evening Col. Isaac Tucker spoke, also John Corbett, Mr. Rarey, H. H. Scofield and others. It is estimated that 85 per cent, of the inhabitants had signed the pledge.

Christian Gayman
1828 - 1896

George Powell
1838 - 1896

Mrs. D. R. Champe, of Groveport, has been one of the most intelligent, persistent and successful temperance workers in this township. Every Sunday afternoon for many years she has gathered the children of the village about her, instilling into their minds the beauty and safety of a temperate life. It is interesting to note that Mrs. Champe was a college mate of "Mother" Stewart, the distinguished temperance organizer. Mrs. Champe's family name was Solomon, and Mrs. Stewart's was Daniels, so at college they were called "Sol" and "Dan," and by these abbreviations they still love to address each other.

The following extract from a letter written by "Mother" Stewart in May of 1900, to Mrs. Champe, reveals somewhat of the spirit and purpose of these devoted women:

"'Sol,' My Darling Old Time Classmate of Marietta Seminary: Oh, what a long, weary journey has been ours. Many a weary mile, over stoney ways that bruised, and thorny paths that pierced our feet. But the service was for Jesus and poor suffering humanity, and without ambition to be seen of men or to overreach others. My work, and yours largely, too, was such as others did not, could not, do, so they had no occasion for jealousy. You and I enlisted 'for service during the war;' we are in it yet, thank the Lord. Our ranks have been so sadly thinned, some by death — many fell by the way. But our disinterested labor is today being remembered and appreciated as never before.

Lovingly, your old-time 'Dan.'"

A local option election was held in Winchester on Saturday, June 15, 1887; the result was 135 votes "dry" and 47 votes "wet." Another local option election was held on April 26, 1895, when 78 votes were cast in favor of local option and 117 against. On April 1, 1895, the voters outside of Groveport and Winchester voted on township local option, when the following vote was cast: For local option, Winchester precinct, 109; Groveport precinct, 178; total for township local option, 287; against, Winchester precinct, 34; Groveport precinct, 84; total against, 118.

The Groveport council passed prohibitory ordinances in October, 1887, and in the spring of 1895. The first of these was soon after repealed, and the latter soon became non-effective.

CHAPTER XXIII
FRANKLIN ACADEMY OF MUSIC

"Music is well said to be the speech of Angels."

Carlyle

During the winter of 1869-1870, Prof. C. B. Hunt conducted a singing school in the M. E. Church at Winchester; recognizing the prevailing desire for a musical education — it is said that one could not be out of the sound of a piano or organ anywhere in town — he interested Prof. A. N. Johnson, who was author of *"The True Choir"* and other singing books, and the president of Allegheny, N. Y., Academy of Music, of which Prof. Hunt was a graduate. The result was the Franklin Academy of Music, organized April 2d, 1870. Prof. A. N. Johnson was elected President, Rev. James Heffly Secretary and Treasurer, and Prof. C. B. Hunt Principal, each having one-third interest. About May 1st, 1870, two pianos and two organs arrived. The hall over the Bergstresser storeroom was occupied as a recitation room and the residence now occupied by Mrs. Selby on Waterloo Street was used for practice rooms; later the Bergstresser residence on West Waterloo Street was occupied for practice.

Prof. Hunt conducted the teaching assisted by occasional visits from Prof. Johnson until the fall of 1870 when Miss Pantha Walcott, of Corning, N. Y., was secured as an instructor; she boarded with Mrs. Mitchell Allen, who lived on lot No. 17, South High Street. She had only been here a day or two until she took sick with typhoid fever and about two weeks later died; the school was dismissed and in a body accompanied the remains to the depot. Her father arrived a few days before her death and took her remains back to their home in New York. Prof. Abraham Brown was then employed and with Prof. Hunt conducted the school until the fall of 1871 when they both resigned and went to Xenia, Ohio, all the students remaining here except Miss Katie Short. Dr. A. Starr, James H. Somerville and Rev. James Heffly then arranged to continue the school and secured Prof. Milton P. Suter and Mrs. Anderson as teachers; this arrangement continued for about a year when Prof. Suter and Mrs. Anderson removed to Pataskala, O., and conducted a school there. Recitals were held every Wednesday evening. Tickets were given to the students, admitting their friends, enough to fill the hall usually attending on these occasions.

The following is a list of the students as far as they can be recalled after a lapse of nearly thirty years: Mary Speaks, Linna Somerville, Clara Cater, Ella Whitehurst, Ella Vought, Sarah Brunner, Jennie Allen, Ella Helpman, Hannah Courtright, Lizzie Courtright, Mary Courtright, Zula Bright, Amanda Schoch, Laura Dildine, Ella Blake, Ollie Hesser, Bettie Decker, Blanch Bergstresser, Flora Triplett, Hulda Whitehead, Maggie Long, Mattie Carlisle, Flora Hunt, Gertie Gerhardt, Susie Smith, Sadie Thayer, Ida Speaks, Emma Doval, Jennie French, Lou Carnes, Mollie Wilkins, Miss ____ Collins, Katie Stevenson, Mellie Whetzel, Alice Baugher, Abigail Gayman, Jennie Wheeler, Ollie Myers, Ada Myers, Miss ____ Ireland, Hattie Rodahafer, Jennie Doval, Emma Cousin, America Showalter, Victoria Campbell and John Ehrenhart, David Saum, Samuel Wilson, Oliver L. Bott, David Fry, Henry Blackwood, Mr. ____ Compton, Mr. ____Richardson.

Hulda R. Whitehead
1839 - 1921

CHAPTER XXIV
JOHN S. RAREY

John S. Rarey
1827 - 1866

In many respects the career of John S. Rarey, the famous horse-tamer — as a horse-trainer he never had a superior and probably never had an equal — is unparalleled in history. He was the youngest of eleven children, a brother of Wm. H. Rarey who laid out the town of Rareys-port and was born December 6th, 1827, in the old log tavern kept by his father, Adam Rarey, just east of Groveport.

When he was but a youth of eight or nine years his skill in horsemanship already attracted attention. On his twelfth birthday his father presented him a pony and so wonderful were the feats and antics which he trained it to perform that his reputation soon extended beyond his neighborhood. He was educated in the district school of his day.

In 1850, in company with some of his neighbors, he went to Cincinnati to attend the first Ohio State Fair. At the time a man by the name of Ovid was giving lessons in horse-training across the river in Covington. Rarey went over and took a lesson and bought a book. Returning home he studied his book and put its teaching into practice with the result that a horse kicked him and broke his leg.

In 1855, in company with Captain Atkinson, an old steamboat man, he went to Texas and set up as a horse tamer. He was not successful in a financial sense, and was looking about for another place when he became acquainted with an English gentleman who was much impressed with his powers and skill and advised him to go to England. Rarey had no money to speak of, but returned to Columbus where he gave public exhibitions. He then wrote and had printed a little book of instructions for the use of his pupils; he charged (10) ten dollars for a lesson, which included a book. Several of these small manuals are yet in the hands of those who attended Rarey's lessons, in this township, but in every instance the owners declined to loan them for inspection, saying, *"We agreed not to show them to anyone."*

In 1856 or 1857 he procured letters of introduction from Governor Chase to the Governor General of Canada, whither he went. His remarkable power soon attracted attention and secured him letters to the army officers of Great Britain. Among them Sir Richard Airy, the Lieutenant General of the English army. The way was at once opened to visit Prince Albert's farm, near Windsor Castle, where Colonel and Lady May Hood received him. Soon an exhibition before Queen Victoria and many other royal spectators followed. His popularity now became world-wide and his exhibitions were attended by crowds of every class, especially by the ladies of the nobility and gentry. The social attentions which he received were among the greatest rewards ever bestowed upon a benefactor. *"Not only the good and great vied with each other in doing him honor but also the active members of the different humane societies of London took an active interest in his fortunes and success."*

John S. Rarey and Cruiser

His skill was so wonderful that many were skeptical and accused him of using drugs or "occult arts." Guy Carlton, Earl of Dorchester, owned a blooded stallion, foaled in 1852, named Cruiser; his breeding—dam, Little Red Rover; sire, Venison—and early work gave promise of a possible derby winner. In 1856 Lord Dorchester sold a half interest in him to the Radcliffe Stud Company for fifteen thousand ($15,000) dollars. Cruiser was a dark bay, nearly sixteen hands high, with black legs, main and tail, with a symmetrical form, and possessing a combination of the best blood in England.

Cruiser had a very bad temper, and it became dangerous for anyone to enter his stall except at the risk of his life; people said he was crazy. Lord Dorchester thinking to put Mr. Rarey's skill to a crucial test, challenged him to manage Cruiser, saying, *"Cruiser, I think, would be the right horse in the right place to try Mr. Rarey's skill; if he can ride Cruiser to London as a hack, I guarantee him immortality and enough money to make a British bank director's mouth water."* Mr. Rarey, in relating this climax in his career, is quoted—by the *Brighton Gazette* of Thursday, September *22d,* 1859—as saying, *"A little over a year ago "Cruiser" was the most vicious horse I ever saw in my life. He had been kept for more than three years in an enclosed box of brick, the door being of solid oak plank. When any one opened the door he would rush*

281

forward to strike or kick him. No one dared to go into his box. I will tell you what happened at my first interview with him. I believe there is some cause for everything a horse does; he acts according to the impressions of his mind. I can myself approach any horse by taking time; not that I have any mesmeric conjuring power, nothing of that kind can tame a horse. The horse has intelligence and affection, which we can cultivate so as to make him kind and gentle. When I first approached Cruiser, I threw open the door and walked in. He was astonished at seeing this, and more so at my exhibiting no fear. Lord Dorchester, his owner, fearful for my safety, advised me to go no farther, but I had too much faith in my principles to recede. At this time he had on his head a large muzzle, lined inside and out with iron. He had to wear this for three years, and till it had almost worn a hole in his head. He has never had it on his head since that time, and he has never tried to bite me since he has been without it. I did not try to hurt him but to establish confidence between us. I don't bring Cruiser here to show as a tamed horse, and to do all manner of tricks, only to show what a gentle creature he has now become, and that instead of rushing at you to strike you, he will even give you his foot at command, and is perfectly docile. Mr. Rarey then asked Cruiser for his foot and it was given him."

In three hours Lord Dorchester was able to mount Cruiser and Rarey became his owner and rode him to London, and his fortune was made. Possibly the most marked compliment Mr. Rarey received was from Queen Victoria (the Queen's death is announced by the daily papers, January 22, 1901, and just while this sketch of Mr. Rarey's life is being compiled), it is one that should be fully appreciated by our readers, for it was the "royal hostess of the most magnificent and august assemblage ever called together to celebrate a wedding," complimenting Mr. Rarey with the acknowledgment that of all the recourses of England to amuse and entertain so select a company his exhibitions were deemed the most worthy. Her Majesty sent Mr. Rarey an invitation to give an exhibition of his skill in the riding school of Buckingham Palace, on the evening before the marriage of the Princess Royal.

Among the spectators were Queen Victoria, the Prince Consort, the Princess Royal, the Prince of Wales — now King Edward VII — Prince Alfred, Prince Frederick William of Prussia, Prince Frederick Charles of Prussia, Prince Albert of Prussia, Prince Frederick Albert of Prussia,

Prince Adalbert of Prussia, Prince Hohenzollern Sigmaringen, the Duke of Brabant, the Count of Flanders, Prince William of Baden, Prince Edward of Saxe-Weimer, the Prince Julius of Holstein Glucksburg and many other distinguished visitors, as also the Duke of Wellington, Major Gen. Sir Richard Airy, Lord Alfred Paget, Col. Hood, Major Groves crown equerry, and others.

The horse submitted to Mr. Rarey on this occasion was a powerful cream-colored horse of state, owned by her majesty, and one that had, from his vicious nature, been discarded as too dangerous for use. The queen herself, with her own hands, applauded his skill. He received an invitation to witness the wedding and a favorable place to witness the ceremony was assigned him at St. James Palace.

Queen Victoria frequently caressed and stroked Cruiser with her own hands.

Naturalists had always contended that a zebra could not be tamed, so it remained for Mr. Rarey to demonstrate the error of this position. It took him four hours to give one its first lesson, after which he mounted and rode it around the ring. Mr. Rarey gave exhibitions before the crowned heads of Sweden and Prussia, where he met Baron Von Humboldt. He tamed a wild horse that the Cossacks had presented to the Emperor and Empress of Russia, much to their astonishment. He tamed Stafford — a noted French stallion, and almost as vicious as Cruiser — in the presence of the Emperor and Empress of France.

Mr. Rarey was presented with many medals and diplomas, which are now in the possession of Miss Lowe, whose mother was a niece of Mr. Rarey. Among the most beautiful of these mementoes is a portfolio presented by the Duchess of Sutherland, the back of velvet, mounted in gold and the front of solid gold inlaid with richly and artistically embossed panels of bronze, accompanied by an elegant inkstand, etc.

At one of his exhibitions before the royalty at Stockholm, the royal family from excitement and admiration all rose to their feet, and at the conclusion, his highness the King of Sweden, presented him a medal of a peculiar social distinction, conferring upon the wearer especial privileges in visiting the royal palaces, being one of the most coveted and gratifying notices that can be received by a Swede.

From a financial point of view, Mr. Rarey's success was also phenomenal. His subscription price for one of his lessons in London was fifty-two ($52.50) and a half dollars, with the understanding that no instruction would be given until the class should number five hundred; this number was soon gained, and by the time these were instructed his list of subscribers numbered more than two thousand. It is estimated that he made a quarter of a million dollars during his four years' stay abroad, one hundred thousand ($100,000) of which he brought home.

He returned home in 1861, at the age of thirty-three years, a rich man with an international reputation. He brought Cruiser and other fine specimens of horses and Shetland ponies with him. A stable was built especially for Cruiser; it stood in the northeast corner of the lawn as long as Cruiser lived, and later was removed to the rear of the house where it stood until recently. Few persons if any ever entered it except Rarey himself. Cruiser was put in the stud and many of his colts were scattered about the neighborhood. Many of these colts inherited their sire's vicious disposition and he soon became unpopular as a sire. For several seasons Mr. Rarey toured the United States with Cushing's Circus and Menagerie, attracting great crowds to his exhibitions. In all his travels "Prince," a very small Shetland pony, accompanied him. Mr. Rarey had also trained a team of elks which he frequently drove in the neighborhood and to Columbus. In 1863 Mr. Rarey built an elegant home — Rarey's mansion — for his mother, on the site of the old tavern, at an expenditure of some twenty thousand ($20,000) dollars; just across the road he laid out a park where the Shetland ponies roamed at will.

"In the flush of youth and favor and fortune" John S. Rarey died at Cleveland, Ohio, October 4, 1866, aged 38 years 8 months and 28 days. His body lies buried in the Groveport cemetery. Shortly before his death he said: "If I could only get back once more to the old farm and put my arms round my dear horse's neck I believe I should get well."

Mr. Rarey is described as "possessing none of the qualities of the gigantic gladiator or the appalling brute force and physical courage with which we are want to picture the horse tamer, but on the contrary he was delicately made, light-haired, self-possessed, good humored, and everywhere admired for his gentlemanly manners and quiet bearing, being especially a great favorite of the ladies."

Mr. Rarey's will made ample provision for Cruiser's care and comfort. It specified that "Cruiser is not to be used for any other purpose than as a stallion nor for any other purposes of exhibition by any one at *any time or place, but is to be kept and remain on the farm where he now is and within the enclosure and stable now occupied by him, or similar ones, as long as he lives; he must be well taken care of and never sold. And I direct that said charge and encumbrance is to be perpetual and run with said farm, whoever may be the owner, so long as Cruiser shall live."*

The farm fell into the hands of strangers and Cruiser's old-time viciousness again returned, for nine years no one ever ventured to enter the enclosure with him. He died July 4, 1875.

Home of John S. Rarey

Mr. Rarey's system was very simple. Its principles were *"kindness, patience, firmness."* The plans laid down in his manual are based on three fundamental principles, as stated by himself:

"First—That the horse is so constituted by nature that he will not offer resistance to any demand made of him which he fully comprehends, if made in a way consistent with the laws of his nature.

"Second—That he has no consciousness of his strength beyond his experience, and can be handled according to our will without force.

"Third—That we can, in compliance with the laws of his nature, by which he examines all things new to him, take any object, however

frightful, around, over or on him, that does not inflict pain, without causing him to fear."

He used a surcingle and two small straps. With one he fastened up the near fore foot of the horse, leaving him the use of only three feet, which prevented him from running or kicking; the other strap he fixed to the ankle of the off forefoot, passing it under the girth-band; with this he could draw up the other forefoot. After a slight struggle the horse would come down on his knees. It was right at this point that Mr. Rarey used to ask his auditors to remain perfectly quiet, saying *"That then all that was wanted was to treat the horse as a child, showing him that resistance was useless, then treat him softly and as gently as possible."*

It is said that a very slight touch will throw a horse on his side when in this position. The horse was controlled so easily and gradually and without violence that he readily yielded to his master and yet recognized him as a friend. It may be added that while Mr. Rarey in all his work practiced the principles of his manual which he taught to others, yet no one ever succeeded with it as he did. Others lacked Rarey's genius.

CHAPTER XXV
CHURCHES

"Where dusky savage wooed his dusky mate.
And through the forest rang his battle cry,

Now stands the arched and temple halls of state,
And gilded steeples pointing to the sky."

Nothing speaks the high regard for civilization, order and intelligence as the prosperity of the church in a community. Among the early settlers were represented almost all the different denominations of the older states, and after a log cabin was erected it was not long until an effort was made to hunt up church people of a kindred denomination with a view to holding services. Often the ministers of the Gospel were among the first to brave the perils and hardships of the unbroken forests. For many years meetings were held at the residences and barns with now and then a camp meeting. The following is a list of the church organizations of the township with their history, more or less complete, owing somewhat to the interest taken by members of the several churches in furnishing data, etc.

Some Old Hymns

With an environment such as we have it is impossible to appreciate the burdens, necessities, loneliness, and dependency which formed the web and woof of the pioneer's forest life. Much less is it possible to enter into the thrill and inspiration that came from singing together the hymns and melodies familiar to them; to do so one must have had their common experience and have heard the sturdy pioneer preacher's exhortations and sermons as they did. Perhaps the best idea we can form of how they were moved is when we meet together and sing our old songs. Few had hymn books, therefore the necessity for "lining" the hymns; this necessity, however, only existed when a new hymn was used for everybody soon committed them. The following stanzas, among many others, were familiar to the pioneers and reveal something of the burden of the pioneer preacher's exhortations—A great "battle field" with heroic "soldiers of the cross," bearing "great burdens" and "terrible tribulations,"

A "lake of fire" to be shun,
"Canaan's happy land" to be won.

"Dearest Jesus, we are here.
To be in Thy word instructed;
Guide our hearts, O Thou who'rt near,
Let our minds hence be conducted,
And from earth be elevated;
Where we wish to be translated."

"By fear was Peter taken,
When he denied his Lord,
But soon his conscience check'd him,
And he went out and cried.
Christ's penetrating eye he felt,
He wept and prayed for mercy,
And Christ did heal his smart."

"He that confides in his Creator,
Depending on Him all his days,
Shall be preserv'd in fire and water,
And saved from grief a thousand ways.
He that makes God his stand and stay.
Builds not on sand that glides away."

"Farewell, dear friends. I must be gone,
I have no home or stay with you;
I'll take my staff and travel on,
Till I a better world do view.
Farewell, farewell, farewell.
My loving friends, farewell."

"O Thou in whose presence
My soul takes delight,
On whom in affliction I call;
My comfort by day,
And my song in the night.
My hope, my salvation, my all."
"Ye weary, heavy-laden souls.

Who are oppressed sore.
Ye trav'lers through the wilderness,
To Canaan's peaceful shore;
Through chilling winds and beating rain,
The waters deep and cold,
And enemies surrounding you
Take courage and be bold."

"Oh when shall I see Jesus,
And dwell with Him above.
To drink the flowing fountains
Of everlasting love?
When shall I be delivered
From this vain world of sin.
And with my blessed Jesus,
Drink endless pleasures in?"

"Tis sure that awful time will come,
When Christ, the Lord of Glory,
Shall from his throne give men their doom,
And change what's transitory;
Who then will venture to retire,
When all's to be consumed by fire,
As Peter has declared."

"Ah, lovely appearance of death!
No sight upon earth is so fair,
Not all the gay pageants that breathe,
Can with a dead body compare."

"Why should we mourn departing friends.
Or shake at death's alarms!
Tis but the voice that Jesus sends
To call them to His arms."

"Come, my soul, and let us try,
For a little season,
Every burden to lay by:

Come, and let us reason.
What is this that casts you down?
Who are those that grieve you?
Speak, and let the worst be known,
Speaking may relieve you."

"The wondrous love of Jesus,
From doubts and fears it frees us,
With pitying eyes He sees us,
A toiling here below;
Through tribulation driven,
We'll force our way to heaven;
Through consolation given,
Rejoicing, on we'll go."

Hopewell Methodist Episcopal Church

The writer of the historical sketch of Hopewell Church in Williams' *History of Franklin and Pickaway Counties* must have personally secured the very interesting and romantic details he relates from Thomas Groom, son of the pioneer, who was then still living. As the story goes, Ezekiel Groom and family came from Virginia in 1804 and settled where Miss Kate Decker now lives. After erecting his primitive log cabin it is said Mr. Groom started out, as was the custom of those days, in search of kindred church members. Going about nine miles south, he found a settler by the name of Bishop, who had also been a member of the Methodist Church in Virginia.

The next morning, which was the Sabbath, they set out together for the old Indian village of Toby Town, near the present site of Royalton, where they had heard there were Methodists living. When near the place they met two men, Broad Cole and Jeremiah Williams, who told them that they were then on their way to class meeting. Mr. Groom wishing to attend the meetings regularly, concluded to find a nearer route than he had taken on his first trip which was some eighteen miles, so in company with a neighbor, William Bush, they went to an Indian camp in the neighborhood and inquired the nearest way of an Indian, whose name was Billy Wyandotte. The Indian held up his eight fingers, signifying eight miles. Mr. Bush and the Indian then took their guns and Mr. Groom his axe, and blazing the trees as they went, thus marking out a path.

Hopewell class was one among the first (perhaps the very first) church organizations in Madison Township. This class was organized by Rev. James Quinn at the home of Ezekiel Groom in 1805, and was then called the "Groom class." At first it consisted of nine persons: Ezekiel Groom, wife and two daughters, Mary and Sarah, Wm. Bush and wife, Mrs. Nancy Burton and two daughters, Lucy and Betsy.

Meetings were held at the homes of Mr. Groom and Jeremiah White until a frame meeting house was erected at the graveyard on Mr. Groom's land and then named Hopewell. The deed is dated June 19th, 1819, and is from *"Ezekiel Groom and his wife, Rhoda, for twenty dollars in specie, to Charles Rarey, Alexander Cameron, and Adam Havely of Franklin County, and Shadrack Cole, William Brown, Daniel Ranier and David Morris of Pickaway County, trustees."* This building continued in use until 1844. The heating was unique; a hearth of loose brick was laid on top of the floor near the center of the room and a charcoal fire built on it which furnished the heating "apparatus" and answered in lieu of a stove, no flue being required.

The old church building stood until in the winter of 1852-1853. On December 22, 1852, Thomas Groom was given permission to take away the old church and if he *"suffers the roof to fall on the fence, he is to repair the same."* It is reported that Isaac Ranier tore it down.

On November 25, 1843, the following persons were present at a trustees' meeting: Rev. J. F. Donohue, Alexander Cameron, Thomas Groom, Isaac Ranier and John B. Moore. *"It was moved that we accept the resignation of the following trustees: Shadrack Cole, Philip Pontius and Charles Rarey, and Bro. Adam Havely, having deceased and the vacancies be filled by Charles Pontius, Moses Groom, Wesley Toy and Jeremiah White."*

The trustees went into the consideration, which would be best at this time, to repair the old meeting house or to build a new one. A motion was made to repair. After being discussed this motion was laid on the table, in order to examine the probable amount it would require to repair, and the following committee was appointed: Thomas Groom, Charles Pontius and John B. Moore, who after examination, reported forthwith, that *"it is not expedient to expend any considerable amount of money on the old house, further than to patch the roof and mend the windows,"* and Chas. Pontius and Moses Groom were appointed to attend to said repairs. A committee of four was appointed *"to draught a subscription"* for the purpose of raising money to build a new meeting house on the county line site, viz.: Charles Pontius, Isaac Ranier, Alexander Cameron and John B. Moore.

At a meeting held on December 23d, it was *"Resolved, that we build a frame church and that it be not less than 35 by 45 feet and 13 feet clear ceiling."*

At a meeting held in the old church on January 20th, 1844, the committee on subscription reported $819.50 subscribed. *"Adjourned until the trustees can examine the site immediately on the east bank of Walnut Creek, north of the county line between the counties of Franklin and Pickaway, to determine whether it is a suitable location to erect the new church on. If so to go on to build with the present subscription. If not to build at the old blacksmith shop, the site previously determined on."* Rev. C. C. Lybrand was present at this meeting.

February 26th. *"The trustees proceeded to examine and view the site on the east bank of Walnut Creek, and having viewed it they decided that the location is eligible for erecting a church on and provided the present subscription can be applied here we will go on to build a church on this site."* Chas. Pontius and Jeremiah White were appointed a committee to ascertain if the present subscribers are willing to apply their subscriptions for building said church on the creek location, and if any part is withdrawn then to solicit sufficient to build with.

On March 10 the committee reported $883.80 subscribed for the creek location, then the board proceeded to form the plans and dimensions of said church, and after consideration the following plan was unanimously agreed upon, that is: *The said church to be in length 46 feet, and 38 feet wide, with good stone or brick foundations three feet high and 18 inches thick. A good substantial frame, to be made of sound timber, said church to be finished off in a good workmanlike manner.*

On March 30th, bids were received and opened. The following proposals were handed in: Mr. Turney's was for $1,370, Patterson Harrison's was for $1,165, Michael Ebright's for $950. and John Groff's for $850. These bids, in the wide margin between the highest and lowest reminds one of some of the modern contrasts in proposals. The proposal of John Groff was accepted, and Alex. Cameron, Thos. Groom and Charles Pontius were appointed a building committee, and the article of agreement was signed up. One Jonas Bichart signing it with John Groff.

Under date of May 31st, the record says, *"We, the trustees, being prepared on our part to make the first payment, and having been informed that the said Groff does not intend to comply with the article of agreement, nor to build said church, resolved, therefore, that we consider ourselves at liberty to put an end to our contract with the said John Groff and Jonas Bichart."*

Under date of August 7th, the minutes says: *"Michael Ebright being present proposes to build and finish off said church for the sum of $1,050 and no less. His bid was accepted and he put up and completed the building."*

At a meeting held at the new church on January 31st, 1845, it was resolved, "That we accept the lamp proposed to be given by Mr. ____Kinear of Circleville," and $36 was paid for two stoves, and the church was accepted from the contractor."

July 17th, 1847, it was recorded *"settled in full with M. Ebright giving him a note for $46.70 to balance."*

Fortunately we obtained an account of the dedication of Hopewell Church, which was written by Chas. Pontius, on the fly-leaf of a little book, three by four inches in size, entitled *"Christian Perfection"* by Rev. John Wesley, published in New York, 1842:

"February 16, 1845, dedication sermon of the new Hopewell meeting house, delivered by Rev. James Laws; text 122d Psalm, 1st verse, "I was glad when they said unto me, let us go up to the house of the Lord."

The following list of members is taken from John Groom's class leaders' book dated August 10, 1835. There were very likely two or three other class leaders' books besides this one. John Groom, Charity Groom, Wm. H. Selby, Mary Selby, Wm. H. Selby Jr., Ivy Decker, James Evans, Huldah Evans, Margaret Evans, Noah Groom, Lucy Groom, Hosea Britton, Tamson Britton, John Giberson, Sarah Giberson, Marenda Giberson, Nancy Burton ("Died in peace October 5, 1836"), Eleanor Burton, John G. Bennett, Melvina Bennett, Isaac Childs, Sarah Childs, Geo. Evans, Oaky Moore, Orlando Fuller, Francis Fuller, Sarah Hunter, Catharine Johnson, Joshua Burton, Susana Burton, Thomas Groom, Nancy Groom, Sarah Ann Groom, Rhoda Groom, Henry Moore, Rebecca Moore, Moses Groom, Catherine Groom, Philip Pontius, Catherine Pontius, Chas. Pontius, Christian Hulva, Henry Bunn,

Elizabeth Bunn, Amos S. Bennett, Mary Bennett, Henry Bennett, Sarah Sawyer, Catharine Sawyer, Nancy Sawyer, Jane Egbert.

Additional names found on roll of membership, 1846: Elizabeth Pontius, Wm. Rarey, Rachel Rarey, Amanda Rarey, Wm. Ranier, Isabelle Berk, Daniel R. Groom, John F. Groom, Christina Groom, Rhoda Groom, Jr., Nancy R. Groom, Louisa Knoderer, Abraham Sawyer, Dr. B. F. Gard (Dr. Gard died in Columbus, July 12, 1849, of Cholera, and was the first adult buried in Green Lawn Cemetery), Elizabeth Pontius Gard, George Rarey, Sarey Rarey, Margaret Rarey, Mary Dildine, Mary Ann Rarey, Enor Ann Moore.

List of 1851: Hester Ann Ranier, Franklin G. Pontius, Margaret W. Rarey, Elizabeth Bunn, William H. Pyle, Rachel Pyle, and in 1854, John Sharp Sr.

Franklin G. Pontius has been a member of Hopewell Church for 51 years and is the only man living who has continuously worshipped here during the whole history of the present building.

The following have been class leaders: Jeremiah White, Isaac Ranier, John Groom, Thomas Groom, Chas. Pontius, for 47 years, and others. The present class leaders are F. G. Pontius, John F. Ranier, Sister Allie Ranier and Harley E. Ranier. In 1850 W. H. Pyle and G. Adel were licensed as local preachers.

In 1851 D. C. Shockley was given a contract to put a new roof on the church and some months later the secretary was authorized to divide a balance of $50 yet due among the trustees, *"as he thinks best,"* then follows this division: Chas. Pontius, $18; Thos. Groom, $15; Moses Groom, $8; A. Sawyer, $3.50; D. J. Groom, $3.50; E. Groom. $2. In 1852, L. Tower was elected sexton at $12 per year. *"He to furnish wood and lard for which he is to be paid market price."*

The lard or fat lamp gave way to the lard oil lamp in 1859, when a hanging lamp and one gallon of lard oil was purchased.

November 25, 1861, kerosene oil was introduced, three gallons being purchased at 50 cents per gallon.

The expenses for the year ending May 1, 1856, were: Lard, $1.29; wood, $3.12; sexton, $12.

Early in the spring of 1901 plans for remodeling the building were being considered. In April the women organized a Ladies' Aid Society with a view to lending financial assistance to the proposed project, and through their zeal and activity, along with the special committee consisting of John F. Ranier, J. P. Sawyer and Lyman P. Moody, extensive improvements were made. The primary Sunday school room and the vestibule were partitioned off from the main room. The large Gothic window was put in the front gable, the new box windows with colored glass took the place of the old 10 x 12 light windows. The furnace compelled the old stoves to yield the space they so extravagantly occupied, new pews took the place of the old ones; these improvements, together with papering, painting and a new carpet were made at an expenditure of $1,350. The building was re-opened with special services on Sunday, January 26, 1902, when $650 was subscribed which amount more than provided enough money to pay for all the improvements.

A Sunday school was organized in 1823 or 1824, with Geo. W. Glaze as superintendent. He continued to hold the position until 1835, when he moved to the west, and Alexander Cameron was elected, serving until 1843. Since then Isaac Ranier, Jeremiah White, James Pyle, Chas. Pontius, Sr., Henry Long, 1854-1864; D. R. Groom, 1875; John F. Ranier, 1877 and 1882; F. G. Pontius, 1878-1881, 1883-1885, 1887, 1888, 1891, 1892; Nathan Whaley, 1886; Harley E. Ranier, 1889, 1890, 1896, 1897; Mrs. Hattie Myers, 1894, 1895; Emma Ranier, 1898-1900; Mrs. Mame Couch, 1901, have served.

Assistant Superintendents: J. F. Ranier, 1875, 1878-1881, 1883, 1886, 1887, 1892; Levi Cavinee, 1877; F. C. Miller, 1884, 1885; Mrs. J. F. Ranier, 1888; F. G. Pontius, 1889, 1890, 1896; H. E. Ranier, 1894, 1895; Miss Hattie Arnold, 1897.

Secretaries: Miss Emma Wright, 1875; F. G. Pontius, 1877; C. R. Pontius, 1878-1880; C. E. Rarey, 1881, 1883, 1885, 1886; F. C. Miller, 1882, 1886; H. E. Ranier, 1884; Miss Eva R. Pontius, 1887; Aggie W. Wright, 1888; Frank C. Ranier, 1889, 1890, 1892; Miss Hattie Arnold, 1891; M. C. Ranier, 1894; E. E. Lincoln, 1895; Edson Ranier, 1896; Miss Mary Flowers, 1897; John Moody, 1900-1901.

An Epworth League was organized during the pastorate of Rev. Prior in 1893. Mrs. Hettie Myers, Miss Emma Rainier and Harly E. Rainier have served as presidents.

Pastors

James Quinn, familiarly known as "Jimmy Quinn," the pioneer Methodist preacher, was born in Washington County, Pennsylvania, in 1775 and was licensed to preach by Bishop Asbury in 1799.

The same year that he was licensed he made his first missionary trip to Ohio, visiting Fairfield County.

May 1, 1803, he was married to Patience Teal, near Baltimore, Maryland, and soon after returned to Ohio, becoming the "circuit rider" of the Hockhocking Circuit, which embraced the valleys of the Muskingum, Hocking and Scioto Rivers. His wife died February 1, 1820, and he followed her in 1847.

Jesse Stoneman, Asa Shinn, John Meek, 1805; James Oxley, 1805; Joseph Hays, 1806; James King, 1806; W. Patterson, 1807; Ralph Lotspeich, 1808; John Bowman, 1808; Francis Travis, 1810; Isaac Quinn, 1811; James B. Finley, 1811; Wm. Lambden, 1812; Archibald McElroy, 1813; Charles Waddle, 1814 & 1824; Michael Ellis, 1815; John McMahon, 1816; Sadosa Bacon, 1818; Peters Stephens, 1818; Abner Gough, 1819, 1820; Henry Mathew, 1819; Charles Thorn, 1820; Wm. Stephens, 1821, 1822; Zarah Coston, 1821; James Gilruth, 1823; J. C. Hunter, 1823; Leroy Swormstedt, 1825; Homer Clark, 1824; James Quinn, 1825, 1826; James Laws, 1826, 1827; Gilbert Blue, 1827; Jacob Young, 1828; C. Springer, 1828; Z. Connell, 1829; H. S. Fernandez, 1829, 1830; Samuel Hamilton, 1830, 1831.

In 1831 the circuit was again divided, and perhaps the following pastors served: Wm. Swazey, Ebenezer Webster, Harvey Camp, Oliver Spencer, Isaac Hunter, Philip Nation and others.

In 1839 Lithopolis Circuit was formed, and in 1848 the name of this circuit was changed to Groveport Circuit. Since 1838, when the Groveport class was organized the pastors have been the same as those mentioned in connection with that church.

Asbury Methodist Episcopal

At about the same time that the Hopewell class was organized a class was organized in the Stevenson settlement. Meetings were held at various residences and barns. Among the first such meetings were those held at the residence of John Stevenson—one of the most active Methodists in that neighborhood—as early as 1806, and continuing on to about 1820, when a log "meeting house" was erected near Mr. Stevenson's house on Blacklick, now owned by Benj. F. Bowman.

Some twenty years later a difference of opinion arose, some favoring the repair of the old meeting house, others, perhaps the majority, selecting the White Chapel site. Those favoring the old site then spent some $75 in repairing the old log building. Many years later Jacob Bowman, Sr., purchased Mr. Stevenson's farm, and in the early fifties, when his residence burned he moved into the old meeting house, where Benj. F. Bowman was born.

Those favoring the new site proceeded to erect a frame meeting house on the Thomas Needels farm, about one mile further west, and on the northwest corner of the intersection of the Bixby Road from the north and the Columbus and Winchester Road. This building was erected in 1842 or 1843, and was known as "White Chapel." The old White Chapel building was sold to W. Leasure, who moved it to Brice and constructed his residence of it.

The present substantial brick building was erected in the summer of 1872 at a cost of about $7,000. It was begun under the pastorate of Rev. C. M. Bethauser, and completed under the pastorate of Rev. H. A. Ferris. It was dedicated in December of 1872, Rev. J. M. Trimble officiating.

Among the early members of Asbury class were: John Stevenson and wife, Philip Hooper and wife, Jacob Algire and wife, Richard Stevenson and wife, Philomen Needels and wife, Zachariah Stevenson and wife, George Powell and wife, John Algire and wife, Richard Derrick and wife. Archibald Powell and wife, and others.

Among the early pastors were: Revs. John Biglow, Charles Waddle, John W. Powers and others. Since 1872 Asbury has been a part of the Winchester Circuit, and the pastors the same as those mentioned in the Winchester congregation.

A Sunday school has been maintained for many years, but we were not able to secure a list of the officers, nor particulars of its history.

Among the superintendents were: James Sandy, Henderson Miller, Jacob Bowman, James P. Kalb, John Pontius, James Fickel, Theo. D. Kalb, E. M. Mills, Clint A. Stevenson and Mrs. Ellen Bowman.

An Epworth League was maintained during the pastorate of Rev. Joseph Clark. The present membership is about 200, and the Sunday school has an enrollment of about 150. Asbury is one of the most prosperous rural churches in this section.

Groveport Methodist Episcopal

This class is an offspring of the Hopewell and Asbury classes, and was organized in 1835 or 1836, and in the same year a brick church was erected on the site of the present one. The brick were made nearby and the clay of which they were made was taken from the lot just west of the church; the clay was mixed by driving cattle around over it during the day and then during the night a number of hogs were turned into the lot and they rooted and mixed it up in their search for the shelled corn that had been scattered over it during the day previous.

In 1839 Rev. Jacob Young (grandfather of ex-Sheriff Wheeler Young) was sent here to form a new circuit. Previous to this, Groveport was in the Circleville Circuit. This circuit included White Chapel, Reynoldsburg, Pickerington, Asbury, Lithopolis, Hopewell, Walnut Hill and Groveport. Among the first members were: Charles Rarey and wife, Mrs. Adam Rarey, Mrs. Margaret Chandler, Mr. J. Watson, Mrs. Harmon Dildine, Mrs. Elizabeth Whetzel, and a few years later Wm. H. McCarty, William and Salem Darnell, Samuel Leigh, Wm. H. Rarey, Parker Rarey, Sr., Jacob Andricks and others.

In 1851 the old church had become too small, when the present large structure was built. A small memorandum book in which the subscriptions were kept has been preserved by Samuel Leigh; this little book reveals the fact that building churches fifty years ago met with the same difficulties and required very much the same sacrifices that building churches does now. Five separate subscription lists circulated at different times were secured. The first one amounted to $2,232.00, the second to $554.00, the third to $295.00, the fourth, a monthly payment plan, $591.00, and the fifth $550.00, a total of $4,222.00. Quite a large amount of these subscriptions could not be collected and are still unpaid. The dates of these different subscriptions are not recorded, but it is safe to infer that some length of time intervened between them. With all this effort it was still impossible to plaster the auditorium, so the basement was used for several years, being seated with the pews from the old church. After the auditorium was plastered, the pews from the old church were still used and did service for several years. Cornelius (Uncle) Black, Sr., has been a member of this class since 1840, and a class leader since 1862.

Presiding Elders*: Jacob Young, 1838; John Terce, 1839-1841; J. M. Trimble, 1842; David Whitcom, 1843, 1844; R. O. Spenser, 1845, 1846; J. W. Clark, 1847-1850; Cyrus Brooks, 1851; Uriah Heath, 1852, 1853; Z. Connell, 1854, 1856-1858; Job Stewart, 1855; J. M. Jameson, 1859, 1860, 1865, 1866; Geo. W. Brush, 1861-1864; C. A. Van Anda, 1867-1870; B. N. Spahr, 1871-1874; A. B. See, 1875-1878; T. R. Taylor, 1879-1882; J. T. Miller, 1883-1886; J. C. Jackson, Jr., 1887-1890; H. C. Sexton, 1891-1895; J. C. Arbuckle, 1896-1901.

Pastors: Many years two and sometimes three pastors served the circuit at the same time, which explains the following long list of the pastors: David Lewis, 1838, 1839; Jacob Young, 1839, 1840, 1852; T. A. G. Phillips, 1840, 1841 ; James Gilruth, 1841; James T. Donahue, 1842, 1843; William Litzenger, 1842; C. C. Lybrand, 1843, 1856, 1857; James Laws, 1844, 1845; _____ Sheldon, 1844, 1845; A. N. Musgrove, 1845; S. Bateman, 1846, 1858, 1859; Andrew Carroll, 1846, 1847, 1862, 1863; Joseph S. Brown, 1847, 1848; Joseph Morris, 1848; James Hooper, 1849; R. Doughty, 1849; E. B. Chase, 1850; Archibald Fleming, 1850; J. S. Vail, 1850; J. W. Clarke, 1851; Lovett Taft, 1851, 1852; S. M. Merrill, 1853; David Young, 1853; F. A. Timmons, 1854, 1855; J. Martin, 1854, 1855; Levi Cunningham, 1856; H. Gartner, 1857; S. Fleming, 1858, 1859; H. H. Ferris, 1860. 1861; F. F. Lewis, 1860, 1861; S. C. Riker, 1862, 1863; James Mitchell, 1864; Samuel Donahoo, 1864; Samuel Tippett, 1865, 1866, 1867; J. E. Moore, 1865, 1866, 1877; Ancil Brooks, 1867; Daniel Horlocker, 1868, 1869, 1870; S. M. Bright, 1871, 1872, 1873; A. C. Kelly, 1874-1876; R. Pitzer, 1877; J. W. Wait, 1877; B. F. Thomas, 1878; J. M. Rife, 1879-1881; J. B. Bradrick, 1882, 1883; W. T. Harvey, 1884-1886; A. R. Miller, 1887, 1888; Geo. W. Lott, 1889-1891; C. F. Prior, 1892-1896; J. W. Atkinson, 1897, 1898; John F. Grimes, 1899-1901.

Rev. John F. Grimes in a list of the Hopewell pastors read at the re-opening of that church in the spring of 1901, includes the names of J. W. Steele (He was a pastor on the Tarlton Circuit in 1851, 1852) and R. W. Musgrove. Rev. Geo. W. Lott included the name of A. N. Musgrove, 1845.

The bell was purchased in 1863. The first organ was purchased in 1869. The following have served as organists; Lillian Horlocker, Mrs.

Flora (Rarey) Peters, Mrs. Mattie (Long) Rarey, Mrs. Lizzie (Long) Eyeman, Mrs. Minnie (Denton) Decker, Mrs. Lizzie (Zinn) Denton, Mrs. J. L. Chaney, Francis Denton, Irenus Denton, Mabel Long, and Nellie Decker.

The Sunday school superintendents have been: Wm. Chandler. 1863; Henry Long, 1864-1881 (Mr. Long served as superintendent at Hopewell and Groveport for twenty-five years); Z. C. Payne, Cornelius Black, Sr., Chas. P. Long, Mrs. John Leigh, Wm. Hutson and Mrs. Mattie L. Rarey, the present incumbent.

Mrs. Hester Ann Long taught the primary class—"Bird's Nest"—for thirty-eight years, 1864-1902.

The Woman's Missionary Society was organized in 1874 with Mrs. Samuel Leigh as president, which position she held until her death in 1898.

The Epworth League was organized during the pastorate of Rev. G. W. Lott in 1890.

A Sunday school was begun in the Leigh school house in about 1847. William English, a brother-in-law of Samuel Leigh, was the first superintendent. Daniel Leigh served one year and Cornelius Black, Sr., for about twelve years. Stated preaching services were also held.

Powell's Methodist Episcopal

A class was organized at an early day, and a church building begun near the Vandemark graveyard. Edward Hathaway was given a contract to erect a frame church in 1823 and he had proceeded so far as to get the frame of the building up, when some of the most active and financially able members died, and so many others were sick that the project was abandoned and the frame allowed to rot down.

In the summer of 1850 a class was organized by Rev. E. B. Chase; the first class leader was Edward Long and the first members Archibald Powell and wife, Jacob Powell and wife, George Powell and wife, Edward Long and wife, and Elizabeth J. Peters. A chapel was erected in 1852 and dedicated in October of the same year.

Among the early pastors were James Hooper, ____Baile, Dr. ____Hoor, Daniel Lewis, John Stewart, Richard Pitzer, Jacob Young, Wm. Filler, Dr. ____Banner and John Longman. Since 1872 the pastors have been the same as those at Winchester.

The present church building was erected in the summer of 1899, and dedicated on December 3d of the same year, Prof. Richard T. Stevenson of Delaware, Ohio, preaching the dedicatory sermon. The building committee consisted of J. B. Powell, H. F. Groves, John H. Motz, Perry O'Roark, and Robert A. McClure. The building cost about $2.500.

A Sunday school was organized in 1850 by Edw. Long who was the first superintendent, followed by J. N. Peters, Calvin Groves, Charles Groves, Amos Medford, Andrew Gray, J. Wilson, Lower, James Wingert, Robert A. McClure, Daniel Springer and Frank Wright.

Winchester Methodist Episcopal

In 1838 Rev. Abner Gough came to Winchester and preached in the United Brethren Church, using the first Psalm as a text. It was on a Tuesday afternoon at two o'clock. Rev. Gough is described as a large man. He only preached here two or three times until conference met, when he was succeeded by Rev. James Gilruth and Andrew S. Murphy, pastors of the Worthington Circuit.

The class was organized in 1838 in the United Brethren meeting house which was occupied by them on alternate weeks until 1850, when the present church building was erected on lot No. 10, West Street. This lot was donated by Dr. J. B. Potter. Jacob Dellinger did the brick work and Bennedum & Kissell the carpenter work.

In 1878 it was enlarged and remodeled — the vestibule and tower being then added. N. J. Wolf did the brick work and Ferdinand Leonard the carpenter work. During the time the repairs were being made, from May until July 28, services were held in Gehm's Hall. Rev. Dr. Trimble conducted the re-opening services. New pews, carpets, and other repairs were added in the summer of 1895.

In the summer of 1901 it was decided to erect a new church building and accordingly a site was secured, being located on West Street, near High Street. The foundation was laid up during October and November under the direction of a building committee consisting of Dr. L. W. Beery, Dr. J. W. Shook, S. H. Tallman, Solomon S. Lehman and Rev. L. S. Fuller preparatory to building in the spring of 1902.

Previously to the building of the church in 1850 the Methodist people of this community attended and took an active part in the Union Sunday school which was held in the United Brethren Church; since then a live Sunday school has been maintained. James B. Evans,

Martin C. Whitehurst, P. R. Mills, L. L. Rankin, Jennie Somerville, Hod Learn and others, and Henry H. Dibble, the present incumbent, have been the superintendents.

An Epworth League and a Society of the King's Daughters add to the efficiency of this congregation. No records whatever of this class were available for our examination.

The first members were Michael Ebright and wife, Joseph Wright and wife and Elizabeth Hathaway. The next winter Agnes and Sallie Hathaway, John Tallman, wife, son David and daughters, Pheba and Nancy, and J. B. Evans—who is still a member— and wife, united with the class.

In 1838 this class was on Worthington Circuit, in the fall of 1839 the circuit was divided and this class became a part of Lithopolis Circuit. Afterwards it was in Pickerington Circuit, then in Groveport Circuit, and since 1872 in the Winchester Circuit, composed of four congregations—Asbury, Brice (Powell's), Lithopolis and Winchester.

An amusing incident is related, as having occurred in about 1855. It happened during a revival meeting; the services had continued quite late and the church had become uncomfortably cold. When Hinton Tallman, the leader of the singing, went back and put his feet upon the tin-plate stove and began to sing:

> *"This is the way I long have sought*
> *And mourned because I found it not."*

Pastors: Previous to 1851 this class was in the same circuit as the Groveport class (Lithopolis Circuit) and the pastors were therefore the same. In 1851 the Pickerington Circuit was formed of which the Winchester class is a part: Archibald Fleming, 1851; David Lewis, 1851, 1852; R. Pitzer, 1852, 1853; Jacob Young, 1853; Job Stewart, 1854, 1855; S. M. Merrill, 1854; C. M. Bethauser, 1855, 1869, 1870; F. A. Timmons, 1856; W. Z. Ross, 1856, 1857; W. P. Grantham, 1857; T. D. Martindale, 1858, 1859; C. C. Lybrand, 1858, 1864; W. S. Banner, 1859, 1860; W. C. Filler, 1860, 1861; H. G. G. Fink, 1861; J. F. Given, 1862; B. Ellis, 1862; E. Sibley, 1863, 1864.

In 1865 the Winchester class was changed to the Reynoldsburg Circuit. S. C. Riker, 1865, 1866, 1867; J. M. Adair, 1865; J. C. Gregg, 1866, 1867, 1868; T. H. Bradrick, 1868, 1869, 1870.

The Winchester Circuit was formed in 1871 and is composed of Asbury, Brice (Powell's), Lithopolis and Winchester classes. Previous to the formation of the Winchester Circuit there had been two pastors. H. H. Ferris, 1871; W. H. McClintock, 1872-1874; W. C. Halliday, 1875-1876; A. C. Kelley, 1877-1879; D. Y. Murdock, 1880-1882; Ralph Watson, 1883-1885; C. W. Bostwick, 1886; Mr. Bostwick died while pastor on July 16, 1891; L. C. Sparks, 1892-1895; Joseph Clark, 1896-1897; W. L. Alexander, 1898-1899; J. W. Mougey, 1900; L. S. Fuller, 1901.

United Brethren in Christ

The United Brethren class of Winchester was organized in about 1815 and was known as Kramer's class. Prior to the organization meetings had been held at the homes of different persons and then at a log school house that stood about half a mile north of Winchester. Lewis Kramer, a local preacher, was one of the most active members, and when he built the log residence on his farm,— the one now owned by Samuel Deitz—with some assistance he included a large room in which to hold their meetings.

In about 1829 or 1830 Mr. Kramer sold his farm to Henry Deitz — father of Samuel—reserving the right to continue the use of the room in which to hold their meetings. It is said that the meetings often got too noisy to suit Mr. Deitz, so three or four years later, in 1832 or 1833, he purchased this privilege and the money was devoted to help erect a church building.

In 1833, the Quarterly Conference met at the residence of Adam Kramer, who lived where Mrs. Mary Brown now lives, and at this meeting it was decided to erect a frame church building on lot No. 4, Columbus Street, the site still occupied. Frederick Frutchey was the "boss" carpenter who with the other workmen boarded with Mrs. Ervin Moore's father—John Kramer, Sr.— a circumstance which she remembers quite well, being then nine years old.

February 1, 1834, the conference met in this new building, Rev. Joshua Montgomery being the pastor and Rev. Wm. Hanby the presiding elder. The circuit was known as the Lancaster Circuit of the Scioto Conference. August 6th, 1834, the circuit was divided and called the Winchester Circuit. In 1850 the frame church building was moved across the street to lot No. 39 now owned by Ervin Moore, where services were held until the brick church was completed.

The first bell in Winchester was put on this old frame church in about 1846. This building was erected in 1851; it was 40 by 50 feet with a basement story. The brick were burned on John Kramer's land just west of Jonathan Rinehard's house. John Kissel did the carpenter work and Jacob Dellinger the brick work. This building was occupied until 1887 when it was torn down to give place to the present neat and substantial building which was erected during that year on the foundation of the old building; the old brick being used in the walls, as were also the joists and floor of the old building. The building committee consisted of Ervin Moore, Henry Will, and George Powell. Mr. Powell personally superintended the construction of the building at an outlay of $4,000 in cash besides the old material and some labor donated.

In about 1828 the United Brethren leased a grove of Lewis Kramer for a term of five years for the purpose of holding camp meetings; as many as fifty "cottages," some of hewn and others of round logs, were erected, and a space in which to hold the services was enclosed with a log wall some four or five feet high. After holding the meetings here for two years, the land was sold to Henry Deitz and camp meetings were then held near where Henry Rush's residence now stands, and in later years meetings were held in John Harmon's woods some four miles north of Winchester.

Among the early members were Rev. Lewis (Ludwig) Kramer, George Harmon, Michael Kramer, who lived on the Shaffer farm, Peter Robinauttz on the Garret Miller farm, Mrs. Francis Beirly on the N. Tallman farm, Peter Earnhardt, Adam Kramer, Sr., on the Brown farm, Adam Kramer, Jr., John Kramer, Sr., where Jerry Kramer now lives, John Kramer Jr., familiarly known as "Uncle Johnnie," a Mr. Coble, John Colman on the corner of West and Liberty Streets, Lewis Kramer at the Kramer mills, Lewis Kramer, Jr., on the Ashbrook farm, George Kramer on the Bruns farm, Jacob Kramer on the Kester farm, Benjamin and John Boyd, Grove Karnes lived at the west end of West Street. Reuben French on the Robt. Thrush farm, Grove French, Elias Smaltz, Elizabeth and Daniel Deitz and Abraham Harrison on the David Martin farm.

An amusing incident once occurred at a meeting led by Lewis Kramer. He had forgotten his glasses, and talking slowly, said: *"My eyes are dim, I cannot see; I left my specks at home,"* hesitating a moment, the congregation thinking he was "lining" a hymn, as was the custom in those days, began to sing, and sang the words through. He then tried to explain by saying: *"I did not say that you should sing, 'I left my specks to home."* Again the congregation sang, much to the embarrassment of the leader.

The presiding elders have been: John Russell, 1833; Wm. Hanby, 1834, 1835; John Coons, 1836, 1837; Elias Vandemark, 1838-1841, 1844, 1853; J. Montgomery, 1842, 1843, 1846, 1847, 1851, 1852, 1857, 1862, 1865; Lewis Davis, 1845; Mathias Ambrose, 1848; Henry Jones, 1849; Wm. Fisher, 1850, 1866, 1867; B. Gillispie, 1854, 1856, 1859; Jos. M. Spangler, 1855, 1858, 1876; David Shrader, 1860; Oliver Spencer, 1861; Wm. McDaniel, 1868, 1869; J. W. Sleeper, 1870, 1871, 1875, 1877; J. H. Dickson, 1873; Daniel Bonebrake, 1874; J. B. Resler, 1878, 1879; E. Bernard, 1884; Wm. J. Davis, 1885; A. Orr, 1887-1889, 1894, 1895, 1898, 1899, 1901; J. A. Crayton, 1890, 1891; W. G. Mauk, 1892, 1893; J. P. Stewart, 1896, 1897.

The following have been the pastors—up to 1863 there were two pastors on this circuit:

James Ross, 1833; Benjamin Moore, 1833; Daniel C. Topping, 1834; Wm. W. Davis, 1834, 1844; Joshua Montgomery, 1835, 1850; Abe Miller, 1835; Jacob Miller, 1835; W. W. Coons, 1836, 1843; Lewis Ambrose, 1836; Elias Vandemark, 1837; David Edwards, 1837; M. Roe, 1838; P. Lamb, 1838; Wm. W. Davids, 1839; Samuel Heistands, 1839, 1840; Wm. Fisher, 1840, 1869; Mathias Ambrose, 1841, 1851; Jesse Wilson, 1841; Wm. K. McKabe, 1842; George Hathaway, 1843, 1848; J. C. Winter, 1844; M. Bitler, 1845: J. Kritzinger, 1846; J. Fink, 1846; Pleasant Brock, 1847; Wm. Furguson, 1847, 1848, 1852; Wm. Walters, 1849; T. J. Babcock, 1849; J. Winn, 1851: Benj. H. Karnes, 1852, 1855; P. Appleman, 1853, 1854; L. D. Ambrose, 1853, 1854; J. H. Drake, 1855, 1856; A. G. Hempleman, 1856; David Shrader, 1857, 1858 1866; L. A. Johnson, 1857; G. L. Johnson, 1858; Oliver Spencer, 1859; Geo. H. Bower, 1859, 1860; Daniel Bonebrake, 1860, 1872; B. Gillispie, 1861; S. Longshore, 1861, 1862; Solomon Zellers, 1862: Jos. M. Spangler, 1863, 1864; Wm. Hanby, 1865; John Y. Potts, 1867; Wm. Brown, 1868; Wm. McDaniel, 1870; J. H. Dickson, 1871; S. F. Altman, 1873, 1874; D. A. Johnson, 1875, 1876; P. L. Hinton, 1877, 1880, 1884, 1885; J. W. Sleeper, 1881; A. E. Davis, 1881; Wm. J. Davis, 1882, 1883; M. S. Bovey,

1886; A. Snyder, 1887-1891, 1896-1899; W. E. Amsbaugh, 1892-1895; H. A. Zuspan, 1900-1901.

A Sunday school has been kept up since as early as 1833, and most likely since 1828 or 1829. In those early days not every one favored Sunday schools. In about 1836 a Union Sunday school was organized in the frame school house which stood on the lot now occupied by J. K. Miller's residence. Joseph Wright was the superintendent and Nathan Wright, Reuben Dove, Matilda Dove, Susan Wright and John Colman were the teachers. About thirty scholars attended. The following rules printed on a card three and one-half by four and a half inches were required to be observed:

1. I must always mind the superintendent and teachers of this school.

2. I must come every Sunday, and be here when the school goes in.

3. I must go to my seat as soon as I come in.

4. I must always be still.

5. I must not leave my seat till school goes out.

6. I must take good care of my book.

7. I must not lean on the next scholar.

8. I must walk softly in the school.

9. I must not make any noise by the school door, but must go in as soon as I come there.

10. I must always go to church; I must behave well in the street when I am going to church; I must walk softly in the church; I must sit still in my place till church goes out; I must go away from church as soon as I go out.

No other records could be found until 1848, but there is reason to believe that this Sunday school was continued from year to year, very likely only in the summer seasons, and grew until on June 11, 1848, according to the record book kept by Chas. B. Cannon, who was then the Secretary, it numbered one hundred and forty-five. The following is the enrollment by classes. The figures following the names gives the age:

Reuben Dove, 49, Superintendent; J. B. Evans, 37, Assistant Superintendent; Chas. B. Cannon, 23, Secretary; W. H. Tallman, 23, Librarian. Class No. 1: M. C. Whitehurst, Teacher, 28; Joseph S. Cater,

15; G. M. B. Dove, 14; W. J. Carty, 13; Herod C. Cater, 17; Reuben S. Bartlitt, 14.

Class No. 2: Hinton Tallman, 37, Teacher: Israel Gayman, 17; Henry Harmon, 13; Philip Game, 12; Chas. Burgess, 12; James Cannon, 9; W. H. Tallman. 8,

Class No. 3: C. W. Carnes, 22, Teacher; John H. Bartlit, 7; Thomas J. Evans, 7; Henry Harbaugh, 10; Thos. Matthews, 10; Wm. Dellinger, 11; Ephriam Gayman.

Class No. 4: John Wolf, 19, Teacher; Moses Gayman, 18; Elijah Kramer, 14; Michael Schrock, 14; Upton Noll, 12; Harrison McCurdy, 12; Thos. Price, 6.

Class No. 5: Lafayette Tallman, 23, Teacher; George Sargent, 11; Jacob Snyder, 7; Henry Robinson, 15; Wm. Helpman, 13; John Colman, 7.

Class No. 6: John Gehm, 19, Teacher; Wm. Cater, 8; Abram Harmon, 10; Peter Brown, 12; Isaac Kramer, 11; Jeremiah Kramer, 7; Chas. Brown, 10; Nathaniel Kramer, 9. It is related that Mr. Gehm would not dismiss his class at the church, but would have them march, two by two, himself forming one of the front twos, in regular military order, up street to Whitehurst and Carty's store, where he clerked, and after a word of advice dismiss them there.

Class No. 7: Israel Knepper, 20, Teacher; Isaac Moore, 13; Martin Samsel, 7; Samuel Harmon, 6; Hanby Kramer, 6; Stephen Robinson, 10; Eli Miller.

Class No. 8; Peter Bolenbaugh,___ , Teacher; Lawrence Carty, Henry Samsel, 11; Wm. Schrock, 8; George Noll, 8; John Line, 10; Irvin Kramer, 13; Chas. Yost, 9; Samuel Dellinger, 14.

Other male scholars, but not classified, were: Emanuel Dellinger, 15; Henry Samsel,___ ; Samuel Carty,___ ; Tallman Slough, 11; David Kramer, 15; Elisha Bolenbaugh, Melvin Schrock, Wm. Schrock, Alex. Harmon, Wm. Boyd, Jacob Fay, 15, Henry Game, Artinesea Osborn, 10, Harrison Tallman, 5, Martin Jeffres, 12. Lafayette Jeffres, 10.

In all these years and on up into the seventies, all the women were seated on the west side of the church and all the men on the east side. The writer remembers well when in the spring of 1869, having just moved from Logan, where a different custom prevailed, he took a seat beside a young lady on the west side. It was only a moment until Mr. Helpman very politely told him *"that is no place for boys."* The result was an embarrassed young man and a snickering audience. The choice seats then for young people were along the middle wall, a solid board partition about three and a half feet high.

The female teachers and scholars follow:

Class No. 1: Elizabeth Lee, Teacher; Louisa Kramer, 11; Emma Colman, 10; Marcella Thompson, 8; Rebecca Line, 13; Alary Jane Helpman, 12.

Class No. 2: Delilah Whitehurst, 21, Teacher: Caroline Cater, 13; Catherine Stevenson, 9; Pheba Tallman, 13; Almira Slough, 12; Francis Tallman, 11.

Class No. 3: Grace Tallman, Teacher; Harriet Cater, 10; Nancy Tallman, 10; Eliza Helpman, 9; Elizabeth Carty, 9; Mary Carty, 9.

Class No. 4: Eliza Tallman, Teacher; Clarissa Line, 8; Mary A. Howard, 9; Pauline Slough, 9; Addie Bergstresser, 8; Diana Carty, 8; Julia Harbaugh, 8.

Class No. 5: Mary Whitehurst, Teacher; Margaret Game, 10; Catharine Myers, 12; Ellen Yost, 11; Margaret Kramer, 14; Catharine Slife, 13.

Class No. 6: Martha Carnes, Teacher; Sarah Brown, 16; Sarah Jane Somerville, 11; Mary Brown, 17; Christina Brown, 15; Sarah Karnes, 11.

Class No. 7: Mary Cannon, Teacher; Francis A. Curtis, 6; Irene Samsel, 7; Irene Helpman, 5; Margaret Cater, 4.

Class No. 8: Eliza Leathers, Teacher: Margaret Samsel, 11; Pheba Adams, ___ ;Lyda Noll, 10.

Class No. 9: Rosanna Herkins, Teacher; Huldy Herrick, 4; Susannah Harbaugh, ___ ; Henrietta Herrick.

Class No. 10: Hannah Shoemaker, Teacher; A. Samsel, Sarah A. Stevenson, Lovina Brown, Caroline Krag, Merion Tallman, 7; Minerva Tallman, 7; Catherine Moore, 13; Jane Moore, 10.

And the following unclassified: Mary E. Fry, Luretta Samsel, Eliza Ebright, Priscilla Howard, A. M. Slough, R. Murry, Augusta Bartlitt, G. Thompson, Minerva Thompson.

In the summer of 1849 the following additional names appear: Lida Noterer, Sarah Pearsall, Louisa Schrock and Mary Kramer as Teachers, and the following scholars: Mary C. Bishop, Delilah Boyd, Sarah Werner, Sarah A. Dellinger, Louisa Werner, Susanna Walters, Polly Samsel, Ellen Johns, Eliza Jane Dellinger, Saluda Fry, Lucinda Pearsall,

Samantha Kramer, Barbara Miller, Mary Price, Sarah McLean, Harriet McLean, and a little later Mary C. Thompson, Caroline Cater, Barbara Bolenbaugh, Amanda Schrock, Mrs. Yost, John Helpman, Samantha Kramer, Sarah Kramer, Eliza Trine, Jacob Moore, P. Kramer, Eliza Boyd, Philo Williams, C. Stevenson, Noah Bannister, Matilda Grub, Rebecca Line, Delilah Boyd, Julia Corner, Rachel Game, Lewis Kramer, Wm. Helpman, Ervin Kramer and John Boyd were teachers and the following additional scholars were enrolled in 1851 and 1852: Lucinda, Sarah and Francis Allen, Adaline Alspach, Harriet Boggs, Jesse Bannister, Chas. Burgess, Katharine Beard, Heber Colman, Alfred Cannon, Chas. B. Cowan, Eliza Decker, Perry Fellers, John Grubb, Mary Hathaway, David Helpman, Geo. Harmon, Melvin Karnes, Orlando Line, John Loucks, Michael Loucks, Joseph Loucks, Henry Mover, Chas. Miller, Thos. Miller, Robt. Moore, Ellen Miller, Katharine Moore, Miss L. Newbour, Herk Price, Edward Root, Daniel Runkle, Collin Schrock, Jacob Snyder, Miss E. Stands, Georgia Yost, David Yost, Augusta Zimmer, Benton Kramer, Sarah Clendening, Elmira Kramer, Elmina Kissell, Benton Kissell, Carson Swisher, Lewis Stands, Milton Schrock, Mary Stands, Amanda Sparr, Catherine Swisher, Malinda Schoch, Thos. Sibel, Henry Sibel, Louise Clendening, A. McComb, Ervin Moore, Wm. Krag, August Krag, Frank Harbaugh, Mary Howard, Leah Ringer, Polly Ringer, Emma Hische, Tena Harmon, Sarah Trine, Wesley Stands.

The officers were as follows—Superintendent: Reuben Dove, 1848, 1852; M. C. Whitehurst, 1849; Levi Kramer, 1851. Assistant Superintendent: J. B. Evans, 1848; Hinton Tallman, 1849; Lewis Kramer, 1851, 1852. Secretary: Chas. B. Cannon, 1848; John Helpman, 1849; Wm. Carty, 1851; Grove Karnes, 1852; refused to serve and Ervin Moore elected. Librarian: W. H. Tallman, 1848; Chas. B. Cannon, 1849; John Helpman, 1851; Levi Kramer, 1852.

This school used *Union Question* and *Union Singing* books. In about 1840 a library was purchased and was in use for many years. The Sunday school was held for a few years after the first brick church was built in the basement, but it was damp and not well lighted so for many years it was used to store wood and finally became the residence of the janitor.

From 1852—when the M. E. started a school of their own— until 1876, no records can be found, so little is known except that Reuben

Dove, John Boyd, John Helpman, J. T. Flinchbaugh and M. C. Whitehurst were active workers, and each at different times was Superintendent.

Since 1876 the following have been Superintendents: James P. Kramer, 1876 to July 29, 1877, when he resigned and John Helpman was elected, 1877-1879; George Powell, 1880; Robt. W. Bolenbaugh, 1881-1892, 1898-1901; Prof. T. M. Fonts, 1893-1895; served only a few months in 1895, when he moved away and Mr. Bolenbaugh, who was Assistant Superintendent, served the remainder of the year; W. D. Boyer, 1896-1897.

Some of the Teachers were: Rev. W. R. Miller, J. K. Miller, J. T. Flinchbaugh, Henry Will, Wm. H. Hische, Ann Helpman, Mrs. Flinchbaugh, Leah Cater, John Helpman, John Boyd, Geo. Powell, B. F. Miller, Ed. D. Winders, Stephen Boyd, Jane Griffith, Susan Leady.

Among the early Secretaries were: Mai Karns, Philip Game, Geo. M. B. Dove, B. Frank Trine, Frank Armpreister (for several years just previous to the starting of the Sunday school by the Lutheran and Reformed in 1865), Wm. M. Game, Wm. L. Walters and others.

The first organ was purchased during the pastorate of Rev. Wm. Hanby in 1865; previous to this John Boyd led the singing. Miss Jennie Hanby was the first organist, followed by Emma Haskell (Mrs. Philip Game), Miss Partridge, Miss Raney, Lola Wright, Ella Vought, Emma Will, Della Tussing, Elida King, Mary Powell, Mae Schoff, Mary Yost and Mrs. C. V. Moore.

United Brethren in Christ

A class was organized in Groveport in the spring of 1856. This organization was largely due to the active members of the Winchester class. A brick church building was erected the same summer at a cost of about $1,400, and dedicated in the following September. Among the most active in this enterprise were the following: John Helpman, Henry Kramer, Ervin Moore, John Kramer, George Nye, Jas. G. Howard and Rev. B. H. Karnes, the first pastor. At one time there were some fifty members, but by deaths and removals the class became so small that services were discontinued after 1869, up to which time regular services had been held. In 1871 the building located on Blacklick Street was sold to the Roman Catholics and the class disbanded.

Truro Presbyterian Church

The name was given this organization in honor and memory of Truro Church at Truro, Nova Scotia. Col. E. L. Taylor, of Columbus, O., says, *"My grandfather, Robert Taylor, came from the town of Truro in Nova Scotia to Ohio in the fall of 1805. The family remained at Chillicothe two years. In 1807 my grandfather built the house on the west bank of Big Walnut Creek in Truro Township, which is still standing, and moved into it in March, 1808. The family were Presbyterians in faith and attended Dr. Hoge's church in Franklin until the Truro church was organized. John Long and brother, also Presbyterians, came some years later to Truro, from Nova Scotia. The town of Truro from which they came is situated at the head of a branch of the bay of Fundy, some forty or fifty miles northwest of the town of Halifax in Nova Scotia. My grandmother has often told me about the great tides in the bay of Fundy—the highest in the world."*

In 1820 Rev. Dr. Hoge organized the Truro congregation and soon after a frame meeting house was built on about three acres of ground given by Wm. Patterson, on the north side of section No. 3, near the Truro Township line, and about this time the graveyard, which in those days was esteemed an essential part of a church property, was laid out. In less than a week Jane Patterson was buried therein.

Among the early members were Robert Taylor, who died in 1828, wife and children, Abiathor Vinton, Matthew, David (Father of the Columbus attorneys, Col. Edward L. and Henry C.), Rebecca and Elizabeth (Married brothers by the name of Long), and Susan (Married Guilbert Green). They all attended Truro when first established, but subsequently Mathew Taylor and his family united with the Seceder church at Reynoldsburg; Guilbert Green's family also united with the M. E. church at Reynoldsburg, Wm. Patterson, Sr., and wife (Jane McComb,, John Sharp and wife (Jane Patterson), Hiram Leonard and wife (Eliza Patterson), Wm. Elder and wife (Martha Patterson), James Patterson and wife, Wm. Patterson, Jr., and wife, Thomas Patterson, "Uncle Tommy", married a Miss Codner and united with the Asbury M. E. church,—Thomas C. Hendren and wife (Mary Turner), for about ten years, when they united with the Baptist church at Groveport; Wm. McCombs and wife (Rebecca Keasley), Thomas McCombs and family, Jonathan McCombs and family, John McCombs and family, Samuel McCombs and wife, Wm. McCombs and wife, David McCombs, Sarah

McCombs Hendren, Robert Cooper McCombs, a minister of the Gospel, father of Prof. P. H. K. McCombs of Hanover, Ind.; Eliza McCombs Forbes, Maria McCombs Marrow, John Cambridge and family, Elias Chester, Sr., and daughters Abigail and Mrs. Louisa Chester Taylor, Freeman Chester and wife, Simeon Chester and wife, Elias Chester, Jr., wife and children, Oscar and wife, Ezra and wife, Thaddeus, a licentiate at his death, Martha, wife of A. T. Hendren and Ann Chester Taylor, Zachariah Paul and sons, John, Robert and William, Elias Guerin and wife, a daughter of John McCombs, Geo. W. Kalb and wife. Among the later members; Miss Lizzie Wheeler, Mathew E. Kalb and wife, Eliza Needels, Cyrus McCombs and wife, George West and wife, James Taylor and daughters, Tip Fahler and wife, Mrs. Zadox Vesey, Jared Forsman, Samuel Carson and others.

No records could be found, so we must be content with the incomplete list of pastors and elders. The successive pastors were Reverends James Hoge, D. D., Mathew Taylor, Abner Leonard, Elias Vandeman, John W. Fulton, Josiah D. Smith, John Scott, John Arthur, Andrew Barr and Wm. Maynard.

Among the elders were Abiathor V. Taylor, David Taylor, John McComb, Geo. W. Kalb, Mathew E. Kalb.

Home of David Taylor
Built in 1842 on the west bank of Big Walnut Creek, Truro Township

In 1835 the frame church was replaced by a substantial brick church. This building was occupied until about 1870 when it was considered unsafe, and in about 1885 on a Sunday afternoon some of the walls fell in. Shortly afterwards Samuel Brown purchased the brick and used them in the erection of some buildings on his farm.

Henry Long
1819 - 1881

Thomas Patterson
1809 - 1901

We are indebted to Henry C. Taylor, Esq., for the following interesting items regarding the purchase of stoves and the sale of pews:

"Truro Church, January 9th, 1836. The congregation met agreeably to public notice. A. Leonard was called to the chair and David Taylor was appointed secretary.

Resolved, That a committee be appointed to procure two ten plate stoves, and such pipes as said committee shall think best for the use of the meeting house. Messrs. David Taylor and Hiram Leonard were appointed said committee.

Resolved, that the stoves shall stand in the broad aisles before the doors, and the pipes suspended from above.

Resolved, that pew No. 1 be designated for the use of the officiating pastor and his family.

Resolved, that eight pews at the east end of the house, viz., two in each row, be set apart as public seats, and the two front block pews for the use of the choir.

Resolved, that a public sale of the pews not otherwise designated, take place on Wednesday, the 25th inst., on the premises at 10 o'clock a. m., and that immediate public notice be given of said sale by the building committee, and that it be published from the pulpit on Sabbath, the 22d inst., in the presence of the congregation, and that a sale of the old meeting house and stoves take place at the same time and place, provided that no pew nor the old house shall be sold at a less value than the appraised price.

> *Adjourned sine die,*
> *Abner Leonard, Chairman*
> *David Taylor, Secretary"*

Also for the very unique copy of a deed in fee simple for a pew:

"David Taylor having purchased and paid fifty dollars in full for pew No. 52 in the Truro Presbyterian meeting house, situated on their lot, being part of the northwest quarter of section No. 3, township 11, range 21, Congress land, in Franklin County, Ohio. In consideration of which payment, the right, title and possession of said pew are hereby granted and conveyed to said David Taylor, his heirs and assigns forever, subject to the conditions on which the pews were originally sold, and to such other regulations as the congregations may hereafter make respecting them. In witness whereof, the undersigned, trustees of Truro Presbyterian congregation, have hereunto put their hands and seals this 30th day of December in the year of our Lord 1837.

> (Seal) John Long
> (Seal) A. V. Taylor
> (Seal) Jonathan McComb
> (Seal) Elias Chester, Sr.
> *Trustees."*

David Taylor also purchased pew No. 31 paying the same price and receiving a similar deed.

"The Truro congregation was for many years one of the strongest in the Columbus Presbytery. The most prosperous period of the church was during the eleven years of the ministry of Rev. Josiah D. Smith. He was a most excellent man and a very able minister and deeply regarded by his congregation. He came from Truro to Columbus to assist Rev. Dr. Hoge in the pastorate of the First Presbyterian Church and afterwards became pastor and built up the Westminster Church. I remember well the time he came to Columbus, which was several years before my father moved to Columbus (David Taylor moved to Columbus in 1857), and the church never prospered after he left it as it had before." (From a letter written by Col. E. L. Taylor).

Like many another rural church, the decline of Truro was caused by the fact that the old substantial members either died or moved away, besides many of the farms in the vicinity of this church have been for many years, largely occupied by tenants instead of by the owners. Then it is reported that *"the coming of the Civil War during the pastorate of Rev. Wm. Maynard caused some dissension."* Very likely these differences were no more serious than in many of the other congregations of the different denominations of those days. While some have distinct recollections of this feeling others cannot recall and even doubt that there was any feeling, indicating that the dissension was not general.

Truro graveyard, for many years one of the best kept and one of the most prominent in the county, has also gone down, and no burials have taken place there for several years. Many of the tombstones have fallen over and some are broken.

The congregation owned a parsonage just north of the church building, but across the line in Truro Township.

A Sunday school was organized at an early day and continued until about the time of the disbandment of the congregation. A Sunday school was also maintained at the "Branch (or Mission) Church," known as the Alum Creek Church. The officers of the Truro Church served both churches, the services at the Alum Creek Church being held in the afternoons. This building was sold in about 1867 or 1868 and still occupies the same lot which is now a part of the Schaff farm on the Columbus and Winchester Pike.

315

Groveport Presbyterian Church

This congregation was organized October 13, 1854 with the following membership: John Begg, Mary Begg, Mrs. Damaris Champe, Jane Coffman, C. Perry Dildine, Mary Ann Dildine, E. A. W. Furgeson, Anna M. Gares, Samuel Sharp, Eliza N. Sharp, Abraham Sharp, Temperance Sharp, Mrs. Ruth Seymour (wife of William), Mrs. Sarah Woodring, Miss Sarah Wright, Miss Jane Wright, and two days later,October 15th—the following, others became members: Daniel McIntire, Clarinda McIntire, Mary Paul, Maria Roberts.

From 1854 until 1860 the following united: John K. Adams and wife, Jane Clark, Mrs. Susan Dildine, Margaret A. Decker, Wm. T. Hendren (entered the ministry in 1864), Geo. L. Hendren, Margaret Long, Mrs. Sarah McCormick, Joseph Rathmell, John R. Smith, Harriet R. Sharp (wife of Abraham), Parmetia Sarber (wife of Leonard), Mrs. Mary Shoemaker, Miss Melvina Sharp, Mrs. Mary Woodring (widow of Perry).

From 1860 to 1870: Solomon Alspach and wife, Sarah Alspach, Miss Jenet Beggs, John Begg, Jr., Mrs. Kate M. Brown (widow of T. M. Brown; Mrs. B. married Rev. John Creath on May 2, 1871), Miss Mary Camerson, Rodney Champe, Mrs. Mary J. Coffman, Elizabeth and Leander Champe, Homer Chester, Andrew F. Dildine and wife, Alpheus H. Davis, Mary, Laura A., Mary Belle and Albert Dildine, Mrs. Mary Decker, Milton Fisher, Miss Sarah J. Fisher, Mrs. Gares, Mrs. Ann Glick, Lewis S. Guerin and wife, John E. Guerin (attending Theological Seminary), Henry Geese, Nancy Hendren (wife of Geo. L.), A. Turner Hendren and wife, Hiram Mealy and wife, Mary E. Moul, Mrs. Christina McIntire, Miss Maggie McIntire (married A. M. Rarey), John McComb, Miss Elizabeth Overdeer, Mrs. Kate Root, Elias Remalia and wife, Mrs. Mary Reese, Mrs. Eliza Steele, Miss Kate Seymour (married John Cox), Chas. J. Stevenson, Thos. Seymour and wife, Welton and Miner Seymour, Leonard Sarber, Wm. P. Sharpe and wife, Mrs. Susannah Senter, Maggie and Ida Ella Seymour, Mrs. Mary E. Sharp, John Wildermuth, Mary A. and Effie Woodring, Mrs. Maggie Peister, Mrs. Martha Wallace, Miss Theodosia Wallace, Mrs. Olive Work, John E. Whitemore and wife, Miss Mahala Whaley, Mrs. Elizabeth Westenhaver.

Between 1870 and 1880: Geo. S. Dildine, Miss Eliza Herr, Virginia F. Hughes, Geo. W. Kalb and wife, Mathew E., Albert and Alice Kalb, Henry Kalb and wife, Jacob C. Knight, Jephtah King and wife, Samuel Kindler and wife, Geo. W. Lisle and wife, Mrs. Eliza Lisle, David Leda, Mrs. Angelina Mansfield, Mrs. Hannah Needels, Mrs. Eliza Needels (wife of Geo. W.), John Pattrick and wife, Mrs. Charlotte Ramsey, A. Miner Rarey, Mrs. Sarah F. Stevenson, Samuel S. Schooley, John P. Sharp and wife, Geo. Seymour and wife, Miss Jennie Seymour, Mrs. Jennie Shockley, Jesse Seymour, Mary Jane Seymour, Mrs. Sarah Seymour, Mrs. Maria Simpson, Mrs. Francis Sarber, Nathan P. Toy and wife, Miss Jennie Thompson, Mrs. Mary C. Van Wormer, Lucinda Van Wormer, Miss Irene Vesey, Mrs. A. J. West, Miss Rosetta M. West, Levi Wagner and wife, Daniel Wagner and wife, Geo. T. Wheeler and wife, Miss Elizabeth Wheeler, Mrs. Margaret A. Whims (wife of Seymour W.). Jacob Wolf, Sr., and wife, Mrs. Elouissa Watkins, Mary L. Woodring, David Westenhaver, Mrs. Catharine Wheeler, Mrs. Nettie Willie, Miss Almeda Barrett, Peter Agew, Mrs. Anna M. Chester, Samuel Cairns, Miss Nancy Cairns, W. A. Chamberlain, Mary A. Champe, Elon Champe, Samuel S. Crist, Sarah A. Crist.

47 persons became members during 1870, many of them coming from the Truro Presbyterian church. Since 1880 the following others have become members: Mrs. Ella Baird, Connetia M. Butterman, Anna Crist (married Rev. S. H. McClenigan), Wm. T. Decker, Dr. Walter Hewetson and wife, John Pattrick, Maggie Pattrick, John Reed, Mrs. Anna Reed, Jacob Reed, Henry Scoffeld and wife, Miss Deaza Senter (wife of C. D. Rarey), Mrs. L. A. Seymour (wife of Miner), Alonzo Strode, J. V. Thompson, Wm. E. Thompson, Mrs. Ann E. Vesey, David M. Willie and Jacob Zimmerman.

Geo. L. Hendren says: *"The present membership is about (40) forty. This congregation has suffered great loss in the last two decades by deaths and removals—seven ruling elders and their families, eleven trustees and their families, and others, making about twenty-five families. The Sunday school has suffered even greater losses. There are more ex-members of this church and Sunday school in Columbus churches and Sunday schools than we now enroll, besides all that have gone far away or died. * * **

"This congregation, in the seventies, could sustain a pastor at a salary of ($1,000) one thousand dollars and give hundreds to missions and benevolence, besides owning a parsonage; now we do well to raise three hundred dollars for all purposes. Surely this has been a mission church, swarming almost to death; but we have a name to live, and in God's hands may yet do much."

The pastors have been: Reverends Samuel Wilson, Wm. Maynard, Irwin Schofield, ____ Creath, ____ Stevenson, ____ Reynolds, ____ Kingery, C. B. Downs 1880, N. R. Crow 1881, E. Thompson 1882. Then Groveport and Lithopolis jointly called S. D. Smith, 1882-1885; A. B. Brice, D. D., 1886-1889; Dr. Brice closed his pastoral labors of fifty years with this church, becoming wholly disabled. He died at Cincinnati June 28, 1892; ____ Hempstead, T. B. Atkins and Wm. Bullock, the present pastor.

Among those served as elders were: Samuel Sharp. C. Perry Dildine, John Begg, Sr., Wm. P. Sharp, L. S. Guerin, Geo. W. Kalb, Samuel S. Crist, Geo. L. Hendren, Miner Seymour, Welter Seymour, A. W. Strode, John McComb.

The church building was erected the same year that the congregation was organized, and about the same time a Sunday school was started. The superintendents have been: Samuel Sharp, C. P. Dildine, Geo. W. Kalb and Geo. L. Hendren.

The present membership of the church is about 40, and of the Sunday school about the same.

Groveport Baptist Church

On August 27, 1808, Ishmael Davis, John Dukes, Wm. D. Hendren, Wm. Clevenger, Mary Dukes, Nancy Chester, Elizabeth Cherry, Eleanor Peterson and Mary Rawlings were constituted into a regular Baptist church, called Bethel, by Elders Wm. Brundidge and John W. Loofborrow.

For several years the meetings were held at the residences of Wm. D. Hendren and Wm. Clevenger. As was the custom of all the pioneer churches of the township, meetings were held but once a month. No meetings were held in November, December and January, in the winter of 1808-1809, on account of the severe weather and high waters. In July of 1809 John Swisher and wife and Jane Puntney become members. In 1815 meetings were held alternately at Bro. Hendren's and Sister Caldwell's. *"On June 22, 1816, by a unanimous vote, Bro. Ishmael Davis was called to exercise his gifts."*

The first church building, a frame, was erected in 1838-1839, about one-half mile west of town, and is now occupied as a residence. Under date of January 14, 1837, the minutes record the following: *"Resolved, that we thankfully accept Bro. Samuel Richardson's proposal for building a Baptist meeting house."* The building committee was Wm. W. Richardson, Jacob Weaver and John Swisher. The first meeting held in this building was on March 16, 1839. Soon after the building was occupied a division arose, some favoring missions and Sunday schools, the others opposing them. On April 18, 1840, Elkanah Simms, Thos. Blakely (an exhorter), Sisters Weaver, Myers, Seymour and Nancy Simms, being opposed to missions and Sunday schools, styled themselves "old school Baptists," and they, having possession of the keys to the church, held the building. *"Having lost our meeting house by fraud"* on August 13, 1842. Thomas C. Hendren, G. W. Simms and Fred Swisher were appointed a building committee—by those favoring missions and Sunday schools—to purchase a lot in Wert's Grove and build a church. This building was erected in 1843 on lot No. 38, at a cost of about $1,200.00, and is still occupied.

"In February, 1846, Elders Madden and Heistand held a *"meeting of days,"* which resulted in the addition, by baptism, of John Swisher, Mary Swisher, Dinah Brown, Elizabeth Brown, Emily Updegraff, Frederick Whitzel, Geo. Whitzel, Emanuel Conklin, Susan Conklin, Catharine Smith, Margaret Tussing, Wm. Rower, Thos. Stickler and Sarah E. Hendren.

In 1880 some $400.00 in repairs and improvements were added under the supervision of Wm. Whims and Frederick Swisher. The following soliciting committee assisting: Miss Sallie I. Settle, Mrs. Mary Turner Hendren and Miss Sarah E. Hendren. And on May 28, 1881, the building was reopened for worship. The re-dedication sermon was preached by Rev. H. L. Gear and Rev. D. A. Randall, D. D., preached in the evening. Miss Irene Vesey of the Presbyterian church acted as organist, and Mrs. Casper Limpert furnished a profusion of plants and flowers for the occasion. The membership had become reduced by deaths and removals to only eight. In 1882 a series of meetings were held at which Rev. A. L. Jordon, of Columbus, assisted, and ten were added to the membership. The candidates were baptized in Blacklick Creek, about a mile north of Groveport, being the first baptism in twenty years. In the fall of 1884 the baptistry was put into the church, and in November Henry Whitzel and wife. Arthur Seymour and Betsey Whitzel were baptized in it.

The pastors have been: Wm. Brundige, 1808; Thos. Snellson, Adam Miller, John Hite, 1816-1819; James Peters, Lewis Madden, 1831-__; Samuel D. Alton (after the division), 1843, (*"John H. Fristoe and John W. Miller were granted clear licenses to preach the gospel on February 11, 1843"*); John W. Heistand, James Harvey, 1848-1852; John W. Miller, 1853—died in 1855, (*"May 6, 1854, M. C. Hendren was licensed to preach the gospel"*); E. Bounds, Mordicai Cloud Hendren, 1861-__; O. Allen, for six years, died in Columbus May 19, 1870; Samuel C. Tussing, 1883.-__; A. L. Jordon (resigned August 1, 1886); A. W. Gale, James W. Miller and M. M. Marlow.

Supply pastors: Geo. Jeffries, A. W. Williams, Dr. D. A. Randall, of Columbus; T. C. Emerson and Geo. D. Rogers.

The following is a list of the officers:

Deacons—Wm. Downing Hendren, Wm. Glasscock, ____ Bolles, Geo. W. Simms, Wm. Cox, Frederick Swisher, Thomas Cloud Hendren, Edward Davis, Chas. Steward, J. W. Mitchell, Wm. Snow Crosby, A. J. Bradfield and Chas. Hattenfels.

Clerks—Wm. D. Hendren (grandfather of Sarah E.), John Swisher, John Fristoe, A. Willie, John Updegraff, Thos. C. Hendren, for 19 1-2 years (father of Sarah E.), and Sarah E. Hendren, for 17 years. The present Board of Trustees is Mrs. Sallie I. Settle Brown, Sarah E. Hendren and Annie McCullock.

Canal Winchester Reformed Church

Among the early settlers in Bloom and Violet Townships, Fairfield County, were many German Reformed people, coming principally from Pennsylvania. The Jobs, Betzers and Glicks congregations (the latter was organized September 15, 1808) were among the very first church organizations in this section. Rev. George Weisz baptized children in the neighborhood of Winchester as early as 1816 or 1817, and in 1830 or 1831 Rev. Weisz instructed a class of about twenty-five children in the Heidelberg catechism preparatory to confirmation, at the residence of Daniel Leckrone, who then lived in a two-story log house that stood on the town lot. The children would bring their dinners and the instruction would begin at eight o'clock in the morning and last until about four o'clock; in this way the catechism would be studied and perhaps committed to memory in one week, and the following Sunday the class was confirmed at Job's church. Preaching services were held in a log school house that stood in the southeast corner of section No. 16, along the Lithopolis and Winchester Road, and in the large room on the Samuel Deitz farm that had been built by Lewis Kramer and the United Brethren people in which to hold meetings. This building was afterwards removed to the southeast quarter of section No. 16, now occupied by Chas. Schacht—and in the building on the southwest corner of West and Washington Streets, now occupied by Mrs. McFadden.

In 1839 in company with the Lutherans, a brick church was erected on lot No. 40, Washington Street. Frederick Fruchey did the carpenter work for $787.50, and Eichelberg & Epply received $784.48 for the brick work. It was occupied some four or five years before it was plastered. The plastering was done by Peter Miller. The first *pews* were slab *benches.*

A memorandum, dated August 1841 says: *"The church is in debt eight hundred and twenty-five dollars and some cents."* Three hundred and fifty dollars of this amount was borrowed from J. B. Wert, the note being dated October 20, 1841 at Werts Grove, O. It seems that this debt hung on for several years. In 1849 and 1850, when Henry Game was one of the Trustees, some two hundred and seventy dollars were paid and on May 8, 1854 a payment of one hundred and sixty-five dollars was receipted for in full.

Samuel Loucks and Philip Zimmer were active Trustees, and each subscribed $50 on the first subscription list under date of May 24, 1839.

In 1861 a new roof was put on the building and a steeple added. The pulpit was located in the east end of the church until the steeple was put up when it was removed to the west end of the room, and the pews faced about.

On March 20, 1863 the bell was put up. In the summer of 1869 the interior of the church was remodeled. The old goblet shaped pulpit with its flight of six or eight steps, the old benches, the Melodeon, the ten plate stoves and other furniture was sold at auction. The old floor was replaced with a new one, a raised platform for the choir and the organ was erected in the rear end, (East) between the doors, new windows and doors and pews were furnished at a total cost of some thirteen hundred ($1300) dollars.

This building was occupied alternately by these two congregations until 1881 when the Reformed people purchased the interest of the Lutherans.

The building was however occupied by both congregations until each of them completed their new churches and later it was occupied by the United Brethren during the time they were building their church in 1887.

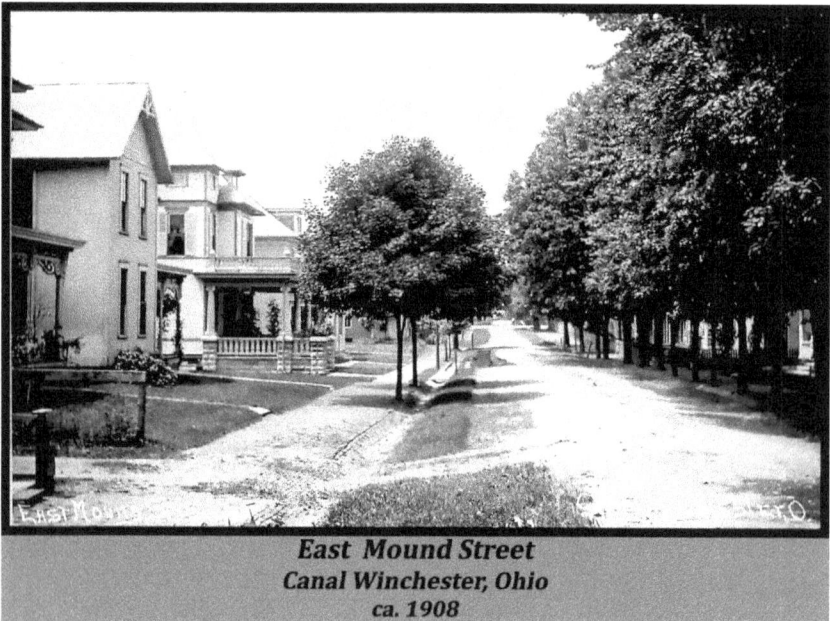

East Mound Street
Canal Winchester, Ohio
ca. 1908

On February 11, 1881 at a congregational meeting called for the purpose *"the Elders, Deacons and Trustees were appointed a committee to see what amount of money can be secured towards putting up a church building,"* and on March 8 this committee made a proposition to the Lutherans to either buy or sell their half interest in the old building at $600.00. After due consideration the Lutherans decided to sell, and on April 2 at a congregational meeting it was voted to build. Several building sites were proposed; one plan was to buy the adjoining lot No. 41 on the south and build on these two lots; some proposed to build on

322

lots No. 19, 20 and 21 on East Waterloo Street then owned by O. P. Chaney, others favored three lots—No. 35, 36 and 37 on East Mound Street then owned by Wm. P. Miller, finally lots No. 24 and 25 on the corner of West and Washington Streets were selected and purchased for $1250, and the following building committee was appointed: John S. Lehman, Chairman; Geo. Loucks, John Brenner, Jacob Bott, and Sam Deitz with Rev. S. P. Mauger Secretary, who served until May 15, 1882 when Geo. F. Bareis was elected Secretary and Elijah Alspach Treasurer.

East Waterloo St · Circa 1908 Canal Winchester O.

The Building Committee visited the Obetz Lutheran church on the Columbus and Groveport Pike and then requested Geo. F. Bareis to prepare plans and specifications for a similar building, which were slightly modified and adopted. The following persons were awarded the respective parts of the work: Ferdinand Leonard, wood work $2225; N. J. Wolf, brick work $2442; James Scanlon, plastering $275; O. J. Lawyer, painting $110; Geo. W. Siegfried, frescoing $250; Watterson and Co., glass $218.

The building alone cost $6600. Other expenditures including the lots, pews, pulpit, carpet, stoves, fence, and bell, (the bell was taken from the old church but its value is included) amounted to $2200 at total of $8800.

The corner stone was laid on August 1, 1881. Rev. J. Vogt D. D. of Delaware preached the sermon, Revs. Geo. H. Leonard, James Heffley and the pastor Silas P. Mager assisting, By September 1 the walls were up to the square and the roof was put on late in the fall. The building then stood until the next spring when the plastering, frescoing, etc. were in turn completed, and on February 18, 1883 the building was dedicated free of all debt. Rev. E. P. Herbuck of Akron preached the dedicatory sermon from Isaiah LI : 1. The following ministers were also present: M. Louck, D. D., James Heffley, W. A. From and the pastor, Austin Henry.

The buildings that stood on the lots were sold at auction on June 4, 1881; Wm. Schrock purchased the house and moved it to Lot No. 36 Dove's 1st Addition and John C. Speaks purchased the stable and moved it to the adjoining lot No. 26. In October 1882 the old church property was sold at public auction to Geo. Loucks for $526, the bell and furniture being reserved.

November 26, 1895 the wind removed part of the roof and soon after Mr. Loucks sold it to Israel Gayman who in 1896 tore down the old building that had become sacred and hallowed by many baptisms, confirmations, funeral and other services.

The following were the early members, perhaps up to 1854: Peter Brown and wife, Chas. Brown and wife, Samuel Loucks and wife, Wm. Leight, Daniel Harmon, Daniel Bergtresser, John Brenner, Henry Harmon and wife, Lydia Miller, George Deitz, Lewis Deitz, Sarah Sunday, Absalom Shoemaker, August Walters, Christina Brown, Rebecca Shoemaker, Eliza Armpreister, Susan Brenner, Solomon Alspach and wife, John Schrock and wife, Henry Game and wife, John Graff, John Wagoner and wife, Jacob Boyer and wife. Of these Mrs. Eliza Armpreister aged 90 years, Mrs. Susan Brenner Hunsicker and Mr. John Brenner are still members.

The following pastors have served this church consecutively:

Rev. George Weisz arrived at Lancaster, Ohio, on October 20th, 1816. He then spent about two months in Fairfield, Pickaway, Perry and Ross Counties, preaching on the Sabbath and often through the week. The people in the localities that he visited importuned him to become their pastor; but not having been licensed and ordained to preach he returned to Philadelphia, Pa., and pursued his studies until the following September, when, at a meeting of the Synod at York, Pa., he was licensed and his call to become the pastor of the people he had visited the year previous was confirmed.

On October 11th, 1817, he again arrived at Lancaster, Ohio, and at once commenced his ministerial labors—organizing congregations, preaching, instructing the young, and engaging in such other duties as were required of the pioneer missionary. At first he supplied thirteen congregations at distances from each other, varying from twenty to fifty-six miles. All the congregations of Lancaster Classes, except Delaware and the two in Columbus grew out of his labors. The rapid increase in the membership and of the number of the congregations, created an imperative demand for more laborers. In the absence of a theological seminary, although burdened with the multitudinous duties of such an extensive field, he still found time to give private instructions to young men desiring to prepare for the ministry. And he also wrote and published a book entitled *"A Short Instruction in the Christian Religion According to the Heidelberg Catechism,"* which he had printed at Lancaster, Ohio, in 1837. The right hand pages were in English and the left hand in German.

During his ministry of nearly forty years he preached 5,144 sermons, baptized 2,940 persons, confirmed 1,464, performed 535 marriages, and attended 736 funerals. He organized this congregation and served as pastor until declining health compelled him to retire in 1854. His home was in Lancaster, Ohio, where he died March 10, 1859, aged 65 years, 8 months, 19 days. Father Weisz is remembered by some of our older people, in his great long overcoat, astride a large black horse, with his saddle bags, and by the fact that bad roads and swollen streams did not prevent him from meeting his appointments unless they were entirely impassible.

Rev. Israel S. Weisz succeeded his father in 1855, at the age of 23 years—to 1860, when he removed to Pennsylvania. He died January 15th, 1894, at York, Pa., where he had preached for the past twenty years. His body lies in Prospect Hill Cemetery at York, Pa.

Rev. James Heffly, December 19, 1860, to September 2, 1871. Rev. Heffly came directly to Winchester from Heidelberg Theological Seminary after his graduation and has lived in Winchester continuously since.

Rev. Eli Keller, D. D., August 25, 1872, to March 30, 1874, when he removed to Zionsville, Pa.: where he served the Reformed Church until March, 1901 when he resigned the pastorate on the account of declining health.

Rev. Eli Keller
1856-1914

Rev. Silas P. Mauger after completing his studies at Heidelberg College and Theological Seminary became pastor April 26, 1874, and served until April 30, 1882, when he removed to Phoenixville, Penn., and for the past several years has served as pastor of the Reformed Congregation at Stone Church, Pa.

Rev. Austin Henry, September 25, 1882, to April 60 1885, when he died at the age of 39 years 5 months and 19 days. His body was buried in Union Grove cemetery, but several years later, November, 1896, after the death of Mrs. Henry and their only child, Bert, his body was removed to Tiffin, Ohio, where they lie side by side, awaiting the resurrection of the dead.

The Winchester charge consisted of the David's, Job's, Zion's and Salem's congregations. A division of the charge had been spoken of at different times; after the death of Rev. Henry, active measures were instituted and a division into two charges effected. David's congregation was constituted one of them and Rev. L. B. C. Lahr became pastor January 1, 1886, serving until April 1, 1890, when he removed to Hillsboro, Ohio, and later to Delaware, Ohio, where he is pastor of the Reformed church.

Rev. John L. Bretz's pastorate began June 20, 1891, and continued until September 21, 1895, when he removed to Millersburg, Ind., and where he died November 30, 1897, aged 45 years 5 months and 3 days.

Rev. J. P. Stahl, the present pastor, began his pastorate on December 1, 1896.

The following is a partial list of persons who have served as elders and deacons:

Elders: Peter Brown, Samuel Loucks. Daniel Bergstresser, Samuel Deitz, Elijah Alspach, Benjamin Alspach, Reuben Bott, Jacob Bott, Geo.

Loucks, Geo. F. Bareis, W. D. Beeks, Chas. Bush, W. T. Heilman, Clinton Alspach.

Deacons: Wm. P. Miller, Emanuel Bott, Daniel Bush, Geo. W. Sponsler, John H. Deitz, Amos Bush, Wm. Palsgrave, John M. Lehman, James A. Alspach, Henry N. Brenner, Chas. F. Dunlop, Jacob Deitz, O. P. Gayman, John H. Barnhart, Philip Weber, Wm. H. Lehman.

The following Sunday school constitution, adopted by the Lutheran and Reformed church, in Violet Township, on July 30, 1843, while not directly in Madison Township, still reveals the methods and practices in vogue in this neighborhood in those days:

Constitution of the Sabbath School Union

Feeling the responsibility we owe toward God and the rising generation, we form ourselves into an union and adopt the following:

Section I. This union shall be called the Sabbath School Union of Job's church; to be held in said church.

Section II. This union shall consist of one superintendent, one assistant (if needed) and three directors.

Section III. It shall be the duty of the superintendent to open the school by reading a chapter or part of a chapter of Scripture, singing and prayer, and give order to teachers and ask questions in general and explain, and devise plans by and with the consent of the directors or a majority of them, and to close by singing and prayer, or cause it to be done.

Section IV. It shall be the duty of the secretary to keep records of all the proceedings and the number of scholars and teachers.

Section V. The treasurer shall receive and keep all moneys received either by subscription or donation, and pay all orders presented to him, signed by a majority of the directors, as far as the funds admit.

Section VI. The librarian shall keep all books belonging to said school, take or cause to be taken to the school room every Sabbath when the school meets.

Section VII. The directors' duties shall be to manage and regulate all the affairs of the school, appoint teachers, regulate the several classes, select and purchase such books as they may think most suitable, and in case of death, resignation or otherwise of any of the officers, fill such vacancy.

Section VIII. There shall be an annual election held on the first Sunday of April each year and elect such officers as specified in section II.

Section IX. No person shall have a vote except he or she is a member of some Christian denomination, and sign his or her name to this constitution."

The first officers were: Samuel Dressler, Superintendent; Michael Ebright, Assistant Superintendent; Jacob Shumaker, Secretary; John N. Slife, Treasurer; H. Nicodemus, Librarian, and John G. Brunner, Jacob Boyer and Michael Ebright, Directors.

The Reformed and Lutheran people started a Sunday school soon after their church building was occupied in about 1840. The Sunday schools of those days were quite different from the modern school. German primers were used in some of the classes, which attracted a number of the citizens—who wanted to learn the German language— to attend the Sunday school for this purpose. Some of the leading members questioned the propriety of conducting the school for this purpose, and as the glass was not yet in the windows and the weather got cold, the school was discontinued.

The Reformed people then attended the Union Sunday school at the United Brethren Church until April 16, 1865, when the Reformed and Lutheran again organized a school with the following officers: Rev. James Heffly and Rev. George Mochel. Pastors; C. Gayman. Superintendent; Jacob Bott, Assistant Superintendent; W. F. Armpreister, Secretary; Geo. Loucks, Librarian; Henry Howard, Assistant Librarian; Geo. Loucks, Treasurer. The treasurer collected $52.00 with which 35 small Testaments, 24 Primers, 36 Hymn books and 44 Question books were purchased. On April 30, 1865, the secretary's report says: *"14 teachers present, total attendance 134."*

On January 23, 1864, a meeting was held to consider the purchase of a melodeon. Miss Hanie was then teaching music in Winchester, and through February and March Daniel and Christian Gayman took lessons of her, practicing on Bergstresser's melodeon. The melodeon was put into the church on Saturday, March 19, 1864, and on the following Sunday, Daniel Gayman played on it at a church service. On the following Sunday Miss Swan, also a music teacher, acted as melodeonist. Of course there was opposition to its introduction, as there was to almost every other innovation. Previous to the purchase of the melodeon Jacob Zarbaugh had for three years led the singing with a clarinet. Miss Barbara Zarbaugh (Bott) was the first regular organist (melodeonist). After a few years the melodeon was replaced by an organ, and soon after the new church was occupied the present organ was purchased. The organists since Miss Zarbaugh have been: Miss Katie Stevenson (Mrs. Rev. M. Loucks), Miss Ollie Hesser (Mrs. Scott), Miss Ella Vought (Mrs. John A. Whitzel), Geo. M. Herbst, Misses Lila Starr, Fannie Lehman, Emma Schoch, Ella Loucks and Ruth Stahl. *Choristers:* Wm. Palsgrove, John H. Speilman, Samuel Foucht, Frank Brown and Wm. D. Beeks.

January 13, 1872, a committee consisting of Rev. Geo. Mochel, Rev. James Heffly, Peter Brown, Wm. C Speilman and Geo. Loucks was appointed to draft a new constitution for the Sunday school, and at a joint meeting on February 3 following, the same was reported and adopted.

Up to this time there had been but one Sunday school, one church choir, one organist, and the best of Christian fellowship prevailed. Many of the members of both congregations being Germans, they had intermarried until it was a common occurrence to find families in which the father and part of the children held membership in one church while the mother and others belonged to the other. It is a curious fact that many persons who were at an early day Lutheran are now Reformed, and that Reformed are now Lutheran.

During the pastorate of Rev. Geo. Mochel the peculiar doctrines of his denomination were emphasized, and then the advent of the Speilman Brothers, prominent and active members of the Lutheran church at Lancaster, culminated in the separation of the Sunday schools in December, 1873, when each denomination organized a Sunday school of its own.

The organization of the Reformed Sunday school took place at the parsonage, Rev. Eli Keller, D. D., being then the pastor; he lived where Elijah Alspach now lives.

The Superintendents have been: Of the joint Sunday school—Christian Gayman, Peter Brown and Moses Gayman.

Since 1873: Peter Brown, Geo. F. Bareis, January 1, 1878, to January 1, 1887; Frank Brown, January 1, 1887, to September 2, 1888; Geo. B. Bolenbaugh, assistant superintendent two Sundays; O. P. Gayman, September 23, 1888, to January 1, 1891; Geo. F. Bareis. January 1, 1891, to date.

The present enrollment of the Sunday School including the Cradle Roll and Home Department is 300.

A Missionary Society was organized May 11. 1879, since which time regular meetings have been held. A Gleaner's Band, a Ladies Auxiliary Society and a Young People's Society of Christian Endeavor represent active auxiliary organizations of the congregation. The present church membership is two hundred and forty.

Rev. John I. Swander, D. D., who was pastor of the Reformed church in Lancaster in 1860-1865 relates the story that *a wolf drove a woman and child out of the old Reformed church in Winchester in the sixties;* the story runs that Lancaster Classis was holding a meeting here, and while a Rev. J. G. Wolfe of Penn was preaching, a small child of Rev. Joel Alspach's began crying, which seemed to annoy him so much that he said, "*I cannot preach with that child crying so, will the lady take it out ?*" As Mrs. Alspach was retiring she is said to have *"glanced back to see if the Wolfe was coming."*

Evangelical Lutheran Church

Previous to 1839 Rev. Pence preached in a school house on the Zimmer farm south of Winchester; later meetings were held in the house now occupied by Mrs. McFadden on the corner of West and Washington Streets. It is not now known definitely when or where the organization of David's congregation was effected further than that in 1839 in connection with the German Reformed Congregation the brick church was erected on Washington Street.

Among the early members were Philip Zimmer and wife, Eli Henry, and George Zimmer, John Overholser and wife, J. B. Ernswiler, George Herbst and wife, Samuel Weller and wife, Daniel Miller, Emanuel Miller and wife, Peter Bott and wife, George Myers and wife, Jacob Schrock and wife, Henry Dellinger and wife, George Lehman and wife, Jacob Bott and wife, Henry Zangmeister, John Low and wife, Henry Eichelberger, Jacob Crooks, John A. Armpreister, Samuel Sunday, John F. Pfundt and wife, Mrs. Rebecca Bergstresser, Jacob Brenner and wife, John Myers and wife, Michael Miller and wife and others. Only two of the above list are still living, Mrs. Bergtresser and Mr. Jacob Bott, both of these are now members of the Reformed Church. For many years services were held but once a month, later on each alternate Sunday.

Some of the early members say: *"One Constitution answered for both churches; the Lutheran members would help elect the Reformed officers and the Reformed members would vote for the Lutherans."* One Sunday School, one organist and one choir worked harmoniously together. This mutual feeling continued until during the pastorates of Rev. George Mochel and Rev. James Heffly when the distinctions became more marked and finally resulted in the organization of separate Sunday Schools. Both congregations continued to occupy the church building on Washington Street until the new Lutheran Church was complete.

In March 1881 the Lutherans sold their interest in the old church building to the Reformed for $600 and at once arranged to build. A lot on the corner of Waterloo and Trine Streets was donated by Christian Gayman but while excavating for the foundation the vats of the old tanyard were discovered, when the question was raised whether a good foundation could be secured except at a large additional cost; finally it was decided to build on another site located on the northwest corner of Mound and Elm Streets where their handsome edifice was erected.

The church was built during the pastorate of Rev. H. J. Schuh, who preached his farewell sermon on the evening of the same day that it was dedicated. The dedicatory services took place on Sunday morning November 19, 1882; the following ministers were present: Prof. Schuette, George Mochel, J. Beck and Henry J. Schuh. Rev. George Mochel preached in German and Rev. Prof. Schuette in English. The frescoing was done in the fall of 1892.

During January 1881 Rev. H. J. Schuh preached a series of sermons on the distinctive doctrines of the Lutheran Church. For several consecutive weeks beginning with the issue of the *"Winchester Times"* of January 26th a discussion was carried on between someone who wrote over the signature *"Enquirer"* and Rev. Schuh, in the issue of the *"Times"* of February 24th Rev. J. S. Mills, of Westerville, a minister in the United Brethren Church addressed an open letter to Rev. Schuh setting forth three propositions and closing as follows: *"Do you hold yourself able and ready to defend these propositions by testimony of the Word of God?"* The controversy, thus began, continued from week to week and finally culminated in a public debate. The following "terms of agreement" fully explains the particulars of the discussion,

"Terms of Agreement for a Public Controversy to be held between Rev. J. S. Mills of Westerville, Ohio and Rev. H. J. Schuh of Canal Winchester, Ohio, May 3, 4 and 5, 1881.

*I. **Subjects**, (a.) That in the Lord's Supper the words 'This is my body' and 'this is my blood' are to be understood and taken in their literal sense, (b.) That the ordinary means of regeneration in the case of infants is Holy Baptism, (c.) That the Evangelical Lutheran Church is the true visible church of Christ on earth.*

*II. **Principles of Discussion**, (a.) The disputants are limited to arguments that are allowed or recognized in the Holy Scriptures, (b.) The words of Holy Scripture are to be understood in their literal sense unless sufficient reasons are found in the Scriptures for assigning a figurative sense.*

*III. **Time**, (a.) The discussion is to take place May 3, 4, and 5. (b.) The morning meetings are to open at 9 o'clock and close at 11, the afternoon meetings open at 2 and close at 4, the evening meetings open at 7 and close at 9:30. (c.) The speeches are to be limited to one-half hour each, (d.) One day and evening to be spent on each proposition, (e.) The affirmative is to have the opening and closing speech on each proposition.*

*IV. **Place**. The discussion is to be held in the United Brethren Church at Canal Winchester.*

*V. **Moderator**. Rev. James Heffly. (Signed) H. J. Schuh, J. S. Mills."*

Rev. Schuh was on the affirmative and Rev. Mills on the negative side.

The seating capacity as well as the standing room of the church was taxed to its utmost during the sessions of this debate, and it ended as such discussions usually do; by the friends and sympathizers of each disputant claiming the victory.

The pastors have been Revs. Pence, John Wagenhals — who moved to Lithopolis from Lancaster, Ohio in 1844 remaining there until 1848 when he again moved back to Lancaster. He was born August 16, 1799 and died at Lancaster on September 12, 1884; Charles Wernle, J. P. Eirich, George Mochel, January 1, 1862 to March 15, 1874, Henry J. Schuh, September 27, 1874 to September 3, 1882; Dr. George H. Shodde — one year while Rev. H. J. Schuh was away on a leave of absence.—Louis H. Schuh, now President of Capital University, April 1, 1883 to February 12, 1890; and the present pastor Theo. H. E. Eich, whose pastorate began in 1890.

In the Baptismal Record of Glick's church we find the names of Rev. M. J. Steck as early as August 24, 1824 to June 21, 1829; Rev. John Wagenhals, September 26, 1829 and at intervals as late as March 12, 1848; Rev. Pence baptized some children May 21, 1843; Rev. C. Speilman, May 24, 1837 to August 4, 1839; Rev. Chas Wernle, January 5, 1852 to February 21, 1857; Rev. P. Eirich, February 1855 to May, 1859.

On April 7, 1871 the congregations composing this charge voted to sell their parsonage located just east of Lithopolis. Rev. George Mochel then built the present parsonage in the same season.

Previous to December 1873 beginning in the spring of 1865 the Lutheran and Reformed churches maintained a union Sunday School. On Jan. 6, 1874 a committee Rev. Mochel and Wm. Speilman representing the Lutheran and Rev. Keller and Peter Brown the Reformed schools — was appointed to divide the property and also a debt of fourteen dollars. A separate Sunday School was then organized with John H. Speilman, Superintendent. Mr. Speilman's successors have been: Christian Gayman, Charles Bachman, about ten years, and John F. Bachman the present incumbent for about ten years. The present membership of the church is about 135 and of the Sunday School about 120.

The Christian Union Church

The Christian Union church was originated and established in Groveport in the fall of 1865 by Rev. James Fowler Given. It was when political excitement ran high and when the partisan spirit was intense that dissentions grew up. Rev. Given and others, Democrats, not being in accord with the stand taken by the Methodist Episcopal church at that time, concluded to form a new denomination (*"The Democratic Methodist"*), which they accordingly did, conducting their services and Sunday school at the school house in Groveport. Among the ministers besides Mr. Given were J. V. Clover and ____ Klick.

Jacob Burgett was Superintendent of the Sunday school, and A. M. Senter, Ida Smith and others teachers.

John P. Given, a son of the founder, says, *"The church flourished until the death of its founder in August, 1867, when some of the interest was lost, and after the death of W. H. Bishop and Jacob Burgett and wife, the organization went down."*

St. Mary's Catholic Church

The St. Mary's Catholic church of Groveport was organized in 1871, when the brick building on the corner of Blacklick and Front Streets was purchased from the United Brethren people.

Michael Corbett and family, Patrick and William Corbett, Thomas Fagan and John Cavinee have been the principal supporters. There has never been a regular pastor located here, but services were held about once a month, and were conducted by ministers from Columbus. Among these supplies have been Rev. X. A. Gallager, L. P. McKeirman, F. J. Campbell, H. Anderson and T. J. Lane.

The Mennonite Church

Beginning about 1843 meetings were held at the residences of George Hoffman (father of Mrs. David Martin), and Abraham Lehman, who were among the first members of this society. Under date of March 6, 1850, Mr. Hoffman deeded a lot to the congregation and a frame meeting house was soon after erected. This building was located about 200 yards east of the Hibernia Road, on the north side of the Columbus and Winchester Pike. Services were held here regularly until the summer of 1898.

On September 15, 1898, the land was sold at auction to Dr. L. W. Beery, and the building to Jones Alspach, who removed it to the west end of his residence. A new meeting house was erected on the farm of Benoni Steman, in Violet Township, Fairfield County in 1890, and services are now held there.

Rev. John Good was the first pastor and John Brenneman the first resident preacher. Jacob Bowman, David Martin and Noah Brenneman have been chosen from among the members as resident preachers; the two latter serving at the present time.

The following was the list of members in 1897: David and Barbara Martin (a daughter of George Hoffman), Noah and Elizabeth Brenneman, Henry and Martha Steman, Benoni and Catherine Steman, Abraham and Mary Lehman, Mrs. Elizabeth Good (a sister of Abraham

Lehman and a daughter of Abraham Lehman, Sr.), Elizabeth Smith, Elizabeth Strohm, Mrs. Hannah Beery, Lydia Steman, Martin Steman and Rachel Steman.

Union Church in Middletown

In the "thirties" a union church was built in Middletown. At first it was the intention to build it near the graveyard, and the framing timber was hauled there, when a peddler, who was stopping in town, proposed to give a cash contribution of ($3.00) three dollars if they would build it in town. Three dollars in *cash* was then considered an item; then the fact of a more convenient location caused a change of plans, and the building was accordingly erected on the north side of the road, about opposite the residence of Esq. Milton Cummins. Various preachers held services here, as they could be secured from time to time. Later it was used as a school house. The building has long since been removed.

CHAPTER XXVI
SECRET AND FRATERNAL SOCIETIES

"Friendship is the only thing in the world concerning the usefulness of which all mankind are agreed."

— Cicero

Lee Lodge, I. S. S. F., No. 386

This organization, named after Grand Master Lee, was chartered May 14, 1867 and instituted the following June by Daniel Fithian, Special Deputy. The first officers and charter members were: Chas. P. Rees, N. G.; John W. Griffith, V. G.; Dr. J. B. Potter, Secretary; James B. Evans, Treasurer; Jesse Brandt, Robt. H. Mason and James H. Cannon.

J. B. Evans is the only one of the charter members still living, being 91 years old. Meetings were held in the Bergstresser Hall until in 1868, when the lodge built the hall over the C. P. Rees store room. They fitted up and furnished this room and occupied it until September 15, 1883, when it was destroyed by fire. All their furniture, regalia, books and records were consumed.

Meetings were then held in the Grange Hall until Mr. Rees rebuilt, when his hall was rented, fitted up and occupied until December 28, 1888, when their present elegant hall was dedicated. After the store room on the northeast corner of High and Waterloo Streets was consumed by fire, they purchased the lot and erected the substantial business block, in the second story of which their hall is located.

The consecutive presiding officers from the lodge's organization have been: Charles P. Kees, J. B. Potter, J. W. Griffith, A. I. Crumley, Philip Game, James Heffley, J. W. Hische, Charles W. Speaks, Peter Zarbaugh, Benjamin F. Hische, Charles L. Brown, Newton J. Wolfe, Henry H. Dibble, J. P. Arnold, John Gehm, James R. Algire, Wm. M. Game, Noah H. Hummel, Lewis W. Ringer, Herk. C. Courtright, John Chaney, Jr., James Palsgrove, Thomas Allely, Brice Taylor, Wm. Schrock, P. C. Tussing, S. C. Swonger, John F. Bauer, J. E. Smith, Peter Brown, Samuel Runkle, Charles Epply, Irvin M. Hart, A. C. Kelley, Thos. Peer, Geo. W. Lisle, Wm. Hesser, J. A. Mathias, J. W. Dewees, John W. Hische, John A. Whitzel, Aaron Smith, Wm. H. Herbst, Geo. Williams, Adam Weber, John M. Lehman, Edw. D. Peer, H. S. Cannon, Chas. S. Smith, S. E. Heller,

Edw. Colman, Wm. Williams, Frank Brenner, Edw. O. Herbst and John Pierson. Several of them have served two or more terms.

Franklin Encampment, No. 142

Franklin Encampment No. 142, I. O. O. F., was chartered May 3, 1871, and instituted June 14 following. The first officers and charter members were : J. B. Evans, H. P.: Dr. J. B. Potter, C. P.; C. P. Rees, S. W.; J. W. Griffith, J. W.; J. W. Hische, Peter E. Ehrenhart and R. H. Mason.

After some years the interest lagged, and in March, 1888, Franklin Encampment was transferred to Columbus. Among the early officers were: J. P. Arnold, James Palsgrove, Thomas Allely, J. W. Hische, Samuel Runkle, John F. Baiters and others.

Daughters of Rebecca, No. I17

Bethel Lodge, D. of R., I. O. O. F., No. 117, was chartered May 15, 1879, and instituted August 15 following by S. K. Bradshaw, Dept. G. M., and C. L. Young, Deputy G. M.

The first officers and charter members were: J. B. Evans, N. G.; Mrs. Emily A. Game, V. G.; Mrs. A. V. A. Heffly, F. S.; Miss Mame Hische, R. S.; Mrs. Catharine Ehrenhart, Treasurer, and Rev. James Heffly, Peter E. Ehrenhart, J. W. Griffith, Mrs. Rachel M. Griffith, J. W. Hische and N. J. Wolfe. The last officers elected January, 1895, were: Blanch Dibble, N. G.; R. M. Griffith, V. G.; Clara Dibble, Treasurer; Bettie Becks, Financial Secretary; Mame Hische, Recording Secretary.

Gordian Lodge, I. O. O. F., No. 205

Gordian Lodge of the Independent Order of Odd Fellows was first instituted February 11, 1853 and was chartered May 16, 1853. The first officers and charter members were George McCormick, N. G.; Jacob Lowe, V. G.; Edmund Gares, P. S.; Geo. P. Champe, Treas.; G. L. Smith, R. S.

Meetings were held in the upper west room of the old brick school house. Many of the former members having moved away, the charter was surrendered in 1864. In 1872 Rev. S. M. Bright and others revived the interest and a lodge was reorganized and on October 12, 1872. the charter was restored with C. F. Needels, G. L. Smith, G. P. Champe, E. Groom, S. M. Bright, Jacob Shirey, J. P. Arnold and S. A. Peters as charter members. The same name and number—Gordian No. 205—was given it. Previous to the occupation of their present hall on the third floor of the Town Hall building, in 1876, the meetings were held in the old warehouse that stood where Vogle's grocery now stands.

Gordian Lodge, I. O. O. F., No. 205
On top floor of Town Hall Groveport

The Noble Grands since 1872 have been S. M. Bright, S. A. Peters, J. P. Arnold, Hunter Rarey, W. L. Powell, Wm. Corbett, Morris Kile, I. R. Earhart, L. T. Sims, N. S. McCormick, C. Black, Jr., W. H. Rager, R. A. Kile, J. F. Kile, J. J. Rohr, Wm. R. Coffman, Albert Young, Wm. Mason, S. Carruthers, Wm. Chandler, W. C. Gill, O. D. Harris, O. R. Mansfield, three terms; G. W. Bigelow, C. F. Needels, George Black, J. P. Rager, Chas. A. Williams, A. M. Senter, Ervin Sallee, Geo. W. Preston, Marion F. Sandy, McC. Seymour, W. H. Zinn, J. A. Kitzmiller, C. F. Baird, John Decker, John C. Coon (two terms), Welton Seymour, Edw. Seymour, Levi Sims, Myron Sallee, H. H. Shipton, W. E. Thompson, Wm. Claffee (two terms), and Samuel Stukey (three terms).

The following is a list of the *deceased members,* with the date of their death: George Rowland, May 8, 1875; S. Allen Peters, April 3,

339

1878; Hunter Rarey, September 1, 1879; John W. Wallace, December 1, 1879; J. P. Arnold, April 21, 1880; Z. B. Bean, August 18, 1884; Thomas V. Decker, January 14, 1885; Miner Seymour, December 28, 1887; S. M. Bright, June 13, 1889; Joseph A. Kitzmiller, March 19, 1892; W. H. Zinn, April 15, 1892; H. H. Shipton, August 16, 1896; E. Grooms, February 17, 1897; G. P. Champe, January 24, 1898. The present membership is 57.

A. A. Short, M.D.
1824 - 1897

Joseph B. Potter, M.D.
1817 - 1897

F. & A. M., No. 240

Groveport Lodge No. 240 was instituted May 11, 1853. The charter members were C. J. Stevenson, Dr. Abel Clark, Chas. Pontius, Jeremiah White, David Sarber, Jonathan Watson, D. C. Shockley and Salem A. Darnell.

The first officers were appointed by Grand Master F. V. Bierce of Akron, Ohio and were C. J. Stevenson, W. M., Abel Clark, S. W. and Chas. Pontius, J. W. The first meetings were held in the brick school house (Rager's Feed Mill) and later in an upper room in the building that stood opposite the town hall, then over Casper Limpert's drug store.

In 1875 when the township and village were building the town hall, it was thought that two lodge rooms could be built on the third floor at a moderate cost and accordingly on July 24th, at an adjourned meeting, a building committee was elected consisting of Wm. Chandler,

S. A. Peters, M. K. Earhart and J. P. Arnold. It was ascertained that a room could be built at a cost of $1,050. The committee was then authorized to contract for the same with the township trustees and the village counsel and also instructed to have the lodge incorporated, which was all accordingly done. In 1876 the hall in the third story, on the west side of the building, was completed and occupied.

The following have been the presiding officers: C. J. Stevenson, 1853-1854; Abel Clark, 1855-1859, 1862; Chas. Pontius, 1856; M. K. Earhart, 1857, 1858, 1863-1868, 1885, nine years; J. B. Young, 1869, 1870; Philip C. Tussing, 1871-1880, ten years; Thos. A. Metcalf, 1881; A. L. Brooks, 1882, 1883; F. S. Rarey, 1884; Wm. Sims, 1886; Chas. P. Long, 1887; C. E. Metcalf, 1888, 1889; Samuel Stuckey, 1890, 1891, 1894; C. R. Clement, 1892, 1893, 1895-1898; J. O. Rarey, 1899, 1900.

The following members have died: Wm. Young, Wm. Blakely, David Baugher, Jonathan Watson, H. C. Cater, J. P. Bywaters, Lapole Rarey, April 4th, 1860; J. F. Groom, May 3rd, 1863; M. Rohr, October 28, 1861; J. B. Young, February 6th, 1875; S. A. Peters. April 3rd, 1878; J. P. Arnold, April, 1880; Henry Long, May 2d, 1881; M. A. Gray, October 19, 1885; Chas. Pontius, May 10th, 1887; P. C. Tussing, January 21, 1886; W. H. Bishop, February 27, 1888; B. C. Sims, January 17, 1891; W. H. Zinn, April 16th, 1892; Martin Codner, May 22, 1895; W. R. Limpert, Dec. 18, 1895; A. C. Finks, 1896; H. H. Shipton, August 16, 1896.

The following members have withdrawn: Wm. Ewing, D. C. Sarber, C. W. Ferington, J. H. Fearn, Rev. H. Gartner, W. S. Durant, A. Zebolt, F. M. Groom, E. E. Decker, John Rodenfels, Chas. Scofield, Rev. A. C. Kelley, S. E. Adams, J. C. Byrne, O. J. Connel, H. K. Brotherton, Robt. Brotherton, A. Clark, H. J. Cox, J. H. Chain, C. J. Stevenson, Salem A. Darnell, H. C. Darnell, M. Davidson, A. R. Fearn, Samuel O. Hendren, A. C. King, Samuel Leigh, J. F. Lincoln, Geo. McCormick, E. D. Northrop, C. Zebolt, A. W. Paul, J. P. Patterson, A. E. Bennett, L. T. Fisher, Rev. J. P. Given, J. Tussing, Peter Teegardin, Samuel Percy, S. M. Sharp, J. F. Bauer, J. H. Saylor, N. H. Garner, C. E. Seymour, J. S. Seymour, S. L. Swisher, S. M. Spurgeon, G. J. Stevenson, C. B. Sullivan and J. White.

In 1863 a public installation was held in the Methodist Church, Virgil E. Show delivering an address, and in 1872 another public installation was held in the Presbyterian Church, Chaplain Byers of Columbus delivering the addresses.

In 1874 an address was delivered in the Methodist Church by L. C. Bailey. In 1878 a quartette from Columbus furnished music and short speeches were made by Brothers Rickley, Coit, Williams, King, and others of Columbus.

Potter Lodge, F. & A. M.. No. 540

Previous to 1885, at different times attempts had been made to secure a dispensation from the Grand Master, for the establishment of a Masonic lodge at Winchester; but the consent of the surrounding lodges that already held jurisdiction over the territory could not be obtained and failure was the result.

During the winter of 1884-1885 their consent was secured and in February, 1885, Grand Master Goodspeed issued his dispensation for the new lodge. The hall in the Lehman block was elegantly fitted and furnished and the first regular meeting was held on Friday evening, April 10, 1885 when the following officers were elected: Joseph B. Potter, W. M.; J. B. Evans, S. W.; B. F. Gayman, J. W.; James Heffly, Secretary; J. M. Bennett, Treasurer: A. C. Kelley, S. D.; Thomas Allely, J. D.; D. H. Cowen Tyler.

The lodge was at first named "Potter Lodge" in honor of its master, Dr. J. B. Potter, but notice was received from the Grand Master that this could not be done during the life-time of the doctor and then the name was changed to "Madison Lodge."

Dr. Potter and B. F.. Gayman were elected delegates to attend the meeting of the Grand Lodge at Cincinnati, on October 20, 1885, to present the claims of the new lodge for a charter.

Their mission was successful, and on Wednesday evening. November 4, 1885, Madison Lodge, No. 540, F. & A. M., was instituted with imposing ceremonies by Past Grand Master Goodspeed of Athens, assisted by a large number of visiting brethren.

After the death of Dr. J. B. Potter, March 27, 1887, the name was again changed back to "Potter Lodge." January 1, 1901, the room over Kramer and Bolenbaugh's store was fitted up, where the meetings are now held. Potter Lodge is in a prosperous condition.

Walnut Chapter, Royal Arch Masons, U- D

In the summer and fall of 1900 Dr. L. W. Beery, R. J. Tussing, Dr. Geo. S. Courtright, John O. Rarey, A. P. Teegardin and a few others began the preliminary movements towards the establishment of a chapter of Royal Arch Masons at Winchester and under date of October 29, 1901, Grand High Priest Levi C. Goodale issued a dispensation under which this chapter would work during its first year. The dispensation authorized the following officers: John O. Rarey, High Priest; L. W. Beery, King, and Geo. S. Courtright, Scribe. These three then appointed the following other officers: Daniel Detwiler, Treasurer; R. J. Tussing, Secretary; John W. Teegardin, Captain of the Host; A. P. Teegardin, P. S.; Levi Dumm, R. A. Capt.; Calvin U. Rose, G. M. 3rd Veil; P. M. Teegardin, G. M. 2d V.; Wm. Becker, G. M. 1st V.; D. H. Cowen, S.

The charter members besides those mentioned above are: M. K. Earhart, J. J. Kershner, Jacob Braun, Levi Teegardin, G. P. Teegardin, F. J. Peters and P. H. Fisher. The following have since become members: C. P. Bauman, Thos. H. Courtright, U. S. Brandt, F. D. Dildine, C. R. Clement, H. L. Rarey, F. P. Creed, Albert Francisco, Paul Alspach, O. P. Gayman, Walter Hewetson and John W. Lehman.

The meetings are held in the Masonic Hall in the Kramer Building.

Knights of Pythias, No. 125

Winchester Lodge No. 125 was instituted December 9, 1880 and worked under a dispensation until May 25, 1881, when it was chartered. It was instituted by Deputy Grand Chancellor Joseph Dowdall, assisted by J. W. Lingo (Chief of Police), J. W. Myers and David P. Boyer of Columbus, and A. Gray, Chas. Miller, J. Crommie and Chas. Scoville of Mt. Pleasant Lodge No. 48, of Lancaster.

A large delegation of Uniformed Knights, headed by the Lancaster Drum Corps, came up from Lancaster and paraded the streets early in the evening. The first officers and the charter members were: Chas. C. Reibe, Past Chan.; John C. Speaks, Chan. Com.; E. E. Geisy, Prelate; C. D. Whitehurst, V. Chan.; E. C. Chaney, M. of E.; B. F. Gayman, K. of R. S.; Geo. A. Whitehurst, M. of F.; Geo. W. Miller, M. of A.; Chas. Kuqua. O. G.; A. J. Decker, I. G.; O. L. Bott, Clark Lechliter, John M. Schoch, Jr., F. H. Arnold, R. C. Caslow. W. E. Chaney, J. W. Ebright, Wm. M. Game, D. D. Gayman, Wm. H. Tallman and John A. Whitzel.

For some years the meetings were held in the Grange Hall, then in the Odd Fellows Hall until January 2, 1900 when they first occupied the hall in the Lehman block, which they purchased in the fall of 1899.

The successive chancellor commanders have been: John C. Speaks, Cary D. Whitehurst, B. F. Gayman, Geo. W. Miller, J. M. Schoch, Jr., N. O. Selby, Geo. A. Whitehurst, Wm. L. Walters, Church B. Tuttle, Jacob W. Baugher, Geo. E. Becker, Wm. M. Game, Dr. J. W. Shook, W. Scott Alspach, Chas. W. Miller, O. L. Dibble, Ed. C. Chaney, Clem. V. Moore, Bent. D. Gehm, Ed. W. Crayton, Wm. H. Herbst, Mart. L. Kemp, W. A. Delong, Wm. H. Lane, Alf. Cannon, Frank Hische, John M. Lehman, W. Scott Alspach, Zach. E. England, Herb. S. Cannon, Jesse Cannon, John C. Kramer, Geo. E. Smith, Wylie Brown, Clem. V. Moore, Arth. A. Chaney, John Hische, Wm. M. Codner, W. E. Sims, Edw. S. Stoz and Wm. Burnett.

The necrology is as follows, with date of death where known: Clark Lechliter, ____; Jeff. L. Bye, June 18, 1889; Isaac B. Wright, December 25, 1892; Thos. A. Arnold, December 8, 1893; Frank Hische (in California), July 2, 1895; W. S. Alspach, December 9, 1897; Cary D. Whitehurst, February 8, 1898; Adrian S. Foor, July 2, 1898; W. H. Kirk (died at Mt. Vernon, Ohio, date not known.

Uniform Rank K. of P., No. 78

At a meeting held on January 31, 1888, the following names were suggested: Winchester, Hermion and Richie. The latter was chosen and on the following February 28th a charter was granted. On May 11, 1888, Richie Division, U. R. K. P. No. 78 was instituted by General Henry Heinmiller of Columbus.

The first officers and charter members were: John C. Speaks, Sir Knight Com.; Chas. W. Miller, Sir Knight Herald; Cary D. Whitehurst, Sir Knight Recorder; Sol S. Lehman, Sir Knight Treasurer; several ballots were taken for the office of Sir Knight Lieutenant but no one was elected until the next meeting when Joe S. Ashe was chosen. Mr. Ashe resigned at the following meeting and Edw. C. Chaney was elected. Joe S. Ashe, W. Scott Alspach, Jerry Alspach. Wm. C. Bailey, Louis W. Boyer, Arthur A. Chaney, N. S. Coon, W. A. Belong, Chas. C. Dibble, Wm. M. Fame, B. F. Gayman, Bent D. Gehm, Wm. H. Herbst, John W. Hische, Wm. H. Lane. John M. Lehman, Geo. W. Miller, Clem V. Moore, Geo. W. Sponsler, Church B. Tuttle, Geo. A. Whitehurst and John A. Whitzel.

Those referred to as the "big four" were Joe Ashe, Scott Alspach, Clem Moore and John Whitzel; these had very close rivals in Bent Gehm, Sol Lehman, Bill Lane and George Sponsler.

Meetings were held in I. O. O. F. Hall and the old foundry was used for practice drills. The Division was disbanded, the last meeting being held on February 25, 1893.

Fraternal Mystic Circle

Madison Ruling *No.* 92 was instituted May 28, 1888 in the Grange Hall by D. E. Stevens, Sup. M. R. and John L. Wilson, S. V. R. of Columbus and R. J. Stoughton, Dept. of Westerville. O. M. L. Kemp was the first member initiated to show the others the workings of the order. The following were the charter members and first officers. The last four named were initiated one week later but were included in the charter which is dated May 21, 1888: B. D. Gehm, Past R.; C. D. Whitehurst, R.; W. L. Walters, U. R.; C. W. Bostwick, Chap.; H. H. Dibble, Recorder; W. D. Beeks, Treasurer; L. W. Berry, Examiner; O. L. Dibble, Warden; Jno. W. Hische, Marshall; William E. Pearsol, Sentry; Thomas Bailey, Out. Gd.: W. L. Arendt, E. V. Bush, A. A. Chaney, M. L. Kemp, Isaac B. Wright, O. P. Gayman, Sam S. Lehman, Clint A. Stevenson and Cyrus W. Stevenson. Later meetings were held in the I. O. O. F. Hall. This Ruling was disbanded in 1894 with all the members dropping out except Wm. L. Walters, whose membership was transferred to another Ruling.

Protected Home Circle

The Protected Home Circle No. 58 of Winchester was chartered May 6, 1895, with the following officers and charter members: J. K. Miller, President; H. H. Dibble, Secretary; O. L. Dibble, Accountant; Wm. L. Arendt, Guardian; Dr. L. W. Berry, Surgeon; Chas. C. Dibble, Conductor; Stephen Boyd, Mrs. J. K. Miller, Simon Shaffer, B. N. Lewis Dr. J. T. Merwin, R. M. Fry, and Z. E. England. The insurance benefit is $1000.00 The officers and membership remains the same as when organized.

CHAPTER XXVII
THE PIONEER'S HOUSE AND HOME LIFE

"We piled with care our nightly stack
Of wood against the chimney back —
The oaken-log, green, huge, and thick —
And on its top the stout back stick;
The knotty fore stick laid apart,
And filled between with curious art.
The ragged brush; then hovering near.
We watched the first red blase appear.
Heard the sharp crackle, caught the gleam
On whitewashed wall and sagging beam,
Until the old rude-furnished room
Burst flower-like into rosy bloom."

The pioneer's first cabin was built of round logs with the bark on. The chimney stood on the outside at one end and was made of sticks and clay with clapboard roof. Many of them had only the earth for a floor. The rafters or beams, as they were called, ran lengthwise of the building and were spaced according to the length of the clapboards.

Some of them had a loft or upper floor. No windows were needed, as the cracks in the roof and between the logs and the big wide chimney admitted plenty of light by day. Often only a blanket or skin furnished the door. All was put together without nail or iron. The following description of the building of the round log cabin is taken from Hill's History of Licking County and has been corroborated to the writer by several of the older citizens of this township, who themselves assisted in the erection of them.

A PIONEER CABIN
Stood on McGuffy's land along the Groveport Road. From a photo taken in 1898

"These round log cabins were often erected ready for occupancy in a single day. The pioneer went 8 to 10 miles to a cabin-raising, arriving early in the morning where not a tree had been felled or a stone turned. Each one had some particular part to see too. Three or four would lay the corner stones and the first logs, two men with axes cut the trees and logs, one with his team of oxen, a "Lizard" and a log chain would "snake" them in; two more with axes and cross-cut saw and frow* would make the clapboards, two more with axes, cross-cut saw and broad-ax would hew out the puncheons for the floor and flatten the upper side of the sleepers. Four skilled axmen would carry up the corners and the remainder, with skids and handspikes would roll up the logs. As soon as the joists were laid on, two men with cross-cut saw went to work cutting out the door and chimney place and while the corner men were building up the attic and putting on the roof, the carpenters and masons of the day were putting down the puncheons, laying the hearth and building the chimney.

In one corner at a distance of 6 feet from one wall and 4 feet from the other the bed post is placed, only one being needed. A hole was bored in the puncheon floor to set this post, which was usually a stick with a crotch or fork in the upper end; rails were laid from this fork to the walls and usually nice straight hickory poles form the bottom, upon which straw or leaves were placed and a blanket put on; this makes a

348

comfortable spring-bed and was easily changed and kept clean. The heavy door was hung on wooden hinges and all that was necessary was to pull the latch string inside and the strong wooden latch held it fast."

*A cleaving tool having a wedge-shaped blade, with a handle set at right angles to it.

The furniture was as simple as the buildings. A cabin contained little beyond the puncheon table with its four sapling legs, its puncheon benches and blocks of wood for stools. Stoves? they had none. A small kettle or two answered the various purposes of bucket, boiler and oven, and when there was company they would take the door off its hinges and thus make an addition to the table. A shelf on two wooden pins held the dishes and pewter-ware. Two wooden hooks over the door held the rifle when not in use. Few had clocks and they were of the "wall sweep" kind. The wearing apparel of the whole family was hung in full view on one side of the house on wooden pins. In the loft, on every beam, hung seeds and roots and herbs, the medicines of those days. On the joists hung dried pumpkins, peaches, apples, beans, etc. The Hominy block sat in one corner; the broom was of split hickory and the "duster" was a wild turkey wing.

These round log cabins stood many years after better houses were erected; they served for stables, sheep-pens, blacksmith-shops, loom-shops, school house, and meeting house. Every one of these first cabins are long since gone and the exact places where they stood forgotten.

Later an improved log house was built. It was made of hewn logs, with sawed lumber for doors, windows and floors, Glass also took the place of greased paper windows sometimes used in the first cabins. Home-made nails were sparingly used; when nails were first used a pound cost a bushel of wheat or two bushels of corn — equivalent to a day's work— the local blacksmith made them out of odds and ends, of old worn out sickles, broken links of chains, pieces of horse shoes., etc.

No house had more than two rooms. One was called the kitchen and the other "the room", if company came they were invited to come in "the room", a little later every family had its "squirrel tail" bake oven. Corn-bread, vegetables, milk, butter, and wild meats constituted the principal subsistence and these were often scarce.

In the summer and fall the mills would stop, for the lack of water and bread-stuffs would get scarce and neighbors would borrow of each other as long as there was anything in the community. Venison and wild turkeys were quite plenty. Squirrels were so numerous that parties were formed to kill them to prevent them from destroying grain when planted and after it ripened. Wild pigeons were so plenty that they literally darkened the heavens in their flight. Coffee and tea were dear and hard to get and as substitutes the early settlers used sassafras, spice-wood and burned rye and wheat for their coffee, using a few grains of coffee to give it flavor. Pounded and lye hominy were common. A half dozen or more kinds of corn-bread were made; then there was the ash-cake, the hoe-cake and the Johnnie-cake. Salt had to be secured at Zanesville and cost ten cents per pound. Sugar and Syrup were made in abundance. Bee trees were plenty. They salted down turkey in troughs as they had no tubs or barrels.

Their wearing apparel was all homemade, — linen and tow in summer and linsey and flannel in winter. The flax, tow and wool were all spun on hand wheels. The weaving was done on hand looms; many of the pioneer girls spun, wove and made their own wedding dresses. The coloring was done with the bark from trees, such as walnut, oak, maple and hickory, as well as with walnut hulls; copperas put into the ooze of these made a variety of shades ranging from yellow to red, black or brown.

Buckskin pants and sometimes vests with the hair on, were common as men's wear. Mr. Almanzer Hathaway for many years a citizen of Winchester relates that his buckskin pants got wet running through the snow and water, and when dry became dry and brittle and broke off at the knees leaving the lower part of his limbs naked for some time before he got another pair. These buckskin pants were made to fit close to the skin and as at that early day no underclothes were worn, it was very much like putting one's limbs into bags of snow on very cold winter mornings. One pair of shoes a year was all any got, so often persons would tie old rags about their feet to save their shoes and to make them last, would carry them until near the meeting house when they would put them on, and after meeting take them off again. Bedding consisted of straw and leaves, a blanket or two and plenty of bear skins. Bear skins were worth 75 cents and deer skins 50 cents. Sometimes the fire went out during the night when someone would have to go to a neighbors for some "live coals" before breakfast could be started.

We found the following among other entries in an old account book kept by "Squire" John Tallman, father of the late Nathaniel Tallman, the dates and prices are suggestive of the pioneer's domestic life.

1818: Edward Hathaway credit by hewing one mantle piece and one pair door hinges $1.00 and by hewing out 1 1/2 pair hames 75 cts.

1818: James T. Pearcy debtor to 2 3/4 yds woolen cloth each $1.75, $4.81: to 1 jacket pattern and trimings $2.62 1/2. 1 3/4 yds. linen at 50 cts., 87 1/2 cts.

1818: Thompson Cross credit by one day's hauling with 2 horses, $1.50; by one day hauling with 4 horses. $3.00.

1818: Andrew Kramer debtor to 2 China pigs at $2.00, $4.00: credit by husking corn one day 50 cts.; by three days husking by boys at 33 1/3 cts. $1.00; debtor to 1 cow, $12.00.

1820: Cristina Kramer credit by 6 pounds wool at fifty cents per pound.

1820: Edith Harrison credit by cleaning 16 pounds of flax at 6 cts. per pound. To 424 lbs. pork at 3 cts. per lb.; 1 day's-rolling at 1 1/2 bushel wheat; cradling 5 acres rye at 1/2 bushel wheat per acre.

1820: Peter Miller, breaking 270 lbs. flax at 1 ct. per lb.; scutching 96 lbs. flax at 3 cts. per lb.

1820: Isaac Lanning, 4 lbs. hog fat at 8 cts. per lb.; 2 lbs. wool at 50 cts. per lb.; 6 lbs. flax at 16 2-3 cts. pec lb.; $ lb. tea at $1.75 per lb.; 1 lb. coffee at 37! cts. per lb.; J bushels salt at $1.00 per bushel.

1820: James T. Pearcy, 327 ft. cherry boards at $2.00 per hundred ft; 1 1/2 bushels barley at 62 1/2 cts. per bushel; 4 bushels rye at 40 cts. per bushel; 2 Gimblets at 12 cts. each; 48 lights 8 by 10 glass at 10 cts. each.

1820: Peter Miller, 1 lb. Tow, 12 1/2 cts.; 1 lb. flax 25 cts; 1 bushel potatoes, 33 1/3 cts.; 4 yds. tow linen at 42 cts. per yard; 2 1/2 yds. flax linen at 62 1/2 cts. per yd.; 7 yds. of cotton cloth at 50 cts. per yd.; 1 pair shoes, $2.25; 2 cuts of stocking yarn at 20 cts. per cut; 1 yd. flannel 62 cts.; 1 dozen buttons 25 cts.; 1 bushel salt, $2.00; 1 pair linsey pantaloons, $1.75; weaving, 2 1/2 yds. at 12 1/2 cts. per yd.; 10 cuts flax thread at 3 1/3 cts. per cut; half-soling pair of shoes, 75 cts.

1821: Edward Hathaway, 7 sheep at $2.50 each; 2 bushel oats at 25 cts. per bushel; 19 1/2 lbs. bacon at 10 cts. per lb.; 37 lbs. pickled pork at 8 cts. per lb.

1822: Anna Scothorn, 40 lbs. flour at 1$^{1/4}$ cts. per lb.; 1 lb. coffee at 40 cts.; 1 set cups and saucers 62$^{1/2}$ cts.; 1/2 dozen tins 50 cts.; 3 bushels wheat at 50 cts. per bushel.

1823: John Cooper, cradling 9 acres of oats at 1/2 bushel wheat per acre; weaving 32 yds. flannel at 12$^{1/2}$ cts. per yd.

1823: Andrew Kramer, hauling 11 bbls. flour to Columbus at 50 cts. per bbl.

1823: James T. Pearcy, 75 lbs. of salt at 2$^{1/2}$ bushels wheat for 1 bushel salt, $1.75.

1823: Edward Hathaway, 1 side of leather 3.12^{1/2}$

1823: Joseph Shannon, hauling one load of lime from Columbus, $4.00; 45 lbs. nails at 12$^{1/2}$cts. per lb.

1823: Elias Huff, making 216 rails at 25 cts. per hundred; making 314 stakes at 16 cts. per hundred.

1827: Zebulon Lee, 1 shovel, $1.50; James Cooper, cradling wheat at 75 cts. per day.

1827: Abraham Harrison, 2 quart whisky, 5 cts.; 1 pint whisky, \\ cts.; 1 pint whisky, 1$^{1/2}$ ct.; 1 qt. whisky, 4 cts.; 1$^{1/2}$ bushel buckwheat at 31$^{1/2}$ cts. per bushel; 2 days mowing at 50 cts. per day; 6$^{1/2}$ days mowing by boys at 25 cts. per day.

1830: John Coleman, 1 cow and calf, $9.00: Almanzer Hathaway, 17 lbs. veal at 3$^{1/2}$ cts. per lb.; 3 bushels wheat at 37$^{1/2}$ cts. per bushel; Wm. A. Green, 1 hide, weight 45 lbs. at 5 cts. per lb. and 1 calf skin, weight, 7 lbs. at 10 cts. per lb.

1830: Wm. Woodcock, 32 lbs. beef at 2 $^{1/2}$ cts. per lb.; 49 lbs flour at 1 $^{1/2}$ cts. per lb.; breaking 87 lbs. flax at 1 ct. per lb., swingling 22 lbs. flax at 2 cts. per pound.

1830: Wm. Riley, 30 lbs. nails at 10 cts. per lb.

Eggs were about 3 to 4 cts. per dozen. Butter 6$^{1/4}$ cents per pound.

CHAPTER XXVIII
INCIDENTS OF PIONEER AND BYGONE DAYS

"Ask who of all our race have shown
The largest heart, the kindliest. hand,
Ask who with lavish hands have strown
Rich blessings over all the land;
Ask who has sown that we might reap,
The harvest rich with ninety years;
And every heart and every voice
Make answer: Madison's pioneers."

Adapted from A. B. Clarke

Under the above heading we present some miscellaneous incidents and expressions that we could not well classify otherwise and that throw light on our pioneer's life. What little money was in circulation at an early day was mostly of Spanish silver. The change was made with "cut money"—thus a quarter cut in two made two nine pence (12$\frac{1}{2}$c), and cut in four pieces made four fi-penny bits (6$\frac{1}{4}$c); quarters, half dollars and dollars were thus cut. It is said that often five fi-penny bits were cut from a quarter, or five nine pences from a half dollar.

A common day's work, from sun up to sun down, was 25c. Harvest hands were paid 50c or more, generally one bushel of wheat for a day's harvesting. This continued to be the price for many years, perhaps until the time of the introduction of reaping machines. It was considered a big day's work to reap and bind forty dozen sheaves of wheat, and only a few could do it.

Blazed trees showed the way from cabin to cabin, even though the distance was short. The woods were very dense and one could easily get lost. Bells were put on the cows and sheep so that they could be found.

Few sheep were kept on account of wolves, and later on account of dogs.

The pioneers were great "meeting" goers. Besides their desire to hear the preaching, it afforded an opportunity of hearing the "news" and meeting the people of the neighborhood. It was no unusual thing to see men coming to "meeting" with their guns on their shoulders, and the crack of the rifle through the woods was almost as familiar on Sundays as on week days.

Within a few years after the settlements began, the hogs strayed off into the woods and became wild, so that in some neighborhoods large droves were found. When a fat hog was wanted the men took their dogs and guns and went hunting them, killing what was wanted.

"Uncle" Johnnie Kramer's mother had to throw his sister Catharine, when a small child (she married Henry Slife), up in the attic to keep the wolves from carrying her off; they had only a blanket for a door; they lived where Jerry Kramer now lives.

George Tongue killed a bear close by a pond, near where Daniel Wright now lives.

Once when John Wright was butchering—they lived where Jeff Mosier now lives—his mother remarked, *"If we had a deer to put in the sausage, it would help its flavor."* It was not long until two appeared and he succeeded in getting them both, and the sausage was flavored.

From 1803 to 1806 township collectors were appointed to collect the chattel tax and county collectors for the land tax. From 1806 to 1827 county collectors collected both land and chattel tax. It was the custom to go from house to house, and later the collector would set a time when he would be at a certain house to receive the tax.

Since 1827 the county treasurer receives the taxes, and is elected; previous to this the collectors were appointed by the commissioners. It was also customary for a time for the assessor to set a time and place where persons owning taxable property would come and have it assessed.

I have before me a tax receipt yellow with age; it is one and three-fourths by seven and one-half inches and reads:

"Received Oct. 16th, 1832, from Henry Deitz six dollars and twenty-five cents and nine mill's, his state, county, township and poor tax, for said year 1832, on the following property, to wit: for four horses, three neat cattle and for one hundred and fifty-nine acres of land, in range 20, township 15, section 31, northwest quarter.

Henry C. Widler, Dept.
Treasurer Fairfield County

The land is the farm on which Samuel Deitz—who is a son of Henry Deitz—now lives.

Some of the plays that were familiar to the young people of the early days were, "*Thus the Farmer Sows His Seed,*" "*Marching to Quebec.*" "*O, Sister Pheba,*" "*Oats, Peas, Beans and Barley Grows,*" "*Passing the Button,*" and others.

The long evenings of the fall brought the "apple cuttings" preparatory to making apple-butter, and the "corn huskings." Forty, fifty or more would gather at a neighbor's at evening. The corn was placed on a huge pile and the men and boys would gather about it, and as the work went on they threw the husks behind them, when the girls would take them away, some with rakes, others in their arms. The boy who found a red ear of corn had the privilege to take a kiss. The girls understood this and as soon as a red ear was brought to light the lucky finder would break for his girl, to the great merriment of all present.

The game of *base*, or, as familiarly called, "*baste,*" was one of the most popular pastimes at school, perhaps from the fact that it was a very lively game and an unlimited number, both of girls and boys, could play at it. Two captains were selected who chose sides alternately; the right to first choice was usually determined by one of the captains spitting on one side of a paddle or chip and then giving it a whirling toss in the air, when the other captain would say either "wet" or "dry".

Two "bases" were fixed—either stumps, trees or stakes—about fifty to seventy-five yards apart, then any one of the players would venture out as near the opposite base as possible, when suddenly one or more of those on the opposite side would try and catch him before he got back to his own base. Others of his own side would then pursue his followers. Now the excitement and noise would be intense. If tagged or caught he was taken and afterwards played with the other side. The game was won by the side who took all the others prisoner. The boys played *bull-pen, town-ball and sockey-up.*

Lee Lodge, I. O. O. F., No. 386, held a festival on Christmas Eve, 1874, at which the following prizes were awarded: To Mrs. John Chaney, most popular married lady, a cake; to Miss Tillie McKelvey, most popular young lady, a card receiver; to Miss Lettie Allen, best looking lady, a silver butter dish. The most spirited contest of the evening was for a gold-headed cane, which was awarded to Wilson (Dad) Somerville, he having more than forty dollars' worth of votes. The net proceeds were over one hundred dollars.

New Year's Calls

In the seventies and eighties especially, New Year's Day was observed as a social holiday when it was customary for the gentlemen to call upon all their lady friends. Usually several of the ladies would join in holding receptions as was done in 1882, at the residence of L. C. Bartlitt, Misses Mame Bartlitt, Louise Olinger, Mary Olinger, Emma Fenstermaker and Laura Fenstermaker; at the residence of Dr. A. A. Short, Mrs. Short, Misses Kate Short, Mary Speaks, Alice Speaks, Mame Hische and Mrs. E. E. Geisy; at the residence of M. C. Whitehurst, Misses Ella Whitehurst, Ida Speaks, Ollie Hesser and Mrs. B. F. Gayman; at the residence of Wm. Hesser, Misses Julia Blake, Anna Cannon, Olie Arendt, Dora Cook, Emma Will, and Sallie Roush; at residence of Wm. M. Game, Mrs. Game, Misses Bell Fornoff, Emma Fornoff, Georgia Fornoff and Lizzie Gaver; at the Merchants' Hotel, Misses Cora Boyer, Lillie Boyer and Ida M. Glover; Mrs. Dr. J. B. Potter and Mrs. E. B. Pollay at the residence of the latter. The calling hours were from 2 to 8 o'clock p. m. *The Times*, in commenting on this reception, says: *"The ladies received by lamplight. Refreshments consisted of cakes, fruits, confections and at several places cold meats. There was an almost entire absence of anything stronger than coffee or chocolate to drink."*

The above comment in reference to strong drink is suggestive of the fact that often on former similar occasions wines and liquors were served and by the time the callers made the circuit, some, at least those who were the most sensitive to the exhilarating influence of the "flowing bowl," would become quite hilarious.

Early Funerals and Burials

The first coffins were made of puncheons (split and hewed plank); they were pinned together with wooden pins, or sometimes each plank was set in the grave separately and after the body was let down the lid was pinned on. Of course there was no hearse; even as late as 1840 it was the custom to use one of the Pennsylvania wagons (Prairie Schooner), usually one with a canvas cover. The corpse and friends would all ride together. The method of getting into one of these wagons was to let the rear end gate— which was on hinges—down, and two strong men, one on either side, would lower it sufficiently that the persons could readily step up, when the gate would be raised level with the bottom of the bed. John Nicodemus remembers when his sister died in 1839, that Jacob LeFever at Waterloo made the coffin which cost one dollar per lineal foot (this was the usual price), and was made of walnut or cherry and varnished (or oiled) and lined with cambric or muslin. In town the corpse was carried on a bier; a familiar sight was to see the funeral procession halt while the pall-bearers rested. In our boyhood days the suggestion came to our minds that, perhaps, it was at such a halt that the Savior called the son of the widow of Nain to life.

The first hearse in this section was the one that Jacob Bennedum made in about 1850. It had a platform with posts at the corners which supported a wooden top; a black curtain with a fringe round the bottom hid the coffin from view. Later Charles Brown and Frank Armpreister built one with glass sides. The running gears of this latter one are still in use by Samuel Saylor.

Among the very earliest physicians in this section was Dr. W. W. Talbott of Jefferson. He came in about 1830. The writer heard him relate that some fifty physicians were now practicing in the territory that he formerly traveled alone. This territory included that now covered by the physicians of Carroll, Pickerington, Reynoldsburg, Groveport, Winchester, Lithopolis, Greencastle and occasional calls even beyond these limits.

Every neighborhood had its female doctor—called grannies—who performed some of the duties now belonging to the physician.

Myatt Wine

Charles W. Speaks, Christian and Daniel Gayman manufactured 58 barrels of Myatt wine in 1866 and about 20 barrels in 1867. The rhubarb plants from which it was made were grown on lots number 77-79 on North Liberty Street. "Myatt" is a very intoxicating beverage.

Moses Seymour
1806 -1877

William Kile
1804 - 1870

The following "Indenditure of Apprenticeship" (found in the records of the town clerk, Groveport) is quite interesting in these days when many of our mechanics simply "pick up" their trade instead of serving a long apprenticeship as was the custom with the settlers of fifty years or more ago:

"The said Samuel Getty, aged nine years, on the thirteenth day of August, A. D. 1850, by and with the consent of Elizabeth Getty, his mother, hath and doth bind himself as an apprentice unto the said John Yourd until the thirteenth day of August, 1862, from the date hereof, to learn the trade or occupation of plastering. And the said Samuel Getty, by his mother, doth hereby covenant to faithfully serve him, and correctly demean himself during the term of his apprenticeship. And the said John Yourd doth hereby covenant that he will teach the said Samuel Getty the said trade and occupation and will provide him, during such apprenticeship with meat, lodging, medicine, washing, clothing, and all other necessities suitable for an apprentice and will give him two years schooling, and at the expiration of said term of service will furnish said Samuel Getty with a new Bible, one good suit of common wearing apparel and one dress suit, a kit of tools sufficient to carry on said business and twenty dollars in money.

July 4th, 1876

The "Centennial" Fourth of July was appropriately celebrated in Kramer's Grove north of Winchester, as the following committees will suggest: J. B. Evans, Mayor, Pres.; Chas. M. Gould, Secy.; with the following Vice Presidents, viz: C. L. Seely, F. M. Senter, Henderson Miller, Geo. Needels, Samuel Hempy, Jesse Seymour, Sr., John A. Armpriester, Wm. T. Conklin, Henry Long, Benoni Steman, Geo. Long, F. G. Pontius, Jacob Bishop, Samuel Leigh, Moses Seymour, John Rager, A. L. Ferrill, James Peters, David Langle, A. H. Morton, John Hisey, A. A. French, Geo. Loucks, B. L. Rees and John G. McGuffey.

Dr. J. B. Potter, reader of the Declaration of Independence; John Gehm, Grand Marshal.

Committee on Finance: Capt. Philip Game, J. K. Miller. Wm. F. Zigler, J. M. Blackwood, Jas. P. Kalb and H. S. Tallman.

Committee on Decorations: Dr. A. Starr, Chas. Epley, F. Leonard, Mrs. J. B. Potter, Mrs. A. Storr, Geo. M. B. Dove, Ed. Speilman, Chas. Zachero, Chas. B. Cowan, C. Limpert, Daniel E. Shultz, Henry Creighton, Mrs. John Chaney, Mrs. Sol. Lehman, Miss Laura A. Schoch, Miss Rachel Gehm, Miss Ida Speaks, Miss Lucy Halliday, Miss Hattie Cater, Miss Ella Rees and Miss Callie Turner.

Committee on Music: John H. Speilman, T. F. Ungemach, John C. Speaks, Robt. F. Dildine, John Oyler, Reuben Blackwood and Wm. Stallsmith.

Committee on Invitations: Benj. F. Bowman, Phil C. Tussing, James Pickering, Albert Young, Wm. Chandler, Willard Powell, I. E. Stevenson, R. Gorham, J. D. Hammel, Chas. L. Brown and Samuel C. Dressier.

Committee on Speakers: O. P. Chaney, Rev. Halliday and W. R. Miller.

Committee on Grove: Jerry Kramer, M. E. Schrock, Jacob Bott, John Miller, James Palsgrove, John Motz and P. C. Tussing.

Committee on Water and Ice: Chas. P. Rees. Aaron Fenstermaker and Chas. Epley.

Committee on Program: Jas. H. Sommerville, John Gehm and Dr. A. Starr.

Committee to Procure a Cannon: C. W. Speaks, H. S. Binkley and John Chaney Jr.

Safe-Guards for the Day: W. R. Miller, Jno. F. Bauer, C. Kuqua, C. P. Rees and Samuel C. Swanger.

CHAPTER XXIX
GRAVEYARDS

"Friend after friend departs,
Who hath not lost a friend?
There is no union here of hearts,
That finds not here an end;
Were this frail world our final rest,
Living or dying, none were blest."

Montgomery

To many, graveyards are hallowed places. Here lies all that is mortal of husband, wife, father, mother, brother, sister or friend; and how common the custom for persons of all grades of cultivation to seek a lonely fellowship with their beloved dead while sitting by their silent tomb.

Who does not cherish the sweet hope that under the willow they are nearer to their departed one than in all the world beside.

"There is a dreamy presence everywhere,
As if of Spirits passing to and fro;
We almost hear their voices in the air,
And feel their balmy pinions touch our brow."

Respect for their memories and for their bodies, ought embalm in our hearts the spot where they lie and constrain us oft to pay our devotions of love there. How sad the feeling, when one visits one of the old burying grounds to see time doing its inevitable work of destruction and decay. Only a few more years and every tombstone that marks the last resting place of the pioneer will be gone and with these sandstone and marble slabs will disappear even the name of these sturdy, simple-lived people. For even now no living person can tell the tone of their silent voice or their form or feature, or the expression of their eye or face. Some of these old burial places we found very badly and disgracefully neglected, many of the stones broken or fallen down, in some cattle and hogs running over them. Those fenced in so overgrown with briars and undergrowth that it was almost impossible to find the graves and often found to decipher the

361

weather-worn inscriptions. We have in our possession as complete a copy of the inscriptions on every tombstone as could be secured in the spring of 1899.

In going about from cemetery to cemetery, transcribing the inscriptions, we were impressed with the fact that even graveyards have marked individualities and that they perhaps reveal somewhat of the estimation of the church and religion held by the friends of those buried there.

In some the silent inhabitants were *dead;* the most hopeful thing said of them is that *"they are gone to the bourne from whence none ever return."* In others the larger number of those buried there were only *"sleeping," "resting," "waiting for the resurrection,"* telling of the life to come in such strains of hope and faith that as we read from stone to stone a feeling steals over our mind that *"to die is gain."*

The following are a few of the more curious and interesting epitaphs:

"The mortal body here is laid
No more to mourn and die,
The living spirit now is gone
To live with God on high."

"Beyond, oh, ye ransomed souls,
Your help is from the sky,
And seraphs guide your fearful path
To yon bright homes on high;
Oh death thou art the gate of heaven
To those who feel their sins forgiven."

"We've laid her lowly in the earth,
The child of hope and love,
The light and music of our hearts
Our own sweet cradle dove."

"Fare well dear friends, if there be room
For memories fond and true,
In the bright world beyond the tomb,
I will remember you."

"His Fight is Faught
His Rase is Run
His Joyes in heaven
Is now begun."

"Weep not my dearest friends,
Nor shed your tears in vain,
My face you'll see no more
Till called to rise again."

"Sleep on sweet babe of rest
For such thy Savior blest."

On John Coleman's marble slab:

"Finish then thy new creation,
Pure and spotless let it be;
Let us see thy great salvation
Perfectly restored in thee,
Changed from glory into glory
Till in heaven we take our place,
Till we cast our crown before thee
Lost in wonder love and praise."

"Stoop down, my thoughts that used to rise,
Converse awhile with death
Think how a dying mortal lies
And pants away his breath."

"The bud had spread a rose,
The Savior, she closed."

"Stop, my friend and view,
The grave allotted you,
Remember all must die.
And turn to dust like I."

"Is this the fate that all must die,
Will death no ages spare?

Then let us all to Jesus fly
And seek for refuge there."

"Go home my friend
Dry up your tears
I will arise
When Christ appears."

"I knew full well the loveliest are always first to go.
To finely wrought they sink beneath the pressure here below."

"Weep not for me my parents dear,
I am not dead, but sleeping here."

"How greatly will my soul rejoice.
How happy will I be.
When I shall hear my Savior's voice
Say, Come unto me."

The following is not a *complete* list of *all* the persons buried in the various graveyards of the township but only such as will recall the names of persons who have lived in the township. The names are alphabetically arranged. Many, very many—perhaps fifty per cent—of the burials are unmarked.*

*BPC has added a list of these names and the Graveyards where their tombsones are located according to this book. Mr. Bareis's statement in regards to names being alphabetically arranged are incorrect. Hopefully this list will help researchers easily find the person th are looking for. Keep in mind this information was gathered by Mr. Bareis before 1902.

Surnames of the Deceased

As compiled by Mr. Bareis and others for inclusion into this book by graveyard. This list shows surnames and the graveyard where their tombstones were located.

SURNAME	GRAVEYARD	SURNAME	GRAVEYARD
Adel	Groveport	Baldwin	Truro
Adell	Union Grove	Ball	Asbury
Agle	Kramer	Ball	Truro
Albert	Groveport	Banck	Huddle
Alder	Asbury	Barkley	Hendren
Algire	Asbury	Barnhart	Groveport
Algire	Union Grove	Barnhart	Union Grove
Algire	Ref. & Luth.	Barrett	Truro
Allen	Groveport	Bastle	Groveport
Allen	Middletown	Baughman	Groveport
Allen	Union Grove	Beals	Union Grove
Allgire	Vandemark	Bechtel	Huddle
Alspach	Powell	Beery	Union Grove
Alspach	Union Grove	Beglin	Middletown
Alton	Hendren	Bennedum	Ref. & Luth.
Anderick	Middletown	Bennet	Hopewell
Anders	Union Grove	Bergstresser	Union Grove
Andrews	Middletown	Bickle	Union Grove
Andrix	Groveport	Bigelow	Groveport
Andrix	Hopewell	Bigerton	Union Grove
Arendt	Union Grove	Binkley	Union Grove
Armpreister	Union Grove	Bish	Powell
Armstrong	Asbury	Bishop	Edwards
Arnold	Edwards	Bishop	Groveport
Arnold	Union Grove	Bishop	Hopewell
Ashley	Union Grove	Bishop	Middletown
Aubert	Huddle	Black	Ref. & Luth.
Axtel	Kramer	Blakely	Groveport
Bachman	Union Grove	Blakely	Middletown
Badger	Union Grove	Blakely	Union Grove
Bailey	Union Grove	Bolenbaugh	Union Grove
Baker	Kramer	Born	Ref. & Luth.
Baker	Truro	Bostwick	Union Grove
		Bott	Union Grove

SURNAME	GRAVEYARD	SURNAME	GRAVEYARD
Bowman	Groveport	Carson	Ref. & Luth.
Bowman	Mennonite	Carty	Union Grove
Bowman	Union Grove	Caslow	Truro
Boyd	Union Grove	Caslow	Union Grove
Boyer	Truro	Cater	Union Grove
Boyer	Union Grove	Cavinee	Groveport
Boyer	Ref. & Luth.	Chain	Truro
Brenneman	Mennonite	Champ	Middletown
Brenner	Union Grove	Champe	Groveport
Brincker	Huddle	Chandler	Groveport
Brown	Asbury	Chaney	Union Grove
Brown	Truro	Chaney	Ref. & Luth.
Brown	Union Grove	Cheeseman	Groveport
Brown	Ref. & Luth.	Cherry	Groveport
Bruner	Groveport	Chester	Truro
Bruns	Union Grove	Childs	Hopewell
Bulen	Asbury	Chilles	Groveport
Bull	Vandemark	Churchman	Groveport
Bunch	Union Grove	Clarbaugh	Groveport
Bunn	Groveport	Clevinger	Hendren
Bunn	Hopewell	Coble	Asbury
Burgoon	Union Grove	Codner	Asbury
Burke	Groveport	Codner	Truro
Burkey	Asbury	Cohagan	Union Grove
Burnside	Union Grove	Cole	Hopewell
Burton	Hopewell	Cole	Middletown
Bush	Ref. & Luth.	Cole	Union Grove
Bye	Union Grove	Colman	Kramer
Byrne	Groveport	Colman	Union Grove
Caldwell	Kramer	Conkle	Powell
Calkins	Groveport	Conkle	Tossing
Cambridge	Truro	Conner	Whims
Cameron	Edwards	Conway	Union Grove
Cameron	Hopewell	Cortright	Gray
Campbell	Groveport	Counckle	Tossing
Campbell	Hendren	Courtright	Gray
Cannon	Ref. & Luth.	Courtright	Kramer
Carder	Groveport	Courtright	Powell
Carney	Groveport	Courtright	Truro

SURNAME	GRAVEYARD	SURNAME	GRAVEYARD
Craig	Groveport	Donaldson	Huddle
Cramer	Asbury	Donaldson	Union Grove
Cramer	Groveport	Dove	Kramer
Cramer	Kramer	Dove	Union Grove
Cramer	Tossing	Dovel	Powell
Cromwell	Union Grove	Dravenstott	Ref. & Luth.
Crook	Kramer	Draygenston	Ref. & Luth.
Cross	Kramer	Dunlap	Union Grove
Cross	Union Grove	Durant	Groveport
Crossly	Hopewell	Durant	Rarey
Crouse	Middletown	Easterday	Asbury
Crouse	Union Grove	Easterday	Truro
Cryder	Truro	Eberle	Groveport
Cummins	Middletown	Ebright	Groveport
Cunningham	Groveport	Edwards	Cox/Sharp
Dagon	Ref. & Luth.	Edwards	Edwards
Darnell	Groveport	Egbert	Hopewell
Dauterman	Union Grove	Ehrenhart	Union Grove
Davison	Middletown	Elder	Welton
Davison	Union Grove	Ell	Groveport
Decker	Gray	English	Hopewell
Decker	Middletown	Entler	Vandemark
Decker	Union Grove	Epley	Truro
Decker	Welton	Epley	Union Grove
Dehority	Groveport	Evans	Hopewell
Deitz	Union Grove	Evans	Truro
Dellinger	Ref. & Luth.	Evans	Union Grove
Denton	Truro	Evans	Vandemark
Derr	Kramer	Fall	Union Grove
Detwiler	Mennonite	Fancher	Union Grove
Dibble	Union Grove	Farrand	Middletown
Dildine	Groveport	Fay	Ref. & Luth.
Dildine	Hopewell	Fearn	Groveport
Dildine	Union Grove	Featheringill	Hendren
Dildine	Welton	Fenstermaker	Union Grove
Dill	Mennonite	Ferrel	Union Grove
Dill	Union Grove	Finch	Rarey
Dochterman	Mennonite	Finch	Union Grove

SURNAME	GRAVEYARD	SURNAME	GRAVEYARD
Finnefrock	Ref. & Luth.	Goodwin	Union Grove
Fisher	Union Grove	Gray	Asbury
Flemington	Hendren	Gray	Gray
Ford	Union Grove	Gray	Powell
Forsman	Truro	Gray	Truro
Fouble	Union Grove	Green	Truro
Fowler	Union Grove	Griffith	Union Grove
Frame	Powell	Groom	Hopewell
French	Kramer	Groom	Welton
French	Middletown	Guisinger	Union Grove
French	Ref. & Luth.	Guthrie	Union Grove
Friend	Asbury	Hainer	Hopewell
Friend	Groveport	Haines	Hendren
From	Union Grove	Hall	Hopewell
Fruchey	Middletown	Halzworth	Hopewell
Fry	Kramer	Hamler	Asbury
Fry	Union Grove	Hamler	Groveport
Fuller	Groveport	Hamler	Huddle
Fullon	Groveport	Hanna	Truro
Furgeson	Mennonite	Hanner	Groveport
Gambler	Groveport	Hanson	Union Grove
Game	Union Grove	Hare	Asbury
Gander	Gander	Hare	Mennonite
Gard	Hopewell	Harmon	Kramer
Gares	Groveport	Harmon	Union Grove
Gares	Rarey	Harpst	Ref. & Luth.
Garey	Groveport	Harris	Groveport
Garrison	Asbury	Harris	Kramer
Gater	Ref. & Luth.	Harris	Union Grove
Gayman	Union Grove	Harrison	Vandemark
Geese	Powell	Hartrum	Asbury
Gehm	Union Grove	Hastings	Union Grove
Geisler	Groveport	Hathaway	Union Grove
Giberson	Groveport	Hathaway	Ref. & Luth.
Giberson	Hopewell	Hathaway	Vandemark
Glit	Groveport	Havely	Groveport
Goettel	Ref. & Luth.	Havely	Hopewell
Good	Mennonite	Havely	Union Grove

SURNAME	GRAVEYARD	SURNAME	GRAVEYARD
Heffley	Union Grove	Hudson	Asbury
Helpman	Middletown	Hughs	Groveport
Helpman	Union Grove	Hull	Groveport
Helpman	Ref. & Luth.	Hulva	Hopewell
Helser	Union Grove	Hurst	Mennonite
Hempy	Union Grove	Iberson	Hopewell
Henderson	Hendren	Jamson	Groveport
Hendren	Union Grove	Jay	Union Grove
Hendron	Hendren	Jeffries	Groveport
Henry	Union Grove	Jenkins	Groveport
Herbst	Union Grove	Jobes	Union Grove
Herkins	Ref. & Luth.	Joes	Groveport
Herman	Union Grove	John	Groveport
Hermon	Groveport	Johnson	Groveport
Herrick	Groveport	Johnson	Truro
Herrick	Mennonite	Johnson	Ref. & Luth.
Herrman	Ref. & Luth.	Justice	Union Grove
Hersh	Asbury	Kalb	Truro
Hesser	Ref. & Luth.	Kalb	Union Grove
Heston	Groveport	Karnes	Middletown
Hewitt	Hopewell	Kauffman	Groveport
Hews	Groveport	Keissel	Truro
Hickle	Groveport	Kelley	Middletown
Hicks	Union Grove	Kelsey	Union Grove
Hicks	Ref. & Luth.	Keys	Asbury
Himrod	Union Grove	Kilborn	Hopewell
Hische	Union Grove	Kile	Asbury
Hockman	Middletown	Kile	Groveport
Hoffman	Mennonite	Kile	Hendren
Holbert	Union Grove	Kile	Kile
Hook	Groveport	Kile	Union Grove
Hooker	Groveport	King	Gander
Hopkins	Vandemark	King	Groveport
Horner	Whims	King	Union Grove
Horning	Mennonite	Kissell	Truro
Horst	Mennonite	Kissell	Union Grove
Hott	Middletown	Kissell	Ref. & Luth.
Howard	Union Grove	Knapp	Truro

SURNAME	GRAVEYARD	SURNAME	GRAVEYARD
Krafft	Ref. & Luth.	Long	Truro
Kramer	Kramer	Looker	Union Grove
Kramer	Middletown	Loucks	Union Grove
Kramer	Union Grove	Love	Hopewell
Kraner	Groveport	Luce	Groveport
Krumm	Union Grove	Lyons	Union Grove
Kuhns	Welton	Mackneyayers	Hopewell
Landon	Union Grove	Mansfield	Groveport
Lanning	Hopewell	Martin	Mennonite
Lanning	Kramer	Mason	Groveport
Lawrence	Ref. & Luth.	Mason	Truro
Leady	Mennonite	Mathias	Union Grove
Leady	Union Grove	Matthews	Ref. & Luth.
Leavel	Tossing	McClaskey	Truro
Leavengood	Hopewell	McClish	Hopewell
Lecrone	Kramer	McClure	Powell
Lee	Middletown	McClure	Union Grove
Lehman	Mennonite	McComb	Truro
Lehman	Union Grove	McCormick	Groveport
Lehman	Welton	McCoy	Groveport
Lehman	Ref. & Luth.	McCracken	Union Grove
Lehr	Ref. & Luth.	McFadden	Union Grove
Leidy	Mennonite	McFarling	Edwards
Leidy	Union Grove	McGarity	Hopewell
Leight	Union Grove	McGuffy	Asbury
Lentz	Middletown	McIntyre	Welton
Leonard	Truro	McKelvey	Union Grove
Lether	Ref. & Luth.	McKelvey	Ref. & Luth.
Limpert	Rarey	McKelvey	Vandemark
Lincoln	Hopewell	McWilliams	Groveport
Line	Union Grove	Medford	Union Grove
Line	Middletown	Meeker	Asbury
Lines	Kramer	Merriss	Truro
Lisle	Cox/Sharp	Meyer	Ref. & Luth.
Little	Groveport	Meyers	Ref. & Luth.
Lockwood	Truro	Michel	Welton
Lohr	Union Grove	Miller	Groveport
Loner	Asbury	Miller	Hendren

SURNAME	GRAVEYARD	SURNAME	GRAVEYARD
Miller	Huddle	Ordel	Middletown
Miller	Kramer	Osborn	Groveport
Miller	Middletown	Overhalser	Ref. & Luth.
Miller	Truro	Painter	Union Grove
Miller	Tossing	Palsgrove	Union Grove
Miller	Union Grove	Parker	Cox/Sharp
Miller	Ref. & Luth.	Parker	Welton
Millisee	Groveport	Patrick	Groveport
Mink	Asbury	Patrick	Welton
Mooberry	Edwards	Patterson	Asbury
Moore	Groveport	Patterson	Truro
Moore	Hopewell	Paul	Groveport
Moore	Kramer	Paul	Truro
Moore	Union Grove	Paynd	Hopewell
More	Hopewell	Perrill	Hopewell
Morris	Groveport	Perrin	Hendren
Morton	Union Grove	Perrin	Vandemark
Mossman	Huddle	Persoll	Ref. & Luth.
Motz	Union Grove	Peterman	Powell
Murphy	Union Grove	Peters	Groveport
Myers	Asbury	Peters	Union Grove
Myers	Middletown	Pickering	Union Grove
Myers	Tossing	Piester	Groveport
Myreir	Ref. & Luth.	Pike	Union Grove
Needels	Asbury	Poland	Groveport
Needels	Kile	Polen	Hopewell
Needels	Kramer	Pontius	Hopewell
Needels	Truro	Pontius	Union Grove
Neff	Groveport	Porter	Cox/Sharp
Nichols	Groveport	Potter	Union Grove
Nickerson	Stevenson	Powell	Asbury
Nicklas	Mennonite	Powell	Powell
Nigh	Groveport	Powell	Union Grove
Nongenecker	Union Grove	Price	Ref. & Luth.
Oakley	Hopewell	Purdy	Stevenson
Ochs	Union Grove	Purdy	Union Grove
Ogborn	Powell	Ramsey	Hopewell
Ogden	Truro	Ramsey	Welton

SURNAME	GRAVEYARD	SURNAME	GRAVEYARD
Ranock	Huddle	Ryne	Groveport
Rarey	Groveport	Sackrider	Truro
Rarey	Hopewell	Sallee	Middletown
Rarey	Rarey	Sallee	Union Grove
Rarey	Union Grove	Samsel	Kramer
Rathmell	Cox/Sharp	Sandy	Union Grove
Rawn	Groveport	Sarber	Groveport
Rawn	Union Grove	Sarber	Union Grove
Reber	Welton	Sarber	Welton
Reckets	Groveport	Satchleben	Union Grove
Rees	Union Grove	Saunders	Union Grove
Reeves	Groveport	Schmitt	Ref. & Luth.
Rexroad	Huddle	Schoch	Union Grove
Rhyan	Hopewell	Schoonover	Kramer
Richards	Asbury	Scott	Rarey
Richards	Truro	Selby	Union Grove
Richardson	Groveport	Senter	Groveport
Rider	Hendren	Sergeant	Ref. & Luth.
Riley	Union Grove	Seymour	Groveport
Ringer	Ref. & Luth.	Seymour	Welton
Robertson	Union Grove	Shaffer	Groveport
Robinson	Asbury	Shaffer	Union Grove
Robinson	Groveport	Shaner	Union Grove
Robinson	Kramer	Shanner	Union Grove
Robnett	Groveport	Sharp	Groveport
Rockey	Kramer	Sharp	Truro
Rohr	Huddle	Shield	Truro
Rohr	Union Grove	Shirey	Groveport
Rose	Hopewell	Shiseden	Asbury
Ross	Groveport	Shoemaker	Union Grove
Ross	Middletown	Shortt	Union Grove
Rossow	Union Grove	Showham	Hopewell
Rowe	Middletown	Shrock	Ref. & Luth.
Rower	Tossing	Shue	Huddle
Rowland	Groveport	Shultz	Kramer
Runkle	Union Grove	Shultz	Truro
Ruse	Union Grove	Shuman	Mennonite
Rush	Tossing	Sidner	Groveport

SURNAME	GRAVEYARD	SURNAME	GRAVEYARD
Simons	Hopewell	Strohm	Mennonite
Sims	Tossing	Suddick	Truro
Skidmore	Asbury	Sunday	Ref. & Luth.
Sleeper	Union Grove	Swanger	Powell
Slife	Kramer	Swayer	Hopewell
Slough	Union Grove	Sweetser	Truro
Smith	Groveport	Swigart	Huddle
Smith	Hopewell	Swisher	Asbury
Smith	Huddle	Swisher	Edwards
Smith	Middletown	Swisher	Groveport
Smith	Mennonite	Swisher	Kile
Smith	Truro	Swisher	Truro
Smith	Union Grove	Swisher	Ref. & Luth.
Soloman	Rarey	Swishser	Hendren
Somerville	Union Grove	Tallman	Union Grove
Sommerville	Union Grove	Tallman	Ref. & Luth.
Sommerville	Ref. & Luth.	Taylor	Asbury
Sparr	Union Grove	Taylor	Kile
Speaks	Union Grove	Taylor	Truro
Speaks	Ref. & Luth.	Taylor	Union Grove
Speilman	Ref. & Luth.	Taylor	Vandemark
Spencer	Truro	Teas	Middletown
Spitter	Union Grove	Teegardin	Union Grove
Sprague	Powell	Thompson	Asbury
Sprague	Truro	Thompson	Middletown
Stambaugh	Truro	Thompson	Truro
Starr	Truro	Thompson	Ref. & Luth.
Steman	Mennonite	Thomson	Groveport
Stevenson	Asbury	Thrush	Middletown
Stevenson	Groveport	Thrush	Union Grove
Stevenson	Powell	Toll	Middletown
Stevenson	Stevenson	Toy	Groveport
Stevenson	Union Grove	Travis	Union Grove
Stevenson	Vandemark	Trine	Union Grove
Stine	Groveport	Trine	Ref. & Luth.
Stott	Union Grove	Trost	Union Grove
Straw	Huddle	Trott	Groveport
Strickley	Tossing	Turner	Truro

SURNAME	GRAVEYARD	SURNAME	GRAVEYARD
Tussing	Union Grove	Whitmore	Hendren
Updegraff	Hendren	Wightman	Edwards
Van Trine	Middletown	Will	Union Grove
Vance	Groveport	Williams	Asbury
Vandemark	Mennonite	Williams	Middletown
Vandemark	Union Grove	Williams	Ref. & Luth.
Vandemark	Vandemark	Willie	Groveport
Vanhorn	Groveport	Wilson	Kramer
Vanwormer	Groveport	Wilson	Truro
Vesey	Truro	Wilson	Union Grove
Veth	Union Grove	Winders	Union Grove
Vought	Union Grove	Winterstein	Kile
Wagoner	Ref. & Luth.	Wolf	Huddle
Wallet	Ref. & Luth.	Wolfe	Union Grove
Walter	Ref. & Luth.	Wood	Truro
Walters	Kramer	Wood	Whims
Walters	Union Grove	Woodring	Groveport
Ward	Truro	Woodring	Welton
Warner	Union Grove	Worrell	Union Grove
Warner	Ref. & Luth.	Wright	Hopewell
Watson	Groveport	Wright	Union Grove
Wax	Edwards	Yost	Union Grove
Weber	Union Grove	Young	Groveport
Welton	Welton	Young	Hopewell
Wernert	Union Grove	Young	Huddle
Whaley	Middletown	Yourd	Groveport
Wheeler	Cox/Sharp	Zachero	Union Grove
Wheeler	Truro	Zahn	Union Grove
Wheeler	Union Grove	Zarbaugh	Union Grove
Whetsel	Groveport	Zarbaugh	Ref. & Luth.
Whimer	Powell	Zebold	Hopewell
Whims	Union Grove	Zimmer	Ref. & Luth.
White	Groveport	Zinn	Groveport
White	Hopewell	Zinn	Union Grove
Whitehead	Truro	Zwayer	Union Grove
Whitehurst	Union Grove		

Asbury Graveyard
Located in Section No. 9.

A.

D. Slices **Alder**, died 1870, aged 24 years.

Isaac D., son of D. S. and M. E. **Alder**, died 1871, aged 3 months.

Zachariah **Algire**, died 1844, aged 30 years.

John, son of Jacob and Sarah **Algire**, died 1841, aged 30 years.

Ernestina, daughter of John and Susan M. **Armstrong**, died 1841, aged 1 year.

B.

Chas., son of Wm. and M. A. **Bulen**, died 18920 aged 26 years.

Samuel **Brown**, died 1897, aged 64 years.

Rebecca E. **Brown**, died 1837, age _____.

Mary A. R., wife of Matthew **Brown**, died 1862, aged 48 years.

Matthew **Brown**, died 1894, aged 83 years.

John **Bulen**, died 1894, aged 75 years.

Mary, wife of John **Bulen**, died 1880, aged 56 years.

Nancy J., daughter of Wm. and M. A. **Bulen**, died 1870, aged 25 years.

Pitts **Brown**, died 1855, aged 56 years.

Nancy, wife of P. **Brown**, died 1859, aged 57 years.

Pitts M. **Brown**, died 1865, aged 21 years.

Malinda A. E. **Brown**, died 1866, aged 27 years.

Mary S., wife of O. J. **Brown** died 1870, aged 28 years.

Amanda, daughter of Joseph and Elizabeth **Burkey**, died 1848, aged 6 years.

John **Ball**, died 1845, aged 19 years.

C.

Margaret, wife of Oliver **Codner,** died 1879, aged 92 years.

Wm. H. **Cramer**, died 1882, aged 41 years.

Wm. **Cramer**, Jr., Co. K, 133d O. V. I.

Lillie M., daughter of Wm. H. and A. **Cramer**, died 1886, aged 16 years.

John **Coble**, died 1887, aged 83 years.

Jane; consort of John **Coble**, died 1843, aged 36 years.

Jacob **Coble**, died 1846, aged 76 years.

Infant son of Robt. and Mary **Codner**, died 1847.

E.

John W., son of H. and M. **Easterday**, died 1852, aged 3 years.

F.

Joseph C. **Friend**, died 1886, aged 22 years.

G.

Evaline, wife of John **Garrison**, died 1852, aged 29 years.

Charlotte, wife of John **Garrison**, died 1858, aged 67 years.

Littleton R. **Gray**, died 1852, aged 47 years.

Anna, wife of L. R. **Gray**, died 1881, aged 74 years.

Leroy S., son of L. R. and A. **Gray**, died at Atlanta, Ga., 1864, aged 23 years.

H.

Bertha C., daughter of J. and J. E. **Hare**, died 1877, aged 1 year.

James W., son of T. and L. **Hartrum**, died 1851, aged 8 months.

Wm. T. **Hudson**, died 1840, aged 1 year.

Julian, daughter of Benjamin and Mary **Hersh**, died 1852, aged 12 years.

Nancy J., daughter of Wm. H. and Lucinda **Hamler**, died 1854, aged 1 year.

K.

Rebecca W., wife of Robt. A. **Kile**, died 1885, aged 98 years.

Lucinda, wife of John **Keys**, died 1850, aged 33 years.

L.

Rebecca, wife of John **Loner**, died __, aged __.

Daniel M., son of John and Rebecca **Loner**, died 1865, aged 24 years.

M.

Sarah **Meeker**, died 1892, aged 80 years.

Cyrus Ray, son of C. R. and M. **McGuffy**, died 1885, aged 6 months.

Lula Olive, daughter of Wm. and Mary **Mink**, died 1888, aged 6 months.

Pauline, daughter of J. and S. I. **Myers**, died 1856, aged 10 days.

N.

Philomon **Needels**, son of Thos. and Sarah Needels, died 1841, aged 70 years.

Sarah, consort of Philomon **Needels**, died 1844, aged 56 years.

Infant son of Philomon and Nancy **Needels**, died 1844.

Rebecca, wife of J. J. **Needels**, died 1847, aged 47 years.

Philomon, son of Thos. B. **Needels**, died 1840, aged 1 year.

Willimet, daughter of W. P. **Needels**, died 1854, aged 2 years.

Heber, son of J. and M. J. **Needels**, died 1877, aged 5 months.

John A. **Needels**, died 1876, aged 62 years.

Nancy, wife of P. **Needels**, died 1854, aged ___.

P.

Miranda, wife of Thos. **Patterson**, died 1881, aged 72 years.

Thomas **Patterson**, died 1891, aged 82 years.

Francis A. R., son of James R. and Matilda **Powell**, died ___, aged 1 year.

R.

Harry L., son of John and I. **Robinson**, died 1884, aged 1 year.

Mary A. **Richards**, adopted daughter of H. M. and M. A. Cryder, died 1847, aged 5 years.

S.

Isaac, son of Robt. **Skidmore,** died 1845, aged 7 years.

Henry C. **Swisher**, died 1894, aged 57 years.

Jacob **Swisher**, died 1890, aged 87 years.

Anah, wife of Jacob **Swisher** and daughter of P. and S. Needels, died 1862, aged 51 years.

Pheba M., daughter of J. and A. **Swisher**, died 1870, aged 27 years.

Phil M. **Swisher**, died at Gallatin, Tenn., 1862, aged 24 years.

Sarah M., daughter of James and Rachel **Stevenson**, died 1852, aged 11 months.

Sarah A., wife of M. G. **Stevenson**, died 1873, aged 44 years.

James E., son of J. and J. **Shiseden**, died 1846, aged 1 year.

T.

Miller F. **Thompson**, died 1891, aged 64 years.

Sarah J., wife of M. F. **Thompson**, died 1890, aged 62 years.

Bennett **Thompson**, died 1888, aged 67 years.

Sarah, wife of M. **Thompson,** died 1884, aged 90 years.

McKee **Thompson**, died 1867, aged 68 years.

Nanny Bell, daughter of Lot B. and M. **Taylor**, died 1886, aged 1 year.

Henrietta **Taylor**, died 1857, aged 54 years.

W.

Elizabeth **Williams**, died 1841, aged 73 years.

Cox (or Sharp) Graveyard
Located on Abner Behm's land, in Section No. 30.

Caleb **Cox**, died 1835, aged 42 years.

Elmer **Cox**, died 1845, aged 75 years.

John **Cox**, died 1873, aged 69 years.

Wm. R., son of Wm. and Sarah **Cox**, died 1841, aged 2 years.

Sarah Dianah, wife of John G. **Edwards,** died 1838, aged 20 years.

Jeremiah, son of Robt. and Abigail **Lisle**, died 1833, aged 4 years.

Simon W. **Parker**, died 1836, aged 35 years.

Katharine, wife of Simon W. **Parker**, died 1844, aged 43 years.

Elizabeth, daughter of James and Jane **Porter**, died 1828, aged 1 year.

Rachel, daughter of Thomas and Mary **Rathmell**, died 1835, aged 19 years.

Catharine, wife of Benjamin **Wheeler**, died 1845, aged 22 years.

Edwards Graveyard
Located on Mary S. Page's and Elmer D. Sharp's land,
In Section No. 18.

Orvilla, wife of Jacob **Arnold** died 1850, aged 33 years.

Henry L., son of Jacob and Mary **Arnold**, died 1860, aged 8 years.

Jacob **Arnold**, died 1870, aged 51 years.

James P., son of Jacob and Orvilla **Arnold**, died 1880, aged 35 years.

Martha J. **Arnold**, wife of D. C. **Wax**, died 1873, aged 25 years.

Mila **Bishop**, died 1837, aged 7 years.

Rebecca **Cameron**, died 1854, aged 64 years.

Lewis H. **Edwards**, died 1845, aged 27 years.

William **Mooberry**, died 1829, aged 76 years.

James W., son of James and Sarah **McFarling**, died 1839, aged 1 year.

Mrs. Rebecca **Swisher**, died 1841, aged __ years.

Ruth, the amiable consort of George **Wightman**, died 1838, aged 63 years.

George **Wightman**, died 1844, aged 84 years.

Gander Graveyard
Located on William Haustine's land, in Section No. 29.

Rebecca, daughter of John and Elizabeth **Gander**, died 1825, aged 8 years.

Lucinda, daughter of J. and E. **Gander**, died 1803, aged 7 years.

Josias, son of David and Lucinda **King**, died 1831, aged 2 years.

Groveport Cemetery

The oldest inscription in this graveyard is the following: "Sacred to the memory of Catharine G., consort of John C. Richardson, M. D., and daughter of Captain Isaac Bowman, all natives of Shenandoah county, Virginia, born December 23, 1787, departed this life January 19, 1809, aged 22 years."

"Oh fairest flower, thy failing breath is gone,
The sense to please no more.
The icy withering hand of death
Has rifled all thy fragrant store.
Calm be thy rest, sweet as the slumbers of a saint,
And mild as the opening gleams of promised heaven."

A.

S. A. **Allen**, Co. F. 90th Regt, O. V. I., died __, aged __ .

Hester A., wife of G. **Adel** died 1880, aged 50 years.

Jacob **Andrix** died 1875, aged 52 years.

James **Albert**, died 1843, aged 17 years.

B.

J. A. **Bigelow**, Co. B, 6th U. S. Cavalry, and Co. K, 14th Regt., O. V. I.

Wm. J. **Blakely**, died 1868, aged 40 years.

Gordila J., wife of Wm. J. **Blakely**, died 1866, aged 35 years.

Melissa, daughter of J. and E. **Brunner**, died 1852, aged 2 years.

Wm. M., son of S. and M. **Bastle**, died 1884, aged 20 years.

John B., son of S. and M. **Bastle**, died 1885, aged 17 years, with this inscription on tombstone: *"Dear son John, who left us so sudden, Father, Mother, Sister and Brother all miss you at home; I trust you are safe in the arms of Jesus".*

Mary D. **Bastle**, died 1894, aged 47 years, with the following inscription on tombstone:

> *"'Tis sweet to die when gone before*
> *The loved ones of my heart,*
> *My angel sons, say, Mother come,*
> *We never more shall part."*

Lewis, son of Solomon and Martha **Baughman**, died 1856, aged 11 months.

Abraham **Burke**, died 1845, aged 68 years.

James Boyd, son of M. and C. **Bishop**, died 1875, aged 8 months.

Washington, son of T. and E. **Blakely**, died 1871, aged 17 years.

Thos. **Blakely** died 1874, aged 59 years.

Mary E., wife of Orange **Barnhart**, died 1870, aged 39 years.

Lida, wife of John **Byrne**, died 1876, aged 27 years.

Harrison W. **Bunn**, died 1866, aged 30 years.

C.

George **Campbell**, died 1853, aged 33 years.

Henry, son of Chas. and Emeline **Campbell**, died 1855, aged 1 year.

Josephine A., daughter of C. and E. **Campbell**, died 1873, aged 23 years.

Emeline **Campbell**, died 1870, aged 41 years.

Wm. Seabury White, son of John and Hannah **Chilles**, died 1854, aged 5 years.

Susannah, wife of ____ **Carder**, died 1837, aged 40 years.

George, son of E. and S. **Carder**, died 1853, aged 29 years.

Henry **Carder,** died 1861, aged 68 years.

Lafayette **Carder**, Co. C, 95th Regt., O. V. I.

E. G. **Carder**, Co. G, 95th Regt., O. V. I., died 1887, aged 41 years.

Alford, son of Riley and Mary Ann **Calkins**, died 1858, aged 4 months.

Ida Melissa, daughter of B. D. and Sarah Jane **Clarbaugh**, died 1859, aged 9 months.

John C., son of Wm. W. and Sarah A. **Cramer**, died 1848, aged __.

Mahala A., daughter of Wm. W. and Sarah A. **Cramer**, died 1847, aged __.

Hugh L., son of G. and M. C. **Cramer**, died 1877, aged 3 years.

Mary E., daughter of W. and E. A. **Cramer**, died 1852, aged 1 year.

David **Craig**, died 1849, aged 50 years.

Jennie M., wife of J. E. **Carney**, died 1857, aged 41 years.

Elizabeth, daughter of I. and R. **Cheeseman**, died 1853, aged 3 years.

Elias **Churchman**, Co. B, 38th Regt., O. V. I.

Wealthy, wife of Elias **Churchman**, died 1868, aged 48 years.

Edgar Allen, son of Wm. and Adda **Chandler**, died 1865, aged 14 days.

Edward M., son of J. C. and J. R. **Cunningham**, died 1869, aged 25 years.

Leander D., son of Geo. P. and D. R. **Champe**, died 1873, aged 19 years, inscription, *"Those hands once so skilled in music here, are now touching the Golden Harp"*.

George P. **Champe**, died 1898, aged 77 years.

Infant son of O. and L. A. **Cherry**, died 1877.

Sarah, wife of Jacob **Cavinee**, died 1883, aged 47 years.

D.

Mary, wife of Hermon **Dildine**, died 1855, aged 65 years.

Harmon **Dildine,** died 1859, aged 72 years.

Henry T. Clark, son of Jesse and Elizabeth **Dildine**, died 1842, aged 2 years.

Sarah E., daughter of Jesse and Elizabeth **Dildine**, died 1853, aged 1 year.

J. H. **Dildine** died 1862, aged 22 years.

Susan, wife of Joseph **Dildine**, died 1855, aged 42 years.

Joseph **Dildine**, died 1855, aged 41 years.

Twin infant sons of Joseph and Susan **Dildine**, died 1843.

Zephaniah, son of E. L. and S. A. **Dildine,** died 1851, aged 1 year.

Wm. E., son of Robt. F. and Mary A. **Dildine**, died 1861, aged 2 months.

Chester V., son of Robt F. and Mary A. **Dildine**, died 1879, aged 11 years.

Ines, daughter of G. M. and F. J. **Dildine**, died 1865, aged 8 months.

Eleanor B., wife of Salem **Darnell**, died 1849, aged 20 years.

James M. P., son of Archibald and Mary **Darnell**, died 1848, aged 9 years.

Larantheadotia, daughter of G. and E. **Darnell**, died 1849, aged 1 month.

Wm. S., son of Wm. S. and A. **Durant**, died 1864, aged 3 years.

Absalom **Dehority**, died 1866, aged 63 years.

E.

John **Eberle**, died 1851, aged 50 years.

Lether, son of D. R. and L. R. **Ebright**, died 1851, aged 1 year.

Mathias, son of John and Elizabeth **Eberle**, died 1851, aged 3 years.

Andrew F., son of I. P. and M. A. **Ell**, died 1852, aged 13 days.

F.

Orlando **Fuller**, died 1836, aged 40 years.

Hannah, wife of Isaac **Friend**, died 1839, aged 27 years.

Geo. W., son of I. and H. **Friend**, died 1839, aged 5 months.

Cora B., daughter of J. H. and C. C. **Fearn**, died 1856, aged 11 months.

Emma, daughter of J. and E. **Fullon**, died 1871, aged 1 year.

G.

Clarinda J., daughter of Thomas and Sarah **Goodman**, died 1848, aged 2 years.

Sarah J. and James H., twin children of Wm. and M. **Giberson**, died 1847.

Chas., son of C. and M. **Glit**, died 1848, aged 1 year.

Samuel **Gares**, died 1859, aged 63 years.

Louisa, wife of Samuel **Gares**, died 1875, aged 77 years.

Samuel J., son of V. A. B. and Jane **Gares**, died 1859, aged 3 months.

John **Gambler**, died 1863, aged 65 years.

Joanna, wife of J. **Gambler**, born 1793 (date of death not given).

Christina **Geisler**, died 1884, aged 65 years.

Wm. **Garey**, Co. B, 128th Regt., O. V. I.

H.

Wm. F., son of Geo. and Angelina **Hook**, died 1836, aged 7 years.

Nancy, wife of Julius **Hull**, died 1843, aged 22 years.

Ann E. **Herrick**, died 1846, aged 21 days.

Wm. C. **Harris**, died 1852, aged *22* years.

Mary C., daughter of Thomas and Christina **Hughes**, died 1846, aged 1 year.

Sarah A., daughter of Thos. L. S. and Adaline **Hews**, died 1851, aged 10 months.

Jonathan **Hermon**, died 1847, aged 23 years.

Susannah, wife of Robert **Hermon**, died 1843, aged __.

Robert **Hermon**, died 1860, aged 72 years.

Walker, son of John P. and Catharine **Heston**, died 1850, aged 10 months.

Francis, son of John and Nancy **Hanner**, died 1857, aged *2* years.

Isaac W., son of J. G. and S. **Howell**, died 1854, aged 1 year.

James G. **Howell**, died 1870, aged 49 years.

Nancy, wife of John **Hickle**, died 1865, aged 48 years.

Elizabeth, wife of Adam **Havely**, died 1877, aged 60 years.

Sarah S., wife of Isaac **Hamler**, died 1888, aged 56 years

Lewis H., son of I. and S. **Hamler**, died 1889, aged 28 years.

A. Burke **Hooker**, died 1857, aged 31 years.

J.

Emily, daughter of John and Mary J. **Jeffries**, died 1849, aged 3 years.

Parley L., son of W. & J. **Jenkins**, died in 1852, aged 4 years.

Luke V. **Jenkins**, died 1871, aged 22 years.

Geo. **Johnson**, Co. F, 18th regiment U. S. infantry.

Harrison R. **Johnson**, died 1883, aged 24 years.

Amanda M. **Johnson**, died 1874, aged 23 years.

Isaac T. **Johnson**, died 1873, aged 18 years.

Francis L. **Johnson**, died 1873, aged 11 years.

Julian Edgar, son of Jacob and Hannah **Joes**, died 1851, aged __.

John Wm. **Jamson**, died 1865, aged 71 years.

Adam **John**, died 1848, aged 41 years.

K.

Addline, daughter of Jeptha and Olive **King**, died 1846, aged 2 years.

America J., daughter of Jacob and Jane **Kauffman**, died 1859, aged 11 years.

Elizabeth C., daughter of Jacob and Jane **Kauffman**, died 1852, aged 21 years.

Henry **Kraner**, died 1858, aged 54 years.

Ann, wife of H. **Kraner**, died 1889, aged 79 years.

Robert **Kile**, died 1877, aged 58 years.

Rhoda, wife of Robert **Kile**, died 1886, aged 57 years.

L.

Henry D., son of Mark and Margaret **Luce**, died 1851, aged 18 years.

Mary C., daughter of J. and S. **Little**, died 1853, aged 9 years.

Lula, daughter of H. and H. A. **Long**, died 1867, aged 7 months.

Henry **Long**, died 1881, aged 61 years.

M.

David **Millisee**, died 1850, aged 26 years.

Ruth, wife of J. **Morris**, Jr., died ___ , aged 67 years.

S. **McWilliams**, died 1871, aged 46 years.

Harmon **Mansfield**, died 1876, aged 67 years.

Fredrick **Mansfield**, died 1876, aged 47 years.

A. F. **Mansfield**, Co. B, 188th regiment, O. V. I.

Jason **Miller**, Co. H. 18th regiment W. S. I., died 1871, aged 25 years.

Hattie D., daughter of Henry and Caroline **Miller**, died 1889, aged 15 years.

Sarah, wife of A. **McCoy**, died 1874, aged 57 years.

Lulu, daughter of Wm. and Mary **Mason**, died 1873, aged 2 months.

Grace L., daughter of Wm. and Mary **Mason**, died 1875, aged 3 months.

Kate G., wife of F. A. **Moore**, died 1881, aged 27 years.

James **McCormick**, Co. B, 118th regiment, O.V. I.

N.

Sylvester **Nichols**, died 1838, aged 51 years.

Margaret J., daughter of L. and L. **Nichols**, died 1841, aged 3 years.

Elizabeth, daughter of D. P. and Hannah **Neff**, died 1840, aged 1 year.

Mahala, wife of George **Nigh**, died 1848, aged 35 years.

James G., son of G. S. and Mahala **Nigh**, died 1850, aged 2 years.

Sarah M., daughter of Geo. S. and Mahala **Nigh**, died 1850, aged 14 years.

O.

Infant daughter of Albert and Martha **Osborn**, died 1839, aged ___.

Clarindae, daughter of Albert and Martha **Osborn**, died 1846, aged 5 years.

P.

Catharine, wife of Richard **Poland**, died 1851, aged 44 years.

Wm. H., son of J. R. and Catharine **Paul**, died 1852, aged 1 month.

Francis W., son of S. A. and C. A. **Peters**, died 1876, aged 15 years.

Silas Allen **Peters**, died 1878, aged 55 years.

Nancy J., wife of John **Patrick**, died 1880, aged 43 years.

John **Patrick**, died 1882, aged 54 years.

Lina May, daughter of J. and L. **Piester**, died 1877, aged 1 year.

J. M. **Piester**, died 1888, aged 40 years.

R.

Children of Adam and Catherine **Rarey**:

Catherina, died 1821, aged 1 year.

Jesse, died 1825, aged 2 years.

Anna C., died 1825, aged 4 months.

Adam S., died 1828, aged 2 years.

Sarah Ann, died 1831, aged 1 year.

Adam **Rarey**, died 1839, aged 53 years.

Mary G., wife of Adam **Rarey**, died 1868, aged 78 years.

John S. **Rarey**, son of Adam and Catherine, died 1866, aged 38 years.

Eliza, wife of Wm. H. **Rarey**, died 1849, aged 40 years.

Catherine, wife of Wm. II. **Rarey**, died 1857, aged 33 years.

Wm. H. **Rarey**, died 1877, aged 65 years.

Ellen G., wife of F. **Rarey**, died 1871, aged 62 years.

Frederick **Rarey**, died 1879, aged 62 years.

Children of F. and E. **Rarey**:

R. B., died 1845, aged 3 months.

M. E., died 1854, aged 10 months.

F. E., died 1858. aged 5 months.

J. C., died 1861, aged 13 years.

Cynthia, wife of C. W. **Rarey**, died 1857, aged 36 years.

Twin infant daughters of C. W. and C. A. **Rarey**, died 1857.

A. B. **Rarey**, died 1881, aged 46 years.

Hannah, wife of Jacob **Rawn**, died 1849, aged 28 years.

Lucius Clark, son of Jacob and Hannah **Rawn**, died 1849, aged 1 day.

Andrew W., son of C. G. and A. **Robnett**, died 1853, aged ___.

Mary E., daughter of P. and A. **Reeves**, died 1852, aged 9 months.

Abagail, wife of Peter **Reeves**, died 1864, aged 38 years.

Infant daughter of P. and H. **Reeves**, died 1867, aged___.

Hannah A., wife of Peter **Reeves**, died 1875, aged 34 years.

Lillie G., daughter of Lida **Robinson**, died 1875, aged 1 year.

George W. **Rowland**, died 1875, aged 45 years.

Dora B„ daughter of Maggie **Reckets**, died 1875, aged 4 years.

Irwin T., son of A. and E. **Ross**, died 1851, aged 4 months.

Owin, son of F. and R. **Ryne**, died 1883, aged 1 year.

S.

Eliza, wife of J. P. H. **Stevenson**, died 1852, aged 25 years.

Harriet A., wife of C. J. **Stevenson**, died 1851, aged 30 years.

Infant daughter of David and Mary C. **Sarber**, died 1854, aged ___.

Infant daughter of Moses and Sarah **Shaffer**, died 1847, aged ___.

Elizabeth A., daughter of D. and J. **Sidner**, died 1851, aged 2 years.

Joseph **Sharp**, died Feb. 16, 1847, aged 32 years;

Sarah Jane, daughter of Joseph and Mary **Sharp**, died March 4, 1847, aged 4 months.

Mary, wife of Joseph **Sharp**, died April 29, 1847, aged 30 years.

Ann, wife of E. **Stine**, died 1850, aged___.

Charlotte, daughter of E. and A. **Stine**, died 1852, aged 16 years.

Rhoda, daughter of Lewis and Elisa J. **Shirey**, died 1858, aged 10 years.

Lewis C., son of Martin and Elizabeth **Shirey**, died 1860, aged 3 years.

Mary Ellen, wife of Adam **Smith**, died 1868, aged 22 years.

L. S. **Senter**, died 1863, aged 45 years. Inscription, *"Positive in his convictions, he made no compromises with expediencies."*

Susannah M., wife of L. S. **Senter**, died 1881, aged 61 years.

Orestes D. A., son of L. S. and S. M. **Senter**, died 1863 aged 16 years.

Chas. A., son of F. M. and **Senter**, died ___ , aged 20 months.

John G. **Sharp**, died 1874, aged 47 years.

Martha, wife of J. G. **Sharp**, died 1876, aged 43 years.

Geo. B., son of J. G. and M. **Sharp**, died 1858, aged 2 years.

Chas., son of J. G. and M. Sharp, died 1871, aged 1 month;

Luther Laflin, son of J. E. and Ellae **Swisher**, died 1871, aged 1 year.

Pearl, son of W. P. and E. G. **Seymour**, died 1878, aged 5 years.

Nettie M. **Seymour**, died 1869, aged 15 years.

Edward **Stevenson**, Co. B, 128th O. V. I.

T.

John E., son of Wm. and Catherine **Toy**, died 1840, aged 4 years.

Catherine, wife of Wm. **Toy**, died 1842, aged 27 years.

Drucilla, wife of Wesley **Toy**, died 1837, aged 30 years.

James, son of Wesley and Drucilla **Toy**, died 1834, aged 13 days.

Sarah E., daughter of Wesley and Minerva **Toy**, died 1846, aged 3 years.

Wesley **Toy** died 1861, aged 65 years.

Minerva, wife of Wesley **Toy**, died 1874, aged 64 years.

Charles **Toy**, died 1835, aged 67 years.

Addison **Toy**, died 1841, aged 27 years.

Wm. Addison, son of Addison and Sarah **Toy**, died 1841, aged 2 months.

May, daughter of C. and M. R. **Toy**, died 1876, aged 6 years.

Wm. M., son of Wm. R. and H. A. **Thompson**, died 1871, aged 1 year.

Claudia Bell, daughter of I. and A. **Trott**, died 1870, aged 3 months.

V.

Josiah **Vance**, died 1852, aged 30 years.

Wm. A., son of A. J. and M. C. **Vanwormer**, died 1865, aged 6 months.

Andrew J. **Vanwormer**, died 1870, aged 51 years.

Linney H, son of H. S. and E. **Vanhorn**, died 1875, aged 5 years.

W.

Eva, wife of William **Watson**, died 1847, aged 53 years.

Margaret, daughter of John and Nancy **Watson**, died 1845, aged 1 year.

Elizabeth, wife of Jonathan **Watson** died 1848, aged 26 years.

James Dixon, son of Jeremiah and Elizabeth **White**, died 1853, aged nine years.

David **Whetzel**, died 1883, aged 73 years.

Elizabeth, wife of David **Whetzel**, died 1887, aged 73 years.

Children of D. and E. Whetzel:

Frederick, died 1847, *aged* 2 years.

Eliza C., died 1848. aged 1 year.

May I., died 1857, aged 5 years.

Martha A., daughter of Augustus and Martha Ann **Willie**, died 1852, aged 3 years.

Clara, daughter of A. and M. A. **Willie**, died 1862, aged 21 years.

Thos. C., son of A. and M. A. **Willie**, died 1865, aged 22 years.

Ellen, daughter of A. and M. A. **Willie**, died 1867, aged 15 years.

Nettie, daughter of David M. and M. A. **Willie**, died 1878, aged 2 years.

Rebecca **Whitestine**, died 1855, aged 34 years.

C. P. **Woodring**, died 1872, aged 40 years.

Henry, son of C. P. and M. **Woodring,** died 1874, aged 17 years.

Solomon **Woodring**, died 1876, aged 71 years.

Y.

Francis Marion, son of John and Mary Ann **Young**, died 1858, aged 17 years.

Lorenzo D. **Young**, died 1853, aged 1 month.

Sousannah H., daughter of J. and E. **Yourd**, died 1874, aged 18 years.

John **Yourd**, Co. H, 95th Regiment. O. V. I., died 1876, aged 50 years.

Z.

Ida J., daughter of M. and T. A. **Zinn**, died 1855, aged 5 months.

Fannie E., daughter of M. and T. A. **Zinn**, died 1861, aged 2 years.

Elizabeth C., daughter of Moses and T. A. **Zinn**, died 1863. aged 11 years.

Abraham **Zinn**, died 1870, aged 44 years;

Elnorie **Zinn**, died 1892, aged 34 years.

Gray Graveyard
Located on L.R. Davis's land, in Section No. 4.

Richard **Courtright**, died August 1851, aged 51 years.

Sarah, wife of Richard **Cortright**, died 1843, aged *57* years.

Mary, wife of John **Cortright**, died 1841, aged 33 years.

Rebecca, wife of John **Cortright**, died 1846, aged 29 years.

Richard, son of John and Mary **Cortright**, died 1831, aged 1 year.

Palmyra, daughter of John and Rebecca **Cortright**, died 1844, aged 1 year.

Aaron L. **Decker**, died 1826, aged 3 years.

Theadogeur, wife of Thomas **Gray**, died 1826, aged 37 years.

Mary, wife of Thomas **Gray**, died 1832, aged 21 years.

Mary, daughter of Thomas and Harriet **Gray**, died 1837, aged 7 months.

Errena, daughter of Thomas and Julian **Gray**, died 1842, aged 10 months.

Hendren Graveyard
Located on Kalita Sallee's land, in Section No. 20.

Nancy, daughter of H. D. and Louisa **Alton**, died 1844, aged 1 year.

Orpha, daughter of Elijah and Rebecca **Barkley**, died 1836, aged 25 years.

Benjamin M. C., son of William and Esther **Clevinger** died 1829, aged 9 years.

Jasper **Campbell**, died 1833 aged 44 years.

John W., son of Jasper and Hetty **Campbell**, died 1831, aged 5 years.

Barret J. **Doherity**, died 1864, aged 34 years.

Sarah K., daughter of B. J. and A. S. **Doherity**, died 1876, aged 21 years.

Thomas **Featheringill**, died 1832, aged 47 years.

Elizabeth, wife of Thos. **Featheringill**, died 1824, aged 50 years.

Joseph **Flemington** died 1801, aged 30 years; (This is the earliest death we found marked in the township.)

Wm. D. **Hendren** died 1826, aged 49 years.

Nancy, wife of Wm. D. **Henderson**, died 1819, aged 62 years.

Benjamin **Haines**, died 1832 aged 51 years.

Sarah, wife of Thomas **Haines**, died 1832, aged 27 years.

389

Robt. **Hendren**, died 1864, aged 42 years.

Matilda H. **Rider**, wife of Mordicai C. **Hendren**, died 1862, aged 27 years.

John W. **Kile**, died 1815, aged 34 years.

John **Kile**, died 1846, aged 71 years.

Mary **Kile**, died 1881, aged 72 years.

Amelia, wife of John **Kile**, died 1849, aged 64 years.

Elizabeth W., wife of Wm. W. **Kile**, died 1848, aged 42 years.

Wm. W. **Kile**, died 1870, aged 66 years.

Rachel, wife of John **Kile**, died 1819, aged 40 years.

Robert W. **Kile**, died 1843, aged 30 years.

Sarah, wife of Robert **Kile**, died 1863, aged 50 years.

Ida L., daughter of John A. and Louisa **Kile**, died 1865, aged 15 days.

Jacob W., son of John W. and Nancy **Kile**, died 1851, aged 2 years.

John W., son of Jacob and Ruth **Miller**, died 1831, aged 1 year.

Martha, wife of Wm. **Perrin** died 1845, aged 49 years.

Eliza, wife of Jacob **Swisher**, died 1829, aged 19 years.

Mary, wife of John **Swisher**, died 1836, aged 54 years.

John **Swisher**, died 1861, aged 79 years.

John L., son of Frederick and Lidie **Swisher**, died 1856, aged 18 years.

John **Updegraff**, died 1851, aged 52 years.

John E. **Whitmore**, died 1876, aged 32 years.

Hopewell Graveyard
Located on Section No. 9, near Hopewell Church.

A.

Francis, daughter of J. and S. **Andrix**, died 1859, aged 7 years.

B.

Clarissa, wife of Morgan **Belford**, died 1823, aged __.

Stephen, son of Wesley and Elizabeth **Bishop**, died 1848, aged 3 months.

Children of Samuel and Mary **Bishop**:

John, died 1834, aged 23 years.

Wesley, died 1847, aged 35 years.

Jackson, died 1866, aged 47 years.

Louisa, wife of A. J. **Bishop**, died 1850, aged 30 years.

Andrew J. **Bishop**, died 1866, aged 47 years.

Clarinda, daughter of Wesley and Elizabeth **Bishop**, died 1839, aged 1 year.

Noah **Bishop**, died 1827, aged 78 years.

Thankful, wife of Noah **Bishop**, died 1832, aged 81 years.

Samuel **Bishop**, died 1842, aged 57 years;

Mary, wife of Samuel **Bishop**, died 1868, aged 81 years.

Thomas R., son of Thomas and Elizabeth **Bennet**, died 1839, aged 1 year.

Joshua **Burton**, died 1835, aged 90 years.

Thomas Becket **Burton**, died 1829, aged 35 years.

Nancy, wife of Thomas **Burton**, died 1836, aged 44 years.

Malinda, daughter of John and Prudence **Bunn**, died 1850, aged 4 years.

Frederick **Bunn**, died 1871, aged 58 years.

Jefferson L,. son of Frederick and Charlotte **Bunn**, died 1883, aged 35 years.

Elizabeth, wife of Henry **Bunn** died 1860, aged 72 years.

Henry **Bunn**, died 1848, aged 68 years.

C.

Anna, wife of Alexander **Cameron,** died 1833, aged 55 years.

Alexander **Cameron,** died 1846, aged 62 years.

Broad **Cole**, died 1831, aged 79 years.

Shadrach **Cole**, died 1845, aged 66 years.

Mary, wife of Shadrach **Cole**, died 1836, aged 56 years.

Polly **Cole**, died 1844, aged 29 years.

Armenta, wife of Wesley **Cole**, died 1853, aged 22 years.

Lydia L., daughter of John and Hanna A. **Childs**, died 1846, aged 6 months.

John **Childs**, died 1830, aged 56 years.

Mary, wife of Wm. **Childs**, died 1835, aged 28 years.

Mary Ann, wife of Henry **Crossly**, died 1871, aged 86 years.

Henry **Crossly**, died 1863, aged 83 years.

D.

Julian, wife of Joseph **Dildine**, died 1842, aged 27 years.

Holman, son of Thomas and Mary **Dildine**, died 1838, aged 49 years.

Andrew **Dildine**, died 1825, aged 46 years.

Robert K., son of Henry and Matilda **Dildine**, died 1834, aged 1 year.

Elisha **Dildine**, died 1833, aged 25 years.

E.

Pheba, wife of William F. **English**, died 1849; aged 29 years.

Jacob B., son of John and Elizabeth **English**, died 1834, aged 15 years.

James, son of John and M. **Egbert**, died 1827, aged 20 years.

Jemima D., daughter of George and Mary **Evans**, died 1847, aged 8 months.

Rebecca J., daughter of James and Huldah **Evans**, died 1832, aged 2 years.

G.

Elizabeth, daughter of Dr. B. F. and Elizabeth **Gard**, died 1846, aged 8 months.

Hezekiah **Giberson**, died 1838, aged 86 years.

Ezekiel **Groom**, died 1836, aged 69 years.

Rhoda, wife of Ezekiel **Groom**, died 1859, aged 86 years.

Moses **Groom**, died 1852, aged 38 years.

Mary **Groom**, died 1849, aged 58 years.

Elizabeth, wife of John **Groom** died 1833, aged 31 years.

Thomas **Groom,** died 1858, aged 40 years.

Noah **Groom**, died 1856, aged 74 years.

Lucy, wife of Noah **Groom**, died 1853, aged 64 years.

David J. **Groom**, died 1858, aged 33 years.

Almira, daughter of Thomas and Nancy **Groom**, died 1839 aged 3 years.

John F., son of T. and N. **Groom**, died 1863, aged 34 years.

Thomas **Groom** died 1881, aged 85 years.

Nancy, wife of Thomas **Groom,** died 1866, aged 70 years.

Daniel R. **Groom**, died 1875, aged 49 years.

Susan, wife of Daniel **Groom**, died 1878, aged 48 years.

Pheba, second wife of Moses **Groom,** died 1816, aged 32 years.

Margaret, third wife of Moses **Groom,** died 1847, aged 23 years.

Catherine, wife of Moses **Groom,** died 1838, aged 21 years.

Hannah **Gameilch**, died 1873, aged 44 years.

H.

Mary Fidela, daughter of Ely and Rebecca **Hainer**, died 1847, aged 2 years.

Emma R., daughter of T. H. and S. **Hall**, died 1853, aged 5 days.

Fannie R.. wife of John **Hewitt**, died 1885, aged 34 years.

John M. **Halzworth**, died 1859, aged 62 years.

Adam **Havely** died 1842, aged 62 years.

Mary, wife of Adam **Havely** died 1832, aged 51 years.

Christina, wife of Josiah **Hulva**, died 1842, aged 32 years.

Mary M., daughter of J. and Elizabeth **Hawkins**, died 1847, aged 1 year.

Daniel W., son of F. J. and Elizabeth **Hawkins**, died 1843, aged 1 year.

I.

John **Iberson**, died 1816, aged 48 years.

K.

Dr. J. H. **Kilborn**, died 1834, aged 26 years.

L.

William C., son of William and Margaret **Love**, died 1838, aged 10 years.

Jacob **Leavengood**, died 1849, aged 72 years.

Mary, wife of Jacob **Leavengood**, died 1861, aged 76 years.

Sarah R. **Lanning,** died 1821, aged 56 years.

John Lanning, son of Susan **Lanning**, died 1831, aged 18 years.

John F. **Lincoln**, died 1855, aged 11 months.

M.

Thomas **Mackneyayers**, died 1859, aged 56 years.

Lucy J., daughter of G. H. and E. **Miller**, died 1877, aged 14 years.

Rebecca, wife of Henry **More**, died 1843, aged 80 years.

Oake **Moore**, died 1839, aged 68 years.

Sarah, wife of John **Moore**, died 1823, aged 26 years.

Nancy, daughter of J. A. and Patience **McClish,** died 1832, aged 1 year.

Sarah **McGarity**, died 1877, aged 65 years.

Elizabeth, wife of Wm. **McGarity**, died 1850, aged 44 years.

William **McGarity**, died 1879, aged 70 years.

O.

William C., son of Jeremiah and Charity **Oakley**, died 1843, aged 27 years.

Margaret, wife of Thomas A. **Oakley**, died 1848, aged 23 years.

P.

James W., son of W. H. and S. A. **Paynd**, died 1861, aged 10 years.

Raleigh C. **Perrill**, died 1891, aged 48 years.

Joseph W., son of Z. H. and R. C. **Perrill**, died 1847, aged 1 year.

John, son of Wm. and M. **Polen**, died 1888, aged 13 years.

Philip **Pontius**, died 1845, age 61 years.

Catherine, wife of Philip **Pontius**, died 1854, aged 75 years.

Charles **Pontius**, died May 10, 1887, aged 75 years.

Elizabeth, wife of Charles **Pontius**, died April 30, 1887, aged 75 years.

R.

Elizabeth C., daughter of Jacob and Mary **Rhyan**, died 1851, aged 1 year.

Jacob **Rhyan**, died 1875, aged 47 years.

John Florence **Rarey**, died 1864, aged 35 years.

George **Rarey,** died 1850, aged 55 years.

Jane, wife of George **Rarey**, died 1836, aged 30 years.

Sarah, wife of George **Rarey**, died 1872, aged 65 years.

Henry **Rose**, died 1844, aged 64 years.

Clarence E. **Rarey**, died 1890, aged 25 years.

Sarah, wife of Daniel **Ranier**, died 1820, aged 52 years.

Daniel **Ranier**, died 1842, aged 77 years.

Abigail, second wife of Daniel **Ranier**, died 1823, aged 55 years.

Hulda, third wife of Daniel **Ranier**, died 1840, aged 73 years.

Amelia, wife of Daniel **Ranier**, died 1854, aged 71 years.

Children of Daniel and Sarah **Ranier**:

Daniel, died 1836, aged 23 years.

Abraham, died 1831, aged 31 years.

Sarah, died 1821, aged 18 years.

Rebecca, died 1823, aged 18 years.

Isaac **Ranier**, died 1863, aged 69 years.

Mary, wife of I. **Ranier**, died 1871, aged 74 years.

Willie, son of J. F. and A. **Ranier** died 1864, aged 6 months.

Jane, wife of Lockhart **Ramsey**, died 1847, aged 38 years.

S.

Mary E., daughter of Stephen and Abigail **Smith**, died 1877, aged 11 months.

Abraham **Swayer**, died 1876, aged 63 years.

John **Swayer**, died 1864, aged 56 years.

Sarah, wife of Andrew **Swayer**, died 1855, aged 78 years.

Thomas and Susan **Showham**, *Father died July 30, 1865, aged 73 years and Mother died July 18, 1865, aged 72 years.*

Stephen **Simons**, died 1856, aged 74 years.

Mary, wife of Stephen **Simons**, died 1845, aged 59 years.

W.

Agnes, wife of Wm. **Wright**, died 1830, aged 62 years.

Mary Bunn, wife of J. P. **Wright**, died 1868, aged 25 years.

Wm. W., son of Orin and Lucinda **White**, died —, aged 4 months.

Y.

Adam **Young**, died 1849, aged 29 years.

Charity, daughter of Thomas and Sarah **Young**, died 1831, aged 2 years.

Robert F., son of A. and E. **Young**, died 1849, aged 3 years.

Z.

Sophia, wife of Andrew **Zebold**, died 1860, aged 19 years.

Huddle Graveyard
Located on Margaret and Wesley Huddle's land, in Section No. 6.

Chas. **Aubert**, died 1865, aged 38 years.

Claudius B. **Aubert**, died 1863, aged 66 years.

Chas. M., son of G. and E. **Banck**, died 1866, aged 1 year.

John W., son of S. and E. A. **Brincker**, died 1861, aged 21 days.

Hiram, son of Samuel and Susannah **Bechtel,** died 1856, aged 18 years.

Matilda **Donaldson**, died 1876, aged 47 years.

Emma A., daughter of B and E. C. **Donaldson**, died 1876, aged 2 years.

Catherine, daughter of Jacob and Elizabeth **Hamler**, died 1835, aged 19 years.

Jacob **Hamler**, died 1832, aged 46 years.

Wm., son of T. and M. **Miller**, died 1862, aged 27 years.

Joshua **Miller**, died 1849, aged 25 years.

John, son of John and Margaret **Miller**, died 1852, aged 23 years.

John R. **Miller**, died 1848, aged 53 years.

Margaret, wife of John **Miller**, died 1853, aged 46 years.

Elizabeth, daughter of Robert and Mary **Mossman**, died 1823, aged 7 years.

Catherine, daughter of Samuel E. **Ranock**, died 1853, aged 16 years.

Elizabeth **Rexroad**, died 1853, aged 20 years.

Susannah, wife of Jacob **Rexroad**, died 1861, aged 70 years.

Infant daughter of George and Catherine **Rohr**, died 1826.

George, son of Wm. and Elizabeth **Rohr**, died 1833, aged 1 year.

Joseph, son of Chas. and Mary **Rohr**, died 1841, aged 2 months.

Martha, daughter of M. and S. A. **Rohr**, died 1853, aged 19 years.

Elizabeth C., wife of George **Rohr**, died 1854, aged 69 years.

George **Rohr**, died 1862, aged 76 years.

Walter G., son of Absalom and Rhoda **Rohr**, died 1866, aged 1 year.

Michael **Rohr**, died 1861, aged 39 years.

Infant daughter of Wm. and E. **Rohr**, died 1853, aged 11 months.

Maria, wife of Michael **Rohr**, died 1823, aged 67 years.

Michael **Rohr,** died 1818, aged 62 years.

Margaret, wife of John **Rohr**, died 1839, aged 49 years.

Jefferson **Rose**, died 1854, aged 7 days.

Rosanna **Shue**, died 1879, aged 57 years.

Elizabeth, wife of Joseph **Shue**, died 1868, aged 80 years.

Catherine, wife of John **Straw**, died 1853, aged 45 years.

John **Straw**, died 1860, aged 68 years.

Elizabeth **Swigart**, died 1835, aged 55 years.

Elizabeth **Smith**, died 1859, aged 77 years.

John **Smith** died 1819, aged 41 years.

Catherine, wife of Mathias **Wolf**, died 1850; aged 65 years;

Mathias **Wolf,** died 1839, aged 50 years;

Katherine, wife of Philip **Wolf,** died 1838, aged 84 years.

Hannah, wife of P. **Wolf**, died 1871, aged 73 years.

Sarah, wife of Chas. **Young**, died 1868, aged 19 years.

Kile Graveyard
Located on John W. Kile's land, in Section No. 9.

James A. **Kile**, died 1855, aged 46 years.

Sally Ann, wife of James A. **Kile**, died 1880, aged 70 years.

John Wesley **Needels**, died 1862, aged 38 years.

Sally Ann, daughter of John W. and Abigail J. **Needels**, died 1853, aged 1 year.

Pheba, wife of Jacob **Swisher**, died 1849, aged 60 years.

Theresa M., daughter of Israel and Rachel **Swisher**, died 1875, aged 22 years.

Sally A., wife of A. J. **Taylor** died 1864, aged 17 years.

Sally A., daughter of A. J. and S. A. **Taylor**, died 1864, aged 5 months.

John **Winterstein**, died 1850, aged 66 years.

Abigail, wife of John **Winterstein**, died 1867, aged 75 years.

Kramer Graveyard
Located on B. F. Ashbrook's land, in Section No. 31.

A.

Amzi **Axtell**, died August 27, 1840, aged 42 years.

Casanda, wife of Amzi **Axtell**, died July 13, 1840, aged 34 years.

Henry S., son of J. and R. **Agle**, died 1853, aged 1 month.

B.

_____ daughter of Isaac **Baker**, died 1824, aged ___.

C.

James **Caldwell**, died 1865, aged 73 years.

John **Colman,** died 1848, aged 51 years.

Mary, wife of John **Colman,** died 1835, aged 37 years.

Luiza, wife of Jacob **Cramer**, died 1837, aged 35 years.

Wm., son of Geo. and Rachel **Crook**, died 1851, aged 4 years.

Chas. **Cross**, died 1830, aged 59 years.

Elizabeth, wife of Chas. **Cross**, died 1822, aged 52 years.

Emily Jane, wife of Israel **Cross**, died 1844, aged 34 years.

Israel **Cross**, died 1853, aged 44 years.

D.

Christina, wife of Reuben **Dove,** died 1838, aged 38 years.

Children of Reuben and C. **Dove**:

Enoch and Elizabeth, died 1825, infants.

Elijah, died 1825, aged 4 months.

Samuel J., died 1830, aged 1 year.

Henry H., died 1832, aged 9 months.

Moses and Aaron, died 1837, infants.

Wm. H., died 1838, aged 2 months;

Barbara, wife of Geo. G. **Derr**, died 1853, aged 33 years.

Elizabeth **Derr**, died 1846, aged 37 years.

Barbara, wife of John **Derr**, died 1843, aged 54 years.

F.

Matilda, wife of John Fry, died 1844, aged 22 years.

Matilda, daughter of John and M. **Fry**, died 1844, aged 8 months.

Wm. W., son of Reuben and Sarah **French**, died 1836, aged 14 years.

H.

Eliza, daughter of Geo. and Sarah **Harmon**, died 1842, aged___ .

Sarah, wife of George **Harmon**, died 1855, aged 63 years.

Kizia, daughter of Philomen and Jane **Harris**, died 1823, aged 1 month.

K.

Susannah, wife of Daniel **Knepper**, died 1850, aged 22 years.

Mical, son of old Adam and Crestena **Kramer**, died 1823, aged 43 years.

Jacob **Kramer**, died 1866, aged 64 years.

Lewis **Kramer**, died 1847, aged 69 years.

Margaret, wife of Lewis **Kramer**, died 1863, aged 87 years.

Martha, wife of Lewis **Kramer**, died 1853, aged 23 years.

Sarah, daughter of George and Catherine **Kramer**, died 1849, aged 2 years.

Barbara, wife of Adam **Kramer,** died 1823, aged 23 years.

Sarah, wife of Jacob **Kramer**, died 1860, aged 44 years.

Edward, son of David and Elizabeth **Kramer**, died 1831, aged 3 weeks.

Philip, son of Ludwig **Kramer**, died 1812, aged 6 years.

Samuel, son of Adam and Abigail **Kramer** (no date):

Adam **Kramer** died 1815, aged 63 years.

Elizabeth Andrix, wife of John **Kramer**, died 1827, aged 24 years.

L.

Elizabeth, wife of Elias **Lines**, died 1842, aged 31 years.

Elias **Lines**, died 1843.

Cisley, wife of Isaac **Lanning**, died 1823, aged 38 years.

Catherine A., daughter of Daniel and Sarah **Lecrone**, died 1838, Aged ___ .

M.

Conrad **Miller**, died 1846, aged 66 years.

Hannah, wife of Conrad **Miller**, died 1821, aged 45 years.

Elizabeth, third wife of Conrad **Miller**, died 1849, aged 70 years.

Emeline, daughter of Levi and Margaret **Moore**, Jr., died 1847, aged 2 years.

N.

Elizabeth, daughter of Philomen and Sarah **Needels**, died 1813, aged 12 years.

Amanda, daughter of J. W. and A. J. **Needels**, died 1848, aged 9 days.

R.

Stephen **Robinson**, died 1836, aged 34 years .

Daniel B. **Rockey**, died 1845, aged 29 years.

S.

Paul **Samsel**, Jr., died 1851, aged 34 years.

Sarah Ann, wife of Henry **Samsel**, died 1852, aged 44 years.

Mary Ann, wife of Henry **Samsel**, died 1854, aged 29 years (*her twin sons sleep with her*).

John M. **Samsel**, died 1835, aged 23 years.

Elizabeth, wife of Paul **Samsel**, died November, 1834, aged 44 years.

Sarah, wife of Paul **Samsel**, died November, 1835, aged 38 years.

Mary Ann, wife of James **Samsel**, died 1844, aged 26 years.

Minerva, wife of James **Samsel**, died 1847, aged 23 years.

Elizabeth, daughter of James and Margaret **Samsel**, died 1842, aged 4 years.

John M. **Samsel**, died 1835, aged 24 years.

Sarah W. **Samsel**, died 1852, aged 32 years.

James, son of Paul and Cyrena **Samsel**, died 1849, aged 11 years.

John S. **Slife**, died 1844, aged 53 years.

Wm. S. **Slife**, died 1848, aged 31 years.

Polly, daughter of Henry and Catherine **Slife**, died 1849, aged 11 years.

Delia, daughter of J. S. and M. M. **Slife**, died 1849, aged 18 years.

Rachel A., daughter of S. and M. **Slife** (no dates).

Henry **Slife** (balance of inscription faded).

Wm. H., son of Jacob and Ann Maria **Shultz**, died 1842, aged 4 years.

Henry **Schoonover,** died July 7, 1833, aged 40 years.

Perry, son of Henry and Sarah **Schoonover**, died July 12, 1833, aged 7 years, *victims of the cholera*.

Elizabeth, wife of John **Schoonover**, daughter of John and Margaret **Courtright**, died 1822, aged 72 years.

Mary, daughter of Abraham and Margaret **Schoonover**, died 1823, aged 4 months.

Sally, wife of John **Schoonover**, died 1827, aged 25 years.

W.

Samuel **Walters**, died 1831, aged 97 years.

Samuel **Wilson**, died 1842, aged __.

Middletown Graveyard
Located on Section No. 1, near Oregon.

A.

Jacob **Anderick**, Sr., died 1812, aged 48 years.

Henry Clay, son of Jacob and Nancy **Anderick**, died 1842, aged 2 years.

Sophia, wife of Martin A. **Andrews**, died 1871, aged 66 years.

Martin **Andrews**, died 1863, aged 50 years.

Mary, wife of Wm. **Allen**, died 1852, aged 27 years.

Margaret J., daughter of Elizabeth **Andrews**, died 1860, aged 28 years.

B.

George **Bishop**, died 1840, aged 57 years.

Catherine **Bishop**, died 1866, aged 77 years.

Louisa **Bishop**, died 1869, aged 21 years.

Jacob **Bishop,** died 1884, aged 70 years.

John **Bishop**, died 1846, aged 47 years.

Arabelle, daughter of John and Nancy **Bishop**, died 1827, aged 4 years.

Geo. **Blakely**, died 1828, aged 44 years.

Sally, wife of Geo. **Blakely**, died 1855, aged 67 years.

Thomas **Blakely**, died 1824, aged 44 years.

Sabina, wife of James **Blakely**, died ___ , aged ___.

Elizabeth, wife of Michael **Beglin**, died 1873, aged 45 years.

C.

Sarah Ann, wife of Thos. M. **Champ**, died 1849, aged 23 years.

William **Cummins**, died 1833, aged 42 years.

Abigail, wife of Daniel **Crouse**, died 1864, aged 59 years.

Daniel, son of Ruthy and Major **Cole**, died 1831, aged 13 months.

D.

Andrew **Decker**, died 1832, aged (scaled off).

Isaac **Decker**, died 1836, aged 47 years.

Elisha, son of Isaac and Eleanor **Decker**, died 1823, aged 1 year.

Mary, wife of Isaac L. **Decker**, died 1845, aged 26 years.

Lydia **Decker**, died 1834, aged 40 years.

Katherine, wife of Elias **Decker**, died 1824, aged 64 years.

Mahala, daughter of Daniel and Margaret **Decker**, died 1830, aged 11 days.

Eleanor, wife of Isaac **Decker**, died 1823, aged 45 years.

____ **Decker**, formerly widow **Bishop**, died 1822 aged (indistinct).

Isaac, son of John and Rachel **Decker**, died 1814, aged 18 days.

Lucinda, daughter of Jacob T. and Sarah A. **Decker**, died 1845, aged 1 year.

Algernon **Davison**, died 1861, aged 35 years.

Sarah, daughter of A. and Abigail **Davison**, died 1861, aged 3 months.

F.

Reuben **French**, died 1833, aged 43 years.

Mary, wife of Hezekiah **Farrand**, died 1845, aged 57 years.

Catherine, wife of H. **Farrand**, died 1877, aged 46 years.

Mary, wife of Fredrick **Fruchey**, died 182_.

Sarah Ann, daughter of Fred and Polly **Fruchey**, died 1836, aged 12 years.

H.

Almira, wife of Henry **Hott**, died 1853, aged 31 years.

Christneth, daughter of Simon and E. **Helpman**, died 1830, aged 7 days.

Rebecca Ann, daughter of Elias and Nancy **Helpman**, died 1833, aged 16 days.

Joseph **Helpman**, died 1816, aged 18 days.

Anna, daughter of S. and E. **Helpman**, died 1824, aged 2 years.

Sary Ann, daughter of Jacob and Angelina **Hockman**, died 1820, aged 2 months.

K.

Nancy, wife of Philip **Kramer,** died 1831, aged 25 years.

Eliza J., daughter of Adam and S. **Kramer**, died 1816, aged 5 years.

Geo. A. **Kelley**, died 1824, aged 44 years.

Eliza Jane, daughter of Adam and Secolahy **Karnes**, died 1846, aged 5 years.

L.

Jonathan **Lee**, died 1814, aged 48 years.

Electhy, wife of Zebulon **Lee**, died 182_. (Last figure gone).

Katherine, wife of Peter **Line**, died 1817, aged 34 years.

Elizabeth, wife of Peter **Line**, died 1839, aged 52 years.

Peter **Line**, died 1842, aged *77* years.

Barbara E., daughter of Wm. J. and A. E. **Lentz**, died 1860, aged 1 year.

M.

Eleanor, wife of Daniel **Miller**, died 1833, aged 43 years.

Joseph **Myers**, died 1869, aged 65 years.

O.

George **Ordel**, died 1854, aged 62 years.

Catherine, wife of Geo. **Ordel**, died 1861, aged 65 years.

Florence, daughter of J. D. and C. A. **Ordel**, died 1872, aged 14 years.

Chas. G. **Ordel**, died 1891, aged 20 years.

R.

William **Rowe**, died 1844, aged 16 years.

Sally, wife of Alexander **Ross**, died 1825, aged 20 years.

S.

James L. **Smith**, died 1830, aged 2 years.

Infant daughter of Geo. C. and K. E. **Sallee**, died 1888.

T.

John B. **Thompson**, died 1851, aged 43 years.

Eliza Jane, wife of Samuel **Thrush**, died 1859, aged 39 years.

Eleanor, daughter of Wm. and Sarah Ann **Toll**, died 182_, aged 7 months.

John, son of John and Sarah **Teas** (dates all gone).

V.

Julian, wife of David **Van Trine**, died 1835, aged 40 years.

W.

Sarah, daughter of George and Sarah **Whaley**, died 1824, aged 4 years.

Four children of J. M. and R. **Williams**, died 1871-74.

Mennonite Graveyard
Located on David Martin's land, in Section No 24.

Manasseh, son of John and Sophia **Brenneman**, died 1849, aged 14 months.

Sarah, daughter of J. and M. **Bowman**, died 1849, aged 14 months.

Jacob **Bowman** died 1884, aged 71 years.

Mary, wife of Jacob **Bowman** died 1888, aged 81 years.

Catharine, wife of Noah **Brenneman**, died 1883, aged 45 years.

Lydia, wife of Noah **Brenneman**, died 1889, aged 46 years.

Anna, wife of Samuel **Detwiler**, Jr., died 1863, aged 25 years.

Isaac, son of S. and E. **Detwiler**, was killed at the battle of Stone River, Tenn., 1862, aged 21 years.

Elizabeth, wife of Samuel **Detwiler**, died 1854, aged 49 years.

Samuel **Detwiler**, died 1874, aged *77* years.

Infant son of J. K. and C. **Dill**, died 1877.

Magdalena, wife of Jacob **Dochterman**, died 1862, aged 59 years.

Jacob **Dochterman**, died 1877, aged 72 years.

Jacob, son of J. and M. **Dochterman**, died 1859, aged 23 years.

Mary, wife of Levi **Dochterman**, died 1873, aged 46 years.

Adaline, daughter of S. and W. **Furgeson**, died 1857, aged 1 year.

John **Good**, died 1862, aged 44 years.

Elizabeth, wife of John **Good**, died 1897, aged 72 years.

John, son of J. and E. **Good**, died 1866, aged 12 years.

Anna P., daughter of Absalom and L. M. **Good**, died 1889, aged 2 years.

Catharine, daughter of Jacob and Anna **Horning**, died 1851, aged 14 days.

Barbara, wife of Henry **Hoffman**, died 1855, aged 24 years.

Adda, *Weib von* George **Hoffman,** *starb, Januar* 21, 1845, *ist alt worden* 42 *Jahre,* 6 *monate,* 19 *Tag. This is the first burial in these grounds.*

Geo. **Hoffman**, died 1857, aged 54 years.

Susannah, daughter of David and Mary **Horst**, died 1848, aged 4 weeks.

Henry M., son of D. and M. **Hurst**, died 1848, aged 10 months.

Susannah, wife of P. **Hare**, died 1865, aged 35 years.

David **Hare**, died 1882, aged 31 years.

Samuel **Hare**, died 1876, aged 67 years.

Christina, wife of Samuel **Herr** died 1848, aged 48 years.

Samuel, son of S. and C. **Herr**, died 1869, aged 29 years.

Ida E., daughter of Jacob S. and Emeline **Lehman**, died 1867, aged 3 years.

Abraham **Lehman**, died 1868, aged 68 years.

Catharine, wife of Abraham **Lehman**, died 1878, aged 72 years.

Lemuel S., son of A. S. and M. **Lehman**, died 1888, aged 15 years.

John **Leidy** Co. F, 1st Ohio Cavalry.

John **Leady**, died 1881, aged 72 years.

Eliza, wife of J. **Leady**, died 1869, aged 54 years.

Elizabeth, wife of David **Martin**, died 1888, aged 58 years.

John, son of D. and E. **Martin**, died 1863, aged 9 months.

Peter **Nicklas**, died 1851, aged 38 years.

John, son of P. and E. **Nicklas**, died 1852, aged 1 year.

Simon B., son of Geo. and Lydia **Steman** died 1863, aged 2 years.

David **Steman**, died 1893, aged 58 years.

Catharine, wife of Nicolas **Steman**, died 1877, aged 75 years.

Nicolas **Steman**, died 1878. aged 76 years.

Nicolas **Steman**, died 1896, aged 67 years.

Martha, wife of Henry **Steman**, died 1900, aged 75 years.

Mary G., daughter of J. and M. **Shuman**, died 1869, aged 5 years.

Jacob, son of H. B. and E. **Strohm**, died 1878, aged 5 years.

Catharine, wife of J. **Strohm**, died 1888, aged 85 years.

H. B. **Strohm**, Co. F, 159th O. V. I..

Lydia, daughter of E. and H. **Strohm**, died 1892, aged 28 years.

Samuel, son of E. and H. **Strohm**, died 1899, aged 32 years.

Infant son of Amor and Leah **Smith**, died 1887.

Infant daughter of G. G. and M. J. **Vandemark**, died 1875.

Powell Graveyard
Located near Brice, on Section No. 25, Truro Township.

Ruth, wife of Joe **Alspach**, died 1879, aged 33 years.

John **Bish**, died 1864, aged 36 years:

Clarina A., wife of John **Bish,** died 1867, aged 38 years.

Gertie A., daughter of L. and S. **Conkle**, died 1864, aged 1 year.

Malinda A., wife of Ira L. **Courtright**, died 1849, aged 30 years.

Catherine, wife of John **Dovel**, died 1878, aged 91 years.

Daisy D., daughter of A. P. and T. A. **Frame**, died 1877, aged 5 years.

Clarisa A., daughter of H. and C. **Geese**, died 1858, aged 16 days.

Clarisa E., daughter of Alford and Rachel M. **Gray**, died 1862, aged 16 years.

William A., son of Joseph A. and Sarah A. **Gray** died 1868, aged 4 months.

James **McClure**, died 1889, aged 60 years:

Minnie E., daughter of Wm. V. and Elizabeth **Ogborn**, died 1874, aged 4 years.

Joseph **Powell**, died 1863, aged 76 years.

Archibald **Powell,** died 1868, aged 83 years.

Lucinda T., wife of J. B. **Powell,** died 1870, aged 28 years.

Nancy O., daughter of G. and N. **Powell**, died 1857, aged 1 year.

Infant daughter of J. and E. H. **Powell**, died 1847.

Home of Joseph B. Powell

Lovina J., daughter of W. E. and M. A. **Peterman**, died 1876, aged 33 years.

John **Swanger**, died 1862, aged 52 years.

Lily F., daughter of W. M. and M. A. **Swanger**, died 1878, aged 2 years.

Rebecca, wife of George **Stevenson**, died 1857, aged 65 years.

Rena A., daughter of O. F. and R. M. **Sprague**, died 1863, aged 1 year.

Matilda, wife of Wm. **Whimer**, died 1873, aged 65 years.

Rarey Graveyard
Located on Rachel Rarey's land, in Section No. 4.

Chas. W. H., son of James W. and Ann **Durant**, died 1841, aged 11 months.

Juliette I., daughter of E. H. and E. M. **Finch**, died 1851, aged 3 years.

Allie, daughter of E. and A. **Gares**, died 1866, aged 7 years.

Amanda, wife of Edmund **Gares,** died 1866, aged 34 years:

Infant son of Casper and Synthea **Limpert**, died 1843.

Laypole **Rarey,** son of Chas. and Mary, died 1860, aged 42 years.

Willis L., son of Laypole and Mary **Rarey**, died 1860, aged 2 years.

Francis Marion, son of Nicolas and Sarah **Rarey**, died 1848, aged 1 year.

Parker **Rarey**, died 1870, aged 76 years.

Sarah **Rarey**, died 1875, aged 76 years.

Carrington H. **Rarey**, died 1879, aged 39 years.

Caroline L. **Rarey**, died 1877, aged 34 years.

Gamaliel **Rarey**, died 1891, aged 63 years.

Rev. Chas. **Rarey**, died 1847, aged 63 years.

Mary, wife of Chas. **Rarey**, died 1868, aged 75 years.

Wm. **Rarey**, died 1848, aged 49 years.

Rachel, wife of Wm. **Rarey**, died 1894, aged 88 years.

Sarah M., daughter of Parker and Sarah **Rarey**, died 1837, aged 10 years.

Edmund, son of Benjamin and Mary **Rarey**, died 1826, aged 3 years.

Servitue, son of Benjamin and Mary **Rarey**, died 1855, aged 17 years.

Elizabeth, daughter of Chas. and Mary **Rarey**, died 1826, aged 5 years.

Sarah E., daughter of Chas. and Mary **Rarey**, died 1851, aged 17 years.

Laura Ann, daughter of Laypole and Mary **Rarey**, died 1815, aged 1 year.

Parker **Rarey**, died 1853, aged 35 years.

Benjamin **Rarey**, died 1841, aged 51 years.

Chas. **Rarey**, died 1826, aged 82 years.

Margaret **Rarey**, died 1839, aged 74 years.

Rev. John F. **Solomon** died 1848, aged 63 years.

Christina, wife of Rev. J. F. **Solomon**, died 1860, aged 75 years.

Alexander **Scott,** died 1867, aged 36 years.

Stevenson Graveyard
Located on B. F. Bowman's land, in Section No. 11.

Hannah, wife of Uzzie **Nickerson**, died 1835, aged 41 years.

Elizabeth, consort of Wm. **Purdy**, died 1835, aged 38 years.

Rebecca Richard Dirrick, daughter of J. and M. **Stevenson**, died 1816, aged 27 years.

Matilda Ann, daughter of Peter and Hannah **Stevenson**, died 1832, aged 7 years.

William, son of R. and R. **Stevenson**, died 1848, aged 19 years.

John W., son of James Q. and Rachel **Stevenson**, died 1844, aged 2 years.

Richard **Stevenson**, died 1875, aged 55 years.

Joshua, son of J. and M. **Stevenson**, died 1856, aged 52 years.

John **Stevenson**, died September 11, 1851, aged 72 years.

Mary, wife of John **Stevenson**, died September 4, 1851.

Truro Graveyard
Located on C. M. Chittenden's land, in Section No. 3.

B.

Archibald K. **Baldwin**, died 1834, aged 21 years.

Peter **Brown**, died 1844, aged 50 years.

Hezekiah E., son of L. and L. **Boyer**, died 1877, aged 2 years.

Geo. W., son of G. and Jane **Barrett**, died 1852, aged 7 months.

Thomas **Baker**, died 1849, aged 50 years.

Littleton G., son of Thos. and Elizabeth **Baker**, died 1843, aged 22 years.

Chas. W., son of G. T. and C. E. **Ball**, died 1851, aged 3 years.

C.

Franklin B. **Chester**, died 1845, aged 47 years.

Mary Ann **Chester**, died 1853, aged 51 years.

Elias **Chester**, Sr., died 1850, aged 77 years.

Hannah, wife of Elias **Chester**, died 1853, aged 80 years.

N. Horatio Nelson, son of S. **Chester**, died 1828, aged 23 years.

Ann, wife of Samuel **Codner**, died 1832 (age not given).

Oliver **Codner**, died 1862, aged 61 years.

Daniel **Caslow,** died 1853, aged 32 years.

John **Courtright**, died 1848, aged 85 years.

Esther, wife of John **Courtright**, died 1832, aged 48 years.

Esther, daughter of John and Esther **Cambridge**, died 1844, aged 29 years.

Matthew **Chain**, died 1838, aged 30 years.

Calista, wife of James **Carson**, died 1865, aged 57 years.

James **Carson**, died 1854, aged 58 years.

Ethel Hope, daughter of W. L. and M. **Carson**, died 1870, aged 2 years.

Oswy Floy, son of S. and M. E. **Carson**, died 1869, aged 1 year.

Jefferson **Cryder**, died 1839, aged 37 years.

D.

Florie N., daughter of J. and M. R. **Denton**, died 1862, aged 13 days.

E.

Peter **Epley**, died 1894, aged 72 years.

Wm. I., son of James and Cracy **Evans**, died 1846, aged 6 years.

Isaac **Evans**, died 1847, aged 57 years.

Sarah **Easterday**, died 1827, aged 37 years.

F.

Abraham S., son of J. and A. **Forsman**, died 1852, aged 22 years.

Robt. S. **Forsman**, died 1858, aged 67 years.

Martha, wife of R. S. **Forsman**, died 1856, aged 67 years.

G.

Belinda, wife of Gilbert **Green**, died 1835, aged 26 years (*daughter of Aaron and Mary Harrison*).

Robt., son of Gilbert and Susannah **Green**, died 1835, aged 2 months.

Gilbert **Green**, died 1878, aged 73 years.

Susan **Green**, died 1886, aged 77 years.

Wm. Henry **Green**, died 1868, aged 38 years.

Aaron Harrison, son of W. H. and J. B. **Green**, died 1863, aged 2 years.

Littleton **Gray**, died 1838, aged 69 years.

Thomas **Gray**, died 1863, aged 62 years.

Mary, wife of Thomas **Gray**, died 1832, aged 22 years.

Julian Ann, wife of Thos. **Gray**, died 1856, aged 41 years.

H.

Matilda, wife of Wm. **Hanna**, died 1874, aged 76 years.

Wm. **Hanna**, died 1857, aged 62 years.

J.

Susannah, wife of Thomas **Johnson,** died 1836, aged 48 years.

Thomas **Johnson**, died 1839, aged 79 years.

K.

Lewis, son of F. and H. H. **Keissell**, died 1852, aged 8 months.

Jane P., wife of G. W. **Kalb** died 1876, aged 64 years.

Alice M., wife of M. E. **Kalb**, died 1878, aged 40 years.

Margaret, wife of Geo. W. **Kalb**, died 1853, aged 47 years.

Hannah K., daughter of Walter and Drucilla **Knapp**, died 1848, aged 12 years.

Chas. Eugene, son of J. W. and H. **Kissell**, died 1853, aged 9 months.

L.

Nancy **Leonard**, died 1833, aged 55 years.

Isaac **Leonard**, Esq., died 1833, aged 80 years.

John, son of A. and S. **Lockwood**, died 1845, aged 7 years,

James **Long**, died 1843, aged 30 years.

Robt. A. **Long**, died 1845, aged 24 years.

John **Long**, died 1844, aged 60 years.

Harriet, daughter of John and Elizabeth **Long**, died 1826, aged 8 years.

John A., son of John W. and Leah **Long**, died 1842, aged 1 year.

Infant daughter of Edward and Catherine **Long**, died 1848.

M.

Eli **Miller,** died 1856, aged 48 years.

Sopha **Miller,** died 1852, aged 36 years.

Sarah S., wife of Eli **Miller**, died 1851, aged 36 years.

David T., son of Eli and Sopha **Miller**, died 1851, aged 5 years.

Sarah, wife of Joseph **Mason**, died 1831, aged 33 years.

Infant daughter of Joseph and Lucinda **Mason** died 1832.

Christina, wife of Solomon **Mason**, died 1850, aged 32 years.

Wm. **Mason**, died 1845, aged 53 years.

Lucretia H., wife of Jonathan **McComb**, died 1847, aged 56 years.

Rebecca A., wife of Wm. **McComb**, died 1848, 86 years.

Wm. **McComb**, died 1835, aged 78 years.

Elizabeth, wife of C. E. **McComb**, died 1854, aged 19 years.

Cyrus E. **McComb**, died 1872, aged 41 years.

Martha Louisa, daughter of Dennis and Emilia **McClaskey**, died 1843, aged 1 year.

Ellery S. **Merriss**, M. D., died 1857, aged 29 years.

Wm., son of E. S. and H. P. **Merriss**, died 1857, aged 1 year.

N.

Jane, wife of John C. **Needels**, died 1846, aged 28 years.

O.

Andrew, son of Elias and Huldah C. **Ogden**, died 1831, aged 12 years.

P.

Jane, wife of Wm. **Patterson**, died 1821, aged 40 years.

Wm. **Patterson**, died 1846, aged 71 years.

Mary, wife of John **Patterson**, died 1834, aged 35 years.

Levi Lewis, son of Thos. and Maryandy **Patterson**, died 1832, aged 3 years.

Sarah, daughter of Wm. And Mary **Patterson**, died 1828, aged 2 years.

John **Paul**, died 1879, aged 64 years.

Eliza, wife of John **Paul**, died 1846, aged 32 years.

Olive, daughter of J. and H. **Paul**, died 1872, aged 19 years.

Zachariah **Paul**, died 1859, aged 75 years.

Sarah, wife of Zachariah **Paul**, died 1841, aged 46 years.

R.

Sarah Ann **Richards**, died 1847, aged 7 years.

S.

Pheba, wife of Moses **Starr**, died 1844, aged 54 years.

Moses, son of John and Rachel **Starr**, died 1835, aged 55 years.

John **Sharp**, Jr., died 1849, aged 23 years.

Ansen **Sprague**, died 1856, aged 75 years.

Austin E. **Sprague**, died 1830, aged *27* years.

Frederick **Sprague**, died 1839, aged 76 years.

Fredrick J., son of Jacob and Mary M. **Sprague,** died 1841, aged 1 year.

Wm. **Shield**, died 1830, aged 43 years.

Abraham **Swisher**, died 1856, aged 73 years.

Margaret, wife of Abraham **Swisher**, died 1862, aged 85 years.

John **Swisher**, died 1877, aged 70 years.

Lydia, wife of Isaac **Swisher**, died 1845, aged 35 years.

Elizabeth, wife of Samuel **Sharp**, died 1845, aged __.

John **Sweetser**, died 1834, aged 41 years.

Mary C., wife of J. L. **Spencer,** died 1863, aged 25 years.

Mary S. **Suddick**, died 1874, aged 82 years.

Sarah Jane **Sackrider**, died 1844, aged 2 months.

Louisa C., wife of Rev. J. D. **Smith**, died 1846, aged 24 years.

Susan W., wife of Rev. J. D. **Smith**, died 1848, aged 22 years.

Edward Hynes, son of Rev. J. D. and L. C. **Smith**, died 1846, aged 8 months.

John Vinton, son of S. and E. **Sharp**, died 1848, aged 13 years.

John **Stambaugh**, died 1860, aged 63 years.

Elizabeth, wife of John **Stambaugh**, died 1861, aged 60 years.

Isaac R. **Stambaugh**, died 1863, aged 28 years.

Balser **Shultz**, died 1832, aged 60 years.

Hanna A., daughter of Solomon and Lovina **Shultz**, died 1844, aged 9 years.

Joseph Roof, son of John and Jane P. **Sharp**, died 1851, aged 4 years.

T.

John **Turner**, died 1827, aged 51 years.

Washington **Turner**, died 1840, aged 29 years.

Ellis, wife of Joseph **Turner**, died 1839, aged 52 years.

Jean, wife of John M. **Thompson**, died 1824, aged 25 years.

Fannie J., daughter of J. H. and W. **Thompson**, died 1861, aged 7 months.

Robert **Taylor**, died 1828. aged 69 years.

Mehitable **Taylor**, died 1857, aged 92 years.

Margaret C. wife of A. V. **Taylor**, died 1838, aged 44 years.

A. V. **Taylor**, died 1853, aged 70 years.

Infant son of Abiathan and Margaret **Taylor**, died 1824.

Margaret R. **Taylor**, died 1836, aged 25 years.

John M. **Taylor**, died 1856, aged 26 years.

Herbert Fletcher, aged 3 years, and Mary Ellen, aged 1 year, children of P. W. and F. S. **Taylor**, died 1851.

Nancy J., daughter of D. and M. R. **Taylor**, died ___ , aged 7 months.

Nancy P. **Taylor**, died 1881, aged 22 years.

V.

Infant daughter of Zadok and C. **Vesey**, died 1848.

Catherine, wife of Z. **Vesey**, died 1878, aged 62 years.

W.

Ruth, wife of Silas **Whitehead**, died 1840, aged 76 years.

John **Wood**, died June 12, 1878, aged 66 years.

Elizabeth, wife of John **Wood**, died August 22, 1878, aged 53 years, Inscription on above tombstone, *"Loved in life, in death not divided."*

Martha A., wife of Robert **Wood**, died 1863, aged 24 years.

John V., son of Samuel and M. L. **Ward,** died 1853, aged 2 years.

George T. **Wheeler**, died 1874, aged 86 years.

Anna, wife of Geo. T. **Wheeler**, died 1876, aged 83 years.

Josiah S. D., son of G. and A. **Wheeler**, died 1845, aged 21 years.

George T., son of G. and A. **Wheeler**, died 1876, aged 11 months.

Levi **Wilson**, died 1843, aged 82 years.

Tossing Graveyard
Located on C. R. McGuffey's land, in Section No. 23.

George, son of Jacob and Elizabeth **Rush,** died 1827, aged 8 years.

Wm. Henry **Counkle**, died 1846, aged 1 year.

Margaret, wife of George **Cramer**, died 1830, aged 36 years.

Peter **Miller,** died 1845, aged 99 years.

John H., son of Geo. B. and Mary A. **Myers**, died 1866, aged 5 years.

Gabriel **Leavel**, died 1841, aged 27 years.

Mary J., daughter of Gabriel and Mary **Leavel**, died 1842, aged 2 years.

Elizabeth, **Rower**, died 1846, aged 56 years.

Mahala Rower, died 1858, aged 18 years.

Geo. W. Sims, died 1844, aged 49 years.

Judah, wife of Geo. W. **Sims**, died 1845, aged 48 years.

James L. **Sims**, died 1851, aged 29 years.

Geo. A. **Sims**, son of Geo. W. and Judith A. **Sims**, died 1849, aged 18 years.

Asenath, daughter of Geo. W. and J. A. **Sims**, died 1842. aged 16 years.

Elizabeth, wife of Wm. **Strickley**, died 1845, aged 36 years.

Henry, son of Nicholas and A. **Tusing**, died 1831, aged 1 year.

Union Grove Cemetery

The Union Grove Cemetery Association of Madison Township is organized under the general laws of the state, passed February 24, 1878, providing for the incorporation of cemetery associations.

Prior to the organization of this association, the burials about Winchester were made in the Lutheran and Reformed graveyard, although it was recognized as an unsuitable place of interment. During the wet seasons it was often necessary for someone to dip the water from the grave even up to the time when the funeral cortege entered the gate to the grounds.

No particular person other than the Trustees had charge of the grounds, but when a death occurred neighbors would volunteer to dig the grave.

At the Annual Joint Meetings of the two congregations, when the election of Trustees for the old graveyard came up, would also come up for consideration *"under drainage of the old"* or the *"establishment of a new burial place."* and on several occasions the Trustees were instructed to call a meeting of the citizens to consider the selection of a more suitable site.

Finally a meeting for the purpose of forming an association was held in the Public Reading Rooms at Canal Winchester, on the evening of November 19, 1877, at which the following citizens were present, viz: James H. Sommerville, Philip Game, Oliver P. Chaney, Peter E. Ehernhart, James B. Evans. Elisha B. Decker, Michal E. Schrock, John S. Lehman, Chas. P. Rees, Martin C. Whitehurst, Christian Gayman, J. Kidwell Miller, and Rev. Jas. Heffly. After adopting the articles of incorporation the following persons were elected to serve as Trustees for one year, viz: E. B. Decker, O. P. Chaney, Philip Game, P. E. Ehrenhart and J. S. Lehman, and at the meeting of the Trustees held on December, 4th, the following organization was effected: Philip Game, President; Rev. James Heffly, Secretary; and E. B. Decker, Treasurer.

The cemetery consists of thirteen acres and was purchased April 5, 1878 from Nathaniel Tallman for two thousand dollars. On August 14, 1888 the Trustees purchased the tract in the northeast corner, that Mr. Tallman had reserved in the former purchase and known as the Hughes graveyard, paying therefore one hundred dollars. The grounds are admirably located and adapted for the purpose and were platted by the late John H. Speilman during the summer of 1878, and on the 6th day of September of the same year were dedicated with appropriate ceremonies. A residence for the use of the Superintendent was erected on the grounds in the spring of 1879.

The Superintendent's have been: John Deitz, February 4, 1879 to February 1884; J. A. Crabbs, February 1884 to February 1888; Stephen Boyd, February 1888 to February 1898; Oscar E. Taylor, February 1898 to September 1900; Geo. H. Zwayer, September 1900 to June 15, 1901; since which time Stephen Boyd is serving.

The Secretaries of the association have been: James Heffly, from the organization to January 1888; Philip Game, January 14, 1888 to April 1890; Al. F. Crayton, April 1, 1890 to June 1891; S. E. Bailey, June 6, 1891 to May 1895; since May 7, 1895 J. K. Miller has served.

The Trustees and date of election have been: John S. Lehman, 1877, 1885, 1888; Philip Game, 1877, 1879, 1881, 1891 ,1893, 1895; Elisha B. Decker, 1877, 1879; Peter E. Ehrenhart. 1877, 1879, 1884; Oliver P. Chaney, 1877, 1880; George Loucks, 1879; John Rohr Jr., 1879, 1880; John Helpman, 1880, 1882; James P. Kalb, 1881, 1883; John Brenner, 1881, 1883, 1892, 1894, 1896; Irwin E. Stevenson, 1882; George Powell, 1883, 1886, 1891, 1893; James P. Kramer, 1884; John

Nicodemus, 1885, 1887, 1889; William Leidy, 1885; Jacob Bott, 1886, 1896; John A. Whitzel, 1886, 1887; Robert Thrush, 1887; John H. Deitz, 1888, 1890, 1892, 1894; George L. Hendren, 1889; Erwin Moore, 1889; S. H. Tallman, 1890; George Delong, 1891; Albert Bachman, 1893, 1895, 1897, 1898-1902; J. K. Miller, 1895, 1897, 1898-1902; R. J. Tussing, 1897, 1898; Robert W. Bolenbaugh, 1898-1902; William M. Game, 1899-1902; Philip Weber, 1901, 1902.

Burials in Union Grove Cemetery

Those followed by an **"R"** were removed from other burying grounds as well as all others who died previous to 1878. The first burial was Mrs. Philip C. Tussing June 6, 1878.

A.

Edwin V. **Adell**, died 1893, aged 36 years.

Mrs. Mary **Algire**, died 1901, aged 70 years.

Mitchell **Allen**, died 1868. aged 48 years.

Elizabeth, wife of M. **Allen** died 1873, aged 41 years.

Jane **Allen**, died 1853, aged 67 years.

William **Allen**, died 1898, aged 87 years.

Susan **Ashley**, died 1886, aged 65 years.

Henry **Arnold**, died 1886, aged 70 years.

Mrs. Kate Dowdall **Alwine**, died 1890, aged 25 years.

Simeon H. **Arendt**, died 1890, aged 67 years.

Rachel P. **Arendt**, died 1901, aged 76 years.

Elijah **Alspach**, died 1901, aged 78 years.

John **Alspach**, died 1893, aged 104 years.

Robert G. **Alspach**, died 1891, aged __ years.

Henry **Anders**, died 1892, aged 74 years.

Joshua **Alspach**, died 1895, aged 71 years.

Winfield Scott **Alspach**, died 1897, aged 45 years.

Hannah **Alspach**, died 1898, aged 92 years.

Rachel, wife of Elijah **Alspach**, died 1899, aged 76 years.

Benjamin A. **Alspach**, died 1899, aged 75 years.

Amos **Alspach**, died 1899, aged 55 years.

Frederica, wife of _____ **Anders**, died 1899, aged 78 years.

Lucy, wife of Henry **Arnold**, died 1900, aged 77 years.

John A. **Armpreister**, died 1893, aged 92 years.

Eliza **Armpreister**, died 1901, aged 91 years.

B.

Mrs. Martha E. **Bachman**, died 1901, aged 39 years.

Jacob **Bachman**, died 1889, aged 58 years.

William **Badger**, died 1898, aged 64 years.

Libby, wife of Thomas **Bailey**, died 1890, aged 33 years.

George M. **Barnhart**, died 1901, aged 32 years.

George **Barnhart**, died 1900, aged 67 years.

Effie H., wife of Grant S. **Barnhart**, died 1899, aged 32 years.

John J. **Beals**, died 1900, aged 47 years.

Amos **Beery**, died 1895, aged 70 years.

Daniel **Bergtresser,** died 1876, aged 66 years.

M. V. Blanch, son of Daniel and M. R. **Bergtresser**, died 1887, aged 28 years.

Susan, wife of Christian **Bickel**, died 1891, aged 62 years.

Mary M. **Bigerton**, died 1899, aged 18 days.

Henry S. **Binkley**, died 1899, aged 73 years.

Dr. Geo. W. **Blake**, died 1877, aged 54 years.

Charles D. **Blake**, died 1890, aged 37 years.

Susan G., wife of Daniel **Bolenbaugh**, died 1899, aged 74 years.

Daniel **Bolenbaugh**, died 1888, aged 62 years.

Vinton, son of Daniel and Susan **Bolenbaugh**, died 1892 aged 25 years.

Rev. C. W. **Bostwick**, died 1891, aged 44 years.

Rachel M., wife of Jacob **Bott**, died 1899, aged 61 years.

Reuben **Bott**, died 1893, aged 60 years.

Sarah, wife of Absalom **Bowman,** died 1895, aged 52 years.

Absalom **Bowman,** died 1885, aged 45 years.

Jacob L. **Bowman**, died 1890, aged 46 years.

Elizabeth, wife of John **Boyd,** died 1874, aged 64 years.

John **Boyd**, died 1891, aged 78 years.

Milton, son of John and Betsy **Boyd**, died 1881, aged 32 years.

Homer, son of William and Sarah **Boyd**, died 1898, aged 31 years.

Benjamin **Boyd**, died June 15, 1833, aged 55 years.

Mary, wife of Benjamin **Boyd**, died June 22, 1833, aged 50 years.

Isaac, son of B. and M. **Boyd**, died June 26, 1833, aged 5 years.

Sarah, daughter of B. and M. **Boyd**, died June 27, 1833, aged 3 years.

Elizabeth, daughter of B. and M. **Boyd**, died 1835, aged 17 years.

Tessa A., daughter of David and **Boyer**, died 1899, aged 30 years.

David **Boyer**, died 1900, aged 70 years.

Edward D. **Brenner**, died 1879, aged 29 years.

Mrs. Mary **Brown,** died 1900, aged 92 years.

Jefferson L. **Bye**, died 1889, aged 32 years.

Augustus **Bruns**, died 1887, age 76 years.

John F., son of Joseph and **Burgoon**, died 1879, aged 8 years.

Matsy Ann **Bunch**, died 1899, aged 52 years.

Sarah, wife of Andrew **Burnside**, died 1899, aged 52 years.

C.

Diana, wife of Jacob **Carty**, died 1874, aged 58 years.

Samuel **Carty**, died 1875, aged 38 years.

Jacob **Carty,** died 1897, aged 92 years.

Anna, wife of Peter **Caslow**, died 1880, aged 58 years.

Peter **Caslow**, died 1885, aged 71 years.

Wm. H. **Cater**, died 1888, aged 48 years.

Edward K. **Chaney**, died 1875, aged 48 years.

Clinton C. **Chaney**, son of E. K. and Eliza Chaney, died 1879, aged 8 years.

James L. **Chaney**, died 1896. aged 78 years.

Geo. W. **Cohagan**, died 1894, aged 76 years.

Wm. H. **Cole**, died 1901, aged___.

Jesse **Colman**, died 1901, aged 26 years.

Elizabeth **Conway**, died 1901, aged 61 years.

Richard Thos. **Cromwell**, died 1882, aged 42 years.

John **Cross**, died 1842, aged 63 years.

Daniel **Crouse**, **R**, died 1882, aged 61 years.

Wm. **Crouse**, **R**, died 1879, aged 7 years.

D.

Jacob **Dauterman**, died ___, aged___.

Mary P. **Davis**, died 1900, aged 25 years.

Ethel **Davis**, died 1901, aged 6 years.

Elisha B. **Decker**, died 1879, aged 61 years.

I. L. (Fay) **Decker**, died 1898, aged 78 years.

Sarah E, wife of E. B. **Decker,** died 1863, aged 41 years.

Samuel **Deitz**, died 1901, aged 85 years.

George, son of Samuel and Elizabeth **Deitz**, died 1892, aged 27 years.

Calvin **Dibble**, died 1883, aged 73 years.

Leroy S. **Dibble**, died 1900, aged 63 years.

Daniel **Dildine**, died 1897, aged 68 years.

E. P. **Dildine**, died 1901, aged 37 years.

Catherine, wife of James K. **Dill,** died 1901, aged 58 years.

Henry **Donaldson**, died ___.

Reuben, **Dove**, died 1857, aged 58 years.

Nevin L. **Dunlap**, died 1900, aged 2 years.

Mrs. Sarah **Dunlap**, died 1901, aged 76 years.

E.

Wm. E., son of John and Sallie **Ehrenhart**, died 1879, aged 1 year.

Peter E. **Ehrenhart,** died 1888, aged 75 years.

Henry J. **Epley**, died 1887, aged 74 years.

Elizabeth, wife of H. J. **Epley**, died 1888, aged 70 years.

Henry J., son of Charles and **Epley**, died 1895, aged 13 years.

Hannah **Epley**, died 1890, aged 70 years.

Christina, wife of James B. **Evans**, died 1870, aged 57 years.

F.

Lizzie W. **Fall,** died 1879, aged 13 years.

Evaline **Fancher**, died 1897, aged 72 years.

Williametta, daughter of Wm. and Louisa T. **Fenstermaker**, died 1883, aged 10 years.

Darias **Fenstermaker**, died 1886, aged 29 years.

Jesse R. **Fenstermaker**, died 1891, aged 21 years.

Elizabeth **Ferrel**, died 1886, aged 30 years.

Ellenora **Finch,** died 1896, aged 78 years.

Wm. **Fisher**, died 1881, aged 44 years.

Jerome **Fisher**, died 1898, aged 44 years.

Mrs. Ivy **Ford**, died 1898, aged 22 years.

Ruth W., wife of John A. **Fouble**, died 1887, aged 68 years.

John A. **Fouble**, died 1891, aged 80 years.

Zachariah **Fowler**, died 1889, aged 56 years.

Harry **Fowler**, died 1900, aged 14 years.

Arthur, son of Geo. W. and **From**, died 1897, aged 19 years.

Wm. **Fry**, died 1854, aged 39 years.

Pheba, wife of Wm. **Fry,** died 1850, aged 30 years.

G.

Henry **Game,** died 1851, aged 44 years.

Philipena, wife of Henry **Game,** died 1848, aged 41 years.

Henry **Game** Jr., died 1864, aged 21 years.

Wm. Stanley, son of Philip and Emma **Game,** died 1881, aged 10 years.

Philip **Game**, died 1902, aged 65 years.

Daniel **Gayman,** died 1898, aged 77 years.

Catharine, wife of Daniel **Gayman,** died 1888, aged 65 years.

Mary A. **Gayman**, died 1885, aged 28 years.

Christian **Gayman**, died 1896, aged 68 years.

Simon **Gayman**, died 1865, aged 9 years.

A. E. **Gayman**, died ___, aged __.

Edwin **Gayman**, died ___,aged __.

John **Gehm**, died 1890, aged 56 years.

Mary, wife of John **Gehm**, died 1865, aged 28 years.

Wm. **Goodwin**, died 1892, aged 44 years.

John W. **Griffith**, died 1887, aged 40 years.

Cyrus D. **Guisinger**, died 1899, aged 75 years.

Mrs. Sarah **Guthrie**, died 1901, aged 84 years.

H.

Martha **Hanson**, died 1885, aged 79 years.

Wesley **Harmon**, died 1901, aged 70 years.

Harvey D. **Harris**, died 1889, aged 61 years.

Margaret **Hastings**, died 1885, aged 67 years.

Eliza O., wife of A. **Hathaway**, died 1899, aged 80 years.

Almanzor **Hathaway**, died 1888, aged 82 years.

Wm. P. **Havely**, died 1895, aged 43 years.

Harry U., son of Rev. James and A. V. **Heffly**, died 1865, aged 2 years.

John **Helpman**, died 1883, aged 70 years.

Sarah **Helpman**, died 1894, aged 77 years.

William **Helpman**, died 1899, aged 65 years.

Mrs. Ephraim **Helser**, died 1902, aged 52 years.

James D. **Helser**, died 1892, aged 19 years.

Samuel **Hempy**, died 1897, aged 80 years.

Adam Turner **Hendren** died ___, aged ___.

Thos. C. **Hendren,** died 1870, aged 64 years.

Rev. Austin **Henry,** died 1885, aged 40 years. (removed to Tiffin, Ohio, November, 1896.)

Henry **Herbst**, died 1889, aged 67 years.

Mrs. Anna Y. **Herbst**, died 1901, aged 44 years.

Catharine **Herman**, died 1900, aged 84 years.

Mrs. Delilah **Hicks**, died 1899, aged 56 years.

George **Himrod**, died 1887, aged 78 years.

Esther **Himrod**, died 1887, aged 76 years.

Benjamin F. **Hische**, died 1878, aged 28 years.

Ellen E., wife of Wm. H. **Hische**, died 1888, aged 38 years.

Lewis, son of J. W. and Mary **Hische**, died 1899, aged 45 years.

Chas. O. **Hische**, died 1900, aged 40 years.

Julius W. **Hische**, died 1883 aged 59 years.

John **Holbert**, died 1864, aged 48 years.

Rebecca **Holbert**, died 1884, aged 72 years.

87, aged 76 years.

Leah **Howard**, died 1863, aged 20 years.

J.

Samuel Edwin **Jay**, died 1880, aged 39 years.

Abraham **Jobes**, died 1898, aged 74 years.

J. R. **Justice**, died 1898, aged 81 years.

K.

Geo. W. **Kalb,** died 1882, aged 80 years.

Jeremiah **Kalb**, died 1891, aged 80 years.

Joshua **Kelsey**, died 1861, aged 73 years.

John W. **Kile**, died 1894, aged 59 years.

Mrs. Ellen **King,** died 1899, aged 61 years.

John **Kissell**, died 1883, aged 62 years.

Christopher **Kramer**, died 1878, aged 59 years.

Aner **Kramer** died 1881, aged 80 years.

Hannah, wife of John **Kramer**, died 1890, aged 79 years.

John (Uncle Johnnie) **Kramer**, died 1891, aged 82 years.

Elizabeth **Kramer**, died 1890, aged 81 years.

David **Kramer**, died 1859, aged 54 years.

John **Kramer**, died 1853, aged 71 years.

Catharine, wife of John **Kramer,** died 1873, aged 86 years.

Peter **Kramer**, died 1835, aged 22 years.

Mrs. Chas. J. **Krumm**, died 1891, aged 62 years.

L.

W. V. **Landon**, died 1890, aged 32 years.

Irene Ann, wife of Geo. **Leady**, died 1879, aged 37 years.

Aner L., wife of John S. **Lehman**, died 1899, aged 60 years.

Sarah M., wife of Solomon S. **Lehman**, died 1899, aged 48 years.

William **Leidy**, died 1898, aged 74 years.

William **Leight**, died 1879, aged 68 years.

Wm. **Line**, died 1850, aged 27 years.

Rachel **Line**, died 1848, aged 23 years.

Mary **Lohr**, died 1901, aged 41 years.

Noah **Looker**, died 1899, aged 66 years.

Mrs. Caroline **Looker**, died 1899, aged ___.

Neil B. **Loucks**, died 1900, aged 1 year.

Elijah **Loucks,** died 1865, aged 22 years.

Samuel **Loucks**, died 1862, aged ___.

Julia **Lyons,** died 1900, aged 73 years.

M.

Harley, son of Joshua and _____ **Mathias**, died 1897, aged 9 years.

Thomas E. **Mathias**, died 1901, aged 20 years.

Infant of Robert. A. **McClure**, died 1899.

Elihue **McCracken**, died 1844, aged 69 years.

Mary **McCracken**, died 1862, aged 92 years.

Elihu **McCracken**, died 1874, aged 62 years.

Rebecca **McCracken**, died 1878, aged 59 years.

Samuel B. **McFadden**, died 1882, aged 46 years.

Lena, wife of James **McKelvey**, died 1898, aged ___.

Matsy A. **Medford**, died 1896, aged 72 years.

Amos **Medford**, died 1899, aged 52 years.

Winfield G., son of Wm. P. and Mary **Miller**, died 1853, aged 1 year.

Flora, daughter of J. K. and Emma **Miller**, died 1878, aged 1 year.

John **Miller**, died 1880, aged 65 years.

Garrett W. **Miller,** died 1888, aged 57 years.

Oscar E., son of Rev. W. R. and **Miller**, died 1893, aged 40 years.

Rev. Wm. R. **Miller**, died 1895, aged 79 years.

Sarah A. **Miller**, died 1901, aged 79 years.

Lizzie, daughter of Jacob and Samantha **Moore**, died 1888, aged 19 years

John K. **Moore**, died 1857, aged 54 years.

Samuel P. **Moore**, died 1863, aged 24 years.

George **Moore**, died 1850, aged 39 years.

Abaline **Moore**, died 1876, aged 36 years.

Samantha, wife of Jacob **Moore**, died 1899, aged 64 years.

Anthony W. **Morton**, died 1879, aged 51 years.

Elizabeth **Morton**, died 1890, aged 90 years.

Charlotte E. **Morton**, died 1899, aged 36 years.

Mary J. **Morton**, died 1899, aged 54 years.

Floyd **Motz**, died 1900, aged 2 years.

Martin **Murphy**, died at Traction Company Camp 1901, aged __.

N.

Abraham **Nongenecker**, died 1857, aged 6 years.

O.

Hallet Chaney, son of Wm. G. and Maud **Ochs**, died 1890, aged 1 year.

Minerva J. **Olinger**, died 1880, aged 38 years.

P.

Joseph **Painter**, died 1892, aged 79 years.

Tillman N. **Palsgrove**, died 1899, aged 5 years.

J. A. **Peters**, died 1898, aged 42 years.

Floris **Peters**, died 1899, aged 1 year.

Florence E. **Peters**, died 1901, aged 25 years.

Florence E. **Peters**, died 1901, aged 25 years.

Minerva J., wife of James **Pickering**, died 1885, aged 45 years.

Eleanor **Pike**, died 1873, aged 78 years.

Jarvis W. **Pike**, died 1854, aged 59 years.

Clara J., wife of Franklin G. **Pontius**, died 1900, aged 53 years.

Philip **Pontius**, died 1901, aged 61 years.

Dr. Joseph B. **Potter**, died 1887, aged 70 years.

George **Powell**, died 1896, aged 58 years.

Wm. **Purdy**, died 1901, aged 72 years.

R.

John Rohr Jr.
1818 - 1900

Maggie C., wife of A. M. **Rarey,** died 1892, aged 44 years.

Jacob **Rawn**, died 1888, aged 31 years.

Charles P. **Rees**, died 1893, aged 58 years.

Nancy **Riley**, died 1846, aged 31 years.

Martha H. **Robertson**, died 1896, aged 48 years.

John **Rohr Jr.**, died 1900, aged 82 years

Sophia **Rossow**, died 1892, aged 70 years.

Frederic **Rossow**, died 1898, aged 79 years.

Elizabeth Ellen **Runkle**, died 1852, aged 30 years.

Geo. W. **Ruse,** died 1887, aged 55 years.

Eliza Ann, wife of G. W. **Ruse**, died 1889, aged 51 years.

S.

Kalita **Sallee**, died 1900, aged 86 years.

Sarah, wife of James **Sandy**, died 1900, aged 73 years.

Christian **Sarber**, died 1848, aged 59 years.

Anna **Sarber**, died 1846, aged 51 years.

Leonard **Sarber**, died 1880, aged 61 years.

Jemima J. **Sarber** died 1880, aged 65 years.

Dortha **Satchleben**, died 1895, aged 56 years.

Elizabeth **Saunders**, died 1899, aged 48 years.

John M. **Schoch**, died 1888, aged 76 years.

Jane B., wife of John M. **Schoch**, died 1894, aged 69 years.

Nannie A., wife of Wm. **Schroch**, died 1889, aged 47 years.

Mrs. Susan **Scotts,** died 1890, aged 47 years.

Edward M. **Selby**, died 1884, aged 39 years.

John **Shaffer**, died 1888, aged 66 years.

Julia A., wife of Frank **Shaffer**, died 1899, aged 45 years.

Wm. A. **Shaffer**, died 1899, aged 16 years.

Sarah, wife of Adam **Shaner,** died 1900, aged ___.

Adam **Shanner**, died 1897, aged 70 years.

George **Shoemaker**, died 1887, aged 87 years.

Isaac **Shoemaker**, died 1881, aged 70 years.

Henrietta, wife of Isaac **Shoemaker**, died 1877, aged 65 years.

Susan, wife of George **Shoemaker**, died 1844, aged 36 years.

Olive S., wife of Dr. A. A. **Shortt**, died 1894, aged 70 years.

Dr. Azro A. **Shortt**, died 1897, aged 73 years.

Ben. C. **Simms**, died 1891, aged 63 years.

Erwin E., son of Benjamin and Belinda **Simms,** died 1898, aged 24 years.

Walla J., daughter of Rev. J. W. and **Sleeper**, died 1882, aged 13 years.

Rev. J. W. **Sleeper**, died 1890, aged ___.

Frederick **Slough**, died 1846, aged 36 years.

Mary **Slough**, died 1853, aged 41 years.

Lida, wife of Frank M. **Smith**, died 1897, aged 23 years

Sarah Jane **Somerville**, died 1891, aged 46 years.

James H. **Somerville**, died 1879, aged 60 years.

Evelyn **Sommerville**, died 1899, aged 45 years.

Elizabeth, wife of James H. **Sommerville,** died 1899, aged 73 years.

Mary Ann, wife of John **Sparr**, died 1887, aged 31 years.

Emanuel **Sparr**, died 1899, aged 79 years.

Wm. H. **Speaks**, died 1901, aged 35 years.

Charles W. **Speaks**, died 1884, aged 70 years.

Harriet M. daughter of Chas. W. and Sarah **Speaks**, died 1890, aged 42 years.

Jesse **Spitter,** died 1892, aged 54 years.

Sarah **Stevenson**, daughter of Joshua and Mary Glanville, died 1835, aged___.

Joshua S. **Stevenson,** died 1900, aged 86 years.

Mrs. Mary B. **Stevenson**, died 1901, aged 80 years.

John **Stott**, died 1895, aged 69 years.

Alonzo **Strode** Jr., infant, died 1901.

T.

Nathaniel **Tallman**, died 1888, aged 78 years.

John **Tallman**, died 1857, aged 69 years.

Elizabeth, wife of John **Tallman**, died 1854, aged 62 years.

Catharine B., wife of Nathaniel **Tallman**, died 1893, aged 73 years.

Sarah, wife of Benjamin **Tallman**, died 1836, aged 20 years.

Mrs. Luella **Taylor**, died 1901, aged 22 years.

Infant of P. M. and Marilla **Teegardin**, died 1898.

Robert **Thrush**, died 1899, aged___.

Samuel **Travis**, died 1900, aged 73 years.

John R. **Travis**, died 1901, aged 45 years.

Henry **Travis**, died 1901, aged 74 years.

Herbert **Travis**, died 1902, aged 22 years.

Susannah, wife of Reuben **Trine**, died 1890, aged 80 years.

Reuben **Trine,** died 1891, aged ___,

John F. **Trost**, died 1889, aged 63 years.

_____, wife of John F. **Trost**, died 1897, aged 75 years.

Phebe, wife of Philip **Tussing**, died June 4, 1878, aged 41 years.

Margaret **Tussing**, died 1855, aged 60 years.

Nicholas **Tussing**, died 1850, aged 71 years.

Archie E. M. W., son of James N. **Tussing**, died 1894, aged 8 years.

V.

Jacob W. **Vandemark**, died 1889, aged 48 years.

Louisa E. **Veth**, died 1899, aged 21 years.

Luther P. **Veth**, died 1900, aged 2 years.

Malinda, wife of Jonathan **Vought**, died 1884, aged 55 years.

W.

John D. **Walters,** died 1886. aged 25 years.

Adam **Warner**, died 1899, aged 66 years.

Margaret, wife of Peter **Weber**, died 1879, aged 55 years.

Peter **Weber,** died 1890, aged 67 years.

Adam **Weber**, died 1897, aged 46 years.

Philip E., son of Philip and Irene **Weber**, died 1897, aged 2 years.

Louisa, wife of Charles **Weber**, died 1900, aged 63 years.

Adam D., son of Philip and Irene **Weber**, died 1900, aged 7 years.

Adam M. **Wernert**, died 1899, aged 2 years.

Henry **Wernert**, died 1900, aged 78 years.

Geo. T. **Wheeler,** died 1898, aged 62 years.

Margaret **Whims**, died 1900, aged 64 years.

Andrew **Whims,** died 1891, aged 73 years.

Martin C. **Whitehurst,** died 1893, aged 73 years.

Cary D., son of M. C. and Delia **Whitehurst**, died 1898, aged 44 years.

Daniel, son of Henry and Hannah **Will**, died 1898, aged 31 years.

Lucy O., daughter of Henry and Hannah **Will**, died 1877, aged 7 years.

Wm. **Wilson**, died 1879, aged 26 years.

Nettie, daughter of M. **Winders**, died 1881, aged 14 years.

Percy M., son of M. J. and Almina **Wolfe**, died 1876, aged 1 year.

Mary A., wife of John **Worrell**, died 1899, aged 66 years.

John **Wright**, died 1887, aged 82 years.

Nancy **Wright**, died 1886, aged 71 years.

Isaac B. **Wright**, died 1892, aged 45 years.

John R. **Wright**, died 1891, aged 78 years.

Delia E. **Wright**, died 1883, aged 28 years.

Joseph **Wright**, died 1855, aged 74 years.

Mary **Wright**, died 1866, aged 79 years.

Susan, wife of John R. **Wright,** died 1855, aged 39 years.

Martha E., wife of John R. **Wright,** died 1878, aged 58 years.

Maggie C., wife of Daniel **Wright**, died 1900, aged 51 years.

Y.

Lulu Ellen, daughter of Chas. F. and Mary J. **Yost**, died 1878, aged 8 years.

Mary Jane, wife of Chas. F. **Yost**, died 1901, aged 65 years.

Z.

Jennie, wife of Chas. **Zachero**, died 1880, aged 26 years.

Martin **Zahn**, died 1895, aged 58 years.

Caroline **Zahn**, died 1895, aged 54 years.

Ruth E., daughter of Jacob E. and Florence **Zarbaugh**, died 1896, aged 4 years.

Jacob E. **Zarbaugh**, died 1899, aged 34 years.

Priscilla, wife of Chas. **Zarbaugh,** died 1898, aged 58 years.

Jacob **Zarbaugh,** died 1900, aged 71 years.

Peter **Zarbaugh**, died 1901, aged 75 years.

Wm. H. **Zinn**, died 1892, aged 37 years.

Catherine M. **Zwayer**, died 1890, aged 2 years.

Welton Graveyard
Located on Josiah Flattery's land, in Section No. 2.

Elizabeth, daughter of Daniel and Elizabeth **Baker**, died 1849, aged 4 years.

Langdon **Decker**, died 1864, aged 32 years.

Infant son of Langdon and Margaret A. **Decker**, died 1855.

Elias **Decker**, died 1839, aged 38 years.

Andrew **Dildine**, died 1839, aged 39 years.

Mary M., daughter of Andrew and Jane **Dildine**, died 1839, aged 14 years.

Eliza, wife of Perry **Dildine**, died 1840 aged 21 years.

Henry **Dildine,** died 1861, aged 87 years.

Effy, wife of Henry **Dildine,** died 1862, aged 86 years.

Wm. **Elder**, died 1831, aged 66 years.

David, son of William and Margaret **Elder**, died 1825, aged 16 years.

Rebecca, wife of James **Elder**, died 1838, aged 27 years.

Thomas **Elder**, died 1847, aged 50 years.

Infant of Thomas and Annie **Elder**, died 1826.

David **Groom**, died 1867, aged 55 years.

Philip M. son of P. and M. E. **Kuhns**, died 1868, aged 3 months.

Mary, wife of G. W. **Lehman**, died 1866, aged 18 years.

Henry D. son of Jacob and Effy **Lehman**, died 1847, aged 11 months.

Infant son of Jacob and Effy **Lehman**, died 1862, aged 10 months.

Daniel **McIntire**, died 1861, aged 45 years.

Aaron **Michel,** died 1824, aged 33 years.

Solomon **Parker**, died 1826, aged 27 years.

Thomas **Patrick,** died 1838, aged 50 years.

Mary, wife of Thomas **Patrick**, died 1834, aged 42 years.

John **Patrick**, died 1880, aged 75 years.

Samuel **Ramsey**, died 1847, aged 83 years.

J. W., son of Charles and Belinda **Reber**, died 1838, aged 4 months.

Palemia, wife of Leonard **Sarber**, died 1867, aged 42 years.

Mary, wife of Wm. **Seymour**, died 1823, aged 21 years.

Mary, wife of Jesse **Seymour.** died 1838, aged 33 years.

Elizabeth, wife of George **Seymour**, died 1832, aged 61 years.

George **Seymour**, died 1839, aged 77 years.

Felix, son of Jesse and M. A. **Seymour**, died 1850, aged 13 years.

Infant son of Jesse and Mary **Seymour**, died 1824.

Bennie, son of Wm. and Elizabeth **Seymour**, died 1844, aged 15 years.

Henry **Seymour**, died 1857, aged 37 years.

Susannah A., daughter of Henry and Elizabeth **Seymour**, died 1860, aged 9 years.

Elizabeth, wife of William **Seymour**, died 1850, aged 42 years.

William **Seymour** died 1855, aged 54 years.

Marion, son of Geo. and Sarah L. **Seymour**, died 1863, aged 9 years.

Robt. L. **Seymour,** died 1860, aged 29 years.

America, daughter of Moses and Nancy **Seymour**, died 1833, aged 3 years.

Allena E., daughter of S. S. and Rebecca **Seymour**, died 1860, aged 3 years.

Jane, daughter of John and Francis **Welton**, died 1815, aged 5 years.

Francis, wife of John **Welton**, died, 1838, aged 56 years.

John **Welton**, died 1850, aged 72 years.

Isaac, son of John and F. **Welton**, died 1845, aged 37 years.

Susan T., wife of John **Welton**, died 1845, aged 25 years.

Effy, wife of Jesse **Welton**, died 1832, aged 28 years.

Andrew **Welton**, died 1852, aged 20 years.

Henry F. **Woodring**, died 1863, aged 24 years.

Catherine, wife of Solomon **Woodring**, died 1841, aged 32 years.

Lucinda, second wife of Solomon **Woodring,** died 1846, aged 42 years.

Sarah, wife of Solomon **Woodring,** died 1864, aged 65 years.

Infant son of C. P. and Nancy **Woodring**, died 1854.

Infant daughter of C. D. and Mary **Woodring** died 1857.

Reformed and Lutheran Graveyard
Located at Canal Winchester.

The first burial was Leah **Brown** a sister of Chas. Brown.

A.

George, son of Amon and A. M. **Algire**, died 1854, aged 8 years.

Milton **Algire**, died 1866, aged 15 years.

B.

Five young children of Joseph and Mary Ann **Bennedum**, died 1849 to 1853.

Philip **Born**, died 1854, aged 37 years.

Lydia, wife of Solomon **Boyer**, died 1846, aged 30 years.

Daniel, husband of Sarah **Boyer**, died 1848, aged 49 years.

Betsey M., daughter of H. and P. **Black**, died 1846, aged 10 years.

Albert L. son of G. and H. **Bush**, died 1868, aged 1 year.

C.

James **Cannon,** died 1852, aged 51 years.

Wm. M., son of Leo F. and Matilda **Carson**, died 1862, aged 21 years.

Bertha, daughter of J. and S. C. **Chaney**, died 1863, aged 2 years.

D.

Martha E., daughter of Chas. and Susannah **Dagon**, died 1856, aged 5 years.

Chas. E., son of Wm. and Mary E. **Dellinger,** died 1857, aged 5 months.

Sarah, wife of Jacob **Dellinger**, died 1855, aged 47 years.

E. L. **Dellinger**, died 1854, aged 25 years.

Catherine, wife of H. **Dellinger**, died 1873, aged 85 years.

Margaret daughter of Jacob, and Elizabeth **Dravenstott**, died 1843, aged 4 years.

Mary, daughter of Jacob and Elizabeth **Draygenston**, died 1841, aged 5 years.

F.

Henry E., son of J. M. and S. E. **Fay** died 1870, aged 7 years.

Mayella, daughter of Hiram and Eleanor **Finch** died 1843 aged 18 days.

Joseph D. son of Geo. A. and Francis J. **Finnefrock**, died 1849, aged 4 months.

Pheba, wife of Patrick **French**, died 1849, aged 23 years.

G.

Susannah, wife of Timothy **Gater**, died 1848, aged 61 years.

Henry, son of John and Carolina **Goettel**, died 1851, aged 17 years.

H.

Mary E., daughter of Edward and Sarah A. **Harpst**, died 1857, aged 15 days.

Emily Amanda, daughter of Almanzor **Hathaway**, died 1846, aged 9 months.

Sarah **Hathaway**, died 1853, aged 75 years.

Agnes **Hathaway** died 1862 aged 79 years.

Wesley, son of Edward and Elizabeth **Hathaway,** (balance of inscription obliterated,)

Caroline J. wife of Wm. **Helpman**, died 1877, aged 38 years.

Josephus, daughter of A. B. **Helpman** died 1848 aged 5 years.

Sylvester B., son of David and Catherine **Herkins**, died 1846, aged 19 years.

John, son of Henry and Phillipin **Herrmann**, died 1847 aged 6 months.

Daniel, son of Henry and Phillippin **Herrmann**, died 1866, aged 3 years.

Henry **Hesser**, died 1865, aged 40 years.

John **Hesser**, died 1858, aged 60 years.

Franklin, son of William and Mary **Hesser** died 1858, aged 2 years.

George W., son of J. R. and M. **Hicks**, died 1855, aged 1 month.

J.

Martha, daughter of Joseph B,. and Nancy S. **Johnson** died 1842, aged 6 years.

Infant children of J. B. and S. N. **Johnson,** died 1844, aged 10 days.

K.

John, son of John and Elizabeth **Kisse**l, died 1850.

Chas. H., son of John and Elizabeth **Kissel**, died 1855, aged 5 months.

Oliver **Krafft**, died 1855, aged 25 years.

Frederick **Krafft**, died 1851, aged 21 years.

L.

Elizabeth, wife of James **Lawrence**, died 1865, aged 63 years.

James **Lawrence**, died 1877, aged 74 years.

George **Lehman** Sr., died 1859, aged 60 years.

George **Lehman,** died 1856, aged 24 years.

Elizabeth, wife of George **Lehman,** died 1861, aged 30 years.

Magdalena, wife of George **Lehman** Sr., died 1864, aged 64 years.

Wm. J. H., son of E. and M. **Lehr**, died 1871, aged 1 year.

Susannah, wife of Daniel **Lether**, died 1856, aged 66 years.

Daniel **Lether**, died 1857, aged 69 years.

Sarah **Lether**, died 1871, aged 69 years.

Daniel, son of Chas. and Catherine **Lether**, died 1842, aged 1 year.

Wm. J. H., son of E. and M. **Lehr**, died 1871, aged 1 year.

M.

Chancey, son of Simeon and Pheba Jane **Matthews**, died 1841, aged 1 month.

David J., son of Simeon and Pheba **Matthews**, died 1847, aged 7 years.

Mary, wife of James **McKelvey** died 1856, aged 28 years.

Maria E., daughter of Henry and Catherine **Meyer**, died 1847, aged 2 years.

Infant son of Henry C. **Meyer,** died 1847, aged 2 days.

Daniel **Miller**, died 1846, aged 55 years.

Pheba, wife of Joseph **Miller**, died 1860, aged 45 years.

Eleanor, daughter of George and Margaret **Myers**, died 1842, aged 12 years.

George **Myers**, died 1844, aged 56 years.

John **Myers**, died 1850, aged 27 years.

Sarah C. **Myers**, died 1850, aged 25 years.

Anna B. **Myers**, died 1850, aged 30 years.

Lucretia **Myers**, died 1850, aged 18 years.

Catherine, daughter of Abraham Stump, and widow of John **Myers**, died 1847, aged 91 years.

Andrew **Myreir**, died 1844, aged 31 years.

O.

Peter **Overhalser**, died 1844, aged 61 years.

P.

Mary, wife of Benjamin **Persoll**, died 1842.

Philip **Price**, died 1867, aged 49 years.

Jemima, wife of Philip **Price,** died 1857, aged 38 years.

Emily A., daughter of Philip and Amanda **Price**, died 1861, aged 5 months.

R.

Edward son of Jonas and Sarah **Ringer**, died 1858, aged 18 years.

Sarah, wife of Jonas **Ringer**, died 1865, aged 50 years.

S.

Frederick **Schmitt,** *geboren* November 2, 1801, *gestorben* September 24, 1854.

Franz **Schmitt,** died 1854, aged 20 years.

Emily A., daughter of Jacob and Elizabeth **Schrock**, died 1847, aged 11 months.

Ann, daughter of John and Lydia **Sergeant**, died 1845, aged 2 years.

Elvira A., daughter of James H. and Elizabeth **Sommerville**, died 1853, aged 3 years.

Geo. W., son of Chas. W. and Sarah A. **Speaks**, died 1852, aged 9 months.

Eddie C., son of John H. and Catherine **Speilman**, died 1873, aged 1 month.

Nicholas, son of Peter and Hettie **Swisher**, died 1845, aged 10 years.

Daniel, son of A. and S. **Sunday**, died 1844, aged 4 months.

T.

Oliver C., son of Henton and A. M. **Tallman**, died 1859, aged 1 year.

Emily Adaline, daughter of Henton and Amanda M. **Tallman**, died 1846, aged 1 year.

Geo. McC., son of John B. and Mary Ann **Thompson**, died 1819, aged 2 years.

Lucy A., daughter of R. and S. **Trine**, died 1853, aged 1 year.

Eliza A., daughter of B. F. and M. **Trine**, died 1870, aged 1 year.

W.

Martin B., son of John and Margaret **Wagoner**, died 1845, aged 6 months.

Elizabeth M., wife of John **Wagoner**, died 1851, aged 28 years.

Daniel, son of Daniel and Rebecca **Wallet,** died 1849, aged 2 years.

Lydia, daughter of H. and E. **Walter**, died 1849, aged 6 years.

Henry, son of John and Mary **Werner**, died 1849, aged 3 years.

Elleni, daughter of G. W. and M. J. **Williams**, died 1855, aged 7 months.

Z.

Elizabeth, daughter of Peter and Martha **Zarbaugh**, died 1854, aged 6 years.

Henry **Zimmer**, died 1852, aged 32 years.

John H., son of Eli and Leah **Zimmer**, died 1853, aged 2 years.

Laura, daughter of Eli and Leah **Zimmer**, died 1862, aged 1 year.

Philip **Zimmer**, died 1856, aged 69 years.

Elizabeth, wife of Philip **Zimmer**, died 1846, aged 61 years.

Vandemark Graveyard
Located on George Vandemark's land, in Section No 18.

Mary Jane, wife of Wm. K. **Allgire**, died 1866, aged 40 years.

Wm. J. S., son of Wm. K. and M. J. **Allgire**, died 1866, aged 16 years.

Charles **Bowen**, died 1831, aged 43 years.

Wm. W. son of Chas. and Mary **Bowen**, died 1831, aged 16 years.

Billingslea **Bull**, died 1824, aged 52 years.

Sarah **Entler**, died 1835, aged 32 years.

Mary, daughter of James B. and Nancy **Evans**, died 1838, aged 1 year.

Grasey **Harrison**, died 1825, aged 37 years.

Losey **Harrison**, died 1831, aged 4 years.

Edward **Hathaway,** died 1824, aged 49 years.

Mary, wife of Eleazor **Hathaway**, died 1825, aged 77 years.

Nicholas **Hopkins**, died 1824, aged 26 years.

Sarah A., daughter of Nicholas and Ann **Hopkins**, died 1848, aged 23 years.

Mary J., daughter of Wm. S. and Hannah J. **Hopkins**, died 1848, aged 2 months.

George **McKelvey**, died 1841, aged 21 years.

Jemima **McKelvey**, died 1835, aged 4 years.

Wm. **Perrin,** died 1855, aged 76 years.

Rachel **Perrin**, died 1836, aged 60 years.

Mary Ann, wife of Wm. **Perrin,** died 1848, aged 34 years.

Wm. J. son of Stephen S. and Eleanor **Russel**, died 1846, aged 12 years.

Gideon **Stevenson**, died 1840, aged 31 years.

Sarah, wife of Abram B. **Stevenson**, died 1847, aged 22 years.

George, son of Rev. Geo. S. and Caroline M. **Stevenson**, died 1855, aged 4 years.

M. A. **Stevenson**, died 1871, aged 54 years.

Catherine, wife of G. K. **Stevenson**, died 1867, aged 74 years.

Rebecca, wife of Wm. L. **Stevenson**, died February 23, 1863, aged 46 years.

William **Stevenson**, died January 24, 1863, aged 49 years.

Sarah E., daughter of Wm. L. and Rebecca **Stevenson**, died February 10, 1863, aged 21 years.

Geo. King, son of M. L. and Rebecca D. **Stevenson**, died 1888, aged 2 months.

Ann B., wife of J. S. **Stevenson,** died 1873, aged 73 years.

Samuel **Taylor**, died 1842, aged 53 years.

Mary, wife of Samuel W. **Taylor**, died 1862, aged 66 years.

Mary A., wife of Geo. **Vandemark**, died 1835, aged 66 years.

Chas. **Vandemark**, died 1844, aged 93 years.

Whims Graveyard
Located on Minnie M. Whims's land, in Section No. 18.

John, son of John and Mary **Conner**, died 1826, aged 54 years.

James **Horner,** died 1848, aged 49 years.
Mrs. Elizabeth **Wood**, died 1818, aged 51 years.
Elizabeth, wife of Charles **Wood**, died 1840, aged 50 years.
Charles **Wood**, died 1838, aged 47 years.

THE END

'Tis grievous parting with good company."

--George Eliot

INDEX

A

Beedle, Elisha W., 240

Beeks, W. D., 122, 156, 163, 167, 252, 274, 327, 345

Beeks, Wm. D., 29, 121, 124, 151, 329

Beery & Gayman, 167

Beery, Dr. L. W., 125, 153, 163, 166, 218, 266, 301, 334, 342

Beery, Harry, 108, 167

Beery, L. W., 343

Beery, Mrs. Hannah, 335

Beery, Noah, 167

Begg, John, 95, 316, 318

Begg, Jr., John, 316

Begg, Mary, 316

Begg, Thos., 232

Beggs, David C., 217

Beggs, John, 268

Beggs, John G., 92

Beggs, Miss Jenet, 316

Behm, A., 234

Behm, Abner, 95

Behm, Chas. R., 179

Behm, E., 243

Behm, E. G., 234

Behm, Edward, 96

Behm, John, 42, 45, 48, 95

Behm, John H., 95

Behm, Joseph, 45, 96

Beirly, Mrs. Francis, 304

Belford, Morgan, 35

Bell Telephone Line, 188

Belong, W. A., 344

Belt, Miss Emma, 111

Bemisdorfer, Emanuel, 243

Benbow, John, 240

Benedum, A. D., 214

Benedum, John, 249

Benj. Gares,, 182

Bennadum, Joe, 227

Bennadum, Peter, 136

Bennedum & Kissell, 301

Bennedum & Mathews, 158

Bennedum, Aaron, 98, 105

Bennedum, Jacob, 357

Bennedum, Joseph, 158

Bennedum, Peter, 157

Benner, Jacob E., 240

Bennett, A. E., 93, 341

Bennett, Amos, 225

Bennett, Amos S., 294

Bennett, C. C., 250, 252

Bennett, E. J., 185

Bennett, Ed. J., 249

Bennett, Edward J., 107

Bennett, Henry, 294

Bennett, J. B., 243

Bennett, J. M., 96, 342

Bennett, John, 225

Bennett, John G., 82, 88, 293

Bennett, Joseph W., 83

Bennett, Mary, 37, 294

Bennett, Melvina, 293

Bennett, Miss, 112

Bennett, Nathan, 37

Bennett, T. B., 236, 239

Bennett, T. J., 43, 96, 194

Bennett, W. C., 216

Bennett, Wallace, 243

Bennett, Wm., 93

Benninghoff, Christ, 243

Benson, Daniel, 162

Berger, George, 184, 186

Berger, Lewis W., 97

Bergstresser Building, 144, 147, 150

Bergstresser Corner, 163

Bergstresser, Addie, 308

Bergstresser, Blanch, 120, 122, 123, 124, 278

Bergstresser, D., 214

Bergstresser, Daniel, 47, 135, 158, 159, 160, 162, 197, 198, 237, 240, 242, 326

Bergstresser, Mrs. Rebecca, 330

Bergtresser, Daniel, 324

Berian, W. Lea, 162

Berk, Isabelle, 83, 294

Bernard, E., 305

Bernard, Wm., 236

442

Blair, Jesse, 37, 40
Blair, John, 38, 40
Blair, Jr., Wm., 185
Blair, Sr., Wm., 181
Blair, W. D. H., 234
Blair, Wm., 181, 185, 227
Blair, Wm. H., 173
Blake, Chas., 248
Blake, Dr., 136, 237
Blake, Dr. G. W., 118, 157, 159, 160, 162, 197, 237, 239, 242
Blake, Dr. Geo. W., 154
Blake, Ella, 120, 121, 278
Blake, G. W., 118, 230
Blake, Geo. W., 101
Blake, Julia, 356
Blakely, Eliza, 244
Blakely, G. W., 234
Blakely, George, 225
Blakely, Jackson, 238
Blakely, James, 225, 227
Blakely, R., 38, 40
Blakely, Samuel, 37
Blakely, Thomas, 35, 225
Blakely, Thos., 44, 47, 319
Blakely, William, 227
Blakely, Wm., 181, 232, 234, 341
Bland, Frank, 246
Bland, Wm., 55
Blinn, Mathias, 243
Blue Goose, 140
Blue, Gilbert, 296
Boggs, Harriet, 309
Boggs, R. M., 111
Boham, Burr, 236
Boham, Geo., 236
Bolen, ____, 185
Bolenbaugh, A. D., 167
Bolenbaugh, Albert, 108
Bolenbaugh, Barbara, 309
Bolenbaugh, Daniel, 91
Bolenbaugh, Elisha, 307
Bolenbaugh, Geo. B., 329
Bolenbaugh, Mrs., 81

Bolenbaugh, Peter, 158, 159, 227, 307
Bolenbaugh, R. W., 103, 122
Bolenbaugh, Robert W., 103, 416
Bolenbaugh, Robt. W., 104, 124, 144, 163, 310
Bolenbaugh, Wilmot, 108
Bolenbaugh, Wm., 167
Bolles, ____, 320
Bond, P., 46
Bonebrake, Daniel, 305
Bonebrake, Lou D., 93
Bonham, L N., 266
Bonham, L. W., 265
Bonhorst, Dr. Von, 273
Bope, A., 249
Bope, H. J., 249
Borland, John, 204
Borland, W. R., 240
Born, Conrad, 195
Bornstein, H., 182
Boroughs, Wm., 240
Bostwick, C. W., 303, 345
Bostwick, Homer Z., 107
Bostwick, Mrs. C. W., 139
Bostwick, Mrs. Rev., 167
Bostwick, Rev. C. W., 125, 245, 253, 254
Bosworth, John, 90
Bott & Epply, 161
Bott, Emanuel, 239, 327
Bott, Jacob, 81, 98, 104, 148, 197, 198, 323, 326, 328, 330, 359, 416
Bott, Oliver L., 140, 147, 278
Bott, Peter, 43, 198, 240, 330
Bott, Reuben, 326
Bounds, E., 320
Bourne, Philip "Dutch Philip", 66
Bover, Chas. L., 124
Bover, David, 152
Bover, Louis W., 138
Bovey, M. S., 305
Bowen, Chas., 41, 236
Bowen, J. W., 151

Brown, Mrs. Kate M., 316

Brown, Mrs. Mary, 46, 303

Brown, Mrs. Sallie I. Settle, 320

Brown, O. B., 217

Brown, O. J., 198, 236, 243

Brown, Owen J., 239

Brown, Peter, 85

Brown, Pitts, 43, 214

Brown, S., 45, 299

Brown, Samuel, 25, 199, 236, 243, 313

Brown, Simon, 155, 161, 162

Brown, Waldo F., 267

Brown, Wiley, 153, 249

Brown, William, 291

Brown, Wm., 46, 160, 161, 273, 305

Brown, Wylie, 344

Broyler, R. C., 249

Brundidge, Wm., 318

Brundige, Wm., 320

Bruner, A., 118

Brunner, John G., 197, 328

Brunner, Sarah, 278

Bruns, A., 47

Brush, Geo. W., 299

Buck, G. W., 105

Buckingham, Cheney, 253

Buckingham, Ebenezer, **10**

Buechler, Frank A., 162, 164

Bulen, Wm., 198

Bull, Billingsly, 25, 35, 70

Bull, Katherine, 38, 40

Bullock, Wm., 318

Bunn, Elizabeth, 83, 294

Bunn, Fred, 44, 84, 260

Bunn, Frederick, 44, 84, 95, 224

Bunn, Fredrick, 25

Bunn, Henry, 37, 40, 83, 88, 293

Bunn, J. L., 47, 49

Bunn, Lew, 232

Bunn, Lewis, 47

Bunn, N. H., 47

Bunn, Samuel E., 107

Bunns, Frederick, 44

Bunton, W. H., 93

Burden, Ed., 234

Burdette, Bob, 126

Burger, Jacob, 232

Burgess, Chas., 307, 309

Burgett, J., 174, 178

Burgett, Jacob, 173, 174, 181, 333, 334

Burgey, George, 183

Burgey, Wm., 183, 187

Burgoon, Joseph, 46, 253

Burk & Foster, 189

Burk, Madison, 255

Burke & Foster, 180

Burke, Madison, 255

Burkett, C. W., 266

Burkey, J., 42, 45

Burkey, Joseph, 42, 44, 95

Burkholder, Samuel, 118

Burky, Jacob, 243

Burman, G. W., 242

Burnett, Wm., 166, 344

Burnham, Mrs., 244

Burnham, R. E., 234

Burnham, Robt., 183

Burns, James, 232

Burnside, Andrew, 253

Burnsides, Andy, 151

Burnsides, Samuel, 254

Burr, Harriet, 106

Burton, Eleanor, 293

Burton, Joseph, 83

Burton, Joshua, 38, 88, 293

Burton, Mrs. Nancy, 291

Burton, Nancy, 293

Burton, Susana, 293

Burton, Thornton, 83

Busch, Edw. V., 151

Busch, Frank, 249

Bush, Amos, 30, 46, 230, 242, 327

Bush, Charles, 230

Bush, Chas., 239, 242, 327

Bush, Daniel, 43, 238, 242, 327

Bush, E. V., 166, 345

Bush, Ed. V., 164

Bush, Edw. V., 153

449

Chaney, H. L., 176, 196, 232

Chaney, Hal. V., 122

Chaney, Hugh L., 185

Chaney, Ida, 124

Chaney, J. K., 125

Chaney, J. L., 113, 125

Chaney, James K., 179

Chaney, John, 28, 30, 33, 35, 43, 46, 69,
72, 97, 100, 103, 139, 145, 151, 152,
158, 161, 163, 192, 193, 196, 197,
213, 214, 236, 238, 239, 240, 242,
243, 248, 259, 355, 359

Chaney, John L., 72, 98, 104, 125, 179,
266

Chaney, Josephine, 104, 106, 107

Chaney, Jr., John, 337

Chaney, Luda E., 107

Chaney, Madge, 108, 252

Chaney, Maude, 116

Chaney, Miss Jesse, 166

Chaney, Miss Jessie, 252

Chaney, Mrs. J. L., 129, 252, 300

Chaney, Mrs. James K., 129

Chaney, O. P., 29, 30, 46, 68, 104, 136,
145, 148, 154, 159, 161, 163, 166,
180, 196, 230, 237, 239, 260, 267,
274, 323, 359, 415

Chaney, Oliver P., 103, 243, 265, 415

Chaney, W. E., 343

Chaney's Run, 33

Chapman & Smith, 180

Chase, E. B., 299

Chase, Rev. E. B., 300

Cheeseman, J., 47

Cherry, Elizabeth, 318

Cherry, J., 109

Cherry, John, 246

Cherry, Joseph, 172, 173, 177, 178, 181

Cherry, Noah, 139, 165

Cherry, Wm., 86

Chester, Abigail, 312

Chester, Ezra, 312

Chester, Freeman, 312

Chester, Homer, 316

Chester, Jr., Elias, 312

Chester, Mrs. Anna M., 317

Chester, Nancy, 318

Chester, Oscar, 312

Chester, Simeon, 312

Chester, Sr., Elias, 312, 314

Chever, _____, 118

Childs, E., 114

Childs, Isaac, 293

Childs, John, 172

Childs, Sarah, 293

Chiles, John, 38

Chillicothe Road, 192

Cholera, 65, 294

Christ, Samuel S., 47

Claffee, Wm., 339

Clapham, Mr., 90

Clark, A., 109, 341

Clark, Aaron, 55

Clark, Abel, 172, 185, 340, 341

Clark, Carrie L., 111

Clark, Chas. T., 253

Clark, D. A., 93

Clark, Dr. A., 178

Clark, Dr. Abel, 108, 109, 112, 172, 173,
174, 176, 340

Clark, E. E., 244

Clark, Homer, 296

Clark, J. W., 299

Clark, Jane, 316

Clark, Jeremiah, 195

Clark, Joseph, 303

Clark, Mana, 112

Clark, Mathew, 55

Clark, Miller, 255

Clark, Miss Julia A., 111

Clarke, J. W., 299

Claypole, George, 97

Claypole, Jacob, 54

Claypool, Jacob, 193

Clellan, Capt. Webb, 124

Clelland, Addie, 128

Clelland, D. W., 161, 165

Clement, C. R., 185, 189, 341, 343

450

Commercial Hotel, 138, 142, 144, 160, 167, 203
Comp, Jacob, 160, 162
Compton, Mr. ____, 278
Compton, W. N., 127, 128
Conaway, James, 240
Conaway, Rebecca, 244
Condit, Burton, 90, 105
Condit, Lizzie, 91
Condon, J. K., 92
Condon, John K., 93
Conklin, Emanuel, 319
Conklin, J. V., 72, 175, 186, 255, 256
Conklin, J. W., 185
Conklin, Mrs. Mattie, 184
Conklin, Susan, 319
Conklin, W. T., 104
Conklin, Wm. T., 104, 152, 359
Conn House, 139
Conn, A. C., 139
Conn, A. I., 232
Conn, Al. C., 138
Conn, C. Al., 165
Conn, John, 180, 182
Connel, O. J., 341
Connell, O. F., 177
Connell, Z., 296, 299
Conover, Alonzo, 240
Consumers' Gas Co, 167
Consumers' Gas Company of Canal Winchester, 149
Converse, Geo. L., 46, 48
Conway, James, 90
Conway, James I., 89
Cook, Dora, 356
Cook, G. W., 249
Cook, Gotleib, 230, 242
Cook, Isaiah, 181
Cook, Luella, 112
Cooken, James, 31
Coon, C. B., 93
Coon, J. C., 179
Coon, John C., 172, 179, 182, 184, 186, 339

Coon, N. S., 344
Coons, John, 305
Coons, W. W., 305
Cooper, John, 352
Cooper, John H., 108
Copeland, Col. L. F., 126, 130
Copeland, George, 256
Copeland, Lizzie, 256
Copeland, R., 256
Copeland, Richard, 72, 179, 188, 255
Copeland, Sadie, 115
Copland, R., 255
Corbett Hotel, 186
Corbett, Frank P., 115
Corbett, James, 127
Corbett, John, 178, 234, 275
Corbett, John T., 248
Corbett, Katharine A., 115
Corbett, Katharine T., 115
Corbett, M., 46, 108, 128, 186, 232, 261
Corbett, M. Leo, 115
Corbett, Michael, 169, 171, 180, 199, 334
Corbett, Mrs., 244
Corbett, Nora, 115
Corbett, Pat, 232
Corbett, Pat., 171
Corbett, Patrick, 171
Corbett, William, 232, 334
Corbett, Wm., 108, 169, 339
Cornell, F., 232
Corner, Chas. D., 157
Corner, Julia, 309
Corner, Stewart, 38
Corothers, John, 240
Corwin, Marion, 128, 167, 169, 182
Coston, Zarah, 296
Couch, Mrs. Mame, 295
Courtright, Dr. G. S., 125
Courtright, Dr. Geo. S., 253, 342
Courtright, Edward, 68, 71, 192, 193
Courtright, G. C., 249
Courtright, Geo. S., 343
Courtright, Hannah, 278

452

453

Evans, Ruth, 86
Evans, Thomas J., 307
Evans, W. H., 92
Evans, Wm., 28
Evans. Mrs. Sarah D., 162
Eversole, ____, 157
Eversole, Geo. W., 94
Ewers, Carrie, 91
Ewing, Thomas, 213
Ewing, Wm., 234, 341
Eyeman, L. E., 180
Eyeman, Mrs. Lizzie, 300

F

Fagan, Jas., 236
Fagan, Thomas, 199, 334
Fagan, Thos., 46, 47, 48, 234
Fahler, Tip, 312
Fairbanks, Alf., 122, 124
Fairchilds, J. B., 111
Falhaber & Black, 182
Falhaber, Theo., 182, 255
Fame, Wm. M., 344
Farley, 25
Farnsworth, W. W., 266
Farrand, George, 230
Farrand, Henry, 232, 239
Farrand, William, 230
Farrell, Jacob, 242
Farrington, Chas. W., 86
Farsee, John, 118
Faskett, George, 214
Fassett, Joseph, 55
Faulhaber, Theo., 175, 179
Fay, Cyrus, 195
Fay, Jacob, 307
Fay, James, 242
Fearn & Watson, 181
Fearn, A. R., 341
Fearn, Al., 181
Fearn, Geo. W., 172
Fearn, George, 181
Fearn, J. H., 71, 113, 182, 234, 260, 341

Fearn, Jennie, 90
Feasel, Jacob, 38
Feasel, John, 236
Featheringale, Thos., 38
Featheringgill, Thomas, 35
Federal Gas and Fuel Co., 149
Feistkorn, Chas., 162
Felch, Allen S., 240
Fellers, Aaron, 159
Fellers, Perry, 309
Fellows, Barnhart, 193
Fenstermaker, Aaron, 138, 142, 214, 359
Fenstermaker, Darius, 248
Fenstermaker, Emma, 356
Fenstermaker, Laura, 356
Fenstermaker, Mrs. L., 162
Fenstermaker, Mrs. Louise, 164
Fenstermaker, Wm., 163
Fenton, T. E. W., 89
Ferall, John, 242
Ferguson, Samuel, 198, 236
Feringer, Alfred, 243
Ferington, C. W., 341
Fernandez, H. S., 296
Ferrill, A. L., 359
Ferrington, C. W., 234
Ferris, H. H., 299, 303
Ferris, Rev. H. A., 297
Fickel, Alice M., 115
Fickel, E. M., 93, 94, 267
Fickel, Edwin M., 93
Fickel, J. C., 92, 96
Fickel, J. Collins, 115
Fickel, James, 255, 256, 297
Fictone, Henry, 27
Fictore, Henry, 197, 214, 227
Filler, Miss S. E., 106
Filler, Susie E., 94
Filler, W. C., 302
Filler, Wm., 300
Fink, H. G. G., 302
Fink, J., 305
Fink, Milton, 44

460

Gander Hill, 81, 84

Gander, Jacob, 25, 38, 70, 84

Gander, John, 38, 40, 84

Gard, Dr. B. F., 294

Gard, Elizabeth Pontius, 294

Gardner, R. W., 93

Gares & Taylor, 180, 195

Gares, Anna M., 316

Gares, Ed, 188, 232

Gares, Ed., 44, 109

Gares, Edmund, 172, 173, 176, 188, 338

Gares, Edward, 44, 95, 112, 113, 186, 261

Gares, Florence, 115, 128

Gares, Jane, 244, 382

Gares, Miss Florence, 129

Gares, Mrs., 316

Gares, Mrs. Ed., 129

Gares, Snyder, 183

Gares, Wm., 127

Garling, David, 227

Garner, N. H., 111, 127, 341

Gartner, H., 299, 341

Gates, J. B., 89

Gates, Mamie J., 115

Gaver, Lizzie, 356

Gay, Miss _____, 90

Gay, R. L., 91

Gayman, A. E., 122, 163, 165

Gayman, Abigail, 272, 278

Gayman, Al., 274

Gayman, Allie, 274

Gayman, Allie E., 121

Gayman, B. F., 70, 123, 124, 147, 151, 152, 163, 166, 199, 257, 266, 267, 273, 274, 342, 343, 344

Gayman, Benj. F., 147

Gayman, Benjamin F., 68

Gayman, C., 101, 102, 103, 104, 107, 141, 149, 152, 158, 159, 160, 163, 166, 197, 198, 218, 230, 237, 239, 242, 328

Gayman, Carrie, 94, 106

Gayman, Carrie A., 92, 107

Gayman, Charles W., 107

Gayman, Chas. W., 92, 122, 167

Gayman, Christian, 91, 141, 151, 328, 329, 331, 333, 357, 415

Gayman, D. D., 343

Gayman, Daniel, 159, 160, 161, 165, 197, 214, 230, 239, 242, 328, 357

Gayman, David, 91, 144, 159, 197, 239, 242, 273, 274

Gayman, Dr. W. S., 153, 166, 252

Gayman, Edwin C., 107

Gayman, Edwin S., 125, 163

Gayman, Eliza, 167

Gayman, Ephriam, 307

Gayman, Ida, 124

Gayman, Israel, 83, 90, 91, 160, 161, 165, 166, 238, 253, 307, 324

Gayman, Jess A., 92

Gayman, Jess. A., 107

Gayman, John, 167

Gayman, Jonn C., 107

Gayman, Katie, 106

Gayman, Mary E., 106

Gayman, Mollie, 92, 94, 122

Gayman, Moses, 161, 165, 166, 230, 271, 307, 329

Gayman, Mrs., 244

Gayman, Mrs. B. F., 356

Gayman, Mrs. C., 32

Gayman, Mrs. David, 272

Gayman, O. P., 122, 124, 125, 148, 166, 252, 327, 329, 343, 345

Gayman, Oliver P., 147, 151

Gayman, Rose, 93, 106, 107, 122

Gayman, Sarah, 122

Gayman, Sol., 227

Gayman, Solomon, 118

Gayman, Wm. S., 249

Gayman's Store, 136, 140, 144

Gear, Rev. H. L., 319

Geary, Joan, 196

Geese, H., 42

Geese, Henry, 316

Gehm, B. D., 148, 152, 166, 345

463

464

Goss, J. D., 42
Gossage, Nicholas
  "Yellow Nick", 26
Gough, Abner, 296, 301
Gould, Charles M., 147
Gould, Chas. M., 161, 359
Grabowsky, John A., 110
Graff, John, 324
Graham & Eckert, 163
Graham, A. A., 125, 265
Graham, Carrie, 94
Grantham, W. P., 302
Graves, John Temple, 126
Gray, A., 198, 343
Gray, Alfred, 42, 45, 96, 255, 256
Gray, Andrew, 301
Gray, C. H., 45
Gray, Dr. G. J., 166
Gray, J. A., 234
Gray, James F., 255
Gray, M. A., 45, 341
Gray, P., 198
Gray, R. S., 45
Gray, Thomas, 26, 55, 198
Gray, Thos., 25, 38, 39, 40, 42, 45
Great Eastern, 140, 165
Green, ____, 185
Green, Andrew, 55
Green, Guilbert, 311
Green, John, 242
Green, W. G., 266
Green, Wm. A., 352
Greenleaf, ____, Saloonist, 273
Gregg, Geo., 159
Gregg, J. C., 302
Griffith, J. W., 337, 338
Griffith, James, 160, 161, 165
Griffith, Jane, 310
Griffith, John W., 152, 337
Griffith, Mrs. Rachel M., 338
Griffith, Nobel, 248
Griffith, R. M., 338
Griffith, Rachel, 125
Grimes, John F., 299

Groff, August, 159
Groff, John, 292, 293
Groom,, 83
Groom, Augustus, 83
Groom, Catherine, 293
Groom, Charity, 293
Groom, Christena, 83
Groom, Christina, 83, 294
Groom, D. R., 295
Groom, Daniel R., 294
Groom, David, 83
Groom, E., 44, 294, 338
Groom, E. E., 44
Groom, Ezekiel, 25, 38, 224, 260, 290,
  291
Groom, F., 341
Groom, Ferdinand L., 240
Groom, Hosea, 83
Groom, John, 38, 293, 294
Groom, John F., 83, 294
Groom, Lucy, 293
Groom, M., 44, 177, 341
Groom, Mary, 84
Groom, Miner, 83
Groom, Moses, 44, 84, 224, 291, 292,
  293, 294
Groom, Nancy, 83, 293
Groom, Nancy R., 294
Groom, Noah, 293
Groom, Rebecca, 83
Groom, Rhoda, 83, 293, 294
Groom, Sarah Ann, 293
Groom, Thomas, 47, 84, 290, 291, 293,
  294
Groom, Thos., 38, 44, 292, 294
Groom, Wm., 38
Groome, E., 47
Groome, Thomas, 48
Grooms, E., 340
Grosvenor, Col. C. H., 203
Grove, Frank, 249
Groveport Brass Band,, 188
Groveport Road, 56, 88
Groves, ____, 254

Harmon, George, 214, 304

Harmon, Henry, 307, 324

Harmon, Samuel, 230, 307

Harmon, Tena, 309

Harmon, Wm., 182

Harold, Wm., 253

Harpst & Prentiss, 161

Harpst, Frank, 248

Harpst, G., 43

Harpst, G. M., 124

Harpst, Henry, 159, 197, 230

Harpst, John, 163

Harpst, Mary, 124

Harpst, Wm. H., 152, 163

Harris, Abe, 43

Harris, Abraham, 25, 41, 44

Harris, Abram, 214

Harris, Alva, 182

Harris, Chas. A., 105

Harris, Geo., 227

Harris, Harvey D., 244

Harris, J. H., 175

Harris, John, 227

Harris, O. D., 96, 255, 256, 265, 269, 339

Harris, P. C., 230, 239, 243

Harris, Phil. C., 47

Harris, Sarah E., 47

Harrison, Abe, 32

Harrison, Abraham, 54, 304, 352

Harrison, Chas. E., 242

Harrison, Dixon A., 89

Harrison, Edith, 351

Harrison, Greazy, 25, 35

Harrison, J. R., 232

Harrison, W. H., 44, 47

Harrison, Wm., 194

Hart & Armpreister,, 139, 161

Hart, Irvin M., 337

Hart, James A., 91

Hartin, Jeremiah, 240

Hartsaugh, W. H., 148

Hartsough, W. H., 106, 148, 257, 265, 266

Harvey, W. T., 299

Harwood, Henry, 242

Harwood, T. F., 111

Harwood, T. J., 234

Haskell, Emma, 120, 310

Hasting, William, 105

Hasting, Wm., 91

Hastings, John, 225

Hatfield, Benj. F., 162

Hathaway, A., 103, 118, 152, 197, 214, 237, 271

Hathaway, Agnes, 302

Hathaway, Almanzar, 137

Hathaway, Almanzer, 99, 350, 352

Hathaway, Almanzor, 15

Hathaway, Edward, 25, 35, 41, 300, 351, 352

Hathaway, Elizabeth, 41, 302

Hathaway, George, 305

Hathaway, Mary, 309

Hathaway, Nancy, 41, 81, 136

Hathaway, Rev. George, 139

Hathaway, Sallie, 302

Hathaway, Sally, 136

Hatten, Chas. "Black Charlie", 26

Hattenfels, Chas., 255, 320

Havely, Adam, 25, 38, 44, 45, 47, 89, 95, 180, 225, 232, 261, 291

Havely, Hester A., 111

Havens, Miss A. M., 111

Hawks, J. A., 203, 204

Hawks, W. B., 203

Hawkstage Coach Line, 138

Hawood, T. J., 91

Hays, George, **11**, **70**

Hays, Hiram F., 253, 254

Hays, Joseph, 296

Headley, Aaron C., 67

Headly & Eberly, 180

Headly, A. C., 172, 176, 178

Heath, Uriah, 299

Hedges, J. E., 153, 167

Hedren, Robert, 234

Hedrick, L., 181
Hedrick, Levi, 234
Hedrick, Mrs., 244
Heffinger, Frederick, 43
Heffley & Bott, 147
Heffley & Gayman, 147
Heffley, James, 105, 323, 324, 337
Heffley, Minnie M., 107
Heffley's Drug Store, 150
Hefflinger, F., 232
Hefflinger, John, 232
Heffly, Bertha, 93
Heffly, Bertha B., 107
Heffly, James, 102, 230, 342, 415
Heffly, Mrs. A. V. A., 338
Heffly, Rev. James, 98, 103, 104, 147,
    152, 153, 197, 267, 277, 325, 328,
    329, 331, 332, 338, 415
Heffly, Rev. Jas., 415
Hefley, Rev. James, 94
Heil, John, 42, 45, 96, 198, 234
Heil, M., 96
Heil, Michael, 234
Heilman, W. T., 106, 327
Heinmiller, General Henry, 344
Heise, Simon, 255
Heise, T., 250
Heistand, Elder, 319
Heistands, Samuel, 305
Heller, E. S., 106
Heller, S. E., 337
Helpman & Shaffer, 159, 160
Helpman, 'Bricky', 274
Helpman, Alary Jane, 308
Helpman, Andrew, 118
Helpman, Ann, 310
Helpman, Anna, 272
Helpman, 'Bricky', 274
Helpman, David, 309
Helpman, Elias, 261
Helpman, Eliza, 308
Helpman, Ella, 123, 278
Helpman, Irene, 308

, 26, 70, 71, 97, 101, 102,
103, 104, 118, 122, 138, 140, 142,
150, 151, 156, 159, 161, 163, 165,
196, 197, 214, 237, 238, 239, 243,
244, 247, 248, 273, 274, 309, 310,
415
Helpman, Mrs. Sarah, 272
Helpman, Simon, 41, 161
Helpman, Wm., 118, 253, 254, 274,
307, 309
Helpman, Wm. (Bricky), 163
Hels, Otto, 243
Helsel, Adam, 45, 234
Helsel, Daniel, 42
Helsel, G. W., 45, 234
Helsel, J. E., 93
Helsel, John, 42
Helsel, Mettie, 93
Helsel, Nic., 234
Helsel, Philip, 42, 45, 96
Helsel, S. R., 45, 48, 96, 238, 269
Helsel, Samuel R., 234
Helsel, T., 45
Helsel, Wm., 42
Helsel, Wm. H., 42
Hemler, Isaac, 243
Hempleman, A. G., 305
Hempstead, ____, 318
Hempstead, C., 162, 164
Hempted, Mary, 105
Hempy Bros., 166
Hempy, Frank E., 97
Hempy, S., 42, 45
Hempy, Samuel, 29, 237, 242, 359
Hempy, Wm., 90
Hendersheit, Frank, 166
Henderson, Arthur, 92
Henderson, L. C., 43
Hendren Jr., S. O., 230
Hendren, "Puss", 91
Hendren, A. T., 46, 271, 312
Hendren, A. Turner, 316
Hendren, Arthur, 115
Hendren, B., 46

468

Hendren, Cyrus, 95
Hendren, D. C., 225
Hendren, Dr. Geo., 160
Hendren, G. L., 96, 234
Hendren, Geo. L., 86, 90, 266, 269, 316,
    317, 318
Hendren, George L., 416
Hendren, H., 196
Hendren, Hattie L., 94
Hendren, L. C., 91
Hendren, M. C., 320
Hendren, Mary, 92
Hendren, Mary E., 93
Hendren, Minnie, 91
Hendren, Mordicai C., 86
Hendren, Mordicai Cloud, 320
Hendren, Mrs. Mary Turner, 319
Hendren, Nancy, 85, 316
Hendren, Nancy M., 90
Hendren, R., 46, 260
Hendren, Rev. H., 43
Hendren, Robert, 43
Hendren, S. E., 46
Hendren, S. O., 44, 95, 196
Hendren, Sam O., 243
Hendren, Samuel, 85
Hendren, Samuel O., 44, 47, 48, 97,
    239, 341
Hendren, Sarah E., 86, 319, 320
Hendren, Sarah McCombs, 312
Hendren, T. C., 43, 46, 96, 97, 238, 260
Hendren, Thomas, 97, 98
Hendren, Thomas C., 85, 311, 319
Hendren, Thomas Cloud, 320
Hendren, Thos. C., 43, 85, 88, 320
Hendren, Turner, 97
Hendren, Turner C., 225
Hendren, William D., 25
Hendren, Wm., 85, 86, 234
Hendren, Wm. D., 38, 70, 318, 320
Hendren, Wm. T., 86, 316
Hendricks, John, 226
Hendricks, Wash, 118
Hendricks, Wm., 157

Hendron, Hiram, 68
Henley, James, 163
Henry Steman, 334
Henry, Austin, 124, 324, 326
Henry, Eli, 330
Henry, Fred, 248
Henry, Michael, 244
Henry, Rev. Austin, 124, 326
Hensel, Geo., 96
Herbst, Edw. O., 338
Herbst, G. M., 153, 167
Herbst, Geo. M., 329
Herbst, George, 330
Herbst, Henry, 155, 160, 162, 165, 239,
    242, 421
Herbst, Wm. H., 337, 344
Herbuck, Rev. E. P., 324
Herkins, Rosanna, 308
Herr, Albert, 115
Herr, Miss Eliza, 317
Herr, Ray, 115
Herrick, Chas., 185
Herrick, Henrietta, 308
Herrick, Henry S., 227
Herrick, Huldy, 308
Herrick, Jason, 227
Herrick, Mary, 244
Hersey, Dr., 131
Hershiser & Gibson, 175
Hertly, Jonathan, 38
Hesser, Henry, 230, 239
Hesser, Mary, 244
Hesser, Ollie, 120, 121, 122, 123, 124,
    278, 329, 356
Hesser, Wm., 245, 253, 254, 274, 337,
    356
Heston, John, 224, 227
Heston, John H., 72
Heston's Independent Company, 227
Hetchins, Alex, 234
Hetzell, Daniel, 38
Hetzell, John, 38
Hetzell, Philip, 38
Hewetson, Dr. Walter, 317

469

I

J

K

Kalb, Alice, 317
Kalb, G. W., 96, 97, 171, 179, 237, 239
Kalb, Geo., 25, 38, 41, 271
Kalb, Geo. Jr., 38
Kalb, Geo. W., 43, 46, 273, 312, 317, 318
Kalb, George, 81
Kalb, H. H., 238
Kalb, Henry, 317
Kalb, I., 45
Kalb, Isaac, 43, 96, 214, 225, 239, 242
Kalb, James P., 73, 96, 97, 266, 268, 297, 415
Kalb, Jas. P., 166, 359
Kalb, Jeremiah, 225
Kalb, Jerry, 43, 45, 243
Kalb, John, 25, 38
Kalb, M. E., 96, 236, 239
Kalb, Mathew E., 239, 312, 317
Kalb, Mrs. Geo. W., 273
Kalb, Roxie, 108
Kalb, T. D., 81, 96
Kalb, Theo. D., 96, 98, 268, 269, 297
Kalies, G. H., 46
Kallies, L., 182
Kanamaker, George, 195
Kanode, Madge, 106
Karnes, B. H., 234, 310
Karnes, Benj. H., 305
Karnes, D. F., 91, 92, 93, 94, 112, 176, 179, 188
Karnes, D. Fisher, 127
Karnes, G. G., 230
Karnes, Grove, 309
Karnes, Grove G., 242
Karnes, John, 230, 243
Karnes, Mal B., 159
Karnes, Melvin, 309
Karnes, Sarah, 308
Karns, Grove, 91
Karns, Grove G., 240
Karns, John, 153
Karns, M. B., 90
Karns, Mai, 310

Karns, Melville, 90
Kartzholtz, Christian, 268
Kauffman, Jacob, 180
Kauffman, W. R., 72, 181
Kaufman, W. R., 178
Keane, Sarah M., 165
Keasley, Rebecca, 311
Keelan, Wm., 232
Keichle, Geo., 65
Kelchner, Daniel, 243
Kelchner, John, 43
Kelkner, John, 96
Keller, Jess A., 92, 93
Keller, Jess. A., 95
Keller, Michael, 180
Keller, Mr., 179
Keller, Rev. Eli, 326, 329
Kellerman, W. A., 266
Kelley & Coon, 182
Kelley & Kile, 182
Kelley & Vogle, 182
Kelley, A. C., 303, 337, 342
Kelley, J. M., 94, 125, 181, 183, 186
Kelley, M. A., 47
Kelley, M. H., 95, 176
Kelley, Rev. A. C., 274, 341
Kelley, Wm., 182
Kelly, A. C., 299
Kelly, George A., 35
Kelly, Joseph, 182
Kelly, M. H., 47, 97, 184
Kelly, Myrtle, 128
Kelly, Rev. A. C., 247
Keltchner, Daniel, 239
Keltchner, John, 239
Kemerer, Elias, 214
Kemmerle, Fredrick, 244
Kemp, M. L., 345
Kemp, Mart. L., 344
Kemp, Martin L., 165
Kemp, O. M. L., 345
Kemp, Thomas, 118
Kennoder & Denig, 175
Kentz, G., 47

King, M., 110
King, Miss A. I., 167
King, Miss Elizabeth, 267
King, Mrs. M. S., 266, 267
King, Philip, 38, 158
King, Phillip, 25
King, Sarah, 38
King, Truman, 38
King, Wm., 38
Kingery, ____, 318
Kinnear, Josiah, 262
Kinney's Run, 33
Kinsel, Geo., 86
Kinsler, Peter, 118
Kirk, W. H., 163, 344
Kissel & Brown, 161
Kissel, Aaron, 248
Kissel, Eph., 234
Kissel, Isaac, 236
Kissel, Jeremiah, 43, 96, 239
Kissel, Jerry, 236
Kissel, John, 138, 153, 159, 161, 197, 236, 239, 304
Kissel, Jonas, 236
Kissel, Mina, 154
Kissel, Simon, 230, 239
Kissell, Benton, 309
Kissell, E., 243
Kissell, Elmina, 309
Kissell, Jeremiah, 237
Kissell, John, 159, 227, 230, 242, 272
Kissinger, Mary, 90
Kitzmiller, J. A., 339
Kitzmiller, Joseph A., 112, 265, 340
Klamforth, Fred, 47
Klein, Fred, 204
Klick, ____, 333
Knepper, Israel, 307
Knepper, S., 243
Knight, Jacob C., 317
Knoderer, Louisa, 294
Koble, Jacob, 238
Koch, Malcolm, 230, 239
Koebel, Geo., 95

Koebel, Wm., 95
Koffits, Chas. F., 249
Kohlstein, Frank, 234
Komp, Jacob, 165, 166, 234
Komp, Jacob C., 243
Komp, Wm., 249
Kooper, John, 38
Korn, August, 159
Krabbs, George, 230
Krag, August, 309
Krag, Caroline, 308
Krag, Mr., 99
Krag, Peter, 138, 144, 145
Krag, Peter T., 97, 103, 157, 214
Krag, Wm., 309
Kramer & Bolenbaugh, 167
Kramer & Fenstermaker, 161
Kramer Bros., 164
Kramer Jr., Wm., 234
Kramer Mill, 159
Kramer, Aaron, 225
Kramer, Adam, 32, 35, 118, 303, 304
Kramer, Andrew, 351, 352
Kramer, Benton, 238, 309
Kramer, Bert, 249
Kramer, Catharine, 244
Kramer, Cristina, 351
Kramer, Daniel, 25, 38, 166
Kramer, David, 43, 118, 214, 307
Kramer, Elijah, 230, 307
Kramer, Elizabeth, 238
Kramer, Elmer, 249
Kramer, Elmira, 309
Kramer, Ervin, 309
Kramer, Geo., 38, 44, 97
Kramer, George, 304
Kramer, Hanby, 307
Kramer, Henry, 43, 230, 238, 310
Kramer, Irvin, 307
Kramer, Isaac, 159, 307
Kramer, J. B., 92
Kramer, Jacob, 25, 230, 238, 304
Kramer, James P., 152, 162, 310, 415
Kramer, Jas. P., 102

478

479

482

Myers, Sister, 319

N

Naftzger, Christ, 234
Naftzger, Josiah, 234
Nafzger, G., 72
Nafzger, J., 183
Nafzger, Jacob, 195
Nafzger, John, 224
Nailer, Joseph, 181, 186
Nash, Dr. ____, 162
Nation, Philip, 296
Nau, Anna, 94
Nau, J., 47
Nau, Jacob, 95
Nau, John, 46, 234
Neckerson, Uzzi, 38
Needels, A. P., 234
Needels, Adda, 92
Needels, Almira, 45, 93
Needels, Andrew, 25
Needels, Blanche, 115
Needels, C. F., 32, 47, 95, 234, 261, 338, 339
Needels, C. Fay, 261
Needels, Cubbage, 25
Needels, E. Ann, 86
Needels, Eliza, 312
Needels, Enoch, 238
Needels, G. W., 96, 234, 238
Needels, Geo., 45, 359
Needels, Geo. W., 45, 198
Needels, George, 42, 48, 115, 198
Needels, J. A., 45
Needels, J. H., 234
Needels, J. J., 72, 118
Needels, James, 41, 42, 43, 96, 260
Needels, Joel, 96, 98
Needels, John, 38
Needels, John A., 42
Needels, John W., 96, 225
Needels, Joseph, 42
Needels, L. J., 45

Needels, M. A., 45
Needels, Miss ____, 111
Needels, Mrs. Eliza, 317
Needels, Mrs. Hannah, 317
Needels, Perry, 92
Needels, Phil, 86
Needels, Philoman, 38
Needels, Philomen, 39, 40, 41
Needels, Rhoda, 90, 91
Needels, Rhoda M., 105
Needels, S. A., 45
Needels, S. T., 125, 148, 166
Needels, Sarah Ann, 45
Needels, Stanton T., 96, 148
Needels, T., 43
Needels, Thomas, 25, 198, 297
Needels, Thos., 42, 43, 45, 88
Needels, Thos. D., 38
Needels, W. D., 42, 45, 96
Needels, Wm. D., 32, 42
Needles, James, 44, 198
Needles, Wm. D., 42, 198
Neil, Wm., 44, 202
Nelson, Marcus, 232
Neville, H. H., 93
Nevons, John S., 83
Newberry, C. L., 266
Newberry, F. P., 93
Newberry, M. A., 92, 94
Newberry, M. J., 95
Newbour, Miss L., 309
Newcomer, John, 240
Newell, Harris W., 175
Nichols, John, 181, 234
Nichols, Wm., 225
Nicodemus, H., 103, 328
Nicodemus, Henry, 70, 157
Nicodemus, John, 357, 416
Nigh, G. S., 183
Nigh, Geo. S., 172
Nitterhouse & Pitzer, 180
Noah Brenneman, 334
Noderer, Louisa, 83
Noecker, H. T., 166

490

Race, Job, 86
Race, John, 86
Race, Wm., 86
Rader, Carrie A., 93
Rager, Adam, 236, 239
Rager, J. P., 248, 339
Rager, John, 25, 29, 38, 43, 46, 48, 95, 196, 225, 238, 239, 359
Rager, Joseph P., 72
Rager, Solomon, 95
Rager, W. H., 46, 187, 339
Rager, Wm. H., 236
Rager's Run, 56
Rager's Saw Mill, 189
Raha, L. C., 249
Railroad Street, 135
Rainer, Harley E., 269
Rainier, Daniel, 35
Rainier, Edson F., 115
Rainier, Harlan E., 107
Rainier, Harly E., 295
Rainier, M. Clark, 115
Rainier, Miss Emma, 295
Rainier, Rebecca, 35
Ramsey, James Jr., 38
Ramsey, Charlotte, 317
Ramsey, Chas. W., 160, 162
Ramsey, James, 38
Ramsey, Rebecca, 243
Ramsey, Robert, 25
Ramsey, Samuel, 38
Ramsey, Wm., 38
Ramsey, Wm. R., 244
Randall, Dr. D. A., 320
Randall, Rev. D. A., 319
Raney, Miss, 310
Ranier, Daniel, 291
Ranier, Edson, 295
Ranier, Emma, 295
Ranier, Frank C., 295
Ranier, H. E., 295
Ranier, Harley E., 294, 295
Ranier, Hester A., 83
Ranier, Hester Ann, 294

Ranier, Isaac, 291, 292, 294, 295
Ranier, J. F., 295
Ranier, John F., 294, 295
Ranier, M. C., 92, 295
Ranier, Mrs. J. F., 295
Ranier, Sister Allie, 294
Ranier, Wm., 83, 294
Rankin, L. L., 106, 302
Rarey & Dildine, 184
Rarey Academy, 31, 108, 189
Rarey Brothers' Drug Store, 188
Rarey, A. B., 47, 48, 175, 180, 189, 232
Rarey, A. M., 125, 172, 176, 255, 316
Rarey, A. Miner, 317
Rarey, A. Minor, 234
Rarey, Adam, **13**, **32**, **38**, **54**, **55**, **86**, **169**, **170**, **279**
Rarey, Adel & Co., 182
Rarey, Alfred, 83
Rarey, Alice, 115
Rarey, Amanda, 83, 294
Rarey, Ann Katharine, 195
Rarey, Anna, 116
Rarey, Benj., 38
Rarey, Benjamin, 83, 86, 169
Rarey, C., 260
Rarey, C. D., 128, 129, 189, 317
Rarey, C. E., 295
Rarey, C. W., 43
Rarey, Charles, 25, 291, 298
Rarey, Charles D., 72
Rarey, Chas., 38, 41, 108
Rarey, Chas. D., 67, 72, 113, 114, 128, 171, 172, 176, 179, 183, 188
Rarey, Chas. Jr., 38, 39, 40, 41
Rarey, Clarinda, 83
Rarey, Courtright & Co., 31, 180, 183
Rarey, Daniel, 225
Rarey, David, 83
Rarey, Elizabeth, 83
Rarey, Emma, 114
Rarey, F., 46
Rarey, F. S., 110, 113, 176, 180, 184, 341

491

Rees, C. P., 155, 158, 159, 167, 230, 239, 242, 337, 338, 359
Rees, Carrie, 122
Rees, Chas. P., 102, 104, 145, 160, 164, 337, 359, 415
Rees, Ellen, 120
Rees, Hattie, 112
Rees, J. H., 234, 260
Rees, Jacob H., 43
Rees, Miss Ella, 359
Rees, Mrs. C. P., 272
Rees, T. L., 92
Reese, Ben L., 68
Reese, Jacob, 97
Reese, Mrs. Mary, 316
Reeves, Abigail, 244
Reeves, Jane, 256
Reeves, Mrs. Peter, 129
Reeves, Peter, 182, 255
Rei, George, 181
Rei, Mrs. G., 244
Reibe, Chas. C., 163, 343
Reicelt, John, 234
Reiling, John, 234
Reiner, Clara, 107
Reinhart, Phil, 234
Remaley, C., 244
Remalia, Eli, 181
Remalia, Elias, 316
Rempel, Col. Ferdinand F., 203
Resler, J. B., 305
Reutsch, L., 96
Rev. S. P. Manger, Mrs., 272
Reynolds, ____, 318
Rhoads & Glatfetter, 166
Rhoads, Jacob, 25
Rhoads, John, 29
Rhoads, John A., 230
Rhodes, Riley, 159
Richards, ____, 165
Richards, Ebenezer, **11**, **70**
Richards, Mr., 106
Richardson, Marcus, 225
Richardson, Mr. ____, 278

Richardson, Samuel, 319
Richardson, W. H., 54, 55
Richardson, Wm., 38, 39, 40, 41, 108
Richardson, Wm. H., 28
Richardson, Wm. W., 319
Richardson's Academy, 108
Ricketts, A. C., 93
Ricketts, Alvin C., 94
Ricketts, Ira, 214
Ricketts, Mr. A., 106
Ricketts, W., 91
Ricketts, Wm., 90
Ridgeway & Co., 195
Rife, J. M., 299
Riggs, Spillman, 126
Riker, S. C., 299, 302
Riley, Dr. Wm., 25
Riley, Wm., 25, 30, 158, 159, 195, 352
Rind, Jacob, 38
Rind, Jacob Jr., 38
Rinehard, Jonathan, 166, 304
Rinesmith, Noah, 268
Ringer, A., 122
Ringer, Anaxy, 254
Ringer, Anexy, 122
Ringer, Leah, 309
Ringer, Lewis W., 337
Ringer, Polly, 309
Ringer, W. L., 248
Riskad, Daniel, 193
Rivers, Peter, 243
Roads, Jete, 38
Roads, John, 38
Robb, C. M., 94
Robb, Geo. W., 92, 93, 94, 112
Roberts, James F., 251
Roberts, James P., 249
Roberts, Maria, 316
Roberts, Owen, 38, 81
Robertson, Effie, 93
Robinauttz, Peter, 304
Robinold, Peter, 41
Robinson, Henry, 307
Robinson, James, 230, 242

S

494

Shipton, H. H., 94, 111, 266, 339, 340, 341

Shirey, Jacob, 338

Shirey, Lew, 178, 234

Shirey, Lewis, 43, 172, 181, 195

Shirey, M., 181

Shiry, Mart., 232

Shisler, Aaron, 105

Shock, Dr. J. W., 136

Shockley, Mrs. Jennie, 317

Shockley, Pierce, 183

Shockley, R., 109, 172

Shockley, Wm., 127, 234

Shockley. D. C., 109, 294, 340

Shockly, S. M., 91

Shodde, George H., 332

Shoemaker, A., 70, 108, 112, 113, 172, 176, 178

Shoemaker, Abraham, 39, 173

Shoemaker, Abram, 195

Shoemaker, Absalom, 324

Shoemaker, B. B., 243, 268

Shoemaker, Benj., 227

Shoemaker, Billingsly, 225

Shoemaker, Chas., 122, 248

Shoemaker, Chas. H., 249

Shoemaker, Geo., 248, 249

Shoemaker, Hannah, 308

Shoemaker, Isaac, 157, 159

Shoemaker, J. H., 161

Shoemaker, Jacob, 41

Shoemaker, John, 85, 120, 225

Shoemaker, L., 46

Shoemaker, Mrs. Mary, 316

Shoemaker, P., 42

Shoemaker, Philip, 85, 225

Shoemaker, Rebecca, 324

Shoemaker, S., 96, 160

Shoemaker, Samuel, 46, 236, 243

Shoemaker, W., 248

Shook, Dr. J. W., 124, 152, 153, 163, 166, 252, 301, 344

Shook, Elias, 44, 268, 269

Shook, J. W., 123, 124, 152, 153, 163, 166, 257, 301, 344

Shook, Kate, 252

Shook, Rebecca, 268

Shorn, Dr. A. A., 102

Short, Dr., 98

Short, Dr. A. A., 67, 153, 162, 163, 197, 238, 243, 356

Short, Kate, 356

Short, Katie, 120, 123

Short, Miss Katie, 277

Short, Mrs. A. A., 272

Shortie's Minstrels, 128

Shortt, A. A., 230

Shortt, Chas. E., 249

Shortt, Dr. A. A., 42, 103, 104, 160, 166, 239

Shortt, Katie, 120

Show, Virgil E., 341

Showalter, America, 278

Shrader, David, 159, 160, 305

Shrader, Rev. David, 104

Shrader, Rightly & Miller, 159

Shride & Weber, 164

Shride, A. L., 103, 104, 180

Shrigly, Miss ____, 112

Shuh, Louis H., 163

Shultz, Daniel E., 359

Shultz, Jacob, 195

Shumaker, Ed, 236

Shumaker, Jacob, 328

Shuman, Geo., 161

Shuman, John, 236, 239, 243

Siball, Hiram, 158

Sibel, Henry, 309

Sibel, Thos., 309

Sibley, Alice, 106

Sibley, Dr. N. B., 163

Sibley, E., 302

Sickles, Andrew J., 204

Sidener, John, 255

Sidner, John, 180

Siegfried, Geo. W., 323

Sigler, Rhoda E., 112

Simms, Belinda, 46
Simms, Benjamin C., 269
Simms, Della, 115
Simms, Edw., 251
Simms, Elkanah, 319
Simms, Ervin, 250
Simms, F. Scott, 115
Simms, G. W., 319
Simms, Geo. W., 320
Simms, Irvin E., 252
Simms, J. T., 46
Simms, J. W., 46
Simms, James, 115
Simms, Nancy, 319
Simms, Nannie, 116, 188
Simms, P. W., 46
Simms, W. E., 115
Simms, Wash, 182
Simms, Wm. M., 46
Simons, F. D., 217
Simons, Samuel, 224
Simons, Thos. A., 217
Simpson, Mrs. Maria, 317
Sims, A. C., 92, 93
Sims, B. C., 46, 72, 196, 232, 341
Sims, Benj. C., 71, 184
Sims, Benjamin, 227
Sims, E. M., 91
Sims, Elk, 85
Sims, Geo. A., 83
Sims, Geo. W., 82, 88
Sims, Gilbert, 182
Sims, J. T., 236
Sims, James L., 83
Sims, John, 179
Sims, John T., 239
Sims, Joseph E., 83
Sims, Juliet A., 83
Sims, L. A., 188
Sims, L. T., 339
Sims, Levi, 339
Sims, T. S., 94
Sims, W. E., 92, 93, 94, 344
Sims, Wm., 71, 96, 236, 341

Sims, Wm. E., 152
Sims, Wm. M., 239
Sipe, Jacob, 253
Sites, M. F., 47
Skinner, Rhoda, 244
Sleeper, J. W., 305
Sleeper, Rev. J. W., 144
Slife, Catharine, 308
Slife, Daniel, 41
Slife, Henry, 41
Slife, J. N., 118
Slife, John, 41
Slife, John N., 328
Slife, Ulrick, 41
Slosser, Frank, 177, 181, 187, 188, 255
Slough, A. M., 308
Slough, Almira, 308
Slough, Charles, 250
Slough, Chas., 249
Slough, Fred, 138
Slough, Pauline, 308
Slough, Tallman, 105, 138, 307
Smalley, H., 256
Smaltz, Elias, 304
Smith Bros., 165
Smith, ____, 181, 246
Smith, A., 55
Smith, A. J., 234, 255
Smith, A. R., 266
Smith, Aaron, 166, 274, 337
Smith, Aaron S., 254
Smith, Adam, 196, 236, 239, 243
Smith, Amor, 268
Smith, Amor R., 73, 266, 268
Smith, Archibald, 39
Smith, C., 91, 111, 178
Smith, C. G., 94
Smith, Catharine, 319
Smith, Chas. S., 337
Smith, David, 39
Smith, Dildine & Co., 180
Smith, Dr. G. L., 44, 72, 113, 176, 178, 196, 260
Smith, E., 47, 166, 337, 344

Smith, Ebenezer, 39
Smith, Eber, 89
Smith, Elizabeth, 39, 335
Smith, Francis H., 107
Smith, G. L., 46, 47, 48, 185, 232, 338
Smith, G. Paul, 124
Smith, Geo., 25, 128
Smith, Geo. E., 210
Smith, Geo. W., 152, 254
Smith, Henry, 111
Smith, Ida, 128, 333
Smith, Ida L., 114
Smith, J. R., 125, 181, 216
Smith, Jackson, 196, 239, 243
Smith, Jacob, 236
Smith, James A. D., 240
Smith, Jane, 43
Smith, Joe, 47
Smith, John, 196, 236, 249
Smith, John R., 173, 316
Smith, Joseph, 21, 46, 47, 48, 171
Smith, Josiah D., 312
Smith, Laura, 107
Smith, Letitia, 89
Smith, Martha, 89
Smith, Mary, 39
Smith, Melisa, 244
Smith, Philip, 181
Smith, S. D., 318
Smith, Simon, 234
Smith, Stephen, 47
Smith, Steve, 232
Smith, Susie, 278
Smith, W. E., 257
Smith, W. R., 114, 179, 186, 188
Smith, Warren J., 267
Smith, Wm., 39, 40, 43, 66, 248
Smith, Wm. R., 72, 113, 127, 128, 180, 184, 188
Snellson, Thos., 320
Snider, Rev. A., 125
Sniffin, Anna, 93
Snively, Rufus, 204
Snively, Rufus J., 216

Snyder, A., 306
Snyder, A. S., 92, 94
Snyder, Alice, 167
Snyder, G. C., 249
Snyder, J., 109
Snyder, J. H., 92
Snyder, Jacob, 307, 309
Snyder, Miss Alice, 252
Snyder, P. D., 94
Snyder, Rev. A., 252
Snyder, Van A., 249
Sodel, S. D., 91
Solomon, D. R., 111
Solomon, Jacob, 243
Solomon, John, 32, 82
Solomon, John B., 39
Solomon, John L., 39
Solomon, John T., 172
Somerville, James H., 157, 159, 160, 197, 277
Somerville, Jas. H., 162, 230, 237
Somerville, Jennie, 120, 272, 302
Somerville, Linna, 278
Somerville, Mrs., 272
Somerville, Warren, 124
Somerville, Warren C., 248
Somerville, Wilson, 356
Sommerville, J. H., 100, 239
Sommerville, James H., 97, 138, 152, 415
Sommerville, Jas. H., 102, 103, 104, 359
Sommerville, Jennie, 106, 154
Sommerville, Miss Lynn, 166
Sons of Veterans, 122, 123, 254, 256
Sorrel, Morgan, 44
Sourden, John, 86
Southward, Johnnie (Burnie), 144
Southworth, John, 249
Southworth, John (Burnie), 163
Spade, David, 195
Spahr, B. N., 299
Spangler, D., 45
Spangler, David, 234
Spangler, F., 45

Stewart, Chas., 110, 249, 271
Stewart, Edmund, 194, 195
Stewart, J. E., 108
Stewart, J. P., 305
Stewart, Job, 299, 302
Stewart, John, 300
Stewart, Samuel, 47
Stickler, Thos., 319
Stimmel, J. F., 92
Stimmel, Jacob, 72, 176, 177, 195
Stimmel, Peter, 86
Stimmel, Sadie, 94, 115
Stinchcomb, Major J. W., 147, 161
Stinchcomb, Will, 161
Stine, Elisha, 185
Stine, Letis, 171
Stipher, Wm. A., 244
Stirling, John, 195
Stockman, G. W., 266
Stone, Alfred P., 195
Stone, Dwight, 195
Stoneman, Jesse, 296
Storr, Mrs. A., 359
Storts, Abe, 95
Stott, John, 255
Stotts, John, 245
Stotzenberger, J., 195
Stoughton, R. J., 345
Stout, Claude, 251
Stout, Wm., 42
Stoutzenbarger, Jacob, 46
Stoz, Edw. S., 344
Strader, Cyrus, 184
Strang, David, 90
Strayer, D., 91
Strickler, F. M., 179
Strickler, Frank, 183, 187
Strickler, G. W., 93
Strickler, J. M., 255
Strickler, J. Russel, 115
Strickler, Jacob, 195
Strickler, John M., 182, 186, 256
Strickler, W. G., 94
Strickler, W. Grant, 115

Strode, A. W., 94, 268, 269, 318
Strode, Alonzo, 317
Strode, Alonzo W., 92
Strode, E. M., 72, 97, 232
Strode, H., 44
Strode, Ida, 269
Strode, James, 179, 188
Strohm, Elizabeth, 335
Strohn, Henry R., 246
Strong, Frank, 164
Stroud, Samuel, 39
Strunk, Samuel S., 254
Stuart, A., 83
Stuart, Amassa, 89
Stuckey, Samuel, 176, 187, 341
Stucky, Samuel, 183
Stukey, John, 163, 167
Stukey, Samuel, 72, 339
Stukey, Tessa, 115
Stulzig, John L., 243
Stutser, Mr., 204
Suddick, A. L., 234
Suddick, J. A., 42, 96
Suddick, J. M., 96
Suddick, James, 193
Suddick, Richard, 39, 234
Suddick, S. P., 234
Sullivan, C. B., 341
Sullivan, C. H. B., 182
Sunday, Chas., 249
Sunday, John, 248, 253
Sunday, Samuel, 330
Sunday, Sarah, 324
Suter, Milton P., 277
Suter, Mr. _____, 162
Swain, A. C., 178
Swaine, A. E., 180
Swaine, John, 180
Swan, Miss, 328
Swander, Rev. John I., 330
Swanger, F., 251
Swanger, J., 42
Swanger, Samuel C., 359
Swanker, H. M., 236

504

Valentine, Dr. M., 162, 163
Valentine, Dr. Milton, 253, 254
Valentine, Dr. V. A., 162, 163
Van Anda, C. A., 299
Van Buskirk, F. M., 250
Van Gundy, Samuel, 255
Van Home, Simon, 232
Van Horn, S., 174
Van Horn, Simon, 172
Van Horne, Mrs., 244
Van Trump, P., 203
Van Wormer, Lucinda, 317
Van Wormer, Mrs. Mary C., 317
Vance, ____, 180
Vance, J. L., 55, 135, 136, 157
Vance, Jacob L., 55
Vance, Joseph, 172, 192, 224
Vance, Nathan, 232
Vance, Wm., 46, 232
Vandeman, Elias, 312
Vandemark, Elias, 305
Vandemark, Geo., 236, 239, 242
Vandemark, Gideon, 194
Vandemark, J. R., 45
Vandemark, Jacob, 236, 239, 242
Vandemark, Joseph, 42, 239, 243
Vandemark, Noah, 236, 242
Vandermark, Rev. Elias, 118
Vanoay, John, 39
Vanwormer, A. J., 180, 183
Varner, Chas., 165, 167
Vaughn, G. W., 256
Vaughn, Geo., 255
Vaught, Mrs. Jonathan, 272
Vause, N. P., 269
Veiler, William, 240
Vesey, Miss Irene, 317, 319
Vesey, Mrs. Ann E., 317
Vesey, Mrs. Zadox, 312
Vesey, Zadok, 45
Vessy, Zadok, 48
Vickers, Anna, 125
Violet, Chas. G., 249
Vogle, W. B., 182, 186

Vogt, Rev. J., 323
Vorhis, Abraham, 39
Vory's Bros., 175
Vought, Ella, 122, 124, 278, 310
Vought, Jonathan, 101, 153
Vought, Miss Ella, 329

W

W. H. & J. P. Rager, 181, 185
W. R. Miller & Co., 160
W. R. Miller & Son, 161, 164
Waddle, Charles, 296, 297
Wagenhals, Dr. F. S., 217
Wagenhals, John, 332, 333
Wagner, D., 43
Wagner, Daniel, 88, 317
Wagner, David
   (Waggoner?), 89
Wagner, Jacob, 180
Wagner, John, 89
Wagner, L. Herman, 251
Wagner, Levi, 317
Wagner, Miss ____, 111
Wagoner, John, 324
Wagoner, W. P., 250
Wahley, Nathan, 232
Wait, J. W., 299
Walcott, Miss Pantha, 277
Walcutt, J. M., 257
Walden, E. H., 105, 106, 197, 230
Walker, James, 162
Wallace, Anna, 183
Wallace, Chas., 126, 127, 232, 240
Wallace, Ella, 127
Wallace, J. W., 244
Wallace, John, 126, 127, 181, 182, 256
Wallace, John W., 340
Wallace, Miss Theodosia, 316
Wallace, Mrs. Martha, 316
Wallace, R. H., 267
Wallis, H., 250
Waltermire, Mart., 232
Walters, Alva B., 249

Welton, J., 44, 47
Welton, Jesse, 44, 225
Welton, John, 39
Welton, Moses, 176
Wender, Jacob, 39
Wendling, Geo. R., 126
Wenger, Henry, 198
Werner, Chas. A., 249
Werner, Louisa, 308
Werner, M. M., 257
Werner, Sarah, 308
Wernle, Charles, 332
Wernle, Rev. Chas., 333
Wert, J. B., 170, 173, 180, 183, 189, 321
Wert, Jacob B., 31, 170, 171
Wert, Julia A., 171
Wert's Grove, 170, 172, 176, 208, 319
Wesley, Rev. John, 293
West, George, 312
West, Miss Rosetta M., 317
West, Mrs. A. J., 317
Westenhaver, D., 171
Westenhaver, David, 232, 317
Westenhaver, Mrs. Elizabeth, 316
Whaley, Miss Mahala, 316
Whaley, Nathan, 47, 295
Whaley, Wm., 47, 239
Wharton, J. P., 96
Wharton, Mary, 90
Wheeler, David, 242
Wheeler, G. T., 214
Wheeler, Geo., 39, 254
Wheeler, Geo. T., 43, 46, 95, 193, 198,
    238, 245, 253, 254, 317
Wheeler, Jennie, 278
Wheeler, L. B., 256
Wheeler, Lucinda, 244
Wheeler, Miss Elizabeth, 317
Wheeler, Miss Lizzie, 312
Wheeler, Mrs. Catharine, 317
Wheeler, S., 236
Wheeler, Samuel, 43, 46, 49, 95, 198,
    239, 243
Whetzel, D., 46

Whetzel, David, 43
Whetzel, Henry, 25, 43, 44
Whetzel, Louis, 204
Whetzel, M. E., 45
Whetzel, Mellie, 278
Whetzel, Mrs. Elizabeth, 298
Whetzel. H. Jr., 43
Whims, A., 43
Whims, A. J., 236
Whims, A. K., 45, 48, 90
Whims, Allen M., 236
Whims, Andrew, 43, 225, 236
Whims, Chas., 236
Whims, Lydia, 271
Whims, Minnie, 92
Whims, Mrs. Margaret A., 317
Whims, Oscar, 89
Whims, S. H., 45, 48, 71, 236
Whims, Seymour H., 96
Whims, Wm., 42, 43, 45, 48, 96, 198,
    319
Whitcom, David, 299
White, Geo., 193
White, J., 341
White, Jeremiah, 13, 70, 71, 82, 84, 88,
    89, 176, 178, 291, 292, 294, 295, 340
White, John, 88
White, John A., 39
White, Orrin, 254
White, W. Hinton, 126
Whitehead, Hulda, 278
Whitehead, Pauline, 89
Whitehurst & Carty, 157, 158, 159,
    198, 216, 242
Whitehurst and Carty Warehouse, 154
Whitehurst, C. D., 104, 125, 148, 153,
    166, 343, 345
Whitehurst, Cary D., 104, 152, 216, 344
Whitehurst, Ella, 125, 278, 356
Whitehurst, Gehm & Co., 159
Whitehurst, Geo. A., 165, 343, 344
Whitehurst, Laura, 272
Whitehurst, Lehman & Carty, 145, 161

Willie, Nettie, 256, 317

Willie, R. L., 232

Willie, Roy, 251

Wills, W.H., 91

Wilson, A., 106, 216, 232

Wilson, Andrew, 47, 48, 71, 97, 196

Wilson, Della, 92, 94, 112

Wilson, Edward, 242

Wilson, Elizabeth, 90

Wilson, F. L., 46

Wilson, Homer T., 126

Wilson, J., 301

Wilson, James W., 240

Wilson, Jesse, 305

Wilson, John A., 140, 165, 197

Wilson, John L., 345

Wilson, Mark, 273

Wilson, Mrs. Mary, 155, 272

Wilson, Rev. Samuel, 44

Wilson, Robt., 39

Wilson, Samuel, 278, 318

Wilson, Sat. A., 106

Wilson, William L., 230

Wilson, Wm., 29, 118, 159, 207, 242, 249

Winchester and Carroll Road, 33

Winchester Brass Band, 124, 266

Winchester Dramatic Club, 121

Winchester Milling Co., 166

Winchester Protectors, 155

Winchester Telephone Exchange, 167

Winchester Vocal Society, 124

Windel, ____, Saloonist, 273

Winder, M., 139

Winders, Ed., 164

Winders, Ed. D., 310

Winders, M., 162, 163, 164

Wingert, J. W., 45

Wingert, John, 97, 242

Wingert, Lower, James, 301

Winn, J., 305

Winter, J. C., 305

Winterstein, John, 39

Winterstein, Widow, 42

Winterstine, John, 88

Winzell, B. Frank, 127

Wiris, Hannah, 90

Wirt's Grove, 171

Wise, Amaziah, 158

Wise, Frank, 180

Wise, Rev. Geo., 158

Wiseman & Speilman, 163

Wiseman, J. P., 103

Wisenjan, J. P., 104

Wm. Hanby, Rev., 303, 310

Wolenzine, Chas. F., 249

Wolf Sr., Jacob, 317

Wolf, Hannah, 47

Wolf, John, 41, 158, 307

Wolf, Matthias, 25

Wolf, N. J., 165, 301, 323

Wolfe & Zackero, 102

Wolfe, N. J., 162, 338

Wolfe, Newton J., 337

Wollenzein, Charles F., 107

Woman's Relief Corps, 256

Wood, Chas., 39

Wood, Geo., 39, 40

Wood, John, 39, 239, 243

Wood, Morgan, 126

Wood, Thos., 39

Woodall, J. D., 240

Woodbridge, Mary A., 274

Woodcock, Mr., 65

Woodcock, Wm., 65, 352

Woodring & Cherry, 180

Woodring & Sarber, 182

Woodring, C. P., 232, 243

Woodring, Effie, 316

Woodring, H. F., 174, 234

Woodring, Mary A., 316

Woodring, Mary L., 317

Woodring, Mrs. Mary, 316

Woodring, Mrs. Sarah, 316

Woodring, Solomon, 44, 45, 95, 178, 225, 260

Woods, Adaline, 47, 92

Woolcoat, Robt., 39

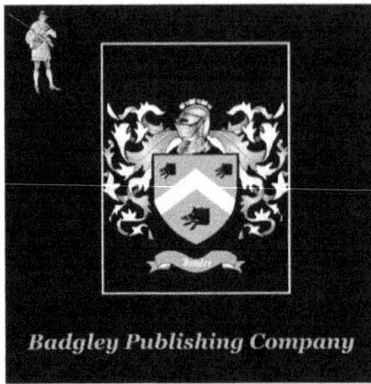

Badgley Publishing Company

For more great stories from our past, visit the Historical Collection at our website:

www.BadgleyPublishingCompany.com